British
Parliamentary Papers

POLICE OF THE METROPOLIS
[1812 (127) VOL II]
[1816 (510) VOL V]
[1817 (231) VOL XVII]

Crime and Punishment

Police 1

IRISH UNIVERSITY PRESS SERIES

OF

British Parliamentary Papers

REPORTS FROM SELECT COMMITTEES
ON THE POLICE OF THE METROPOLIS
WITH APPENDICES
AND EXTRACTS FROM THE EVIDENCE
OF REV THOMAS THIRLWALL

Crime and Punishment

Police

1

SHANNON · IRELAND

© *1969*

Irish University Press Shannon Ireland

Microforms

Microfilm, microfiche and other forms of micro-publishing
© *Irish University Microforms Shannon Ireland*

SBN 7165 0362 X

Irish University Press Shannon Ireland
DUBLIN CORK BELFAST LONDON NEW YORK

Captain T M MacGlinchey Publisher

Robert Hogg Printer

Contents

REPORT

On the Nightly Watch and Police of

THE METROPOLIS.

Ordered, by The House of Commons, *to be printed,* 24 March 1812.

THE COMMITTEE appointed to examine into the State of the Nightly Watch in THE METROPOLIS and the Parishes adjacent, and farther into the State of the Police; and who were empowered to report their Observations, from time to time, to The House;—and to whom several Petitions of Licensed Victuallers, Publicans, within the Cities of *London* and *Westminster*, and its Environs, were referred;——HAVE proceeded in pursuance to their Instructions, and agreed upon the following REPORT:

YOUR Committee first directed their enquiries to the state of the Nightly Watch. They were induced to pursue this course in their investigations, as well from a desire to conform to the order in which the several subjects submitted to their consideration are classed by the House in the terms of their appointment, as, from conceiving this branch of the subject to be of itself of the higheft importance, and in consequence of late occurrences, to be pressed upon their attention with more urgency than any other.

Had they found the defects in this part of the system of our Police to have been such, at this moment, as to have demanded the immediate interposition of the Legislature, they would have hastened to have made an early Report; but they had the satisfaction of observing, that the apprehensions which had been excited had produced such a degree of activity and vigilance in many Parishes and Districts, and such a conviction that the former means of security were insufficient, that all immediate alarms on this head had been in a great measure removed.

In some Parishes, indeed, the zeal and energy of the Inhabitants appears to have been moft exemplary and meritorious; they have agreed to take upon themselves, in rotation, the duties of Superintendents of the Nightly Watch, to visit and inspect the Watch-houses, the Constables, Beadles, Patroles and ftationary Watchmen, so as to ensure the perpetual vigilance and activity of every class of persons on duty during the night, within their parish; and a system of the Nightly Watch, thus introduced by the voluntary exertions of the Householders, has been so effectual, that Your Committee think it necessary only to recommend such measures to be enforced by Legislative enactment, as would give an uniformity and permanency to such a system, and secure its activity by a constant superintendence and controul.

Your Committee finding, that, owing to these and similar means of security, no immediate dangers were to be apprehended, were desirous, indeed they felt it to be their duty, to endeavour to obtain a more detailed as well as a more comprehensive

127.   view

view of the various circumstances which influence and affect the state of the Metropolis as to its Police, the manner in which its local Limits are divided, the various Laws
applicable to such divisions, the various public Bodies, or individuals, in whom powers
are vested, for the purpose of watching over and regulating the means by which its
security and good order is to be maintained, and the mode in which such powers are
executed.

With reference to this view of the subject, the Metropolis may be considered as
divided into Three Parts:

The City of LONDON, properly so called, and the Liberties thereof.

The City of WESTMINSTER, and the Liberties thereof.

The several PARISHES which are neither within the City of *London* and its
Liberties, or the City of *Westminster* and its Liberties.

The City of London is governed by various ancient Charters and Statutes. The
Statute of the 13th of Edward I. called *Statutum Civitatis London*, is one of the most
ancient; and as it is not to be found in the ordinary editions of the Statutes, Your
Appendix, Nº 1.   Committee have inserted it in the Appendix. But the principal Act of Parliament,
which at this time regulates the Nightly Watch of the City of London, is the
10 Geo. II. c. 22.

By this Act, the Lord Mayor, Aldermen, and Common Council, are directed yearly
to make Regulations on this subject, and the Aldermen and Common Councilmen in
each Ward are to carry these Regulations into effect, and make such minor Regulations
as to details, as they may judge necessary.

Appendix, Nº 2.   The Act specifies the duties of the Constables and Watchmen, and prescribes the
mode in which they are to be punished for misconduct or neglect.

As this is one of the principal Acts respecting the duties of Watch and Ward,
Your Committee have also inserted an Extract from it in the Appendix.

Your Committee have not failed to observe, that the City of *London,* from the nature of its Magistracy, the description of its various public Officers, the gradation
and subordination of their various classes, the division and subdivision of its local
limits, affords an example of that unity, and of that dependence of parts on each
other, without which no well constructed and efficient system of Police can ever be
expected. If such a system could be successfully imitated in *Westminster* and its Liberties, and within the other adjacent Parishes which have hitherto formed an unconnected
mass of scattered and uncontrouled local Authorities, considerable benefit might be
expected to ensue; for Your Committee are disposed to concur in opinion with
several of the witnesses, that a well arranged system of Superintendence, Vigilance,
and Controul, would tend more to the prevention of crimes, by rendering it difficult to
commit them, than any degree of activity in the pursuit and conviction of criminals
after the crime has been committed : at all events, however, the two systems are not
only not incompatible, but would necessarily afford mutual aid and assistance to each
other.

This system of Watch and Ward, adapted by the Legislature to the City of
London, is not a dead letter, but is kept alive and in action by the constant superintendence of the Marshals of the City, with their Assistants, who every night visit the
different Wards and Precincts, and take care that the Constables, Beadles, and
Watchmen of all descriptions, are alert and do their duty. Morning Reports are
made to the Lord Mayor, as Chief Magistrate; deficiencies are noticed, as well
as any disorders or irregularities, or other occurrences of the night.

In ancient times, when the whole of the Metropolis consisted of little more than the
City of London (properly so called) such a system might have been abundantly sufficient for its good government and security.

The

The City of *Westminster*, owing to its having never been incorporated, is not provided with the same means, and the same gradations of its public Officers, to ensure the unity and efficiency of its exertions for the prevention of crimes, by the same system of controul and superintendence.

But Your Committee have to observe, that by the Statute of the 27th of Elizabeth, presiding and subordinate Officers are appointed, and powers given to the Dean and Chapter, and to the High Steward and others, to make Regulations for the good government of the City of Westminster. It appears that Lord Burleigh was appointed the first High Steward, and a Code of Regulations was introduced by him, and a division of its local limits into twelve Wards, for the purpose of a more perfect superintendence.

Your Committee have inserted this Statute of Queen Elizabeth in the Appendix, together with the original Regulations introduced by Lord Burleigh. Appendix, N° 3.

This Statute is specifically referred to, and its powers enlarged, by the 29 Geo. II. c. 25. and by the 31 Geo. II. c. 17. and a unity and gradation of authority are endeavoured to be established ; and the High Constable is directed to obey the orders of the High Steward, and the Petty Constables to obey the High Constable.

The duties and superintendence of the High Steward have fallen into great disuse, although very important duties are imposed on him.

It appears, however, that on great occasions of ceremony, he has from time to time personally interfered, and put himself at the head of the whole Civil force of the City of Westminster, marshalling and arranging the subordinate Officers.

The present High Steward, the Marquis of Buckingham, is stated to have so interfered at the funerals of Lord Nelson and Mr. Pitt.

The Statute of 14 Geo. III. c. 90. seems to have superseded this system, and is of such pre-eminent importance with reference to the subject matter of present investigation, that Your Committee have inserted large Extracts from it in the Appendix. It is a local Act applicable to the City and Liberties of Westminster, and certain other Parishes therein named ; and, with great detail, prescribes the duties of Constables, Beadles, Patroles and Watchmen. It is not founded upon the principle of 10 Geo. II. c. 22. which relates to the City of London, and which entrusts to the Lord Mayor and others the whole of the details of the Nightly Watch as to numbers, distribution, wages of the Watchmen, and other particulars, but it limits the discretionary powers of the different parochial Authorities, and, with the most scrupulous minuteness, prescribes the exact manner in which the various descriptions of persons employed must discharge their duties, and defines the smallest number which each Parish is to employ, and the lowest amount of wages to be paid. It details the manner in which misconduct and neglect is to be punished, and meritorious exertions rewarded. It is observable, that both these Statutes refer to the ancient Statute of Watch and Ward, the 13th Edward I. and recognize the principle, that the protection of every District is a compulsory duty incumbent on the Inhabitants; and therefore, an express clause is inserted in each of these Acts, to discharge from this duty such Inhabitants as shall contribute to the Rate for defraying the expense of such Watch and Ward. Other Parishes or Hamlets are governed by particular Acts of Parliament, authorizing the raising of Rates for Watching and Lighting, and vesting powers in certain Commissioners or Vestries for carrying these purposes into effect; but in many cases, the execution of the Law is extremely defective, and in some cases the power of raising Money is inadequate; in others the full amount is not levied; the mode of Watching generally bad, and the men employed, both in number and ability, wholly inefficient for the purpose. Appendix, N° 4.

In other Parishes there is no Legislative provision, and upon the whole, no uniform system prevails ; and neither the Magistracy, or the Government, have at present any connection whatever with the state of the Watch, and no controul or superintendence over it.

It

It would appear that this Statute of the 14 Geo. III. c. 90. has been very little known, or very loosely examined and considered, for many of the Witnesses whom we have examined, and many of the projects which have been submitted to our consideration suggest, as valuable improvements, the very principles, and very details, which are enforced by substantive enactment in this very Statute.

Your Committee feel that much would be done by merely extending the provisions of the 14 Geo. III. to the adjacent Parishes in and near the Metropolis, which should be particularly described, provided it were duly executed; but they are convinced that it may receive very beneficial amendments, for the details of which they would Appendix, N° 5. refer to the Appendix, stating here only, that, in many instances, it may be absolutely necessary to give powers for levying a higher Rate than is now allowed, in order to defray the expense arising from an increase of the numbers or wages of the persons employed in different capacities in the Nightly Watch; Your Committee being strongly impressed with the opinion of the expediency, if not necessity, of relieving the Watch once at least in the night.

But the main improvement of this Law would consist in creating a superintending Power, to whose discretion should be entrusted, the dismissal of the persons appointed by the Parochial Authorities in cases of misconduct, negligence or inability, and to whom it should belong to enforce generally, if necessary, the due execution of this Act; for, with all the other proposed amendments, it cannot escape observation, that the system would still remain imperfect, and very inferior in efficacy to that which subsists within the City of London (properly so called); there still would remain that want of unity, that want of dependence of parts on each other, that want of a general superintendence and controul, without which every system of government must be imperfect.

Your Committee, considering with this view whether there are any public Bodies or individuals already known to the Laws, and vested with judicial and adminiftrative powers, and on whom might conveniently be impofed the duty of connecting in fome degree the scattered Parochial Authorities, have naturally found their attention directed to the several Boards of Magistracy which have been created by the 32 Geo. III. c. 53.

This Act, reciting that a regular attendance of fit Magistrates at certain known places, and at stated hours, was much wanted, establishes seven Boards of Magistracy in various parts of the Metropolis.

These Boards of Magistracy have in common parlance obtained the name of Police Offices, although neither by the provisions of this Act, nor by the nature of their duties as Justices of the Peace, have they any superintendence whatever in matters of preventive and parochial Police, or any neceffary knowledge of the principles on which the several independent unconnected Parishes act, or of the details by which the Peace and good Order of the Metropolis are endeavoured to be maintained; nor have they any means of obtaining this knowledge, except incidentally, in consequence of persons being brought before them charged with disorderly conduct, or suspected of having committed crimes. They merely constitute the first stage in the administration of Criminal Jurisprudence. It would seem to be extraordinary, that in such a Metropolis as London, there should be no Office in which information is collected, from which intelligence can be obtained as to the state of the Police. The Secretary of State for the Home Department has not, neceffarily, any knowledge on this subject, nor has he the means of obtaining any such knowledge, except with reference to crimes committed, or of disturbances which have arisen, or of the number of informations or committals which have taken place during any given period.

Your Committee are therefore persuaded, that the greatest advantages would arise from making use of these Boards of Magistracy, even if it were for no other purpose, than as constituting centres to which information might habitually and constantly be communicated, and daily Reports made from the several Parishes situated within the District, which, for the sake of mutual convenience, is considered Appendix, N°. 6. as assigned to each of these seven Police Offices.

The

The details of these Reports, and the various subject matters to which they should refer, are comprized in a Project inserted in the Appendix, which seems not unworthy of confideration.

Appendix N° 7.

By means of this system of daily Report, detailing the number and description of the persons employed on the Watch during the preceding night, and the occurrences which may have taken place while they were so on duty, the Magistrates would be informed as to the manner in which the proposed Act of Parliament had been complied with; and also of the state of order, or disorder, which might prevail in the various Parishes within their District.

But Your Committee further propose as a means of superintendence and controul, and for the purpose of verifying in some degree the correctness of such Reports, and of ascertaining the fitness as well as good conduct of the persons so employed, that it should be the duty of some of the principal Officers attached to the several Boards of Magistracy (generally known by the name of Police Officers) to go rounds according to some rotation, to be settled during the night, and to visit the several Watch-houses within their district, and report in the morning to the office to which they are attached as to the vigilance, good conduct and fitness of the Conftables, Beadles, Patroles and Watchmen, on duty during the night.

It is also proposed that it should be the duty of the High Constable within the several divisions, occasionally to make similar visitations and Reports, and with this view, it might perhaps be advisable to attach to them a certain number of Assistants, who might be stipendiary officers, to be paid out of the County Rate, or out of some Rate to be levied within each respective division to which they belong.

Nor are these the only means by which it is proposed to furnish the Boards of Magistrates with information respecting the state of the Metropolis as to its Police, and as to the manner in which the parochial Authorities execute the powers entrusted to them; but it is further recommended, that the excellent provisions of the Statute of 14 Geo. III. c. 90. should be extended.

This is the Statute which Your Committee have before alluded to as applicable to the City and Liberties of Westminster, and certain other Parishes therein named, and which, after having prescribed the general outline of the manner in which Watch is to be kept, directs that the several parochial Authorities shall meet, and make more detailed Rules and Regulations for the instruction and guidance of the Constables, Beadles, Patroles and Watchmen.

These detailed Instructions are directed to be written or printed, and delivered to each of such persons respectively.

Your Committee would further propose, that copies of such Rules and Regulations should also be transmitted to the Police Office of the district for their information, that the principal Officers attached to each Office may, in their nightly visitations, be able to judge whether such Regulations are properly complied with. Copies also of these Regulations should, in some convenient manner, be affixed to the walls in each Watch-house.

By means such as these, the several Boards of Magistrates would acquire such a degree of knowledge, as would enable them to give instructions to their principal Officers for their conduct during their visitations, and would enable them further to exercise, with correctness, the power which should be given them, of displacing such of the Watchmen or Patroles as appear to be unfit from bodily infirmity, or from negligence or misconduct.

Having thus collected at each respective Police Office a great mass of information, as to the principles and details by which the good order and security of their district is endeavoured to be maintained, and having thus called into activity the attention of a great number of persons as to matters of preventive Police, and introduced that system of superintendence and controul which may keep alive and continue the activity and

vigilance

vigilance which has thus been excited, it would still appear that the system would be imperfect unless this information, thus collected at each of the seven respective Boards of Magistracy, was accumulated at some one central point, in order that there may be the means of comparing the occurrences and transactions and circumstances of the various parts of the Town, and of forming estimates from the comparison of such facts, of the probable means for the effectual prevention of crimes, or for the detection, pursuit, apprehension, and conviction of criminals.

It should seem, that the Office at Bow-street, which is wholly unconnected with either of the seven Offices, might form the proper centre, to which this various information should be transmitted.

It would probably be necessary, considering the great pressure of business which devolves on that Office, to attach to it some fit person, whose immediate duty it should be to compare and digest such information, for the purpose of being communicated to that Board of Magistrates, and also to the Secretary of State of the Home Department.

Your Committee have dwelt the longer on this branch of the subject, as they deeply feel the necessity of introducing some system which may give unity and connection to the scattered parts of which the Metropolis consists; and which may, by introducing more means of superintendence, and more means of knowledge, secure a due execution of the Laws, and above all things, may secure that active vigilance and precaution which may lessen the number of Criminals, by rendering it difficult to commit crimes.

Although Your Committee consider this part of the subject to be of pre-eminent importance, and as some of the witnesses have said, to be all in all, yet there are several other measures which may come in aid of this System, and may conduce materially to the prevention of crimes.

With this view, Your Committee advert to the Police Office which has been established at Wapping, called *The Thames Police Office*, for the detection of felonies &c. committed on the River Thames. The Magistrates of this Office have also a jurisdiction co-extensive with the other Magistrates.

Your Committee are fully convinced of the beneficial effects which have been derived from this Establishment; the increased protection which has been afforded to every species of property on the River, furnishes the strongest proof of its utility. But it is stated to Your Committee, that the Funds of this office are at present inadequate for such an increased Establishment as would be necessary to guard the valuable property on the various wharfs and line of River from London Bridge to Battersea; added to which, at certain periods of the tide, the communication between the parts of the River above and below London Bridge is so interrupted, that during several hours the upper part of the River is consequently open to great depredation. It is therefore recommended that an additional number of boats should be provided, locally applicable to that part of the River above the Bridge.

It has also been represented, that the great and increasing population in the neighbourhood of Greenwich requires another Police Office on that side of the River. Your Committee are informed, that it is now in the contemplation of Government to remove the Thames Police Office to the Surrey side for that purpose: this might then be made the office for an eighth division, comprehending Greenwich and the other surrounding Parishes.

It has also been represented to Your Committee, that the most notorious Pickpockets and other reputed Thieves are permitted to frequent the public avenues of the Town with impunity, notwithstanding the provisions of 32 Geo. III. made for the purpose of their apprehension: but the Law, as it now stands, does not authorize the Officer to apprehend them, unless, first, they are seen in some public avenue; secondly, unless they are reputed theives; and thirdly, unless they are on the spot with the intent to commit a felony: this can be proved only by some overt act which

they

they are seen to commit, such as hustling, attempting the pocket, or the like. It has been suggested, that if further powers were given by the Legislature, the apprehension of these offenders would be greatly facilitated; but on the other hand, it has not occurred to Your Committee that the powers already given could be enlarged consistently with the general liberty of the subject. Doubts, however, have arisen on the construction of this Act, and the subsequent Act of 51 Geo. III. whether they extend to the City of London (properly so called), which is stated to Your Committee to be at present the resort of many reputed thieves, from the shelter afforded by the operation of the Act being understood to be so limited; it seems therefore desirable that it should be amended for this purpose.

It is at present very difficult to prosecute to conviction the Receivers of stolen goods; but Your Committee think that the evil would be much checked, and less facility would be afforded in the removal of stolen property, if the Law with respect to the execution of Search Warrants were amended, and the Officer enabled to put them in force as well by night as by day, under the direction of the Magistrates; which Your Committee beg leave to suggest to the future consideration of the House.

It has been proved to Your Committee, that Hackney Coaches frequently are used for the conveyance of stolen property in the night, and, to avoid detection, the iron plate with the proper number of the coach is frequently taken off, and another substituted during the time they are in waiting; this might in some degree be remedied by directing the proper number to be painted on the pannel of the Coach, or by some similar regulation.

Your Committee fully agree in the recommendation of a former Committee (28 Report Finance) that the Magistrates should have further means of rewarding their different Officers for any extraordinary activity and exertions, in such a manner as the circumstances of the case might require. If this power was given to a limited extent, it appears to Your Committee, that the Police Officers might be precluded in future from participating in the rewards given by Act of Parliament. The rewards are usually divided between the prosecutor and all the witnesses; the Police Officer has only a small share of them; but this circumstance sometimes operates against his credit as a witness, and to the defeat of public justice: it seems desirable therefore, that as a public Officer, he should be free from any such imputation, and that his services would be best rewarded by the Magistrates, without depending on the conviction of the Offender.

The great increasing expense attending all criminal prosecutions has been truly stated to be a great source of the impunity, and consequently of the increase of crimes; and it seems highly deserving the attention of the Legislature, whether the expenses of prosecution to a limited extent, and in particular cases, which may be specified, might not with propriety be defrayed out of the Parish Rates, or some other general fund. Your Committee think that such a Regulation would materially tend to an increased activity in the prevention and prosecution of offenders, and the great relief of individuals on whom these depredations are committed.

The Petitions from the licensed Publicans, with regard to the stealing of Pewter Pots, having been referred to Your Committee, they have heard evidence on the subject, and find the extent of the evil to be great, notwithstanding the severity of the existing Law; but it does not occur to them, that the interest of the Petitioners can be so well guarded by any new Act of the Legislature, as by Regulations which they are competent to make among themselves.

Having thus adverted to these subjects, which are most of them more or less intimately connected with the immediate object of their enquiries, Your Committee cannot conclude their Report without mentioning the incongruity which subsists in the system for the government of the Metropolis, owing to the Chief and other Magistrates of the City of London, which is situated in the centre of the Metropolis, being unable to pursue, by their warrants, beyond the local limits of the City of London (properly so called) goods which may have been stolen within the limits of the City,

and

and may have been removed beyond these limits. Your Committee conceive, that the warrant of the City Magistrates should have operation, without being backed by any other Magistrate, within a circle of five miles from the Royal Exchange; and that warrants signed by County Magistrates, within five miles of the Royal Exchange, should operate within the local limits of the City, without being backed by the City Magistrates. Your Committee conceive, that such an intercommunity of jurisdiction could not be considered as affecting any of the valuable exclusive Rights and Privileges of the City, particularly if it was limited to definite cases.

Whatever the feelings or opinion of the Legislature might be upon this point, Your Committee have conceived that they could not avoid, after the evidence they had received, directing their attention to the subject.

Your Committee are aware that there are many other points which may be considered as intimately connected with the subject of Police, and to which they might have directed their attention; there are many branches of the Criminal Law, many circumstances connected with the modes in which such Law is administered; the periods for which offenders may be imprisoned, the places in which they may be confined, and the manner in which they may be returned again upon the community 'after the period of their imprisonment may be elapsed; all which subjects may be considered as intimately connected with Police, as they operate strongly both on the dispositions which induce men to commit crimes, and on those previous arrangements of precaution by which crimes may be prevented.

But as these subjects have been referred to other Committees, Your Committee have conceived it to be their duty to confine their Investigations and their Observations to those leading principles of preventive Superintendence and Controul, and to that system of provident Vigilance, which, by watching assiduously over the interests of the Community, may maintain, without interruption, its good Order and Security.

Appendix,
N° 8. N° 9.

Since Your Committee framed their Report, two Reports, made in the years 1770 and 1772, on the same Subject, have been referred to; and Your Committee think it their duty to bring them, at this time, to the notice of the House, in the Appendix to this Report.

24 March 1812.

CONTENTS OF APPENDIX.

Appendix, No. 1.

(From the folio edition of "The Statutes of the Realm." Printed in 1810 by Command of His Majesty; under the Direction of the Commissioners on the Public Records.— Vol. I. page 102.

Anno 13° EDWARDI I. A. D. 1285.

𝔖tatuta 𝔠i𝔟itatis 𝔏on𝔡on.

STATUTES for the CITY of LONDON.

Ex magno Rot. Stat. in Turr. Lond. m. 42. in Cedula.

CES sont les Articles le queus nr̃e Seign͛ le Rey Comaunde q̃ bien seient gardez en sa Citee de Loundres, p͛ sa pes garder e meyntenir. Primeremēt p͛ ceo q̃ multz des mals com des murdres, Robberyes, e homycides ont este fetz ca en arrere deinz la Citee de nuyt e de Jour, e gentz Batues e mal tretes, e aut͛s div'res aventures de mal avenuz encontre sa pes; Defendu est q̃ nul seit si hardi estre troeve alãnt ne wacraunt p my les Ruwes de la Citee, ap's Coeverfu psone a Seint Martyn le gãnt, a Espeye ne a Bokuyler ne a autre arme p͛ mal fere, ne dount mal supeciõn poet avenir; ne en autre man'e nule, sil ne seit gãnt Seign͛ ou altre prodome de bone conysaunce, ou lour c'teyn message q̃.d els serra garaunty q̃ vount li un a lautre p conduyte de Lumere. E si nul seit trove alant encontre la fourme avantdite, ou q̃ il seit encheson de tart venir en vyle, seit p's p les Gardeyns de la pes e seit mys en Le Tonel, la quel p͛ tiels meffesours est assigne, e Lendemeyn seit amene e p'sente devant le Gardeyn ou le Meyre de la Citee q̃ p͛ tens serra, e devant les Aldermans, e solong ceo q̃ il troveront qil eit trespasse e a ceo seit coustumers seit puny. E pur ceo q̃ tiels meffesours avauntditz, alant nutauntre, communalment ont lour Recet e lour Covynes,

127. e font

THESE be the Articles which Our Lord the King doth command to be well kept in his City of London, for the keeping and maintenance of his Peace.

First, Whereas many evils, as Murders, Robberies and Manslaughters have been committed heretofore in the City by Night and by Day, and People have been beaten and evil intreated, and divers other Mischances have befallen against his Peace; it is enjoined that none be so hardy to be found going or wandering about the Streets of the City, after Curfew tolled at St. Martin's le Grand, with Sword or Buckler, or other Arms for doing mischief, or whereof evil suspicion might arise, nor any in any manner, unless he be a great man or other lawful Person of good repute, or their certain Messenger, having their Warrants to go from one to another, with Lanthorn in hand. And if any be found going about contrary to the form aforesaid, unless he have cause to come late into the City, he shall be taken by the keepers of the Peace and be put into the place of confinement appointed for such Offenders; and on the morrow he shall be brought and presented before the Warden, or the Mayor of the City for the time being, and before the Aldermen; and according as they shall find that he hath offended, and as the Custom is, he shall be punished.

And whereas such Offenders as aforesaid going about by Night, do commonly resort and have their Meetings and hold their evil talk

talk in Taverns more than elsewhere, and there do seek for shelter, lying in wait, and watching their time to do mischief; it is enjoined that none do keep a Tavern open for Wine or Ale after the tolling of the aforesaid Curfew; but they shall keep their Tavern shut after that hour, and none therein drinking or resorting; neither shall any man admit others in his House except in common Taverns, for whom he will not be answerable unto the King's Peace. And if any Taverner be found doing the contrary, the first time he shall be put in pledge by his Tavern drinking cup, or by other good pledge there found, and be amerced forty-pence; and if he be found a second time offending, he shall be amerced half a mark; and the third time ten Shillings; and the fourth time he shall pay the whole Penalty double, that is to say, Twenty Shillings: And the fifth time he shall be forejudged of his Trade for ever.

None shall teach fencing with Buckler in the City.

Also, forasmuch as Fools who delight in mischief, do learn to fence with Buckler, and thereby are the more encouraged to commit their follies; it is provided and enjoined that none shall hold school for, nor shall teach the art of fencing with Buckler, within the City, by night or by day; and if any so do, he shall be imprisoned for forty days.

Offenders shall be discharged only by the Mayor, &c.

And whereas Malefactors taken and arrested for Trespasses, as for Batteries, spilling of Blood, and other Offences against the Peace of our Lord the King, and for evil suspicion, are often delivered too easily, by reason whereof, others the less dreading such punishments are encouraged in their follies, and in often transgressing against the Peace, in expectation of such easy deliverance; it is provided that no man so imprisoned shall be delivered by the Sheriff, nor by any Officer under him, without the award of the Warden or Mayor for the time being, and of the Aldermen; unless the Trespass be very small; and then good and solemn mainprize shall be taken, and of Persons justiceable before the Bailiffs of the City, that he do appear before the said Warden or Mayor, and the Aldermen, at a certain day, to receive award and judgement according to his Trespass.

Aldermen shall secure Offenders in their respective Wards.

Moreover it is provided, that every Alderman in his Wardmote shall make diligent enquiry concerning such Malefactors, resorting to and abiding in his Ward; and if any such be found by presentment or indictment of the good Men of the Ward, or by evil suspicion, they shall straight be attached by their Bodies, and brought before the Warden or Mayor, and the Aldermen, and be arraigned of that whereof they are indicted or presented; and they who cannot acquit themselves, shall be punished by imprisonment, or other Punishment, at their discretion, and according to what the Trespass requireth.

Foreigners shall not be Inn-keepers, unless made free of the City.

And whereas divers Persons do resort unto the City, some from Parts beyond the Sea, and others of this Land, and do there seek shelter and refuge, by reason of Banishment out of their own Country, or who for great offence or other misdeed have fled from their own Country; and of these some do become Brokers,

---

e font lour mauveyses purparlances en taverne plus q̃ aillours, e illoekes querent umbrage attendanz e geitant lor tens de mal fere; Defendu est q̃ nul ne tiegne taverne overte de Vyn ne de Cerveyse ap's le Coeverfu avantdit p'sone; mes q̃ il tiegne sa taverne close ap's cel houre, e nul leinz Bevaunt ne recettant ne en sa mesoun hors de Communes tavernes nul ne recette p' quy il ne voillit estre respoignant a la pes le Rey. E si nul tav'ner seit trove q̃ autrement faceo, primerement seit degage p soen Hanap de la Tav'ne, ou p altre bon gage leinz trove, e seit am'cye a quaraunte deniers; E si altre fiez seit trouve q̃ ceo faceo, seit am'cye a demy mark e a la tierce fiez a dys souz; e a la quarte fiez paie tute la peyne double, cest asav' vynt souz. E la quynte fiez seit fors-jugge del mestier p' tutz jourz. Ensement p' ceo q̃ fous, q̃ sei delitent a mal fere, vount ap'ndre Eskirmye de Bokyler, e de ceo plus sei abaudissent defere lour folyes; Purveu est e defendu q̃ nul ne tiegne escole ne aprise de Eskirmye de Bokyler, dedeinz la Citee de nuyt ne de jour, e si nul le faceo eit la Prison de xl. jours. E p' ceo q̃ mals fesours p' trespas com de Bateryes, sanc espaundu, e autres malfetz encontre la pes nr̃e Seign' le Rey, e p mal suspicioun, pris e arestutz, sovent sont delivres p trop legiere manere, p queyautres meyns doutantz tiels punyssementz sei abaudissent en lour folyes e en souvent mesprendre, encountre la pes, p beiaunce de tiele eyse deliveraunce; Purveu est q̃ nul en tiele manere enprisone seit delivres p Viscounte ne p Mynystre de south ly sanz agard del Gardeyn ou del Meyre q̃ p' tens serra, e de les Aldermans si le trespas ne seit mult petit, e adunks seit prise bone meynprise e sollempne, e des gentz justizables a les Bayllyfs de la Citee, q̃ il seit devant le dit Gardeyn ou Meyre e les Aldermans a certyn jour a receyvre agard e juggement solong soen trespas. Derichief p'veu est q̃ chescun Alderman, en soen Gardemot ententivemēt enquerge de tiel meffesours repeirantz e demorantz en sa Garde; e si nuls tiels seient trovez p presentemēt ou enditement des bones gentz de la Garde ou de male suspicioun, tantost seient attachez p lour cors, e veignēt devant le Gardeyn ou Meyre e les Aldermans, e seient aresonez de ceo dont il sont enditez, ou sour eus presentez; e cels qe aquiter ne sei poent seient punyz p enprisonement, ou autre punyssemēt, p lour descretion, e solong ceo q̃ le trepas demaunde.

E p' ceo q̃ akunes gent soent repeirantz en la Citee, acuns des t'res de outre mer e acuns de la t're meismes, e illoesks querent umbrage e refu p' Bannyssement hors de lour pays ou p' g'nt trespas ou autre forfet sei sont de lour pays aloignez; e des tiels les uns sei font abrocours

abrocours hostillurs e herberjours denz la Citee des privez e des est{a}nges, si avant com il fuysseient bons e leals de la f{a}nchise de la Citee : e les uns riens ne font fors q aler sus e jus p {my} les Ruwes, plus de nuyt q de jour, e sont bien atirez com de vesture e munture, e sei font pestre de deliciouses vyaundes e coustouses ; ne il ne font mestier ne mar-chaundise nule, ne t'res ne tenementz ne ount de quei vyvre, ne amy q les trove, e des tiels avenēt multz des perils en la Citee sovent, e multz des mals, e les uns ont apte mauveytez sont trovez, com des Robberyes e Brusures des mesons de nuytz, murdres, e autres mals : Purveu est, q nul dest{a}nge t're ne altre dont q il seit, ne seit reseant herberjour ne hostiler denz la Citee sil ne seit f{a}nc home de la Citee, receu e a ferme devāt le Gardeyn ou Meyre e les Aldermans, com bon home e leal ; e q il eit bone testmoignance, del luy dunt il s'ra venu, q il seit bien e lealmēt depty e trove saufs plegges justizables a les Bayllifs de la Citee destre respoignant a la pes le Rey, e les Citeyns e la Citee garder sanz dam-mage. Ne nul Abrocour ne seit denz la Citee for ceaus q seent receuz e jures devāt le Gardeyn ou Meyre e Aldermans. E touz ceus q sont Herberjours, Hostiliers, e Abro-cours en la Citee encontre la fourme avant-dite, del jour qe ces Articles sorront Lus e pubbliez denz la Citee, [desks a un moys[1]] sei demettēt e retreient q mes ne le facent e si nul seit trove q le faceo ap's la dist meys, ou altre de quy len eit [male[2]] suspeceoun p soen mauveys port com p mauveyse Com-paignye ou p bone testmoignance del vygne, tantost seit arestu p soen cors p le Gardein ou Meyre ou les Viscontes, ou par Alderman en qui garde il serra trove, e solong ceo q il serra trove cont{e}venāt la fourme avantdite ou en altre trespas seient punyz ; Cestasav', les Herberjours e Hostilliers, e Abrocours seient noun receivables a la franchise pur tutz jours, e a la prisone ajuggez ; e les altres seient punyz p enprisonement ou en alt{e} man'e, selong ceo q le trespas demaunde.

Le Rey, q veut la pes de sa Citee estre bien garde entre tutes gentz, ad entendu q ses distz Articles ne sont poynt tenuz, ne estre ne poent, p{r} ceo q ses mynystres sovent ont este enquerelez e grevement punyz de-vant ses Auditours des pleyntes, e aillours en ca Court, p{r} enprisonementz e altres punys-sementz de meffesours e de suspecionous de mal, pur ceo q il ne eurent de Rey garaunt a ceo fere ; dont les ditz mynystres ont este e sont meyns osez a chastier e punyr les meffesours, e p tant sei abaudissent de mef-fere, e donnēt as altres ensample de mau-veyste, a g{a}nt peril de la Citee e g{a}nt nurture des mals ; Veut e comande q desormes nul de ses Mynystres seit enquerele devant ses Au-ditours des pleyntes ne aillours en sa Court.

[1,2] Interlined on the Roll.

Brokers, Hostelers, and Innkeepers within the City, for Denizens and Strangers, as freely as though they were good and lawful Men of the Franchise of the City ; and some nothing do but run up and down through the streets, more by night than by day, and are well attired in cloathing and array, and have their food of delicate meats and costly ; neither do they use any craft or merchandize, nor have they Lands or Tenements whereof to live, nor any Friend to find them ; and through such Persons many perils do often happen in the City, and many evils, and some of them are found openly offending, as in Robberies, breaking of Houses by night, Murders, and other evil deeds ; it is provided that no Man of Foreign Lands, or other Per-son whatsoever, shall be a resiant Innkeeper or Hosteler in the City, unless he be a Free-man of the City, admitted and at farm before the Warden or Mayor, and the Alderman, as a good Man and true, and that he have good testimony from the Parts whence he cometh, that he hath well and lawfully departed ; and that he find safe Pledges justiceable before the Bailiffs of the City, to be answerable to the King's Peace, and to save the Citizens and the City harmless. And there shall be no Broker in the City, except those who are admitted and sworn before the Warden or Mayor, and Aldermen. And all that are Innkeepers, Hostelers, and Brokers in the City, contrary to the form aforesaid, from one month after the day when these Articles shall be read and published in the City, shall forego the same, and withdraw themselves that they do so no more ; and if any be found offending herein after the said month, or any other of whom there is evil suspicion for his ill behaviour, as for bad Company or by good evidence of the Neighbourhood, he shall forthwith be arrested by his Body by the Warden or Mayor, or the Sheriffs, or by the Alderman in whose Ward he shall be found, and shall be punished according as he shall be found to have transgressed the Form aforesaid, or to have otherwise offended ; that is to say, Innkeepers and Hostelers, and Brokers, shall be for ever inadmissible to the Franchise, and awarded to Prison ; and the others shall be punished by Imprisonment, or otherwise, according as the Offence re-quireth.

THE KING, who willeth that the Peace of his City be well kept among all Persons, having been informed that his said Articles are not observed, neither can be, by reason that his Officers have been many times ac-cused and grievously punished before his Auditors of Plaints, and elsewhere in his Court, for imprisoning and otherwise punish-ing Offenders and suspected Persons, for that they had not the King's Warrant for so doing ; whereby the said Officers have been and are less bold to chastise and punish Offenders, and these do become so much the more daring to offend, and do give unto others the example of evil doing, to the great peril of the City and great encouragement of Offences ; he doth will and command, that from henceforth none of his Officers shall be complained of before his Auditors of Plaints, or elsewhere in his Court, for any imprisoning

Admission of Brokers.

Punishment of Persons acting as Brokers, Innkeepers, &c. contrary hereto.

Officers execut-ing this Act in-demnified.

ing or other punishing of Offenders or Persons suspected of evil; unless it be that any Officer should do so of open malice and for his own revenge, or for the revenge of another that maliciously procureth the same, and not for the keeping of the Peace.

And the King willeth that these provisions, and the additions, be well and surely kept in the aforesaid City, for the maintenance of his Peace, with the amendments thereof when it shall please him to make such, for the profit of his City.

pur nul enprisonement ou altre punyssement de meffesours ou souspecionous de mal: Si eus ne seit q̃ mynystre le face p apte malice e sa ppre venjeaunce, ou p̃ venjaunce de autri q̃ p malice le procure, e ne mye p̃ la garde de sa pes.

E le Rey cestes purveaunces e ajoustementz vent q̃ en lavantdite Citee seient bien e sauvemēt gardez, p̃ sa pes meyntenir, ove les amendementz q̃nt il li plerra quil mettre pur le proffist de sa Citee.

Appendix, No. 2.

ANNO DECIMO GEORGII II. REGIS.

An ACT for the better regulating the Nightly Watch and Bedels within the City of London and Liberties thereof; and for making more effectual the Laws now in being, for Paving and Cleansing the Streets and Sewers in and about the said City.

Preamble.

WHEREAS the well ordering and regulating a Watch in the Night time within the several Wards in the city of London, is of very great importance, for the preservation of the persons and properties of the inhabitants thereof, and very necessary to prevent Fires, Murders, Burglaries, Robberies, and other Outrages and Disorders; and whereas by the Laws now in being, no effectual provision is made for the establishing, ordering, or well governing of such a Nightly Watch, or for levying and collecting any sums of Money for defraying the necessary charges thereof, and of the Bedels who shall be appointed to take care of the same; for the effecting of which good purposes for the future, and to the end that a due application and just Account may be had and taken of the Money which shall hereafter be levied and collected by virtue of this Act, for the purposes aforesaid, May it please Your most Excellent Majesty, at the humble Petition and Desire of the Mayor, Aldermen, and Commonalty of the City of London, in Common Council assembled, that it may be enacted; and be it enacted by the King's most Excellent Majesty, by and with the Advice and Consent of the Lords Spiritual and Temporal, and Commons, in this present Parliament assembled, and by the Authority of the same, That the Mayor, Aldermen, and Commons of the said City in Common Council assembled, shall and they are hereby impowered and required, between the first day of October one thousand seven hundred and thirty-seven, and the twentieth day of November next following, and so in every year ensuing, between the first day of October and the twentieth day of November in each succeeding year, to order and appoint what number of Watchmen and Bedels they shall judge necessary and proper to be kept within each of the several Wards of the said City and the Liberties thereof for one whole year, commencing from the twenty-fifth day of December next ensuing the said order; and shall then and there direct how they ought to be armed, how long they are to watch, what Wages and Allowances shall be given to the said Watchmen and Bedels for their attendance; and shall also order and direct what number of Constables shall attend every night in each respective Ward; and shall make all such other Orders and Regulations as the nature of each particular service shall seem to them to require.

Common Council to determine the number of Officers, and make Orders for the Nightly Watch,

And for the better raising and levying of Monies for paying the Wages of the said Watchmen and Bedels, and other charges incident thereto, be it further enacted by the authority aforesaid, That the Mayor, Aldermen and Commons of the said City, in Common Council assembled, every year as aforesaid, shall then and there, and they are hereby authorized and impowered to determine and direct what sum and sums of Money shall be raised and levied upon each respective Ward for answering the purposes aforesaid; and for raising the said several sums of Money, to direct the Alderman, Deputy, and Common Council Men of each and every of the respective Wards in the said city of London and Liberties thereof, or the major part of them, to make an equal Rate and Assessment upon all and every the person and persons who do or shall inhabit, hold, occupy or enjoy any Land, House, Shop, Warehouse or other Tenement, within their respective Wards (regard being had in making the said Rate, to the abilities of, and likewise to the Rent paid by the said several Inhabitants and Occupiers so to be rated and assessed), and the Aldermen, Deputy, and Common Council Men of each Ward of the said City, or the major part of them, are hereby authorized and required to make such Rate and Assessment for their respective Wards, in such manner and form as shall be so directed by the said Court of Common Council; which said Rates or Assessments so to be made, and all arrears due upon the same, shall be collected quarterly from the several Inhabitants or Occupiers, in each of the said several Wards, by the several Constables for the time being of the several Precincts,

and to appoint Rates,

to be collected quarterly.

Precincts, or by the Bedels in each of the said respective Wards, as the Alderman, Deputy and Common Council Men of each Ward, or the major part of them, shall direct and appoint ; and in case any of the said Inhabitants or Occupiers shall refuse or neglect to pay **Distress on Nonpayment,** the sum so rated or assessed upon him her them, it shall and may be lawful to and for such Collector or Collectors, by Warrant under the hand and seal of the Lord Mayor of the said City for the time being, or the Alderman of the Ward wherein the premises for which such Inhabitants or Occupiers shall be rated and assessed shall be situate (which Warrant the said Lord Mayor or Alderman is hereby authorized and required to grant, upon Oath made before him, by the said Collector or Collectors, of the party or parties so refusing or neglecting to pay), to levy the same by distress and sale of the Goods and Chattels of the party or parties so neglecting or refusing, rendering to him her or them the overplus (if any be) the reasonable charge of making the said distress and sale being first deducted ; and for **or Imprisonment.** want of such distress, by like Warrants to commit the party or parties so neglecting or refusing to one of the Compters of the said City for the space of one month, or until payment thereof.

Provided always, and it is hereby Declared, That in case any person or persons shall **Appeal in case of Grievance.** think him her or themselves aggrieved, by any Rate and Assessment to be made as aforesaid, it shall and may be lawful for them respectively, within the space of twenty days after the sum so rated and assessed shall be demanded, to appeal to the Court of Lord Mayor and Aldermen, whose decision shall be final and conclusive.

And be it further Enacted by the Authority aforesaid, That the Alderman, Deputy, and **Aldermen, &c. of each Ward to make Orders and Regulations within their respective Wards.** Common Council Men of each Ward, within the said City, or the major part of them, whereof the Alderman or Deputy to be one, fhall within fourteen days after the number of Watchmen fhall have been so appointed as aforesaid, assemble at some convenient place within their respective Wards, yearly and every year ; and shall nominate and choose such honest and able-bodied men, to be employed as Watchmen within their respective Wards, as they shall think best qualified for the service ; and shall then order and set down in writing, at what Stands it is fit for the said Watchmen to be placed, and in what manner and how often it shall be required of them to go their Rounds ; and shall then make such other Orders and Regulations, concerning the Watchmen and Bedels, as the nature of each particular service shall appear to them to require ; and if any of the said Watchmen, so by them appointed, shall die within the time for which they are appointed to serve, or shall be negligent in his or their duty, or guilty of any misbehaviour, or if it shall be found necessary to repeal, amend, or alter any of the Nominations, Appointments, Orders or Regulations by them made, it shall and may be lawful for the respective Aldermen, by and with the advice and consent of their respective Deputies, and the Common Council Men of each Ward, being convened by due notice, or the major part of them, who shall be there present, at any intermediate times of the year, to remove any of the said Watchmen so by them appointed, and to nominate and appoint one or more person or persons fitly qualified, in the room and stead of him or them so dying, or of him or them who shall be removed for misbehaviour, as aforesaid : and also to make such further Orders and Regulations, for the better government and direction of the said Watchmen and Beadles, within their respective Wards, as they shall think proper : Provided, that such Orders and Regulations be not repugnant to the Regulations and Orders which shall be made by the Mayor, Aldermen, and Commons, in Common Council assembled.

And be it further Enacted by the Authority aforesaid, That a true Copy or Transcript, **Copy of Orders, &c. to be given the Constables ;** as well of all the Orders and Regulations made by the said Court of Common Council, as of all such Nominations, Appointments, Orders and Regulations, as shall be so made from time to time as aforesaid, for the better direction and government of the Watchmen and Bedels, by the Aldermen, Deputies and Common Council Men of the said respective Wards, shall be fairly written and signed by the Alderman or his Deputy, and the major part of the Common Council Men of each Ward, and shall be delivered to all and every the Constables of the several Precincts within the said respective Wards ; and that from and after the **Their Charge.** twenty-fifth day of December one thousand seven hundred and thirty seven, one or more of the said Constables of each of the said Wards as shall be judged necessary by the said Court of Common Council to be held as aforesaid, shall attend every night by turns, and shall keep Watch and Ward within their respective Wards, in manner following ; that is to say, from the said twenty-fifth day of December to the tenth day of March following, from the hours of nine in the evening, till seven the next morning ; and from thenceforth yearly and every year the said Constables shall attend from the tenth of March to the tenth of September, from the hours of ten in the evening, till five the next morning ; and from the tenth of September to the tenth of March, from nine in the evening, till seven the next morning ; and the said Constables shall, in their several turns or courses of Watching, use their best endeavours to prevent Fires, Murders, Burglaries, Robberies, and other Outrages and Disorders ; and to that end shall, and they are hereby impowered and required, to arrest and apprehend all Night-walkers, Malefactors, and suspected persons, who shall be found wandering or misbehaving themselves, and shall carry the person or persons who shall be so apprehended, as soon as conveniently may be, before one or more Justice or Justices of the Peace of and for the said City, to be examined and dealt with according to Law ; and shall twice or oftener, at convenient times in every night, go about their respective Wards, and take notice whether all the Watchmen perform their duties in their several stations, according to such Orders and Regulations as shall have been made for that purpose by the Lord Mayor,

127.   Aldermen,

Aldermen, and Commons of the said City in Common Council assembled, or by the Aldermen, Deputies, and Common Council Men of the respective Wards ; and in case any such Watchman shall misbehave himself, or neglect his duty, the said Constables, or one of them, shall, as soon as conveniently may be, give notice thereof to the Alderman, or his Deputy, for the time being, of the Ward to which such Watchman shall belong, to the end that the Alderman, Deputy, and Common Council Men may be forthwith summoned, for the examination and punishment of such offence.

Penalty of 20 s. for Default. And be it further Enacted by the Authority aforesaid, That if any of the said Constables shall wilfully neglect to attend any night in his or their turn, to keep Watch and Ward within their respective Wards, or shall not come to keep Watch or Ward at the respective hours appointed by this Act for his and their attendance thereon, or shall depart from, or leave keeping Watch and Ward, during the respective hours appointed by this Act for the keeping the same, or shall neglect in any night of his and their Watching to go about his and their respective Wards, twice at the least in each night of his or their watching, for the purpose of this Act, or shall otherwise misbehave himself or themselves against the duty prescribed to them by this Act, in each and every of the said cases the person or persons so offending shall respectively forfeit the sum of Twenty Shillings for every such offence.

Watchmen's Charge. And be it further Enacted by the Authority aforesaid, That it shall and may be lawful for the said Watchmen, or any of them, in the absence of the Constable, and they are also hereby authorized and required in their several stations, during the time of their keeping Watch and Ward as aforesaid, to apprehend all Night-walkers, Malefactors, Rogues, Vagabonds, and all disorderly persons whom they shall find disturbing the public peace, or shall have just cause to suspect of any evil designs, and to deliver the person or persons so apprehended, as soon as conveniently may be, to the Constable of the Night, who is hereby required to carry him, her or them, as soon as conveniently may be, before one or more Justice or Justices of the Peace of the said City, to be examined and dealt with according to Law.

£. 10. Penalty on Collectors refusing to act. And be it further Enacted, That if any of the persons who shall from time to time be directed and appointed Collectors of the several Rates and Assessments, to be made in pursuance of this Act, shall neglect or refuse to take upon him or them the said office, or duly to execute the same, according to the true intent and meaning of this Act, he or they shall respectively forfeit the sum of Ten Pounds, and shall continue liable to be appointed into the said office again the year following ; and in case of his or their refusal, they shall be again liable to the like penalties, as often as he or they shall refuse to take upon him or them the said office; and upon every such refusal of any person or persons so to be appointed Collector or Collectors as aforesaid, to take upon him or them the said office, or in case of death after such appointment, it shall and may be lawful for the Aldermen, Deputy, and Common Council Men of such Ward, or the major part of them, to direct and appoint any other person or persons inhabiting in such Ward, to be Collector or Collectors in the room or stead of such person or persons who shall so refuse to take upon him or them the said office, or shall die after such appointment; and in case such person or persons so directed and appointed shall refuse to take upon him or them the said office, he or they shall be liable to the like penalties as hereinbefore are appointed for any Constable or Bedels, who shall refuse to take upon him or them the said office.

Collector's Duty ; And be it further Enacted by the Authority aforesaid, That all and every the Collector or Collectors of the Rates and Assessments aforesaid, of every Ward, shall collect the same quarterly, and shall severally enter in some book or books, to be by them respectively kept for that purpose, the several sums which they shall from time to time receive on account of the said Rates and Assessments, and likewise the names of the persons from whom, and the particular times when they received the same ; which book and books they shall at all convenient times produce upon demand, and shew to the Deputy or Deputies of their respective Wards ; and they shall pay the Money by them respectively received on account of the said Rates and Assessments, into the hands of such Deputy, as he or they shall receive the same, and in such manner as that such Collector shall never have a sum exceeding Five Pounds so collected at one time in his or their hands, by the space of five days ; and if any of the said Collectors shall neglect to make such entries, or shall refuse to produce and shew to the Deputy of their respective Wards, the book or books hereby directed to be by them respectively kept for the purposes aforesaid, (the same having been demanded of them, or if any of them shall keep or retain in his or their hands more than **and Penalty on Default.** the said sum of Five Pounds, longer than five days, in each and every the said cases, the person or persons so offending shall respectively forfeit the sum of Forty Shillings for every such offence ; and on payment of every such sum of Money into the hands of such Deputy of each Ward, such Collector or Collectors shall take a Receipt for the same from the said Deputy, in which Receipt shall be specified and expressed the name of such Collector or Collectors, the sum paid, and the name of the Precinct and Ward wherein the Money hath been collected ; and the respective Deputies for the time being shall be obliged, and he and they is and are hereby required to give such Receipt without fee or reward ; and such Receipts shall, by the Collector or Collectors, be produced to the Alderman of the Ward at the time he and they shall settle and adjust his and their yearly Account and Accounts, and shall by the said Alderman be taken and allowed as a full and sufficient discharge for all and every such sum and sums of Money such Collectors shall have received and paid to such Deputies respectively

respectively as aforesaid ; and the said several Collectors shall, within twenty days next after the end of every three months, after their severally taking upon themselves the said office of a Collector, produce and deliver to the Alderman of the said Ward, or such person as he shall appoint to receive the same, the book and books in which they entered the sums by them severally received on account of the said Rates ; and shall at the same time give and deliver to the said Alderman, or such person as he shall appoint to receive the same, a true account in writing of all such persons as shall have neglected or refused to pay the said Rates and Assessments, to the intent that the same may afterwards be recovered and levied.

AND, to the end that the payment of the said Rates and Assessments for the purposes aforesaid, may be effectually enforced ; BE it further Enacted by the Authority aforesaid, That every Freeman of London, liable to pay the Rates and Assessments aforesaid, who shall have neglected or refused to pay the said Rates and Assessments to the person or persons authorized and impowered to collect and receive the same (the same having been lawfully demanded) or shall have desired to be excused from paying such Rates and Assessments, shall be under the same incapacity of voting at Elections within the said City of London, as any person or persons now is or are, who do not pay their Scot and Lot to the several yearly Rates and Taxes, to which the Citizens of London are at this time liable. *Persons not paying the Rates incapacitated to vote at Elections.*

And be it further Enacted by the Authority aforesaid, That the Deputy of each Ward of the said City for the time being shall and may, and he is hereby authorized and required to pay all and singular the Orders and Draughts on him to be made by the Alderman of such Ward, with the advice of the major part of the Common Council Men of each Ward respectively, in discharge of the Watchmen and Bedels, and other incident Charges in relation to the Watching of such Ward, in pursuance of this Act ; and the said respective Deputies of the Wards for the time being shall and they are hereby required to keep regular and plain entries, in a book to be for that purpose by them severally provided, of all and singular the receipts and payments they shall make, on account of the Nightly Watch and Bedels, within their respective Wards as aforesaid, and other Charges incident thereto ; which books shall be produced yearly at the Wardmote in each Ward, if required ; and also that the Deputies respectively for the time being shall have the same Account audited and passed between the first day of February and the first day of March yearly, by the Alderman and the major part of the Common Council Men of each Ward, in which the Money so to be accounted for shall be collected. *Deputy's Charges.*

And be it further Enacted by the Authority aforesaid, That it shall and may be lawful to and for the Lord Mayor for the time being, or any two or more Justices of the Peace for the said City, to hear and determine any of the offences which are made subject to and punishable by any pecuniary penalties directed to be levied by this Act ; and the said Lord Mayor, or such Justices of the Peace, are hereby authorized and required, upon any information exhibited, or complaint made in that behalf, within ten days after such offence committed, to summon the party or parties accused, and the witnesses on either side ; and in case the said party or parties accused shall not appear on such summons (and after oath made of the commission of any of the offences above mentioned, by one or more credible witness or witnesses) to issue a Warrant or Warrants for apprehending the party or parties offending in the said city of London ; and upon the appearance of the party or parties accused, or his or their contempt in not appearing, upon the proof of notice given, to proceed to the examination of the witness or witnesses upon oath (which oath he or they are hereby authorized, impowered and required to administer), and to give such judgement, sentence or determination, as shall be just and conformable to the tenor and true meaning of this Act ; and where the party or parties accused shall be convicted of such offence, either upon such information as aforesaid or on confession of the party or parties accused, it shall and may be lawful for such Lord Mayor or Justices to issue a Warrant or Warrants for levying the pecuniary penalties and forfeitures so adjudged, on the goods and chattels of the offender or offenders, and to cause sale to be made thereof in case they shall not be redeemed in five days, rendering to the party or parties the overplus (if any there be) after deducting the reasonable charges of such distress and sale upon demand ; and in case any person or persons shall be so convicted as aforesaid, and no goods or chattels of such person or persons so offending can at the time of such conviction be found, then and in such case it shall and may be lawful to and for the Lord Mayor or Justices of the Peace before whom such person or persons shall be convicted as aforesaid, to commit such offender or offenders to the House of Correction, there to be kept to hard labour for any time not exceeding the space of three months, or until such pecuniary penalty or penalties shall be paid. *Lord Mayor, or Justices of Peace, are to try Offences against this Act ; and to levy Penalties by Distress,*

Provided nevertheless, That it shall and may be lawful to and for such Lord Mayor, or Justices of the Peace, from time to time (where they see cause) to mitigate, compound or lessen, any of the said forfeitures or penalties as he or they in their discretion shall think fit (so as such mitigation do not extend to remit above one moiety of the penalty or penalties inflicted and directed to be levied by this Act), and every such mitigation shall be a sufficient discharge to the person offending respectively, for so much of the said penalty or forfeiture as shall be so lessened, mitigated or remitted. *or mitigate them.*

Provided also, That if any person or persons shall find him her or themselves aggrieved, or remain unsatisfied in the judgement of the said Lord Mayor or Justices, then such person or *Appeal from the Lord Mayor to the Justices at their Quarter Sessions.*

127.

or persons shall and may, by virtue of this Act, complain or appeal to the Justices of the Peace at the next Quarter Sessions to be held for the said city of London; who are hereby impowered and required to summon and examine witnesses upon oath, and finally to hear and determine the same; and in case of conviction, to issue a Warrant or Warrants for levying and compelling, by such means as aforesaid, the payment of the said penalties and forfeitures.

Penalties how to be applied.

And it is hereby further Enacted by the Authority aforesaid, That all the Penalties to be levied by virtue of this Act shall be paid and applied in manner following; that is to say, one moiety thereof to the person or persons who shall inform and prosecute for the same, and the other moiety to the Alderman of the Ward where such offence shall be committed, to be by him paid and applied for and towards defraying the charges and expenses of the Nightly Watch and Bedels, and other charges incident thereto within such Ward.

Deficiency in Rates, how to be supplied, &c.

Provided always, and be it further Enacted, That in case there shall be any deficiency in any one year's rate or assessment so to be made as aforesaid, in any of the Wards within the said City or Liberties thereof, either by Houses, Shops, Warehouses, Buildings or other Tenements being empty, or by the insolvency or removal of any of the Inhabitants, Tenants, Occupiers or otherwise, for which or upon whom such Rates and Assessments are respectively charged or chargeable by this Act, so that the Wages and Allowances to Watchmen and Bedels, and other incident charges, cannot be fully satisfied, paid and discharged, in that year; then and in such case the deficiency so happening in the said Ward, shall be paid out of the next succeeding years Rate and Assessment; and if there shall happen to be any surplus money collected by such Rates and Assessments as aforesaid, in any of the said Wards in any one year, such surplus shall be carried on to the credit of the Account of the next years Rate and Assessment, and shall be applied for such uses and in such manner as the Rates and Assessments collected in such Ward are by this Act directed to be laid out and applied, and to no other use or purpose whatsoever.

Houses let out in Lodgings, how to be assessed.

AND whereas many Houses in several of the Wards of the said City are, by the several Landlords or Owners thereof, let out in Lodgings or Tenements, to divers Tenants, whereby it will be difficult to rate and assess such Houses, or to recover such Rates and Assessments when made; for remedy whereof, BE it Enacted by the authority aforesaid, That from and after the twenty-fifth day of December, which shall be in the year of our Lord one thousand seven hundred and thirty-seven, it shall and may be lawful to and for the Alderman of each respective Ward, by and with the consent of his Deputy and Common Councilmen, or the major part of them, from time to time, and at all times when they are directed by the Lord Mayor, Aldermen and Commons of the said City, in Common Council assembled, to make any Rate and Assessment on the Inhabitants of their respective Wards, to rate and assess the Owner or Owners of all such Houses or Tenements as shall be let or occupied by three or more Tenants, which Rate and Assessment shall be paid by one or more of the Occupiers of any part or parts of such Houses; and in case any Occupier or Occupiers of any part of such Houses or Tenements shall refuse to pay the same, then the said Rate and Assessment shall be levied by distress and sale of the goods of him her or them so refusing to pay the same, which distress and sale shall be made in like manner as distresses and sales of the goods of other parties neglecting or refusing to pay the Rates and Assessments imposed and directed to be imposed by virtue of this Act, are directed to be made; and such Occupier and Occupiers of such Tenements are hereby required and authorized to pay such sum and sums of Money as shall be so rated, imposed or assessed on the Owner or Owners thereof, in pursuance of this Act, and to deduct the same out of the Rent thereof; and the Landlord or Owner or Owners thereof are hereby required to allow such deductions and payments upon receipt of the residue of their Rents; and every Tenant paying such Assessment or Assessments shall be acquitted and discharged for so much money as the said Assessment or Assessments shall amount unto, as if the same had been actually paid to such person or persons to whom his her or their Rent should have been due and payable.

Persons rated not liable to any Watch.

Provided always, and it is hereby Enacted and Declared, That no person or persons who shall be rated and assessed, and pay to any Rate and Assessment to be made in pursuance of this Act, shall be liable to any Watch or Ward, by virtue of the Statute commonly called the Statute of Winchester, made in the thirteenth year of King Edward the First, or any other subsequent Statutes relating thereto, but shall be and are hereby discharged of and from the same.

Act 22 & 23 Car. II.

AND whereas by an Act of Parliament made and passed in the twenty-second and twenty-third years of the reign of his late Majesty King *Charles* the Second, intituled, An Act for the better paving and cleansing the Streets and Sewers, in and about the city of London, it is enacted, (among other things) That from thenceforth the sole power and authority of ordering, designing and regulating of the pitching and paving all the Streets, Lanes and Passages whatsoever, within the said City and Liberties, with the order and manner thereof, should be and remain in the Mayor, Commonalty and Citizens of the said City, to be executed by such persons as by the said Mayor, Aldermen and Commons, in Common Council assembled, should be appointed, or by any Seven or more of them, being all Members of the said Court; and it is also thereby further enacted, that for the better enabling the said Mayor, Commonalty and Citizens to perform the works by the said Statute appointed to be done, and for defraying the charge thereof, it should be lawful for the said persons so to be authorized, or any Seven of them, as often as need should be, to impose any reasonable

Tax

Tax or Assessment, as well upon the Tenants and Occupiers as also upon the Owners of Houses, Shops or other Tenements or Hereditaments, whereof there should be no present Occupier, to be levied by distress and sale of the goods of the parties refusing or neglecting to pay, as by the said Act more fully may appear; but inasmuch as it frequently happens that no distress can be found upon Ground, Houses, Shops or Tenements, that lie vacant or untenanted, whereby the necessary Taxes or Assessments for paving the Streets, Lanes or Passages, lying before such vacant Ground, Houses, Shops or Tenements, cannot be levied, by reason whereof such part of the said Streets, Lanes and Passages, often remains unpaved, to the great nuisance of the Public; for remedy whereof, BE it Enacted by the authority aforesaid, that from and after the twenty-fourth day of June one thousand seven hundred and thirty-seven, it shall and may be lawful to and for the said persons now authorized, or hereafter to be authorized, by virtue of the said Statute as aforesaid, or any Seven or more of them, to order such parts of the respective Streets, Lanes and Passages, as lie before such vacant or untenanted Ground, Houses, Shops or Tenements, as often as need shall be, to be well and sufficiently paved, cleansed and amended, and to impose such Tax or Assessment on the Owner or Owners thereof, as shall be necessary for the doing the same; all which Taxes and Assessments shall be paid for and upon the account of such Owner or Owners thereof, by him her or them, who shall from time to time be the next and first Occupier or Occupiers of such Ground, Houses, Shops or Tenements, after the making or imposing such Tax or Assessment; and in case such Occupier or Occupiers shall refuse to pay the same, then the said Taxes and Assessments shall be levied by distress and sale of the goods and chattels of him her or them so refusing to pay the same; which distress and sale shall be made in such manner as distresses and sales thereof are directed to be made by the said Statute; and all and every such first Occupier and Occupiers are hereby required and authorized to pay such sum and sums of Money as shall be so rated, imposed or assessed on the Owner or Owners of such Ground, Houses, Shops or Tenements in pursuance of this Act, and to deduct the same out of the Rent thereof; and the Landlord or Landlords, or Owner or Owners thereof, are hereby required to allow such deductions and payments upon receipt of the residue of their Rents; and every Tenant paying such Taxes or Assessments, shall be acquitted and discharged for so much Money as the said Taxes or Assessments shall amount unto, as if the same had been actually paid to such person or persons, to whom his her or their Rent should have been due or payable.

Assessments on untenanted Grounds, &c. how to be made.

AND to the end that all and every the Pavements lying before any vacant or untenanted Ground, House, Shop or Tenement, in any of the Streets, Lanes or Passages, may from time to time be effectually amended, Be it further Enacted by the Authority aforesaid, That the Chamberlain of the said City for the time being shall pay all and every the Taxes and Assessments which shall be imposed or assessed upon the Owner or Owners of such vacant or untenanted Ground, Houses, Shops, or Tenements, during the time the same shall so continue vacant or untenanted, out of the City Cash; but in case, after such payment by the said Chamberlain, any of the said Taxes or Assessments shall be paid or levied by or upon the Tenant or Tenants thereof, who shall afterwards occupy the same, then and in every such case the same shall forthwith be repaid into the Chamber of the said City.

Taxes on vacant Grounds, &c. to be paid out of the City Cash,

and repaid by the next Occupiers.

AND whereas, from the great increase of Coaches, Carts, and other Carriages, and their frequent passing through the Streets, Lanes, and Passages of the said City, it is become necessary, for the safety and convenience of all persons passing within the said City, that Posts should be set up in many Streets, Lanes, and other Passages, where now there are none, to preserve a Foot-passage; BE it therefore Enacted by the Authority aforesaid, That from and after the twenty-fourth of day June one thousand seven hundred and thirty-seven, it shall and may be lawful for the said persons authorized, and to be authorized as aforesaid, or any Seven of them, to order, design, and set up Posts in all or any the Streets, Lanes, and Passages whatsoever, where need shall be, within the said City and Liberties, to preserve Foot-passages; which power shall be exercised in the same manner as the power vested in them by the said Statute, For the better paving and cleansing the Streets and Sewers in and about the said City; and for enabling them to execute and perform the Works last-mentioned and appointed to be done, it shall also be lawful for them, or any Seven of them, to make such Taxes and Assessments as shall be reasonable, to be charged and levied in the same manner as the other Taxes and Assessments may be and are directed to be charged and levied by the aforesaid Statute, or by so much of this present Act as relates to the paving of the said Streets, and in as full and ample manner to all intents and purposes whatsoever, as if the same was herein particularly recited.

Posts to be set up for Foot Passages.

And be it further Enacted by the Authority aforesaid, That if any Action or Suit shall be brought or commenced against any person or persons, for any matter or thing to be done in pursuance of this Act, then and in such case the Action or Suit shall be brought or commenced within six months next after the fact committed, and not afterwards; and shall be laid and brought in the city of London, and not elsewhere; and the Defendant or Defendants in such Action or Suit to be brought shall and may plead the General Issue, and give this Act and the special matter in evidence at any trial to be had thereupon; and if the Plaintiff or Plaintiffs shall become nonsuited, or discontinue his her or their Action or Actions, Suit or Suits; or if upon demurrer, judgment shall be given against the Plaintiff or Plaintiffs, the Defendant or Defendants shall and may recover Treble Costs, and have such remedy for the same as any Defendant or Defendants hath or have in any other cases by Law.

Limitation of Actions.

Treble Costs.

127.

And

Public Act.

And be it further Enacted by the authority aforesaid, That this Act shall be deemed, adjudged, and taken to be a public Act; and be judicially taken notice of as such by all Judges, Justices, and other Persons whatsoever, without specially pleading the same.

Appendix, No. 3.

Anno XXVII ELIZABETHÆ, Reginæ.

An ACT for the good Government of the City and Borough of Westminster, in the County of Middlesex.

The Preamble of the Act.

FORASMUCH as by erection and new building of divers houses, and by the parting and dividing of divers tenements within the city or borough of Westminster, and the liberties of the same, the people thereof are greatly increased, and being for the most part without trade or mystery, are become poor, and many of them wholly given to vice and idleness, living in contempt of all manner of officers within the said city, for that their power to correct and reform them is not sufficient in law, as in that behalf were meet and requisite; Be it therefore ordained by the Queen's most Excellent Majesty, the Lords Spiritual and Temporal, and the Commons, in this present Parliament assembled, and by the authority of the same, That the said city or borough of Westminster, the Liberties, Territories, and Precincts of the same, shall be, and for ever hereafter continue severed and divided, as it hath been accustomed, into Twelve several divisions, to be called or known by the names of Wards, the same to be and continue by such limits, metes, and divisions, as heretofore hath been commonly taken or known.

The City or Borough of Westminster, and Liberties thereof, shall be divided into twelve Wards.

And for the better ordering and government of the people inhabiting and being within all and every the wards aforesaid, and for repressing and rooting out of vice there used; Be it further ordained by the authority aforesaid, That the Dean of the Collegiate Church of Saint Peter's of Westminster, or his successors, or the High Steward there for the time being, or his lawful deputy, shall upon Thursday in Easter-week next after the end of this Session of Parliament, and so yearly for ever hereafter, nominate and elect Twelve sufficient persons, being merchants, artificers, or persons using any trade of buying or selling within the said city or borough, or such other persons as shall be willing thereunto and inhabiting within the said city or borough, and the liberties of the same, which shall be called by the name of Burgesses; unto the government of every which Burgesses, one of the said twelve wards shall be, by the said Dean, and High Steward, or his lawful deputy for the time being, appointed and limited; which said Twelve, and every of them, shall accept their election, and shall continue in his said room for one year next ensuing, and so from year to year during his or their natural lives, if they shall so long inhabit there, except for some offence or misgovernment by them or any of them committed; (and unless for cause reasonably proved) they shall be displaced by the Dean of Westminster or High Steward there for the time being; and if any person or persons resiant, and so nominated, shall refuse to accept the said room, he shall forfeit Ten Pounds to the use of the poor within the said city or borough of Westminster, and to be levied by the Bailiff of the liberties of the said Dean and Chapter, by way of distress, to be taken and justified to the use aforesaid; which said Twelve Burgesses, and every of them, shall receive as well the usual Oath of Supremacy, as also a corporal Oath to him to be ministred by the said High Steward, or his deputy, in open Court, to do and execute all things to them appointed and authorized by this Act.

The Dean of Westminster, or High Steward or his Deputy, shall yearly on Thursday in Easter week for ever, nominate and elect twelve persons to be Burgesses.

The qualification of the persons to be chosen Burgesses.

The Dean and High Steward, or his Deputy, shall appoint the government of a Ward to every of the twelve Burgesses.

They shall accept their election, and continue for one year, and from year to year during life.

A Burgess not to be removed but for offence or misgovernment.

The Dean or High Steward may displace a Burgess for good cause shewn.

A resiant refusing to accept the place of a Burgess shall forfeit Ten Pounds to the poor of Westminster.

The Bailiff of Westminster shall levy the forfeiture by distress.

The Burgess shall take the Oath of Supremacy, and an Oath to execute the power of this Act.

And for the more aid and assistance to perform that which by the true intent of this Statute is meant to be performed, Be it ordained by the authority of this present Parliament, That the said Dean, or his successors, or the said High Steward, or his lawful deputy, with the said twelve Burgesses, or the more part of the said Burgesses, shall within ten days after the election and choice of the said twelve Burgesses, nominate and elect twelve others, able persons, inhabiting within the said city or borough, and the liberties thereof, being merchants, artificers, or using any trade of buying or selling within the said city or borough, or any other being willing thereunto as aforesaid, to be Assistants to the said twelve Burgesses; and that they shall accept the same charge upon payment of Five Pounds, to be levied of every of them that shall refuse the said room in form aforesaid, to be employed as aforesaid, with like oaths as is aforesaid; and shall be called by the names of Assistants unto the said twelve Burgesses nominated to the aforesaid twelve wards; unto every of which said wards one of the said Assistants shall be appointed for the government of the same with the said Burgess; which said twelve Burgessess, and the said twelve Assistants, and every two of them, within the several wards to them appointed and limited, viz. every Burgess, together with his Assistant, shall and may, by virtue hereof, do and deal in every thing and things as Aldermens deputies in the city of London lawfully do or may do; and every of the said twelve Assistants shall continue in their said office for and during one whole year

The Dean, High Steward or his Deputy, with the Burgesses, shall, ten days after their election, nominate twelve to be Assistants.

The qualification of the twelve persons to be Assistants.

The Assistants shall accept the charge, on the penalty of Five Pounds.

They shall take the Oaths before mentioned, and be called Assistants to the Burgesses.

To the government of every Ward, one Assistant shall be joined to the Burgess.

Each Burgess and Assistant in his Ward, shall have the power of Aldermens Deputies in London.

The Assistants shall continue in their office one whole year if they live in Westminster or the Liberties.

then

then next ensuing, if they shall continue their habitation within the said city or borough, or liberties of the same; and if any of the said twelve Burgesses or Assistants shall happen to die, or otherwise, upon reasonable cause, to be removed or displaced from his said office, that then the said Dean or his successors, and the High Steward for the time being, or his lawful deputy, shall, from time to time, at their wills and pleasure, nominate and appoint any other meet able person or persons of like estate, faculty, and quality, as aforesaid, inhabiting within the said city or borough, and the liberties of the same, to supply the place or places of such of the said Burgesses or Assistants as shall so die, or be moved, or displaced, who shall continue in the said room until the Thursday in Easter-week then next following; and that such person or persons so nominated and elected, shall accept and exercise the same, upon pain of Five Pounds, to be levied and employed in form aforesaid, and with like oaths, as is aforesaid.

Burgesses or Assistants dying, or being removed or displaced, may be supplied by the Dean and High Steward, or his Deputy.

The person so put in, shall continue till the Thursday in Easter week next succeeding his choice; and shall accept and exercise the office, on the penalty of Five Pounds, and shall take the like Oaths as others.

And be it further Enacted by the authority aforesaid, That the said Dean and his successors, or the High Steward, or his lawful deputy, for ever hereafter yearly upon Thursday in Easter-week aforesaid, shall nominate and appoint two persons out of the twelve Burgesses, to be called and known by the name of the Two Chief Burgesses, to continue in office for one year then next following; which office they and every of them shall accept upon pain of Ten Pounds aforesaid, to be paid as aforesaid, and to be levied by way of distress to the use aforesaid, as is before limited.

The Dean and the High Steward, or his Deputy, shall every Thursday in Easter week for ever appoint two Chief Burgesses out of the twelve Burgesses. The two Chief Burgesses shall continue in their place for one year, and accept thereof, on pain of Ten Pounds to the use aforesaid.

And for due reformation of the inconveniences and disorders which shall or may happen within the said city, borough or liberties, Be it ordained by the authority of this present Parliament, That as well the said Dean, or his successors, the High Steward aforesaid, or his deputy, as also the said two chief Burgesses, the other ten Burgesses, or any four or three of them, whereof the said Dean, High Steward, or his deputy, or one of the said two chief Burgesses, to be one from time to time for ever hereafter, to be appointed during their said office, shall and may, by virtue of this Act, within the said city or borough, or the liberties thereof, hear, examine, determine, and punish, according to the laws of this Realm, or laudable and lawful custom of the city of London, all matters of incontinencies, common scolds, and of inmates, and common annoyances; and likewise that they shall have authority to commit to prison such persons as within the said city shall offend against the peace, and thereof shall give notice within four and twenty hours after to some Justices of Peace within the county of Middlesex.

The powers of the Dean, High Steward or his Deputy, and the two Chief Burgesses, with the other ten Burgesses;

To hear, examine, determine and punish, according to the laws or the customs of London, incontinencies, common scolds, inmates, and common annoyances.
They may commit to prison such as offend against the peace, but to give notice to some Justice of Middlesex, in twenty-four hours.

And be it further Enacted by the authority aforesaid, That all good Orders and Ordinances to be made by the said Dean and High Steward, with the assent of the Burgesses and Assistants for the time being, or the more part of them, for or concerning the government of the said inhabitants, not repugnant to the Queen's Majesty's prerogative, nor the laws and statutes of this Realm, shall, by virtue of this Act, stand in full force and strength.

All Ordinances to be made for the government of the inhabitants, not repugnant to the prerogative of the Crown, or the laws of the Realm, shall be of force.

Provided, that this Act, or any thing therein contained, shall not be prejudicial to the Steward, Marshal, or Coroner of the Queen's Majesty's Household, nor to the authority of Justices of Peace within the county of Middlesex, nor to the Dean and Chapter of Westminster, or their successors, nor to the High Steward there, or his deputy for the time being, nor to the Mayor, Society, and Clerk of the Staple, High Constable, Bailiff of the Liberty, Town Clerks, nor to the Clerk of the Market, nor to any search to be made by any other officer in the said city or borough of Westminster now being, or that at any time hereafter shall be, not being contrary to the true meaning of this present Act.

The Act shall not prejudice the Marshal of the Queen's Household, nor the Steward or Coroner thereof; nor the authority of Justices of Peace of Middlesex; nor the Dean of Westminster; nor the High Steward or his Deputy; nor the Mayor and Clerk of the Staple, High Constable, Bailiff of the Liberty, Town Clerks, nor Clerk of the Market. The Act shall not prejudice no search to be made by any Officer in Westminster, not contrary to the Act.

And be it Declared by the authority of this Act, That they and every of them, their deputies and assigns, shall and may have, take and enjoy all the privileges, authorities, benefits and profits, unto them or their said office belonging, from time to time, for ever hereafter in as ample wise, as they or any of them have had, taken and enjoyed the same at any time heretofore, not being contrary to the true meaning of this present Act.

The Officers before mentioned, and their deputies, may enjoy all their rights in as ample manner as heretofore, if the same be not contrary to this Act.

Provided always, That if it shall happen at any time hereafter, that the Dean of Westminster aforesaid, or his successors, and the said High Steward for the time being, and his lawful deputy, and every of them, be remiss or negligent in choosing and nominating of the Burgesses aforesaid, at the time before limited, that then it shall and may be lawful for two Justices of Peace within the county of Middlesex, whereof one to be of the Quorum, to nominate and choose the said Burgesses, being such persons as aforesaid; who being so nominated and chosen by the said Justices, shall occupy and enjoy the said rooms, upon the pains aforesaid, and have and enjoy such liberties in all respects, as if they had been nominated and chosen by the said Dean and High Steward as aforesaid.

If the Dean, &c. be remiss in choosing Burgesses, two Justices of Middlesex may choose them.

Burgesses chosen by Justices, shall have such liberties as those chosen by the Dean, &c.

Provided also, That all such Burgesses as aforesaid, which hereafter shall be chosen as aforesaid, to serve in any of the said rooms or places, shall not be compellable by this Act to remain in the said office or room above the space of one whole year next after such choice or election; and all such persons as shall for refusal of any of the said offices, pay any the sums aforesaid, shall not be

Burgesses chosen in the rooms of others, shall not be compelled to serve more than one year.

Persons refusing to be Burgesses, and paying the sums therefore imposed, shall not be nominated in five years.

be nominated again to any of the said places within the space of five years then next following.

The Dutchy of Lancaster.

And forasmuch as there be divers houses, tenements and buildings within the liberties of the Dutchy of Lancaster, of the which said houses, tenements and buildings there are certain which are lying and being within the city or borough of Westminster, and divers of the same are next adjoining to the said city or borough, and yet the inhabitants within the said liberties of the said Dutchy are not subject to the government or jurisdiction of Westminster, but have liberties and franchises distinct and divided by themselves: And to the intent that one uniform government may be in both the said Liberties of Westminster and the Dutchy in the places aforesaid; Be it Enacted by the Authority of this present Parliament, That the Chancellor or Steward of the Dutchy for the time being, shall have the like power and authority by virtue of this Act in all things, as the Dean of Westminster, and the High Steward of the same have by virtue of this Act, for the better government of the inhabitants within the liberties of the said Dutchy, being and next adjoining to Westminster as is aforesaid.

The Chancellor or Steward of the Dutchy of Lancaster shall have like power as the Dean of Westminster, &c. within the Dutchy Liberty.

The Act not to extend to the College or Close of Westminster, for any offence within the circuit thereof.

Provided always, that this Act, or any thing or matter therein contained, shall not extend to the Church or College of Westminster, nor to the Close of Westminster, nor to any person or persons inhabiting within the site, circuit, or precinct of the said Church, College or Close, for any offence or misgovernment to be committed by them or any of them within the site, circuit, or precinct of the said Church, College, or Close, or city or borough of Westminster; and that this Act, nor any thing therein contained, shall extend to give any authority, jurisdiction, or power to the said Burgesses, to hear, examine, and determine any thing by virtue of this Act, without the consent of the said Dean, or of the said High Steward, or his lawful deputy, or in the absence of the said Dean, High Steward, or his lawful deputy, then with the only presence and consent of the Town Clerk there for the time being, and not otherwise.

The Burgesses shall not hear or determine any thing without the Dean, or High Steward or his Deputy or the Town Clerk in their absence.

And that this Act to continue unto the end of the Parliament next following.

The Searcher of the Sanctuary shall have execution of process within the Sanctuary, as he might do before the making this Act.

Provided also, That the Searcher for the time being of the Sanctuary of Westminster, shall have and enjoy within the Sanctuary of Westminster, the execution and serving of all process, commandments, and warrants, and the attachments, and apprehensions of all manner of offenders within the Sanctuary aforesaid, and within the site, circuit, and precinct thereof, in as ample manner and form as if this Act had never been had or made.

Civitas sive Burg. Westm. 27th Eliz. 1585.

Certain ORDERS and ORDINANCES* made the 27th day of May in the 27th year of the reign of our Soveraigne Lady Elizabetha, &c. by the Right Honorable Sir William Cecill, of the Most noble Order of the Garter, Knight, and Baron of Burleigh, Lord Treasurer of England, and High Steward of the City and Burrough of Westminster; and the Right Worshipful Mr. Gabriel Goodman, Doctor of Divinity, Dean of the Collegiate Church of St. Peter's in Westminster aforesaid; with the assents of Thomas Fowler and John Fisher, then being Chief Burgesses of the said City or Burrough; and alsoe with the like assents of the other Ten Burgesses; and alsoe with assents of their Assistants, according to the Statute lately made and provided for the good government of the said City or Burrow of Westminster: —Viz.

Inmates.

1. Item, That all and every person or persons which at this present have dwelling or inhabiting within any his her or their house or houses, or in any part or parcel thereof, any inmates or under-tenants, the said inmates or under-tenants and every of them shall avoid and quietly depart from every such house and houses at or before the feast day of St. Michaell the Archangell next ensuing, upon pain, that every person and persons that shall keep or suffer any such inmate or under-tenant to inhabit or dwell in any his her or their house or houses after the said feast day, shall forfeit and pay for every week offending, touching the premises, ten shillings.

Unlawful Weights and Measures.

2. Item, If any person or persons useing the trade of buying and selling any victuals or wares by any weights or measures, and shall be found to have at any time hereafter, either false or unlawfull ballance, or false or unlawfull weights or measures, against the laws and statutes of this Realm, the same shall then by the officer finding the same be defaced; and the owner thereof shall be committed to prison, there to remaine by the space of twenty-four hours, and to pay for every time soe offending twenty shillings.

3. Item, If any Baker or Brewer shall put to sale any bread beer or ale within the said City or Burrough, not being lawful or good, or wanting in weight, or in assige contrary to the weight and assize therein commonly used and allowed within the city of London, that then every such Baker or Brewer shall receive and have such condigne punishment and such

---

* It is hoped that the House will excuse the length of the following Ordinances, as they are extremely descriptive of the plain simplicity and integrity of our Ancestors, as well as capable of affording much useful information for the present time.

such fine and amerciament as shall be assessed for every time soe offending, according to the laws and statutes of this Realme, and alsoe according to the custom used within the city of London in those cases from time to time.

Amerciament, according to the City of London.

4. Item, If any Collier shall put to sale any coals in sacks, and the same sacks not being lawfull, or if his sack or sacks should be found to be lawfull, and not being filled with coals accordingly, that then every such Collier, for every such time soe offending shall be committed to prison, there to remain by the space of twenty-four hours; and all his defective and unlawfull sacks shall be burned in the market place, and to receive for every time soe offending such further punishment as is used within the city of London.

Colliers.

Punishment is 24 hours imprisonment, and his sacks to be burnt.

5. Item, If any Woodmonger or Bargeman shall put to sale any kind of wood or fuell within this said City or Burrough, and the said wood wanting of the assige allowed by the Statute, that then every such Woodmonger and Bargeman shall receive and have such condign punishment, and pay such fine for every time so offending, as by the Statute and the custume of the city of London in these cases are lawfully used.

Woodmonger and Bargeman.

According to the custume of London.

6. Item, That the Burgesses and their Assistants of the City or Burrough, and every of them, according to their severall divisions, shall, every Saturday during all the time of the market, attend and peruse the same, and then and there to take diligent care and heed, that the Queen's Majestie's people may well and duely be served of all such victuals as they and every of them shall buy in the said market; and if any of the said Burgesses or Assistants shall make default in not performing the premises, that then he soe offending shall forfeit and pay for every time soe offending, without just cause or lawful lett xijd.

Burgesses and Assistants.

7. Item, If any person or persons shall receive or take into his or her service any servant without a lawfull testimoniall in writing, or that shall put away such servant without giving to him or her lawfull warning, according to the Statute, that then every such person offending herein shall forfeit and pay, for every time so offending herein, as by the Statute is provided; and alsoe, if any servant shall depart from the service of his or her master or mistress, without just cause or giving lawfull warning, or not having a lawfull testimoniall, shall then be punished according to the said Statute.

Servants Testimoniall.

Warning.

8. Item, If any person or persons shall at any time hereafter forestall, regrate or ingrosse any victuals, or any kind of fuell, either in the market, or being brought towards the same, that then every such offender shall receive and have such condign punishment as by the Statute in that case is made and provided.

Regrators.

9. Item, If any Butcher or any other person or persons shall cast or lay any thing into any common sewer, which may be to the decay or hurt of the same, or that shall cast or lay any noisome thing or things into any common street, to the annoyance of any of the Queen's Majestie's people, that then every such person for every time offending in any of the premises, shall be committed to prison, and there to remain by the space of twenty-four hours together.

Laying of Soyle in the Common Sewer or Street.

10. Item, That noe person or persons that now keepeth or that hereafter shall keep any cooke's shop, shall alsoe, keep a common alehouse (except every such person shall be lawfully licensed thereunto) upon pain to have and receive such punishment, and to pay such fine, as by the Statute in that case is provided.

Cookes.

11. Item, It is alsoe ordered, That from the feast of Saint Michaell the Archangell next ensuing, there shall be within the said City or Burrough the number of one hundred common alehouses, and noe more at any one time; viz. in the parish of St. Margarett's sixty, in the parish of St. Martin's-in-the-Fields twenty, and in the parish of St. Clements and Savoy or Strand, within the liberties of Westminster, twenty.

Victuallers 100, and noe more. [At present there are upwards of 1,200.]

12. Item, If any cause of variance shall happen to be ministred between any the neighbours of this City or Burrough, upon any uncharitable speeches, or other annoyances, that then the party grieved shall make his or her complaint to the Burgess or his Assistant of the same ward, and not to commence any action or suite in law for any such cause, without the lycence of the said Burgess and his Assistant, upon payne of imprisonment.

Controversies.

None to commence actions, or to arrest without leave.

13. Item, That every Burgess and their Assistants, and all and every other person and persons, using any trade of victualling or keeping any common alehouse, shall yearly and every year hereafter, from the feast of All Saints untill the feast of the Purification of the Blessed Virgin Mary, find and keep one convenient Lanthorne, with a candle being light in the same, in the street, at every their street-doors, viz. from six of the clock in afternoon untill nine of the clock then next following, every night nightly (except those nights as the moon shall then and at that time shine and give light) upon paine to forfeit and pay for every time offending herein four pence.

Lanthorne and candle light.

14. Item, That all other the inhabitants of the City or Burrough shall find the like Lanthorne and candle-light, in manner and form as aforesaid, and as they and every of them from time to time shall be assessed by the Burgess and Assistant of that ward where any of the said inhabitants shall then dwell, upon pain to forfeit and pay for every time offending therein four-pence.

Lanthorne light.

15. Item, That noe Tavern-keeper or Inn-keeper shall keep any cookes-shop, upon pain to forfeit and pay, for every day offending herein, two shillings.

Vintner and Inn-keeper.

127.

16. Item,

Offenders punished.

16. Item, That if any person or persons after he she or they shall happen to be punished and banished from this City or Burrough, for any incontinency of life or such like, and shall return againe to the City or Burrough, to the intent there to inhabit and dwell, that then every such person and persons shall be whipped naked at a cart's tayle throughout the said city, for every time so offending contrary to this order.

Rogues and sturdy Beggars.

17. Item, If any constable or constables shall willingly permitt and suffer any rogue or rogues or sturdy beggar to wander in the streets, and doe not apprehend them, according to the Statute, that then every such constable shall forfeit and pay six shillings and eight-pence.

Tenants to bring tes-timoniall.

18. Item, That noe person or persons shall accept or take any tenants into any his or her messuage tenement or cottage within this City or Burrough, except every such tenant doe first bring with him or her a sufficient and lawfull testimoniall in writing, touching every such persons good behaviour and conversation of life from the place of his or her last abode, and the same party shall deliver the said testimoniall to the Burgess and Assistant of the same ward ; and alsoe that every such tenant shall live by some lawfull science or manuall occupation ; and if any person or persons shall accept and take any other tenant, contrary to this order, that then he or she for every time soe offending shall forfeit and pay forty shillings.

Keeping clean with water the Streets.

19. Item, That the inhabitants of the City or Burrough, yearly and every year hereafter, from the feast-day of the Annuntiation of the Blessed Virgin Mary untill the feast-day of Saint Michaell the Archangell, viz. every day at six or seven of the clock in the forenoon, shall, either by themselves or some others, with clean water, wash and sweep the kennels and gutters near unto every of their dwelling-house, upon paine to forfeit and pay, for every day making default, four-pence.

Laying of Soyle.

20. Item, That no person or persons shall cast or lay any soile or things noisome, either in the Old Palace, or near unto Henry the Seventh his Chappell, or in any church-yard, upon payne to forfeit for every time offending in any the premises four-pence.

Scavengers.

21. Item, That the scavengers or carter shall well and duely make clean and carry away the soyle of the streets upon every such day, and in such convenient order, as it hath here-tofore been lawfully used and accustomed, upon paine of imprisonment, and there to remaine during the space of twenty-four hours, for every time offending in this order.

Keeping clean the Streets.

22. Item, That no person or persons upon the same day after that the scavenger or carter shall have made clean any street as aforesaid, shall cast or lay any soile or sweeping of any house, or other rubbish, or make any heaps of such like things in the same street, and especially upon any Saturday or Sunday, upon paine to pay for every time four-pence.

Keeper of the Queen's Bridge Watergate.

23. Item, That the Gate which leadeth to and from her Majesties bridge in Old Palace, shall be kept locked during the time of Divine Service, every sabbath day and other usuall holy daies, upon paine that the Keeper thereof shall forfeit for every time offending contrary to this order, twelve-pence.

Hoggs, Tuthill.

24. Item, If any hogg or hoggs shall at any time be found upon the Common of Tuthill, and not being ringed or pegged, or shall be found wandering in any street or church-yard, that the owner of every such hogg shall forfeit and pay for every such hogg, and for every time offending in any of the premisses, twelve-pence.

Soyle, Sand, Turf.

25. Item, That no person or persons shall cast or lay the soyle of the streets, or any other noisome thing or things whatsoever, in or upon any part of the Common of Tuthill, but onely in such place or places, and in such convenient order as from time to time shall be appointed by the two Chief Burgesses for the time being; nor that any person or persons shall digg or take away any sand or turfes of and from the said Common of Tuthill, without the lawful lycence of the Dean of Westminster, or his Officers, upon payne that every person that shall happen to offend in any of the premisses, and for every time offending shall be committed to prison, and there to remaine for the space of twenty-four hours, and to pay such fine as shall be assessed by the Burgesses*.

Butchers, Poulterers, Fishmongers.

26. Item, That if any Butcher, Poulterer, Fishmonger, or any other person or persons, shall put to sale within this City or Burrough, any corrupt or unlawful flesh or fish meat or poultry ware, that then the said corrupt and unwholesome meat shall be consumed with fire, or otherwise by the discretion of the Burgesses and Assistants with the consent of the Searchers ; and the owner thereof shall be committed to prison, and there to remain for the space of twenty-four hours for every time soe offending, and to pay such fine as shall be assessed by the Burgesses.

Butchers.

27. Item, If any Butcher shall put any flesh meat to sale in the market upon any market day, and having his shopp in King-street, that then every such Butcher shall forfeit and pay for every time soe offending three shillings and four-pence.

28. Item,

---

* Many of these Regulations are become impracticable, and others unnecessary ; but that above is extremely wanted at this moment, from the pernicious custom of laying all the filth of the Town in a place so well inhabited.

28. Item, That no Butcher, or any other person or persons, shall put to sale any flesh-meat in the market, but only upon Saturday in the forenoon, viz. untill twelve of the clock at noon, according to custom used within the city of London, upon payne to forfeit and pay for every time offending herein, three shillings and four-pence. *Butchers.*

29. Item, If any Butcher, or any other person or persons, shall put to sale any veal, mutton or lamb, wherein shall be used any indirect or deceitful dealing, contrary to the orders therein taken amongst the Butchers of London, or that shall put to sale the flesh of any ewe or lamb at any time or season contrary to the said orders, or that shall kill any kind of flesh meat in any place within this city, contrary to the said orders and custome of the city of London, that then every such person offending in any of the premisses, shall forfeit and pay for every time offending in this order, or any part or parcell thereof, three shillings and four pence. *Butchers.*

30. Item, That no Butcher or Butchers, or other person, shall scald any hoggs in any place contrary to the orders and custome aforesaid, nor shall put to sale any pork at any time or season contrary to the custome of the said city of London, upon payne to forfeit and pay for every time offending in any of the premisses three shillings and four pence. *Butchers, for scalding hoggs,*

31. Item, That no Butcher, Poulterer, Fishmonger, or any other person or persons using the trade of selling and uttering of victualls or wares whatsoever, shall have his or their shopp window or windowes open upon any Sabbath-day, or upon other usuall holyday, or that shall make any open shew of any victuals or wares without his or their shopp or shopps upon any the daies aforesaid; or that if any Butcher or Poulterer make open shew of any flesh meat or poultry-ware upon any other fasting daies, contrary to the custom lawfully used within the city of London, that then every person offending in any of the premisses, shall forfeit and pay for every time offending in any part of this order three shillings and four pence. *Butchers, Poulterers, Fishmongers.*

32. Item, To avoid all such abuses as may be committed by the said Butchers and others, there shall be chosen and sworn at the Leet Court next after Easter yearly, and every year hereafter, three discreet persons haveing skill and knowledge in the said occupation, and shall be called by the name of Searchers, who upon their oaths shall be authorized to sarch the butchers meat and poultry wares, as well in the Butchers and Poulterers shops as in the market, upon market daies, and others bringing any kind of victualls to the said market; and that the Searchers may doe and deal as the Searchers in London are authorized touching the premisses; and if any person being appointed to the said office of Searcher, and shall refuse to serve the same by the space of one whole year, every such person soe refusing shall pay for his time twenty shillings. *Searchers and Over-seers.* *Leet Court.*

33. Item, That no person or persons shall receive or take into his or her house, any sick person being infected with the plague, without the consent of the Burgess and Assistant of that Ward; and if any persons shall happen to be sick of the said infirmity, that then as well the owner of every such house as his and her houshold and family, shall forbear to come amongst any other company, but to keep themselves within every such houses being infected as aforesaid, by the space of one and twenty daies next after the death of any such infected person, (except one person to fetch necessary provision for their reliefe) and not to hang or lay forth any infected clothes out of any such house during the time aforesaid, upon paine of open imprisonment in the Stocks by the space of twelve hours, and to receive further punishment by the discretion of the Burgesses and Assistants. *Plague.*

34. Item, The Burgesses and Assistants shall, in convenient order every Sabbath Day in the forenoon come to the Collegiate Church of St. Peter in Westminster, and there to be present all the time of the sermon, upon paine every one of them for every time makeing default without just cause shall forfeit and pay fourpence. *Burgesses and Assistants, for comeing church.*

35. Item, All the said Burgesses and their Assistants shall repair and come to the Court House in Westminster every Tuesday (except the same shall be a holiday) viz. in the term time at one of the o'clock in the afternoone; and out of the term, at eight of the clock in the forenoon, and then and there to hear and examine such causes as they, by virtue of the said Statute be lawfully authorised, upon paine, that if any of the said Burgesses or Assistants makeing default in not appearing at the houses and places appointed, shall forfeit and pay for every time soe offending without just cause or lawfull lett twelve-pence; and that they nor any of them shall at any time determine any thing without the consent of the Dean of Westminster, or the High Steward or his Deputy Steward, or the Town Clerk, according to the Statute in that case provided. *Burgesses and Assistants, their Court daies.* *Dean, Steward, Town Clerke.*

Appendix,

Appendix, No. 4.

ANNO DECIMO QUARTO, GEORGII III. REGIS, Cap. XC.

EXTRACTS from 14 Geo. III. Cap. 90, intituled " An ACT for the better Regugulation of the Nightly Watch and Beadles within the City and Liberty of Westminster and Parts adjacent; and for other Purposes therein mentioned."—1802.

Trustees, Directors, &c. to set up substantial Watchboxes.

AND be it further Enacted by the authority aforesaid, That it shall and may be lawful to and for the said Vestries, Trustees, Directors or Governors of the Watch, Governors and Directors of the Poor and other persons chosen and to be chosen as aforesaid, within their several and respective Parishes, Liberty, Precinct and Places respectively, from time to time, to set or fix up and place a sufficient number of substantial Watchboxes, at and in such convenient parts of each of their said several and respective Parishes, Liberty, Precinct and Places, as they or the majority of so many of them as shall be assembled at any of their public Meetings respectively, shall judge necessary or convenient; which Watchboxes so set or fixed up and placed, or any of them, shall not be taken down or removed by any person or persons on any pretence whatever, without the order or consent of the said Vestries, Trustees, Directors or Governors of the Watch, or Governors or Directors of the Poor, or the majority of so many of them as shall be assembled at some such public meeting.

Penalty, if any Person destroy the Watchboxes, not exceeding 20s.

And be it Enacted by the authority aforesaid, That if any person or persons shall wilfully break, take down or remove, damage or destroy any or either of such Watchboxes, every person so offending, being thereof convicted upon the oath or oaths of one or more credible witnesses or witnesses, or upon his her or their own confession, before any one or more of His Majesty's Justices of the Peace for the County of Middlesex, or the City and Liberty of Westminster, as the case may be, (which oath such Justice and Justices is and are hereby authorized and impowered to administer), shall, for every such offence forfeit and pay any sum not exceeding twenty shillings, over and above the necessary charges of replacing, repairing or making good such Watchbox or Watchboxes, or any damage done

besides the charge of replacing them.

thereto, together also with all such necessary charges as aforesaid, to be ascertained before such Justice or Justices, in such manner as he or they shall think fit, and in his or their discretion in that behalf require.

First Meeting of the Trustees for the several Parishes where to be held; who are to appoint a sufficient number of Watchmen for the year ensuing, under the following Restrictions;

And be it further Enacted by the authority aforesaid, That the Trustees to be nominated and chosen in and for the said Parish of Saint Mary le Strand, and the said Precinct of the Savoy, shall severally assemble and meet together at the several usual places of meeting for transacting the public business of the said Parish and Precinct; and every of them respectively shall then and there appoint what number of Watchmen they shall judge necessary to be kept and employed in each and every of their said Parishes, Liberty, Precinct and Places for the year then next ensuing, specifying particularly how many of such Watchmen are to have certain beats and stands, and at what places, and how many of them are to patrol and have no certain stands, under the following restrictions and limitations; (that is to say), in the said united Parishes of Saint Margaret and Saint John the Evangelist, the number of Watchmen having beats and stands, to be forty or more, and the Watchmen to patrol to be six at the least; and in and for the said Parish of Saint Martin in the Fields, the Watchmen to have stands and beats to be forty or more, and the Watchmen to patrol to be six at the least; in the said Parish of Saint James, the Watchmen to have stands and beats to be fifty or more, and the Watchmen to patrol to be eight at the least; in the said Parish of Saint George Hanover Square, the Watchmen to have stands or beats to be sixty or more, and the Watchmen to patrol to be eight at the least; in the said Parish of Saint Anne, the Watchmen to have stands and beats to be twenty or more, and the Watchmen to patrol to be four at the least; in the said Parish of Saint Paul Covent Garden, the Watchmen to have stands and beats to be eighteen or more, and the Watchmen to patrol to be four at the least; in the Parish of Saint Clement Danes, as well within as without the Liberties of the said City, the Watchmen to have stands or beats to be twenty or more, and the Watchmen to patrol to be five at the least; in the said Parish of Saint Mary le Strand, as well within as without the Liberties of the said City, the Watchmen to have stands and beats to be not less than two and one to patrol; and in the said Precinct of the Savoy, to be one Watchman; in the said united Parishes of Saint Giles in the Fields and Saint George Bloomsbury, the Watchmen to have stands and beats to be thirty or more, and the Watchmen to patrol to be six at the least; in the said united Parishes of Saint Andrew Holborn above the Bars, and Saint George the Martyr, the Watchmen to have stands and beats to be thirty or more, and the Watchmen to patrol to be six at the least; and in the said Liberty of Saffron Hill, Hatton Garden, and Ely Rents, the Watchmen to have stands and beats to be twelve or more, and the Watchmen to patrol to be two at the least; and the said Trustees, Vestries, and other persons so met, shall then and there direct and set down in writing at what places particularly the stands or Watchboxes shall be fixed or put, and the

extents

extents, limits or boundaries of the several beats of every such Watchmen and Patroles; and shall also then and there, or at some other meeting of the said Truftees, Vestries, or other persons, to be held within fourteen days then next following, nominate and appoint such number of Beadles as shall be kept within each of the said Parishes, Liberty, Precinct and Places, in proportion to the extent of each respective Parish, Liberty, Precinct or Place, and to the monies which can be raised therein by the Rates to be made pursuant to the directions of the said former Acts and of this Act; and shall also nominate and chuse such honest and able-bodied men to be employed in the offices of Beadles and Watchmen, as they shall find best qualified for the same; and also shall and may order what wages and allowances are to be paid and given to the said Beadles and to the said Watchmen respectively, as well Patroles as others, for their services and attendances, under and subject nevertheless to the limitations and restrictions hereinafter expressed and directed; and also may and shall order and direct what Pound Rate shall be made for defraying the charges and expences of such Nightly Watch and Beadles.

Provided nevertheless, and it is hereby Enacted and Declared, That the wages of every Watchman appointed to patrol as aforesaid, shall not be less than one shilling and three pence per night, during such time as he shall be employed, and that the wages of every Watchman who shall be appointed to a stand or beat, shall be regulated, so that such wages shall not be less than eighteen pounds five shillings in every year; and that the wages of any of such Watchmen shall not be more than four weeks in arrear at any one time.

Proviso for appointing the Wages of Watchmen.

Provided also, and be it Enacted by the Authority aforesaid, That no such Assessment or Assessments to be made in any one year shall exceed sixpence in the pound, of the yearly value of the houses, tenements, shops, warehouses, cellars, or other buildings, to be assessed and charged by virtue of any of the said former Acts, or of this Act.

No assessment to exceed 6d. per Pound in one year.

And be it further Enacted by the Authority aforesaid, That each of the said Watchmen as well those who shall be appointed to patrol as those who fhall have ftands and beats, shall be furnished with a Rattle, and such other accommodations, and shall be armed with a Staff, or such other weapons, or arms, to be provided at the expence of each of the said parishes, liberty, precinct and places, as the said Vestries, Trustees, or other persons authorized to put this Act, or the said former Acts, in execution, shall direct; and that each Watchman to be appointed to a stand or beat shall provide himself a Lanthorn, to be numbered in such part and manner as from the light within may most effectually tend to make such number distinguishable in the night-time; and that each and every such Watchman, being appointed to a beat or stand, shall be and appear at his stand every night before the hour of ten, or such earlier hour as the said Vestries, Trustees, Governors or Directors shall order, direct and appoint; and shall keep watch at his stand or in his beat or round from the said hour of ten, or such earlier hour as shall be so appointed as aforesaid, until five in the morning during all the months of May, June, July, and August, and from ten or such earlier hour as shall be so appointed as aforesaid, in the evening, until six in the morning, during all the months of September, October, March, and April, and from the hour of ten in the evening or such earlier hour as shall be so appointed as aforesaid, until seven in the morning during all the months of November, December, January and February; and every such Watchman shall appear and be at the Watchhouse belonging to each respective Parish, Liberty, Precinct and Place at least half an hour before he is to be at his stand, to receive his Rattle and Arms, or other accommodations, and shall return to the Watchhouse next morning, when the time for his keeping watch is expired, to the end that both at night and morning his name may be called over, and the condition of his Arms, Rattle and Lanthorn, may be examined by the Constable or Beadle of the Watch or other person to be appointed for that purpose; and that each and every the Watchmen who shall be appointed to patrol, shall appear at and shall set out from the Watchhouse of the Parish, Precinct or Place in and for which he is employed in the evening of the first day of October and every evening afterwards, until and upon the last day of April in every year, at eleven of the clock, and shall (not singly, but two together, and not more) patrol the whole of the said Parish, Liberty, Precinct, or Place, or such parts or divisions thereof as shall be directed and appointed in each respective Parish, Liberty, or Place, where two or more Patroles are directed continually from that hour, until six of the clock in the morning, during the whole of the several months of December, January and February, and until five of the clock in the morning during the several months of October, November, March and April, and until four of the clock in the morning during all or so much of the other months as such Patrol Watchmen respectively shall be employed.

Watchmen how to be armed and accommodated;

and the time when they are to do duty.

And be it Enacted by the Authority aforesaid, That the Watchmen appointed to patrol the said Parish of Saint Mary le Strand, shall in company, and together with one of the Watchmen appointed to patrol the faid Parish of Saint Clement Danes, patrol the whole of said Parish of Saint Mary le Strand, and the Precinct of the Savoy, and such part of the said Parish of Saint Clement Danes as lies westward of the said Parish of Saint Mary le Strand, and of the said Precinct of the Savoy; and that the Trustees for the Watch to be nominated and chosen for the said Precinct of the Savoy shall, and they are hereby authorized, directed and required from time to time, to bear and pay to the Directors or Governors of the Nightly Watch and Beadles of the said Parish of Saint Clement Danes for

Patrols appointed;

and Payments, how to be made

the

the time being, or to such person as shall be by them appointed to receive the same, one-fifth part of the wages and charges of such Watchman of the said Parish of Saint Clement Danes, so to patrol in company with the Watchman of the Parish of Saint Mary le Strand, and shall also pay to the Truftees for the Watch to be nominated and chosen for the said Parish of Saint Mary le Strand, or to such person as they shall appoint to receive the same, one-fifth part of the wages and charges of such Watchman, so to patrol in company with the Watchman of the said Parish of Saint Clement Danes.

When the Patrol Watchmen are to be employed.

Provided, and it is hereby Declared, That the said Vestries, Trustees, or other persons, or any of them, are not required, nor shall be compellable to employ any such Patrol Watchman for any other parts of any year than during the several months of October, November, December, January, February, March and April, and within the said Liberty of Saffron Hill, Hatton Garden and Ely Rents, during the several months of November, December, January and February only.

£. 5. penalty for assaulting a Watchman.

And be it further Enacted, That if any person or persons shall assault or resist any Watchman whilst in the execution of his office, or shall promote or encourage the same, every such person shall, for every such offence, forfeit and pay any sum not exceeding Five Pounds.

Constables duty.

And be it further Enacted by the Authority aforesaid, That the Constables appointed and to be appointed in and for the said Parishes of Saint Clement Danes and Saint Mary le Strand, shall watch in the Watchhouses of the said Parishes, as well within as without the limits of the Duchy of Lancaster, alternately and by turns, in a rotation to be settled by the said Directors or Governors of the Watch for the said Parish of Saint Clement Danes, and the Trustees to be chosen in and for the Parish of Saint Mary le Strand as aforesaid, jointly, at some meeting of the said Directors or Governors and Trustees, to be held for the purposes of this Act, and as if such Constables were or had been chosen Constables for all parts of both the said Parishes; and all and every such Constables in the said Watchhouses and in each and every other of the Parishes, Precincts and Places subjected to the powers of this Act, (the Precinct of the Savoy only excepted), each and every of the Constables and Headboroughs shall watch in the Watchhouse of the Parish, Liberty, Precinct or Place in and for which he shall serve as Constable or Headborough, alternately and by turns, in a rotation to be settled and ascertained by the said Vestries, Trustees, or other persons aforesaid, and shall continue so to do throughout the year, during all the hours herein and hereby appointed, for the Watchmen having stands or beats to watch and continue on duty; and shall take charge and dispose of according to Law, all such persons as shall be brought before such Constables or Headboroughs by any of the Watchmen or Beadles, in manner herein and hereby directed.

List of the Constables to be given to the Clerk of each Parish; also to Magistrates.

AND for the more easy ascertaining and settling the rotation or turns in which such Constables and Headboroughs are to watch as aforesaid, BE it Enacted, That the High Constable for the City and Liberty of Westminster for the time being, and the High Constable for Holborn Division in the County of Middlesex, for the time being, shall, and they are hereby required, within four days next after the appointment of Constables and Headboroughs in and for the several Parishes, Liberty, Precinct and Places, respectively included in this Act, within their respective Districts, to make and return to the Vestry Clerk of each of the said Parishes, Liberty, Precinct and Places, a true List of the Constables and Headboroughs so appointed for such Parish, Liberty, Precinct or Place respectively.

Watchman's Duty.

And be it further Enacted by the Authority aforesaid, That every Watchman (other than and except such as are appointed to patrol) shall, every night, twice in every hour, during his whole time of watching, go round his walk or beat and loudly and as audibly as he can, call or proclaim the time of the night or morning, and every such Watchmen, and every other Watchman appointed to patrol as aforesaid, shall carefully observe and try whether the houses, shops, warehouses, or other buildings in his respective beat or walk, are safe and well secured; and in case he shall discover and perceive that any doors, shutters, windows, or other parts of any such house, shop, warehouse, or building shall not be shut and fastened, he shall forthwith give notice thereof to the occupier, or other person or persons inhabiting or being therein, to the end every such door, shutter, window, or other part of such building may be properly secured, and shall give his best assistance in or toward securing the same; and each of the said Watchmen, as well Patroles as others, and every Beadle shall during his respective time of watching, to the utmost of his power, endeavour to prevent, as well all mischiefs happening by fire, as all murders, burglaries, robberies, affrays, and other outrages and disorders; and to that end, during the time of watching, each and every of them shall and may, and is hereby authorized and empowered to arrest and apprehend all Night-walkers, Malefactors, Rogues, Vagabonds, and other loose, idle and disorderly persons whom he shall find within his beat or walk, or within any part of such Parish, Liberty, Precinct, or Place, for which he shall be Watchman, Patrolman, or Beadle, disturbing the public peace, or that he shall have cause to suspect of any evil designs, and all persons lying or loitering in any square, street, court, lane, mews, yard, alley, passage or place; and to deliver the person or persons so apprehended, as soon as conveniently may be, to the Constable or Headborough of the Night, at the Watch-house, in order that such person

or

or persons may be there, or in some proper place of safety secured and detained, until he she or they can be conveniently conveyed before some or one of His Majesty's Justices of the Peace in and for the County of Middlesex, or City and Liberty of Westminster, as the case shall be, to be dealt with according to Law.

And be it further Enacted by the Authority aforesaid, That in case any one or more of the said Watchmen shall want any assistance to enable him or them to perform any part of the duty herein and hereby required to be by him or them done, then and in every such case any other of the Watchmen of the same or any adjoining Parish, Precinct or Place, having knowledge or notice thereof by the rattle or other signal, outcry or otherwise, shall and may, and is hereby required, immediately to repair to and assist such Watchman or Watchmen wanting assistance, by the best ways and means in his or their power, and as the case may require; but that no Watchman during the time of keeping watch as aforesaid shall be absent from his particular stand, beat or walk, on any pretence whatever, except on some such occasion or occasions as is or are above expressed, nor longer on any other occasion as before expressed than the necessity of the case shall require, nor shall go into any ale-house or other public house during the aforesaid times of watching, unless called there to on or account of an affray, breach of the peace, or of the apprehending some Malefactor or disorderly person.

Watchmen to assist each other in each Precinct.

And be it further Enacted by the Authority aforesaid, That one or more Beadle or Beadles, on every night of his and their watching, shall twice or oftener go and patrol in and through all the squares, streets, and places, in the Parish, Liberty, or Precinct in which he shall watch, and shall see to the behaviour of the Patroles and other Watchmen; and shall twice or oftener in every such night of watching make true and just returns and reports to the Constable, Headborough of the Night, or to such other Person as shall be appointed to receive the same, of all misbehaviours and neglects of duty (if any) of such Watchmen, as well Patroles as others, who shall be found negligent or remiss in the duty of watching, or misbehaving in any manner howsoever; and such returns or reports shall enter, or cause to be entered in a book or books to be kept at the Watch-house for that purpose, by such Beadle or Beadles, or other person to be appointed to keep and take care of the same; and that each and every of the said Patroles shall also twice or oftener in every night watch and see to the behaviour of the other Watchmen, and shall make true and just returns or reports to the Constable, Headborough, Beadle of the Night, or to such other person as shall be appointed to receive the same, of all neglects of duty, or other misbehaviour (if any) of all the Watchmen, and shall enter or cause to be entered such returns or reports in the said book or books, which book or books shall be laid before the said Vestries, Trustees, Directors or Governors of the Watch, and Governors and Directors of the Poor for the time being, and before the Committee, and to be appointed, as herein directed, at every of their meetings, to the end all such neglects of duty and misbehaviours may be enquired into and punished, pursuant to the powers of the said former Acts, and of this Act.

Beadles to patrol through the Streets or Places.

And be it further Enacted by the Authority aforesaid, That if any of the said Watchmen shall misbehave himself or shall neglect his duty, upon complaint thereof made to the said Vestries, Trustees, Directors or Governors of the Watch, Governors and Directors of the Poor, at any of their meetings, or to the Committees to be appointed as herein directed at any of their meetings, every Watchman so misbehaving or neglecting shall for every such misbehaviour or neglect forfeit such sum or sums of money as the said Vestries, Trustees, Directors or Governors of the Watch, Governors and Directors of the Poor, or the majority of them, or the said Committees or the majority of them, at any such meetings assembled, shall adjudge and think fit to exact and require, not exceeding Ten Shillings, to be retained and deducted out of the Wages then due or to become due to such Watchman.

Penalty on Watchmen neglecting their duty.

And be it further Enacted by the Authority aforesaid, That if any Victualler or Keeper of any Public-house or Cellar shall knowingly harbour or entertain or permit any Watchman having a stand or appointed to patrol, to abide or remain in his or her House or Cellar during any part of the hours or times of watching herein and hereby appointed, or if any Constable or Headborough shall make default of watching, and shall not watch and abide in the Watch-house during all the hours and times hereby directed and appointed for keeping watch, every such Victualler or Keeper of any Public-house or Cellar, being convicted by his or her own confession, or by the oath of one or more credible witness or witnesses, of knowingly harbouring and entertaining or permitting any such Watchman so to abide or remain, and every such Constable or Headborough making such default of watching as aforesaid, being thereof convicted by his own confession or by the oath of one or more credible witness or witnesses, before any one or more Justice or Justices of the Peace for the County of Middlesex or City and Liberty of Westminster, as the case shall be, (which oath such Justice or Justices is and are hereby authorized and empowered to administer) shall forfeit and pay the pecuniary forfeitures hereinafter expressed and directed; that is to say, every such Victualler or Keeper of a Public-house or Cellar, for the first offence, shall forfeit and pay the sum of Twenty Shillings, and for the second offence shall forfeit and pay the sum of Forty Shillings, and for the third and every subsequent offence shall forfeit and pay the sum of Five Pounds; and every such Constable shall forfeit and pay for every such default of watching or absence from the Watch-house any sum not exceeding Twenty Shillings nor less than Five Shillings.

Penalty on Victuallers, or Publick Housekeepers, harbouring Watchmen; or Constables making Default of Watching.

AND,

None but a Householder to be admitted a Constable in Westminster.

AND, for the more effectually preventing the appointment of improper persons to be Deputy Constables within the City and Liberty of Westminster, BE it Enacted, That from and after the passing of this Act, no person whatever shall be appointed a Deputy Constable in and for the said City of Westminster, or Liberty thereof, who shall not, at the time of such appointment, be an Householder, and resident in the Parish, Liberty, Precinct or Place, for which he shall be appointed, and who shall not produce a certificate or testimonial in writing, signed by the Churchwarden or Chapelwarden of such Parish, Liberty, Precinct or Place, signifying that he hath been approved at some Vestry, or other public meeting of the inhabitants, having a right to assemble in Vestry in such Parish, Liberty, Precinct or Place, in and for which such person shall be so appointed a Deputy Constable.

Power of the Vestrymen and Trustees.

And be it further Enacted by the Authority aforesaid, That the Vestrymen of the said Parishes of Saint Giles in the Fields and Saint George Bloomsbury, jointly as one Vestry, or any seven or more of them, in and for the whole of the said united Parishes, and the Trustees to be elected and chosen as aforesaid, in and for the said Parish of Saint Mary le Strand, or any five or more of them, and the Trustees to be elected and chosen as aforesaid in and for the said Precinct of the Savoy, or any three or more of them, in and for the said Parishes and Precinct, severally and respectively fhall and may, and are hereby impowered and required, from time to time to use and exercise the same or like powers, to make Rules, Orders and Regulations, to be observed by the Constables, Headboroughs, Beadles, and Watchmen; and to cause copies or transcripts of all such their Rules, Orders and Regulations, to be written or printed, and signed by the Vestry Clerk of the said several Parishes and Precinct respectively, and delivered to such person and persons respectively; and to make and assign Assessments on such persons, and to be allowed in the same manner, and to appoint such Collector and Collectors thereof, and to order payment of any monies in the hands of any Collector or Collectors, and to apply or direct the application of monies levied, raised or collected upon or by virtue of any Rate or Rates so to be made, and the surplus money collected on any Rate or Rates, to carry on and apply, and to carry on the deficiency of any Rate or Rates; and to cause to be kept such books of account of the total sums assessed, collected, and received, and of all monies paid and disbursed for or any way concerning the Nightly Watch and Beadles, and charges incident thereto; and to do, perform, and execute all such other powers, authorities, and matters and things, about and concerning the Nightly Watch and Beadles, and the assessing, raising, levying, and collecting monies to defray and discharge the necessary and reasonable charges thereof, within their several and respective Parishes of Saint Giles in the Fields and Saint George Bloomsbury, and Saint Mary le Strand, and the said Precinct of the Savoy, as the Trustees elected and chosen, and to be elected and chosen by virtue and in pursuance of the said Statute of the Tenth year of His late Majesty's reign, or any seven or more of them, are by the said Statute and this present Act impowered or required to use and exercise, nominate or appoint, make and sign, order or direct, do, perform and execute, in and for the said Liberty of Saffron Hill, Hatton Garden, and Ely Rents, at such time and times, and in the same or like manner, and as fully and effectually to all intents and purposes as if the same powers and authorities thereby enacted and given to the said Trustees elected and chosen, and to be elected and chosen in and for the last-mentioned Liberty were herein expressed, enacted and given to the said Vestrymen for the said united Parishes of Saint Giles in the Fields and Saint George Bloomsbury, to be by them, or any seven or more of them, used and exercised in their said united Parishes, and to the Trustees to be elected and chosen as aforesaid, in and for the said Parish of Saint Mary le Strand, to be by them or any five or more of them, and to the Trustees to be elected and chosen as aforesaid, in and for the said Precinct of the Savoy, to be by them or any three or more of them, used and exercised within the said Parish of Saint Mary le Strand and the said Precinct of the Savoy respectively.

Directors and Governors of the Watch to meet annually, or oftener;

Provided nevertheless, and be it Enacted by the Authority aforesaid, That it shall and may be lawful to and for the said Directors or Governors of the Watch for the said Parish of Saint Clement Danes, and the Trustees to be elected and chosen in and for the said Parish of Saint Mary le Strand, if they, or the majority of them, shall agree and so think fit, to assemble and meet together, attended by the Vestry Clerks of both the said Parishes, annually or oftener, in the Vestry-room of the said Parish of Saint Clement Danes, by general summons of the whole of them, or other notice, to be agreed upon at the time or times in and by the said Statute of the fourth year of His present Majesty's reign, appointed for the making general rules, orders, and regulations, for the government of the Nightly Watch and Beadles within **and to make Rules and Orders.** the said Parish of Saint Clement Danes; and the said Directors, or Governors and Trustees, or the major part of them so assembled, may and shall, if they shall so think fit, join together, and, as one body, make and set down in writing, such and the same rules, orders, and regulations, to be observed by the Constables, and by the Nightly Watch and Beadles of and in both the said Parishes of Saint Clement Danes and Saint Mary le Strand, as well all such parts thereof as are and lie in the Duchy of Lancaster, in the County of Middlesex, as in the Liberty of Westminster, during their respective times of watching, as at every such meeting shall be agreed upon by the major part of such Directors, or Governors and Trustees, then and there assembled; and to cause copies or transcripts of such Rules, Orders and Regulations, to be fairly written or printed, and signed by both the said Vestry Clerks, to be delivered to the Constables and Beadles of the said Parishes.

And

And be it further Enacted by the Authority aforesaid, That the said Vestries, Trustees, Directors or Governors of the Watch, Governors and Directors of the Poor of each and every of the Parishes, Liberty, Precinct, and Places aforesaid, at their several and respective meetings for appointing the number of Watchmen and Beadles, to be employed as aforesaid, or the major part of such of them as shall be then met and assembled, shall and may, if they shall so think fit, nominate and chuse any number of them the said Vestrymen, Trustees, Directors or Governors of the Watch, or Governors and Directors of the Poor, as they respectively shall think fit, not exceeding ten, nor less than five, to be a Committee, to have continuance for one year from thence next ensuing, and no longer; and that the said Vestries, Trustees, Directors, or Governors of the Watch, and Governors and Directors of the Poor, may and shall meet four times in every year, or oftener, if they shall see fit; and that the said Committee shall meet at the usual place of meeting for transacting the public business of each and every of the said Parishes, Liberty, Precinct and Places, within the first week in every month, or oftener, if they shall think fit, and as well the said Vestries, Trustees, Directors or Governors of the Watch, and Governors and Directors of the Poor respectively, or the majority of them, present at every their said quarterly or other meetings, as the said Committees or the majority of them present at every their said monthly or other meetings, may and shall and are hereby empowered to summon or call before them all and every the Constables, Headboroughs, Beadles, Patroles and other Watchmen, and to examine into their behaviour respecting the Nightly Watch, and reward or censure them accordingly; and to hear and redress complaints, and to give all necessary and occasional directions, and to see to the due payment of the wages and allowances to be made and given to such Patroles and other Watchmen, and to encourage the attendance of supernumerary Watchmen, to the end such Supernumeraries (if thereto required) may go upon duty as Watchmen, instead of such of the more constant Patroles, or other Watchmen, as by means of sickness, or for any other cause, shall not attend, by making to such supernumerary Watchmen, whether they shall be so employed or not, such pecuniary allowances as they respectively shall judge fit and reasonable for their attendances.

Vestries, etc. to chuse a Committee annually

How often Meetings are to be held. Place of Meetings, and Powers of the Committee.

Provided nevertheless, and it is hereby enacted and declared, That all and every the Acts, Orders and Directions of every the said Committees respectively, shall be subject to the controul, alteration or revocation of the said Vestries, Trustees, Directors or Governors of the Watch, and Governors and Directors of the Poor respectively, at their next or other subsequent meetings, and shall continue in force until such meetings, and no longer, unless approved of and confirmed by the said Vestries, Trustees, Directors or Governors of the Watch, and Governors and Directors of the Poor respectively, or the majority of them present at their next meeting, after the making such Acts, Orders and Directions.

Acts, Orders, &c. of the Committee to be under the Controul of the Directors, &c.

Provided also, and it is hereby further enacted and declared, that every such supernumerary Watchman, during all such times as he shall watch, and be employed and go upon duty, instead of any Patrol or other Watchman, shall have like powers and authorities in all cases as are given to any Patroles or other Watchmen, and shall be subject and liable to the same Rules, Orders and Regulations, and to the like forfeitures for misbehaviour and neglect of duty, as the Watchmen and Patroles to be appointed by any of the said former Acts, or this Act, are hereby subjected and made liable to.

Supernumerary Watchmen, when on Duty, vested with the same Powers as the other Watchmen, etc.

Provided always, and it is hereby enacted and declared, that no person or persons, who shall be rated to and pay any Rate or Rates to be made in pursuance of this Act, shall be liable to Watch or Ward by virtue of the Statute commonly called The Statute of Winchester, made in the thirteenth year of the Reign of King Edward the First, or any other subsequent Statute relating thereto, but shall be and are discharged of and from the same.

No Person rated to be liable to the Statute 13 Edw. I.

Appendix, N° 5.

AMENDMENTS proposed to the Act 14 Geo. III. c. 90.

THE new Act to extend to all Parishes and Liberties within a circle of   miles from the Royal Exchange, according to the particular description and name of each.

The powers of all former Parochial and District Acts relating to the Watch and Lighting to be repealed, as far as they are inconsistent with the provisions of this Act.

That an Assessment be allowed to the amount of one shilling in the pound for the Watch only, and sixpence in the pound for Lighting.

That the powers of rating, paying the Watchmen, and appointing the Trustees, be continued as in 14 Geo. III. c. 90.

That a sufficient number of Watchmen be appointed in each Parish or District, and that the Trustees do appoint such persons as are competent for the situation.

That the night be divided into two watches, and the Watchmen relieved once every night.

That

That the Watch be set every night at the Watchhouse by the Beadle and Constable of the night.

That the hours of watching be fixed from an hour not later than eight to seven during the months of November, December, January and February, from an hour not later than nine to six in March, April, September and October. and from an hour not later than nine to five in May, June, July and August.

That the Watchmen have regular beats assigned to them, and power to act in adjoining Parishes so as to protect the frontiers of each.

That a Patrole of one or more persons be appointed to perambulate the Parish, or part of the Parish assigned to them, to superintend the Watchmen, inspect the Alehouses and state of the Lamps, and report these, and all other occurrences of the night, to the Constable of the night at the Watchhouse, and enter them in a book there. This Patrole to be on duty all the night.

The Patrole and Watchmen to be armed.

That a copy of the entries in the books at the Watchhouse be sent to the Police Magistrates of the District every morning, and another copy laid before the Trustees of the Parish at their meeting.

That the Parishes to be comprized in the Act be divided into Eight Districts, and that a District be assigned to each Police Office, including the Thames Police Office.

That the Magistrates be empowered to hear any complaint against the Watchmen for misconduct or incapacity, and discharge them either from their own view, or on such complaint; and certify the same to the Trustees of the Parish, who are to find other competent persons.

That a Constable of the Parish or Precinct do attend every night at the Watchhouse, to receive and take charge of all persons brought in there, and also receive the Report of the Patroles, and transmit them to the Magistrates the next morning, and also to the Trustees: one-half only of the Constables to go out of office every year.

That there be appointed two Assistant High Constables in each Parish, to superintend and visit the Watchhouses occasionally, and see that the Constables do their duty. These Assistants to be paid out of the Parish Rates.

Appendix, No. 6.

DIVISION OF DISTRICTS by POLICE OFFICES.

— 1. —

Police Office, Hatton Garden.

A RETURN of the Local District established for the convenience of the said Office, and Number and Names of the Parishes that the said District contains.

LOCAL DISTRICT.

The East Side of Gower Street, of Charlotte Street, and of Drury Lane, St. Andrew (Middlesex) St. Sepulchre (Middlesex) St. James Clerkenwell, Liberty of the Rolls, Liberty of Saffron Hill, Islington, St. Luke Old Street, West Side of Golden-Lane, and Bunhill Row, including the Western Sides of those Streets, and St. Martin-le-Grand.

Names of the Parishes, &c. within the said District:

St. James Clerkenwell.
St. John Clerkenwell.
St. Luke Old street.
St. Martin-le-Grand.
St. Sepulchre (Middlesex).
Liberty of Saffron Hill.
United Parishes of St. Andrew Holborn, and St. George the Martyr.
United Parishes of St. Giles in the Fields, and St. George Bloomsbury.
St. Clement Danes, within which is the
                    Duchy Liberty, and
                    Westminster Liberty.
Liberty of the Rolls.
St. Pancras, within which is the Southampton Estate,
                    Foundling Estate,
                    Harrison's Estate,
                    Doughty Estate,
                    Hampstead and Highgate Road Trust in part,
                    Somer's Town,
                    Skinners Estate, and
                    Lucas Estate.

                                        R. Ford,
                                Chief Clerk to the Magistrates
February 8th, 1812.   at the said Office.

— 2. —

Public Office, Queen-Square, Westminser,
8th February 1812.

The understood local District of the Public Office Queen Square Westminster, comprizes the south side of Picadilly, in the Parish of Saint James's ; also, the south side of the weftern Road in the Parishes of Saint George Hanover Square, Saint Luke Chelsea, and Kensington : that part of the Parish of Saint Martin in the Fields west of Leicefter Square, to Coventry-street, and the whole of the Parishes of Saint Margaret and Saint John the Evangelist.

When the seven Public Offices were established in 1792, the Justices then appointed, at a General Meeting, described Limits, comprising a certain space surrounding each Office, without regard to the Parishes. The object at the time was to promote the convenience of the Public as much as possible, and it has been generally the practice to discourage the applications of persons preferring complaints where the offence was committed, or where the parties resided, out of the understood District so described; but in many instances this practice has not been adhered to.

— 3. —

Public Office, Worship-street, Shoreditch,
8th February 1812.

In obedience to the order of the Honourable the Committee of the House of Commons, on the Nightly Watch and Police of the Metropolis, dated the 6th of February instant, we herewith return the number and names of Parishes contained in this District; viz.

1. The Parish of St. Leonard Shoreditch.
2. The Parish of St. Luke Middlesex.
3. The Parish of St. Mary Islington.
4. The Parish of St. John Hackney.
5. The Parish of St. Mary Stoke Newington.
6. The Parish of St. Mary Bethnal Green.
7. The Parish of Christ-Church (Middlesex) Spital Fields.
8. The Hamlet of Mile End New Town.
9. The Liberty of the Old Artillery Ground.
10. The Liberty of Norton Falgate.

JOHN GIFFORD.
JOSEPH MOSER.
W. PARSONS.

— 4. —

Union-Hall, 8th February 1812.

The Magistrates of the Police Office, Union Hall, have the honour of stating to the Chairman of the Committee on the Nightly Watch and Police of the Metropolis, that the local District of this Office contains fourteen Parishes :

Saint Saviour.	Christ Church.
Saint George.	Bermondsey.
Saint Olave.	Rotherhithe.
Saint John.	Camberwell.
Saint Thomas.	Clapham.
Newington.	Streatham.
Lambeth.	Manor of Hatcham.

— 5. —

Public Office, Great Marlborough-street,
8th February 1812.

A Return of the Local District established for the convenience of this Office, and the number and names of Parishes that District contains; viz.

1. The parish of St. James Westminster.
2. St. George Hanover-square.
3. St. Mary-le-bone.
4. Pancras, west of Tottenham Court-road.
5. St. Giles in the Fields and St. George Bloomsbury.
6. St. Anne Westminster.

P. NEVE.
One Magistrate absent,
One (vacant.)

— 6. —

Public Office, Shadwell, 8th February 1812.

A RETURN of the Local District established for the convenience of the above Office, and the number and names of Parishes, &c. which the same contains:

Parish of St. George Middlesex.
St. John Wapping.
St. Paul Shadwell.
St. Ann Limehouse.
Hamlet of Ratcliffe. ⎫
Poplar, and ⎬ in the Parish of St. Dunstan Stepney.
Blackwall. ⎭

EDW. MARKLAND.

— 7. —

Police Office, Whitechapel, 10th February 1812.

A RETURN of the Local District established for the convenience of the above Office, the number and names of Parishes therein contained.

The District of this Office commences at the extremity of the City of London, at Whitechapel Bars, and extends on both sides of the Great Eastern Road to Bow; from thence southward to Bromley; returns westward by Stepney Church, to the Commercial Road; then by Cannon-street Road, and Cannon-street, to Ratcliff Highway, Upper and Lower East Smithfield, Saint Catharine's, both Tower Hills, and that part of the Minories which lies in the Liberty of the Tower, and comprizes,

Five Parishes.
Two Hamlets.
Three Precincts, viz.

The Parishes of St. Mary Whitechapel.
St. Botolph without Aldgate.
Trinity Minories.
St. Mary Stratford Bow.
Bromley Saint Leonard.
The Hamlets of Mile End Old Town,
Mile End New Town.
The Precincts of Saint Catharine,
Tower Without,
Wellclose.

M. Thompson,
Chief Clerk.

Appendix, No. 7.

Parish of N.

REPORT of the Constable of the Night to the Parochial Vestry, and also to the Police Office.

Detail of Watch.						Special Instructions.	When Beadles and Patroles went rounds.	When Visited.
Constable.	Beadle.	Conductors.	Patroles.	38 { Watchmen.	2 Supernumeraries.	To keep an eye on new Buildings at the corner of Street; to see that no suspected Persons lurk in the areas. D° on low shed in ( ) Mews that none get over Wall	Viz. at at at	By Police Officers at 3. By High Constable at 12. D° by Assistants at 5. By High Steward's Assistant at 1.
1	1	2	8	40			Deficiencies. Board of general Regulations defaced. Fire-shovel broke. Broom wanted.	

Relief came on.

At 1.
2 Patrol absent sick.

Special

Special Occurrences.

Police Officer said he should report (   ) Watchman as old and infirm.

(A. B.) Patrole stopped hackney-coach at 4 o'clock corner of (   ) mews with empty sacks; coachman ran off.

(C. D.) Watchman reported 4 lamps out in (   ) Lane at 2 o'clock.

(E. F.) Patrole apprehended a man with small saws, wrenching chissel, and picklocks in pocket; taken before Police Office at 9.

(G. H.) Watchman observed lad getting over wall into garden in (   ) Street, sprang rattle, and passed word to adjoining parishes; lad escaped.

(I. K.) Reported disorderly persons drinking at Red Lion at 2 o'clock.

(Signed)   JOHN THOMAS,
Constable of the Night.

The following short Remarks made by F. RAINSFORTH, High Constable, on Friday Night, the 23d March 1770.

SAINT MARGARET's.

Three quarters past 11; Constable came after I was there; Houseman and Beadle on duty; 41 Watchmen, with St. John's united, at $8\frac{1}{4}d$. per night, with one guinea at Christmas, and one guinea at Lady-day, and great coats as a present. Their beats large; was obliged to take a Soldier into custody for being out of his quarters and very insolent, with several more Soldiers in the street at 12 o'clock; called out "Watch," but could get no assistance from them.

SAINT GEORGE's.

Half-past 12; Constable and 4 Housemen on duty; 57 Watchmen at 1 s. per night, and great coats. Two men had attempted to break into Lady Cavendish's house near Hyde Park Corner, but was prevented.

SAINT JAMES.

One o'Clock; Constable and Beadle on duty; streets very quiet, meeting with no disorders; 56 Watchmen at 1 s. per night for 5 months, and 8 d. for 7 months, with coats, lanthorns, and candles.

SAINT ANN's.

Half-past 1; Constable gone his rounds; 23 Watchmen 1 s. per night 6 months, and 9 d. the other 6, with candles; no disorders.

SAINT MARTIN's.

Two o'clock; Constable, Regulator, and Beadle on duty; 43 Watchmen at £.14. per annum, candles and great coats; every thing quiet; beats large.

ST. PAUL's COVENT-GARDEN.

Half-past 2; Constable, Housekeeper, and Beadle on duty; 22 Watchmen at 1 s. per night, down to $8\frac{1}{2}d$.; no disturbance.

ST. CLEMENT DANES.

Past 3; no Constable on duty; found a Watchman there at a great distance from his beat; from thence went to the Night Cellar facing Arundel-street in the Strand, which is in the Duchy, and there found 4 of St. Clement's Watchmen drinking. St. Mary-le-Strand no attendance, having only 2 Constables, which only attends every other night; 3 Watchmen, Duchy included, at 1 s. each. A very disorderly Cellar near the New Church for selling saloop, &c. to very loose and suspected persons; St. Clement's Watchmen 22, at 1 s.

SUMMARY of WATCHMEN.

St. Margaret's and St. John's - - - - -	41	Watchmen.
St. George's - - - - - - - -	57	D°
St. James - - - - - - - -	56	D°
St. Ann's - - - - - - - -	23	D°
St. Martin's - - - - - - - -	43	D°
St. Paul's Covent Garden - - - - -	22	D°
St. Clement Danes - - - - - -	22	D°
St. Mary-le-Strand - - - - - -	3	D°

267 in all.

Appendix, No. 8.

REPORT (in 1772) from a Committee of the House of Commons, appointed to enquire into the several Burglaries and Robberies committed in *London* and *Westminster*.

> THE COMMITTEE appointed to enquire into the several Burglaries and Robberies that of late have been committed in and about the Cities of London and West-minster, and to consider of more effectual methods to prevent the same for the future; and to report the same, with their opinion thereupon, to the House, have, pursuant to the order of the House, enquired accordingly; and

Sir JOHN FIELDING, knight, being asked what number of houses have been broke open in and about the Cities of *London* and *Westminster*, and whether it is a growing evil? said, that all robberies with the circumstances attending them, and particulars of goods stolen, are registered at his office, and from that register informations are grounded, and offenders are detected several years after the offences are committed; and he delivered in lists of houses broke, with computations of the goods stolen, from Michaelmas 1766 to 14th March 1770, in half-yearly periods; by which it appeared, that from Michaelmas 1766 to Lady-day 1767, 13 houses had been broke open, and goods stolen to the value of £. 280.; from Lady-day 1767 to Michaelmas 1767, 36 houses, value £. 627.; from Michaelmas 1767 to Lady-day 1768, 52 houses, valued £. 569.; from Lady-day 1768 to Michaelmas 1768, 48 houses, value £. 1,332.; from Michaelmas 1768 to Lady-day 1769, 35 houses, value £. 1,448. 15s.; from Lady-day 1769 to Michaelmas 1769, 63 houses, value £. 1,616. 6¼.; from Michaelmas 1769 to 14th March 1770, 104 houses, value £. 4,241. He further informed the Committee, that it is supposed the last 104 houses were broke open by a number of housebreakers, not exceeding twenty, and few of them more than 20 years of age, 16 or 17 of whom are in custody, with little probability of their being convicted. That the evil increases amazingly, and never was at so great a height as since last Michaelmas. Being asked, what is the cause of this increase of housebreaking? he said, that felons formerly carried their goods to pawnbrokers, but by the present method of quick notice to pawnbrokers, silversmiths and others, that plan is defeated; and the Housebreakers now go to Jews, who melt the plate immediately, and destroy other things that might be evidence, which in burglary can be nothing but the goods, though in other cases the person may be sworn to; that they disguise jewels by knocking them out of the sockets, so that they cannot be sworn to; that the present gang of housebreakers are sons of unfortunate people, and of no trade; that they began when boys as pickpockets, but turned housebreakers when they grew up, in order to procure a greater income to supply their increased expenses. And he informed the Committee, that for twenty years a footpad has not escaped; that highwaymen cannot escape, upon account of the early information given to the aforesaid office, and the great number of prosecutors who always appear against them, which he thinks must in time put an end to that evil. He then said he had detected several persons in Duke's Place with plate, and has offered a reward of five guineas for apprehending one person in the same place. Being asked, what he thought of the present method of watching the town? he said, the watch is insufficient, their duty too hard, and pay too small; that he has known serjeants in the Guards employed as watchmen, that the watchmen are paid 8¼ per night in Saint Margaret's Parish, and a gratuity of two guineas a year, out of which they find their own candle; that as they are paid monthly, they borrow their money of an usurer once a week; that in other parishes the watch are paid from 10d. to 1s. per night; that the watch in Westminster is in every parish under the direction of a separate commission, composed of persons who have served the offices of Churchwarden and Overseer; that Commissioners of the respective parishes appoint the beats of their Watchmen, without conferring together, which leaves the frontiers of each parish in a con-fused state, for that where one side of a street lies in one parish, and the other side in another parish, the watchman of one side cannot lend any assistance to persons on the other side, other than as a private person, except in cases of felony.

JAMES SAYER, Esq. Deputy High Steward of Westminster, confirmed the above evidence, and added, that St. Margaret's Parish has a Select Vestry, the majority of which is composed of tradesmen; that they will pay no more than 8¼d. a night to their Watchmen, and have no way of punishing them for neglect of duty than by dismissing them, which in fact is not a punishment, for they find it difficult to get men to serve in that office; and he further said, that their number is not sufficient.

Being asked the reason for changing the Constables from being parochial to be Con-stables for the whole City and Liberty, he said, That before 29th Geo. II. Constables were parochial; that he apprehended the reason for the change was, that a Constable could not execute any official act out of his parish without being specially authorized so to do; he mentioned an instance of a Constable's being killed when he was serving a warrant out of his parish, that the person who killed him was tried and found guilty of manslaughter only, though he would have been guilty of murder if it had happened in the parish to which the Constable belonged.

Sir JOHN FIELDING being asked, what remedies he could suggest, to prevent the
                                                                                    above

above evils? he produced two papers, relating to Constables, Watchmen and other Officers; which were read to and confirmed by him; and are as follow; viz.

Watchmen too old—should be from 25 to 50—their beats too extensive—should not exceed twenty houses, one each side of the way—Watchmen too few—the sum raised for the watch too little, being only fourpence in the pound—should be sixpence.

Ward Officers to be chosen out of those inhabitants that have served the office of Constable, and to have a good salary.

One half of the Constables to be discharged within the year, so that one half remaining two years, will be able to instruct the new Officers, and the whole duty will be done well.

If the new provisions for the Watch can be established by the Commissioners remaining where they are, it will save trouble, for then the Money may be raised by them as it now is, and every parish may pay and cloath their own Watchmen, so that the appointment, distribution, direction, wages, number and punishment of the Watch may be in the Magistrates by a new commission, and the paying and cloathing be in the present Commissioners.

The words " a Constable of the City and Liberty of Westminster," to be placed over the Constables doors; the words " Ward Officers" over the Ward Officers doors. Beadles by name to be discharged, and the necessary part of the duty they now do, to be performed by the Ward Officers.

That it would be right to confine the intended improvement and Constables to Westminster only, as the Watch in the adjoining parishes of Middlesex remain on the same footing as is originally settled by the Statute of Winchester.

Second Paper.

1. The Watch of Westminster is extremely defective—the number ought to be increased, their pay augmented, and the whole direction of them put under one commission, and that commission should be Magistrates of the City and Liberty of Westminster—the Watch should be attended by Ward Officers, and relieved in the night, a whole night's duty being too hard.

2. The Roundhouses should be capacious—no liquor should be sold in them—publicans should be punished for permitting Watchmen to tipple during their duty, and Watchmen should be particularly rewarded for diligence, and punished for neglect by the Civil Power.

3. High Constables should not quit their office at the end of three years—Constables should be increased—half the number only discharged annually—the Constable of the Night should be considered for his attendance on that duty, and punished for neglect.

4. The power of raising money at present for the Watch is too confined, it should be enlarged, raised by the present Commissioners—the Watchmen paid by them, but their number, direction and appointment, be by the new Commission of Magistrates.

5. Receivers of stolen goods, especially of those taken by burglary or highway robbery, should be made principals, with a power of mitigation in the Judge.

JAMES SAYER, Esquire, being again examined, approved of Sir John Fielding's plan, and added that the Beadles are an unnecessary set of men, advanced in years, and servants to the Churchwardens and Overseers—are forty in number over the whole City and Liberty—they have an allowance of £. 20. per annum a piece, which they may make up £, 30.—that he apprehends if the number was increased to sixty, and the City and Liberty divided into so many Divisions, a Beadle to each Division, and the object of their duty to take up Vagrants, they might be of great service—that if the Beadle was to have two shillings for every Vagrant he took up, and four shillings was given to any other person who should apprehend one, the one half to be deducted out of the Beadle's salary of that District, where the Vagrant was apprehended, it would have a good effect.

Sir JOHN FIELDING being again examined, said he thought the name of Beadle should be abolished, and that they should be called Ward Officers.

Mr. S. RAINSFORTH, High Constable of Westminster, being examined, said he had been in office twelve months—that he had visited the different night Watchhouses in the City and Liberty of Westminster, frequently from twelve to three in the morning—found many of the Peace Officers upon duty, some were not—that there is a general complaint of Peace Officers neglecting their duty, from which neglect it is owing that the Watchmen and Beadles are not present, and this general neglect, he apprehends, is the reason why so many houses are robbed.—That he has frequently found seven or eight Watchmen together in an alehouse, he thinks that the High Constable should visit the Roundhouses in the night-time once a month at least, or oftener if required, and agreed with Sir John Fielding as to the number and pay of the Watchmen.

JAMES

JAMES SAYER, Esq. being again examined, said that Constables are appointed under Acts 29 and 31 Geo. II. which Acts are in many articles defective; that eighty Constables, which is the number, limited, are not sufficient ; that they are appointed by the Leet Jury, which has been attended with great partialities, for the Leet Jury being composed of the Overseers of the several Parishes of the preceding year, they protect each other from serving the office of Constable; that in general opulent inhabitants are excused, and young tradesmen returned ; that if a rich man is now and then returned, he is generally got off by pleading age or infirmities ; that deputies are generally hired men, and though they cannot be appointed unless approved of by the Deputy High Steward, yet as it is impossible for him to get a true character of the person nominated, he finds many unfit persons are ap-pointed, who he is informed make a trade of serving the office ; for remedy of which he proposed, that the number of Constables should be increased to one hundred and twenty; he thinks the burthen of serving the office of Constable should not lay wholly on the trading inhabitants, as it does by the late Act ; that by Common Law every person able and fit is liable to serve; that the fine for not serving the office should be enlarged from £.8. to £.20. which fine should be distributed among those that do serve ; and he added, that twelve being obliged to attend daily during the session of Parliament, as long as either House sits, the duty comes round to each individual every sixth day, eight being excepted, who may be sick or kept in reserve ; during which attendance the Constables must necessarily neglect their own business. With respect to the High Constable, he said; it is an office of great burthen and trust ; that by Law he the witness is obliged to appoint a substantial tradesman to that office ; that the person appointed is not to continue in office above three years, and is liable to a penalty of £.20. for refusing to serve, which penalty goes to the Poor of the Parish ; upon which he observed, that the High Constable should not be a tradesman, because his power enables him to oblige the keepers of public houses to deal with him, or those with whom he is concerned in his way of trade ; that the penalty on persons refusing to serve the office should be increased ; that the High Constable should have a reward for his service, and that the Constables of the Night should have a reward also.

Mr. RAINSFORTH, the High Constable of Westminster, being again examined, said he was of Mr. Sayer's opinion.

Sir JOHN FIELDING being again examined, said that Ballad-singers are a greater nuisance than Beggars, because they give opportunity to Pickpockets, by collecting people together; that the songs they sing are generally immoral and obscene ; the people themselves capable of work, and the lowest and most abandoned order of people : for remedy of which, he proposed that all Ballad-singers should be considered as Vagrants, and be made liable to the same punishments, no person being a Vagrant now, but who comes within some one of the descriptions of vagrancy in the Vagrant Act ; and the High Constable being again examined, informed the Committee, that he has often had Warrants for taking up Ballad-singers; that he has apprehended a great many, notwithstanding which their numbers in-crease, and they are become a very great nuisance ; they have often been dispersed, but still continue the practice.

Sir JOHN FIELDING being again examined, said that the City of Westminster is a fran-chise under the Dean and Chapter of Westminster; that the Common Gaol thereof is called the Gatehouse, to which offenders of every kind, apprehended within the Liberty of Westminster, have been usually committed for some years back, to the number of 600 or 700 annually ; that in this Gaol there is little or no allowance or provision for the Prisoners, but what arises from the charity of Passengers, seldom amounting to more than five or six shillings a week, the greatest part of which is given to the Beggar at the window for the day ; that the said Gaol appears, from experience of the Magistrates, to be too small for the number, and too weak for the safe custody of Prisoners; that to this Gaol, persons in execution for debts recovered in the Court of Conscience are committed; and he said he believed this is the only Gaol in England where there is not some provision for poor distressed Prisoners; and he added, that when a Magistrate commits a man to that Gaol for an assault, he does not know but he commits him there to starve ; for these reasons, as well upon the principles of humanity as of civil policy, this ought to be remedied ; and that on account of the vast increase of inhabitants, property, and number of offenders, there ought to be in Westminster a strong, capacious, and useful Gaol, and there is no such thing at present ; that the said Gaol, called the Gate-house, is a very old building, subject to be repaired by the said Dean and Chapter, who appoint the Gaole; that the supposed original use of this Gaol was for the purposes of committing Clerks Convict ; the Commission of Magistrates of Westminster is not later than Charles the First's reign ; they began first to commit offenders to this Gaol, rather by sufferance than by right; and he observed, that however proper it may have been for its original purposes, it is unequal to the present occasions, and, as he apprehends, cannot be altered without a Law ; and he further informed the Committee, that the Magistrates of Westminster have represented this mischief to the Dean and Chapter, who acknowledge it, are willing to pull it down, and to give a piece of ground in their Royalty, in Tothill Fields, to build a new Gaol upon, and to subject the same, with every thing thereunto belonging, to the Magistrates of Westminster, under such regulations as the Legislature shall think proper, provided a sum be granted by the Public for building the same ; and he added, that Estimates have been

made,

made, by which it appears that a very effectual Gaol may be built for the sum of £.2,500.; in order therefore to remedy the inconveniences above mentioned, he proposed that such Gaol should be built and kept in repair out of the County Rate, which he said may be done without injury to the County at large, for this reason, that there is but one Rate at present for Middlesex and Westminster, near one-third of which is paid by the latter, since the increase of buildings there; that this proportion is much greater than the expenses required by the Act for County Rates would subject Westminster to; and he added, that the Gaol called the House of Correction in Westminster is repaired by the Magistrates of Westminster, and the expense is paid by virtue of their orders on the County Treasurer; that the same thing, if allowed by Parliament for the repair of the proposed new Gaol, will answer the purpose without separating the Rate.

JAMES SAYER, Esquire, being again examined, concurred with Sir John Fielding in every particular.

Sir JOHN FIELDING being again examined, informed the Committee, that about six or seven years ago, the Magistrates of Westminster had no other Court-house but a place at the bottom of the stairs, leading to the House of Commons, called Hell, to keep their Sessions in; the increase of business, and of offences in Westminster, made it impracticable to carry on the business there. The nuisance was represented by the Magistrates to the Lord Lieutenant, Lord Northumberland, who said he had then applied for redress, and told the Chairman that it could not be taken up by Government then, but would be in future considered; in the meantime, at his own expense, amounting to £.800. he directed the Chairman to prepare a large house in King-street Westminster, which was formerly a Tavern, to be made proper for a Court-house; that the Magistrates for their Sessions, the Burgesses for their Courts, the Lieutenancy for the Militia, Commissioners of Sewers for the execution of their business, Grand Juries for the Counties of Middlesex, Writs of Enquiries for the Sheriffs, and Meeting of Inhabitants for nominating their Representatives, should use the said building; for all which purposes it has been constantly, effectually and conveniently used; that it is scarce possible for the above business to be transacted without it, and the establishment of it is as essential to the Civil Power as any thing that has been mentioned; that the purchase of the said building, and fitting it up, cost the Duke of Northumberland near £.4,000. and he added, that this building also might be kept in repair by the County Rate, at an average of £.30. or £.40. a year.

JAMES SAYER, Esquire, confirmed the aforegoing Evidence: And

Sir JOHN FIELDING said, he thinks the acting part of the Magistrates in Westminster is in as good a state as it ever was, and more free from imputations or neglect of duty; that it would be useful to have some persons of rank and condition in the Commission of the Peace for Westminster, who would attend at the Quarter Sessions, where they would become acquainted with the conduct of the Magistrates in general, give a dignity to the commission, support the acting Magistrates in great occasions, and give encouragement to such of them as discharged their trust becoming the honour of the commission, and discountenance those who did not; and he added, that for the last two or three years the Magistrates of Westminster have gone through very painful duty, and have been very diligent in it; and having been sensible of the necessity of their attendance, have mutually agreed to attend at any time or place, upon the least notice from their Chairman.

JAMES SAYER, Esquire, being again examined, admitted that the Magistracy at present is composed in general of persons of character, and that justice is administered with activity, diligence and skill; but alledged that it has been otherwise formerly, and may be the case hereafter, and therefore he was of opinion, that a regulation in the Magistracy of Westminster is necessary; that there should be a qualification of Justices; that they should have a reward for acting, as the most part of their time will be devoted to the public Service; that the fees to be taken by their Clerks, should be appropriated to some public Service, such as a Vagrant Hospital; that there should be certain Rotation Offices established by Law; that as he apprehends one such Office might be sufficient, if properly regulated; that the Rotation office should do all the business, except in emergent cases; and that the private offices of Justices of the Peace should be abolished, because it sometimes happens that a man committed for a notorious bailable offence, is carried to another justice, who bails him, without knowing the enormity of his offence: And

Sir JOHN FIELDING said, that in criminal offences that nearly regard the Public, it is impracticable to use a Rotation Office, as there are many things that are necessary to be kept secret; and though the whole of the circumstances must be known to the acting Magistrates, yet they cannot be known by a fresh Magistrate who attends in rotation.

And he added, that the great number of brothels and irregular taverns, carried on without licence from the Magistrates, are another great cause of robberies, burglaries and other disorders, and also of neglect of Watchmen and Constables of the Night on their respective duties; that these taverns are kept by persons of the most abandoned characters, such as

127.   bawds,

bawds, thieves, receivers of stolen goods, and Marshalsea Court and Sheriffs Officers, who keep lock-up houses; the principal of these houses are situate in Covent Garden; about 30 in St. Mary-le-Strand; about 12 in St. Martin's, in the vicinity of Covent-Garden; about 12 in St. Clement's; five or six at Charing-Cross, and in Hedge-lane about 20; that there are many more dispersed in different parts of Westminster, in Goodman's-Fields and Whitechapel, many of which are remarkably infamous, and are the cause of disorders of every kind; shelter for bullies to protect prostitutes, and for thieves; are a terror to the Watchmen and Peace Officers of the Night; a nuisance to the inhabitants in the neighbourhood, and difficult to be suppressed by prosecution, for want of evidence; and, in short, pregnant with every other mischief to society. That any person desirous of gaining a livelihood, by keeping a place of public entertainment, who is of good reputation, can obtain a license with ease from the Magistrates to keep such house; when a public house in any neighbourhood happens to be vacant, that has been licensed before, the Magistrates of Middlesex and Westminster have long held it to be a rule essential to the public good rather to diminish than increase the number of public houses; that persons of abandoned characters, by applying to the Commissioners of the Stamp Office, may obtain a licence for selling wine; by virtue of such licenses it is that the taverns above described are kept open; for the aforesaid Commissioners are empowered by Law to grant such licenses to whom they shall think fit. That licences for selling spirituous liquors by retail are not granted by the Commissioners of Excise, unless the parties produce to them a licence under the hands and seals of two Justices of the Peace to sell ale. That Magistrates cannot by Law authorize any person to sell ale without a certificate of such person's being of good fame, and sober life and conversation; so that producing this licence to the Commissioners establishes their character with them, and takes away the necessity of any enquiry. For remedy of which, he proposed that wine licences should be placed by Law under the same restraints as the licenses for selling spirituous liquors now are. This remedy, he apprehends, might probably reduce the revenue of wine licenses; if confined to the Bills of Mortality, it would, in his opinion, diminish it no more than £.400. per annum; but if extended to Portsmouth, Plymouth, Chatham, and other Dockyards, it may lessen it £.200. more. He added, that he thinks it more necessary to correct the evil in those parts, as it has a direct tendency to corrupt and destroy the very vitals of the Constitution, the lives of the useful seamen, who, by means of these houses, become the objects of plunder as long as they have any money, and are induced to become robbers when they have none. And he informed the Committee, that there is another great evil, which is the cause of these disorders, namely, the immense number of common prostitutes, who mostly from necessity infest the streets of the City and Liberty of Westminster and parts adjacent, attended by common soldiers, and other bullies, to protect them from the Civil Power; these prostitutes, when they have secured the unwary customers, lead them to some of the aforesaid taverns, from whence they seldom escape without being robbed. The cause of this evil, as he apprehends, is the great difficulty, as the Law now stands, to punish those offenders, they being, as common prostitutes, scarce, if at all, within the description of any Statute now in being; and, he added, that this subjects Watchmen, Roundhouse-keepers, Constables, and even the Magistrates themselves, to prosecutions from low Attornies. That the remedy, in his opinion, should be to declare that persons walking or plying in the said streets for lewd purposes, after the Watch is set; standing at the doors, or appearing at the windows of such taverns in an indecent manner for lewd purposes, shall be considered as Vagrants, and punished as such. That as to the circumstance of street beggars, it never came to his knowledge that they are under contribution to the Beadles.

Mr. RAINSFORTH, the High Constable, being called, delivered in a paper called the State of Watch in Westminster, which paper is hereunto annexed, and said, That all the Watchmen being assembled at Guildhall, on Saturday the 24th of March, to see the House-breakers, they appeared to him in general very infirm, and unfit to execute that office. Then

Mr THOMAS HEATH, a Burgess of the Duchy of Lancaster, being examined, said, that both the Constables and Watch within the said Duchy are very insufficient and defective.

Upon the whole of which matter the Committee came to the following Resolutions; viz.

Resolved, That it appears to this Committee, that since the 29th day of September last, 104 houses within the Cities of London, Westminster, and the parts adjacent, have been broke open, and plate, jewels, and other goods stolen therefrom, to the amount of £.4,241.; that the said evil hath increased very much of late years, and is likely still to increase, unless some effectual provision is made to prevent it.

Resolved, That it is the opinion of this Committee, that to put a stop to the said evil, the number of Constables in the City and Liberty of Westminster, St. Martin's le Grand, and such parts of the Duchy of Lancaster as are within the said Liberty, should be increased; and that all persons being householders within the same, other than the Members of both Houses of Parliament, acting Justices of the Peace, and certain other Officers and persons, should be made liable to serve as Constables, or pay a penalty for refusing to serve the said office; and that a new mode of appointing and discharging them should be adopted.

Resolved,

Resolved, That it is the opinion of this Committee, that the number of Watchmen in the said places should be increased; more able persons appointed; their pay augmented; another method adopted for appointing them; that their beats or districts should be less extensive; their duty be made general, and that they should be put under one general direction.

Resolved, That it is the opinion of this Committee, that the Beadles in many Parishes are not at present of sufficient service; that they should for the future be employed under another name, and under some general direction as Regulators of the Watchmen, and to take up Vagrants and other disorderly persons in their respective Wards; and that their number should be increased.

Resolved, That it is the opinion of this Committee, that the duty of Constables and Watchmen, and of Beadles under another name, should be regulated with proper encouragements for doing their duty, and penalties for their neglect of it.

Resolved, That it is the opinion of this Committee, that the receiving Stolen Goods, particularly Gold and Silver Plate and Jewels, should be made more penal; and the Receivers of them, particularly of those taken by Burglary or Highway Robbery, be made principals.

Resolved, That it is the opinion of this Committee, that provision should be made for transporting Criminals, which now are transported to America, to the Coast of Africa and to the East Indies.

Resolved, That it is the opinion of this Committee, that common Ballad-singers, by collecting great numbers of people about them, give opportunities for picking pockets, and are a great nuisance, and that some effectual provision should be made for suppressing them.

Resolved, That it is the opinion of this Committee, that the present unrestrained method of granting Licences to sell Wine in and about the City and Liberty of Westminster, gives an opportunity to persons of the most abandoned characters to open houses for the retailing of Wine to be drank in the said houses as taverns, which are frequented by every species of disorderly persons, and is a great cause of robberies and other disorders; and that the said method should be restrained.

Resolved, That it is the opinion of this Committee, that the house in King Street, Westminster, called Guildhall, which is now the property of his Grace the Duke of Northumberland, and was some years ago fitted up by him at his own expense, hath been of great benefit in the holding the Sessions for the said City and Liberty, and for doing other essential public business regarding the same, and is absolutely necessary for those purposes.

Resolved, That it is the opinion of this Committee, that the Prison called the Gatehouse, in the City of Westminster, to which a great number of criminals and debtors are committed, is too small, and totally unfit for the purposes of a Common Gaol in the present increased state of the said City and Liberty thereof; and that there is no certain allowance for the maintenance of the prisoners committed thereto.

Resolved, That it is the opinion of this Committee, that a strong and capacious Gaol for the City and Liberty of Westminster should be built in another place, and some provision be made for the maintenance of the Prisoners which are or shall be committed to the Gatehouse, and to the said new Gaol when built.

Resolved, That it is the opinion of this Committee, that larger and more convenient Round-houses should be provided in the said City and Liberty of Westminster, and in St. Martin's Le Grand, and that part of the Duchy of Lancaster which is within the said Liberty, and that no liquor should be sold therein.

9 April 1770.

Appendix, N⁰. 9.

REPORT from Committee (1793) on Westminster Nightly Watch.

THE COMMITTEE who were appointed to enquire into the State of the Nightly Watch within the City and Liberty of Westminster, and to report the same, with their Opinion thereupon, to The House, have, pursuant to the Order of The House, enquired accordingly; a State whereof, together with the Resolutions of the Committee, are as followeth; viz.

YOUR Committee, in order to proceed in a regular manner, directed the several Parishes to lay before them the amount of the Watch Rate, with the number of Men employed on that

service

Service, and their Ages and Pay; in pursuance whereof they received several Returns, and from which the following Observations are extracted.

N° 1. St. Paul's, Covent Garden, who collect about £.646. per annum; they employed twenty-two Watchmen, who are paid, for the Winter months 1s. 2d. per night, for the Summer 10d. and for the Spring and Autumn 11d. they Act under the direction of Act 9 George the II.

N° 2. St. Giles in the Fields, and St. George Bloomsbury. Your Committee received from these Parishes two Returns, one of which gave the account of the united Parishes, and the other of St. George Bloomsbury only; from whence it appears that they are under no particular Act of Parliament, but exercise their authority under the Statute of Winchester; that the Constables collect the money from the inhabitants, who pay what they please, and that the Constables never account for the same; that the above Statute relates only to inhabitants keeping Watch and Ward: above 200 inhabitants do not pay any thing, and most of them are so dissatisfied with this mode of watching, that they have entered into voluntary subscriptions to pay other Watchmen than those provided by the Constables.

The Committee think proper to represent to the House, that during the course of their enquiry relative to these Parishes, some of the inhabitants of St. George's gave evidence, that they apprehended they ought to be considered in the article of watching, distinct and separate from St. Giles, and Your Committee taking the same into consideration, an Act made in the 10th year of Queen Ann, for enlarging the time given to the Commissioners for building fifty new Churches, was read, whereby it appears that the said two Parishes were to be united as to the Poors Rates, Church Rates, Highway Rates, and other Parish Rates, but no mention is made of a Watch Rate, therefore think the words (other Parish Rates) does not comprehend the Watch Rates.

That there are two Divisions, and two Constables, whose jurisdiction extends equally over the whole Parishes.

N° 3. St. Andrew's Holborn above the Bars, and St. George the Martyr; the Watch Rate, at 4d. in the pound, amounts to £.856.; that they employ 30 Watchmen and six Patrole men, who are armed; that the pay of the Watchmen is 1s. 3d. per night in Winter, and 1s. in Summer; the pay of the Patrole men 1s. 6d. per night in Winter, and 1s. 3d. per night in Summer; that the Fourpenny Rate, which they are limited to by Act of Parliament, will not defray the expenses, the deficiency whereof used to be made good out of the surplus of the Rate for Cleansing and Lighting, which is now appropriated to another purpose; that the Parish is so well satisfied with the above Regulations of Patroles as well as Watchmen; that a voluntary Subscription has been raised for providing Great Coats and Hats for the Watchmen and Patroles.

N° 4. Liberty of Saffron Hill. The rate at 5d. in the pound, amounts to about £.280. per annum; they employ 13 Watchmen all the year, and two Patrole Men for four Winter months; the pay of the Watch is 1s. 2d. per night in Winter, and 1s. in Summer, and the pay of the two Patrole Men is 10s. 6d. per week each. The Watch and Beadles are regulated by Act 10th Geo. II. which appoints 40 Trustees to manage the affairs of the Parish.

N° 5. St. James Westminster. The collection last year was £.1,497.; they employ 56 Watchmen, at 1s. 1d. per night in Winter, and 9d. in Summer, and 11d. in Spring and Autumn.

N° 6. St. Clement Danes. The collection last year was £.670.; they employ 25 Watchmen, at 1s. 2d. per night in Winter, and 10d. in Summer; they are empowered to raise no more than 4d. in the pound.

N° 7. St. Ann Westminster; the rate at 5d. in the pound amounts to £.809.; they employ 25 Watchmen, at 10d. per night in Winter, and 8d. per night in Summer.

N° 8. St. George, Hanover-square. The collection from Midsummer 1770, to Midsummer 1771, was £.1,431.; they employ 61 Watchmen at 1s. per night each, and four Patrole Watchmen.

N° 9. St. Margaret and St. John the Evangelist. The collection last year was for both Parishes, £.1,250.; at 6d. in the pound, and the inhabitants charged at rack rent; they employ 48 Watchmen at 1s. 2d. per night in Winter, and 10d. per night in Summer.

N° 9. St. Mary le Strand. The collection the last year was £.89.: they employ three Watchmen, at £.18. 5s. per annum each; and the remainder of the money collected is retained by the Beadle, for providing an apartment as a Watchhouse, Fire and Candles therein, superintending the Watchmen, and collecting the Money.

N° 11. St. Martin in the Fields. The collection at 4d. in the pound amounts to £.894.; they employ 85 Watchmen at £.18. per annum each.

N° 12. Precinct of the Savoy. The collection at 4d. in the pound amounts to £.17. per annum; they employ one Watchman at 1s. 2d. per night in Winter, and 10d. per night in Summer

Your

Your Committee, having considered the above particulars, find, that the mode of watching and pay of the men is very irregular and various; that in some parishes they employ Patroles, and in others Watchmen; and that the Statute of Winchester, being very obsolete, is a very improper Regulation.

Upon the whole matter, the Committee came to the following Resolutions.

Resolved, That it is the opinion of this Committee, that the present mode of watching, and pay of the Watchmen, within the City and Liberty of Westminster, is very irregular and various, and ought to be put under proper Regulations.

Resolved, That it is the opinion of this Committee, that it would tend to the safety of the inhabitants of the said City and Liberty, if a regular and uniform Watch, with Patroles, was established under proper Regulations.

Resolved, That it is the opinion of this Committee, that it will be necessary to levy a Rate upon the inhabitants, to answer the above purposes.

Resolved, That it is the opinion of this Committee, that in levying the said Rate, the two Parishes of St. George Bloomsbury, and St. Giles in the Fields, ought to be considered as one Parish, in like manner as they are in the collection of Poor and Church Rates.

Resolved, That it is the opinion of this Committee, that Constables of the Night should be appointed, who, as well as the Beadles, Watchmen, and Patrole Men, should be under the directions of proper Persons in each Parish, to be called directors of the Watch.

15 February 1773.

REPORT

ON THE

Nightly Watch and Police of

THE METROPOLIS.

Ordered, by The House of Commons, to be printed,
24 March 1812.

127.

R E P O R T

FROM THE

COMMITTEE

ON THE

State of the Police of The Metropolis :

WITH,

THE MINUTES OF EVIDENCE

TAKEN BEFORE THE COMMITTEE;

AND,

AN APPENDIX OF SUNDRY PAPERS.

Ordered, by The House of Commons, *to be Printed,*
1 *July* 1816.

510.

REPORT.

———

The COMMITTEE appointed to inquire into the State of The Police of The Metropolis, to report the same, with their Observations thereupon, to The House ; and who were empowered to report The Minutes of the Evidence taken before them;—— Have considered the Matters to them referred, and agreed upon the following REPORT:

———

Your Committee have gone into Evidence, to a considerable length, on the Police of The Metropolis ; a Copy of which they have annexed to this Report: They however consider it as a Subject, by no means exhausted ; and they trust that, in the ensuing Session of Parliament, they will be permitted to resume their labours ; having no doubt they shall be able to submit to the consideration of the House, Measures resulting from their Inquiry, the adoption of which they would consider as highly advantageous to The Public.

1 *July* 1816.

WITNESSES.

MINUTES OF EVIDENCE

TAKEN BEFORE

The Committee on the State of the Police of The Metropolis.

Veneris, 26° *die Aprilis,* 1816.

The Honourable HENRY GREY BENNET, in The Chair.

Sir *Nathaniel Conant,* called in, and Examined.

YOU are Chief Magistrate of the Police Establishment at Bow-street?—I am.

How many Justices are there?—There are two besides myself; three Justices.

What are the hours of attendance?—The hours of attendance are not directly prescribed; but we take them in analogy to the Act of Parliament made for the seven Police Offices.

In point of fact, what is the nature of the attendance?—There is an attendance, all night as well as all day, of certain Police officers and constables, to be ready if any disturbance of the public peace oceurs; and the Magistrates, when they leave the office, give orders to have immediate notice if any exigency arises. There is a clerk also, resident in the house, to act and give directions as occasion may require.

The practice then is in conformity to the statement you have just made?—It is.

What is the regular attendance of the Magistrates themselves each day?—The office opens with the clerks and officers at ten in the morning, and earlier if circumstances require; the Magistrates make a point of being there about eleven, the clerks having prepared matters which are to come before them.

How many Magistrates attend?—One engages himself to be there on each day, at the hours that are named.

How long do they sit?—They sit much oftener till near four o'clock than any other hour; but three is the nominal time, if the business is entirely done. They return at seven; but if there is any pressing occasion, or any expectation of urgent business, the Magistrates always go to the office without regard to the hour.

Till what time does the Magistrate stay?—He leaves the office soon after eight, if there is no business expected: but before the Magistrate leaves the office in the evening, inquiry is made at the public theatres and other places, whether every thing is quiet; if not, he stays till twelve o'clock, or all night, if necessary.

How often do you attend personally?—There are three Justices, and we take two days a week each. In case of the illness of any one, the others take his turn; and during any short vacation, the two Magistrates agree to accommodate the third by taking his duty during his absence. We are subject to no positive regulations, but take the attendance always with a view to the public exigency. I have been myself, in times of riot and disturbance, in constant attendance, both night and day, for a fortnight together, without ever seeing my own house.

In case of any subject of importance being brought before the Police, does more than one Magistrate feel it his duty to attend?—All three, if the exigency requires, or if we have any idea that occasion may arise.

What number of regular Police officers have you in your establishment?—There are 87 patroles attached to the office, and 13 conductors of that patrole,

making

Sir Nathaniel Conant.

making together 100 patrole ; and eight Police officers besides, who have general duties.

Duties of inspection ?—No, not regarding the patrole at all.

What are the salaries of those different officers?—The eight I have mentioned have one guinea per week each ; the patrole are paid 2 *s.* 6 *d.* per night for their patrole, and the conductors 5 *s.* per night.

Have the conductors any perquisites or other sources of emolument besides the salary you have mentioned ?—None, as conductors of the patrole ; but individuals of them have, in the day-time, employments under the Office.

Of what nature are those employments ?—Door-keeper and messenger ; they receive the salaries specified against their names in the Return which I have made out by order of the Committee.

Have those conductors any profits in the nature of a share of rewards on convictions?—Nothing from the establishment at all ; but in common with other persons who are within the distribution of rewards upon conviction by Act of Parliament, they, for a person they may have apprehended in the course of their duty, would, from the Judges at the time of the trial, receive a certificate for the rewards which the Acts of Parliament give them : they are not excluded from that by their appointment. We allow, in another way, all the patrole attached to the office, 5*s.* a day for their trouble in attending Courts of Justice to give evidence, and for special duty in the day ; and we do it upon this principle, we look upon them as engaged to us for their night duty of patrole, and what arises to be done in the day-time (which is their own time) we give them occasional allowance for.

Do you speak now of the conductors, or the patrole ?—I speak of the whole body of the patrole, who are specially engaged for night duty only.

The patrole have the same share of rewards arising from conviction, as the conductors or any other individual?—Precisely, as it arises out of the general law of the country.

Have the Police officers any profits arising from being employed by individuals for the detection of robberies committed ?—Yes.

In what manner are those rewards paid ?—They are paid by the parties themselves, subject, sometimes, to a reference to the Magistrates ; but in general the parties themselves induce the officers to assist them in their objects, and they pay them according to their private dispositions.

Is it not the practice for an individual robbed, to come before the Police, and offer large rewards for the apprehension of the offender?—It is very common for an individual who has suffered any great injury, to offer rewards of a very large amount ; a banker will sometimes offer £.500. for the apprehension of his clerk, who may have absconded with thousands ; and persons otherwise injured and extremely interested in a detection, will advertise to the public large sums : this the Police officers take into their view, and naturally are stimulated in their exertions by the hope of obtaining it.

Do you not think the effect of that is to lessen the exertions of the Police in those cases where the reward is not offered ?—I think not, according to my apprehension of the particular character of the men who are employed as officers at this time in Bow-street ; I think, though they would be stimulated by the view of greater reward, the exertion of their ordinary duty is not relaxed by the absence of it.

If they were excited to a very great exertion by the hope of a reward, must not other things be neglected in consequence ?—I was distinguishing the motives : they would go into a speculation at private expense to get the 500 *l.* which was the lottery of their success ; but I do not think they would lessen their ordinary efforts under the orders of the Magistrates, because that advantage was not provided.

Do you not think those large rewards being offered by individuals, act in the nature of expedition money paid in some public departments, by which, though one particular case may be forwarded, the general effect would be that of throwing back all the others ?—It certainly does in some degree ; but the impediment towards the public is not very great, while other officers remain to execute the other business.

Is it not the case that people let crimes go unpunished, because they are sure that, unless great rewards are offered, there is little chance of the detection of the
offender ?

offender?—I think naturally those motives operate in a certain degree; but I do not think, from my observation, that the class of men immediately employed upon this establishment would forego the exercise of their general duty because no particular reward was offered.

Your opinion upon that subject is founded more upon the particular character of the present officers of Bow-street, than upon any general principle?—I think men of bad character will prefer their interest to their duty, their personal safety to the hazard of any personal danger.

So that if in any one of the establishments, either at Bow-street or at the seven Police Offices, there should be any individual employed whose character would be considered as bad, in the same proportion his exertions would be relaxed?—Certainly; a man of such character would avoid personal danger and extraordinary exertion, would be destitute of that esprit de corps which actuates men engaged in this employ to pursue public depredators at the hazard of their lives independent of any pecuniary consideration.

From what class of persons are those Police officers chosen, and what testimonies of character are required?—If I speak of the eight officers of Bow-street, they are selected by long observation of their general character; some of them have been conductors of the patrole, or in some such employ within the view of the Magistrates, for a great length of time; they have in some instances been otherwise recommended, but not within my time; but always with characters that the Magistrates thought would answer the purposes of the public.

Those persons are to be understood as generally collected from men who had already served a sort of apprenticeship under the Police in inferior offices?—I should always look to the establishment, and to the conductors in the first instance, in the appointment of the eight Police officers: Some men also would possibly present themselves from other Police offices, whose characters and qualifications were particularly desirable.

When any of the officers receive the money allowed on the conviction of a felon, in what proportion is it divided?—In rewards given by Act of Parliament, the Court where the offender is tried settles the distribution, and an order goes to the Sheriffs to pay it.

Is the distribution made by the Court, or is only the sum of money awarded by the Act of Parliament ordered by the Court to be paid?—At the Old Bailey, the Recorder appoints a time for all claimants to attend him at the end of the Sessions. The Act of the 4th William III. provides, if there is any dispute among the claimants, the Judge shall apportion the reward in such way as he shall see just; and the certificate specifies what share each party is to receive.

In what proportion are those rewards paid that are offered by the Secretary of State, and who settles that proportion?—The advertisements in the Gazette by the Secretary of State, have two objects; a reward, which is generally specified to be paid by the party injured, and a pardon to any accomplice who informs: these rewards are settled privately between the parties.

Is it not customary to give what is technically called a " Tyburn Ticket" on some occasions?—Persons apprehending a burglar are entitled, by Act of Parliament, to an exemption from parochial duties in the parish where the offence is committed.

Those Tyburn tickets are sold?—They are once assignable, and persons receiving them assign them to some inhabitant of the place, to whom only they are valuable.

When an officer receives what is called a Tyburn ticket, is not it sold, and the money arising from the sale divided?—If there is any dispute, there is an apportionment by the Judge, as in the case of the 40 *l*; and when sold, each claimant gets his share.

Do you know what they generally sell for?—I have some notion of having heard that 20 *l*. is about the sum.

Under what Act of Parliament are persons entitled to a Tyburn ticket?—Under an Act of the 10th and 11th King William.

For what services do they become entitled to it?—Discovering or apprehending any burglar, horsestealer, or shoplifter.

Is that superadded to the money that is paid by the statute of William and Mary, amounting to 40 *l*. on the conviction for certain offences?—In burglary, both certificates are given.

510.   Is

Is it common for an officer, belonging to the office, to be joined with the prosecutor in the prosecution; and if so, for what purpose?—The party aggrieved is generally the person bound over to prosecute; but, in the Police Offices, if no other person is ostensible for that object, we always bind over one of the Police officers, or a constable, to do it; if he is a witness in any part of the case, he is bound over of course: but the apprehender is the person entitled to the reward.

So that the Committee are to understand, that an officer is never bound over unless there is a deficiency of evidence, from the failure of the person injured?—Always, if he is a witness in any part of the case; but he is not bound over to prosecute, if, on the commitment of the offender, we find the person aggrieved, for then we compel him to prosecute, and we bind over all the witnesses who can give evidence in the prosecution.

That is to say, you force them to attend as witnesses, but you do not join them in the prosecution, if the person aggrieved is ready to come forward?—No, never to prosecute, unless we see a failure of justice likely to occur, and then we bind over a Police officer.

The Police officer so bound over is entitled, for convicting of certain offences, not only to a Tyburn ticket, but also to the money settled by the statute, or a part of it?—The Court would not give it him merely because the Justice had bound him over, and he could not be entitled unless he apprehended or discovered the offender.

Is it not common for officers, so joined, to obtain the conviction money, or a share of it?—If they are witnesses within the statutes.

But not if prosecutors?—But not as prosecutors.

Do not the officers regularly ask persons for money, on account of the time they have given up in their endeavours to find an offender?—I apprehend they do.

Do not they ask money of prosecutors for the time they have taken up in the apprehension of an offender?—For their time and trouble and expenses in the apprehending offenders, I believe they apply to the parties employing them, for recompence.

If either of those cases came to your knowledge, should you think it part of your duty to reprimand the officer for taking money for the execution of his duty?—I generally do restrain it.

But you cannot say that you restrain it effectually?—Nor should I always: If a banker came to me and said, that out of a mail-coach five or ten thousand poundsworth of bills had been taken the night before, and he wished I would do every thing I could to discover it, or rather to get his property, for that would be the primary object, I should send perhaps six or eight officers in different directions, either to check the circulation of those notes, or to search for and apprehend the felons; and for the expenses of that I should not think of burthening the public; but I should tell the person, he must be at the charge of this expensive exertion: on the contrary, in all cases of great public concern, I should, without any second consideration of any kind, direct the officers to use every exertion, with no view or expectation of other recompence than I might see occasion to give.

Is it not, in point of fact, the constant practice for the officers of the Police to ask for money from every individual who applies to the Office in consequence of having suffered any injury to his person or property?—No, I believe not at all universally. There is a fee of one shilling for executing a warrant, and this increases according to the distance; but there is a general disposition in every person who applies to another to exert himself in objects personally interesting, to give some gratuity for the trouble and loss of time they occasion.

Do you think the officer is entitled to demand from the party prosecuting, any emolument, as payment for extra trouble, in serving warrants and summonses, going journeys after offenders, and so on?—I think he is entitled to say, I receive one guinea a week in my engagement as a Police officer, and because a person wishes that I should go twenty miles off, at a minute's notice, and employ all my time, I do not think that guinea is the retainer for such excessive duty, possibly at the hazard of my life, and certainly at some expense.

Would you think he was warranted in refusing to go any distance of that sort, supposing the party refused to pay?—I have told them a hundred times, I will have the duty done upon all occasions of public concern.

Without

*Sir
Nathaniel Conant.*

Without putting the extreme case, of his going out of town, would a Police officer consider himself as legally entitled, or by practice entitled, to receive money of a person complaining at the office, for doing the duty within the precincts of the establishment of that office?—The Magistrates always expect them to do the duty, whether they are paid or not; if it is done under the private direction of the parties aggrieved, they expect to receive the ordinary fee of one shilling for serving the warrant; but the Magistrates always require the duty to be done independent of that.

For what do they consider they receive their guinea a week?—As a general retainer for the objects of Police, which they are subject to perform night and day, and do perform it.

But if they receive from each individual complainant a fee for the execution of their duty, the guinea a week seems to be paid by the public, and no duty performed for it?—It is not at all universal that they take private rewards from individuals, and the Magistrates always control them wherever they can, and recompense them from other funds.

Do you think that the system of the payment of rewards for the detection of offenders is one productive of public benefit?—Yes; I think that every inducement that can be held out for the detection of offenders is desirable, and the expectation of pecuniary reward for their trouble is the greatest that can be; and the Magistrates always reward them, where it is not expedient that they should have it from individuals.

Do you not think that if the sum paid was proportioned by the Justices to the nature of the duty done, it would be a better mode of rewarding the exertions of the police agents, than that at present adopted under the Act of Parliament, which affixes to the conviction for certain offences certain rewards?—I see no difference in the expediency to the public.

Do you not think that there being no reward for the conviction of persons committing small offences, does in point of fact make it the interest of the officers of the Police to pay little attention to the detection of such offenders?—I do not observe it in practice.

Do you think that it is, or not, the practice at the present moment, of officers to let offenders continue in the career of small crimes in which they are engaged, till they commit some felony by which the officers or persons connected with the Police can take their share of the 40 *l.* settled by the statute on their conviction?—I think, certainly not; I have not the least idea that any person whom I have ever seen employed in the Police had that kind of speculation.

Do you not think that the common interests and motives that govern the actions of mankind would weigh with a police officer as well as with any one else, so as to induce him to be more active where he was to gain something, than he would be if he was to gain nothing?—He would be more active in the detection of important offenders; but I think he would never carry that expectation of gain to the extent of lying by till greater gain was to arise from detecting the offender in riper crimes. It has been often thought that criminals are nursed up till they come to great offences; but I think the Police officers always take the merit of detecting offenders in the present offence, and never lie over upon a speculation of greater offences in future; I have never discovered this, in my experience.

Is it not a common cant phrase, that "such a person is not worth conviction?"—I have heard it said, that an offender was not yet ripe for detection.

That " he does not weigh 40 *l.* yet?"—I have often heard that expression, but have no knowledge of it in practice; and never knew any individual employed in the detection of offenders neglect to take them, where there was evidence to be found against them, upon such a speculation.

You have stated, that the pecuniary rewards offered by individuals are great stimulants to the exertions of the officers?—They certainly are.

Why then do you think that the absence of the pecuniary rewards for the detection of small offences should not operate precisely in the inverse ratio?—The officer would rather employ his time where he could gain, than where he could not; and therefore a reward for detecting small offences would operate

Of course the officer would rather be employed in detecting offenders where he could be gaining money, than where he gained nothing?—Certainly.

Then of course the rewards being paid only on the conviction of felonies, must

directly

directly operate to the officer not paying the same attention to the conviction of offenders for small crimes?—If he had the two objects before him at the same time, it would; but I think he would not be employed at all in the Police Establishments if he was the sort of person upon whom that consideration would operate in exclusion of other duties.

Do you think it would be an improvement of the present establishment of the Police, to allow the Magistrates to give small rewards for the detection of persons guilty of inferior offences, picking of pockets, &c.?—I think it would, but it would be a great burthen on the public account.

Do you not think it would be better to leave in the Magistrates a power of giving specific rewards for specific services, than the present practice arising under the Statutes, which is technically called " Blood-money?"—I do not think it would operate to the same extent; the persons described in the Statutes as objects of reward, are persons not employed by the Magistrates in the capacity of Police officers, it is the party prosecuting or detecting, and frequently not a peace officer.

Supposing the party lodging a complaint be poor, or that no prosecutor is to be found, can you state any other way in which the expenses of the prosecution can be defrayed?—If the party injured is extremely poor, and incapable of carrying on his own prosecution, the Magistrate will, and frequently does at his own private expense, direct a constable to carry on the prosecution, and in some instances even to maintain the party injured, till the time of the trial; I have known that done in many instances.

Can you at all state to the Committee what is the ordinary cost of a common criminal prosecution?—If the prosecutor has to maintain the witnesses during the time of the trial (which at the Old Bailey often requires an attendance of six or seven days) which he is not bound to do, but witnesses are not willing to stand at the door of a Court of Justice eight or ten hours in a day, for days together, without receiving refreshment, which will frequently cost the prosecutor four or five pounds; and if he employs counsel and an attorney, which is seldom absolutely necessary, it will cost him more than double that sum; I should say from ten to twelve pounds.

You would consider four or five pounds as the minimum of the expense?—Yes, if the witnesses are to be maintained, and are long in attendance, but that is not compulsive; and the necessary expense would only be, the indictment and a fee for swearing the witnesses, and these expenses are allowed by the Court, and also loss of time to poor witnesses, if applied for. In this view, the necessary costs of a prosecutor in felony, is nothing. The charge upon the County of Middlesex, for the allowances at the Old Bailey, is more than 4,000*l.* a year.

Supposing the officers, who now receive a guinea a week, were to be allowed a larger sum by the public, and to be allowed their expenses, at the discretion of the Magistrates, for going into the country, not being permitted to take any reward from individuals; do you think the ends of justice would be thereby promoted?—Whatever facilitated the demand for Police officers, especially to a distance, would require the number of Police officers to be greatly increased, and I much doubt whether the advantage to the public would be adequate to the expense.

Do you not imagine there would be a discretionary power vested in the Magistrates, as to whether those officers should or should not be so employed?—That is the case now, for we never stop a moment in case of a serious offence to the public; if a person at the farthest end of the neighbouring counties gave notice of a murder or any atrocious offence being committed, I should send one, two, or three officers immediately to the spot for information, and send others in all directions to search out the offenders, and no party would ever be applied to for the expense.

In every case in which the assistance of a Bow-street officer is demanded, do you always grant it?—Near home we do; but where much expense is to be incurred, we hold a discretion over the application, and the applicant is told it must be at his own expense, the case not being sufficiently a public concern to incur large expenses. All the expenses the Magistrates countenance are the officers journey backwards and forwards by the stage coach, and perhaps a guinea a day for his other expenses and trouble.

You

Sir Nathaniel Conant.

You would be guided, in giving the assistance of a Bow-street officer, a good deal by the power of the party to pay the expenses of the officer?—By the disposition of the party to pay the expenses; but to the poor, or in cases purely of a public nature, no charge is ever countenanced by the Magistrates.

Is the establishment at Bow-street to be considered as a central establishment for the Metropolis, or a Police establishment connected with all parts of the kingdom?—The provision of the Office in Bow-street, applicable to distant objects, is eight constables or Police officers, and three Magistrates, always upon the spot to use their best endeavours for the furtherance of the public security: our legal powers are confined to the county of Middlesex and neighbourhood of the Metropolis, but we extend our endeavours towards the preservation of the public peace, and the apprehending of felons, to every part of the kingdom, whenever it is found desirable.

Do you keep up a constant correspondence with the seven Public Offices, and with the City establishments of Police, in respect of the Police of the Metropolis?—We have communications upon all the pressing occasions, but not as to lesser offences, or by any regular system.

Does the Bow-street Office act independently of those Offices, and do they all act independently of each other?—They all act independently of each other, except where special circumstances may call for general co-operation.

Does your Office communicate with the Secretary of State on any public matter? —I personally do every day; and indeed all the Police Offices communicate to the Secretary of State all matters of deep public interest.

Do you not think that it would be a great improvement in the Police establishment of the Metropolis, to have one central head Police Establishment, which might be the organ to the Government, and under which all the other different establishments should be considered to be; by which means there would be formed a regular system of communication from all the different inferior Police establishments in the Metropolis, directed to one object?—If that was confined to objects of great atrocity or great importance, it would be well; but if you are to have every sort of offence that is committed and brought to the offices, sent over to a central point, the lesser offences (although, perhaps, felonious) would be infinitely the greater number, and there could be no practical benefit from their being communicated from one end of the town to the other; and it would throw a cloud over the whole transaction, and the few important cases would be obscured by the number of indefinite communications.

The question referred to a superintendent establishment, that would have all the greater offences committed in the Metropolis laid before it; that would keep up a communication with the different inferior establishments; that would proceed upon one unity of plan; that would have before it the various crimes that were committed, and the extent and nature of them; that would have a register of the principal offenders as well as of offences; and that would be considered as a superintending establishment of Police over the whole Metropolis, having of course its branches of correspondence through all parts of the kingdom?—I do not think it would have great practical benefits adequate to the expense, because these things, where they are of any importance, are universally known through the newspapers, and the communications which already take place between the officers, so as in my opinion to answer the end in all matters of deep public concern; but I say this with some hesitation.

Is there not considerable practical inconvenience arising from the conflicting power of the different Police Establishments in the Metropolis, not only of the seven Polices Offices, but the exclusive jurisdiction exercised by the City?—It has always been thought that the City of London, and the other parts of the Metropolis (the City of London being very jealous of their privileges) impeded the search after felons to a certain degree; but in point of fact, the City Magistrates have always been very desirous of facilitating the pursuit of offenders, and to a degree that greatly removes the public inconvenience.

Is it not necessary that a warrant issued by one office, should be countersigned by the Magistrate of the neighbouring office before it can be executed within his jurisdiction?—Not in respect of offices, but in different jurisdictions it is necessary; but in cases of atrocious felonies every body may take the offender by force and carry him before a Magistrate, and the effect is answered without a warrant.

510.

You

Sir
Nathaniel Conant.

You do not think the substantial justice of the country is much impeded by the different obstructions thrown in the way by the various powers the different Magistrates have?—I do not think that, practically, it is much impeded.

Do you not think that the public justice would be materially advanced, if the different Justices of Peace at the Police Offices had a power over the four counties surrounding the Metropolis?—Every Magistrate engaged in the Police is included in the Commission of those four counties.

Has a Magistrate belonging to any one of the Police Offices a power to issue a warrant that will run through those four counties?—Yes; there is an Act of Parliament which says, that a Magistrate resident in one county adjoining another, and being in the commission for both, shall exercise his jurisdiction, whether he is locally resident in the one or the other, and he captions his warrant accordingly; a Magistrate for two adjoining counties may issue his warrants into both.

Does the Office in Bow-street keep up a correspondence with Magistrates in provincial towns, and in different parts of the country?—I think it of the greatest importance that Magistrates should be on the best terms with one another, and therefore in every opportunity of communication with them I am desirous of promoting it.

In point of fact, is there a regular communication kept up between the Office and different parts of the country?—No regular communication; but where the Country Magistrates wish to describe an offender who has escaped, or to have any other aid, they write to the Office in Bow-street, and we do all we can to promote the object.

Do you not think that if that correspondence was more extensive and more regular, it would be the means of preventing the necessity of the Police officers being so often taken, as they now are, from their regular town duty and sent into the country?—Such a correspondence does now exist in important cases, and perhaps it could not, by any system, be beneficially extended; it does not very frequently happen, even among the offences in the Metropolis, that such a communication could be useful, and in distant places the advantages of the communication would be less.

How often does your Office make a regular Report to the Secretary of State?—Every month, and the other Police Offices the same.

Is it a general Report, or does it enter minutely into the number of commitments and the number of convictions?—So many murders, and the names of the parties; so many burglaries, and the name and situation of the house in each district; so many larcenies, as far as they have come to the knowledge of the Office; and so of other offences.

And that Report, so made by your Office and the other Police Offices, comprises the whole of the County of Middlesex and of the Metropolis, with the exception of the City?—Exactly so.

All within the County?—Of all the offences within the Counties of Middlesex and Surrey, so far as they are known to the Offices. A great many things will happen without their being known to us; if the butler of any gentleman took away part of his plate, the complaint might not be carried to a Police Office; and so of other offences.

Are those Reports made in a general way, or is there a distinct Copy of the Information Book laid before the Secretary of State?—The Return is made upon a broad sheet of paper, upon which the offences are separately specified; the offences are named in the margin, and the names of the parties aggrieved; and the number of offenders, either discharged or committed, particularly specified.

Has any plan ever suggested itself to you by which a general communication could be kept up between the Office in Bow-street and the different Magistrates through the kingdom, touching the state of the Police, the crimes, the extent of crimes, and their nature?—I have often thought upon that subject; but it never has struck me that a communication of that kind would have any great practical benefit, either as to the detection of the offenders, or with respect to any speculation of Police.

The Magistrates in different districts meet once a fortnight or once a month; do you not conceive it would be of great advantage to have an account of the proceedings at such division meetings transmitted to Bow-street, and that the Magistrates at Bow-street should communicate with the Magistrates at those

meetings

Sir
Nathaniel Conant.

meetings on subjects of Police?—I think in general the objects before those division meetings of Magistrates in the country, are such as would not at all touch the general policy of the kingdom; the commitments for important felonies of a whole county, in a year may not amount to twenty, and those upon matters chiefly local.

If such communications were to be confined to cases of felonies, would benefit arise?—I think a report of common larcenies would be of no effect; if it was a highway robbery or a burglary or a murder, if the parties suspected could be described, and had escaped, such a communication might be useful; in cases of consequence we generally now have these communications.

If any offence arises in a district, with whom do the Magistrates communicate; with the officers at your Office, or the Secretary of State?—Sometimes with both; there are a great many letters come to the Secretary of State, almost every post, which I frequently see; but if there is any thing important, perhaps the Magistrate writes to Bow-street, giving a description of the offender, and desiring that if such a person is found they may have notice of it; perhaps this has almost the same practical benefit as if an institution of the nature alluded to was established.

Is there not a Gazette, in the nature of a Hue and Cry Gazette, which is sent to all the different Magistrates?—There is; it is sent to all the Magistrates in the kingdom, who desire it, and to the Clerks of the Peace of the counties, and Mayors and Functionaries of the great towns: It describes offenders, whose description has been sent, from all parts of the kingdom, by advertisement.

Under whose control and direction is that Gazette?—There is an editor appointed by the Secretary of State; the present editor is the chief Clerk in Bow-street.

Is it in the power of any individual to insert another's name in that Gazette, without the control or check of the Magistrates?—The Magistrates never see it; it undergoes the inspection of an editor, who would throw out any matter that he thought exceptionable, and inspects the advertisements that are sent, before their insertion.

Does he act under the superintendence and control of the Magistrates?—I think he would do nothing that he thought there was difficulty in, without consulting me; but he has no such specific order.

Does he receive money for the insertion?—There is money paid for the insertion of advertisements.

Is the profit his?—No; he is paid, I think, 70 l. a year as editor; and the printer has his bill.

To whom does the money go, that is received for advertisements?—The printer charges for the printing, and gives credit for the money received for advertisements, and the bill, like any other tradesman's, is paid. The balance of the account is paid out of the funds of the Office, and is charged in the account of the Office.

Have the expenses of Bow-street Office increased of late years?—The establishment has increased of late years; the number of patrole, and of course the expense: I think the expense for many years was about 12,000 l. and now about 14,000 l. but that includes occasional repairs; the Office was once burned down and rebuilt.

How many Police Clerks are there in your establishment?—There are three, and an extra one occasionally.

Do any of them practise as attornies?—Yes.

Is it your opinion that they are induced to take the office of clerks, from the prospect it holds out of obtaining them business?—I think not.

For what reason are they selected as attornies for a prosecution?—They are selected as clerks, being persons more in the habit of legal proceedings, and better qualified than other persons; but I know nothing of their employ in prosecutions.

Do you know whether in point of fact it brings them business?—I think that in point of fact they may in the Office in Bow-street, and in other offices, be frequently employed as attornies by parties resorting to the Office.

Is

Is it not true that when the Police clerks act as attornies, the office-business is at times not well attended to, because the clerk is called away by his professional engagements, and his duty devolves to inferior clerks, who are in many instances not adequate to the duty ?—It does not occur to my recollection that the Clerks at Bow-street have at any time within my observation been so employed as attornies as to impede the public service in any way. When I was at Marlborough-street, and concerned in the conduct of that Office, the Clerk there occasionally, certainly had business that abstracted him from the duties of his office in a certain degree; at the same time I do not think the public service was ever impeded for a moment.

Do you not think it would be a better plan, that sufficient salaries should be given to induce intelligent men to fill these situations, who would devote all their time to the duties of the office, and would not devote any part of their time to other business for private emolument?—I do not see that any evil results from it at present in the Office in Bow-street, nor has in my time; but I think in general it would be better if they were not so employed.

Might it not happen, that if a clerk was employed to conduct the case of a prosecutor as an attorney, that he might have an opportunity, if his views were to harrass the prisoner, which sometimes is the case, to afford an improper facility, by advice given to the Magistrate to remand the prisoner for frequent examinations, and ultimately commit for trial, when perhaps there might be no prospect of conviction?—I think it very unlikely that the Magistrate could be influenced by such conduct in the clerk.

Of course it is not meant to suppose that if the Magistrate became acquainted with the motive of the clerk, he could be so influenced; but might not the situation in which the clerk was placed, acting as attorney for the prosecution, give him the power, without the Magistrate discovering his motive, of advancing what he might think the interest of his client, contrary to the substantial justice of the case ?—The interests of the prosecutor, as he is before the Magistrate, are the interests of the public, and therefore the clerk being concerned for the prosecutor, could not be detrimental to the public; if he was on the part of the defendant, he might make a use of that knowledge of the prosecution which he has in his office against the public interest.

Do you not see that there are two interests, the public interest and the interest of the party accused; though the public interest might not be interfered with, might not the private interest be oppressed; might not the clerk make an accused individual, supposing him to be innocent, suffer, where otherwise, if the party prosecuting had not that situation, he could have no facility for so doing ?— I think the duty of the Magistrate, in giving the legal protection to the offender, would prevent the clerk from introducing that evil; but it is certainly desirable to avoid it.

Might he not, from his situation as clerk and attorney for the prosecutor, obtain an advantage detrimental to the interest of the prosecuted?—I really do not think he could; I think the Justice would look to his own duty, and could not be governed by such interference.

Are not the Clerks consulted occasionally by the Magistrates, upon questions of law that may arise, as to the correctness of the informations ?—Yes, certainly.

Those clerks, then, acting as attornies, prepare sometimes the informations themselves?—It is their duty, it is their direct employment.

So that they may be called upon to give their opinion upon a document prepared by themselves ?—Beyond a doubt.

Do they not prepare informations, which are lodged by the officers, to recover pecuniary penalties ?—Yes.

Do they participate in any part of the money received?—Never.

Have you ever had any instances before you, of complaint to that effect ?— Never the least; I never suffered a clerk to appear nominally as the informer, or have any thing to do with the interests of the informer in any respect; he receives a fee, and that not to his own pocket.

Did you ever know that any of the clerks participated in any portion of the penalties recovered ?—I never knew an instance of it.

Would

Sir
Nathaniel Conant

Would there be any difficulty in establishing a weekly or monthly communication of offences, from the Clerks of District Meetings in the country, and from the Magistrates in London, to a superior Office of Police, which should be in constant communication with the Secretary of State?—There could be no difficulty in doing it; I think I could point out a mode in a moment, by writing to the Clerks of the Peace, requesting they would desire the Clerks of the Division Meetings in their county, to send the requisite return to any particular place, (the Secretary of State's, or any where else;) the Clerks of the Division Meetings would then consult the Magistrates, and make the return immediately: writing one letter to each Clerk of the Peace would be sufficient.

Would there be any difficulty in getting the Offices in London to communicate with a superior office?—Not the least.

Do you not think benefit would arise from a monthly report of the different species of offences committed in different parts of the kingdom, divided into different classes, by which legislative provisions might be applied to one offence which might be found to be more prevalent in one county than in another, or more prevalent in one year than in another?—It might have a beneficial effect; but the crowd of lesser offences which exist in all places, and whether they exist in one proportion or another, the knowledge of the fact can answer no end, that I can imagine.

Might not the return be confined to offences of a certain class, and thereby, in consequence of this return, a comparative view given of the improving or deteriorating state of morality in the country at large?—The returns from the Courts of Justice contain all that; the returns from the Assize and from the Quarter Sessions, already come in regular course to the Secretary of State, and there is an analysis of them, which will show the comparative numbers at all times.

What is your opinion of the advantages which would arise from the establishment of a superior Board of Police in London, in constant communication with the centre of the other Police Offices in London?—I am apprehensive that a general return of that kind would be so voluminous, (99 items out of 100 being of no use) that it would rather cloud a general view of police than elucidate it: but I think a communication of this kind, upon important objects of immediate pursuit, would be beneficial.

Do you not think great advantage would arise from the other seven Police Offices being under the direction and control of one superior Police Office?—I think that every matter that can apply to the detection of offenders, in matters of any material consequence to the public, already has its effect without a head office; for, in the first place, where the Magistrates think it will in the least assist in such detection, there is such a communication sent to the Bow-street and to other Offices, and a description of the persons suspected and of the things stolen; all this is done without any regular system of daily communication; all the Magistrates look to the same general object, the apprehension of persons who may have committed particular offences, and they have a knowledge of the offences from the parties, or from the Police officers, or from the public newspapers, which last mode of communication is the most universal of any, and in some measure supersedes any other system.

Could not the complaints made at the eight different Offices be concentrated into one point, so that one office would be able to give an account of all which had taken place in all the various parts of the Metropolis, instead of having seven or eight offices to resort to?—Such an Office might be formed, and when you despaired of apprehending any offender, or had got him in custody, the registry would be at an end; there would be a great system of registering cases, and there they would sleep.

Do you not think that if the matter collected at the different Offices was accumulated at one office, so that there was an opportunity presented of comparing the transactions and circumstances at the various parts of the town, that would afford means for the apprehension of criminals, or for the prevention of crimes?—I see the theory very well, but I do not think the practical uses arising from it will tend materially to a detection of offenders, or will tend to the prevention of offences in any material degree.

You

Sir Nathaniel Conant.

You never find inconveniencies arise from the isolated character of the Police Offices at present?—I think they lie so within the compass of each other, and the officers are so well known to each other, that every thing disturbing the public peace is as much known as it would be by a centre of communication.

You never knew any jealousies arising in the Officers belonging to the different Offices against each other?—I do not think there are now; I think at the beginning of the establishment, one officer would do his own business without communication, in order to prevent others from having the credit or the profit, or whatever it might be, of detecting it; but I think now that jealousy is wholly over.

You never knew of any inconvenience occurring from the want of immediate communication between Office and Office?—In individual cases, I think, it must often have happened; I have seen myself that such a communication would have been desirable at one part of the town, of an offence committed at another; because they would possibly have discovered an important offender, who was afterwards found to have escaped into that neighbourhood.

Do you think that would have been forwarded, if there had been a daily report to a central office?—I think it might in that instance; and there must have happened particular instances in which, if every Police officer in London had known of a particular offender being suspected to have committed a certain offence, he would have been taken, but, for want of such communication, he escaped; but it is not in one offence in twenty that the person is known who has committed it. I have often thought that such communication, but for the expense attending it, would have a beneficial effect. I have thought of recommending, that one of the Clerks of every Office, at three in the afternoon, should put upon paper a minute of important offences, and send it in the Penny-post to each Office: it would reach the Offices in two hours, and would answer many useful purposes.

Is not there some sort of pre-eminence in Bow-street; some sort of control that the Magistrates at Bow-street have, over the other Offices?—Not the least; nothing can be more distinct. Every Magistrate aids and assists in the general object, without the least idea of superiority or importance in one more than the other. I am not quite sure that I did not feel my own importance as great when I was an individual Magistrate at Marlborough-street, as now that I am entitled the Chief Magistrate in Bow-street, excepting that it brings me more immediately within the confidence of His Majesty's Government.

Is it not the practice for several Magistrates of the County to attend, besides the regular Magistrates, at Bow-street?— It has been matter of great satisfaction to the Magistrates at Bow-street, and, I believe, at all the Public Offices, that other Magistrates should attend with them.

Has there been often attendance at Bow-street of other Middlesex Magistrates?—They look in, as private friends and as County Magistrates, to communicate and confer with the Magistrates at this Office upon matters which have occurred in their neighbourhood: many Country Magistrates also frequently look in, for the same end.

Martis, 30° *die Aprilis,* 1816.

The Honourable HENRY GREY BENNET, in The Chair.

———————

[THE following printed Paper was delivered in, and read.]

" Tyburn Ticket.—To be Sold, a Tyburn Ticket, for the parish of Ash, in the county of Surrey.   Apply to A. B. (post paid) No. 11, Grange-walk, Bermondsey-square.   The purchaser of the above Ticket will have the valuable privilege of being excused serving any parish offices; and any person, although at present chosen, by purchasing before they are sworn in, will be equally excused."

Sir *Nathaniel Conant,* again called in, and Examined.

Sir Nathaniel Conant.

IN your evidence on Friday last, you state, that it is not at all a general practice that the Police officers should take private rewards from individuals, but that the Magistrates always control them whenever they can, and recompense them from other funds; what funds are those to which you allude?—I charge them in the current account of the Office to the Government.

Have you an unlimited power to do that?—None; but in the examination of the accounts they are generally allowed.

Do they amount, in the course of the year, to any considerable sum?—Not very great; but in the Accounts of the two last years, which I have now to deliver, all that has been done in the two last years is specified, with the names of the officers.

[Sir *Nathaniel Conant* delivered in the Accounts.]

The sum of 470*l.* is charged in the account, for expenses and trouble incurred by the different officers and patrole in the execution of their public duty, in one quarter; was this money paid in the nature of travelling expenses, or in the nature of rewards for the apprehension of felons?—It is a bill made by them individually, including one guinea a day for the trouble of any of the eight police officers, and half-a-guinea a day to the conductors of patrole who are so employed.

Then in this account there is no money charged in the nature of reward for the apprehension of felons?—No.

Is there any separate sum allowed to the different individuals in the Office, beyond what is paid by Act of Parliament for that purpose?—The guinea a day is supposed to include a gratuity for the specific service; if an officer is wounded, a surgeon is provided for his cure.

In point of fact there is no allowance made to the Police officer, nothing given in the nature of present or gratuity, for any important service that he may render in the execution of his public duty?—I do not recollect any.

In your evidence on Friday, it appears that the Editor of the Hue and Cry Gazette is appointed by the Secretary of State, and that it is customary to send it to all the different Magistrates in the kingdom who desire to have it?—I was in no instance applied to for that Gazette to be sent to any Magistrate, that I did not immediately do it.

Who pays for the Gazette?—It is sent gratuitously.

When a person taken upon suspicion is brought before you in Bow-street, is his person searched?—The officer always thinks it his duty to search his person for the discovery of the stolen property, and against the danger of his being armed.

Is it customary to take from him not only the stolen property, but what money, &c. he may have in his pocket?—They do that at discretion; but the Magistrate always has it produced at the moment of his examination, and restored to him, excepting where it is likely to furnish evidence, and then other money to the same amount is given him as an equivalent.

You

You mean prior to the committal of a person to prison, so that he shall take the money found in his pocket with him to support him in prison?—Always.

Has it never occurred that persons who have had their property taken from them, have been sent to prison without a penny in their pockets?—Never, unless it appears to be the specific property taken in the offence.

You have answered that before, by stating that a sum to the same amount is given to the party committed; does that always happen?—I know of no instance in which any criminal went from me to a prison that was not satisfied in that respect.

Has it never happened that persons who have been discharged from prison, either by proclamation or under an acquittal, have come to the Office to demand property that has been so taken from them, which has been refused?—In many instances, where at the time of their examination they have denied the property to be theirs, as for instance, that they have found it, that they kicked their foot against it in going along the street, and picked it up: on being acquitted, they have come and demanded that property; that has been denied them, because it would be an encouragement to theft.

You undertake to say, that in no other case but the denial of property, or property proved not to be theirs, the money in possession of the accused party, at the time of his committal, is never withheld?—Never to my knowledge, and I am always open to every appeal of that kind.

Have complaints of that sort often been made?—They come, after their acquittal, or send, after their conviction, people to the Office, who buy of them, I suppose, the privilege; and in all those cases I endeavour to see every justice done: the Sheriffs will send to claim too.

What becomes of the property; into whose hands does it fall?—It remains in the hands of the prosecutor; it is generally given in the Court to the prosecutor, who in evidence claims it.

Does any share of it ever fall to the Police officers; do they gain any advantage by the seizure of such property?—Never by any arrangement of the Magistrates, and never within their knowledge.

You feel it your duty either to reprimand or to discharge a Police officer for such robbery?—I should reprobate it in the highest degree.

But it is an event which never has occurred within your knowledge?—Never.

Are public-houses licensed at Bow-street?—The houses within the parish in which that Office is situated, but not by the Magistrates in the office only, but such others as may be within the district.

Have you any principle upon which those licences are granted, by which you guard against their falling into improper hands?—With the extremest care, and sometimes approaching to injustice, as it respects the interests of the proprietor of the house.

Do you limit yourselves at all as to number, taking special care that there should not be a greater number in any given street than are absolutely necessary? —It is difficult in respect of the property to suppress a house, excepting for very flagitious mismanagement; but it is a leading object with us, never to increase their number; a public-house has never, I believe, for years, been added in that district.

Is not the Strand within the district of Bow-street?—Not for the licensing.

In what district is that?—The Liberty of the Duchy of Lancaster principally; some part in the parish of St. Martin, and some in the Savoy.

Is Bedford-street within your district?—It is.

Are there not three new gin-shops set up in that neighbourhood, one formerly the Wheatsheaf Chophouse, the corner of a court, one down an alley in the Adelphi, and the Cock and Bottle public-house?—I think they must be old licensed houses; I am certain that no new licence can have been granted and continued at Bow-street to a house so employed.

What is the nature of the security you demand, or the examination as to the character of the party, before you license a public-house?—The Act of Parliament has described the certificate for that purpose.

To which you scrupulously attend?—No licence was ever granted without that certificate.

Or renewed?—Not the certificate every year, but every year a recognizance,
with

with two sureties, is requisite : the certificate is of the Clergyman and Overseers, or three substantial inhabitants.

Which certificate is constantly demanded as a matter of course ?—It is always brought as a matter of course ; the petition cannot be seen without it ; it is a part of the Act of Parliament.

Have there not been repeated complaints of outrages having occurred, and riot, and the most profligate scenes of debauchery and vice, in the Rose public-house, in Rose-street Covent-garden, near Long-Acre?—I have given orders to all the officers in Bow-street, to be particularly watchful of that house, within this fortnight.

Was not that house verbally presented, by the Magistrates at Clerkenwell, last year ?—That house, I think, was denied its licence the last year but one, on the first day of the licensing.

Do you recollect why it was granted afterwards ?—The keeper of the house was changed, and a reputable man brought in.

Does it not occur to you, that there is no fraud so easy to be practised, and that in point of fact there is none so uniformly practised, as where a complaint is laid against a house, that there should be a nominal abandonment of it by the tenant ; and have you not heard that the phrase that is used is, that " the stone walls carry no sin ;" and that if the tenant is changed, the license is renewed, and the old practices, before complained of, still continue ?—The term is entirely new to me ; but if a house gets completely reformed, and there is an expectation of the house getting completely reformed, and the keeper of it is removed, in tenderness to the property the license is frequently continued.

Are there not at **this** present moment, in the immediate district of the Police Office, many houses where the worst and lowest description of people assemble, which are the common receptacle of thieves in the day-time, and of thieves and prostitutes at night, which are kept open the whole night long, and which must of course be known to every Runner or Patrole at Bow-street?—Whenever a house so conducted has been presented to me, I have uniformly, as far as my own influence went, endeavoured to suppress it : I do not now speak merely of the district of Covent-garden, which is a very confined one.

Have you any doubt that at this present moment, if the Bow-street Officers did their duty, a great proportion of those small public-houses or gin-shops, from the thieves that are harboured there, and the crimes that are daily and nightly committed, ought to be shut up ?—I always desire notice to be given me of any house so conducted, and I exert my utmost endeavour to have it completely suppressed.

Do you not believe that there are at this moment a great number of houses, such as the question describes, within your district ?—There are public-houses not very regularly conducted ; but whenever they can be brought within the correction of the law, whenever they come to the knowledge of the Magistrates, such prosecution is directed.

Do you not know that there have been houses licensed for years, that have had for years the worst possible character ?—Certainly not within my knowledge.

Will you take upon yourself to say, that for the last two years there has not been any house licensed at Bow-street, which has a character such as has been before given to it ?—Round about Covent-garden Market, where persons arrive at very early hours in the morning or late hours at night, for the objects of the market, houses are opened which perhaps may be abused to licentious purposes ; but at the time of licensing, we always reprove or correct, or suppress them, so as in our expectation to create a reform.

You have stated, that the clergyman of the parish always signs the certificate of his knowledge of the good character and conduct of the person claiming the licence ?—The clergyman or three inhabitants ; that applies to the character of the person petitioning for a licence to open a new house.

Is it not within the cognizance of the Police ; and if it is within their cognizance, how do you account for the neglect that there are public-houses within the immediate vicinity of Bow-street, in which the most abandoned women and thieves, as well as boys who are in the training of those thieves, assemble, and who nightly sally forth from those resorts to commit their depredations?—There are three grounds upon which public-houses are later in the neighbourhood of Covent-garden than any where else : one reason is, the market,

which

which is a nightly resort; another, the public theatres, which are open at late hours; the third, the watering-houses of hackney coachmen, which the theatres bring in great number from every part of the town; into those houses persons of the description named in the question naturally intrude themselves; but the Magistrates are daily in the habit of checking and reproving the keepers of them, and at the licensing time, unless they have reason to expect a reformation, the houses themselves would be suppressed.

Have you in point of fact, the last licensing day, taken away any number of licences for the misbehaviour of the persons holding those houses; or have you in fact had them punished in any way, practically putting your threats into execution?—I have sat in Bow-street for licensing only two years: I am not quite in the recollection of how many; but I am sure some houses have been suppressed, and others entirely reformed; for I recollect now a house that was turned into an inn, that was before a gin-shop and a house of ill-fame: I remember that the Rose public-house was stopped at one time, though I cannot recollect the circumstances, more than above stated.

Are there not two houses, the one in Drury-lane and the other in Wild-street, which have been over and over again reported to the Bow-street Office, as being the resort of thieves?—I do not recollect the case; but I am persuaded there are houses in Drury-lane which are open to complaint every hour of the day and night, and the difficulty of correcting them is very great; people are put in by the proprietors of the estate, who it may be hoped will conduct themselves with propriety: but the places now named are in the County, not in the city of Westminster.

Are there many public-houses in London in the hands of the brewers?—The brewers and distillers, either as security for the money advanced to the tenant upon his coming in, or for the liquor they intrust him with, and perhaps sometimes to obtain a preference in the custom, get possession of the leases, and those are very numerous; the worst conducted houses are often the most valuable, on account of the greater consumption.

Do you conceive the stopping the licensing of houses which are the common receptacle of thieves and vagabonds, would promote the well-being of society?—I so entirely think so, that, having been acting more than thirty years as a Magistrate in this county, I have uniformly endeavoured to suppress houses of such resort.

Can you state to the Committee any change or alteration in the law, in that respect, which you would think advisable?—Every person who behaves well while he is there has so much right to go into a public-house for his refreshments, that I know of no legislative provision that could reach the evil of the bad associations that may arise, till they break into riot.

Do you not think that if regular information was laid before the Magistrates, of such and such houses being the resort of thieves and people of the worst description, some mode of proceeding might be found out to put a stop to those evils, and to the assemblage of persons otherwise than the law prescribes?—If such houses are kept open at late hours, or attended with riots or disturbances, the present laws would reach them, and they are at the licensing time brought under the correction of the Magistrate.

You must be aware that there might be a period of many months, during the whole of which scenes of riot and licentiousness might go on in those public-houses, and there would then be no remedy against them till the licensing day; do you not think that some plan might be devised by which those scenes of riot and licentiousness might be stopped during that period?—There is a Clause in the licensing Act of Parliament, 26 Geo. II. which says, That if any house is conducted so as to involve a forfeiture of the licence, any Magistrate may adjudge that, and return a record of it to the next Sessions, where the Justices with a Jury may carry that forfeiture into effect, and the licensed person is rendered incapable of keeping a public-house for three years from that time.

Since you have been in Bow-street, have you ever known that law put in execution?—Not in Bow-street; but I have often threatened it, and heretofore put it in execution.

Are you aware that there are certain public-houses within your district which are not frequented by respectable persons, but by thieves and prostitutes?—Respectable persons are not those only for whom public-houses are provided:

people

Sir
Nathaniel Conant.

people may be reduced to their last penny, who may want refreshment; they are open for the poor more than the rich, and laborious persons more than any other description.

Are there not houses which are solely opened for thieves and prostitutes, in which they live; not that they go there for the purpose of occasional refreshment, but in which they pass their time?—There is not a district in this county where the Magistrates would not immediately suppress such a house.

Then you take upon yourself to say, that there is no house within your district subject to such objection?—The moment they came to the knowledge of the Magistrates they would be suppressed.

Could they exist with a hundred patrole, without coming to the knowledge of the Magistrates?—If they came to the knowledge of the Magistrates, the law would be put into force immediately, or at the general licensing time they would be suppressed.

Do you believe that they exist, and you not know of them?—If they existed in a shape amenable to the laws, I think I should know of them; and I am sure I should suppress them as far as the law enabled me.

Then, to the best of your knowledge, they do not exist amenable to the laws?—I think houses calculated for the succour of the poor, or the laborious part of the community, will necessarily, almost, fall into abuses.

Do you not know that there are some called " Flash-houses," solely used by thieves and prostitutes?—I do not know that there are; and if I did, I would, as far as the law enables me, immediately suppress them.

Is it not an established known fact in the Police Office, that there are houses, such as have been described, which are frequented by thieves, and people of the worst description; and to which resort the Police officers go just as regularly as a gentleman goes to his preserve, in his manor, to find game?—If I say the officers look to those places, it implies that those places exist; but I believe they do not exist upon system: I think the Magistrates, I am sure I myself would, by every contrivance find out evidence that should justify the Magistrates in their suppression of such houses; and I believe the Magistrates are extremely desirous of discovering an opportunity to do it at all times. I would go any lengths to obtain the evidence. I send Police officers to every licensing meeting, to give evidence against houses that have come to my knowledge as encouraging a resort of thieves. There is no feeling in Bow-street to nurse such places, either in the Magistrates or Officers.

Do not the Police officers frequent those houses, knowing them to be the assemblage of thieves?—They go into them, to seek for thieves whom they know are likely to associate at a particular place. A man discharged at the Old Bailey, yesterday, for a robbery, would go the same night to the place where he was last taken into custody; probably to see his old associates, and to receive their congratulations, or, perhaps, if he is distressed for a little money; or he will go there to be treated by his friends; and, I fear, more commonly in furtherance of his former crimes.

Is there not a sort of understanding uniformly kept up between the Police officer and persons of that description, thieves, at houses of this kind, so that when they want them, they know where to find them?—They may keep up an understanding with the master of such a house, to say, " Let me know if Bill such a one drops in here, for I *want* him;" that is their cant expression.

Is it not a matter of notoriety that they sit drinking at the same table, and are considered as boon companions, till just that moment arrives when they are to be seized?—I do not much understand their art; but I think one mode of it would be, if they wanted to know the offences of one offender, as applicable to the particular object in view, they would be very glad to get themselves into company with another who was likely to be in his confidence; but it is a part of the mystery, or of the art, or of the policy, which I can neither understand or explain.

Are the houses to which those thieves resort more particularly noticed for riotous proceedings?—Houses of bad association are most riotous; but I cannot think there is any house kept for separate association of thieves; I am certain if there was it would be immediately suppressed, as soon as the Justices have notice of it.

How long did the Rose public-house, against which there were such repeated complaints,

complaints, continue unchecked?—I think the Rose more than a year ago was denied its licence; I cannot take upon myself to recollect the particulars.

How long had the complaint been made against it?—I rather think it was a general complaint against the character of the man that kept it.

Had not the Magistrates at Clerkenwell made a verbal presentment of it?—It was in consequence of that, that the impediment to the licence took place.

I think you have stated before, that the licence was granted in consequence of the change of the landlord?—I think that was the reason.

In what state is the house at present?—I am fearful it is not reformed, and unless it is, the licence I believe will not be continued; but the actual licensing of that house is not in Bow-street, it is in the Parish of St. Martin.

Is it part of the duty of the patrole to attend to the state of Covent-garden during the night?—We have a small part of the patrole in waiting at the Office through the night, and by my directions they go out into the neighbourhood to secure the public quiet.

Have complaints ever been made to you, that the booths of Covent-garden are the nightly resort and shelter of boys and women of the worst description, who flock there by some hundreds nightly?—I think not less than fifty persons of that description have been before the Magistrates within a month past, and many of them have either been, if very young, placed within the government of those who were likely to protect them, or committed to the prisons.

Does that search take place nightly?—No; occasionally, we try to deter them; by thus disturbing them, it gets clear for a short time, and afterwards they return again, and we deal more severely with those who are the fittest for example.

Do not you think it would further the objects of police, if the watchmen were instructed nightly to examine and clear those places from such assemblage of persons?—They have those general instructions, both from the Magistrates and from the Watch Committee.

Do you believe that they execute them?—They do it more by driving them away than by taking them into custody.

When a person is given in charge to the watchman, what is the mode of securing him?—He is kept in the watch-house through the night, unless he is a person of apparent responsibility, or sends for somebody to be answerable for his coming forward the next morning before the Magistrates.

Is it not common for the Police officers to confine persons in watch-houses, without entering any charge in the charge-books against them?—If the officer is known, perhaps they will take them in for safe custody for a few hours; but the constable of the night generally writes down the name of the prisoner, and of the person who brings him, and the charge, felony, or whatever it may be.

Have they orders to do that?—They have; it is the defence against the charge of false imprisonment.

They have a charge-book?—Yes; it is generally signed by the person who gives the charge, unless it is a constable who is well known.

Is it a fact within your knowledge, that the leaves of those books are defaced or torn out sometimes?—I think not; I see those books every day, they are brought before me, with the prisoners.

Are not the charges frequently written on loose paper?—Not frequently; if the charge-book happens to have been carried to the Watch Committee, and not brought back, they will write it on a loose piece of paper, and stick it into the book afterwards.

Are there not more charges taken to the watch-houses on the Saturday night than on any other?—There are more charges before the Justices on the Monday morning than any other, for that includes two nights; and there are more disturbances on the Saturday night than any other; first, because Sunday is a leisure day, and they have no work to look to early in the morning; and another reason is, that labouring people are paid that night, and drunkenness is one of their recreations.

Do you not believe that it may arise from the watchmen being able to obtain somewhat more money from the parties, to prevent their being detained during the Sunday?—I think not, because the parishes at whose expense the watch-houses are kept would restrain such a practice, and the Constable of the night would discover it.

Are you not aware that there is a constant understanding between the watch-

men

Sir Nathaniel Conant.

men and the women of the town, and the idle and the profligate people who are about all night?—The Watch are a class of men who are willing, for fifteen pence, to undertake that laborious duty, for it is one beginning at eight o'clock at night, and lasting till seven in the morning; such men must be open to temptation, but I think it is less than one might reasonably expect.

When a dangerous person is taken up, how is he secured; is there not a place technically styled a "dungeon" in some of those watch-houses?—There are strong rooms in the watch-houses.

Some without light, and almost without air?—They are better secured by being half under ground, and the light comes in at the grating.

In those places people may remain from Saturday till Monday, at the pleasure of the watchman who seizes them?—At the pleasure of the Constable of the night; but complaints of real grievance are not frequent.

Are you acquainted with any public-houses, the notorious character of which, for the resort of thieves, is such, that there are strong rooms in which they can be confined when they are seized by the officers of the police?—There was a public-house in Bow-street, where all the prisoners were carried for security before they went to gaol; but for more than two years past, a place of that kind has been provided within the Office at Bow-street; and there is no place of confinement of that kind in Bow-street now, or in the neighbourhood of any of the Police Offices.

Has any plan ever struck you as feasible, by which that disgrace to London, to its police, and its morals, the crowds of women, some in a state of intoxication, infesting the streets and annoying the passengers during the best part of the night, could be prevented?—It would be ten times worse if the Police officers and watch-men did not take them up or drive them away, as they do at present; that might be done certainly more universally than it is, but the gaols would be filled, without hope of reforming them, to a degree that would not be expedient. The punishment by law is long imprisonment (for corporal punishment of another kind, with women, is out of the question) and the instant they came out they must be committed again; for this degraded condition has no resource, even to friends or employment. There is a woman who for ten years past has been much the greater portion of the time in prison, but is always in the streets the moment she is out; and the same is the case of some beggars, but these are more easily restrained.

Do you not think that some means might be found, by which the outrageous nuisances might be put an end to, which prevent women of another description from walking through the streets without the protection of men?—These insults are visited with such severity by the Magistrates whenever they are brought before them, that I do not think they exist in any very great degree at this time; such insults are now unfrequent.

Do you know that amongst the great capitals of the Continent, Paris in particular, no such evil as exists in the streets of London is to be found?—I think a severity of Police similar to that in the countries alluded to, would suppress the evil here; but the lenity of the English law does not allow it to be carried to the full extent that it is in those countries; besides, this class of women in France are not in the use of spirituous liquors.

Do you not think that the employment of a more efficient race of watchmen, and at higher salaries, would be productive of much benefit in that respect?—I think the mode of watching might be improved, but at an expense that would be grievous to those who pay the parish rates.

Do you think that the Police of the Metropolis would be under better management if the parish watchmen were placed under the superintendence of the Police?—I have not the least doubt that a system of watching at greater expense might be established under the Police, with better effect than the parish watch, as now provided, furnishes.

Do you not think that at the same expense which is now incurred by the parishes, supposing the watch was under the control of the Police, it would be better managed?—I fear not; and I am sure it would be attended with great dissatisfaction to those who have the local benefit of it, and supply the expense.

Why do you think it would not?—I should think the small payment given at present to watchmen, would not provide better men.

Are

Sir Nathaniel Conant.

Are you not of opinion, that by more effective men being employed, the number might be reduced ?—I do not think the number should be reduced, and any increase of their qualifications would be attended with an expense little to the satisfaction of those who pay it, or are benefited by it: I have sometimes thought, if you could get the lower description of housekeepers to engage in the watch, the one during the first part of the night, and the other towards the morning, it would double the number of watchmen in the dangerous part of the night, by their crossing each other in going to duty and returning home, and would increase the respectability of the watch ; but such people would not go out for less than half-a-crown for the half night, and that is an expense which would not be satisfactory to those who have to pay it: I suppose the number of watchmen in the Metropolis is as one to about seventy or eighty houses.

That is generally an old man ?—Yes, and he is dosing in his watch-box in the interval between crying the hours and when he is moving ; men cannot walk for ten hours together ; a thief will watch him to one corner of the street, while the intended depredation is perpetrated round another corner, and the lantern he carries shows where he is at a great distance.

Is it within your knowledge that the general management of the Police of the City, both as to the proportion of burglaries, and by the removal of women who infest the streets at the East end of the town, is much better than the Police of this part of the Metropolis ?—I think within the present year the removal of the prostitutes from the streets in the City has been much greater than we have been able to effect in this part of the town, and also drives them here ; but they are diminished, even in the Western part of the town, greatly in their numbers, and very materially in their conduct, which was formerly, I believe, more obnoxious.

Do you not know that the public-houses, for instance, in the City, are shut up at a much earlier hour, and that greater care is taken that they should be so shut, than in this part of the Metropolis ?—In the Western parts of the Metropolis all public-houses are required nominally to be shut at eleven o'clock, excepting the watering-houses for the hackney coaches, and those in the immediate vicinity of public places, which are open later ; but these are perpetually restrained by the Magistrates in every possible way.

Is not it universally true that no houses are open, either as public-houses or gin-shops, during the whole or the best part of the night, except in that confined district, or for those limited purposes you have mentioned ?—Never, without the immediate check of the Magistrates, whenever they know it.

Do you know that the Proprietors of the hackney coaches have presented a petition to the Lord Mayor of London, or have they presented a similar one to your Office, praying that those houses might be shut up, for that they were productive of great injury to them ?—I have had no such petition, but have frequently heard from the proprietors of hackney coaches that they should have no objection to such an arrangement.

What then would be the objection to enforcing the law, by shutting up those houses ?—I have endeavoured to enforce the law in that respect, and frequently check the keepers of those houses ; when they have applied for a licence, it has been my opinion that it would be better there should be none of them ; better for the horses, better for the men, and better for the public who seek the accommodation of the coaches.

Then if such is your opinion, and that of your brother Magistrates in your own district, there appears to be no reason why the law should not be carried into effect ?—I see no reason, and have a wish that it should be ; though the vicinity of the theatres makes some difference.

Is it not true that many of the keepers of the lowest order of brothels in the Metropolis take out a licence for selling wine, and are thus enabled to keep open those houses ?—Formerly, the wine licences by the Excise were obtained without the intervention of the Magistrates ; by a late law, a person must carry a certificate of licence by the Magistrates, before he can obtain one for wine. I have never known a new licence granted to a house of the description named in the question, since that arrangement has taken place.

Do you not know that in point of fact many of the houses, such as have been described, hold licences granted before the law passed, and who annually come for a renewal ?—With respect to low brothels, certainly not ; but with regard

regard to a higher kind of hotels, kept for the reception of men and women, for purposes which one cannot be blind to, I think they may have been continued; but in no instance, within my knowledge, in any Division in which I have acted.

Are not the persons who principally keep the houses, such as have been described, notorious thieves who have " retired," according to their own phrase, " from doing business, because the times are hard?"—I think such a man would never have got a licence of any kind whatever from the Magistrates, at any time or in any place.

You mean to say, that to the best of your belief there are no houses of the description referred to in the question, held by any persons?—I have known no persons of that character ever receive a licence, unless a prize-fighter is considered as within the description; I have known two or three of those men keep public-houses.

You know no one answering that description, who at present holds a licence?—Indeed I do not; and if I did, if it was within any fair influence of mine, he would not be licensed next September.

Mercurii, 1° die Maii, 1816.

The Honourable HENRY GREY BENNET, in The Chair.

Sir *Nathaniel Conant*, again called in, and further Examined.

YOU stated in your evidence on a preceding day, that the Justices regularly attend at eleven o'clock in the morning and at seven in the evening?—Those are the times settled in their own minds for their attendance.

Can you take upon yourself to say, that within your own knowledge there has been any exception to that rule?—As a rule, certainly none; as a practice by accident perhaps, not very unfrequently it has been later than that by a quarter or half an hour; but in general, I should think, nearer seven has been the time.

Will you say it has never happened that there was no Justice at all present any one evening?—Yes, I think it may have happened, particularly in the times of the Quarter Sessions or other distant duty.

Were you in attendance, or was it your turn of attendance, on Wednesday the 17th of April last?—In general, the Wednesday is not a day on which I am in attendance at all, or considered to be so.

You do not know whether a man taken at four o'clock on the Wednesday, was not examined before two on the Thursday following, in consequence of there being no Justice present?—I cannot say that at all; I can say something perhaps leading to it, which is, that I know the Magistrate who takes generally the duty on Wednesday, was at that time in a very ill state of health; I speak of Mr. Nares.

You cannot say that the same thing did not happen two days before?—I cannot say that it did not; it might have happened in my own person, but it hardly could, because I always provide some Magistrate to be there when I cannot attend myself; but it might happen in my own person, arising from public duty in a distant place, or I was in the vicinity, and had given orders to be sent to.

How long has Mr. Nares been ill?—Mr. Nares has been under the care of physicians and surgeons, in great extremity both of pain and danger very frequently, every year for the last fifteen years; he is frequently taken, and his disorder is attended with great temporary danger.

He may be considered, then, as a person in a bad state of health?—In a very hazardous state of health.

Not as an efficient person to act as a Magistrate?—His energies are extremely useful as a Magistrate; he is very capable and active.

He has been a long time in the situation of a Magistrate?—I think he has acted as a Magistrate more than fifteen years.

It has been stated, that a very great defect in the arrangement of the Police

Sir Nathaniel Conant.

is a want of ready and certain means in seeking the protection of a constable, in cases of street-robbery or unprovoked personal insult?—There is not a time, night or day, that Police officers cannot be found at the establishment at Bow-street, at the moment; and they have the orders of the Magistrates to give immediate assistance to any person when required.

Are you aware that there is a practice at Newcastle, and in other towns in the North of England, which is considered there as facilitating very much the execution of public justice, namely, the having written against the front of the residence, a large legible inscription, painted on a board, three or four inches long, " William Williams, Constable?"—I was not aware that that practice existed.

Should you not think that a very wise plan, to be universally adopted?—I do not know how any man, in the situation of a constable, could be compelled to deface his residence by putting out such a sign; the Lord of the Leet appoints him, under a penalty of 20*l.* or 30*l.* to take upon him the compulsory office of a constable; to deface his dwelling, if he felt it a defacement, by any order that might be made upon him of this kind, he would naturally resist: notwithstanding, I think the regulation would be useful.

Why should you think persons would be more tender on that subject in the South of England than they are in the North, where it is almost universally the practice?—They may be hired substitutes. I think that a constable here would not wish to invite customers; it is a compulsive and laborious duty.

It has been suggested by some Magistrates in the country, that it would be a very advisable plan to compel every publican to set up in his bar, fairly and conspicuously, the names of two or three of the nearest constables; should not you think that an advisable plan?—I think it would be very proper if every body knew that by going into a public-house he could learn the residence of a constable, it would be a useful plan; every notoriety of the residence of a peace officer must be desirable.

You have stated in your evidence, that though some of the Clerks in the Bow-street Office practise as attornies, yet no public inconvenience has been found in consequence of their private business interfering with their public?— I believe I rather in that answer might have said, that no public inconvenience had arisen in the concerns of the Office. It must be admitted that just as much as a man is absent on his private avocations, or his mind is engaged in them, just in that degree his public duty is suspended.

In point of fact, are the Clerks who are solicitors often absent on their duty?— Speaking of the Clerks now employed in Bow-street, at times they are, but not greatly to the public inconvenience, because those remaining, and the Magistrates together, do the business without public detriment.

Has Mr. Stafford any other engagement besides that of attending his duty as first Clerk of the Office?—He has.

Has Mr. Francis Thomas any other occupation?—I believe not.

How long has he been in the Office?—I can hardly tell, but I suppose the best part of 20 years; he is rather declining in his energies.

Has Samuel Keene any other employ?—Samuel Keene is often absent from the Office, when he thinks there is any person remaining there to do the duties, having considerable business as an attorney.

There is an extra Clerk, of the name of William Woods; what circumstance led to the appointment of an extra clerk?—I was not attached to the Office at his original appointment, but I fancy his skill in accounts and writing, which has given him an insight into the duties of a clerk that almost compensates the absence of others.

If there were three Clerks who devoted the whole of their time and attention to the business of the Office, would they be sufficient to conduct the whole of the business?—Beyond a doubt.

Have you any means of knowing, from any record which is kept in the Office, or otherwise, at what hour persons are apprehended in the course of the day, and at what hour they are examined?—If a person is brought to the Office in custody, and a Magistrate is sitting, that person is immediately brought before him, or as soon as the business in hand will permit; but it will often happen when a person is brought in custody, that the prosecutor and witnesses are not arrived, and then he stops till that necessary delay is over.

There

There therefore exist in the Office no means by which it could be known whether it was true that a person was apprehended on one day at four o'clock, and not examined until four o'clock the next day, if such a thing happened?—I hardly think that such a thing ever happened, unless the absence of necessary witnesses occasioned it; there is no entry made of the time at which a person was apprehended, and the hour at which he is examined; till he is brought before the Magistrate, the constable is responsible for the confinement.

Would it not be possible to make an entry of the time when he arrived at the Office, and the time when he is ultimately examined?—The constable is responsible for bringing his prisoner before the Magistrate as soon as he can, and till he brings him before the Magistrate, the accusation takes no shape; but the hours might be noted if required.

What check have you upon the exercise of that responsibility by the constable?—Only as the individual case arises; if the prisoner makes any complaint to the Magistrate, he goes into a strict inquiry as to the neglect, and would in a flagitious case order the constable into a course of responsibility; I would call it a false imprisonment, and make him amenable to an indictment.

Is not the time of his being taken into custody entered into the charge-book, which you have stated is kept in every watch-house?—Not always; I have frequently recommended it, and frequently observed upon it when it has not been so, when the watch-house book has been produced.

According to your opinion, that would be a very advisable regulation?—I think it would, even for their own indemnity.

What is the nature of the fees that are paid at the Office at Bow-street?—Upon the taking out a warrant, there is a written information, and a warrant issues upon that, each attended with a fee of one shilling; that is all that ever is taken by the Clerks; there is no instance of any extortion, I believe.

Those fees are paid over by the Receiver General quarterly?—Those fees are virtually paid over, they are carried into the account, and deducted from the incidental charges, and the Receiver settles the balance as it appears upon the accounts.

In point of fact, each Clerk quarterly makes out his account, and pays to the Receiver of the Police the money he receives?—The account is made out altogether, and the balances are paid over or received according to the fact; the quarterly balance is about 3,000 *l.* generally, including salaries and the patroles.

What is that account made up of, entirely of fees?—The fees received in the Office are placed against the account of the expenditure, and the balance is brought by the Receiver as soon as he gets the issues from the Treasury.

You stated yesterday, that pains were taken at the Public Offices to ascertain the character of persons petitioning for licences; and that the persons so petitioning, brought with them the recommendation, either of the Clergyman, or of two resident housekeepers?—The statute requires that, to obtain a new licence.

Are you aware that it is stated by Mr. Colquhoun to be within his knowledge, that those recommendations are got by the beadle of the parish for a fee of half-a-crown, who gets the signature of the Clergyman?—I have not the least idea that any Clergyman would certify such a matter upon such a mode of application.

Is it a matter of much solicitation, the obtaining those recommendations from third persons to the Magistrates?—They are extremely pressing; individuals carry it on almost as a canvas; I have heard the merits discussed at the Justices' Meeting, on a single licence, for an hour.

You stated in your evidence yesterday, that you thought it would be advisable if some regulations were established for shutting up gin-shops at an early hour of the night; do you not think a similar advantage would arise if gin-shops were prevented selling liquor every Sunday morning before church-time?—This might countenance their legality; but every restraint on the trade of a gin-shop would be beneficial, and I could wish that no spirits were sold in very small quantities, except to persons who went through the general tap-room of an ale-house, properly so called, to the bar: I have done every thing for twenty years, that I could do, consistent with a just regard to the property, both in my Police appointment and in the capacity of a county Magistrate, and almost all the Magistrates have the same view and feeling on the subject, namely, to prevent any gin-shop, not being an alehouse, to be kept open.

510.   You

Sir
Nathaniel Conant.

You say you have done all that lay in your power to suppress houses selling gin alone, and that you have been twenty years engaged in that endeavour; are you not of opinion that gin-shops are more numerous now than at any former period?—No; every opportunity of suppressing them the Magistrates have availed themselves of: when they see a public-house turned into a gin-shop, they insist upon their wholly changing the features of the house, and going back into the ostensible appearance of a beer-house; universally at every licensing meeting that I have attended, the having two doors, a bar-door and a public-house door, is objected to; and licences are withheld, to the amount of twenty at a time, till that complete reform has taken place. I speak particularly of the Holborn Division.

Do you believe that practice to be confined to the Holborn Division, or to be general?—In the City of Westminster it is not so much attended to.

Are you aware of any public-houses in London with two doors, the one for entry and the other by which they go out, passing by a bar, where they take their glass of gin, deposit their money, and take their departure; the consequence of which has been, that on a Sunday morning, between half past six and eight o'clock, an opposite neighbour counted 165 persons pass through one house?—I think it probable; but if that was made a formal complaint of to the Justices at any licensing meeting, the licence would be withheld till the building was reformed, or denied altogether.

The object of the construction of the gin-shops in the Metropolis is to have but one room where the liquor is retailed, and a small apartment inside, where the family live, in many instances with no second story, solely devoted to the sale of spirits; should you license a house of that description and character, if it was applied for?—Never; I never saw a pretence to get a licence for a new house that had not the capacities of an alehouse conspicuously belonging to it.

What opportunities have the Magistrates of obtaining the form of the house; do they visit it before they license it?—I do not know what they do in other divisions, but for many years past I have gone with the Chairman of the Holborn Division round to every new house that was petitioned for, to examine into the local circumstances; and many other Magistrates do the same.

Is there any regular inspection as to the form of the gin-houses, by which the proprietors would be prevented, after they had obtained their licences, from changing the form at their convenience?—If they do, if they turn them into gin-shops, they hear of it the next time; and generally it is an absolute reason for denying the licence a second year.

Has that been often done?—I have always done it as far as I could, and many other Magistrates have the same feeling.

Do you mean to state that no alehouse can be converted into a gin-shop without information coming to the Magistrate?—The high constable is always in attendance upon the Magistrates; we never begin a licensing without the high constable and petty constables of the Division being convened; and we question them (on oath too, which may be extra-judicial) whether any house is misconducted in their respective districts, both as to general management, or as having been converted into gin-shops. Those that are pointed out, undergo a candid examination at an adjournment day, generally a fortnight afterwards; and I believe this is the practice in other Divisions. The Magistrates attend to this duty with the utmost diligence.

Have you any doubt that the great prevalence of those gin-shops contributes, more than any other cause you can name, to the early corruption of both sexes?—I think them mischievous to the last degree, in every point of view.

Have you any doubt that, from those shops not having tap-rooms, persons reputably dressed, women particularly, are induced to go there to drink spirits, who would be ashamed to pass through a room which was crowded with men?—That is the reason why I wish the opportunity of obtaining spirits in small quantities should be through a public room.

What is the course you pursue in your Division, to limit the increase, or to put an end to gin-shops?—By requiring the high constable to present at the licensing meetings, all the houses that are carried on as mere spirit shops distinct from victualling houses, and by suppressing them wherever we find an opportunity.

Do you believe he is faithful in the execution of that order?—They have been so, so, I think, in general; there are a great number, in the parts of the town where they most prevail, suspended on the first day of licensing, to the amount perhaps of twenty at a time, and the bricklayer and carpenter are set to work to alter them, and the painter to put up the chequers, which is the sign of beer, and the house carries another form : we very often find them the next year going on in the old way, and then, without giving them an opportunity of explanation, deny the licences ; but generally the high constable gives them warning beforehand.

Is it not an obligation by law, that persons should take out a beer licence before they can get from the Excise a spirit licence?—Yes.

Is not that in many cases only nominal, and no beer is sold?—When a new licence is applied for, for a tavern or coffee-house, or hotel or eating-house, if it happens to be in a neighbourhood where we could suspect it might be converted into a gin-shop, from the failure of their present speculation, we have of late years introduced an indorsement upon the back of the licence, that that licence is granted for a coffee-house, or whatever it may be, upon condition that it is used as such only, and not to be converted into a shop for the sale of spirits ; we do that because of the injury, if an assignment was to take place, to the person who might purchase it, not knowing the condition imposed at the time of granting it.

You have no doubt that the practice alluded to takes place?—It certainly does, and it requires extreme caution to prevent it, otherwise the mischief would be greater than it is ; and after all, the practice prevails in a considerable degree.

Have not the licences increased, the last year?—The licences in the neighbourhood of London increase just as the new buildings increase ; if 100 houses are built, there will be one or two licences granted, and half a dozen denied.

Is there any account kept in your Office, of the number of persons brought before the Magistrates in the course of a year, and of the proportion committed, to those who are discharged?—For the lesser offences, of assaults, and casual disturbances in the streets, though in general the names of the parties are entered in the book of occurrences, and how they are disposed of, whether discharged or bailed, or committed, they undergo no summing up ; although, if occasion required, they might be collected at any time.

You are speaking now of the smaller offences ; is there any account kept of those charged with capital offences?—Yes, and of any evidence that any witness offers on the subject.

Do you think that an account could be furnished to the Committee of that number?—There could be an account given of every such person brought before the Magistrates, distinguishing how they are dealt with, and all the circumstances of their case : an abstract of such an account goes to the Secretary of State's Office every month.

You have stated, that you have been in Bow-street only two years and a half? —Yes.

From what you have seen yourself in that Office, in your capacity as a Magistrate, do you think that the crimes that are committed in the Metropolis have considerably increased within these few years?—The atrocious offences have been less, for the last three or four years ; the number of larcenies have increased ; I think the number of pickpockets and street-robbers are less frequent.

Has there not been a very considerable increase of juvenile depredators, commencing almost at the earliest age?—I think they increase, even to the present moment ; but at all times offenders under twenty years of age have been as numerous as those above it.

The question does not refer to offenders under twenty years of age ; but have you not brought before you, charged with crimes of all descriptions, children of the early age from six and seven years to fifteen?—For pilfering and privately stealing, to an alarming number.

Can you state to the Committee any reason that has suggested itself to your mind, why there should, within these few last years, have been that alarming increase of crimes among children?—I cannot impute it to the increased profligacy and poverty of their parents (for I do not think that cause has increased ;) but the exposure of goods at shop-doors, the opportunity of bad association from increased population, are the principal causes that occur to me at present.

Do you not think that the limited opportunity for education is also one of

the

the most efficient causes?—I think both the improvement of the mind, and the restraints attending education, go greatly to diminish crimes in young people, very much indeed.

Do you think, speaking generally of the lower classes in the Metropolis, that their habits are more vicious, or that their poverty is greater, than they were ten years ago?—No, I do not think they are.

Then, if the increase of crimes which is allowed to exist is to be traced to the poverty and vice, which have not increased, how can you account for the additional number of crimes which is allowed on all hands to have taken place in the Metropolis?—I know no way of accounting for that, unless some of it is imputable to the exposure above-mentioned, and the neglect of those to whose care property is intrusted; and perhaps some of it may be imputable to the greater vigilance of Police in the parishes as well as offices, in the apprehending of offenders; and I rather think that the number of crimes has not so much increased in fact, as the number of offenders discovered.

Do not you think it is partly attributable to the increased size of the town, and the increased population?—I do: the population probably has increased within the last five or six years. In the former ten years, I believe, there was an increase of 150,000 persons, between the returns of population in the Metropolis of the years 1801 and 1811.

You are inclined to believe that the increased number of crimes that appear to have taken place within the last few years, is more the result of the vigilance of the Police, in detecting them and apprehending the offenders, than the positive result of there being a greater number of crimes committed?—I can account for it in no other way.

Do you think that if the principal places of confinement in the Metropolis were placed in a situation different from what they are, in which a proper classification of offenders took place, and in which the infant could be separated from the adult, one of the causes of the increased number of criminals would be removed?—The infant, under proper discipline, without the bad example of the adult, must be greatly amended; and the other classification must be beneficial.

Have you any doubt that the principal places of confinement, so far from effecting the correction and reformation of the criminal, tend to send him back, at the expiration of the period of his imprisonment, more confirmed in vice?— I think he comes out generally worse than he went in, but perhaps still with a fear of getting there again that may lessen his future offences; for though he comes out worse, he is afraid of going in again, having experienced the miseries of a gaol: the worst of them hate the restraint; though they are free from labour, and fed, they have not those licentious occupations and strong liquors that are necessary to their idea of happiness.

Do you not think, among the various predisposing causes for vitiating the people of this Metropolis, the Lottery establishment is a very efficient one?— That evil is at present very much restrained.

As far as it goes, is not its whole operation on the morals of the public, bad?— It leads to theft, to supply the deficiency occasioned by their losses and disappointments in the Lottery.

Have you not constantly brought before you informations for illegal insurances, on the drawing of the Lottery?—Frequently.

Are not persons brought before you, the accused as well as the accuser, amongst the lowest orders of society?—Among them there are persons of the lowest order; they are the greater number. There are people in the back ground, that have got 40 or 50,000*l.* by that traffic, who employ people of the lowest order, and give them a commission for what they bring; there is a wheel within a wheel.

Is not the evidence by which those informations are supported, generally that of persons of the most abandoned character?—As far as my observation goes, they are generally persons who have been sufferers in that sort of lottery, actuated either by resentment or by the object of future gain.

They receive from three to five pounds a piece for each information, do they not?—I cannot tell the amount; it sometimes comes out in evidence that they receive for their general employment, not for the particular case that is brought forward, for then the Magistrate would throw the evidence aside at once.

Do not those persons form a class of persons who gain a livelihood, and who

derive

derive a trade, by lodging informations upon this subject; are not their faces almost as well known at your Office as those of your own Runners?—Yes; and they seek a knowledge of the offender and then the offence, and then give evidence of it.

Have you not had cases before you, in which it has been quite manifest that the persons lodging the information have wilfully perjured themselves, for the purposes of the money they were to gain by it?—I do not remember an instance of that.

Had you not a case, not many days back, in which a woman deposed against another person for making an illegal insurance, and who being questioned whether she had not been tried at the Old Bailey for forgery of a seamen's will under another name, denied the fact; upon which a solicitor who was accidentally present at Bow-street, and who had conducted her defence, gave testimony to the fact, and the consequence was that the Magistrates dismissed the information?—I think it must have been before other Magistrates; I do not recollect that I was present at the hearing of such a case, but I think it is very likely to have occurred, I am sure that result would have followed upon the circumstances stated.

Do you not, then, think that the facility that this mode of rewarding the informers against those who make illegal insurance affords, is one of the most fruitful means by which the poorer classes of the people can suffer wrong, and that the parties lodging the information can gain a livelihood by perjury?—I hardly know how to answer that question; because in nine cases out of ten that those people bring forward, the party appears, from other circumstances attending the case, to have been guilty; they generally fix upon the right person, although they may be induced to support it by false testimony.

Do you believe that in nine cases out of ten brought before your Office, for illegal insurances, the party is really guilty?—Indeed I do, in some such proportion.

Do you not know that there are persons now under sentence of confinement, convicted of perjury, who have for years past been in the frequent habit of lodging informations against individuals, to the amount of sixteen or eighteen cases per annum, and who have derived their livelihood from that trade?—I know nothing of their habits, excepting when they are brought forward to give their evidence, and as it comes out in cross-examination.

Of course one conviction before your Office, of an attempt to perjure themselves, would preclude altogether the evidence of that person from being again received?—I think it ought; it is not at all uncommon for the offenders solemnly to deny the fact, but before they leave the Office to confess it; and I have known many cases in which they have set up false alibis.

Do you not think that the system of pawnbrokers in the Metropolis, and the facility with which any thing that is stolen can immediately be disposed of, is also one of the great causes of the multiplication of thefts?—The facility with which stolen goods are got rid of, is a great encouragement to theft; but the business of a pawnbroker is of infinite accommodation to the poorer classes of people, and a great means by which they carry on their most profitable and honest pursuits; a woman can pawn her garments, and with the produce of that pledge can go to Billingsgate and buy mackarel, and afterwards fruit, and, by the sale, keep her family for three days.

Has any plan suggested itself to you, by which those shops could be placed more under the inspection and control of the Police, without interfering with those beneficial results which you have just stated?—The law is already strong upon that point. It is a profitable trade, and the persons who carry it on are not disreputable, or uninclined, as far as I have seen, to aid the detection of thieves.

Do you not think there is a class of persons who may be considered as pawnbrokers, who are in fact neither more nor less than the receivers of stolen goods, and who gain their livelihood by their connexion with thieves?—They have not come to my knowledge.

Do you think they could exist to any considerable extent in this Metropolis, without coming under the eye of the Police?—Where a pawnbroker is at all understood to be the encourager of thieves, or there is even well-founded suspicion of it in evidence, they have been indicted as receivers of the stolen goods, and this deters them.

510.   *Patrick*

Patrick Colquhoun, Esquire, LL.D. called in, and Examined.

THE Committee, seeing in the evidence which you gave before the Committee of the House of Commons in the year 1798, that, turning your attention to the means of improving the Police of the Metropolis, you suggested the plan of a central Police Board, which should have under its control the different Police Establishments of the Metropolis, wish to know whether the experience of the number of years which have passed since that opinion was first given, has confirmed you in it?—My experience has most unquestionably confirmed the opinion I then entertained of the propriety and utility of that measure, and I never can sufficiently lament that it has not been carried into execution, as a means of preventing many crimes which have since been committed in the Metropolis.

State to the Committee the general outline of your plan.—In reply, I beg leave to present to the Committee a printed Abstract, which contains the general outlines of the system, and which perhaps will be found more correct than any answer I can give verbally from mere recollection at this distance of time.

[The Witness delivered in a book, entitled, " A general View of the National Police System recommended by the Select Committee of Finance to the House of Commons, and the Functions of the proposed Central Board of Police Revenue; with Observations on the probable Effects of the general design, in the Prevention of Crimes, and in securing the Rights of the peaceful Subject.

By P. Colquhoun, LL.D."]

Was that plan, so proposed by you, ever in the contemplation of His Majesty's Government?—Certainly it was; I have understood its adoption was at one time determined upon.

Do you know for what reasons it was abandoned?—I do not know; I never heard any reason assigned.

What were the leading advantages of that plan over the present system ?—The present system extended no advantages whatever in the way of improvement, beyond that of a purer and perhaps a more intelligent Magistracy; the improvements proposed had not only for their object the diminution of crimes, and the consequent lessening of the demand for punishment, but also the relieving the finances of the country of the expenses of the Police establishment.

Do you think that the positive expenses of the Police would have been thereby considerably diminished?—They would at all events have been diminished to the extent of that revenue, and would certainly go very far beyond the expenses of the proposed new system.

Have you any reason to think that that mode of collecting the revenue, stated in the plan you have given in, has become less practicable than at the period in which it was proposed?—It is equally practicable at this period, in my opinion, as before, with this difference, that it is now more imperiously called for, and is likely to be more productive.

Do you not think that there are considerable practical obstructions to public justice, from the separate and unconnected and uncorresponding Establishments of the Police in this Metropolis?—I certainly think so; my opinion is not altered since my examination before the Committee in 1798.

So that it might happen that a criminal under a better system of Police would be immediately apprehended, whereas now he almost as certainly escapes?— I conceive that it would give more energy generally to the Police system, and would tend in a great degree, not only to the detection, but also more particularly to the prevention of crimes, which has always been my great object, and which I consider as the very essence of Police.

Do you not think that one of the best modes for the prevention of crimes would be the speedy apprehension of any criminal, the moment he commits the offence?—It would be one of the modes, but I do not conceive the best that could be adopted, for the prevention of crimes.

What are those modes to which you give a preference?—The great features of the plan of Police which I suggested in the year 1798, had for their object the prevention of crimes in a greater degree than exists at present, but also the means of a more speedy detection when crimes were actually committed.

In

P. Colquhoun, Esq.

In what manner would you suggest that crimes could be prevented more easily than in the present practice, namely, that of seizing the offender as soon as he commits the crime?—I conceive that seizing the offender the moment it is practicable after he has committed the crime, is one of the readiest methods of bringing him to justice, and this I conceive would be one of the effects of the proposed system ; to permit criminals to go at large for a certain length of time would be highly injurious, and a great breach of duty on the part of the officers of justice. The positive remedies for the prevention of crimes, appear to me to be, first, a revision and consolidation of the criminal law of the country ; secondly, to adopt checks and regulations such as have been recommended by the Select Committee in 1798, and other improvements, which a full consideration of the subject might suggest ; thirdly, to improve the laws relative to vagrants ; fourth, to consolidate the poor laws, and render them more applicable to the present state of society, and to the object originally intended ; and, fifth, to promote emigration of our surplus population to the colonies, since, from its rapid increase and the introduction of machinery, the supply of labour has for a length of time appeared to me, in almost all branches of industry, to be greater than the demand, and hence the vast number of individuals on the parish funds in the middle stations of life.   I conceive also that the increase of the population, partly arising from vaccination, and partly other causes, has introduced into society a vast number of infants of both sexes left orphans, *destitute*, and the progeny of indigent and profligate parents, who cannot find employment for them, and have not the means of binding them out as apprentices to trades, especially where under more favourable circumstances it is difficult to find masters ; and hence I account for the mass of infantine criminal delinquency which prevails at present.

The Committee understand you then to state, that prior to the introduction of those means by which infantine life has been prolonged, the number of children who reached the years of maturity was considerably less than at present ?—I certainly think so, I can account for the great increase of infantine profligacy in no other way.

And consequently that there are a greater number of children thrown as it were into the market of vice, without the means of finding honest employment, than existed formerly ?—Yes, I think so.

Is it your opinion that the crimes in the Metropolis have increased in a positive proportion, or only in the proportion of the increase of the number of inhabitants, arising from the causes you have just mentioned ?—It appears to me that both causes have tended to the increase that appears upon the public reports that have been made ; an additional cause of late is, the number of persons discharged from the army and navy without the means of subsistence.

Do you think that the number of offences have increased, or only that the Police has been more active in detecting them ?—The Police certainly, as far as it can be called a Police, has been as active as the nature and organization of the present system will admit, in detecting offences ; and I cannot attribute their increase to any other than the causes I have already stated.

Do you think that the morals of the poorer and middling classes of the inhabitants in this Metropolis have deteriorated, or improved, within these last ten years?—With regard to the middling classes, their morals are unexceptionable ; those above poverty may be considered as stationary, and generally good ; with regard to the lowest ranks of society, I think there has been a progressive retrograde from the commencement of the revolutionary French war, particularly in all the large towns, in the course of the last twenty-four years.

Then in that view of the subject you would be led to conclude that there has been a positive increase of the number of crimes, arising from the morals and habits of the lower orders of the people having become worse?—The increase of crimes is partly to be traced to that source.

Have you a general Table there of the increase of crimes within the last ten years?—I have a general Table stating what the crimes were in 1805, and from 1810 progressively to 1815 : the results are,

    In 1805 - - 3,267 males - - 1,335 females - - total 4,602 in the whole country, that is, upon a population then of 8,872,980 resident in England and Wales.

         In

P. Colquhoun,
Esq.

In 1810 - - males 3,733 - - females 1,413 - - total 5,146
In 1811 - - males 3,859 - - females 1,478 - - total 5,337
In 1812 - - males 4,891 - - females 1,685 - - total 6,574
In 1813 - - males 5,433 - - females 1,731 - - total 7,164
In 1814 - - males 4,826 - - females 1,564 - - total 6,390
In 1815 - - males 6,036 - - females 1,782 - - total 7,818

Total during the last six years, from 1810 to 1815 - 38,429

Out of what population?—A population of about 10,500,000, making an increase of 2,000,000 from the former return, excluding the soldiers and seamen in both instances. In order to form a correct opinion of the general state of the country in these respects, you must look not only to the actual amount of criminals who come under the cognizance of Courts of Justice, but also to the numbers that are discharged, after their punishment expires, without character or the means of subsistence ; to which is to be added, those who float in and out of gaols in the metropolis and in the country, charged with offences without sufficient proof. The number imprisoned under summary convictions, and bailable offences, disorderly persons charged with assaults, disorderly prostitutes, assaults, and other petty delinquents, are extremely numerous, and make up part of the criminal catalogue of offenders, although they do not appear in the registers of the Courts of Criminal Justice. You can therefore draw no accurate conclusion from the number of offenders sent for trial, without also adding thereto the number of other delinquents who pass through the gaols periodically from year to year. The total amount, male and female, may be ascertained to a point, by calling on the gaolers of the different counties to make returns of prisoners (not sent for trial) who have been committed and discharged in each year. I calculate in round numbers, that about 5,000 individuals, not sent for trial, float in and out of the gaols of the metropolis in the course of every year ; but keeping in view those that are acquitted, you must consider also those sent for trial but not prosecuted, who amount in this Table exhibited to 14,067, besides those that are imprisoned and discharged within this period, amounting to 16,035. Supposing that those that have been committed and discharged by the Magistrates amount to 10,000, and those committed for minor offences were 12,000, you will have a total of upwards of 50,000 floating delinquents arising from discharges from prison after the expiration of their sentences, from acquittals, from liberation for want of prosecutors at the gaol deliveries, from the temporary commitments and dis-charges of Magistrates. It is from this general view only that the actual number of criminal delinquents can be estimated ; and even this will not be accurate, since almost innumerable larcenies are committed, which never come under the view of Magistrates or Courts of Justice.

Do you not think the facility with which any person who steals an article of property, from the greatest value to the smallest, is enabled to dispose of it, furnishes a great encouragement to the commission of thefts?—I certainly do.

Have you been able to obtain any information as to the number of places that may be considered as opened for the reception of stolen goods in the Metropolis?—I have understood that they amount at the present time to about eight thousand, principally kept by persons dealing in old iron and other metals, marine stores, rags, second-hand apparel, old building materials, and piece-brokers selling remnants of cloth; besides private receivers of every species of stolen property, who do not keep open shops.

You mean in your number of 8,000, that there are 8,000 places existing in the Metropolis alone?—In the Metropolis, and in the environs thereof.

Comprising Southwark?—Yes, comprising the Bills of Mortality, with Saint Pancras and Mary-le-bone, and streets adjacent.

Is there any check, in the nature of licence, to the existence of those houses? —None whatever.

Do you think that it would be advisable to propose any thing in the nature of a licence, which would operate as a check to their existence?—I have stated this fully in my examination before the Select Committee in 1798, and I am more and more confirmed in the opinion since that period, that it would be highly desirable to establish some check by a licence, or other regulations, applicable

P. *Colquhoun,*
Esq.

applicable to the class of dealers, including itinerant Jews and other purchasers of old clothes, persons erecting or setting up any cutting engines for cutting round blanks by force of a screw, or any stamping-press, fly, rolling-mill, or other instrument for stamping, flatting, or marking metals or Bank notes, or which, with the assistance of any matrix, stamp, dye, or plate, will stamp coins or notes, so as to prevent the enormous evils constantly experienced by the coinage of base money and the counterfeiting of Bank notes; a regulation whereby the criminal part of ingenious artists could be kept under the immediate view of the Police, and those offences in a great measure prevented.

What are the other remedies that you allude to, that you would propose in addition to the check of a licence, as applicable to those 8,000 houses?—Those are particularly detailed in the Report of the Select Committee in 1798, and in the printed " View " now presented to the Committee, but more particularly in a Bill drawn under my inspection in the year 1799.

Are not those houses now constantly within the superintendence and care of the Police?—Those houses where old metals are sold, upon information given that stolen metals or other goods are deposited, may be visited by a warrant from a Magistrate, and all suspected articles removed, and the parties brought before him, to prove that they came into their possession in the regular way of fair trade; if such proof cannot be adduced to the satisfaction of two Justices, the goods are forfeited, and a penalty of forty shillings is inflicted upon the offender for the first offence, four pounds for the second, and six pounds for the third. There is no other check; no warrant can be granted, or shop visited, unless by previous information upon oath that stolen goods are suspected to be there deposited or concealed.

Do you think that the existence of those houses, as affording the means to thieves for the sale of goods that are stolen, is known to the Police?—The existence of the houses is certainly known to the Police, because they are open shops, and the fact of their being the receptacles for stolen goods is certainly very notorious.

Are complaints often lodged against those houses at the different Boards of the Police in the Metropolis?—As far as my knowledge goes, they are very frequently lodged, it is so where I sit as a Magistrate, and very large quantities have often been seized, of lead and other metals, and sometimes goods and apparel of various descriptions.

Can you specify to the Committee any of the leading improvements that you would suggest for the remedy of the evils which you state?—It does not occur to me that any material regulations beyond what are contained in a Bill already mentioned, which was drawn under my direction about seventeen years ago, would be necessary.

The Magistrates are empowered by a late Act of Parliament to commit to the House of Correction persons who are proved before them to be reputed thieves?—They are.

Is that power, to your knowledge, much exercised by the Magistrates?—I believe it is never exercised but in case of notorious offenders.

Are there frequent instances?—The instances are not very frequent in my practice.

The mode of proceeding is to commit them to the House of Correction, is it not?—Upon proof of their being reputed thieves, found in the avenues leading to places of public resort, and not giving satisfactory account of their way of living, one Justice, on the oath of one or more credible witness or witnesses, may adjudge them to be rogues and vagabonds within the intent and meaning of the 17th Geo. II. and to commit them to the House of Correction until the next General or Quarter Sessions of the Peace, there to be farther dealt with according to law. It is, however, a bailable offence, and if they find bail they are liberated till the Sessions; then the Sessions either affirm or quash the conviction of the Magistrates, and give them a further punishment by imprisonment under the authority of the Act of the 17 George the Second, commonly called the Vagrant Act.

That is only in case the conviction is appealed from?—No; the Magistrates conviction goes to the Session, and, according to the form of the conviction inserted in the Act, " there to be further dealt with according to law."

Are not the Magistrates authorized, on the oath of one person, to commit

for

for six months?—The Magistrate may, on conviction, commit the offenders even for a less time than until the Sessions. The power of committing for six months belongs only to the General or Quarter Sessions. This Act has existed since the year 1792, when a purer and better informed Magistracy were appointed to sit at the different Offices then established. It has certainly tended in some degree to intimidate persons of evil fame, and to prevent their attending public places; although, upon the whole, its preventive operation has not perhaps been so extensive as had been anticipated.

What number of instances, in the course of a year, are there of that description?—Speaking from my own knowledge, I should say very few indeed; there are a good many from Bow-street, I believe. The number, during the last 24 years, can easily be ascertained by calling for a return of the convictions at the different Public Offices.

Jovis, 2° die Maii, 1816.

The Honourable HENRY GREY BENNET, in The Chair.

Mr.
John Stafford.

Mr. *John Stafford*, called in, and Examined.

WHAT is your situation?—Chief Clerk at the Public Office in Bow-street.

Do you hold any other situation besides that?—Yes, I have other situations, but not under Government; I am Clerk of Indictments on the Home Circuit and at the Middlesex Sessions.

Do you practise as a solicitor?—No; I am not a solicitor, I am admitted of the Society of the Inner Temple, and practise as a Crown draughtsman.

How many days are you, in consequence of holding those two first situations, necessarily absent from the Office?—I think, upon an average, the two Circuits in the year require about eight weeks absence; my attendance at the Sessions never entirely prevents my attending at the Office, because I have a clerk to assist me at the Sessions, and I go backwards and forwards during the day, as I find necessary; if the business presses at the Sessions, I am a longer time there; if I find it necessary to be longer at the Office, I am so.

There are eight Sessions in the year?—Yes.

How many days do they generally last?—My attendance is never required but while the Grand Jury are sitting, that is generally five or six days each Session, and no evening attendance is necessary.

When you are not attending your duty at Bow-street Office, who does it for you?—There are two other Clerks upon the establishment, a Second and Third clerk, and also an assistant clerk.

In point of fact, is it not the Extra Clerk, as he is named in the return, who does a great part of the business of the Office?—He certainly is of most material service, for Mr. Thomas, the Second clerk, from illness and infirmities, is not so competent now as he was formerly to do the business. I originally took the appointment of Chief Clerk at Bow-street, with an understanding that I was to be permitted to go the Circuit. I previously had the appointment of Chief Clerk at Union Hall, and a vacancy having taken place at Bow-street, Sir Richard Ford, at that time the Chief Magistrate there, offered me the appointment, which I was glad to accept, as the Magistrates at Union Hall had found some fault with my absence on the Circuit; but Sir Richard Ford, so far from objecting to my going the Circuit, said, he thought I might derive from it much information that might be useful to the Office.

Do you not think that if the three Clerks did daily their duty, confining themselves solely to the business of the Office, the necessity of the employment of the extra clerk would no longer exist?—I have my doubts about that; the business of the Office is a great deal more than people in general have any conception of; and I believe that none but persons belonging to the Office are aware of the great labour required from the clerks by the great quantity of business.

You

You must be aware that if you are absent such a number of weeks in the course of the year, if the Second clerk is in a state such as you have described, and if the Third clerk rarely comes to the Office, that supposing all the three Clerks did regularly and punctually their duty, there could be no necessity for an extra clerk?—I certainly think that the three Clerks, by having nothing else to engage their attention but their duty at the Office, and by constant attendance to it, might be enabled to get through the business, but it would be with very hard fagging; there is a great deal of business to do; my time is frequently taken up for hours in answering persons who come to ask questions and seek advice in various matters. There is one duty thrown upon us by two recent Acts of Parliament with respect to the subsistence of soldiers wives and children, and making out routes and passes for them; that takes up almost one person's time.

Is the attendance of the Magistrates at Bow-street regular and uniform?— Our Magistrates certainly do not consider themselves exactly bound to the particular hours specified for the attendance of the Magistrates at the Police Offices; but, generally speaking, the attendance of the Magistrates at Bow-street is regular.

In point of fact does one of the Magistrates daily attend at eleven o'clock?— Yes.

And again at eight o'clock in the evening?—The attendance in the morning is uniform and regular; in the evening sometimes it happens that they do not attend; sometimes it occurs that a Magistrate from another Office will attend for them: Mr. Nares some time ago was in a very bad state of health, he is better now, and attended so late as last night, but when he was in ill health he sometimes absented himself in the evening, and got a Magistrate to attend for him.

Is not the attendance of those Magistrates who may be considered as volunteer Magistrates, receiving no salary, more regular than the attendance of the Magistrates who are paid by the Public?—No; and I beg to state, that the Magistrate who attends in an evening occasionally for him whose turn it is, is generally either one of our own, or one of the Police Magistrates; we have very little attendance indeed at our Office of foreign Magistrates.

Does it ever happen that a person is kept under charge all night, in consequence of there being no Magistrate in attendance to receive the information against him?—It is possible such a thing may have happened, but I do not know of any instance of it within my own recollection.

Were you in attendance on Wednesday the 17th of April last?—I cannot bring to my recollection whether I was or not; but Wednesday is one of the days of Mr. Nares's attendance, and I think it is possible that in the evening there might have been no Magistrate there.

So that it might have happened that a person who was taken up at four o'clock on Wednesday afternoon, was not examined before a Magistrate till between two and three on Thursday?—That might happen; but the lateness of the examination on Thursday could not arise from the non-attendance of a Magistrate. It very often happens, where prisoners are taken in an afternoon, that their examination cannot be gone into in the evening, the officers not being able to procure the attendance of the necessary witnesses so soon; therefore though the Magistrate might be absent, and the prisoner remain in custody, it does not necessarily follow that it was occasioned by the absence of the Magistrate.

You must be aware that though it does not necessarily follow, he could not be examined if there was no Magistrate?—Certainly.

And you are also aware that it is the duty of the Magistrate to be there?— Certainly.

Do you recollect whether the same thing happened a few days previous, in the preceding week?—That I cannot say.

In point of fact is it not a circumstance of common occurrence, that there is not that attendance on a night that there ought to be, on the part of the Police Magistrates?—The only nights that I am aware of any thing like it having happened, are the nights that I have already mentioned, when Mr. Nares should have been there, and another Magistrate has not attended for him; and therefore it has happened that there has been a failure of attendance sometimes in an evening.

510.   Are

Mr.
John Stafford.

Are you at all concerned with the licensing of public-houses at Bow-street?—In the district that is licensed at Bow-street, I am so far concerned as to be joint licensing clerk with the vestry-clerks of the respective parishes we license at Bow-street; which are, the parishes of St. Clement Danes, St. Mary-le-Strand, St. Paul Covent-garden, and the Liberty of St. Martin's-le-Grand.

What pains are taken, prior to the granting of the licence, to ascertain that the person petitioning for a new licence is one to whom such licence ought to be granted?—It has very rarely happened that any new licence has been granted within the district of Bow-street; the Magistrates are anxious rather to lessen the number of public-houses than to increase them. When a person applies for a licence, it is by petition; he states his name, residence, trade or business, and what his reasons are for wishing to take a public-house; and sometimes also the inhabitants send a memorial, stating that the house is necessary or unnecessary, as the case may be; and the Magistrates inquire into all the particulars, and exercise their discretion upon the subject.

Are the certificates generally signed by the clergyman of the parish, or by the parishioners?—I think they are generally signed by some of the parish officers, and some of the parishioners who are substantial housekeepers; in some instances the clergyman signs, but generally the overseers and churchwardens, and some respectable inhabitants.

Are you aware that it is stated by Mr. Colquhoun, that it is a common practice for the beadle to get the certificate of the clergyman, he (the beadle) receiving a fee of half-a-crown, and that those certificates are given as a matter of course?—No, I am not aware of any such practice, nor does it exist in the district I have any thing to do with; we never grant a licence, or even a transfer, without sending for the vestry clerk, who regularly attends, and states that the inhabitants are satisfied with the account they have had of the incoming tenant.

Are not you aware at the Office of the existence of many houses which are known by the name of "Flash houses," where there is a nightly assemblage of bad and low people of both sexes?—No, I do not know of any in our district.

Were you not aware of a house in Rose-street, Covent-garden, against which complaints were made at the Office, and against which a presentment was made by the Magistrates at Clerkenwell?—The house alluded to, I apprehend, is the sign of the Rose, situate in the parish of Saint Martin in the Fields; I am aware of complaints having been made against it: It was kept by a man of the name of Kelly, of bad character, and it was understood that it was frequented by improper persons; the licence was taken away: it has been since granted to another person, and I believe the house now is a very well regulated house.

Will you take upon yourself to say that within your district there are no houses such as have been described, in which nightly meet thieves, persons of the most notorious character, of both sexes, in which they live, and which they use as their dwelling-house; and where the Bow-street Officers go when they wish to look after a thief, knowing that there are his haunts?—To the first part of the question, No, there are none in our district. There is a house, the nearest I know any thing of, known by the name of The Wheat Sheaf, in Drury-lane, situate in St. Giles's in the Fields; we have nothing to do with the licensing of that, but I know that the licence was taken away some time ago, and that the parish indicted the occupier for keeping a disorderly house; the house was afterwards relicensed, and there has been a change of tenants since: I have not heard lately of complaints being made against it, but I have reason to believe that it is now nearly as bad as ever. I do not know of any of our Officers going and associating with the company there.

The question is, whether they do not go there, knowing that there they shall find their prey?—I have no reason to believe that they do.

Do you mean to say that the Police Officers of Bow-street do not know that there are particular-public houses which the thieves in the Metropolis, whose character and whose persons they know, frequent?—Certainly there are houses in the Metropolis that the officers must know and do know are frequented by thieves.

Should you not think it a sufficient objection to warrant the Magistrate refusing the renewal of a licence for the masters of those houses, that the houses themselves are receptacles for thieves?—Most undoubtedly; I should think that

when

when it was established before the Magistrates, that the house was frequented by thieves and persons of evil fame, or that the house was in any other respect a disorderly house, that the Magistrates would consider it a sufficient ground for refusing the licence.

Do you not know that nightly, in the neighbourhood of Drury-lane and Covent-garden, all the small public-houses and gin-shops, of which there are many, are scenes of the greatest debauchery?—No, I do not know it; neither do I think the fact can be established.

Did you ever pass on an evening through any of the streets or alleys in which these public-houses are situate?—I have passed on an evening through all the streets and alleys in the neighbourhood of Covent-garden, and certainly there are many houses open, and there is more bustle in that part of the town than in other parts, in consequence of the vicinity to the theatres; and a great number of persons employed at the theatres, labourers, mechanics, and others, go to those public-houses for necessary refreshment after their business is done.

Is it not a matter of public notoriety, that those houses are the receptacles of every species of vice?—No, certainly not.

Do you consider it as a part of the duty of the Bow-street patrole, to clear the streets and the market of disorderly people, during the night?—"Disorderly people" is such a general term, that I hardly know how to answer; I take it a person must be doing some specific act that will authorize the patrole to interfere, before they can meddle with him.

Do you not know the market itself is a place where boys and women of the town promiscuously sleep?—I never heard of women of the town sleeping in Covent-garden market; I have certainly heard that boys slept there, and idle fellows, and even labourers and porters, previous to commencing their work in the morning, which begins as early as three or four o'clock on market mornings.

Then the Committee are to understand you to state, that the public-houses and gin-shops, and places of that description, in the neighbourhood of Covent-garden and Drury-lane, are generally conducted in a manner that meets with the approbation of the Magistracy?—Perhaps I should be going too far if I was to state that they were conducted in a manner that meets with the approbation of the Magistracy; but I have no hesitation in saying that nothing like the scenes referred to have taken place at those houses, within my knowledge, and I believe many publicans are extremely anxious to keep their houses as orderly as possible. When the licence for the Rose was stopped, some of the people that used to go there, went to another house, the Green Man, and I know that the landlord of that house applied to a Magistrate for advice as to what means he could take to prevent such people coming to his house. Some of the houses are necessarily kept open to a late hour in the night, from the vicinity to the theatres; and the accommodation of persons frequenting the market, requires other houses to open very early in the morning; then there is a description of houses which have sprung up of late years, and are more mischievous than the public-houses, over which the Magistrates have no summary power, they are called coffee-houses or coffee-rooms, and open at eleven, twelve, or one at night, and remain open during the whole of the night, so that when idle people are driven out of the public-houses, they first find a harbour in those places, and can afterwards go to the early market-houses.

Are they obliged to take out a licence?—No, there is no licence at all. Even some eating-houses or cook-shops have got into the way of keeping open almost all night, in which hot victuals, roast pigs, and joints of meat are provided, and people, men and women of any description, are received; I have seen them open till four in the morning.

Do they not there sell liquor?—No, not spirituous liquors; they sell spruce beer and ginger beer, and those sort of things.

Have you ever had any complaints at your Office, of any disorders at those houses?—Yes.

What steps were then taken?—We sent a party of our Patrole with a search-warrant, and took the whole of the people found there at a late hour in the night into custody, considering that they came under the description of idle and disorderly persons, and such as they would be authorized by their warrant to apprehend.

Were

Were any of them in the situation of reputed thieves?—No, I do not recollect that they were.

What did you do with the parties?—They were brought before the Magistrate the next morning; a great proportion of them were discharged; I am not sure whether any were held to bail: Some stated that they were journeymen printers, and that they were employed on the morning papers, which required early attendance; some said they were fishmongers, men going to Billingsgate; and a variety of accounts were given by others. They all said, that seeing the house open, they went in for refreshment. I think the women taken amongst them were sent to prison.

There is a statute 54 Geo. III. (c. 37,) in which it is provided, " that Constables may apprehend suspected persons, that is, persons of ill-fame or reputed thieves; and if such person or such persons shall not be able to give a satisfactory account of themselves, the Magistrate shall have the power of committing them to the House of Correction;" is that Act often acted upon in your Office?—Yes, daily almost: but it requires three things to convict a man under that Act; he must first be a reputed thief, he must be found in one of the places the Act describes, then he must be proved to be there with an intent to commit felony upon the persons or property of His Majesty's subjects, and not be able to give a satisfactory account of himself or of his way of living.

Then one Magistrate can commit him to gaol?—Yes, if he does not appeal at the time of conviction, and offer bail; and as there is no fraction of a day in this respect, he has the whole day to procure bail; but if he does not offer bail till afterwards, we do not accept it.

Can you state to the Committee the number of persons whom the Magistrates at Bow-street have committed within the last year under this Act?—No, I cannot from memory.

Should you think a considerable number?—Yes; I should think there are some committed to every Sessions; perhaps, on the average, four or five to each Sessions, there being eight Sessions in the year.

Do you believe that informations are ever laid against the keepers of public-houses, in order to extort money from them?—I am not aware of it; that has never appeared from any cases brought to the Office in Bow-street.

Do you believe that offences to any extent are committed in the licensed houses, that are not heard of at the Police Office?—No, I do not believe there are.

Do you believe those houses, which are the resort of thieves and loose characters, assist, or otherwise, the Police, in the detection of those thieves?—I think that in some measure they assist; not but that the evil tendency of them more than counterbalances any good they do; but they may assist in this way, that the Officers may go and look into those houses, and by that means they get a knowledge of the persons, of those who are suspected, that they otherwise might not obtain.

Do you not think that, though you are thereby enabled to seize upon one offender, by the general corruption of morals which of course must result from the assemblage of that class of persons together, young and old, more injury is suffered by the community than gained by the punishment of the criminal?—The injury to the community must far exceed any benefit that can be obtained, in my opinion; but I beg leave to say that it very rarely happens that our Officers go there to apprehend thieves.

Is it not a common cant phrase on the part of the Police officers going to one of those houses that he knows will be the resort of the man he seeks for, that he is gone to such a place because he " wants " him?—It may be so amongst some officers, but it certainly is not among ours; and I beg to say I consider our Officers a very superior class of men to some of those who are employed at the other Offices.

Do you speak of those more generally denominated the " Bow-street officers," or the patrole?—I speak of the eight Officers; not but that we have some very respectable men among the patrole.

Is there any difficulty in well-regulated public-houses obtaining a renewal of their licences?—I know of none; at the licensing time, the regular course is for the constable of each ward (for in Westminster the parishes are divided into wards) to bring a list of the houses who require to have their licences renewed;

the

Mr.
John Stafford.

the Magistrate puts the constables upon oath, and asks them such questions as he thinks necessary, and among others, whether the conduct of the house has been such in the neighbourhood as to occasion any complaints, whether the inhabitants have made any complaints, and whether the constable has gone round and observed the conduct which has taken place in the houses ; and if he reports well of them, and there are no objections made by other persons, the renewal of the licence is a matter of course.

What is the practice in case of a complaint being laid against a victualler on the licensing day ?—The practice is to suspend the licensing from the first day, which is generally held early in the month, until the adjourned meeting, and in the mean time take into consideration any petitions or representations made relative to the complaint, and to send the officers, or the Magistrates go themselves, to ascertain whether there is any truth in it.

And that is the invariable practice, however trifling the complaint is ?—It is.

Are there not among the low public-houses in the courts and alleys in the vicinity of the theatres, public-houses that are kept by persons who nominally take out a licence, but whose real trade is the keeping of a brothel ?—No, I do not know any house, myself, that is licensed in our district, that might come under that denomination, except one, which is a very respectable house in point of appearance, and I never heard any complaint against it, but nobody can doubt for what purpose the house is kept; I do not know of any other.

The question refers to that class of houses kept by reputed thieves, who are well known to have been thieves, and to have retired from the trade, considering it as dangerous, and to have set up under the plea of keepers of a public-house, but in reality keepers of brothels ?—I do not know any thing of the kind ; there are brothels in the neighbourhood of Covent-garden, which the occupiers call taverns and hotels, but in fact they are not licensed.

Do you think that it is possible that such a practice as that described should have taken place without its being known at your Office ?—I think not.

Should you not consider it as very culpable remissness on the part of the persons employed in the Office, if it was so ?—If such houses were kept under the colour of a licence in the neighbourhood of the Office, I should think certainly there was culpable remissness in the persons belonging to the Office being unacquainted with it.

Have you the means of telling the Committee where those miserable women, that you see prowling about the streets in such numbers in the vicinity of the theatres at all hours of the night, lodge ?—In all parts of the town ; many of them, I believe, come from Saint George's Fields and from the lower parts of Westminster, from Saint Giles's, Saffron-hill, and every part of the Metropolis inhabited by persons of that description ; the number of people frequenting the theatres necessarily draw many other persons after them ; certainly the bulk of the women do not reside in the neighbourhood of the theatres, the greater part come from a distance.

Does it come within your observation that there has been a great increase, of late years, of juvenile depredators ?—I think there has been an increase.

Can you assign to the Committee any reason for that increase ?—The principal reason that strikes me is, I am sorry to say, a general laxity of morals among the lower orders of people, which has appeared of late years ; they are not so attentive to their religious or moral duties as they used to be ; and I attribute the increase of crimes of the younger branches of the community to the laxity of those whose duty it is to instruct and look after them.

Do you think it is the result of poverty, and that the situation of the lower classes of the people has been considerably deteriorated within the few last years ?—I think in some instances it may arise from poverty, but more generally from a carelessness and negligence of the duty which attaches to parents to take care of their offspring ; many men and women might take care of their children, and bring them up in religious and moral habits, if they were so inclined themselves.

Do you not know that a great proportion of the children brought before you are persons who have been deserted by their parents, and left to seek their subsistence in the streets ?—In some instances they have been deserted by their

parents,

Mr.
John Stafford.

parents, and in others corrupted by their juvenile companions and others, and induced to run away from school or from their parents.

Has it fallen within your observation to ascertain whether the number of schools which have been established, has had any effect in preventing a greater increase, than the state of public morals, such as you have described, would have led any one to consider to be the case?—I am not able to answer that question further than by stating, that I have not observed any material alteration lately.

Do you think that the non-observance of the Sunday has any effect upon the public morals among the lower classes of society?—No doubt of it; I think if they were taught regularly to observe the Sunday, that would have a great effect upon them; but instead of that, they are suffered to go and play about in courts and alleys, and in the fields, and get into bad company, instead of going to church.

Do you think Sunday Papers have any effect upon public morals?—I think not; I think Sunday Papers are not much read by the lower classes of society; sometimes they induce the mechanic to go to a public-house and drink a pint of porter, to read the news, but not further than that.

Do you think the trading in Sunday Papers has any effect to deteriorate public morals?—I cannot say it has; but it certainly is an improper thing, sounding horns and selling them about the streets as they do, on Sundays.

Have you had occasion to notice the number of boys playing in the fields on a Sunday?—Frequently.

What is your opinion of the effect of that habit?—If they are boys that are employed all the week, I think the effect of that habit is likely to lead them to improper courses and to get into bad company; if they were sent to church and kept proper company, they would get much better habits, no doubt.

Has it fallen within your observation that there is a greater degree of sobriety, and of anxiety for information, amongst the journeymen workmen and mechanics, than existed ten years ago?—I have no doubt of there being greater habits of sobriety; how far that may tend to induce them to wish for information I have no means of saying; but I have no doubt that the manners of the lower classes of society are much better than they were ten years ago, those excessive scenes of drunkenness which I have formerly observed are not by any means so frequent.

You think that while the morality of the lower classes of society has been improving, their negligence of their children has grown greater?—I think their drunkenness has been less, and yet the negligence of their children greater

It appears upon the Report of the Committee on Mendicity last year, that there were above 6,000 children in the Metropolis who were mendicants; do you not think that that number might very materially account for the great increase of juvenile depredators which has lately taken place?—I should certainly think that it might; but from my own observation, if I may be permitted to give an opinion, I do not think that any thing like that number exists.

Do you think that if the watchmen in the different divisions of the Metropolis were placed under the control of the Police Magistrates, the town would be considerably better guarded than it is at present?—There cannot be a doubt that it would improve them a great deal; but I should be inclined to think that Police Magistrates have already pretty well as much to do as they can manage

To what is it owing, that the Police Officers at Bow-street are of a higher class than at the other Offices?—Owing to the carefulness observed in selecting and appointing them, and to their having a better school for instruction, and to their being brought up to regular habits. When a man solicits employment at Bow-street, he is placed at first upon the patrole; and after having been there for some time, and his conduct being approved of, he may succeed to the appointment of Conductor, or perhaps be selected for an Officer, and that gives them those habits which are not to be acquired elsewhere, and operates as a stimulus to their exertions. There is a great deal of regularity in the management of the patrole, and we have no instance of any of the officers being induced from venal or corrupt motives to swerve from or betray the confidence reposed in them; and I attribute that to their considering themselves a better description of men, and to their being more generally respected, and in many instances better paid, than at the other Offices; those circumstances altogether make them more anxious to do their duty correctly.

You

Mr.
John Stafford.

You have heard those circumstances respecting the officers of other Establishments?—Certainly I have. As to the patrole, I have a small printed book, containing Regulations, which I beg leave to put in.

Are those peculiar to Bow-street?—Yes, to the foot patrole of Bow-street.

[The Witness delivered in the same.]

Are those Regulations you have given in, uniformly acted upon?—Yes; wherever they are not attended to, and it is discovered, the men are constantly punished, by suspension from pay or by being dismissed.

From your experience in the Office, should you think it all advisable that the Magistrates should be empowered to give rewards for the apprehension of small offenders; you being now aware, of course, that there is no reward paid, unless a person is found guilty of one of those crimes, to the apprehension and discovery of which the Act of Parliament has affixed a reward?—I am no friend to rewards; I think that if men are well paid, and their expenses in looking after offenders allowed under the direction of the Magistrate, it would answer better by exciting in them a general wish to do their duty, rather than to look to conviction only for reward; for there are many instances where the officers act most meritoriously, and where, speaking in a pecuniary point of view, their labour is lost if they are to look only to the conviction for their reward.

Do you not think it would be a change greatly for the better, if the Magistrate was at liberty to reward the special service of an officer, rather than the present system?—Yes. The present system sometimes induces a Jury to discredit the officer, in consequence of observations made upon this subject; the reward is called " Blood-money," and the officers are charged with having it always in view, although frequently the officers benefit very little by the reward, for the Judges on the Circuits, and the Recorder of London at the Old Bailey, in apportioning the rewards, attend to the situation of the parties; and if the prosecutor is poor, or has had a great loss, I understand they give him the larger proportion of the reward; sometimes the officer gets it, but not frequently.

Should you not think, without meaning to imply any censure on the Officers in your department, supposing them to be governed by those motives which ordinarily govern men, they would of course be more remiss in discovering offenders where there was no reward, than they would be in cases where they would receive a large reward?—No, I do not think it would operate upon them in that way: I should not be against rewards being offered in specific cases, for a crime of any magnitude, particularly any one relating to the public, where it became a material object to secure the offender; I think then as a stimulus, not only to our officers, but to officers in general, and to the public, holding out a reward for the apprehension of such a person does good, and that a reward might be offered with considerable effect: the thing I have been speaking of is the parliamentary reward, paid on conviction for particular offences; whether there has been any merit in discovering and apprehending the offender or not, the same reward is paid in those cases.

Do you not think that the parliamentary reward which is given, has a tendency to make the Police officers neglect those crimes which are not worth the reward, as it is stated?—No; speaking of our Officers, I should say decidedly no, I do not think the reward operates upon them in that way.

Your opinion is formed more upon the character of the individuals belonging to your Office, than upon the motives that would operate upon and govern the conduct of ordinary men?—Undoubtedly; but speaking generally, I take it the motives that would operate most on men's minds, would be the motives of gain; and that they would be more anxious to apprehend offenders for whom they were to have a reward, than those in respect of whom they were to have none.

Of course, then, it might have this effect, that an offender might be permitted to pursue his criminal career, from the commission of a small crime, through all the stages, till he committed a great one, he not being worth conviction in the first instance, though he might be worth conviction in the last?—No, I do not think that; I do not think there are any of the officers so venal as to overlook an offender if he was within their reach, and not apprehend him because they knew that there was no reward given by Act of Parliament for the conviction; I meant it to go no further than this, that I think the reward would produce in some

instances

instances a greater stimulus, but I do not think they would neglect to apprehend an offender because there was no reward.

Do you not see that, supposing a Police officer, who, like any other person, might be worse or better than his neighbour, was worse, he would have his inducement, namely, that he would make money by the conviction of one man, when he would not make any thing by the conviction of the other?—Undoubtedly, if you once admit the principle of gain to act exclusively upon the man's mind.

Mr. Samuel Keene, called in, and Examined.

WHAT Office do you hold in Bow-street?—My situation is Third Clerk of the Police Office Bow-street.

What is the attendance you are expected to give in that Office?—The Magistrates take two days in the week for their attendance, according to their agreement; it has been sometimes suggested, that the Clerks should take particular days in the week with particular Magistrates, but that has not been adhered to, and the attendance of the Clerks has been rather more promiscuous.

There are three Clerks in the Office, besides an extra Clerk?—Yes.

Is there sufficient business to keep the three Clerks and the extra one in daily employment?—Yes, I think there is; the incidental business of the Office has latterly increased very much.

What is the nature of your personal attendance in that Office?—It is to attend the Msgistrates, and to take the depositions of persons brought before them for offences; it is the custom of that Office for the Clerks to take down the evidence in an occurrence book; I do not believe that in the Police Offices that is adhered to, I believe the Magistrates in some of the Police Offices take down the evidence themselves, and that the depositions for the Judges at the Old Bailey are made out from the book by the Clerk; but it is the custom in Bow-street, and has been ever since I have known the Office, for the Clerk to take down the evidence.

How often do you attend at the Office yourself?—My days of attendance are Tuesdays and Saturdays, more particularly; I very frequently attend there on other days.

Do you in point of fact attend regularly on every Tuesday and Saturday?—Yes, and very frequently on other days.

Do you attend the whole of those two days?—Yes.

Do you think that if the three Clerks attended constantly, throughout the year, their duty, there would be any occasion to have an extra Clerk?—I think there would, because there is the business of making out the monthly reports, which are transmitted from our Office to the Secretary of State; there is at Bow-street Office an immense number of persons who come to make affidavits, particularly officers in the army and navy on half-pay, and there are a number of other incidental matters, which made it necessary an extra Clerk should be established.

You were appointed by the Secretary of State?—Yes, during Sir Richard Ford's time.

Do you act as a solicitor?—Yes, I occasionally act as a solicitor.

Are you not more employed upon your own private affairs as a solicitor, than you are upon the public affairs of Bow-street Office?—No; I have a share of business as a solicitor and attorney; at any time that I am prevented from attending, either Mr. Thomas or Mr. Stafford has occasionally done my duty when I have been called away on particular business, as I have done theirs on similar occasions.

Have you ever heard any remonstrances made on the part of the Magistrates, that your attendance was not as regular as they thought it should be?—The Magistrates have mentioned, when I have been absent, that they required a stricter attendance; when I was originally appointed to that office by Sir Richard Ford, it was within his knowledge, and the knowledge of the Magistrates, that I was a solicitor, and the small salary I obtained would not have induced me to attend wholly and solely at the Office; it was within Sir Richard Ford's knowledge that I was to be at liberty to attend to my professional business.

Did you consider it as advantageous to your business as a solicitor, to become a clerk in that Office?—Originally it increased my business a little in criminal proceedings, I have had very little of that lately.

Do you act as solicitor to persons brought before the Office for offences?—No, very

very seldom; I have occasionally, on particular prosecutions, been concerned, but very seldom.

Of what nature were those prosecutions?—Felonies and burglaries, and any thing of that kind; but I have not had any thing of that lately; the Magistrates, I believe, conceive it to be unfit and improper that a clerk should be concerned in those prosecutions.

Do you know whether it is the practice of the other Clerks in the Office to be concerned as solicitors for offenders?—I believe in some of the other Police Offices the principal clerks are professional men: when they were established, I believe the major part of the clerks were attornies, and that it is the case with several of them now.

You say Sir Richard Ford understood you were to attend to your own business occasionally; did he understand you were to attend the Office only two days a week?—It was not, I believe, at that time mentioned, that there should be any particular days, but it was a regulation the Clerks adopted from what the Magistrates did; Sir Richard Ford was made acquainted with my situation at that time, which was about fifteen or sixteen years ago; my salary was 100 *l.* it is now increased to 130 *l*; it was always understood that I should attend to my own business also.

Should you decline acting as a Clerk of that Office, if you were told to attend daily the duty there upon your present salary?—I should certainly decline my situation if I were told that I was to attend regularly every day with the salary I receive for it; it is inadequate to any professional person, or any person whether professional or not, who was adequate to the duty of clerk to the Magistrates.

You consider your situation of Clerk to the Office as a secondary consideration to the situation you hold as a practising solicitor?—Yes.

Was the appointment a verbal appointment?—It was a letter, I believe, written by Sir Richard Ford to the Duke of Portland, who was then Secretary of State.

The duties you were to perform were not pointed out by Sir Richard Ford, but only generally, that you were to attend to your business during part of the time?—I was to be allowed to do that; and if any thing particular occurred on those days, Mr. Thomas or Mr. Stafford have done my business for me, and I have done the same for them.

Who fixed Tuesdays and Saturdays as your days?—It has never been adhered to, as the Magistrates adhere to their days; it was proposed by Mr. Stafford, but has never been adhered to; but there are two days in the week that it is considered that I attend more regularly than the other days.

Was it considered that, there being three Clerks, one was to attend on one day, and one on the other?—There is a great deal of business besides the business before the Magistrates, the taking affidavits and so on in the Clerks' office.

Which are Mr. Stafford's two days?—Mr. Stafford considers his days as Mondays and Thursdays; those are the days that Sir Nathaniel Conant attends.

Does Mr. Stafford only attend on those days?—He attends other days promiscuously, like myself and Mr. Thomas; we do not adhere strictly to certain days, as the Magistrates do.

Patrick Colquhoun, Esquire, LL.D. again called in, and Examined.

HOW many Clerks are there in the Office over which you preside?—There are two clerks upon the establishment; and there is another young man, who has been there for a considerable length of time, not upon the establishment, nor paid by the establishment, the Chief Clerk pays him.

Have those Clerks any other employment besides their attendance there?—The Chief Clerk (who is a very able, excellent, and valuable man) is in the law; but he does not let that interfere with his official duties; he is there every day, with

510.   a very

P. Colquhoun,
Esq.

a very few exceptions in term time, and then this person, who is very competent, and has been a long time with him, assists in the business in his absence.

Do you conceive that independently of the personal character of the Chief Clerk in your Office, it may be a disadvantage that the clerks should be employed as attornies?—If he was a man that had not a strong sense of duty, as many may not have, it would be certainly a disadvantage; but in the present case, we have never felt it any inconvenience; whenever there has been any thing of the least importance requiring his attendance, he has always been punctual and regular, we never have felt his occasional absence, which was but seldom, the smallest degree injurious to the public service.

Do you think it is considered as an advantage to the parties in a cause, to employ a clerk in the Police Office as their attorney?—I cannot really say that it can be an advantage, or that it may not; there are other attornies who are generally employed in those cases, who turn their attention particularly to the Crown Law, and who are generally employed in criminal cases. I recollect no instance where the chief Clerk at the Queen-square Office has been so employed.

Do you conceive, at their present salary, you could obtain competent persons to act as Clerks in the Police Offices, without their being at liberty to act as attornies also?—I should think, at their present salaries we could not obtain very competent persons for the situation, unless he had permission to employ his leisure hours in a way to increase his emolument.

Have you ever formed an opinion in respect of the propriety of the present system of rewards given to the officers of the different Police Offices?—The legislative rewards certainly have an effect to excite a good deal of vigilance on the part of officers, where the reward is considerable. Hitherto, in the seven legislative Offices established in 1792, the Magistrates have had no fund, nor any power, to grant rewards to officers performing meritorious services. On some occasions, where they have been sent into the country, and incurred an unavoidable expense to a small amount, the Magistrates have made an order for such expenses; it has amounted only to a trifle in the course of the year. My opinion has been, decidedly, from the beginning, that it would be of importance that the Magistrates should have a power to a certain extent to reward officers who were vigilant and successful in detecting and apprehending offenders; and to mark those who were not vigilant, and less attentive to their duty, by depriving them of any of those pecuniary benefits which the Magistrates might have it in their power to grant. There is a great diversity in mankind; and although there are always many candidates for the situation of Police constables, it is difficult to find men in all respects calculated for the duties that are required; and therefore the power of discriminating between the one and the other would be important to the public interest, and might excite a greater degree of vigilance in those that are less attentive to the important duties assigned them.

Do you think it would be more advantageous that the whole system of rewards should be apportioned at the discretion of the Magistrate, according to the circumstances of the particular case, or that they should be adjudged as they are by law, to the particular nature of the crime for which the criminal has been convicted?—The Crown rewards are generally distributed here by the Recorder of London, and by the Clerks of Assize, under the control of the Judges, in the different counties: They have been of old standing; and they apply not only to the officers of justice, but to all persons contributing to the conviction; it would not be expedient, perhaps, to disturb that system, although it may be susceptible of improvement. The rewards that are in contemplation to be given by Magistrates would be confined entirely to the officers under their immediate control, who were most active and vigilant in detecting felonies and other offences, and in apprehending offenders, and in recovering stolen property.

Do you think that the present system of rewards has ever induced, or that it is likely to induce, officers to neglect those crimes for the discovery or conviction of which no reward was given?—Suspicion had been excited at a very early period, and even previous to Sir John Fielding's time, that many officers in those days were not anxious to apprehend a criminal person till he was worth 40 l. I cannot say, as far as my own experience has gone, that it seems to have operated much in latter times, though it is very difficult to decide upon the impulses of the officers that have been at different times under my control.

I have

P. Colquhoun,
Esq.

I have found always, when any felony has been committed, a considerable degree of eagerness to discover and apprehend the offenders.   Perhaps in some instances, where an extensive burglary has been committed, where a reward might be offered or expected from opulent sufferers, a greater degree of zeal and activity might have been manifested; but upon the whole, I must confess that it has not appeared to me that the non-expectation of legislative rewards has in any material degree influenced the conduct of Police officers in exercising their zeal and activity in apprehending persons for minor offences.   It very frequently happens that they expect the offence will turn out a burglary, where in the result of the trial they are disappointed.   Upon the whole, the rewards they obtain in that way have not tended to enrich many of them, as far as I have seen.

Do not you think that it is very difficult to discover how far such a circumstance might influence them?—It is very difficult; but if you judge from the nature of man, they will be naturally more anxious when they are to gain a great advantage, than when the advantage is less, or there is none at all.   I must also add, that it is the practice of the Court at the Old Bailey to allow a moderate sum for loss of time and expenses incurred by Police officers in the prosecution of offenders.   Those expenses are generally (comparatively speaking) liberal; so that they have a chance in almost all cases, more or less, of getting something.   When it comes to be a burglary or a highway robbery, where, in the latter case, it amounts, including what they call the Tyburn Ticket, to about 50*l.* they are remunerated in a much greater degree.   But still, under every circumstance, all who contribute to the conviction, and even the prosecutor himself, when he is not a gentleman or a man of property, as well as the witness, participate in the reward, and hence the share allotted to the Police officers is always considerably reduced.

It is a custom at some of the Offices, for persons of fortune, that wish to employ officers, to give them certain presents, according to the duty they are to perform?—I must say the officers are, with perhaps some exceptions, rapacious enough, for I have sometimes had occasion to check them for that rapacity. When they conceived they were doing a service for a person of fortune, I have uniformly told them they must leave it entirely to the gentleman, and must not presume to set a price upon services they are under any circumstances bound to perform; otherwise, they would lose their situations that instant.   This brings me to mention, that many years ago I drew up and framed a distinct system, applicable to the Office at Queen-square, both with regard to the functions of the Magistrates, and the duties of the Clerks and Constables, stating what fees they were entitled to demand, with full instructions respecting the various duties which the constables were expected to perform, and on every circumstance which was likely to occur.   A copy of these Instructions are delivered to every officer on his appointment.   If it is the wish of the Committee, I will produce the book on a future day; it will throw some light on the nature of the present Police system, as conducted at the Office in Queen-square Westminster.

Do not you think it would be advantageous that all the Police officers should be forbidden from receiving any fees or presents of any sort, from the persons by whom they are employed?—I have no difficulty in saying, that if they can be sufficiently remunerated through the medium of the Magistrates, it would be infinitely preferable that no person suffering the loss of property should be called upon to give any remuneration whatever, unless he chose to advertise a reward, or, from a sense of the benefits he had derived, to make a voluntary present, subject to the approbation of the Justices.   But I should wish to see it in the power of the Magistrates to remunerate them where they have been diligent, and that it should not be understood as expected, except in extreme cases, that any of them should receive money from those persons who call upon them to execute their duty, either in the recovery of their property, or the apprehension or prosecution of the offenders.

Do not you think cases may occur in which officers may be equally deserving of reward, though a conviction may not take place?—I certainly do; since convictions are not always obtained, although the persons may be guilty.   I believe

P. Colquhoun,
Esq.

a very considerable proportion of those who go to trial would be convicted, if there was a prosecutor for the Crown; very few Magistrates send persons accused of offences to trial, where they do not consider the proof sufficiently strong to obtain a conviction.

Are there within your jurisdiction any houses notoriously the resort of thieves and abandoned persons?—There are certainly in the district of Westminster several houses that are notorious as the rendezvous of criminal persons: those in the higher scale generally go to the houses about Drury-lane, and parts adjacent, all of which are well known; they are an inferior class of petty thieves who generally frequent the houses in and about what is called the city of Westminster.

Can you give any reason why the licence of those houses has not been taken away?—Whenever it is found that they are disorderly or notoriously bad, in the District in which I act, we certainly stop their licenses or compel the Proprietor to find a more proper person to occupy the house. It has been frequently stated that the existence of such houses is necessary for the purpose of enabling the Police officers to know where to find criminal persons accused or suspected of having committed specific felonies; and it must be acknowledged that it frequently happens that the landlords or occupiers of those houses do give useful information to the officers.

Then in fact there are houses which are overlooked by the Police, for the purpose of gaining information?—I cannot exactly say they are overlooked; I speak of houses where there is no particular disorder, except that they are frequented by reputed thieves; if such houses merely on this account are put down, others will rise up immediately, and there would be no useful practical result. If they excite disorder by assembling a number of prostitutes, or otherwise, we certainly take notice of it.

Do you not think that the existence of houses of resort for thieves, from the combination which they occasion of one with another, encourage the habits of the people who frequent them?—I certainly do think so; the conclusion is obvious. One of my reasons for wishing very much to have a register of lodging-houses not paying above a certain rent, was, that an eye might be kept on profligate characters and thieves who associate in the habitations of common prostitutes; the possibility of their being considerably reduced or regulated might arise from that circumstance: if they were licensed as lodging-houses, we could have perhaps a more correct view, not only of the number, but of the characters and pursuits, of the persons who inhabit or resort to them. Most of the thieves reside with prostitutes.

You think that at present the law does not give sufficient power to touch the greater proportion of those houses?—The law, I think, at present is defective as to houses of bad fame, they can only be touched by an indictment; it is very difficult to prove what they call " bawdry," and they are generally convicted on the proof of their being disorderly houses; if there was a summary jurisdiction, I think it would be much more effectual.

Do you think young offenders become more instructed and initiated into the system of crime by visiting these houses?—Undoubtedly; it is the first stage of corruption of morals, young men getting connected with these women.

Do you know of any houses within your District, particularly set apart as great lodging-houses for juvenile depredators of both sexes?—There are various streets in Westminster, where there are a number of those houses which lodge prostitutes; and the youths who naturally mix with that class of people have immediate access to them in their apartments; and these facilities to an illicit intercourse with the sexes at an early age, prevails I believe in every quarter of the town more or less.

Do you think there any lodging-houses which receive almost exclusively boys and girls of bad character?—I am not aware of any that *exclusively* receive boys and girls of bad character; if there were, we certainly should (if we were aware of it) order them to be indicted immediately.

You have mentioned, that you thought it would be advantageous to proceed against houses by summary conviction; in what way would you suggest that

that

P. Colquhoun,
Esq.

that proceeding should take place?—By summary convictions, with a power to inflict smaller penalties or a shorter imprisonment, the law would reach a vast number of persons keeping disorderly houses, which it is impossible to do in the circuitous and expensive mode of indictment.

Is not the law defeated by the difficulty of obtaining the names of proprietors of houses of ill fame?—There is a very considerable difficulty in prosecutions of this nature; although the offence is notorious, it must be proved that the occupier of the house pays the taxes; there are a variety of other legal niceties; and these people or their advisers are adepts in all of them, and are perfectly aware of the difficulties that stand in the way of procuring a conviction. Upon the requisition of two housekeepers to the constable, they may be, and are frequently, prosecuted at the expense of the parish; but the expense of prosecutions, and the difficulty of finding the necessary proof to procure a conviction, in a great measure prevents the suppression of offences of this nature. All efforts have hitherto failed in remedying the evil; when driven from one spot, they resort to another.

Do you think persons of feigned names are given in as the proprietors of those houses?—Every trick that it is possible for the wit of man to devise, is resorted to for the purpose of defeating the law in cases of this sort.

Do you think that the difficulty in prosecuting with effect the proprietors of houses of ill fame, deters many persons from attempting it?—Although the prosecutions may be carried on by the parishes upon the requisition of two housekeepers, it seldom happens that individuals trouble their heads about it, except where they are particularly annoyed by the nuisance.

Are parishes deterred from prosecuting, in many cases, on account of the difficulty of conviction?—The parishes must prosecute if two housekeepers will require the constable to do so; but the prosecutions are certainly less frequent than the evil to be remedied requires.

Are prosecutions frequently defeated by the artifices of the keepers of those houses?—Unless in very notorious cases, they are.

Then it is entirely owing to the difficulty of putting the law into execution, and not to the *choice* of the Magistrates, that such a number of houses of ill fame exist?—The difficulties (as already mentioned) of putting the law in execution, and perhaps the expense, may have deterred the parishes: they cannot well refuse it when they are required, but persons may be deterred from calling on the parish to prosecute, in consequence of the trouble and difficulty of bringing forward the witnesses; these difficulties may deter many persons from applying, since they must prove the offence.

Do you think the system of permitting public-houses, which are the resort of thieves, for the sake of gaining information, is really necessary to obtaining such information?—Upon the general principle that every thing that can contribute to the detection and apprehension of thieves, may be useful in bringing criminal offenders to justice; if one house of this description is put down, another will immediately rise up.

Are you of opinion the detections would be as frequent and as speedy, if the licences of those houses to which they resort, were taken away?—I should doubt it.

Are the Police officers in the habit of resorting to those houses, and living in communication with the thieves, for the purpose of obtaining information?—They do mix with them occasionally, in order to obtain information, and they send persons unknown to the thieves, to mix with them, for the purpose of gaining information, more especially when great offences have been committed; under such circumstances, every expedient must be resorted to for the detection and apprehension of the delinquents.

Are you not aware that the number of spirit licences which have been granted have very much increased?—On or about the years 1744 or 1745, when multitudes of men and women were rolling about the streets drunk, in consequence of the number of gin-shops, the physicians were consulted upon it, and then an Act was passed, that no person should be entitled to a spirit licence that could not previously produce an ale licence. The object was, that there should be *no gin-shops whatsoever*. In spite of this, however, when the Magistrates were less vigilant than they are now, they found means to get ale licences, merely to entitle them to obtain a spirit licence from the Excise, and thereby enable them to open

gin-

P. Colquhoun,
Esq.

gin-shops. We are in this District (and the Magistrates who license in other divisions of the Metropolis) particularly attentive to this object; and it is a rule very generally established, to refuse ale licences to every person, unless where a considerable quantity of beer is sold as well as spirits, and unless also there is a bar in the centre of the tap-room, so that no person shall come in to drink gin without being seen by every body there; no private bar is allowed in this District. When I first acted as a licensing Magistrate in 1792, in the great district of the Tower Hamlets, I found 1100 public licensed houses, and, I think, in two years we suppressed eighty-seven gin-shops.

It is a well-known fact, that in no other Capital in the world is there the same outrageous behaviour on the part of prostitutes infesting the streets, which there is in this City; have your ever thought of any means by which that great evil might be checked?—I have turned my attention to this excessive evil many times. I certainly think that as the laws now stand, it is not possible to do much towards the diminution of this mass of profligacy and delinquency; and I am sorry to say it appears to increase, not only in the Metropolis, but in all the principal towns in the Kingdom, and in many where no prostitutes were at all, forty years ago. It appears to me, that in addition to the increase of prostitutes, there is also a great increase of profligacy of manners among that class of unfortunate females. In addition to this, the major part of them derive a considerable portion of their subsistence by the robbery of those who come in contact with them, of their watches and money; a vast proportion of them are associated with thieves, who actually live with them, and who follow them in the streets, not only to tutor them in the way they are to commit robberies, by pulling out watches, money, &c. &c. but also are near at hand, ready to attend them when they commit those robberies, in order to receive the booty and run off.

To what circumstance do you attribute this increase of profligacy?—I certainly must attribute it to a deficiency in the laws to aid the Police; and to a variety of other causes, *the profligacy of parents, the total want of education, the want of means of putting them into reputable service at the time they arrive at a certain age; the death of parents, leaving them destitute orphans, growing up, who have no resource but to go upon the town; to a love of dress, and to the seduction of innocence.* The numerous fairs that are held in different parts in and near the Metropolis, and in the villages round about, tend infinitely to the corruption of the morals of females, and ultimately to their seduction.

Would it be difficult, by directions given to the existing watchmen and patroles, and perhaps by employing occasionally officers for that particular purpose, to prevent the misbehaviour of the prostitutes in the street to a certain degree, in holding the language they do, and seizing people as they do?—It is not understood, according to law, that a watchman can seize a prostitute, unless she is in some shape disorderly; if she is riotous, drunk, or disturbing the neighbourhood, they are uniformly instructed, and by law they may then take them up as disorderly persons, and bring them before the Magistrates, which is very frequently done; but what is the result? I generally admonish them, inquire where their parents live, commit them for seven days, endeavour to send for their parents or relations, if they have any in town, or offer them a pass to go into the country from whence they originally came, if their settlement is not in the Metropolis. But it appears to me that all we can do is hopeless, as a remedy; it does not tend to diminish the evil.

Have you thought of any plan for removing prostitutes from the public streets?—I have been consulted upon that subject by various respectable people residing in streets where they are much annoyed by the clamour of the disorderly prostitutes; and it occurred to me, that if an asylum were established in each parish, where all women known to be prostitutes could be sent by an order and under the authority of Magistrates, after full examination, and ascertaining that they were living by prostitution alone, that means might be found through that medium, and by the aid of religious and moral instruction, and introducing labour, to produce a reform, and in some instances to reconcile many of them to their friends, or to find them employment after being reformed.

Do

P. Colquhoun, Esq.

Do you mean that persons should be sent to those asylums, if they do not belong to the parish in which they are found?—If it is discovered on due examination that they do not belong to the parish in which they are found, there shall be a power to remove them to that parish where an asylum is fixed, if in the Metropolis, so that each asylum shall only be burdened with those prostitutes who have a legal settlement; in cases where they have no legal settlement in the Metropolis, it was proposed that after a certain time they should be sent to the parish in the country to which they belonged, with a certificate of good behaviour, and with a recommendation to the parish officers, to endeavour to get them employed; it was proposed also, that those asylums should be supported partly by the labour of the females, as far as it will go, and partly by the respective parishes, and perhaps, that they should have some assistance from the general revenues of the State.

In stating that the increased profligacy is owing to a deficient Police, do you mean a deficiency of law, or of the establishment of Police?—I must state to the Committee, that there has been no establishment of Police at all, in consequence of any Act of Parliament that has passed; the Act of 1792, which established the seven Offices, did no more than establish a purer Magistracy, excepting merely that a clause in the Act authorized the apprehension of persons of evil fame and reputed thieves, in the avenues of public places.

Do you think it would be advantageous if the law was put more in execution in respect of persons who are recognized by the law as reputed thieves?—I confess, myself, I should not be very willing to extend that much further than it is; it is a strong measure; it has certainly done good, it has in some degree frightened criminal persons, but it does not appear to have materially lessened the evil. I am desirous of finding out the means generally of preventing crimes, by throwing every impediment in the way, by means of the Police regulations already detailed in my examination.

Have you thought of any plan for the summary conviction of keepers of houses of ill fame?—I should conceive that the mere evidence of the persons residing in the house, whether they paid the taxes or not, and that they carried on a disorderly house for lodging prostitutes, should be sufficient, and that upon that proof alone they might be convicted, provided the penalty was moderate and the imprisonment short.

Do you mean this to apply to persons in the character of servants, where their employers are not to be found?—Certainly; let the servants be punished, and let any person, keeping servants for such a purpose, have the law apply to him or her by indictment, as at present, where the punishment would be severer, inasmuch as the pillory might be added to imprisonment.

Should you think that the evidence of two respectable housekeepers proving a disorderly house, should be sufficient to convict?—I certainly do.

What in your opinion should constitute a disorderly house?—The evidence of men entering the house with women known to be common prostitutes; and the general character of the house being proved to be a house of evil fame by the neighbours, should be considered as sufficient evidence to obtain a conviction in a summary way, where the punishment would be less severe than by the conviction of a Court of Record.

Veneris, 3° die Maii, 1816.

The Honourable HENRY GREY BENNET, in The Chair.

Robert Raynsford, Esq. called in, and Examined.

YOU are one of the Magistrates of the Police Office in Hatton Garden?—I am.

How long have you been in that situation?—I have been there about two years; I was at Shadwell two years before, making four years altogether that I have been a Police Magistrate.

The date of your appointment appears to be in 1812?—Yes.

Do you hold any other situation of emolument besides that of Police Magistrate?—No other whatever.

Your Office is one of the Offices appointed by the 51 Geo. III?—It is.

What is the nature of the attendance that the Magistrates give in that Office?— The Act of Parliament requires that there should be two Magistrates there every day from ten o'clock in the morning till three, and from six to eight in the evening; it has been the custom to consider ten o'clock as eleven, or a few minutes before; but instead of staying till three, we are often there longer, and do not leave the Office while there is any business before us: we go there again in the evening a little before seven, and stay very frequently till nine, when any business is before us.

Is any Clerk resident in the Office, to give information to the Magistrates in case their presence should be rendered necessary?—Not in the Hatton Garden Office.

Who resides in the Hatton Garden Office?—There is a housekeeper and a messenger; and Mr. Leach is considered as the resident Magistrate; but for the last eight or nine months Mr. Leach has been in an ill state of health, in consequence of which he has a residence at Hampstead.

Who pays the rent and taxes of the house in Hatton Garden?—Government, with an allowance for coals and candles.

It does not appear, in the return, what advantage Mr. Leach gains by living in that house; with the allowances you have stated, that is an emolument?—No doubt of it, for it of course saves rent and taxes, coals and candles; I apprehend it was from a misconception of the heading of the article, it was not considered as an emolument.

How long has Mr. Leach ceased, from the state of his health, to live at that Office?—He has been in a precarious state of health for the last nine months, and been attended by physicians; he is rather better, but in a precarious state of health at this moment.

He is not in a state of health to enable him to do his duty?—Yes, he attends in a morning regularly; but does not attend in an evening, for the reasons I have before stated.

In point of fact, has any inconvenience occurred in consequence of his non-residence in that house?—None whatever, that I am aware of.

Has it ever happened that there was no Sitting Magistrate, either on an evening or a morning, at Hatton Garden?—Not to my knowledge; I can answer for myself, and I can, I think, speak decidedly as to no instance having occurred of there not being a Magistrate there every morning and evening.

The Act of Parliament says there shall be two Magistrates?—The Act of Parliament says there shall be two Magistrates in the morning, but it does not require two in the evening. The business which requires the attendance of two, is by custom brought in the morning; and I do not recollect any instance of business being brought in an evening that required the attendance of two.

How

Robert Raynsford, Esq.

How many Clerks are there in the Office?—There are two Clerks.

Have you an assistant Clerk, who has a salary of 20 *l.* a year?—We have.

What is the name of the assistant Clerk, as his name does not appear in the list?—His name is Robert Ford, he is son of the Chief Clerk; he is not regularly upon the establishment as a clerk, but he has been permitted for the last five years to assist: I found him when I came into the Office.

Is he efficient as a clerk?—He is useful; we do not intrust him as we do the other Clerks, with the material part of the business.

How comes his name not to be inserted, as he receives 20 *l.* a year out of the public purse?—I am not prepared to answer that question.

Who made out that return?—Our Chief Clerk, under our directions; we produced the heading of a paper brought before the Finance Committee in the year 1792, and ordered him to follow the directions of that, according to the orders we received from this Committee, and the heading was prepared from that.

Do the Clerks hold any other situation than that of clerks to your Office?—Our Chief Clerk has no other situation whatever, he gives up his whole and undivided time to it.

Does he practise as a solicitor?—Not at all; he has no other employment.

Has the Second Clerk, John Shearman, any other employment?—He is an attorney.

Does he practise as a solicitor?—I believe he does, but I am not certain.

In the Office?—No; when I say not in the Office, I beg to correct myself; he is sometimes employed for the prosecution, but we never suffer him, on any occasion, if we know it, to be concerned for the defendants.

Does he give daily attendance?—He does, generally.

Is his attendance as constant as that of the Chief Clerk?—They divide the attendance between them; if Mr. Shearman wants to be out of the way, Mr. Ford takes care to be there, and sometimes Mr. Ford wishes to be absent on an evening. I beg to say, that Mr. Ford is a most diligent, efficient Clerk, and unremitting in his duty.

Is Mr. Shearman as unremitting in his duty as Mr. Ford?—I think he is; we have no cause to complain of him; our business never stands still.

Was the appointment of young Mr. Ford owing to a pressure of business beyond the united attention of the two Clerks, or because the private avocations of Mr. Shearman rendered other assistance necessary?—When I came to Hatton Garden, I found Mr. Ford, junior, there, and I am not prepared to speak as to the mode in which he was appointed. Mr. Shearman has been at the Office about two years, but has now left us, being appointed to another situation, I believe that of Governor of the New Penitentiary House. Mr. Shearman is a very worthy, humane man, and a valuable member of society.

Do you think that if the two clerks were as regular in their attendance as Mr. Ford is, there would be any occasion to have an extra clerk?—I should think not.

It appears by the return, that you have eight Officers belonging to your establishment, and that you had ten on the 21st of January 1815; why were the two last dismissed?—They were dismissed in consequence of mal-practices.

Have you filled up their places?—We have not.

What were the practices for which they were dismissed?—To the best of my recollection, for having taken money of some parties who had been delivering coals that were deficient in measure; that those officers were sent for in order to see those coals measured, and we had reason to believe, indeed I rather think we had positive proof at the time, that they had been bribed, that they had taken what is called "hush-money:" the moment that came to the knowledge of the Magistrates at Hatton Garden, we examined into the facts, and finding they had taken money, we discharged them. We wrote (which is our usual way) to the Secretary of State, to inform him we had discharged those two men, and that we thought we could do with a less number, that the eight were sufficient, and therefore there were no others appointed.

Have you often reason to complain of the conduct of the Officers, in the receipt of money from individuals for the purpose of obstructing public justice?—No;

but

Robert Raynsford,
Esq.

but we have very frequent cause to complain of them, they are very ungovernable, we are obliged to admonish them very often; but if it ever came to our knowledge that they had been guilty of corruption in any way, we should discharge them.

Have you in point of fact, often, complaints of their having taken money?—No, we have not.

What is the nature of that misconduct for which you are often obliged to admonish them?—Inattention to the rules we lay down for their attendance; they are not in the way when they ought to be, they are apt to neglect the duty we impose upon them, they make frivolous excuses; we are obliged to admonish them, and threaten them with being discharged if they do not behave better.

The salary they receive is a guinea per week?—It is.

Have they any other emoluments besides those mentioned here; payments for extra trouble in serving warrants and summonses, and for apprehending offenders?—They have a shilling for each warrant and each summons, and a quarterly allowance of 3 *l.* 18 *s.* for extra services, which are understood to comprise their going out of a night for the purpose of looking after offenders after the usual Office hours; they are out till eleven or twelve at night, and I believe that additional allowance is made for those extra services.

Do you consider the twenty-one shillings per week a sufficient payment, with the other advantages, for the services they perform?—Certainly not; it is impossible that they can maintain their families upon such a stipend.

So that the effect of course is, that inferior persons take those situations to what you would naturally look to if there was a higher salary?—There are other modes by which they get money, that very often remunerates them for the small stipend allowed by Government; I mean by that to say (what the Committee are perfectly in possession of) that whenever they bring an offender to punishment for a burglary or a highway robbery, there is a reward by Act of Parliament of forty pounds; now the whole of this sum does not go to the officer, but a part of it goes to the prosecutor, and the rest is divided among those witnesses that are put at the back of the bill, for when a bill of indictment is found, the names of the witnesses are put at the back of it, and when any reward of that kind is given them, the Recorder distributes it in such way as he thinks proper. There are also other modes of their getting money, and I may say fairly getting money. I am afraid that sometimes there may be also such a thing as hush money; but I can assure the Committee, that if it came to the knowledge of the Magistrates, the man who received it would not be suffered to remain one moment in the Office. What I mean by obtaining money fairly, is in cases where persons who have been robbed, and apply for the assistance of an officer; the officer, whether he succeeds or not in the apprehension of the offender, is often put to considerable expense, and for which it is but fair that he should be reimbursed. The officer has certainly no claim as a matter of right to any remuneration for his trouble, but I have reason to believe that they are frequently liberally rewarded on those occasions; and I am glad when I hear that they are so, for, without some recompence in addition to their pay, they could not maintain their families, and support a creditable appearance.

Have you any rules or regulations for the conduct of your officers?—We have.

Are they printed?—They are.

Are they similar to those which are established at Bow-street?—I am not sure. Two of our men are directed to be in attendance every morning to execute the warrants and summonses; the others are supposed to be going into the different parts of the district to keep the peace, or to apprehend offenders, or are doing the business of the preceding day.

Do you consider your Establishment as sufficient to watch over the Metropolis, in that populous part of London which is under its care?—When we had ten, I think it was quite sufficient; since we have been reduced to eight, we do not find any great inconvenience for the loss of those two, and therefore we did not wish to put Government to an expense of two more than we thought the public service required. I do not think we are at present in want of more assistance.

Do you think the mode of payment arising out of the Act of Parliament, giving the forty pounds to be divided amongst the witnesses, and those that

convict

Robert Raynsford,
Esq.

convict an offender, the best mode of bringing criminals to conviction?—I think, without some stimulus to the officers, very few notorious offenders would be brought to conviction. If the Magistrates were empowered to reward the officers according to their merits, when any of them were found particularly active, I think it would be much more likely to produce the desired effect, than the precarious chance the officer has of receiving the share of the forty pounds reward; for although the Officer may have been extremely diligent, and probably run the risk of his life in the apprehension of the offender, still he can receive no reward in the latter case unless the offender is convicted, and we all know how often they escape punishment.

Do you not think that the reward being given solely on the conviction of persons committing certain offences specified by Act of Parliament, has a tendency to render the officers remiss in seizing offenders, till they have committed that offence for which they are to gain some profit by their conviction?—I acted as a Magistrate for some years before I was in the Police, and always entertained the idea that the officers suffered a man to go on committing trivial offences, waiting for the opportunity of his doing something that would entitle them to receive what is technically called "Blood money;" but since I have been in the Police, I am inclined to believe (from the number of persons who are daily brought to the Office charged with petty larceny, and from my observations on the general conduct of the officers) that I entertained an erroneous opinion on that subject.

Do you keep in your Office a register of the persons who are brought before you, and whether they are discharged or sent to prison?—Every first Tuesday in the month, we carry up a report from each Office to the Office of the Secretary of State for the Home Department; in that report, there is a statement of every person brought before us for larceny, the name of the Magistrate who examines him, what is done in consequence, and whether discharged or fully committed; the Magistrates sign their names to this report, and one Magistrate from each Office goes up to the Secretary of State, to whom it is personally delivered, by which means he is put in possession of every occurrence that has taken place within our respective districts in the course of the preceding month.

When persons are either remanded for further examination, or committed to prison, to what prison are they committed from Hatton Garden?—In general, to the New Prison Clerkenwell; but certainly in some instances, where it may happen to be a female, and she has a child in arms, so that it cannot be disposed of, we commit them to the House of Correction in Cold Bath Fields, where they have an opportunity of treating them with more humanity, and they have more comforts than they can possibly have in the New Prison; for that, certainly, of all prisons, is the worst I have seen.

You consider, then, the New Prison Clerkenwell as one of the worst you have ever seen?—I do most conscientiously; at the same time I beg to state, that the Magistrates for the county of Middlesex have lately come to the resolution of laying out several thousand pounds in immediately putting that prison into a proper state of repair; and I believe directions have been given for that purpose.

Are there not persons there confined under sentence?—I rather think not; I speak from memory.

You do not know whether at this moment there are not women confined there under sentence, for perjury?—I do not happen to know it.

Persons are committed there for assaults?—They are committed there for want of finding security to answer to the indictment the prosecutor may bring against them.

There is no allowance, no straw, no blankets, nor no bedding?—Certainly not.

They are all huddled together in one or two large rooms, where they sleep upon the boards, and are often many days without being able to change their clothes, or to obtain any other accommodation, unless they pay for it?—That is perfectly correct, with this observation, that the women are in a separate room from the men; I never commit any respectable female or person of a decent appearance there, that I can possibly avoid; but there are some shocking vagabonds that hardly know the comfort of a bed, and therefore cannot be supposed to endure the same misery for the want of it.

510.   Are

Robert Reynsford, Esq.

Are not boys, or more properly children, committed to that prison, and mixed there indiscriminately with other prisoners?—Not generally; the Magistrates commit boys to the other prison; we are not in the habit of sending felons to the House of Correction, except under particular circumstances; the house is frequently so full that we cannot commit there: I am sorry to say that three-fourths of the offences now committed in this town, as far as my observation goes, are by boys.

What is the length of district, the management of which belongs to your Police?—It consists of the East side of Gower-street, Bedford-square, Charlotte-street, Drury-lane, the parish of Saint Andrew's, the parish of Saint Sepulchre's, Saint James's Clerkenwell, the Liberty of the Rolls in Chancery-lane, the Liberty of Saffron-hill, Islington, Saint Luke's to the West side of Golden-lane, and Bunhill-row, including the Western sides of those streets; that is what is considered the Hatton Garden District.

That district is principally occupied by the middling and lower classes of society?—Certainly.

What is the present state of public morals within that district?—I think it is not worse than it has been; the District has been remarkably quiet all this winter, when we certainly did expect, in consequence of the number of persons discharged from the army and navy, we should have had a great number of serious offences committed, but I can most distinctly state to the Committee, that this winter has been as quiet as I recollect since I have been in the Police.

Do you think that, though the serious offences may have diminished rather than increased, the smaller and petty offences have not considerably increased of late years?—I think that for the last three months the petty offences have increased; but we have no instance, in our district, of any case of atrocity within that period.

Has not the number of juvenile depredators very much increased latterly?—Certainly.

Can you give to the Committee any reason for that increase?—I think the pressure of the times, and the indigence of parents in the lower classes of life, occasion a number of their children to get out from home; having no means of obtaining a livelihood, they go out into the streets, and we all know the young mind is open to be corrupted; they get amongst the common thieves, and they make those young children the instruments of their depredations.

Do you not think that there is a regular plan organized throughout the Metropolis, by which it being known that the laws are not rigidly executed in respect of juvenile depredators, they are used as instruments to those of a more mature age, for the purpose of committing various kinds of theft?—I do think so, and that they are made the instruments of other persons who might be fearful of committing those offences themselves, because they would most likely suffer the punishment of the law; but from the well-known humanity exercised in the administration of justice towards children, they perhaps think that by making a child the instrument, a capital punishment would not be inflicted for the offence, and transportation is not much regarded.

Do you not think that system has very considerably increased within these few years past?—I think most alarmingly so.

At what age do you permit a child to take his trial for felony?—We have some brought to the Office of ten, twelve, and fourteen years of age. Our duty requires us to see whether there is sufficient evidence before us that the child has committed an offence that will justify our sending him for trial; and if that clearly appears, we have no power to do otherwise than commit him, however we may lament the youthful depravity of the party.

Are you not of opinion, the state of the public prisons in the Metropolis, in which there is little or no separation of the young from the adults, contributes very much, by rendering the children worse when they come out of prison than they were when they went in, to increase the number of crimes?—I am most decidedly of that opinion, and I think it a very alarming evil.

Do you not think it would be most advisable to establish, if it were possible, some general plan of a penitentiary house for the children convicts, but in which they could, by habits of industry, and better morals being inculcated, become good members of society, instead of becoming, as they do, worse and worse, till they are either transported or suffer capitally?—I am most decidedly

of

Robert Raynsford,
Esq.

of that opinion; I have seen instances of children that I have been under the painful necessity of committing to prison, shew marks of contrition at the time he has been under examination (as far as one can look into the human mind;) but I have felt if that child could be separated when he got into the prison, and kept distinct from the depraved characters he mixes with, there would be reason to hope, that when he came out again he might be restored to habits of industry, and be a useful member of society; but from the present system of mixing children with the most depraved characters, I consider them as lost to society for ever.

Are you not, as a Magistrate, often compelled, from a mere principle of humanity, anticipating the fatal consequences arising from committing one of those infants to prison, to discharge them?—When a child has been committed for further examination, we do not tell the prosecutor himself, but we find the means of giving him a hint, that if he does not wish to prosecute, he may afford us an opportunity of discharging him, being fully aware that it would be the ruin of that child, and that he would be lost for ever.

Supposing it were made a positive rule, that none of the inferior officers should take fees or rewards from persons for the apprehension or discovery of offenders, and no such fund as that you have hinted at, were established, do you think any material inconvenience would follow?—I think that if those men were merely to depend upon their guinea a week, and the small pittance they get from serving warrants and summonses, they would not be able to live; as to what they receive from persons employing them, it is purely voluntary; we do not authorize them in demanding any thing, the parties do it of themselves.

Do you think the Police of the Metropolis would be improved by placing the parish watchmen under the superintendence of the Police, and having the whole under one head?—At present, as the law now stands, we have no power at all over the parish watchmen; but when this question was agitated on a former occasion, the parishes had so rooted an aversion to the interference of the Magistracy, that I believe there were petitions from most of the parishes; at the same time there are offences committed in the streets, close by a watch-box, and we are told that the watchman was fast asleep, or would give no assistance; we have no power of sending for the watchman, or if we did, we have no power of punishing him; we recommend that the persons complaining shall go to the parish Watch Committee: I think it would be an improvement if they were put under the direction of the Police; but this is matter of opinion, and the subject requires much consideration.

Are the public-houses licensed before your Board of Magistracy?—No, it is done jointly; the Police Magistrates in the district are summoned to attend, with other county Magistrates, on the licensing days; and I occasionally attend on those days, when not prevented by my official duty.

Are you rigid in your examination of testimonials of character, prior to granting the licence to open a new house?—We certainly are, and more particularly as to the necessity of opening a new house, for a certain portion of the Magistrates go round and look at the situation in which the new public-house is proposed to be opened, and see whether there is a sufficient number already to answer the purpose for which public-houses were intended; and if we find there are, in general (without some special reason) it is rejected: our primary object is to reduce the number, except on some occasions where it interferes with private property, and there we are tender.

Is it an objection to a house of that sort, that it is known to be the resort of infamous characters, persons engaged in plunder?—Most certainly; and if it came to the knowledge of the Magistrates, I have no doubt the licence would not be renewed; but with respect to those houses, which it has gone abroad there are a great number of in this town, and which are technically called " Flash Houses," I am free to say that there are houses of that description, and, though certainly it is a great evil to society that such houses should be permitted, yet at the same time as a Police Magistrate I am bound to tell the Committee that many of the most notorious thieves would escape if it were not for those particular places of rendezvous, which afford us the means of getting those offenders into our power. The officers go into those houses at night, where they see and mix with five or six men whom they know to be thieves, and if there has been any information of a robbery having been committed, and they miss one or two of

those

Robert Raynsford, Esq.

those men on a particular occasion, suspicion naturally falls upon them (owing to their being absent from their usual haunts) that they are in some mischief; our officers immediately take the risk upon themselves, and apprehend the parties. Those men, upon being brought to the Office, and notice being given to persons who have been robbed, they are frequently identified, and from no other cause but that of being absent from their place of rendezvous, and being known to the officers as notorious characters. The officers will go into one of those houses, and find six or eight notorious characters assembled; the thieves will say, " Master, do you want me? whom do you want?" Upon receiving an answer, they will go out and suffer themselves to be searched, without any difficulty in the world. At the same time I would wish the Committee distinctly to understand, that if it came to our knowledge that there was any particular public-house that was a notortious receptacle for thieves, we should make a memorandum of that house, and should certainly try to put a stop to the licence; the consequence of that would be, they would be driven from that house and would go to another; and as there always will be thieves, the place of resort for those thieves will naturally be the public-houses; and it certainly is the principal means of our knowing where notorious offenders are to be taken. I have no doubt the public are surprised, when an offence takes place, at the offender being so soon taken into custody; but the cause is explained from what I have stated. I have been told by an intelligent Officer at Hatton Garden, that when thieves quarrel amongst themselves, they often, from a principle of revenge, tell the officer, " Ah! Jack such a one was one of the persons concerned in the burglary the other night, and he was one concerned in another offence;" then away go the officers and take this man up; the consequence is, that the public sometimes are surprised how soon notorious offenders are in custody after committing the offence, but, this circumstance being explained, the mystery ceases.

Do you not think that, though it be true that the advantage to be gained to public justice in seizing the offenders where you know their haunts is considerable, the very establishments of those haunts, by bringing persons together into a society of thieves, particularly by bringing young boys to be trained up by thieves, does more mischief to society than good by the apprehension of the offender?—I can only answer that question by saying, that in my opinion we should very rarely get hold of notorious offenders if every place of this sort was done away.

Is there not in point of fact a regularly understood system between the inferior Police officers, for the maintenance and support of certain public-houses where the thieves are accustomed to resort?—Not that ever came to my knowledge.

Are you not of opinion that though those houses may facilitate the discovery of offenders, they also facilitate the commission of crimes, by being notorious rendezvous for persons disposed to enter into schemes of that sort, and by bringing them acquainted with each other?—There are a great proportion of the public-houses that will not admit persons of this description; at the same time there are a great many that openly encourage them, and I dare say would conceal them if they had an opportunity.

Has it ever occurred to you what might be the effect of shutting individuals of this character out of all public-houses?—I should think it wholly impracticable.

Does it not also occur to you, that the letting them have the free run of those public-houses has a great tendency to increase the evil and multiply thieves, there being no check to the assemblage of those persons?—The officers when they go into a public-house, though they know several persons assembled there to be notorious thieves, unless they knew of any overt act they had committed, they cannot legally take them into custody, but they run the risk of the consequences.

Is it not within your knowledge that persons, on their dismissal from New-gate or Cold Bath Fields, go directly to certain places as their haunts, where they find their associates, and, perhaps the very same night, engage in a plan of robbery?—In answer to that question, I must beg to say that the necessity of the case compels them; the wretched culprit, after he is tried, is turned out of the prison as a marked man in society, without the means of subsistence, and how is that man to find food but by resorting to the same practices.

Does not that man know, on his coming out of prison, a place to which he may go and meet with other persons of the same character?—He does know

that,

Robert Raynsford, Esq.

that, certainly, there are many places to which he may resort and find his former associates; but, from loss of character, no reputable person will take him under his roof, and therefore he is obliged from necessity to return to his former companions and evil habits.

Are the houses which are the resort of thieves, particularly marked for riotous and disorderly conduct of the persons who frequent them?—I am not prepared to answer that question.

Do you not see that the existence of those houses, Flash-houses as they are called, serves the purposes of the discovery, but that at the same time they have a direct tendency to increase the number and facilitate the commission of crimes?—I am decidedly of that opinion.

Is Whitecross-street, Saint Luke's, within your District?—One side is; I am not certain whether the whole is.

It is not a very long street?—I think not.

Do you recollect the number of public-houses and dram-shops there are in that street?—I do not.

A paper before the Chairman states there are twenty-three public-houses and dram-shops licensed in that street, and that the street measures three furlongs thirteen poles; should you not think that number of public-houses and dram-shops most intolerably large?—I should think it very prejudicial.

And much beyond the necessary call?—I should think so.

Are there not many called "Houses of Call," where persons merely step in to take drams and pass on?—Yes.

Is Golden-lane within your District?—One side of Golden-lane is, the other side I think is in the City of London.

It is stated to the Committee, that there are twelve public-houses licensed in that lane, measuring two furlongs and five poles?—I cannot speak to the number.

Within these few years do you think there has been a great increase of dram-shops?—There has. I think the number of dram-shops in this Metropolis is one of the greatest evils existing, and it is always a primary object with me, as far as I am concerned, to endeavour to prevent as many of those from being licensed as possible; for it is not the laborious, hard-working, honest labouring man, that resorts to dram-shops, he generally is content with his porter, but it is the loose and the dissolute who are in the habit of drinking drams, and they drink to such excess as to reduce themselves to a state of partial madness, when they often commit the most desperate crimes.

From your observation, has the vice of drunkenness increased lately?—I think not; I am not in the habit of seeing more drunken men in our district than usual.

According to your observation, are the morals of the journeymen workmen, and lower orders of society, improved within the last ten years?—I should think they are.

Do you not think they are become more domestic, and that there are less habits of drunkenness, and less assemblages for the purpose of drinking, than existed formerly?—I do think so.

Was your Clerk, Shearman, concerned in the prosecution of Eliza Fenning?—He was.

Is he much concerned in criminal prosecutions?—He has been frequently employed, certainly.

Do you consider him to have a good business?—He is a very respectable man in his line; I am not aware of the extent of his business.

Where is the place where you keep persons who are accused, prior to their examination?—In the back yard there is a place fitted up, that was formerly a stable.

How long are they ever lodged there?—If they are committed for further examination, they are generally sent immediately to New Prison or Cold Bath Fields; but they are sometimes kept in the lock-up house at Hatton Garden till the Magistrate goes away at night, and the last thing done then is to send for the officer (who has the custody of them) to inquire whether there is any person in confinement, and if there is, he is immediately ordered to be carried to the prison expressed in the warrant of commitment.

Is it a fit place to confine prisoners?—It is clean.

Is it without windows, and damp, and without a floor?—There are two rooms, one for men and the other for women, who may be brought to the Office of an

evening

Robert Raynsford, Esq.

evening after the office hours, and are examined when the Magistrates come to the Office in the morning; those rooms have strong oak boarded floors, the walls are perfectly dry, and it is a place perfectly clean; I cannot tell any place that can be better, and I have never heard the slightest complaint of it. There is also another room, where prisoners are confined in the day, during the time they are under examination: the floor of that room is not boarded, but is paved with flagstones; persons are never shut up there all night; that is not so clean as it ought to be, but directions have been given to put it in a proper state. I consider those two rooms perfectly sufficient for the wants of the Office.

Is your Office sufficiently large for the purposes for which it is designed?—I think it is; but from the multiplicity of business we have occasionally at Hatton Garden, it is extremely crowded sometimes, and very offensive in consequence of it.

Are not persons who are brought there for examination, carried over to a public-house contiguous to the Office?—No, not to my knowledge; there is certainly no necessity for carrying them there.

Thomas Evance, Esquire, called in, and Examined.

Thomas Evance, Esq.

HOW long have you been appointed a Magistrate at Union Hall?—I was appointed in the year 1801.

Have you any other public situation of emolument besides that you have stated?—None at all.

Do the three Magistrates of your Office attend regularly, according to the Act of Parliament?—They do attend as regularly, I believe, as the Magistrates generally do; there is no cause of complaint.

What are the hours of attendance?—One Magistrate attends from ten in the morning to three, and from seven to eight in the evening; the second Magistrate attends from twelve o'clock at noon, till three in the afternoon, and does not attend in the evening.

So you have two Magistrates from twelve to three in attendance, and one from ten to three?—Yes, one of the two, the other is considered as attending the half day only.

This is the case every day?—It is, generally speaking.

It never happens that either in the daytime or the evening, there is no Magistrate at the Office?—I should hope never.

That never has happened in point of fact?—I am not aware of such a circumstance; a Magistrate may be sent for to the Secretary of State's Office, or called upon other duties of a public nature, where he is obliged to attend; and it might happen in those cases, but not from intentional neglect of the Magistrate, I am pretty sure.

How many Clerks are there?—We have two Clerks.

Have you any assistant?—There is a young man who was brought into the Office, and who is rated and appointed as a constable; the multiplicity of business we have at Union Hall required an assistant.

What is the name of that young man?—Aldred; we have him for copying those examinations where the parties are committed for trial, which are first taken down on paper by the Chief Clerk, to be transmitted to the Sessions or Assizes, that the case may appear on our books; we also find him generally useful in the business of the Office.

Do the two Clerks regularly attend their duty daily?—I should hope they do; but not attending de die in diem myself, I cannot answer for it; it is their duty to do it, and if they are absent at any time, there is an inquiry.

Whenever you attend, you always find the two Clerks present?—In general; they do not immediately come at the same time; the senior Clerk we allow to come an hour later than the junior Clerk, that is the practice at our Office.

Do they hold any other situation besides that of clerks at that Office?—Mr. Kitson, I believe, has some situation as a copying clerk in the House of Lords, which occupies his extra hours.

Do

Do either of them practise as solicitors?—Mr. Reeves practises in a small degree as a solicitor, but so as not to interfere with his attendance at the Office, in which he is very regular.

Does he practise as a solicitor in the Office?—No, that we should not allow.

You would feel it your duty as one of the Magistrates, to protest against any of your clerks acting as solicitor either for the prosecutor or defendant?—Certainly.

If Mr. Reeves the Chief Clerk, and Mr. Kitson the Second Clerk, constantly and regularly attended their duty, would it be necessary to have an extra clerk?—From the multiplicity of business we have it is impossible for us to do without a third person; we take a great quantity of evidence which must be copied to go to Sessions or the Assizes; the business at Union Hall is inconceivable.

You consider a third clerk as absolutely necessary?—We so conceive, but believe the Secretary of State does not think it right to allow the additional expense of a third clerk, and therefore Mr. Aldred is put on the footing of a constable of the Office.

What salary has he?—A guinea a week.

Nominally a constable, and really acting as clerk?—Just so, acting occasionally in both capacities.

You have seven Officers, with Mr. Aldred?—Eight, with him.

Do you consider that number of Officers sufficient for the duties of your Establishment?—If I were to say that many more were desirable, I should not say improperly, for it is impossible, with the extent of the jurisdiction of Union Hall, that the duty of the Office can be sufficiently attended to, by supplying the various demands upon us, without further aid.

What is the extent of the jurisdiction of your Office?—The parish of Christ Church, Saint Saviour's, Saint George's, Saint Olave's, Saint John's, Saint Thomas, the Clink Liberty of Southwark, Saint Mary Magdalen, Bermondsey (the land and water side) Saint Mary Rotherhithe, Saint Mary Newington, Walworth, Saint Giles's Camberwell, Peckham, Dulwich, Saint Mary Lambeth, Vauxhall, South Lambeth, Stockwell and Norwood, Brixton, Denmark Hill, Streatham, Upper Tooting and Baalam, the Manor of Hatcham and the Manor of Saint Paul Deptford: how is it possible that, with only seven Officers, we can be attending to such an immense extent as our jurisdiction includes.

Have you any idea how many miles round it is?—I should think that, commencing from the foot of London Bridge, round the different parishes to the extent of our jurisdiction, and returning through the parishes on the other side to the foot of the bridge, cannot be less than between thirty and forty miles.

Have you any notion of the extent of the population?—From the Statistical Return taken under the 51 Geo. III, in 1811, the amount of the population appears to be, one hundred and twenty-seven thousand three hundred and twelve.

It is your opinion that the strength of your Establishment is not at all equal to the calls that the interest of the public daily make for the protection of the Police?—The business of the Office would be conducted with more desirable energy if the Establishment was increased.

Have you many offences daily brought before the Office?—A great many. The business of the Office arises out of felonies, misdemeanors, breaches of the peace, disputes between masters and labourers, masters and apprentices. A great deal of parochial businesss is brought to the Offices, such as the binding of parish apprentices and settling disputes between them; and differences arising in friendly societies under the Act of Parliament; and a variety of other things, which do not occur to me at this moment.

Can you state to the Committee, upon an average, what are the number of new cases which come before you daily?—I cannot answer that distinctly; but I recollect the other morning, that, independent of other business, I heard nineteen assault causes. My brother Magistrates and myself are constantly occupied in endeavouring to reconcile the different parties, and prevent their going to the Sessions. We frequently find that the lower orders of the people will actually pawn their clothes to take out warrants.

You

You commit to Horsemonger-lane Gaol ?—Yes.

Has any plan ever suggested itself to your mind, by which a division could be made of your extensive jurisdiction, more for the advantage of the public than exists at present?—I never took it into consideration myself, but I have heard that there was once some talk of making a division, by removing the Thames Police Office, and establishing another Office lower down on the Surrey side of the water.

Do you not think that some alteration to lessen the extent of your duties might be useful ?—I do ; or that the number of officers should be proportionably increased.

How long has the Office at Union Hall been established?—From the original establishment of the Police ; previous to that, there was an Office attended by some of the County Magistrates of the Division, and supported at their own expense, in order to do away the improper practices of some persons who, at at that time, made a trade of their office : it was called the Rotation Office.

Do you find the business of Union Hall much diminished since the appointment of an Alderman to sit in Southwark ?—That has, in some measure, diminished the business from a part of the District.

Do you not consider that the parishes you first named, situate in Southwark, are taken out of your jurisdiction by that arrangement?—No, we consider that we have a concurrent jurisdiction ; but we do not usually interfere with those parishes, unless in cases of felonies, or where we are called on, and when the Sitting Alderman is not in attendance.

You do find the business of your Office diminished in those respects ?—Certainly, in a degree.

Do you find that diminution so great as to prevent the necessity for curtailing the extent of your jurisdiction ?—I am not aware of the existence of that necessity, but have only suggested the utility of some increase upon the establishment, more adequate to that extent of jurisdiction.

In the District you describe, there are several resident Magistrates who act, are there not ?—We wish those Magistrates to undertake the parochial business, and there are some who do so.

Has the population of your District increased very much since the establishment of your Office ?—Certainly ; I should think it is more than doubled.

Has not a great deal of land been covered with buildings since the establishment of your Office?—A great deal ; all St. George's-fields, Newington, and several small streets that branch out from those places and from the Borough.

Do you at your Office keep up a constant correspondence with the other six Offices, and the Office at Bow-street ?—We meet once a month, and at those times confer upon any thing we have to communicate ; but the Returns made every month to the Secretary of State give the Magistrates an opportunity of meeting there ; and the Secretary of State enters into the business of the respective Offices, and if any thing particular has occurred, we then report it to him.

You do not make any daily communication of capital offences brought before you ?—No.

Do you not think that it would be very advisable, for the furtherance of public justice, that such a communication should be made by all the Offices to each other ?—I think it might in certain cases ; but then we must have additional hands to do it, and it would be attended with trouble and expense : and in many respects, where privacy is desirable, great mischief might result from it.

Could not that communication be made by the Twopenny-post ?—I think not.

In point of fact, would the trouble be more than the writing each a letter, detailing the capital offences brought before them ?—I hardly know how it would be practicable for that to be done daily, from the multiplicity of business brought before the Office, and, as I have before observed, in many cases unadvisable.

Do you not think that the speedy apprehension of offenders would be considerably facilitated, if the offences that are brought before the cognizance of one Police Office were that very day communicated to all the others ?—I question if it would be possible to accomplish it, unless there was one person appointed specially for that purpose at each Office.

If

Thomas Evance, Esq.

If it were practicable, would it be desirable?—I cannot but say I entertain very serious doubts upon it, and the present bias of my mind is, that it would not.

Has it ever occurred to you that it would be an advisable arrangement to establish one central Police Office, which should be considered as the head, and all the other Offices subordinate, and that a regular correspondence should take place between them?—I should think that might be useful.

At present the seven Police Establishments are independent of each other, and Bow-street independent of them all?—Just so.

What proportion of time do you suppose is taken up by the examination of felons, independent of parish business?—A great proportion of our time is taken up by parochial business; it was formerly confined to one day in the week, but now otherwise, and is much increased by boys brought to be apprenticed by the parishes, and by hearing summonses for not paying the poor rates, sometimes thirty or forty, and the numerous applications for relief made by paupers, all of which upon the average take up, in my opinion, as much time as felonies and other criminal matters.

Do you ever find the public business at a stand because you have parish business to take under your consideration?—No, never at a stand; though it sometimes happens that public business is impeded by it.

Do you consider the time of the Office occupied most by public business or parochial business?—Perhaps about equal.

Do you consider that crimes, felonies and misdemeanors, have considerably increased within these few years?—They certainly have increased, but not to the extent which might have been expected from the disbanding the army and navy.

Are more children and boys brought before you than were formerly?—A great many more.

Have you in your Office an account from which you could give a return of the ages of the accused, under twenty, that have been brought before you, for the last four or five years?—I should think it probable it might be collected, but I cannot speak with any certainty.

Has the number of those of a very young age considerably increased from what it was?—Very much.

Have you them ever brought before you of the early age of eight and nine years?—I think we have.

Can you state to the Committee what, according to your opinion, is the reason for this alarming increase?—There are several reasons which may be assigned for it; there are a number of children who are deserted at an early age by their parents, and many brought before us who appear to be orphans, and without any friends; there are others, where the parents are in indigent circumstances, not capable of providing for them, or able to put them out apprentice. After a certain age the parishes will not keep them, urging that they are big enough to earn their bread; and there are a number of designing thieves constantly on the look-out for children, who are naturally more inclined to be idle than to work, and who commence with petty thefts at the wharfs, and other places where property is exposed; these the confirmed thieves seize hold of, and make them the catspaw in doing those things which they otherwise would themselves, and for which they would probably suffer detection and punishment, hoping that, in consideration of their youth, commiseration may be excited in the breasts of the Magistrates, and that they may be dismissed. I have frequently sent for the parents of such as have been brought before me, and on their solemnly promising they will take care of the children, and punish them themselves for the offences they have committed, I have given them up to them; but it seldom happens to any good purpose, for they get out, and again associate with their thievish comrades, and continue their practices.

Do you consider that the public schools established in the Borough have lessened the number of children that commit crimes?—I am afraid not, because we have had more children brought to the Office latterly than I ever knew or ever heard of before.

You

Thomas Evance,
Esq.

You wish the Committee to understand that the increase of those juvenile depredators is very great?—Certainly.

The number going on from year to year increasing?—Certainly; but I am of opinion that they have not made their appearance till within this last year or two, at such an early period of life. It has often occurred to me, that if a ship fitted up as a Penitentiary were provided, and those young depredators committed to it, and made to work, they would not only be taken away from the bad boys they associate with, and be released from the clutches of the wretches they are now connected with, who have them under tuition, but they might learn and be made to work, and after a certain period of time perhaps become good members of society, and by this mode be kept detached from other bad characters.

Has it fallen within your observation, whether persons who have been discharged from the Hulks, as they are established at present, have, generally speaking, nine times out of ten returned to their old habits of thieving?— I believe nine times out of ten they have; I have heard many instances of it.

Do you consider the detection of an increased number of juvenile depredators at all attributable to an increased vigilance on the part of the Police officers?— It may in some degree be owing to that, but not wholly; those who have been brought before the Office, have been apprehended not only by the attention of the Police officers, but also of parochial constables who are attending at the water-side and the wharfs.

Are you of opinion that it is in consequence of greater vigilance on the part of those parochial constables?—I cannot say that, but certainly many have been brought before us by them.

You would think the increase proceeds from two causes, partly from the increased vigilance of the Police officers, but more particularly from the increased number of crimes?—From the increased number of crimes, chiefly.

Are public-houses licensed at your Office?—No; they are licensed by the Magistrates of the district, of the Hundred of East Brixton.

Are there many houses within your knowledge, that are technically known by the name of " Flash-houses?"—I do not know; but the Magistrates came to a resolution some time ago, that those houses that were avowedly for the purpose of selling spirits, should have their licence taken away, unless they would have accommodation for people, as in a public-house, where there should be a tap-room.

Has that regulation of the Magistrates been attended to?—It is to take place the next licensing. There were several meetings of the Magistrates upon that very point: they were aware of the ill consequences of having so many gin-shops, and they came to certain resolutions, which were afterwards printed, and stuck up in the different houses, with notice, that those who did not change the front of their houses from being mere gin-shops, and have a tap-room for people to go in and take beer, their licences should be rejected when they applied for a renewal of them.

It was formerly the practice for persons to take out a beer licence, which they are obliged to do before they can take a spirit licence, selling no beer?—Yes, merely as a cover to authorize the sale of spirits.

Lunæ, 6° die Maii, 1816.

The Honourable HENRY GREY BENNET, in The Chair.

John Thomas Barber Beaumont, Esquire, called in, and Examined.

YOU are a Magistrate for the county of Middlesex?—I am.

In your capacity as a Magistrate have you ever directed your attention to the general system of the Police of the Metropolis?—I have.

State the result of your opinion?—In my opinion there is too little exertion used in preventing the propagation and growth of crimes, and too much exertion used in punishing them when they arrive at maturity. The children of idle, drunken, and dishonest parents, are suffered to infest the streets in a state of destitution; the first instructions and ideas these little creatures receive are to procure the means of life by begging and thieving. I have seen children not more than seven or eight years of age initiated into the trade of picking of pockets, under the eye of adults, seemingly their mothers. In Covent-garden Market, and other places affording partial shelter, and in private houses in Saint Giles's, and in public-houses in Whitechapel, boys and girls take up their nightly abode in a state of promiscuous depravity. These born and bred thieves I believe are never reclaimed, so long as they are suffered to live; they live by depredations on the public. Where parents thus throw their children on the public, I think the public ought to take such children in immediate charge. By separating them from their parents and other bad connexions, and giving them some education, they might soon be made useful members of society, instead of their continuing for life a burthen and a terror to it. The impunity with which small thefts are committed, is a great encouragement to crime; the first thefts of the children just alluded to, and of the children of well-disposed persons drawn in by their example, take place at too tender an age to fit them for legal prosecution; they rob, are detected, but are unpunished; and when in the next stage of their education they are introduced to Flash-houses, they there see thieves and thief-takers sitting and drinking together on terms of good fellowship; all they see and hear is calculated to make them believe they may rob without fear of punishment, for in their thoughtless course they do not reflect that the forbearance of the officers will continue no longer than until they commit a 40 *l.* crime, when they will be sacrificed. The system of offering great rewards on the perpetration of a capital offence, and no reward or encouragement for the discovery of minor felonies, I think is radically bad; the thief-takers are thus interested in concealing and encouraging rising thieves until their crimes arrive at the highest growth. If rewards upon a small scale were given for the discovery of thieves in their earliest acts, and for the apprehension of reputed thieves when found in suspicious situations, the trade of thieving would even in its first attempts be so exposed to the harassing of informers, and be of so much difficulty and danger, as not to be worth following. Impunity is still further assured to petty thieves by the general indisposition to prosecute; the trouble, loss of time, expense, and the probability that the indictment after all will be defeated upon some legal quibble, discourage even the public-spirited from prosecuting. To lessen the waste of time in attending prosecutions, I think that lists of the causes set down for trial, and numbered, ought to be fixed up in the hall of the Sessions as soon as the bills are found; that they ought to be taken up in regular order, and be marked off as they are disposed of. I think that crimes against the public peace ought to be prosecuted at the public expense, and be conducted by a public officer; this would secure the ends of justice, and prevent collusion between the prisoner and the prosecutor. If this principle however is deemed inexpedient, at any rate indictments ought to be prepared, subpœnas and notices served, and advice given, without fees or other expense to prosecutors; and further, their loss of time and moderate expenses ought to be paid for. There may be danger in offering rewards on successful prosecutions,

510.   but

J. T. B. Beaumont,
Esq.

but there can be none in making the discharge of an important public duty barely not a loss to the prosecutor. To mend the proverbial uncertainty of the law, and secure the ends of justice, I think throughout our whole system of jurisprudence the true interpretation of points of law and rules of practice should be defined precisely and laid down scientifically and systematically in a work under authority, instead of hanging on scattered and varying opinions. Impunity is visibly enjoyed by pick-pockets to a very great extent; gangs of this extensive class of robbers impudently look us in the face year after year, rob us, and continue to elude punishment. One reason of this is, the facility with which adepts in the art pass their booty from one to another, whereby it is difficult to identify the thief when the offence is completed: if he be detected, it must be while he is in the act, and before its completion; it is then only a misdemeanor, and is bailable; the production of two sureties in 40 $l.$ each is usually deemed sufficient to set the felon loose again on the public; he does not appear to his trial, the recognizances are in due course estreated into the Exchequer, but the penalties are not sought after for two years, when, I have authority to state, not one in five hundred is recovered. Indeed the present system of dealing with recognizances is a mere mockery; it sets justice at naught, it leads only to the superadding of perjury to other crimes. A casual transgressor may pine in gaol for want of sureties, but a professed villain is never at a loss for such assistance to set him free; there are men in abundance who make it their business to stand bail for hire; they know at what time the estreat will be in process, when they shift their quarters, and are " non est inventus." I was in June 1814 surrounded by a gang of five or six hustlers, in the Strand; one of these put his hand into my breeches pocket, where I seized it, and with much difficulty secured the man, and took him to the Bow-street Office; he was committed for trial; I attended two days at the next Sessions, when I at length heard that the offender had put in bail, and might not appear until the succeeding Sessions; he appeared no more. I find that to this day no process is issued against his Jew bail, the only penalty inflicted was on myself, in the money I paid for the bill of indictment, &c. &c. and in the time I was confined at the Sessions. Magistrates ought to be well assured that bail admitted in such cases is substantial, that the penalties of the bond are large, and that the prosecutor have notice when bail is put in, that he may not waste his time at the Sessions to no purpose. Formerly, no cause contributed more to the growth of crime than the indiscriminate mixture of, and disorderly practices among, persons committed to prison; great improvements have latterly taken place in the system of imprisonment, but it is not yet on the best possible footing; persons under accusation only, ought to be kept separate from convicted or reputed thieves, and persons imprisoned for assaults ought not to be mixed with convicted or accused felons; then as to the duration of imprisonment, the public are put to an immense expense in keeping convicts in custody, their labour is almost lost to the public during the term of imprisonment, and they rapidly ripen in villany by their intercourse with each other. The objects of imprisonment being to deter by its sufferings, and if possible to work the reformation of the prisoner, I conceive those objects may be achieved with more certainty and at much less expense than is usual, by making the confinement strictly solitary, refusing all access of friends, restricting the diet to coarse bread and to water only, and in aggravated cases adding to the imprisonment a certain number of sound floggings during the term. Subject to this abstinence and discipline, I think one month's confinement would be more dreaded, and more completely subdue daring spirits, than six in the common way and with the customary indulgences; contamination would thus be avoided, and the reformed culprit be exempted from the future contagion and disgrace of prison acquaintances. Discharged sailors have latterly committed many robberies: the interest of these poor fellows has been sadly neglected, and with it the interest of the public; some thousands of these, when paid off, have received sums which, rightly applied, would have secured their remaining days from want, but, as helpless as children in the use of money, they are immediately stript when they reach the shore which their valour has defended, and left to perish through distress, or subsist by plunder. If Government had managed a little for these men who are so unable to manage for themselves, the evil to a great extent might have been averted, and their future services secured to this country. It would not have been difficult with due preparation to have persuaded them to have sunk the greater

part

J. T. B. Beaumont, Esq.

part of their prize-money in annuities (which might have been rendered unassignable;) considering the peculiar hazard of their lives, very high terms might have been afforded, and the political generosity of the State might have added to the computable values by way of increasing the attraction. It is perhaps not yet too late to do some good in this way. Receivers of stolen goods are by no means under effectual checks, although numerous Acts of Parliament have been passed for the suppression of their trade. The subject is one of great importance, for " If there were no receivers, there would be no thieves." It is too complicate and extensive, however, for my present evidence; I will therefore only suggest, that it would throw considerable difficulty and impediment in the way of the receiver's dealings, if it were enacted that no person should purchase second-hand wearing-apparel, linen or piece-goods, iron-mongery or metals, for the purpose of re-sale, without taking out an annual licence for those purposes; that his purchases should be completed at his dwelling-house only ; that the things in which he dealt under the licence, should be described in conspicuous letters in front of his house; and that the Magistrates, or Commissioners, empowered to issue the licences, should be at liberty to withhold them, where the applicant had been found guilty of any felony or misdemeanor, or on any other sufficient cause, subject to any appeal to the General Sessions ; such houses to be open at all times to the inspection of any Magistrate, or person deputed by him. Among the immediate causes of thefts and other offences against the public peace, lotteries hold an undoubted place. It is a scandal to the Government, thus to excite people to practise the vice of gaming, for the purpose of drawing a revenue from their ruin; it is an anomalous proceeding by law to declare gambling infamous, to hunt out petty gamblers in their recesses and cast them into prison, and by law also to set up the giant gambling of the State Lottery, and to encourage persons to resort to it by the most captivating devices which ingenuity, uncontrolled by moral rectitude, can invent. I am now come to a subject of universal influence on the morals of the public: it is decidedly my opinion, that low public-houses, flash-houses, and gin-shops, compose the foundation and hot-bed of nearly all the vices and crimes which disturb the Metropolis ; in these, thousands consume their time, money, and constitution, and acquire insensibility to all the moral duties; from these they sally forth to commit depredations on the public, impelled by destitution and fired by burning liquors. It is lamentable, that public-houses, which are indispensable to public accommodation, should thus be rendered public nuisances. The evil however is inseparable from the law, which gives to certain individuals in their several localities the power of setting up or putting down such houses, subject to no other control than that of their own private wills and unsearchable motives. This despotic power was given by the Legislature for the purpose of more effectually repressing disorderly houses; but in this, as in all similar powers, the abuse supersedes the use. Whatever the object might be, the effect of the law is to throw a very great proportion of the public-houses into the hands of brewers and gin-sellers, whose interest consists in procuring the greatest possible consumption of their liquors, and at the highest price ; the effect also is to exclude from the ownership of such houses, the owners of the surrounding houses to which the public-houses are appurtenant ; the interest of which owners, in diametric opposition to that of the brewers, consists in preventing their public-house from becoming a harbour for drunkenness or disorder, and in promoting industry and sobriety among their tenants. It is capable of full proof, that some brewers procure licences for new houses at pleasure, which the right owners have in vain applied for, and that they are able to preserve licences to old houses of the most disorderly kind; whence the publicans are taught to depend, not on good conduct, but on good interest, for the preservation of their licences. These brewers are men of great wealth and influence, and know how to apply both ; but where the licences are above the brewers influence, which I hope is the case with the great majority of Justices, the procuring of a licence is still so much a work of mean solicitation and intrigue, that an estate owner, who is aware of licensing practices, will not risk his property or commit his independence in erecting a public-house, when one is wanted for his tenants. If then the brewer does not stand forward in his own person, some needy or avaricious intriguer supplies his room, and administers to his objects. My conclusion therefore is, that licensing houses for brewers, should

510. be

J. T. B. Beaumont, Esq.

be prohibited by law; that gin-shops should be speedily abolished altogether; that a preference should be secured to the estate owner, where new neighbourhoods arise and a new public-house becomes necessary; and that licensing decisions should be subject to an appeal to the Quarter Sessions. Lastly, for the preservation of order and decency in the public streets and in public-houses, I am of opinion that considerable benefit would arise if Magistrates and principal Parish Officers were personally to visit the haunts of vice, and personally to direct the apprehension of disorderly persons, instead of leaving all to the frequently interested selection of Police officers, constables, and watchmen.

Has any plan ever struck your mind for the separation of the children referred to in your evidence, from their parents?—Something of the nature of the Philanthropic Reform; I believe that is limited in its objects to the children of convicted felons, if so, it would not reach deserted children, who might be as proper objects as the other: whether it should be a popular society or a Government establishment, I have not made up my mind, but I am satisfied there should be one or the other. My idea is, that the children I have described are born and bred thieves, and they never or scarcely ever are reclaimed; they are therefore a burthen to the public, and they cost more in being employed all their lives as thieves or beggars, than they would by a short education, which would qualify them to be useful members of society.

Are you speaking of children who are convicted of misdemeanors or felonies, or merely children in a state of destitution?—Children generally in a state of destitution; such as the children of low prostitutes, who may be nightly seen about the streets with their mothers, and brought up regularly to every sort of vice.

How do you account for the increased number of juvenile depredators, if you think that the Officers are not induced to apprehend culprits but for the sake of the 40 l. reward?—I am not aware of the fact, that there is an increase of youthful culprits; though that may be the case.

Do you think that, supposing there to be an increase of charges, it is a positive increase arising from there being a greater disposition to commit crimes at present than heretofore; or that it is a merely nominal increase, arising from the increased vigilance of the Police?—I am unable to form an opinion upon that alternative.

From your observation, upon what you have heard from other Magistrates, do you think that the morals of the lower orders of people are better or worse than they were formerly?—I think they are worse.

Do you think that the vice of drunkenness is considerably increased?—I think that, by the profusion of new gin-shops which have been lately set up, drinking of the most pernicious kind has largely increased within these few years, and that the low tippling houses which have been newly licensed, are expressly calculated to promote the view of hard drinking; whether, upon the whole, there is now more intoxication among the lower orders than formerly, I cannot say.

That it has diminished?—Speaking of the lowest orders, I do not think it has, either one or the other; among the middling orders I think it has diminished.

Do you not think the existence of the gin-shops where spirits are sold, and where a beer licence is merely nominal, one of the great causes to which is to be attributed the increase of inebriety, supposing it to exist?—Most certainly I do; perhaps the greatest.

Have you ever been present when the licences were given by the Magistrates at their Petty Sessions?—I have.

In what district?—In the Tower Hamlets and in Kensington Division.

Was there a great facility shown by the Magistrates to granting those licences, or did they make a vigilant examination into the claims of the new candidates, as well as into the conduct of those who applied for a renewal of their licences?—I think not in either district, as regards the claims of new candidates.

Can you state to the Committee any particular case or cases in which such negligence on the part of the Magistrates appeared to you?—I can state several; I will state one, of which I have an intimate knowledge. I have considerable freehold and copyhold estates in the neighbourhood of Stepney, upon which I have lately built, and caused others to build, nearly 100 houses, besides two large manufactories. Part of my land lying between the Mile-end Road and Stepney Church, is planned into streets capable of containing about 500 houses. Whitehorse-lane, a great thoroughfare, passing through these streets, is without any

public-house

public-house in or near to it, although there are more than 350 new and inhabited *J. T. B. Beaumont, Esq.* houses in and by the line, which is about three furlongs in length. At the pressing desire of my tenants, and misled into a belief that my extent of houses would entitle my tenant to a licence as a matter of right, between three and four years since I ordered a public-house to be built midway on this line, to supply the reasonable wants of the neighbourhood. While I was having it built, I was applied to by several persons, the friends or agents of Messrs. Hanbury the brewers, and Mr. Stables and Williams the spirit dealers.

Who are Messrs. Stables and Williams?—They are both near relatives of Sir Daniel Williams; I have heard Sir Daniel speak of Mr. Stables as his nephew.

Is Mr. Williams his relation too?—I have always understood so.

How long have they set up the spirit trade?—About five or six years since. I was asked to enter into an engagement with Messrs. Stables and Williams, for the supply of the house, intimating that if I complied, my house would be immediately licensed, but not otherwise. Conceiving that the wants of the neighbourhood, and my own property there, must ensure a licence for the house without such condition, and being desirous that the house should be a free house, I rejected all these applications. But when the licensing day arrived, in 1813, the house was not even noticed. I then shut up the house for a year, until the licensing in 1814. It was again refused. I shut it up another year, and applied again in 1815, but with no better success. My house still remains unlicensed; and from further applications that have been made to me, and from facts that have come within my own knowledge, independent of general notoriety, I am persuaded that the house will not be licensed, unless I comply with the condition, or previously selling it, or letting it for a term, and much under its value, to Messrs. Hanbury, or use other exceptionable means. In illustration of what I have here asserted, I will name two instances, one of either kind, from among many that may be adduced and proved. In 1813, Mr. Humphreys, now a publican near Stepney, applied to me, and offered to introduce me to a Mr. Stables, who had interest to procure a licence, and would do so if the spirit trade of the house were secured to him; I declined the offer. Mr. Stables, I am informed, is a Clerk to the Commissioners of Sewers, a very near relative of Sir Daniel Williams, brought up at his expense, who, about three years previous to this application, under the support of Messrs. Hanbury was set up as a dealer in their bottled porter, and in spirits; in which trade he was shortly afterwards joined by a Mr. Williams, another near relative of Sir Daniel's; they have since met with extraordinary success, as I am informed among the publicans in Sir Daniel Williams's Division. In August last, I spoke to Mr. Robson, a leading Magistrate in the Tower Hamlets Division, and the confidential friend of Sir Daniel Williams, expressing my hope that a difference which had subsisted between me and the Magistrates in that neighbourhood, would not be the means of preventing the public-house, of which I was the owner, from being licensed. Mr. Robson said, that as a friend, he would advise me to engage the trade to Messrs. Hanbury and Co. for that it was expected the Magistrates wished so serve them. Seeing that it was in vain to contend against this issue, I therefore offered to sell the house to Messrs. Hanbury for what it cost me out of pocket, without interest, or to let it to them on a long lease at a rent yielding me between 5 *l.* and 6 *l.* per cent. interest on what the house cost building: with this they seemed willing to close. I then went to Mr. Robson, at the Whitechapel Office, where he was sitting with Mr. Rice Davies, and told him what I had done, and that I conceived my offer to be accepted. Upon this Mr. Robson expressed his satisfaction, and intimated there would be no difficulty in licensing the house; he freely stated that three of them (whom I understood to be Sir Daniel Williams, Mr. Merceron, and Mr. Robson) met previous to the licensing day, when they predetermined what houses should be licensed: and he added, "if necessary, our friend here (Mr. Rice Davies) will attend." He then proceeded to explain to Mr. Davies the necessity of licensing the house; its remoteness from any other public-house; the very great number of new and inhabited houses around it; the large property I had on the spot, and the circumstance that I had taken down an old public-house, the Marquis of Granby, on the same estate in the Mile-end Road, where public houses were too crowded, while in Whitehorse-lane, the situation of the new house, there was not one; so that the public were greatly benefited by the exchange of place, and obliged to Mr. Beaumont; and he, Mr. Robson, particularly desired that the circum-

stance

J. T. B. Beaumont,
Esq.

stance of my having pulled the old public-house down should be mentioned in the Memorial for licensing the new one. Mr. Davies concurred in all that was said, promised to attend if necessary, and added, It would be a great shame if, holding so much property on the spot, I could not get a house licensed. On the following day, I saw Sir Daniel Williams, and stated to him the terms on which I had offered to part with the house to Messrs. Hanbury, remarking, that I should still lose the interest of my money for three years. Sir Daniel entered with seeming zeal into the argument for licensing the house, and observed that it was no bad thing to get my principal back. A few days before the licensing, Messrs. Hanbury declined taking the house on the terms offered, saying, that an inferior house would be more to their interest. On Monday the 18th of September the Justices met on the business of licensing; present, Sir Daniel Williams, Mr. Rhode, Mr. Story, Mr. Merceron, Mr. Robson, Mr. Windle, Mr. Flood, Mr. Mashiter. The licensing was opposed by Sir Daniel Williams and Mr. Robson, in which they were followed by Messrs. Merceron, Flood, Windle, and Mashiter, who usually vote with them, as I am informed and believe. Mr. Rhodes and Mr. Story appealing strongly against this decision, were shortly answered by Mr. Robson, that it was a better house than necessary, and perhaps never would be licensed. The connexion here evinced, between these Magistrates and Messrs. Hanbury, is made no secret of by the agents of the latter: I had heard it freely avowed by them. At a licensing meeting in 1814, a Mr. Ventom, the broker of Messrs. Hanbury, was introduced to me by Mr. Hubbard, a Lieutenant in the Tower Hamlets Militia, saying, " This is the gentleman to get your house licensed ;" Ventom said, it would be licensed directly, if I gave Messrs. Hanbury the trade ; and in answer to a question, added, " Messrs. Hanbury would not of course be at the expense and trouble of using their influence with the Justices, unless the trade were made sure to them."

Does Major Jackson act in that Division ?—He does.

Does he take any part or interest with Mr. Williams and others in licensing ?—Yes, he does ; they occasionally differ when there is a collision of interests ; but in general he gives way to Sir Daniel Williams ; he has a nephew who set up in the spirit trade.

Do you state it distinctly to the Committee as your opinion, that in the case which you have just laid before them, if you had sold your house to Messrs. Hanbury, or engaged to take their spirits and liquors, there would have been no difficulty whatever in obtaining the licence ?—I am thoroughly persuaded of that.

Have you had any discussions with the Magistrates in that Division, relative to any other houses besides those in which you had an immediate interest ?—No, I have been at their meetings when other cases were considered.

Are those persons who applied to Mr. Hanbury for his interest with the Magistrates to obtain a licence, required to enter into any undertaking with him of a legal nature, that they will deal with him, when their house is licensed ?—I have had numerous publicans who have been with me and stated that, and that when they had done so they had always succeeded.

What is the nature of those agreements ?—The one I have heard of is, that the trade should be assured to them for a term of seven or fourteen years, in consideration of their interest in procuring the licence.

Do you know of any sum of money paid by victuallers to their servants or other persons, in addition to the agreement you have described ?—No, I have never heard of that.

Can you take upon yourself to say, that it is the common fame of that district, that a connexion exists between Messrs Hanbury and the Magistrates, so that those who have the recommendation of Messrs Hanbury, have a preference over any other persons in the licensing of public-houses ?—Most decidedly so.

Do you know whether the near relations of any of the Magistrates are spirit dealers, or hold retail spirit shops?—Messrs. Stables and Williams, whom I have already mentioned ; and Mr. Orange, the nephew of Major Jackson, who keeps a retail spirit shop at the corner of Somerset-street, Whitechapel, as I am informed and believe.

Do you know whether those young men were brought up to the trade ?—I believe none of them ; they were in the Tower Hamlets militia.

Can

J. T. B. Beaumont, Esq.

Can you state to the Committee any thing as to the conduct of the persons who keep the smaller public-houses in the Division; whether they are kept in an orderly condition or not?—Many of them are most disorderly; the worst practices are allowed in them.

Have you ever been present when complaints were laid before the Magistracy, as to the conduct of those houses?—Yes.

What was done?—The complaints were rejected.

Did a minute investigation take place?—No; it was tendered, but overruled.

Do you know whether those houses either belonged to or were supplied by Messrs. Hanbury and Williams?—I do not know that.

Are there any houses that are technically termed " Flash houses ' in that District?—I believe there are many.

Have repeated complaints been made against them?—Yes.

Within your own knowledge do you know any instance of licences having been refused on the licensing day to persons who kept disorderly houses?—No, not of my own knowledge.

Did you ever hear of that having taken place?—Yes; I have heard that it has taken place, but that they have afterwards been revived.

Do you believe that it was a mere fraudulent withdrawing of the name, the old parties having a connexion still in the houses?—From all I have heard, I have no doubt of the original parties connexion with the house still subsisting.

Did the same bad practice that had called down the censure of the Magistracy still continue?—Yes, as I am informed.

Do you know whether complaints were again made against those houses?—Yes, they were, in the licensing in 1814.

Do you recollect what took place then?—I allude to houses in the parish of Shadwell. Mr. Fletcher, the churchwarden, accompanied by the other Parish officers and a large number of very respectable inhabitants, attended in Osborne-street on the adjourned day for licensing: they had previously sent in a memorial, setting forth the bad conduct of certain houses in that division, and they then attended and tendered themselves on oath to give evidence of what they had stated in their memorial, and of other facts in addition; their oath was refused, and their evidence repressed upon points of form. Mr. Fletcher proceeded to give evidence against the landlord of a certain public-house, I think the King's Arms; when it was remarked, that he was no longer the landlord, for that a new man had been lately put in, and the complaints that applied against the former tenant could not be heard against the new one; he professed himself unapprised of that fact, but said in general terms that the conduct still continued the same. It is not an unusual expedient, where a house is of such ill fame that it is known complaints will be made against it, just before the licensing day, for the old tenant to be removed to some other house, or removed from the one in question at least, and a new man put in; in which case there can be no evidence.

You were present at this time?—I was.

Was there a disposition on the part of the Magistracy to inquire minutely into the conduct of those public-houses?—No; on the contrary, there appeared to me a disposition to shut out inquiry.

Had not those particular houses against which Mr. Fletcher made a complaint to the Magistrates, had their licences stopped the year before; and was not that the second year of his making the complaint?—He had complained of several houses the year before, but these were not the houses which had had their licences stopped, these were the houses to which the business had been carried in consequence of those licences being stopped.

To whom did those houses belong?—The worst house, the Duke of York, belonged to Messrs. Meux. When those houses were put down, other public-houses adjacent to them, which previously had been well-ordered houses, became immediately as bad as the houses just put down; and Messrs. Meux, who were the proprietors, or interested in the Duke of York, set up one of those houses, putting a man in for the avowed intention of keeping up the connexion, which was a series of brothels at the back of the Duke of York, kept by the landlord of the Duke of York.

Do you think, as a Magistrate sitting upon the Bench, that the objections

taken

J. T. B. Beaumont, Esq.

taken by the Bench to the evidence of Mr. Fletcher, proceeded from a bias in favour of the publican, or from thinking he had not made out his case?—I think there was a bias against Mr. Fletcher's application, decidedly.

Might not that bias arise, from the houses of which Mr. Fletcher complained, being of that description which it is admitted must be tolerated in that particular District?—It might, certainly.

William Stocker, called in, and Examined.

William Stocker.

WHAT are you?—A licensed victualler.

Where do you live?—I keep the Peacock, on Bethnal Green.

Did you ever hold a public-house, the Admiral Vernon, in Bethnal Green?—I did, five years.

Who was your landlord?—Mr. Merceron.

Who is Mr. Merceron?—A Magistrate of the county.

When did your term expire?—Unfortunately in moving I lost my particulars, so that I cannot tell exactly, but somewhere about 1809.

Had you any reason to believe you would be continued as the tenant?—I had, previous to my time expiring, up to the very day.

Do you know why you were refused?—It is a very nice matter to say that I know why I was refused; there was no complaint against my house.

When the licensing day arrived, what happened?—The first licensing day after my term was out I had my licence, but the second licensing day I was refused it.

What happened?—I was not called, I went to the Clerk of the Court and asked the reason I was not called; and he went over to Mr. Merceron, and he told me that my licence stood over to the adjournment day; and I drew up a petition, stating the circumstances, and that Mr. Merceron had agreed I should continue in my house: after I had agreed with the person that had the renewal, or more properly the collector, under certain terms, who the very night before shook hands with me and wished me success, I was applied to, to give up my house to another man.

Was there any complaint laid against your house?—Not any; I have been a licensed victualler near sixteen years, and never had a complaint against me.

Was any new house licensed instead of yours?—Yes, on the opposite side of the way, about five doors off.

Was that licensed to the person to whom you were asked to give up your house?—Yes.

Under what sign?—Under the same sign that I had, the Admiral Vernon.

You lost your licence without a complaint being made against you; and the person to whom you were solicited to give up your house, and which you refused, gained it in a new house?—Yes, a house that had not been licensed before.

Did you ever learn from Mr. Merceron, or any other of the Magistrates, why your licence was refused?—The only thing I could learn was, that I was told by the Clerk of the Court that I held the estate over in contempt, that I did not give it up at the expiration of my term; that I denied.

Your licence was not refused in consequence of there having been any complaint of any thing in your house?—No, it was not.

You are the proprietor of a new house in Bethnal Green?—In Shoreditch parish.

Whereabout is it situate?—In Haggerston, near Kingsland Road.

For what is it intended?—I believe originally the person that first built it had an intention it should be a public-house.

And you purchased it with a view of making it a public-house?—Yes.

Did you apply for a licence on the last licensing day?—No; I went over to Mr. Merceron, conceiving that I should get an answer, whether it was right or wrong to purchase it when it was first offered me, whether there was any complaint against that house, as I understood there had been a licence petitioned for before; he told me there had been a petition against it formerly, because there were not sufficient houses, but that now there were sufficient houses. I was told the next day, that Mr. Merceron saw the ground landlord, and that I could do nothing without I paid 100*l.* to the ground landlord to get his interest for the licence; so I did not apply the last time.

Who is the ground landlord?—Mr. Whitling; he is surveyor for Mr. Hanbury's brewhouse.

Had

William Stocker,

Had you bought the lease?—I had agreed for the lease, and then afterwards this 100*l.* was required.

Was it understood, in the original purchase you made of the house, that you were to pay 100 *l.* to Mr. Hanbury's surveyor, for his interest to procure you a licence?—No, I did not understand that till afterwards.

After you had agreed to purchase this house in Haggerston, you were told that unless you paid Messrs. Hanbury's surveyor 100*l.* you could not have their interest to gain the licence?—Yes, that is what I was told.

Do you consider yourself liable to pay it?—If I do not pay that, I shall have an opposition against me.

You keep a public-house now?—Yes.

Should you wish, if you followed your own inclination, to deal with the same brewer in this new house that you expect to get licensed, with whom you deal now?—At the moment I purchased this, it was my intention to do so.

What is your reason for changing your intention?—I was led to believe it would be no use my petitioning, for that I should not get it, and that this 100*l.* must be paid before I got the licence.

Who informed you of that?—From the person I bought the lease of, that bought it of Mr. Whitling, and Mr. Merceron saw Mr. Whitling the day before, when I applied to know whether I should be likely to get a licence for the house. I had no communication with Mr. Whitling in the purchase; Mr. Whitling knew nothing of it, nor none of Messieurs Hanbury's people.

Is it generally understood in that District, that a person applying for a licence to a new house, must, if he expects to obtain it, promise to deal with Mr. Hanbury?—I do not know of any house that has been licensed in that District, but what has been opened in Messieurs Hanbury's trade.

It is generally understood that they must deal with Messieurs Hanbury, to expect to be successful in their application for a licence?—It is.

In the first house you held, namely, the Admiral Vernon, did the church-wardens, constables, and principal inhabitants, certify in favour of your good conduct at all times?—The two churchwardens that year, the constable of that year and the year preceding, and several of the other officers and very respectable inhabitants all around there, signed my petition, when the party who got the licence against me had got neither churchwardens nor overseers, nor any of the officers.

Are you bound to take your beer from any particular house?—No, I never did; except that when a person holds a lease of a house under the brewer, he generally continues there.

Do you hold under a brewer now?—Yes.

Who is your brewer?—Mr. Calvert.

The Committee understand you to say, that you hold your house under Mr. Calvert?—Yes.

How long have you been in your house?—Nearly six years I have been in this house; this house orignally belonged to the Peacock brewhouse.

With whom did you deal when you first went into that house?—Mr. John Calvert.

Who is the proprietor of the house you meant to put your son into at Haggerston?—Mr. Whitling was the ground-landlord.

Did the house belong to any brewer?—No.

No brewer owned the house at Haggerston to which you have referred?—No.

It would sustain therefore the character of what is called a Free house?—Yes, it would.

And on the ground of its being a free house, from your partiality to the connexion you had with Messrs. Calvert, you wished they should have supplied your son with his beer?—That was my meaning.

What was the reason that you were prevented from getting a supply from Messrs. Calvert to your son's house?—The reason is, that when I bought the lease I did not understand any thing about the 100*l.* and when I was going to petition for the licence, I was informed that unless I paid the 100*l.* I should not get the licence; I then laid myself under Messrs. Hanbury & Co.

You expect to get the licence to that house next year?—I have been led to understand that I should.

510.

Who

William Stocker.

Who has given you to understand that?—Mr. Aveling, the managing clerk at Hanbury's, and Mr. Whitling, who acts as surveyor for their house.

Those gentlemen have given you to understand, that if you will deal with Mr. Hanbury, they will get you the licence for the house?—I do not remember any thing being said as to my dealing with Mr. Hanbury.

There was no condition annexed?—No.

Do you apprehend that if you had told Mr. Whitling and Mr. Aveling you should not deal with Mr. Hanbury, they would have given you their interest?—No, it is not to be considered that they would.

Do you know Mr. Simpson, a haberdasher in Shoreditch?—I do, very well.

He is also a builder, is he not?—He is.

He has built several houses on the Hackney Road, has he not?—Yes, a good many houses about there.

How many, do you suppose?—I do not know how many, but his connexions have built a great many.

Do you know any thing of an application of his to the Magistrates, to license one of those houses?—I have heard him speak of his applying year after year for the licence for a house he had built in a conspicuous place.

Was he successful at last?—Not till he put it into Mr. Hanbury's trade.

Has the number of public-houses, in the neighbourhood in which you live, increased or diminished within your experience?—On my spot there has a house been licensed where there was none before, but there are very few now; I am not competent to say whether they are generally increased.

Joseph Huxen, called in, and Examined.

Joseph Huxen.

WHAT are you?—A publican now, a carpenter by trade.

Did you build many houses in Rich-street, Limehouse?—I built about six houses.

Was one of them a public-house?—One I built for a public-house, it is now a public-house.

Known by the sign of Lord Hood?—Yes.

Did you endeavor to get that house licensed?—I did.

For how many years?—Six years and upwards without effect, and I strained every nerve I possibly could.

Did you apply to Mr. Reid, the distiller in Aldersgate-street, to get it licensed?—I did.

Did you offer to him the spirit trade?—I offered him the spirit trade for a certain term of years (seven years) if he could get it licensed; he said he was afraid it was out of his power to do it; he recommended me to call on Messrs. Trueman and Hanbury, which I did, and they put me off many times, but at last they said, if I would enter into an agreement to give them a lease of the premises, they had no objection to try what they could do; and I agreed to grant them a lease for twenty-one years, under the agreement that they were to grant me an under-lease.

Were there any conditions attached to the under-lease?—To deal with them.

That was expressed in the condition?—Yes.

Was it then immediately licensed?—No, it was not; the next year following I applied again to them, and entered into a similar agreement with them, as the date of the other did not stand, which I had to pay the licensing clerk for doing; I had to pay the licensing clerk both years; and this house being on my hands so long, I did not know what to do, and I considered it would be of more effect perhaps if I went into a house of theirs, and mortgaged the house to them, which I did for 250 *l.* and I was in the house eighteen months.

Was it then licensed?—No, it was not. Then I left the house, which was a very indifferent house; then they directly called in their mortgage money, and told me they must have it within two months, or they must sell the house to pay them their money; accordingly I advised with a person, who turned out to be their attorney, Mr. Thomson the licensing clerk, and he persuaded me to leave it to their generosity to do as they pleased; accordingly I did, so they agreed to give me 700 *l.* for it, and in two months after that it was licensed, and they said if it was licensed they would give me something more. When I went to apply,

Mr.

Joseph Huxen.

Mr. Aveling said, Why you have soon found out it is licensed now; I said, yes, I had; I said, you promised me a something more, I hope you will be as good as your word now; he said, That is another consideration; the fact is, you sold us the house, and we have sold the house again to liquor-merchants in the city, Messrs. Stables and Williams. I had a house joining, a little house I had built, as I had leisure time to do it, and they wished for this house; this was not a freehold house, but a lease I had taken (having bought this lot of ground, and then thinking there was not sufficient ground) from a friend of mine, who had bought the other ground; they would not give me any thing, unless I would sell them that house alongside of it.

Did you do that?—I did.

What did you get for the whole?—They gave me 250 *l.* for that.

Did Mr. Hanbury's clerk ever call upon you and solicit your orders for spirits, for Messrs. Stables and Williams?—Yes, Mr. Hanbury's clerk called, and left a card of Messrs. Stables and Williams; I believe he is a relation, and that he is in the distil-house now.

Do you know whether there is any connexion between Messrs. Hanbury and Messrs. Stables and Williams?—I have heard there is, but I cannot say further than that.

Was it your opinion that if you dealt with or sold your house to Messrs. Hanbury, you would get a licence, and that if you did not, you could not?—Yes, that was my opinion.

Is that the generally received opinion in that part of the town?—Yes, it is.

Do you keep a public-house now?—I do.

Under whom?—Mr. Calvert.

Are you bound to have your beer of Mr. Calvert?—Yes, it is Mr. Calvert's house.

Do you think that you are worse supplied with beer on account of your living in a brewer's house?—I do not.

Are you in the habit of tasting porter at other houses you know to be free houses?—Yes.

Do you believe the beer at those free houses is better than the beer you have at your own house?—No, 1 do not think it is at all better; I have had but three barrels of beer that were not very good, and that was in consequence of the season.

Is it the custom of the publicans in London to brew for themselves?—No.

Martis, 7° die Maii, 1816.

The Honourable HENRY GREY BENNET, in The Chair.

Robert Raynsford, Esquire, again called in, and Examined.

Robert Raynsford, Esq.

YOU were asked in your first day's examination, whether it ever happened that there was no Sitting Magistrate, either on an evening or a morning, at Hatton Garden; the question was put, not in reference to County Magistrates, but to those Magistrates who are known by the name of Police Magistrates; has it then ever occurred that there ever was *no* Police Magistrate present, either on an evening or a morning, at Hatton Garden?—Never, in a morning; it has occasionally happened that there has not been two, from various causes.

Will you state what those causes are?—County Magistrates are in the habit of attending Police Offices for their amusement; the Police Magistrates, in cases of illnesss, or on other occasions, sometimes ask those Magistrates to sit for them.

Do you consider that it is the mere love of amusement that calls those Magistrates to the Bench; or is it not rather that those persons may be considered as candidates for any vacant seat in the Police Magistracy?—I cannot tell what their object may be, I can only speak to the fact of their attending frequently.

Is there any particular Magistrate that is in the habit more than any other of attending at Hatton Garden?—There is a gentleman of the name of Sellon,

510.   the

Robert Raynsford, Esq.

the brother of Mr. Serjeant Sellon, who is in the habit of giving his attendance very frequently at Hatton Garden.

In point of fact does he attend as regularly as any of the Police Magistrates at the Office?—I think he does.

Is his attendance as regular in the evening, when one or two Magistrates are required by the Statute to attend?—The attendance of two Magistrates in the evening is not required by the Act; Mr. Sellon does certainly attend frequently in the evening.

Do you consider that under the words of the Statute the Police Magistrates are enjoined to attend so many hours each day, or whether the object of the Act is answered by a County Magistrate attending in lieu of one of them?—By the 51st of Geo. III. chap. 119, there is a proviso, that the attendance of one of the Police Magistrates may be supplied (during the hours at which the attendance of two is required) by any other Justice of Peace for the Counties of Middlesex or Surrey respectively; but by the 54th of the King, chap. 37, that proviso is omitted; yet I certainly think the object of the Act is answered by a County Magistrate attending in lieu of one of them, though in point of fact the strict letter of the Act is not complied with.

Robert Baker, Esquire, called in, and Examined.

Robert Baker, Esq.

YOU are one of the Police Magistrates of Great Marlborough-street?—Yes, I am.

The Committee see by the return before them, that you hold no other public situation?—None at all.

What is the extent of your jurisdiction?—We take in several of the parishes around us, the parish of Saint James Westminster, Saint George Hanover-square, Mary-le-bone, part of Pancras, that part West of Tottenham Court Road, Saint Giles in the Fields, Saint George Bloomsbury, Saint Anne Soho, and Paddington, and occasionally business from the out-parishes North and West of the town.

Do the three Magistrates belonging to the Police Office, regularly attend according to the injunctions of the Act of Parliament?—Yes, they do.

Do any of the County Magistrates attend with them?—Yes, occasionally; the Office is always open to other County Magistrates.

Does it ever happen that there is no Magistrate in attendance, either in the morning or the evening?—Very seldom; it may have happened occasionally of an evening, from some accident or another, but never in the morning.

When it happens of an evening, is it the result of the bad health of any of the Magistrates, or any other cause not so good?—I can only answer for myself in that respect; it has never happened to me, except from unavoidable necessity.

In point of fact, it is a circumstance that occurs but seldom?—Very seldom indeed.

Is there a Clerk resident in the Office?—No, not in the Office, but within twenty yards of it.

So that in case any of the Magistrates are wanted during the night, early information can be given them?—Yes, a messenger resides in the house; and I reside there myself.

How many Clerks are there in the Office?—Two.

Is there any extra clerk?—There is a young man who occasionally assists, but he has no pay from the establishment.

Do the Clerks practise as solicitors either in the Office or out of it?—Neither one nor the other.

Is their attendance uniform and regular?—Perfectly so.

Do they attend daily, both the Clerks, or do they take it day and day?—They both attend daily; the business is such, we could not spare them a single hour in the morning.

From your observation, since you have acted as a Magistrate (that is since 1812) do you think that the number of criminals that are brought before you has increased?—I think it has increased in a small degree, but not very much.

What is the principal nature of the crimes?—In the last year, I think they have been of a slighter nature than they have been before, principally common larcenies, shoplifting, and picking of pockets, and street robberies.

Has the number of juvenile depredators increased?—I think it has.

Can you state to the Committee any reason why, according to your judgment,

the

the number of juvenile depredators should have increased?—I am not aware of any reason why it should, except from the population in general having increased.

Robert Baker,
Esq.

Do you think that the morals of the lower orders of people are in a worse state than what they were some years ago?—No, I do not think they are.

Drunkenness has not increased, nor general depravity, has it?—No, I think not.

Has the number of public-houses and spirit-shops increased in your Division?—Public-houses have decreased a little, rather than increased.

With regard to spirit-shops, have they increased?—I think they have decreased, the Magistrates have made it a point that they shall not exhibit the same appearances of gin-shops that they did some years ago: I speak particularly of the Holborn Division, which comprehends Mary-le-bone, St. Giles, Bloomsbury, St. Andrew Holborn, and St. George the Martyr, Pancras, St. Clement's, the Savoy Liberty, Hampstead, and Paddington, in which I attend the licensing. The Committee are perhaps aware that in the parishes in Westminster the public-houses are licensed by the parochial Magistrates in each parish.

Can you say as much for the other parishes, which are attended by the other Magistrates, as you can for those in your own Divison?—I think they have not taken the same pains in the parishes of Saint Anne and Saint James as they have in Mary-le-bone, and some others.

Saint Giles is within your Division, is it not?—Yes, it is.

Do you think that the morals of the lower orders of people who live within that populous part of the Metropolis, are either better or worse, or stationary, for the last few years?—I cannot say I have myself perceived any material alteration in them.

As a Magistrate, do you know whether they are more or less indigent than they were some years ago?—I think they are more indigent, from the greater number of applications we have for relief.

Do you not think that if their morals are deteriorated, you are to look to their indigence as the effective cause?—I think so, in a great measure.

Has there been any recent establishment of Sunday schools in your district?—Not that I know of.

Do you speak of Sunday schools, or those schools that are better known by the name of Lancasterian or National?—Some, I believe, have been established; the schools that I here speak of are confined to females only.

From your observation, should you think that those schools have even as yet contributed to the amelioration of the morals of the children?—I think not materially in that parish; I do not think they have been established long enough to have that effect, nor are they on an extended scale sufficient for that purpose.

Are there many of those houses in the Division peculiarly intrusted to your care, that are technically known by the name of " Flash-houses," houses that are frequented by thieves?—I am not aware of any such houses.

Do you think that, supposing your seven officers to do their duty, that any such houses could exist to any great extent, without a report being made of such to your Office?—I should think not.

In case it was reported to your Office that any public-house was the continued resort of bad characters of both sexes, and that constant scenes of drunkenness and profligacy of various descriptions were practised in them, should you not consider that report as authorizing you to withhold the licence at the next licensing day?—We should consider it incumbent upon us to report at the licensing meeting the conduct of that house.

According to the practice of that meeting, and which you say you have attended, would not the withholding the licence be the natural consequence of that report?—Certainly, I think.

So that the public may now have the satisfaction of knowing, that in the great and populous Division, of which Saint Giles's forms the preceding part, there are none of those houses the character of which has been described in preceding questions?—There is only one house, not in St. Giles's, but in Mary-le-bone, that I recollect at this moment, which comes under that description, and of which house we have a memorandum to report at the next licensing meeting.

Are those houses shut up at any specific hour of the night?—The hour fixed

is

Robert Baker, Esq.

is eleven o'clock in general, on common nights, and twelve o'clock on Saturday nights.

Do you think that, speaking generally, those hours so fixed are attended to by the public-houses?—I think in the generality they are; there are exceptions undoubtedly, one exception allowed is watering-houses for hackney-coaches.

Have any complaints or even any statements been made to you by the masters of those coaches, that they consider the existence of those houses as injurious to their interests?—A representation of that sort was made at the Licensing Meeting in September, two years ago.

What attention was paid to that?—An order was made, that all the watering-houses should be shut at one o'clock.

Do you think that that order is generally attended to?—Not so much as it ought to be.

Is it the business of your different officers, in rotation, to see that those regulations, so properly made for the conduct of publicans, are adhered to?—We consider that a business peculiarly under the High Constable of the Division; it is his business to visit all the public-houses, and to be acquainted with the conduct in them, and to report what is amiss, the officers immediately attached to our own Office are by no means numerous enough to perform that duty. I believe the late High Constable did his duty remarkably well, as far as it was in his power to do it; but the Division is so extremely extensive, that I do not know it was in his power to do it better.

Do you not think that those regulations, relative to the public-houses, are of great importance?—Certainly.

Do you not then think that it is equally important, that means should be furnished to the High Constable, if he has not them already, of carrying into effect those regulations?—Certainly it would be a very good thing if he had, I think.

Has any plan ever occurred to your mind by which so desirable an end could be accomplished?—I think one great point would be to make the High Constable perfectly independent of the publicans, which he is not at present.

What do you mean by the High Constable not being independent of the publicans?—Because he has a very laborious duty to perform, for which he has no pay, and the only way in which he can remunerate himself is by obtaining the custom of the publicans in the articles in which he deals; the High Constable is in general a tradesman.

Can you state in what trade the last High Constable was?—He was a salesman in Saint Giles's, a dealer in second-hand clothes.

Is it not an office of annual election?—No, permanent.

By whose appointment is the High Constable?—By the Quarter Sessions.

Is any representation ever made, to the Sessions, of the impropriety of the High Constable being in that situation?—They have often considered that an independent person should fill that situation.

Are there many candidates for that situation, when it is vacant?—There have been upon former occasions; upon the last occasion, about three years ago, there were ten or twelve.

Can you state to the Committee what is the reason why they should be candidates for an office to which there is no salary attached, and only heavy and laborious duties to perform?—The only reason I can mention is that I have already alluded to, and also the possession of money by the collection of the county rate, which is allowed for some time to remain in their hands; there was an Act of Parliament last Session which will prevent that in future. The High Constable, Mr. Chambers, told me the other day, that he had lost 200 *l*. a year in his business by the active conduct he pursued to suppress the riots on the Corn Bill, by which he offended most of his customers.

Do you know whether the parishes in the Metropolis are in the same situation as to High Constable?—I believe generally so; in my opinion it would be a very good thing if the High Constable was to receive a salary.

Are there no fees of any kind which he receives?—Nothing at all; indeed he has a great deal to do to get what he pays out of his own pocket on public occasions.

The Committee perceive, by the return you have made, that seven Officers are attached to your Office?—There are ten in all; three superannuated.

Do

Robert Baker,
Esq.

Do you consider that number sufficient for the great extent of your jurisdiction?—I think not; we ought to have at least ten effective.

Have you ever made any remonstrances to the Secretary of State upon that subject?—We applied to have the number increased from seven to ten, in consequence of three of our men being, from old age and infirmity, very unable to perform their duties; and those three have been reduced to fourteen shillings a week, in order that the guinea so saved might pay for one of the extra ones.

Has it ever occurred in your Office that suspicions have attached to the officers, as holding a correspondence with those whose conduct it was their duty to control?—No, I do not know of any instance of the kind.

Are they diligent and attentive in the execution of their duty?—Generally speaking they are: I must beg to observe however upon that, if they were better paid, so that they could devote their whole time to the duties of their office, without following any other employ, I think that would be a benefit to the establishment.

Their pay is twenty-one shillings per week, and their total receipt somewhere about seventy-five pounds per annum; what should you think a sufficient pay for them, supposing they devoted their whole time to the duties of their situation?—I think that you could not probably get men, fit for the situation, for less than thirty shillings per week.

What other situations do they hold?—They generally follow some trade; one is a coal merchant, another a glazier, and another a green grocer.

So that some portion of their time, perhaps a considerable portion, may be taken up in the management of their own private affairs, and not in the execution of their public duty?—Some portion, certainly; not a considerable portion.

From what you have seen, as a Police Magistrate, do you consider the manner in which they are rewarded, namely, when they share in those rewards which are paid by Act of Parliament for the conviction of crimes, is a good mode of remunerating them?—I rather think not.

Should you think it a better mode, that the Magistrates should be empowered to reward each officer for the specific duty which he has performed, whether he succeeds in leading to a conviction or not; for you must be well aware that it must repeatedly happen, from one cause or another, that an officer may diligently perform his duty, and yet not be able to succeed in convicting the person whom he has taken?—I think that would be a better thing.

Do you not think that it might happen that a Police officer not receiving any reward till the person he apprehends is guilty of one of those great crimes to which the Legislature has attached a reward, must lead to his neglect of all the smaller crimes that it would equally be his duty to repress?—I think certainly it must have some effect; at the same time I believe that the rewards now given very little influence the officers, because they obtain very little of them; the reward in case of a burglary is forty pounds, but that is divided frequently amongst a great many persons, who contribute, by giving evidence, to bring the criminal to conviction.

Are there any other houses, except public-houses, the resort of thieves and bad characters?—There has lately sprung up a species of coffee-shops for the sale of ready-made coffee, which are kept open all night, and are under no control of the Magistrates, no licence being required; and they are generally resorted to by persons of the worst descriptions, of both sexes, and are become a considerable nuisance.

Are they not so far under the control of the Magistrates, that in case of it being proved that within those houses there were scenes of riot and debauchery, an indictment would lie against them as against any other persons who keep disorderly houses?—Certainly.

Is there not considerable difficulty found in bringing those persons to conviction who keep disorderly houses?—Yes, great difficulty.

Can you suggest to the Committee any remedy to the existing law upon that subject?—I know of none but that enacting they should positively be shut at a certain hour of the night, and that their being open for the reception of company alone, after that hour, should be considered as an act of disorder; but then it would be difficult to draw a line between houses of that description and houses for the reception of higher company.

Do

Robert Baker,
Esq.

Do you not think that the existence of those houses may be considered more as a proof that the love of drinking and assembling at alehouses is diminishing among the middling classes, than the result of a new mode of establishing places of resort for the profligate and the idle?—I believe it arose, originally, from the cheapness of coffee four or five years ago, and they have since become the resort of loose and disorderly characters of all descriptions, at hours when the alehouses are closed; and that this convenience has been the cause of their being so much frequented, rather than the preference given to coffee over spirituous liquors.

Do you believe that spirits are sold in those houses?—Yes, I know for a certainty they are in one particular house in the neighbourhood of Oxford-street.

Of course information has been laid against it?—We have several times taken up parties in the house; on one occasion we took up about thirty, upon a search-warrant, and the parish is now taking measures to indict it.

Did you bind them over for their good behaviour?—Yes, most of them.

Is gambling carried on to any extent in those houses?—No, I do not know that it is in those houses.

Do you believe that gambling has increased among the lower orders, illegal insurances being included in that term?—I have not lately had any instances of that kind.

Are there any houses opened in your District, known by the name of Helis?—Yes, there are several in the neighbourhood of Leicester Fields and Coventry-street.

Of course, if information was laid before you against them, you would feel it your duty to interfere?—Yes; we took up some parties a short time ago in Leicester-street, at a house of that description.

When you commit criminals to prison, to what prison do you commit them?—The general prison is the New Prison in Clerkenwell, called the County Prison, and the prison in Tothill Fields; we commit occasionally to the House of Correction, if we wish particularly that the person shall not see any of his friends.

Are you aware that it is the practice in both places, both the new House of Correction, as well as in Cold Bath Fields, to mix the persons who are kept in custody for re-examination (unless under very particular circumstances, where the object is to keep their evidence secret) with felons, and with persons who are under confinement for crimes?—I apprehend that they are always kept together with prisoners of the same description, unless a specific order is sent to the contrary.

Do you not know that in the New Prison Clerkenwell, as it is termed, that they are all mixed together indiscriminately?—I do not know for a certainty.

Do you ever visit that prison?—I was there some years ago, but have not been latterly.

It is a prison generally known to you by report, as one of the worst which can be stated to exist; are the accommodations bad in every way?—Yes, very bad; some additions are now to be made, by order of the Quarter Sessions.

Those persons that are committed in the city of Westminster, are sent to Tothill Fields?—Yes.

Are you aware that the situation of the prison in Tothill Fields is nearly the same as that of the New Prison Clerkenwell, the young and the old, the accused and the sentenced, the felon and the misdemeanor, and a person guilty of an assault, are all confined together?—There are divisions in that prison, perhaps not sufficient to keep them entirely from each other; there is a railing between the different yards.

Do you not think a great evil arises from this promiscuous intercourse of criminals?—No doubt it does.

Do you not think that it is a most imperious duty of those who have it in their power to make an alteration to that effect, to make it?—If it is practicable, I think they ought.

Do you know any other difficulty than the expense of it?—No.

Does it not often occur to you as a Magistrate, when you are about to commit an infant to one of those prisons, that you are about to send him to a place out of which he will come worse than he went in?—Certainly so; there are no cases in which we have so much difficulty as those in which we have infant prisoners, we do not know what to do with them.

Have

Robert Baker,
Esq.

Have you any doubt that amongst men and women cases must constantly occur, where persons for a first offence are sent to those places which may be termed schools or academies for vice, and out of which they must come corrupted and ruined; whereas if there was that classification and proper separation of the prisoners, they might be reformed?—I think it would tend very much to prevent the entire corruption of the parties who are committed perhaps for the first time, if they could be separated.

Have you any doubt that this intermixture of persons tends most considerably to increase the number of criminals in the Metropolis?—I think it may.

Has any plan ever suggested itself to your mind, by which you think a more speedy and effectual administration of criminal justice in the Metropolis might be attained?—It has struck me it might be attained by having a weekly Sessions at the Old Bailey, for the trial of all offences except murder, forgery, or perhaps one or two others that might be named; and that two days in every week would be sufficient for that purpose, leaving the greater offences to be tried by the Judges once in six weeks, as they are now; that would be infinitely more convenient for the public, to prosecutors, and to the juries both grand and petty, and to every person indeed who is concerned in carrying on the prosecutions there.

Who would you constitute as the Magistrates to try those offences?—I should think, the Recorder and the Common Serjeant.

Do you think that their other avocations would not take up their time to such a degree as to prevent their attendance?—I am not a sufficient judge of their other duties to be able to speak to that; a great many parties are not prosecuted on account of the great inconvenience which prosecutors sustain in loss of time by attending for ten days or a fortnight together at the Old Bailey, and the county is put to a great expense by paying the charges which are allowed by Judges for loss of time in witnesses attending; at the last Sessions the county paid 1000 *l.* for that purpose.

Do you not think that some arrangement might be made at the Sessions, so that the week might be divided, county business on one day, criminal trials and assaults, &c. on others, and a list prepared so that every person would know when his trial was fixed to come on?—That I believe is already done at the Quarter Sessions, as far as it is practicable; the county business is always done on one day, on a Thursday; traverses on the three first days, if the Sessions begin on a Monday; and petty larcenies and other misdemeanors on a Friday and Saturday; it would be impossible to fix a time precisely for each trial.

Do you think that a more minute division could take place in this arrangement?—No, I think not. With respect to the trials at the Old Bailey, it has occurred to me, that if the sentences were carried into execution sooner than they are, it would have a good effect; in general, now, in consequence of no report being made for a considerable time, the remembrance of the circumstances of the crime is forgotten.

Have you fit places at the Office to lodge persons who are detained for re-examination?—Yes, we have.

How long are they ever kept there?—They may be kept there till eight o'clock in the evening, never beyond that.

When they are brought from the prisons, how are they brought?—They are handcuffed and brought along the street walking, unless there are any of them who chuse to pay for a coach.

Mr. *Joseph Fletcher*, called in, and Examined.

Mr.
Joseph Fletcher.

WHAT are you?—A ship owner.

You live in the parish of Saint Paul's, Shadwell?—I do.

Have you long lived there?—About eighteen years.

When were you churchwarden for that parish?—I am so now.

Have you been long in that situation?—Four or five years.

The parish of Saint Paul's, Shadwell, is principally the residence of seamen?—Yes.

Can

Mr.
Joseph Fletcher.

Can you state to the Committee at all the amount of the resident population of the parish?—By the last census, between ten and eleven thousand.

What length is the High-street of Shadwell?—Perhaps not a quarter of a mile.

How many public-houses are there in it?—I really cannot tell from memory.

Is it at the rate of one public-house to every twelve other houses?—It is.

What is the length of New Gravel-lane?—Something shorter than the High-street, rather better than half the length of High-street.

Are there fifteen public-houses in that lane?—There are.

Which is at the rate of a public-house to every other eight houses?—It is.

Is the proportion in Lower Shadwell greater than that?—It is one to every six, I think; I think there were eighty-five.

Are those public-houses generally very disorderly?—Not generally so.

Are there any disorderly?—Some of them very much so indeed.

As one of the Parish officers, did you ever make a complaint against one or more?—I did.

When?—In the year 1814.

What are the names of the public-houses against which you complained?—The Duke of York, the White Hart, and the Paviors Arms.

To whom did you complain?—First to the Magistrates of Shadwell Police Office.

What was the result of your complaint?—They were called before them, and admonished, several times.

Was that all?—The admonition was ineffectual.

Of what did you complain?—Of the indecency and immorality of the scenes that were witnessed in those houses.

Can you state the particulars?—Each of those houses, but particularly the Duke of York and the White Hart, contained large rooms fitted up for the purpose of dancing; they were the constant resort of the lowest class of prostitutes and procuresses; there were sometimes from 150 to 200 women assembled in each of them, and the officers of the parish went several times to remonstrate with the landlords upon the impropriety of their conduct.

Was the conduct of the individuals assembled within those houses, indecent and profligate; or was it merely an assemblage of men and women for the purposes of dancing?—The most profligate and indecent it is possible to conceive.

Having laid your complaint of the conduct of those houses before the Magistrates, and the parties being summoned and admonished, was that conduct changed?—It was not.

Did you expect that the Magistrates at the Police Office would have contented themselves with admonishing the keepers of those houses; or did you expect that some other mode of proceeding would have been adopted?—We did not expect they could do more than they did; the Magistrates of the Police Office did all in their power; the Magistrates before whom they were summoned, were Mr. Raynsford, and Mr. Markland the resident Magistrate.

This was in 1813, was it?—It was; I stated it by mistake to be 1814.

Were the licences that year taken away from the three most notorious houses, the Duke of York, the White Hart, and the Paviors Arms?—They were; a memorial was presented to the Churchwardens by the Parishioners, complaining of the conduct of those houses, and it was made the subject of a public vestry.

Was that in 1813 or 1814?—In 1813.

When the licensing day came in 1814, were the houses re-opened?—They were at the second licensing day.

Did you and other inhabitants and churchwardens oppose that measure, and prefer complaints against the King's Arms and some other houses?- We did.

That was on the 5th of September?—It was the day of appeal, the first day.

Were you ordered to attend again?—We were ordered to attend again on the 19th of September.

Did any thing happen between the 5th of September and the 19th, relative to those houses?—Early in the morning of the 12th September, I was informed by
the

Mr.
Joseph Fletcher.

the resident Magistrate, Mr. Markland, whom I met casually in the street, that the Magistrates were that day coming down to view those houses, the Duke of York, the Paviors Arms, and the White Hart; my answer to him was, " It is impossible, it was the 19th we were to see you, and not the 12th ;" he said, " You are mistaken, we are coming to-day, you had better send up to the Court-House and know the truth." I sent the Vestry Clerk up, to know whether the Magistrates were coming down that day, and his answer was, that they were coming down to view new houses ; immediately the Parish Officers, to whom I sent round to attend, assembled, and were in waiting at the house of one of the officers, which is directly opposite to the Duke of York ; they promised, immediately the Magistrates came, to send for me, which they did. When I came, there was a great crowd of persons assembled, and the Magistrates in the middle of the street; the first I saw was Mr. Markland ; said he, " Did you not tell me that you had memorialled the Magistrates against the re-opening of these houses ?" I said, " Certainly I did, Sir, and it is true, so far as we could do it with any propriety ;" "Then," said he, "go tell Sir Daniel Williams so, for he will not believe me." Sir Daniel was in the middle of the street ; I went up to him and took my hat off, and stood with it off; I said, " the Officers of our parish did not expect to see you here to-day, I believe they were ordered to attend on the 19th, but they are in attendance, and we shall be very happy to state to you what we have to say." Sir Daniel said, " Sir, you are too late, the Magistrates have determined to re-open the houses."

Do you know that the memorial which you and the other parishioners had written against this measure, was presented to the Magistrates ?—I do.

What was your answer to Sir Daniel Williams, when he told you the Magistrates had determined to grant licences to those houses ?—I said, " Sir Daniel, may we not be permitted to attend you personally at the Court-house ?" At that moment Mr. Thurwell came up, and he immediately exclaimed, " Mr. Fletcher, you are acting a most indecent, improper, and unbecoming part; what right have you to interfere with the Magistrates? you are not a magistrate !" I immediately said to Sir Daniel, without at all replying to Mr. Thurwell, " Sir Daniel, have I acted an indecent, improper, or unbecoming part ?" He replied, " Certainly not to me, Sir, certainly not." He appeared very much agitated, and crossed the street, and put his hand against the door of the Duke of York, as if he was going to open it. Mr. Merceron took him by the hand, and said, " Come along, we have determined the case." This passed in the public street, where we were surrounded by prostitutes and the people whom we were endeavouring to check. The Landlord of the Duke of York came out, and said to one of our Overseers, " We have settled the business very pleasantly, I hope." The Magistrates walked on.

On the 19th of September, did the Parish officers attend the Magistrates ?—They did.

Who were present, on that day, of the Magistrates ?—Many more than I knew; but Sir Daniel Williams was in the chair; Mr. Merceron was there, Luke Flood, Mr. Markland, Mr. Storey, and I think Mr. Raynsford was present, and a number of others, about eighteen or twenty in the whole.

Did you request to be sworn as to the facts you were going to state ?—I did.

Were you sworn ?—Sir Daniel Williams said, " We do not chuse to swear you."

Was any thing said about your memorial ?—Yes, a great deal.

Did they acknowledge the receipt of that memorial ?—They did ; when Sir Daniel Williams had said that the Magistrates did not see fit to swear me, and desired me to state what I had to allege against the houses in question.

What houses ?—The houses named in the memorial.

What houses were those ?—The King's Arms, the Black Horse, the Angel, and the Ship.

Did you memorial against those houses for their bad conduct?—We did, and we were desirous of connecting their conduct (which was quite as bad) with the houses which had been shut up, which were the same parties opening under different names.

510.

How

How do you know that?—By the communication that was made to the Church-wardens and the Committee; the detail would be long, or else it would clearly elucidate the connexion.

Were you and the other Parish officers satisfied in your own minds, that they were in point of fact the same parties as kept the former houses?—As kept the former house, the Duke of York, certainly; and we told the Magistrates we had evidence to substantiate our charge.

Did you offer that evidence to the Magistrates?—We did.

Did they take it?—They refused it.

Did they assign any reason for so refusing it, and what reason?—Sir Daniel Williams said I could not be heard, unless I confined myself strictly to the memorial then before them, that the other business had been disposed of.

Did you understand them to say by that, that the Duke of York having been already licensed, no evidence could then be received against the conduct of the keeper of that house?—I understood they would not suffer us to connect the Duke of York with the King's Arms, which was the subject we had to bring before the Magistrates, and they seemed desirous to prevent it.

Are the Duke of York and the Paviors Arms now kept by the same persons against whom the original complaint was made, and for whose misconduct they were shut up?—They are, and have been from the time of their being opened.

Those houses, then, in 1813 were shut up for misconduct?—They were.

They were opened again, and kept by the same parties, in the year 1814?—They were.

What has been their conduct since?—As bad, or worse than before. The Duke of York has been changed in appearance; the dancing-room has been shut up, and changed into a gin-shop, and the prostitutes are going in by shoals all day long.

Are scenes of drunkenness, riot, and debauchery, constantly practised?—I cannot speak to what has been done in the house, because on the former occasion we received insults and ill usage, and have been thus deterred by menaces and threats from going there again.

Did you make any complaint on the 5th of September 1815, against those houses?—We did not.

Why did you refrain, knowing that the same scenes against which you had before complained, at that time existed?—Knowing it externally, and having every evidence of it, the true reason why we did not complain was, that our former complaint and ourselves had been treated with so much contempt, that we considered any further application useless and unavailing.

Can you state to the Committee any reason for this conduct on the part of the licensing Magistrates?—No further than as matter of opinion that there is that which perhaps I am hardly justified in saying, a conviction which cannot be proved, that it appears to me there was some connexion between some of the Magistrates and the brewers who were connected with those houses.

Can you state to the Committee what brewers and distillers either served or were proprietors of those houses?—Meux and Co. served the Duke of York, and Calvert's house the White Hart, I think; I really do not know who served the Paviors Arms, but we had a variety of communications with the representatives of Messrs. Meux and Co.

To what effect?—They came down to request that we would sanction the re-opening of the Duke of York; first, that we would sanction the re-opening of the King's Arms; the persons who presented themselves before us were the Bar-maid of the Duke of York, and an uncertificated Bankrupt.

Can you state whether the principal officers of the parish, and all or most of the principal inhabitants, consider those houses neither more nor less than public nuisances?—I do; and a great number of the most respectable inhabitants were attending the Magistrates on each of the days above mentioned; and there is likewise, which could be laid before the Committee, the paper which was printed and circulated by the direction of the Vestry.

Mr.

William Simpson, called in, and Examined.

WHERE do you live?—131, Shoreditch.

What are you?—A haberdasher and hosier.

Are you a builder also?—I have built a few houses.

Did you ever build any houses for public-houses?—One.

Did you ever make any applications for that house to be licensed?—Yes.

To whom?—To the Magistrates.

To what Magistrates?—Sir Daniel Williams, and others whom I cannot name.

Did you apply very often?—Three or four years, I cannot say which.

And was constantly refused?—Yes.

Were you at last successful?—I was.

By what means?—Continual applications.

Did you apply to any one to intercede with the Magistrates for you?—Not particularly.

Did you form any connexion with any particular brewer, for the purpose of furthering your object?—Not any in particular.

What do you mean by " not any in particular?"—I applied to Messrs. Hanbury and Co.; I asked them if they had any influence with any of the Magistrates, and they said they could not give me any instructions in the least.

Did you put the house in Messrs. Hanbury's trade?—I did.

How soon after you put the house in their trade, did you get your house licensed?—I did not put it in his trade till I got the licence.

Did Mr. Hanbury give you to understand that he would procure you that licence if you dealt with him?—Never.

Did you give Mr. Hanbury to understand that if you got your licence you would deal with him?—No.

Then you mean to tell the Committee, that you went to Mr. Hanbury as a friend, and asked him if he could assist you in getting a licence, he told you he could do nothing in it; and that having made application for three years successively without success, the result of that conversation with Mr. Hanbury (who told you he could do nothing in it) was to get you a licence at the next licensing day?—I did, after three years trying, but it was on account of the neighbourhood increasing, and that there was one wanted.

Having failed in getting the licence for three years, you at last bethought yourself to apply to Mr. Hanbury, and the result of that application to Mr. Hanbury was your getting a licence the next licensing day; do you think he had nothing to do with it?—I applied the very first year to Mr. Hanbury, that was the time I applied.

Did you only apply once to Mr. Hanbury?—I applied several times the first year, but not afterwards.

Mercurii, 8° die Maii, 1816.

The Honourable HENRY GREY BENNET, in The Chair.

John Gifford, Esquire, called in, and Examined.

John Gifford,
Esq.

YOU are a Magistrate, I believe?—Yes.

What Division do you belong to?—Worship-street.

You are the principal Magistrate of Worship-street?—I am the senior Magistrate.

Do you hold any other situation?—None whatever.

How many Clerks are there in the Office?—Two.

Is there any extra Clerk?—No, none at all.

Are the Clerks solicitors?—The senior Clerk is.

Does he practise as a solicitor in the Office?—No.

Is his attendance regular?—Yes.

The attendance of both of them, daily?—Yes.

Is the attendance of the Magistrates daily, according to the Act of Parliament?—I cannot say according to the Act of Parliament, because the Act directs the Office to be opened from ten in the morning till three in the afternoon; but we have found, from experience, that the public service will not be at all forwarded by opening the Office at ten o'clock, and it very seldom happens that we close it at three; it has happened to me within these last two weeks to be sitting constantly employed till within a few minutes of five o'clock.

Are there three Magistrates attend according to the provisions of the Act of Parliament?—Yes.

Have you any assistance from the County Magistrates?—Very little; I think but once within the last twelve months, to the best of my recollection.

Is your attendance regular, in the evening?—Yes.

Does any one sleep at the Office?—I sleep at the Office; I cannot say that I reside there, because residence is impossible, there being only three rooms, and those on the attic story.

Is there any clerk or constable, or housekeeper, sleep there?—Yes, an office-keeper and his family.

So that in case of any request being made for a Magistrate, you can be sent for at a few moments warning?—Yes; when I sleep there, which is frequent, I give constant orders to my officers to call me at any hour of the night, if my assistance should be necessary.

What is the extent of the jurisdiction of the Public Office of Worship-street?—The jurisdiction of the Office is not accurately defined; the parishes which make their general application to us for business are St. Luke's, St. Leonard Shoreditch, Christ Church Middlesex, St. Matthew Bethnal-green, Mile-end New Town, St. John's Hackney, St. Mary Islington, and occasionally parishes much beyond those.

Have you ten constables belonging to the Office?—I think at present only nine.

Do you conceive that you have as many as are requisite for the business of the Office?—I can only say that the constables complain that they are starving; I think more might be beneficially employed.

Have the constables any other occupation besides their situation in the Police Office?—Not to my knowledge.

Are they tradesmen and keep shops?—That is more than I can say; some of them I know do not.

Their salary is one guinea per week?—Yes.

Do you consider that a sufficient salary?—By no means.

What should you consider sufficient to enable you to secure to the Police proper officers?—I should think a fixed salary of something more than a guinea a week, with some contingent advantages, according to the services performed.

Should you not think that those contingent advantages according to the services performed,

performed, are a much better mode of payment than allowing the constables to share in those rewards given by Acts of Parliament for the apprehension and conviction of offenders?—Yes, beyond all doubt.

Have you any doubt that it would be a much better plan for the carrying on of public justice, than the mode now pursued?—Infinitely better.

Do you not think that, judging of the motives of Police officers by the motives that govern ordinary men, they might be induced to let offenders pursue a full career of crime unchecked, till they have committed that crime from which they themselves would share something in the nature of a reward by apprehending the criminal?—Speaking from personal observation, and the experience of sixteen years in that Office where I now act, I have no reason for thinking that such has been the case ; but if I am asked the question as to a general opinion, formed upon a knowledge of human nature, I should certainly think it might produce that effect.

From your own observation as a Magistrate, do you think that the morals of the lower orders of people are ameliorated, are stationary, or on the decline?—Woefully on the decline.

Have you had a much greater number of offenders brought before you of late years, than when you first performed the duty of a Magistrate?—I really have not had an opportunity of referring to papers to ascertain that fact, but certainly the numbers of offenders brought before us within these few months are much greater than they have been for some years past.

Are they for heavy offences, or for petty offences, picking pockets, and other small crimes?—Many for heavy offences.

Have you many persons brought before you for picking pockets?—Not many, except for hustling in the streets, and making a forcible attack.

Are those principally boys, or men?—A large proportion boys.

Are you aware that, of the persons that are committed to the different prisons in the Metropolis, for picking of pockets, a very great majority of them are not brought to trial, by the Grand Jury throwing out the bill?—I am not aware of that fact.

Has the number of juvenile depredators increased of late years?—Certainly ; I am speaking as far as my own observation and experience go.

Can you state to the Committee any cause for that circumstance?—The increased profligacy of the lower classes of people.

Do you think that the habits of drunkenness are much increased amongst the lower orders?—I do believe it, certainly.

Are many public-houses licensed at your Office?—None at the Office, but in the District a great many.

Are you in the District of the Tower Hamlets?—Yes, we are ; we act for it.

Do you take particular care, when an application is made to you to establish a new public-house, to ascertain, by the testimony of reputable householders, or by your own examination, that the wants of the neighbourhood require the establishment of that house, and that the person seeking the licence is one of reputable character and good behaviour?—My avocations at the Office render it impossible for me to attend constantly on the view which Magistrates take of new houses proposed to be licensed; but I do not believe that any such examination for such a purpose takes place.

What knowledge, then, do you obtain of the character of the person soliciting the licence?—From the certificate which is required, signed by the minister, the majority of the parish officers, and other respectable inhabitants.

Are you not aware that it is stated by Mr. Colquhoun, in his book upon Indigence, that it is the ordinary practice in the Metropolis for the minister of the parish to give his signature as a mere matter of form, the beadle receiving a small fee, and the person soliciting the licence obtaining such signature?—I have not read Mr. Colquhoun's book on Indigence, and I am very sure that such is not generally the case.

Do you know that the clergyman and the parish officers bonâ fide know, when they sign the certificate, that the person demanding the licence is qualified to have it?—I can only take it for granted that no man would so far forget the duties of a clergyman as to affix his signature to a fact of which he was not personally cognizant.

Do you require at your Office the signature of the clergyman; are you not aware
that

510.

John Gifford,
Esq.

that the Act of Parliament is satisfied if it is signed by reputable housekeepers?—I am perfectly aware of what the Act of Parliament requires; but I conceive the Magistrates have a discretion, and that in the exercise of that discretion they are to consider what conduces most to the interest of the public, and the preservation of public morals ; and it is likewise in the exercise of that discretion, I apprehend, that the signature of the minister has been thought, if not absolutely necessary, highly expedient and proper.

Does it often happen, when the licence day arrives, that a number of houses are reported to the Bench as being very ill managed?—I believe it does; I have made such reports myself.

Has it often happened that the licences have been taken away?—Scarcely ever.

When a house is reported as of bad character, what part do the licensing Magistrates take upon that report?—I really am not competent to speak to the present time, for I was so dissatisfied with the proceedings of the licensing Magistrates, when I did attend, that I have in a great measure absented myself from that meeting.

Who are the licensing Magistrates in that District?—All the Magistrates living in or acting in it.

Is Sir Daniel Williams one of them?—He is the Chairman of the Licensing Meeting.

And Mr. Merceron?—Yes.

And Major Jackson?—Yes, generally; I am speaking now of the time when I attended.

Is it not the practice on those licensing days to consider the report of the Police Magistrates against any public-house, as a decisive reason, unless such report is contradicted by other evidence, and as authorizing the Magistrates to refuse the licence?—No; I can speak positively to that circumstance, from having last year reported a very disorderly house at no great distance from my own Office, and sent a competent witness to establish the facts; notwithstanding which, the house was licensed.

What was the nature of the complaint that you made against the house?—I have it not in my immediate recollection what the specific complaint was; it was some very gross misconduct, general misconduct, I believe.

Riot, drunkenness, and debauchery?—By referring to notes I can ascertain the fact, but I cannot immediately recollect it.

Were you present during the time that the propriety of granting or refusing this licence was taken into consideration?—I was not; I was detained by unavoidable business at my Office.

Do you know whether the complaints that you made against the bad character and conduct of that house, are now as well founded as what they were when you made them?—No, I do not know that.

Do you know whether the house is in the same condition now as formerly?—No; I have reason to think it is not, because I have had no further complaints against it.

Do you know to whom the house belonged, or who was the person that supplied it with liquor and spirits?—No, I cannot recollect now; but I think it was some person resident in Shoreditch.

Generally speaking, are licences granted and continued in that jurisdiction with a facility that you think prejudicial to the public morals, because granted and continued to houses of bad character?—In my opinion they are.

Are there many houses that are technically called "Flash houses" in that District?—There are some.

In which thieves, and prostitutes, and persons of the worst character, assemble together?—Certainly.

Have repeated complaints been made against those houses to the licensing Magistrates?—I am not competent to say that, for I have not attended them lately.

You did not attend those meetings, because you found that little or no good resulted from that attendance, in refusing the licences of those infamous houses?—Most certainly.

Have you as a Magistrate any authority to shut up a house, or suspend its licence, for notorious bad conduct, between the days of licensing?—None whatever, to my knowledge or belief.

Do you think that it would be advisable that upon a regular conviction before
the

John Gifford,
Esq.

the Sessions, of the house being the resort of notorious thieves, and persons of loose, idle, and profligate character, it would be a very desirable plan that something of that kind should take place ?—Certainly.

Do you not think that one of the great causes of the depravity of public morals in this Metropolis, arises from the extensive spirit-drinking which takes place?— I am as fully convinced of it as I am of my own existence.

At what hours are the public-houses and spirit-shops shut up in your Division ?— The public-houses have orders to shut up at eleven o'clock; but knowing the spirit-shops to be illegal, the Police Magistrates take no cognizance of them whatever as to giving directions.

Do you not think that, according to the Act of Parliament, the taking out a nominal beer licence, and in fact selling nothing but spirits, is decidedly illegal?— Decidedly rendered illegal by the 17 Geo. II.

As you think those spirit-shops are decidedly illegal, why are they not suppressed ?—That is a question I cannot answer; they ought to be suppressed, and licences ought not to be granted.

Is it not within your jurisdiction, as a Police Magistrate, to suppress them ?— No, we cannot act against the spirit-shops, unless an information is lodged before us for selling spirits without a licence; and if the fact were proved before me on the oaths of credible witnesses, that a man, having a beer licence, kept a spirit-shop purely without selling beer at all, I should have no hesitation in convicting him under the 17 Geo. II.

Are there not in point of fact many houses of that nature known to your Office ?—Many houses apparently of that nature; not that I have been able to ascertain them to be entirely so.

Is it a subject of Police regulation to which you have paid particular attention ?— I have paid particular attention to it.

Have any steps been taken by the Magistrates in your Division to ascertain whether those houses do deal in beer or not?—I have particularly desired and indeed directed such inquiries to be made, but as yet no result has been reported to me.

Have those directions been recently given ?—Within these three months; and I have given notice of a motion at the Quarter Sessions on this very subject.

Do you believe that the regulations of the Police, that the public-houses should be shut up at eleven o'clock, are attended to strictly?—I have reason to think they are not.

Under whose care is it placed to enforce those regulations?—I am not aware of any power to enforce them, except that discretionary power vested in the licensing Magistrates of the District to refuse the renewal of any licence to a person who has disobeyed those orders and those regulations which they have issued, and which they think it necessary to enforce.

But as far as your experience has gone, the licensing Magistrates have never paid any attention to ascertain the fact, whether their own regulations are attended to or not?—I am not aware that they have; I cannot say positively that they have not.

Is it not the general belief in that District, that, provided publicans deal with particular individuals for beer, there would be no difficulty in getting their licence on the licensing day ?—Such a belief is certainly prevalent.

Do you not believe it to be the general practice of the licensing Magistrates, upon the day of granting fresh licences, to inquire if any complaints are lodged against the person who applies for that licence ?—It is so.

Are you not of opinion that if the orders given by the Magistrates for the regulation of the licensed houses were not attended to, complaints would be made against the individuals so disobeying their orders?—I do not know; I cannot say there would not; if the instances were very glaring, they would.

Has it not often occurred to you, or is it not within your own knowledge, that complaints have been laid against the conduct of the publicans, which, according to your judgment, ought to have deprived them of their licences, or prevented their renewal, and yet no notice has been taken of them by the licensing Magistrates ?— Instances have occurred where complaints have been made, and the licences renewed; but not to my knowledge, where no notice has been taken of the complaints.

It was meant by the expression " no notice," no punishment in the nature of a deprivation of the licence had followed that report?—Certainly, instances of that kind have occurred.

To

John Gifford, Esq.

To what prison do you commit?—Sometimes to the NewPrison, sometimes to the House of Correction for re-examination, and sometimes to Newgate when fully committed for trial.

What distance is the Public Office Worship-street, from all those three prisons? I should think, from a mile and a half to two miles.

In what way are the prisoners conveyed backwards and forwards?—Sometimes in a coach and sometimes on foot.

If they pay for the coach, they are conveyed in it?—I apprehend that is the case; in some instances I have directed them to be sent by a coach, and ordered the money to be paid.

But, generally speaking, the prisoners are hand-cuffed two and two, and paraded through the streets from the Office to the place where they are committed?—Not having seen them, I cannot say; but I believe that to be the case.

Are you aware that the New Prison at Clerkenwell is one of the worst managed prisons in the Metropolis?—No, I am by no means aware of it.

Do you know that in that prison persons of all ages, and for all offences, are mixed indiscriminately together; that there is no allowance of bedding or blankets, or even straw?—No, I am not aware of that fact, certainly.

Do you attend the licensing of public-houses in the Borough?—I do, occasionally.

Is great attention paid there by the licensing Magistrates to the correction of any abuses that may arise in the public-houses, by refusing to renew licences where complaints of such public-houses have been laid before them?—No.

Do you not think that the neglect of correcting the mismanagement of public-houses, by refusing the renewal of licences, is not, on the part of the licensing Magistrates, doing that which materially affects the morals of the public?—I have no doubt of its influence on the morals of the public.

Is there a regular correspondence carried on between your Office and the different public Police Offices in the Metropolis?—Certainly not.

Do you not think that the public justice would be very much furthered, if such a correspondence was daily carried on, in respect of greater offences?—I think that a frequent communication might be productive of great benefit in the discovery of offences; but the fact is, that the different Police Offices keep their information to themselves, and do not wish to communicate it to others, that they may have the credit and advantage of detecting offenders.

Do you not think it would be advisable to re-model the several Police Establishments of the Metropolis, to make one Central Board, which would hold a general correspondence with all the different Police Establishments within the Metropolis?—I am not prepared to say it would be followed with advantage; I have not considered it maturely enough to satisfy my mind it would be.

But you are prepared to say, that at present there is little or no correspondence going on between the different Offices, and that it would be an advantage to the public if there was?—Certainly it would; there is none at present, further than this, that we take up our monthly reports to the Secretary of State, and which are afterwards sent to Sir Nathaniel Conant, whereby he is cognizant of all the proceedings of the other Offices.

Robert Raynsford, Esq. attended, and delivered in the following Papers:

" Police Office, Hatton-Garden, June 8, 1813.

" RESOLUTIONS of the Magistrates:

Robert Raynsford, Esq.

" 1. That each Officer shall be furnished with a book, in which he shall daily enter the occurrences which arise in the exercise of his individual duty, and produce it by eleven o'clock the succeeding morning to the Messenger, who shall lay it before the Magistrate of the day, upon his first coming into the Office, that he may have the means of examining into the particulars thereof, if he shall so think fit.

" 2. That if any Officer shall presume to demand any reward as the price of doing his duty, from any person or persons whatsoever; or shall attempt to settle any complaint, without bringing it before the Magistrate of the Office, or shall take money for so doing; or shall prevent any person from coming quietly into the Office on their lawful business, or shall in any way ill treat or abuse any person, or shall turn them out, except by the order of the Magistrate; he shall be immediately suspended, without pay; and if he

does

Robert Raynsford, Esq.

does not sufficiently answer for his conduct, and give such satisfaction as the Magistrates shall think proper, he shall be discharged.

" 3. That no Officer shall hereafter become an informer upon any penal Statute, unless with the approbation of the Magistrate of the day, upon pain of expulsion.

" 4. That no Officer shall upon any pretence go above five miles from the Metropolis upon any duty, without the consent and directions of some one or more of the Magistrates.

" 5. That no business shall be postponed to the evening, that can be done in a morning, unless by order of the Magistrate of the day.

" 6. That as it is necessary that no delay shall be occasioned by any Officer in the execution of any summons or warrant, the Information book shall be signed by such Officer to whom its execution shall be assigned, and shall be produced by such Officer, at the hearing such case, to the Clerk, who shall cheque it with the Minute book, that when necessary it may be seen what complaints have not been attended to, and the Officer called upon to account for the delay; who, if in fault, shall be punished by suspension or otherwise, as the Magistrates may think expedient.

" 7. That there shall be two Officers in waiting, each day, who shall be entitled to the summonses and warrants issued on that day; and that if it shall be proved to the satisfaction of the Magistrates that any Officer shall prevent complainants from having free access to the Office, or shall use any means whatever to get warrants or other documents into his own hands, otherwise than according to the tenor of this article, he shall be suspended without pay as long as the Magistrates shall think proper, and, if repeated, shall be discharged.

" 8. That no Officer shall take with him any person not belonging to the Office, as an assistant in the execution of his duty, unless such person as may give information upon the subject, except by the express order of the Magistrate acting upon each respective case, upon pain of suspension or expulsion, as the case may require.

" 9. That as it seems expedient that all persons within the District shall be satisfied of the good intentions of the Magistrates towards them, notice in printed hand-bills (to be delivered in such way as the Magistrates shall direct) signifying that all persons who shall feel themselves aggrieved by the conduct of any one or more Officer or Officers, whether by delay, extortion, incivility, violence, or otherwise, are desired to complain to the Magistrates of any such offences, who will make an inquiry into such complaints, and if found to be just, will afford such relief as the nature of the case shall require.	" *John Turton.*
" *Thomas Leach.*
" *Robert Capper.*"

" Police Office, Hatton Garden, January 5th, 1815.
" Ordered by the Magistrates,

" That the two Officers for the day, and the Messenger, be in constant attendance from ten o'clock in the morning until the Sitting Magistrate quits the Office at night, except at the hour of dinner, during which time only they may relieve each other, after the Sitting Magistrate is gone in the forenoon, and that neither of them be absent without permission of the Sitting Magistrate during that time; it being to be clearly understood that one of such Officers, and the Messenger, are during the hours aforesaid to be ready to take in letters and messages, to keep order and silence, and to see that improper persons do not come into the Office during the absence of the Magistrates.

" That none of the other Officers come into the Magistrates Sitting Room, except when prisoners are under examination, unless he has business or something to communicate to the Magistrates or Clerk.

" Any Officer neglecting his duty in these respects, will the first time be suspended from pay for a fortnight, and for the second omission be discharged from his employment.
" *John Turton.*
" *Rob* Raynsford.*"

Robert Raynsford, Esq.

" Police Office, Hatton Garden, January 19th, 1815.

" IT is Ordered by the Magistrates of this Office, That the Officers thereto belonging shall within twenty-four hours next after they make a seizure of goods or property of any description whatever, deliver the particulars thereof in writing to one of the Clerks, in order that an entry of the same may be forthwith made in the book provided for that purpose ; and that in case any Officer shall neglect to make and deliver such account within the time aforesaid, he shall be immediately discharged.

" *John Turton.*
" *Thos Leach.*
" *Robt Raynsford."*

Baker John Sellon, Esquire, Serjeant-at-Law, called in, and Examined.

B. J. Sellon, Esq.

ARE you one of the Magistrates of Union Hall?—I am.

You are but lately appointed?—In September 1814, I was appointed.

Since you have been in that situation, have you directed your attention particularly to the state of the morals of that District?—Certainly I have, as much as opportunity has allowed me; indeed I may say that since I accepted the situation, I have particularly turned my mind to the state of the Police ; having been several years in the profession, I thought it my duty to do so. With regard to morals, if the question alludes to any increase or decrease of depravity, I really must confess that from my experience in the Police I hardly know how to draw a comparison, because it can only be from the judgment that I must form from what has passed since I have been in the situation, and therefore I am not so able to form any decisive opinion upon that particular point; but, generally speaking, I think latterly it has been in some respects upon the increase.

Have the number of juvenile depredators increased ?—To that particular point it is that I allude ; we have had, undoubtedly, many instances which have been lamentable, with regard to the youths that have been brought before us ; and I must confess, so far as I can speak from my own practice, it is one of the most difficult things that we have to manage; we have even had instances of parents coming with their own children, and complaining that they have been and still are so extremely depraved and incorrigible, as to desire us to send them to prison, with the hope that some amendment may be effected.

You commit to the New Prison Clerkenwell, do not you?—No, to Horsemonger-lane.

From the condition of that prison, are you satisfied that the children, whom you send there, will rather come out better, from the punishment they have received, than worse?—My private opinion is, that children very rarely indeed come out better ; at the same time I must say that I know no prison in a better state than that of Horsemonger-lane ; and I know that the Magistrates of the County have taken a great deal of pains, and have ordered alterations for the separation of offenders, and of having every accommodation to make the gaol as perfect as possible.

Has any plan ever suggested itself to your mind (as you state it to be your opinion that children seldom are made better by imprisonment) by which an establishment in the nature of a Penitentiary might be set on foot, in which the bad conduct of the children might be remedied ?—I have often thought that some plan of that kind would be of great public utility ; there is now a Society (the Philanthropic Society) in St. George's Fields, for the reception of abandoned youth, and we are often indebted to the gentlemen who are subscribers and governors of that Institution, for the recommendation of several youthful prisoners, who have been brought before us, to their notice, and who are sometimes sent there ; and I must confess that I think if there was a plan of that kind, or similar to it, so as to be able upon a more extensive scale to provide for the younger class of the community of this description, it would be a very great benefit.

Your jurisdiction is very extensive ?—It certainly is.

Do you think that the number of officers that you have is at all equal to the demand for them, for the execution of their duty?—I cannot say that I do ; our

number

B. J. Sellon,
Esq.

number at present, I think, is eight, and I conceive it would be of great benefit if it were extended to ten, or even twelve would not be too many.

Are they all efficient officers?—They are at present.

Is not one engaged as an assistant Clerk?—Yes, it is so; in truth we have only seven efficient constables; we have eight nominally, but only seven acting as constables. By the general establishment of the Police Offices, there are but two Clerks allowed in each Office, and our business being very extensive, the Magistrates before my appointment were anxious to have the services of a third, and, not being able to have one regularly appointed, one of the constables acts in that capacity; therefore, in fact, we have but seven efficient constables.

Do the Clerks daily attend their duty in the Office?—Out of the three there are generally two in the morning, very often all three; but they are certainly not at all times able to attend, having other duties to perform.

Do they practise as solicitors?—I understand that Mr. Reeves, the head Clerk, is a solicitor.

Does he practise in the Office as a solicitor?—Not to my knowledge; I never knew an instance of it; he acts merely as clerk to us, and I am not aware of his acting as attorney in the immediate business of the office, I think I must have known it if he had, because people coming before us would naturally have said, Mr. Reeves is my solicitor.

What is the nature of his attendance?—Perhaps, upon the average, about four-fifths of the time; he is often attending the Sessions; and it may be necessary perhaps to explain, with regard to our Office, that it is under peculiar circumstances, and therefore not altogether to be governed by the exact principles which govern other Offices; our Office is the only one in the county of Surrey, and we are quite detached from Middlesex; all our business goes to the County Assizes, and to the Surrey Sessions, and it is absolutely necessary for one of the Clerks and some of the officers to be away on those occasions as witnesses, and on other duties.

If the Clerks always attended the duties of their office, would a Third Clerk be necessary?—I should think it would; especially considering the average of their necessary absences, and the extent of our business.

Do your Officers hold any other situations besides those under the Police?—I believe not, I never heard of it.

Are they tradesmen keeping shops, or do they devote their whole time to the duties of their office?—I cannot answer that of my own knowledge, but I believe some of them have trades; this I can say, with regard to our seven officers, that they do not appear to me, whatever the nature of their trades may be, to be called off so as to neglect the public business of the Office.

The Officers receive as a salary one guinea per week?—Yes, they do.

They share also in rewards for apprehending offenders?—That is a chance matter; so do parish officers and others.

Do you think that that latter mode of rewarding is of advantage to the public interest?—Generally speaking, I think not. In my opinion, there does want some amendment in the mode of rewarding officers generally; I mean upon all ordinary occasions to be at the discretion of the Magistrate, as where officers in bringing offenders to justice, or in making discoveries which, notwithstanding all their diligence, may be frustrated, still deserve remuneration. But I beg leave to add, that in certain cases we do make a return in our quarterly accounts of monies paid to officers for their expenses and attendances upon business specially ordered by the Magistrates, and which returns are signed by two of the Police Magistrates, and always liberally allowed. The above observation therefore only applies to the daily occurrences in more trifling matters; and indeed I doubt whether, upon the fair construction of the Police Act, this is not sufficiently provided for.

Are the Officers permitted to receive rewards from persons who require their services?—Never, to my knowledge; but I have reason to think they do; I only judge of that from the common practice of gentlemen applying, in cases of robberies or on other occasions, for the assistance of officers, and I suppose they sometimes make them rewards for their trouble; that however is totally unconnected with the government of the Office; it does not come before us, nor can I speak from any certain knowledge of the fact.

Are the Officers permitted in any cases to take money from any persons who are brought before the Magistrates charged with committing crimes?—I believe never. But I do not mean to include in that common assaults, because it is the usual practice

for

B. J. Sellon,
Esq.

for the Magistrates, in cases of common assaults, instead of sending a party to prison, or compelling him to be at the expense and trouble of finding bail when the offence itself may be trifling, and yet proved against him, to recommend the parties to talk together, and see if they can make it up, and in such case perhaps to give some compensation to the watchman for his time, or the like, but which the Magistrates never settle or interfere in, only by way of checking any imposition; but I do not mean to say that we are not so far acquainted with this mode of reconciliation as to know that it is done, because we often recommend it.

Do you conceive that any considerable part of the emoluments of Police officers may arise from what they obtain in such cases of assaults?—I do conceive a considerable part of the emoluments of Police officers arises from what they are paid in one way or another, either in that shape or in other ways; and it is for that reason that I think it would be beneficial if some other mode of rewarding officers were adopted.

Do you not imagine that the smallest part of the emoluments which the Police officers receive is their salary?—I answer merely as a matter of opinion, that I should think it was, or in other words, that they get more by their offices, somehow or other, than their salary, for they have families to maintain; and I should think they would not be so desirous of obtaining the situation, if they did not get at least 100 *l.* a year, but in which I include all the fees they are entitled to.

Do you know of any impositions practised by the Officers?—Of my own knowledge I do not, but I have my suspicions; and in order to prevent any such, I certainly think it would be advisable to put the officers upon a more independent footing, by way of salary, in order to raise them if possible above temptation.

To what place are persons sent, previous to their being fully committed?—All persons committed for re-examination, upon a charge of felony, are sent to Horsemonger-lane.

Are they there mixed with other prisoners who are fully committed?—I believe they have been, for want of accommodation in the gaol; but I know that orders have been made by the County Magistrates to make more room in the gaol, in order to prevent any such inconvenience, which orders are being carried into execution.

Are not persons sometimes committed, who are found, upon further examination, to be perfectly innocent of the crimes with which they are charged?—Such instances have occurred. At all events I beg leave to say, that in my opinion all persons committed for re-examination ought to be kept apart from those who have been convicted of offences; and although it has not been done, I know it to be the intent of the County Magistrates to do it, and that immediately, as I have before observed.

Jovis, 9° die Maii, 1816.

The Honourable HENRY GREY BENNET, in The Chair.

John Gifford, Esquire, again called in, and Examined.

DO you wish to explain any part of your evidence given yesterday?—The question to which I refer was, Whether I knew that any licence had been taken away from a public-house in consequence of any complaint of mine to the licensing Magistrates; I now am able to state, that a house in Norton Falgate, called the Blakeney's Head, kept by a Mrs. Elliot, which was constantly filled with thieves, in which house we have frequently apprehended thieves, the licence was refused to be renewed on my application, but on the representation of some of the inhabitants I find that the licence was afterwards granted to the same individual.

Do you know what was the nature of that representation on the part of the inhabitants?—I do not; but I understand it was at the solicitation of the woman, representing the distress she would be subjected to if the licence was not granted to her.

Do you know who those persons were that made that representation?—I understood the same persons who had before signed the petition to the Magistrates not to grant the licence.

Are you aware that that was owing to a more minute examination into the case?—I certainly am not aware of that, because the house was so completely infamous that no subsequent investigation could alter the complexion of those complaints which I felt it my duty to urge against it.

Did you take any notice to the Magistrates, of their licensing the house after the complaints you had made against it, while in the hands of the same person?—I was not aware till this morning that it was licensed.

They made no communication to you?—None whatever.

How long was this ago?—September 1814.

Between September 1814 and September 1815, the house remained unlicensed?—I am not competent to say whether it was in 1814 or 1815 that the complaints were made; but the house remained unlicensed for a twelvemonth.

Have you learnt whether the conduct of that house is the same as it was prior to your laying the complaint against it, or whether it has improved?—The licence has been transferred to another person, and it is now converted into a liquor-shop, with a different sign.

Do you believe that the original occupier holds the house?—Certainly not; I should think the licence was granted to the person against whom the complaints were made, who has now transferred it to the present occupier.

You stated in your evidence yesterday, that you made a complaint against a public-house for some gross misconduct, to the licensing Magistrates, which house was at no great distance from your own Office, and that the complaints were laid the last year, that is, 1815?—Yes.

Can you give to the Committee now an explanation of the whole of that transaction?—The house was the Marlborough, in Holywell-street, Shoreditch, which was kept by Charles Price, who had been convicted on the 9th of November 1813, and fined, for suffering tippling in his house; who had been again convicted, on the 14th March 1814, and fined for the same offence; who had been a third time convicted, on the 22d April 1814, and fined for a similar offence; who had been a fourth time convicted, on the 29th April 1814, and again fined, for a similar offence; and who had once more been convicted, on the 7th of October 1814, and fined for a similar offence; one of those convictions was for suffering tippling on a Sunday. I returned one of these convictions, in form, to the licensing Magistrates, and gave it as my opinion, that the man was in consequence of that conviction incapacitated from keeping a public-house for three years. The licensing Magistrates differed in opinion from me, and ordered a case to be drawn up and the opinion of the Common Serjeant to be taken upon it, whose opinion was certainly different from my own. The man's licence was renewed, and he holds it at this moment.

510.

Who

Who were the licensing Magistrates?—I cannot pretend to say; it was on the general licensing day.

Who was in the chair?—Sir Daniel Williams. Since that time a robbery was committed in that house, upon the person of a Captain Williams, who was robbed during the time he was asleep in the parlour, at the back of the bar, of 100*l.* The landlord, upon having the fact communicated to him, instead of affording the protection which it was his duty to afford to the person who had been robbed, turned him out of doors; this fact was proved on oath before me, on the oath of a person of the name of Williams; the landlord afterwards, however, did all in his power to bring the offenders to justice

Were they brought to justice?—No, they escaped.

Do you know to whom that public-house belongs?—I understand it belongs to a brewer who lives close to it.

Do you know the name of the brewer?—I do not.

Cannot you ascertain whether the date of the robbery was before the last licensing day or afterwards?—I am certain it was subsequent to my complaint at the licensing meeting, because I could not help exclaiming, when the fact came out before me in my Office, that if the Magistrates had refused the licence, this offence could not have been committed.

What is the condition of the house at present?—The house before, I must observe, was very ill conducted, particularly in receiving a great number of boys and girls; I sent repeated remonstrances to the landlord, on this subject, which produced no effect.

It united the two trades, that of a brothel and a nursery for thieves?—No, I do not know that; they went there to drink. I told the landlord frequently I should remonstrate against the renewal of his licence, and I apprehended it could not be granted. I have frequently complained against public-houses; but cannot remember the particulars at present, not supposing I should ever be called upon to state them.

But the general impression upon your mind is, that you have made many complaints of the misconduct of public-houses before the Magistrates, and having found them wholly unattended to, you have yourself ceased, in consequence, your attendance on the licensing days?—I cannot say they have been wholly unattended to; but certainly the general impression on my mind is this, that complaints of a nature which in my humble opinion should prevent the renewal of licences, have not had that effect; and that, perceiving the inutility of those efforts, I have in a great measure refrained from attending those meetings.

You have said in your evidence of yesterday, that there was a general belief prevailing in your district, that where publicans dealt with particular individuals for beer and spirits, there would be no difficulty in getting their licences on the licensing days; do you know any facts that have corroborated that belief in your opinion?—I can state one fact which appears to me to afford some ground for that belief; it is this, that in going round with the Magistrates last year, or the year before, I am not quite sure which, when a house for which a petition was presented for a licence, was pointed out near St. George's in the East, the licence of which had been refused the preceding year, it was now unanimously agreed to grant the licence. I made some inquiry, with a view to ascertain if possible the cause of this change of opinion in the licensing Magistrates, when I discovered, that since the preceding year the house had become the property of another individual.

Who was that individual?—It belonged to Messrs. Hanbury and Co.

Do you know why the licence was refused the preceding year?—From a conviction of its being perfectly unnecessary for the neighbourhood, as I understood.

Was it a new licence?—I do not know whether there had been a licence formerly, or not; but it was a petition for a new licence.

Is a book kept at your Office for the purpose of entering the complaints which are made against the publicans within the district?—It is, and special directions are given to the Clerk to enter all such complaints in the book, to make an abstract of them, and to transmit that abstract to the licensing Magistrates at their general meeting, which is regularly done.

You stated in your evidence yesterday, that you had some information upon the practice of licensing public-houses in the Borough; you attend there occasionally as licensing Magistrate?—I do.

When any complaints are laid before the Magistrates of the Borough, of any specific

John Gifford, Esq.

specific public-house, what is the practice pursued by such Magistrates, in inquiring into those complaints?—The practice, not the constant practice, but the occasional practice, is to postpone the licence till the adjourned days, to afford an opportunity to persons preferring complaints to substantiate them by evidence.

From what you have personally seen, can you say that there exists on the part of the Magistrates in the Borough a disposition to correct the abuses of public-houses that may be brought before them?—I cannot pretend to say whether there does or does not exist that disposition, I can only say that it appears to me that licences are granted with great facility, and far beyond what appears to be necessary for the public accommodation, and in some instances in direct violation of the laws of the land.

Have you ever been present when charges have been made out distinctly, of misconduct on the part of the publicans, and yet the licences have been continued?—I cannot say that I recollect that. I will explain what I mean by licences being granted in violation of the law of the land, I mean licences to shops known to be purely liquor-shops, where the sale of beer has been proved not to exist. I was present at the Quarter Sessions last year, where this subject was taken into consideration by the Magistrates of the County; it there appeared, that two Magistrates had gone to a liquor-shop in the Borough, for the express purpose of ascertaining whether they really sold beer, or not, when the landlord confessed, that if any body applied for beer, he sent out for it to another public-house, and that he kept none in his house; a Magistrate then present declared, that if that very individual who kept that house were to apply to him for a renewal of his beer licence, if he could get any other Magistrate to join with him, he would, even with a knowledge of that fact, grant the licence; and he was one of the Magistrates who had visited that house.

Do you know whether it is the practice of those persons to keep a barrel of beer within the house as a mere matter of form, their trade being exclusively in liquor?—I do not know that precise fact; but it is the full impression on my mind, that a beer licence is obtained for no other purpose, by persons keeping such shops, than to enable them to obtain a spirit licence.

Is the number of spirit-shops in the Borough very great?—Very great indeed.

Can you at all state to the Committee what proportion they bear, in any given quarter, to the number of houses?—No, I am not able to do that.

Should you think the number of those houses much beyond the number requisite for the public accommodation?—Greatly beyond it, I should think.

Do you know whether any of the Magistrates are themselves dealers in spirits by wholesale?—There are some.

Do you know whether any of the Magistrates are either concerned themselves, or concerned through near relations, in any of the great brewery establishments?—One of the Magistrates is himself a brewer; and the son of another Magistrate who constantly attends the licence meetings, is a partner in the same house.

Did you ever hear of any number of licences being granted to that house, in any given district, on any given day?—I have heard, but I do not know it to be the fact, that as many as eleven licences have been granted to new houses belonging to that house, in the half hundred of East Brixton, or in the Borough of Southwark, in one day.

Do you know whether it is the practice to insert clauses in the leases of publicans, by which they are compelled to deal with particular houses, at the time of their being newly licensed?—I do not know it, but I have heard it, and believe it to be the fact; I never saw one of the leases; the leases are generally from twelve to fourteen years, as I have heard.

Were you present, as one of the licensing Magistrates for the county of Surrey, when an application was made, by a man of the name of Pannel, for the licensing of the Lord Wellington in Morgan's-lane, in the Borough; and can you state to the Committee the particulars of that case?—I was present at the License Meeting, I think, in the year 1813, when an application was made to license a house, to be called the Lord Wellington, in Morgan's-lane; most of the parish officers and many very respectable inhabitants appeared to oppose the licence, and it was unanimously refused, it appearing that the local situation of the house was particularly objectionable, and that it could only be supported by the lowest orders of the populace and by prostitutes; information came afterwards to the Magistrates, that, notwithstanding the refusal of that licence, the house was opened and the trade

510.   carrying

John Gifford,
Esq.

carrying on; and on inquiry it appeared that a man of the name of Pannel, who had formerly kept a public-house, called the George, on Cotton's Wharf, which house was pulled down, had taken the licence granted to him for the George to the house in Morgan's-lane, and had with that licence in his hand applied at the Excise Office for a spirit licence. Representations were made, by the two Magistrates who had signed his original licence, to the Excise, explanatory of the fraud committed by Pannel; proceedings were consequently instituted against him by the Commissoners of Excise, and he was fined. At the next licensing meeting this man petitioned for a new licence; I opposed it, on the ground of his conviction for a fraud; but it was carried, and he received the licence.

By whom are the Police constables appointed?—By the Secretary of State.

Do you consider that the appointment by the Secretary of State is agreeable to law?—It is too much for me to say; by the last Police Act the appointments are directed to be made by the Magistrates, with the consent and approbation of the Secretary of State.

But in point of fact the Magistrates do not recommend to the Secretary of State, but the Secretary of State appoints the constables in the first instance?—I can only speak as to my own Office; the Secretary of State has generally appointed constables, without communication with the Magistrates.

Are you aware what steps are taken by the Secretary of State to select proper persons, when the appointment originates with him?—I must suppose the Secretary of State satisfies his own mind that the persons appointed are fit persons to fill the office.

Has it not come to your knowledge that improper persons have been appointed by the Secretary of State?—In one instance, certainly, a man has been lately appointed, who has turned out to be an improper person to fill the office.

Was that man, so appointed by the Secretary of State as a constable, a jew-bail?—I have heard, but I do not know the fact, that he has frequently been bail in considerable sums, and he is now in the King's Bench prison.

Do you not think it would be a furtherance of justice, if the appointment of the constables in the first instance rested with the Magistrates, as was the case formerly during the old Act of Parliament?—I am certainly of opinion that the Magistrates have the best opportunity for ascertaining what persons are best qualified to fill the office of constable in their respective districts.

Why have you returned, in the paper transmitted to this Committee, that constables are appointed by the Magistrates?—Because the return applies to a period antecedent to the passing of the last Police Act.

Do you think that the present Lord Lieutenant of Surrey is more particular as to the persons he appoints as Magistrates, than the former one was?—I believe that no man can more conscientiously discharge all the duties attaching to his high office, than the present Lord Lieutenant of the County of Surrey.

Mr. Thomas Harrison, called in, and Examined.

Mr
T. Harrison.

WHAT are you?—A wine merchant.

What tavern do you keep?—The Bedford, at Camden Town.

Did you ever keep a public-house called the Globe, at the corner of Globe-lane?—No, I did not keep it, the house belonged to me.

Was it in a dilapidated state?—Yes, it was; and I rebuilt it at 2,000*l.* expense.

Had that ever been a public-house?—Yes.

When that house was rebuilt, did you apply for a licence?—Yes.

Did the Justices' Clerk tell you that you must petition as for a new house?—I understood so from some gentleman, but who it was I do not know.

Did you do it?—Yes.

Did you get your licence?—Not that year.

Prior to getting your licence, did you enter into any engagement with Messrs. Hanbury for the trade of your house?—I did enter into an engagement that they should serve the house for seven years, if they gave me their interest.

Did they give you their interest for procuring the licence?—I believe they did; it was unknown to me.

In point of fact, the house was licensed the next licensing day?—Yes.

Did you sell the lease of the house?—I disposed of the lease of the house.

Did you sell it with the condition of purchasing the beer of Messrs. Hanbury?—

Yes;

Yes; the lease was for thirty-one years, and there was a clause in it, when I disposed of it, that Messrs. Hanbury should serve the house for seven years.

Do you think you could have got better terms if it had not been for that clause in the lease?—I might have got something more, no great deal.

Did you not go to Mr. Hanbury and make that voluntary offer on your part, from the general understanding that Mr. Hanbury's interest could procure you the licence of that house?—I understood they could give me some assistance.

In what year was it your house was licensed through the influence of Mr. Hanbury?—In the year 1811.

Mr.
T. Harrison.

Sir *Daniel Williams*, Knight, called in, and Examined.

YOU are one of the Magistrates of the Whitechapel Division?—I am.

You have held that situation since the year 1796?—I have.

What other employment do you hold, independent of that of Police Magistrate?—No other employment, except that of Colonel of the First Regiment of the Tower Hamlets Militia, when embodied.

What is the extent of your jurisdiction?—From West to East, about two miles and a half; from North to South, about two miles: there are five complete parishes within the Division; the Trinity Minories, Whitechapel, Aldgate, Bow and Bromley, part of Spital Fields, Bethnal Green, the Hamlets of Mile-End New and Old Town, the precincts of the Tower, and Wellclose-square; I think those are all.

Is the attendance of the different Magistrates at your Office according to the terms of the Act of Parliament?—Nearly so.

Are you acquainted with any of the County Magistrates?—There are several of the County Magistrates, who are resident near the spot, who occasionally look in at the Office.

So that it never happens that, according to the letter of the Act of Parliament, there is not one of the Police Magistrates present?—I believe, never.

It has never occurred of an evening, for instance, that no Police Magistrate should be present?—I believe not; the resident Magistrate always attends in the evening.

Mr. Davies, I think, resides in the house?—He does.

It is considered as part of his duty to attend every evening at the Office?—Not quite so; Mr. Davies is a very aged infirm man, seldom going out, therefore myself and colleague Mr. Rogers take the whole of the day duty, and he executes the duty of an evening.

In case he should from the state of his health be unable to attend, who does his duty?—One or other of us, certainly.

Then you wish the Committee to understand distinctly, that it has never occurred that the Police Office should be without a Magistrate of an evening?—No, I believe it has never occurred that the Office should be without one Police Magistrate; in case Mr. Davies should be ill, one of those Magistrates who frequently look in of an evening could give us assistance as occasion might require.

The Committee wish to know, in point of fact, whether such is not the state of health of Mr. Davies, that those Magistrates do not attend oftener than is needful?—No; he is constantly at the Office of an evening, and, though he is old and infirm, yet he is not in a state to incapacitate him from his duty.

How many Clerks are there in the Office?—Two.

Is there an extra clerk?—No.

Do those two Clerks daily attend?—Invariably.

Do they hold any other situation; are they solicitors?—The Chief Clerk is a solicitor; but I do not know of any man more correct in his attendance than he is.

Does he practise as a solicitor in the Office?—No, he is a partner with a solicitor in the neighbourhood.

But neither he nor his Partner practise as solicitors in the Office?—Certainly not.

You have eight Constables?—Yes.

Do you consider that number as sufficient for the extent of your jurisdiction?—It has hitherto been sufficient; but I think it would be desirable if there was a small increase.

They receive a guinea a week?—They do.

Do you think that sufficient to enable you to procure persons fit for the purposes of Police constables?—I do, taking into consideration the other emoluments derived from their situation.

Sir
D. Williams, Knt.

510.

How

How much should you estimate those other emoluments to be?—I cannot immediately ascertain, but I will describe them: they receive so much for serving a warrant; they receive three shillings a week from the establishment, a certain number of them, for perambulating the District every night; what occurs during that perambulation is entered in a book, and laid upon the Magistrates' table every morning; they have also an allowance from the County, of three shillings a day for each day's attendance when they have prosecutions to carry on; and they have a similar allowance at the Old Bailey, when attending as witnesses; and of rewards under the several Acts of Parliament, they also receive a proportion, but that is entirely at the discretion and under the direction of the Recorder of London, and is divided between the officers, the prosecutors, and witnesses, according to his direction.

Should you estimate the whole of the receipts drawn from those sources, at fifty or sixty pounds a year?—I should think more; I have not minutely inquired into it, but I should consider it must be eighty or ninety pounds.

You have not taken into the account what they may receive, in the nature of reward, from the party prosecuting, or from persons seeking their assistance at the Office?—It is the general practice, in cases of felony, where a prosecutor is anxious to apprehend an offender, to offer a reward upon their conviction; and I have not taken into the account, when I say eighty or ninety pounds a year, any sum which they might derive from receiving such portion of the reward.

Do you, as one of the Magistrates, or do the Magistrates in general, pay great attention to that part of the subject, under the conviction that considerable abuses might arise from their receiving sums of money?—Bad men would undoubtedly be very prone to betray their trust. I can only speak as far as regards my own people; I consider them to be very fair and honourable men; they are certainly exposed to very great temptation, but I never met with any single instance that had a tendency to criminate any one Officer under our employ.

Do you put any limit to, or do you discourage in any manner, the receipt of those sums of money on the part of the Police Officers, from persons attending at the Office to request their assistance for which they are paid by the Public to give?—They are encouraged and directed to give prompt assistance whenever it is required; and whenever they receive information that a felony has been committed, it is their duty, under our immediate inspection, instantly to make every exertion in their power, and never wait for any stimulus or reward.

Do you think that, as far as the Constables of the Whitechapel Division are concerned, the receiving or not receiving the reward makes any difference in the pains they take in apprehending an offender?—I should consider not; where a reward is offered, it most probably will create additional exertion.

Is it your opinion that the present laws, proportioning the reward for the apprehension and conviction of offenders, is the best mode of rewarding Police officers; or would it not be better if a discretionary power was vested in the hands of the Magistrates, enabling them to give rewards for specific services?—I am inclined to believe that if the law was altered, and gave that power into the hands of the Magistrate, it would be beneficial to the Public.

You have been a Police Magistrate twenty years?—I have.

Has it fallen within your observation, that the morals of the public, in your Division, are better or worse, or stationary, since that period?—I think that their morals during that period have somewhat amended; I do not think they are worse, if it is taken into consideration the nature of the employments and the situations of those who reside in that extensive district; they are comprised of the labouring Irish and their families, who are poor and distressed; when they receive money for their labour, they are improvident, and do not apply it to benefit their families, but in general indulge in intoxication, and the consequence of that is, it breaks out sometimes into riots of some consequence. Another portion of the inhabitants, and a very great proportion, are the lower class of Jews; they are a sober set of people, in point of drinking, but they are addicted to gambling, and in consequence of their indulgence in that vice are reduced to great necessity, and the consequence of that is to induce them to make depredations upon the public. I beg leave to observe, that there is an increase of offenders of the juvenile branch, which is very considerable, and they are frequently trained up to such pursuits by their relatives and connexions; during the last two years, I think, that class of offenders has very much increased.

You think, then, that within these few years there has been a system carried on to employ

employ children in the commission of crimes?—I am afraid so; I have no positive proof of it, but my mind is made up that it is so.

The great mass of inhabitants within your district, you describe as persons quite of the lowest condition of life?—The major part.

Are their habits less dissipated and drunken than formerly?—I think they are.

Can you state to the Committee what proportion the public-houses and spirit-shops in that district bear to the number of houses?—I really cannot with any degree of accuracy; I could tell the number that is contained within the Tower Hamlets; there are 1000, and that comprises a great extent of ground.

Do you mean by public-houses, spirit-shops?—I mean the general mass of both; the Magistrates have for a great number of years past endeavoured as far as was within their power to lessen the number of what were termed gin-shops, being in themselves contrary to law, and the parties being liable to penalties by the existing law.

Do you attend as one of the licensing Magistrates, when licences are granted?—I have executed the duties of Chairman of that Meeting for the last seventeen or eighteen years past.

What is your practice when an application is made to you for the licensing of a new public-house?—The practice is, that a petition for a new public-house must be presented on the day that the public-houses in the parish where the new house is situated are applied for; all the petitions received are taken into consideration on what is termed the "adjourned day;" the applications for renewals of licences that have not been licensed the year before are then decided; the applications for new houses are personally visited by the Magistrates, who upon the spot determine whether it is proper that the house should be licensed, and whether the public convenience requires a new house, or whether it would be injurious to the houses in the neighbourhood to create a new one.

Do you inquire into the character of the applicant?—The character of the applicant is not personally inquired into by the Magistrates licensing; they are by law compelled to bring a certificate from the parish where the house is situate, signed by the overseers and churchwardens.

Do you require the signature of the minister?—We do not specially require that the minister should sign it, we are as well satisfied with the signature of the church-wardens and overseers, because we consider we are more likely to have his conduct specified; the minister generally receives his information from the beadle or churchwardens.

Is it your opinion that, generally speaking, or if not generally, it has sometimes happened, that those signatures on the part of the churchwardens are mere matters of form?—I believe so, frequently, and it was upon that principle that the Magistrates of the Tower Hamlets some seventeen years ago thought it right personally to view every situation where a new house was applied for, that they themselves might judge of its fitness.

Do you recollect whether in the last year, 1815, you licensed many new public-houses?—I think not; to the best of my recollection, not above three or four.

Did you license one that was near St. George's in the East?—There was one licensed in that parish.

Perhaps you may recollect, that a request for a licence was made the preceding year, and was refused?—Yes, there was.

Do you know why that licence was refused the preceding year?—I should consider, upon the personal view of the Magistrates, and not considering it necessary.

If they refused it in the year 1814, why would you think they granted it in the year 1815?—There might be a variety of causes; there might be an increase of inhabitants, or an increase of buildings.

Do you in point of fact recollect that any circumstances of the sort you have mentioned, appeared in this instance, namely, an increase of inhabitants, or an increase of buildings?—I cannot take upon myself to recollect.

Is there any register kept of the proceedings of the licensing Magistrates?—Yes, but in which there are no reasons assigned, merely stating that such licences were refused, but not stating why they were refused.

You do not then recollect any particulars upon this subject?—No, I do not.

Why the licence was granted one year and refused the preceding?—No, I do not.

Did it ever come to your knowledge that the house had changed its proprietor during that period?—No, it did not.

Did

Sir
D. Williams, Knt.

Did you know at the time the licence was granted, who was the proprietor ?—No, it was the person whose name was contained in the petition which was presented.

In point of fact do you, when you license the houses, inquire who are the proprietors of them ?—No.

You do not then in this instance know who was the person who had bought the house in the preceding year?—I should be able to answer that more accurately if it was pointed out to me where the house was situated.

Is there a house in that neighbourhood called the Duke of York ?—There are several houses of that sign in the Tower Hamlets.

Do you recollect whether the house in question bore that sign ?—No, I do not.

When complaints are made against the conduct of publicans at the licensing day, what is the practise of the Magistrates in examining into those complaints ?—It is the practice of the Magistrates at the Office I am in, in the course of the year, whenever any circumstance occurs of ill-conduct on the part of the publican, to make a register of that conduct, and then to lay before the Magistrates, at the re-licensing time, the several complaints against the several publicans.

Is it the practice of you, who sit as the Chairman of the licensing Magistrates, to consider those complaints taken upon oath before a Magistrate (whether he is a Police Magistrate or not) unless rebutted by the defendant, as conclusive evidence against the propriety of his having a licence ?—Those complaints are never taken upon oath, and they arise from a personal view of the conduct of the publicans, in some cases that they have violated the law laid down for their observance.

But in case evidence was offered to you, that came from any Magistrate, which had appeared upon oath, or any record of conviction, should you not consider such evidence of such misconduct as conclusive against the propriety of granting the licence ?—Yes.

Were you present when the keeper of the Marlborough public-house in Holywell-street, a person of the name of Charles Price, applied for his licence to be renewed, in the year 1813 or 1814 ?—I cannot recollect.

Do you recollect that complaints were laid against his house by the Police Magistrate, Mr. Gifford, and that it was proved in evidence that he had been convicted five or six times of suffering tippling in his house within the space of a few months?—I do recollect a gentleman coming from the Office in Worship-street, stating such a circumstance, which was laid before the Magistrates ; whether that man was re-licensed, I do not know.

Should you not consider that such complaints laid by a Police Magistrate, resting upon a conviction or upon evidence on oath, would compel the Magistrates to refuse such application or licence?—I think it undoubtedly would ; but this man must have been re-licensed, if he was so (but I have no recollection of it) in consequence of his being heard upon his defence ; and therefore the effect of that defence must have been, that the Magistrates were of opinion there was no sufficient ground why the licence should be refused.

Should you think that any defence that could be made by a publican who had been convicted for allowing tippling in his house six times in the course of a small number of months, one conviction being for suffering tippling during divine service on a Sunday, as resting upon sufficient good grounds to warrant the Magistrates in re-licensing the house ?—I should think not ; such a character ought not to be re-licensed.

The natural inference would be, supposing the Magistrates present on that day having had before them the record of those convictions, the licence of that house, had it needed it in your opinion, they were not warranted in granting ?—From motives of delicacy, I should not choose to reprobate the conduct of Magistrates acting in that situation, considering that they did act from the purest motives.

But you have stated, that the record of conviction you thought was sufficient reason why the person should not have had the licence ; the question was, that if he had the licence, upon the record of conviction having been produced, whether you did not think that the Magistrates ought not to have granted it?—I think when a man has been guilty of repeated acts of immorality, he ought not to be suffered to have a licence.

In this particular instance, do you not think that the licence ought not to have been granted ?—I have not a full recollection of that case before me ; if it was as it has been stated, I think it ought not to have been granted.

The house is now a gin-shop ?—I do not know the house.

Then perhaps you do not know that since the period of licensing, a robbery has
been

been committed in the house under very suspicious circumstances on the part of the landlord?—No, I do not; it is not within my District.

Are there within your District many of those houses which are technically known by the name of " Flash-houses?"—There are in my District a great number of low public-houses, which are resorted to by persons of the worst description.

Houses of resort of reputed thieves, and other infamous characters?—Yes.

If complaints are made at your Office of the conduct of publicans in permitting such scenes of vice and debauchery to take place in those houses, should you not feel it your duty to report the same to the licensing Magistrates?—Certainly, and it is invariably done; I observed before, we had a register, in which any complaints arising from the ill conduct of persons keeping public-houses were kept.

Have you in point of fact taken away the licences of many houses, in consequence of such complaints?—Several.

Is it the duty of the constables in your Office to watch over the conduct of those public-houses, and to report the same to you?—I think not; whenever, in the execution of their duty, any circumstances should arise, as that of men keeping public-houses acting improperly, it is their bounden duty to report such conduct to the Magistrates.

Is it not the custom of constables in your Office to go to those public-houses to look for thieves whom they want to apprehend?—I have no doubt but it is; I consider it to be their duty, if a criminal is to be apprehended, immediately to go to the most likely places to find him.

It would then come immediately within the purview of the constables, the existence of those houses in the state and condition which has been described?—Certainly.

Would it not then be their duty to make a report to you?—With respect to those sort of houses, the officers know perfectly well who are the persons who resort there, but, so long as there is no flagrant outrage committed by the landlord of that house, they are not the subject of animadversion.

Did not many of those houses unite the double trade of a brothel and a public-house?—I do not know that there are any in my District of that description.

Have you any doubt that in that District of London there are houses that are technically known by the name of the " Cock and Hen Clubs?"—There are some, certainly.

And those clubs are held at public-houses?—Certainly; considering that that part of the Metropolis has all the disadvantages attending a great sea-port, that there is constantly a prodigious influx of seamen; and it is very well known that when seamen arrive and receive money, they are profligate in their expenditure, and that a great number of women associate with those men when they do arrive, and that they accompany them to public-houses and other places of resort, the landlords of which are very glad to receive them, from the quantity of money they have to spend.

Is it not a circumstance of nightly occurrence, that in those obscure public-houses there are scenes of riot, breaches of the peace, drunkenness, and debauchery of every description, and that they are the dwelling-place of reputed thieves and prostitutes?—I do not know that that is the case; flagrant breaches of the peace are very rarely committed, and the very instant that such outrage is known, one of the Officers is sent to quell it, and take the parties into custody.

Is there no regulation issued from your Office for the shutting up public-houses at any given hour of the night?—They are generally given to understand that it would be very reprehensible on their part to keep their houses open after eleven o'clock at night.

Do you believe that this is acted upon?—I do believe it is; there are some exceptions, certainly.

Does it at all fall within the duty of any of the constables of your Office, to see that the public-houses are not kept open after that hour?—Yes, it is; those whose duty it is to perambulate the streets nightly: in case they saw a publican who did not conform with the regulations laid down, they would report it to the Office, and that report would be entered in a book, and laid before the licensing Magistrates.

Are those reports often made?—Those omissions and commissions are frequent, and they are invariably reported every year.

Should you consider the repeated disobedience of that regulation as a sufficient ground to warrant you in refusing to continue the licence?—I should consider it

was

Sir
D. Williams, Knt.

was sufficient; the practice has been, that when a party has so offended, he has been at first reprimanded; if he has continued in that line of conduct, his licence has been refused.

Then the Committee are to understand, that it is the general practice, with few exceptions, of all public-houses and spirit-shops in that neighbourhood, to close their doors at eleven o'clock?—I believe it is.

Of course, with the character that you have given of the Officers in your department, it could not be otherwise?—If they executed their duty, it could not be otherwise.

And you consider them as persons of good character, and good officers, and you believe they do their duty?—I verily believe they do.

Is there any High Constable of the Division?—There is.

How is he nominated?—He is nominated at the County Court, by the Magistrates at large.

Does he receive any salary?—None.

What is his duty?—His duty is upon special occasions to summon the head-boroughs; upon a breach of the peace, he is to summon them to attend upon him; it is his duty to see that the publicans do their duty upon the quartering of soldiers, and for providing waggons for the transport of baggage, &c. and collecting the county rate.

Has he any thing to do in the control of the Police; it is not meant by that, with your department, but what may be considered the Police of the Division?—I think he has.

Does he in point of fact attend to the watchmen, or to the execution of any of those parish regulations which are of great importance?—I should think not; the watch is superintended by the constable of the parish, his is a paramount control over that constable.

Does the constable receive a salary?—None.

The offices of high constable and petty constable being offices of great trust and laborious duty, and receiving no salary for doing that duty, do you know whether they are paid in any other manner?—There are certain expenses that the law allows them, which of course they receive, but they have no stipend; it is a duty imposed upon them by lot in the parish.

Is the situation of High Constable much sought after?—It is a situation that is considered a very respectable one, and I believe whenever it is vacant there are candidates sufficient to fill it.

Do you believe that the reward for the labour that belongs to that situation is alone confined to the respectability that attaches to it, and that there is not in point of fact some money reward, of which it may be difficult to find altogether the trace, but of the receipt of which there can be very little doubt?—I do not know how to answer that question; I have no knowledge of it.

You are not aware then of any emolument, either direct or indirect, which the High Constable receives?—None, except what is allowed by Act of Parliament.

There are no sources of profit beyond that belonging to the office?—None, excepting as before mentioned.

Is it an annual office, or held during good behaviour?—During good behaviour.

Who appoints the Police Officers?—They are all appointed by the Secretary of State for the Home Department.

[Attendance of witness required for the following Session]

Veneris, 10° *die Maii,* 1816.

The Honourable HENRY GREY BENNET, in The Chair.

———

Mr. *William Crush,* called in, and Examined.

WHAT are you ?—A victualler.

Do you keep a public-house?—Yes, the Marquis of Granby in Vine-street, Westminster.

Had you ever any other public-house in any other part of London ?—Yes, in Whitechapel.

Had you any difficulty in getting that house licensed ?—Yes, I had.

How many years were you in making application for a licence, before you obtained one?—I did not obtain one at all for that situation ; I was an applicant for five years.

Was the situation of the house eligible for a public-house ?—Yes, most particularly so ; I was encouraged by a Magistrate to buy the house for that purpose.

Was it fitted up for a public-house to sell beer, for or a shop to sell spirits ? —Both.

Had you a tap-room?—The house not being licensed, was not fitted up as a public-house.

Did you part with that house in consequence of not being able to obtain a licence ?—Yes.

Who to ?—To a Mr. Brown ; I sold to him a lease for fourteen years.

Then it is let upon lease to Mr. Brown?—Yes.

Did he obtain a licence for it the first year he applied?—He never applied for a licence.

Who is the present occupier of it?—Mr. Brown.

Is the house licensed ?—No, it is not; no application has been made since.

What do you consider the reason why the house has not been licensed ?— It rested wholly with the Magistrates. I made application to the Rev. Mr. Robinson before I purchased the house in the shell ; he rather encouraged me by saying the situation was proper, and he thought commanded a licence ; when I got it finished, I made application for a licence, I tried in September, I forget the date, and it was not obtained. I then took another public-house, and that was shut up for fifteen months. I then tried again on the following September ; the licence was not obtained then, the reason was, because I did not live in it : I went and I lived in it, and tried again the following September, and made sure of it from the encouragement that I had met with from the Magistrates, for I attended them all ; I had a list of their names, they all gave me good encouragement, and as I was living in the house I fully expected the licence ; however it was not obtained : I tried again on the following September, and I then made personal application to more of the Magistrates of the Tower Hamlets, and they all encouraged me very much ; I waited upon Mr. Jackson in particular; he was a gentleman that pretended to be my friend, and recommended me ; I told him I was reducing my circumstances by living there, and that I must be obliged to sell it ; he recommended me not to sell it, and asked me who was my brewer ; I told him, from being out of business I had no brewer in particular; I told him I had made application to Mr. Calvert's house for their assistance ; he told me I had done wrong, and that I should have gone to Mr. Hanbury. " Sir," said I, " I have been to Mr. Hanbury, and likewise to Mr. Aveling, and Mr. Hanbury seemed not to wish to have any thing to do with it, unless the house was his *in toto.*" He said, " You must go to him again, and give my compliments to him, and tell him that he must interfere, and the house must be licensed." I accordingly went to Mr. Hanbury again, and I delivered the message from Mr. Jackson to Mr. Aveling, who said, he had no disposition to have any thing to do with it. I then went to another Magistrate, whose name I do not recollect, who said he had nothing to do with it. " The time," I said, " is not yet arrived; it will be on such a day." Says he, " I have nothing at all to do with it: but let me put you to rights; all houses are determined on to be

licensed."

licensed." " Sir," said I, " you do not comprehend me; the day is not arrived for houses to be licensed." Says he, " I must put you to rights; all the houses have been surveyed, and they have determined in the Tower Hamlets what houses shall be licensed." " Sir," says I, " you have set me to rights, for I saw Mr. Aveling surveying the houses on such a day;" and then I bid him good morning.

Did Mr. Hanbury engage with you to take the house?—No, he did not; on the first application I made to him, he said they had no inclination to have any thing to do with it.

Did they give you to understand that if you transferred the house to them, the house would be licensed?—No; they said they would have nothing to do with it, unless I sold it to them; I said, as I had finished the house at a great expense, I did not like to part with it.

Was it in your belief that if you had sold the house to them, it would have been licensed as a matter of course?—I have no doubt of it.

Is it a general opinion in that neighbourhood, amongst the publicans, that a house that deals with Mr. Hanbury can be licensed with great facility?—For years past there have been very few licensed, except those in Mr. Hanbury's interest.

Sir *Daniel Williams*, Knight; again called in, and Examined.

DID you attend the licensing of public-houses in the years 1814 and 1815?—I did.

There were complaints laid against particular public houses by the churchwardens and some of the principal inhabitants in that district, in both those years, were there not?—I think there were.

Particularly against the public-houses known by the names of the Duke of York, the White Hart, and the Paviors Arms?—I think there were.

Did you know in the year 1814, that the officers of the parish had complained of those public-houses to the Magistrates of the Shadwell Police Office?—I did not know of it.

Was there not a memorial presented to you and the rest of the Magistrates, stating the scandalous, indecent, and licentious conduct which daily and nightly took place in those houses?—There was.

That was in the year 1813?—I cannot say what year it was in.

In consequence of those complaints, you took away the licences of some of those houses?—All three.

The next year a petition was presented by the parties, to have the houses re-opened; was not that the case?—There was such a petition presented, and also a petition from certain inhabitants, praying that the licences might be restored.

Was there not also a representation on the part of the parish officers, as well as by many of the respectable inhabitants of that place, praying that they might not be restored?—The parties praying that they might not be restored, and the parties praying that they might be restored, were both called in together, and heard in each others presence what they had to say.

The houses that were objected to in the year 1814 were not the same houses that were shut up in the year 1813 of course, they being the King's Arms, the Black Horse, the Angel, and the Ship?—I do not recollect their names at all.

Did you receive a memorial, signed by the parish officers, against those houses?—I do not recollect.

Do you recollect whether evidence was offered to be tendered to the Magistrates, that the same parties were connected with those houses, who were connected with the former houses, the Duke of York, the White Hart, and the Paviors Arms?—No, I do not recollect that.

You do not recollect whether any evidence to that effect was offered to the Magistrates?—I cannot charge my memory; whatever evidence was offered, was necessarily received.

Did you not at the time know, when the licences were granted and the houses re-opened, that the Duke of York and the Paviors Arms were kept by the same parties against whom the original complaint was made?—To the best of my recollection, two of the persons were restored their licences, and I believe it was upon this ground: the principal complaints against them were, that they had what was mentioned as cock and hen clubs, and that they had a long room for the reception of those persons; a representation was made, that those long rooms were totally destroyed, and the Magistrates personally went, and saw that that was the case.

Was

Was it not offered to be proved to you, that though, in the Duke of York particularly, the long-room had been shut up as a dancing room, yet that it had been changed into a gin-shop, and that there were shoals of prostitutes and drunken persons going in and out at all hours of the day?—I believe that all those houses united under the same roof a gin-shop and a public-house, a tap-room for the reception of those who thought proper to go there, and a bar for those who thought proper to go there.

Was it not offered to be proved before you, that scenes of drunkenness, riot, and debauchery, were constantly practised in those houses?—I believe that such evidence was given of such circumstances having occurred there.

Having shut up the houses for their being the resort of infamous characters of both sexes, and there being scenes of riot, drunkenness, and debauchery, constantly practised therein, why did you permit them to be re-opened while in the hands of the same persons?—The Magistrates determined they should.

Can you state, as one of the Magistrates present, what were the motives that governed your own conduct on that occasion?—I did not take a particular part; I was merely the chairman of the meeting, and therefore did not personally interfere.

Was the question then decided unanimously?—I do not recollect; I should hardly suppose it was.

This was a subject that created considerable discussion amongst the Magistrates, was it not?—I consider not at all.

Was it not a question in which there was much matter of dispute between the Magistrates on this subject, and the churchwardens, at the head of whom was Mr. Fletcher?—No, certainly not.

Were not Mr. Fletcher and the other churchwardens extremely anxious that those houses should not be re-opened?—Mr. Fletcher, and the party at the head of which he was, were anxious that they should not be re-opened, and another party of very respectable inhabitants were anxious that they should be.

Mr. Fletcher was one of the churchwardens?—I do not recollect whether he was in office or not.

In point of fact did not the officers of the parish resist the opening of the houses? —Some of them might, but I do not know that it was unanimously resisted by the parochial officers; the parties in that parish had been in a state of dissension for some time past.

Do you think it was a party spirit that led to the opposition to the opening of those public-houses, or that it was a disposition on the part of the parish officers to check those scenes of riot and disgusting debauchery that assailed the eyes and ears of the inhabitants and other persons every hour of the day and night?—I cannot say what were their motives; I suppose their motives were pure.

Have any complaints been laid before you as a Magistrate, since that period, of the conduct of those houses?—It is not in my district.

Then you cannot say whether the same scenes, which were so reprehended, continue?—No, I cannot say. There is one thing I wish to observe, that the greatest care and attention is paid by the Magistrates to the moral conduct of publicans; and taking the whole class of publicans in the Tower Hamlets, I do not know that there is a better regulated set of people in the Metropolis; they are never at a licensing meeting without receiving an admonition from the Chairman respecting their conduct; and that no one in that situation might plead ignorance of what the law is, and how it stands at present, the Magistrates at their own expense have printed a short abstract of the laws respecting public-houses, and distributed one to each publican.

Do you recollect whether Mr. Joseph Fletcher tendered himself to be sworn to give evidence in order to prove the charges that were laid against the houses above mentioned?—I do not know that he did; very probably he might.

You do not recollect having refused to receive it?—No.

The Committee are to understand that the conduct of the publicans in your Division is in general praiseworthy?—Most certainly.

You were asked yesterday, whether you could give the Committee any information relative to the licensing of the Marlborough public-house, Holywell-street, Shoreditch, kept by a man of the name of Charles Price?—I have inquired since I was before the Committee yesterday, and was informed, that about five or six years since the landlord's licence was suspended in consequence of a complaint of his having been repeatedly convicted of permitting tippling in his house; the landlord petitioned, and was heard in his defence, and the Magistrates restored his licence,

and

and he is now, as I understand, keeping the same house : About the character of Price I know nothing.

Are you sure it was five or six years ago, and not in 1813 or 1814 ?—Upon inquiring of one of the licensing Magistrates' Clerks this morning, I have learnt it was five or six years ago, and according to the best of my recollection it cannot be less.

Do you not recollect that it was not one conviction for tippling, but that there were four or five, and one for suffering it during divine service ?—It was very likely so.

Have you any recollection that the house was stated to be very disorderly, and the landlord a person of very indifferent character ?—No, I have not.

The Committee have before them a copy of the informations laid at the Public Office Worship-street, Shoreditch, against Charles Price, and it appears from them, that he was convicted for suffering tippling in his house, by Joseph Moser, Esq. in November 1813, in 10 s. penalty ; by John Gifford, Esq. on the 14th of March 1814, in 10 s. penalty ; by Sir William Parsons, on the 22d of April 1814, in 10 s. penalty ; by John Gifford, Esq. on the 29th April 1814, in 10 s. penalty ; by Ditto, on the 17th of October 1814, in 10 s. penalty ; it appears, therefore, that instead of its being five or six years ago, it is only two years ago ?—Whether those are the identical convictions upon which the man's licence was suspended, I do not know ; but I can only say that I know nothing as to the facts ; it was in consequence of a representation from that Office that the man's licence was suspended ; there was a petition to have the licence restored, it was heard, and in consequence of that he was restored, and is now landlord of the house.

Was it not known to the licensing Magistrates at the meeting, that the Magistrates at Worship-street set their faces directly against the licensing of that house ?—I do not know that they set their faces against that house or not ; the representation from that Office was laid before the meeting of Magistrates, and the licence suspended in consequence of that representation : the man petitioned, and was heard upon his petition, and what he had to urge in his defence ; and upon due consideration the Magistrates determined to restore the licence, which was accordingly done.

Should you not think, acting as a licensing Magistrate, that if in the course of eleven months a person was five times convicted of breaking the law before a Magistrate, in suffering tippling in his house, that he was a person to whom you would not feel yourself justified in regranting his licence ?—If such a circumstance came before me as a Magistrate, I should have felt myself bound to have indicted him upon his recognizance, and if he had been found guilty upon that indictment, he would have been incapacitated from keeping a public-house for three years.

The question that was asked, was not what you would have done by way of augmenting the punishment, but that, whether a man being guilty of those offences, for which he had been fined by three different Magistrates in the course of eleven months, you would not think that a sufficient cause to warrant the licensing Magistrates in refusing to re-license his house ?—Certainly.

Should you not think that a house licensed, with those convictions against the publican, an act, to say the least of it, highly irregular ?—It would ill become me to call in question the judgment of other Magistrates.

You are asked, as a Magistrate, whether you would think it within your duty to license a house against which there had been five convictions ?—It would all depend upon such circumstances as might occur in the defence of the individual, as to the extenuation of the offences.

Then you have no doubt that this person made out such a case before the Magistrates, as to warrant them in passing over the five different convictions that he had received in the course of that preceding year ?—I have no recollection of the circumstances of the case ; doubtless the Magistrates felt themselves justified, or they would not have done it.

There was another case, of which you said you would inquire, namely, the licensing a house in St. George's in the East ?—I stated at the time, that unless I could be informed of the name of the street, and also the sign of the house, it would be impossible for me to speak to it.

Then you do not know any thing more upon that subject than what you knew yesterday ?—Certainly not.

It has been stated to the Committee by different witnesses that have been summoned before it, that there is a general prevailing opinion in the Whitechapel Division,

Division, that a publican applying for a licence for a new house, finds the greatest impediments thrown in his way by the licensing Magistrates, unless he comes with the recommendation of Messrs. Hanbury and Co. ?—I believe that it is not true; it is to be considered that there are twenty-six licensing Magistrates, that a great portion of them attend at the licensing time, and it is not likely that the minds of those men would be pervaded with any such unjust principle.

Do you mean to state, that the fact itself is not true, or that the opinion is not true?—I am perfectly convinced that the fact as stated is not true.

It has been stated, not only that the fact is true, but that there is a generally received opinion that it is so; the fact you deny ?—Certainly.

Has it ever come to your knowledge that there was that impression on the minds of the publicans of your district?—No; excepting that I have heard people say, that if they had applied to the house of Messrs. Hanbury for their interest, they would perhaps have had better success.

Do you know, or can you furnish the Committee with an account of, the number of new houses that have been licensed, for a certain number of years?—No, I do not; but licences have been dealt out with a very sparing hand; the account required will be furnished as soon as the licensing clerks can make it out.

In point of fact, have there been many applications made to the Board of Magistrates by Messrs. Hanbury, for licences?—None by themselves personally, I believe.

Have their agents, Mr. Aveling, or any one else employed by them, made applications to the Board for licences?—I think not; it is not probable.

Then it never became a question at all discussed at the Board, as to the recommendation of particular individuals to receive their licences?—Never.

Then the sole question you have to discuss, and the sole question you do discuss is, whether the neighbourhood wants the public-house, and whether the character of the individual soliciting to establish one, is good or bad?—The principal object of Magistrates in licensing new houses, is first of all to see whether the neighbourhood requires such a house, and they decide upon the spot.

And the principle of that decision is, whether the neighbourhood wants the house?—Whether it is an accommodation that the public requires.

Then you take it upon yourself distinctly to say, that the influence and authority of Messrs. Hanbury & Co. and Messrs. Stables & Williams, in that district, has no more weight or effect over the Board of licensing Magistrates, than that of any other brewer or spirit dealer in the Metropolis?—I certainly so conceive it; because there are several other brewers and distillers in that District who are proprietors of public-houses.

Has it ever come to your knowledge that by far the greater proportion of those houses in that neighbourhood are held by Messrs. Hanbury, or that Messrs. Hanbury & Co. furnish them with beer?—I have never made inquiry into that subject.

Have you in point of fact ever heard that it is the case?—No, I have not. It is natural to conclude that a brewer of such eminence as Mr. Hanbury, residing upon the spot, will have more houses upon that spot than any other brewer.

Are Messrs. Stables and Williams, who are distillers, any relations of yours?—Messrs. Stables and Williams were not distillers.

What were they?—They were wine merchants, but are not now in business; the partnership has been dissolved about a twelvemonth.

Are they any relations of yours?—Mr. Stables is a nephew of mine.

Was their trade set up at your expense, or at Mr. Hanbury's expense?—I believe Mr. Hanbury never supplied an iota towards it in any way whatsoever.

Then it is within your knowledge that Messrs. Hanbury are the proprietors of most of the public-houses in that neighbourhood; that if not proprietors, they furnish them with liquor?—It is not within my knowledge any such thing.

Did you ever hear that such was the case, or do you believe it?—No, I do not believe it is the case.

Had you ever any conversation with Mr. Beaumont upon the subject of licensing a house in Whitehorse-lane Mile-End Road?—Mr. Beaumont has applied for the licensing two or three houses in that neighbourhood.

The Marquis of Granby is the one which is alluded to?—He applied for it, and it was refused.

Did you ever learn that he had offered that house to Messrs. Hanbury and Co.?—No.

510.   Did

Did he ever tell you he had offered to part with the house to them?—I do not recollect any such conversation; I have very little intercourse with Mr. Leaumont.

Have you never heard that terms were proposed by him to Messrs. Hanbury for the parting with that house?—No.

That he had received something in the nature of an understanding that the house would be licensed if Mr. Hanbury bought it, and that in consequence of that being declined by Mr. Hanbury, it was refused to be licensed?—I know of no such occurrence; the Magistrates assemble upon the spot, and determine whether such house shall be licensed.

It is not then the custom of the Magistrates to settle beforehand what houses they will license or not?—Certainly not.

Are you accustomed to meet the day before the licensing day, to determine what houses you will license or not?—Never any such meeting takes place; they are advertised, and a notice is sent to the different licensing Magistrates of the days of meeting and the time of meeting.

Then there is no meeting between particular Magistrates, of which you are one, the day before the licensing day, in order to determine what houses you will license or not?—No.

And that has never happened?—Never.

You have stated, that the partnership between Messrs. Stables and Williams is dissolved?—It is.

Do they carry on business separately?—No, they have retired from business.

When you commit persons to prison, where do you commit to; to what prison?—If they are for further examination, generally to the New Prison Clerkenwell, unless there is some particular circumstance that makes it necessary to keep them separated from others, and in such cases we send them to the House of Correction.

What is the distance from your Office to Clerkenwell?—I should suppose about three miles.

How are the prisoners conveyed backwards and forwards?—They are conveyed by an officer attached to the office, who executes the duties of gaoler, either in a coach or otherwise.

But generally they are marched two and two through the streets?—Yes.

Hand-cuffed?—I suppose so.

Did you ever examine the prison of Clerkenwell yourself?—Yes, I have.

What is your opinion of the condition of that prison?—That the greater part of it ought to be pulled down; that it should be extended, in order to accommodate the number of prisoners that are committed there. I should suppose it is known to the Committee that a meeting of the Magistrates did take place, in order to report to the County the state of that prison; and that Report was accordingly made, and a Plan annexed, for the removal of such buildings as were thought proper, and of making an additional building to hold 200 more than the building now contains.

Do you not know that in that prison there is no classification of prisoners at all, with the exception of the separation of male from female?—Certainly there is not.

Do you not consider that persons sent there for the first offence are rendered worse members of society when they come out than they were when they went in?—I certainly think they would not be improved.

Do you not consider that the prison, in the state in which it is now, is discreditable to the Metropolis?—I do; I have already expressed that as my opinion.

Do you think the vice of drinking to excess has very much increased within the last twenty years?—No, I do not think it has; in my own opinion I should think there has been a considerable diminution of that vice.

Do you not think there is a much less consumption of spirits than there was twenty years ago?—I should consider that the consumption of spirits must be much decreased; I have no doubt of it; and that the vice of intoxication among the lower ranks is not so frequent.

Jovis, 30° *die Maii,* 1816.

The Honourable HENRY GREY BENNET, in The Chair.

John Harriott, Esq. called in, and Examined.

WHAT is the nature and extent of your jurisdiction, as a Magistrate of the Thames Police office?—It comprehends the four counties of Middlesex, Surrey, Kent, and Essex, it extends all over these counties. Our powers are very large. We sometimes send into the Downs, and take people from ships of war; and sometimes send even to Harwich in Essex : in short it extends all over the four counties. We are under a specific Act of Parliament, and are distinct from all the other Police Offices.

John Harriott, Esq.

What is the extent of your establishment; I mean the strength of it?—The strength of our establishment is as follows : one principal surveyor, at a salary of 150 *l.* per annum; three surveyors at 90 *l.* per annum each; four surveyors at 80 *l.* each; three surveyors at 75 *l.* per annum each; and six surveyors at 65 *l.* per annum each. I must beg leave to observe here, that this rate of payment has been established only within the last twelve months, in consequence of an arrangement which has taken place at my recommendation to the Secretary of State, to make a distinction in the salaries to be paid to different classes of officers; for otherwise all the surveyors, except the chief, would have had no more than 65 *l.* per annum, and in rewarding them, no reference could be had to the question, whether they were of late or of long standing upon the establishment; no distinction could be made, whether their services were more or less meritorious, when they were all at one salary; I represented, therefore, to the Secretary of State, that I could not warrant our having such good officers, if we were not enabled to increase their allowances according to their merits. In consequence of that representation, the scale of allowance was extended; and I have the satisfaction to say that the arrangement has been attended with considerable advantage. It struck me that there would be no encouragement for exertion, if the principal surveyor was to have a large salary, and all the rest were to remain at 65 *l.* per annum, for in that case, no distinction would be made between the old and the new surveyors.

What is the nature of the duties of the surveyor?—All the surveyors are boat officers; they command a boat with a crew of two, three, or four men, according to their rate of standing, and abilities.

Be so good as to state what are the other officers of the establishment?—There are 43 watermen, at 23 *s.* per week; they are obliged to be paid weekly; two waterside watchmen, at 20 *s.* per week; five land constables, a messenger, and an office keeper, all at the same salary of 20 *s.* per week : the total strength of the establishment, therefore, amounts to 69 individuals. There are two clerks, and three magistrates.

State what the salaries are of the clerks and the Magistrates?—The Magistrates salaries are 600 *l.* per annum each; as to the clerks, I think the senior clerk's has been raised to 150 *l.* and the junior's, I believe, but I will not say exactly, is from 100 *l.* to 120 *l.*; that is the whole establishment as it now stands.

Do any of the Magistrates reside in the Office?—I do myself.

Do either of the clerks reside in the Office?—No.

There is an office-keeper, does he reside there?—Yes, there is an office-keeper, but he does not reside there; the clerks and the office-keeper merely attend in the day; I am the only person that resides in the Office. This establishment is quite distinct from all the other Offices, it proceeds upon what is called the *preventive* system; I speak of it from being the original founder and projector : it is a constant moving Police on the River, regularly changing their watches.

The Committee are then to understand that there is a regular watch, day and night, which watch is continually inspected at uncertain hours; and the greatest attention is paid, so that the different officers employed by the establishment shall be on their posts in the strict discharge of their duty?—Yes; a report is made to me every morning by the inspector : and if any fault is to be found, the officer is

suspended,

John Harriott, Esq.

suspended, or the case is put off to a further hearing, according to any case that is made out against the parties.

How long has this system, so acted upon, been established?—It has been established eighteen years, next June.

You were the founder of it?—I was the original projector of it; I suggested the idea, first to Mr. Colquhoun, and he first wrote to the Duke of Portland, to know whether it would be attended to or not: I first imparted the plan to Mr. Colquhoun, and he was so pleased with it, that he said if I would give him a copy of it, he would propose it to the Government; which I did, and he accordingly wrote to Mr. Dundas at that time upon the subject. It was laid before that minister, and then taken up for two years, under the sanction of Government, without being authorized by an Act of Parliament. The benefit appeared so great during that time the system was made permanent, and was reduced to an establishment by Act of Parliament, and has been continued from that time to the present.

Then you have found the greatest benefit arising from this establishment?—It would not so well become me to speak of its advantages; but the great commercial bodies bear the strongest testimony in its favour; the East-India Company, the Corporation of the Trinity-house, and all descriptions of men, down to the most insignificant, who are connected with property on the River, speak highly of it; indeed they have been wishing to extend our strength, and a great many applications have been made for the purpose of extending our power beyond the reach of our arm.

Do you mean by extending your strength, the increase of your number of officers, or the enlargement of your jurisdiction?—The jurisdiction must be the same, for it cannot well be extended beyond the four counties I have named.

Then what is meant by increasing your strength, is increasing your numbers?— When these gentlemen upon the River, to whom I have alluded, had suffered so much from the great number of robberies committed lower down the river, particularly below Blackwall, as well as above, they put in a plan, which was delivered to the Secretary of State, for increasing our strength, which plan now lies before the Government, and I believe the objection is, that it would be too expensive; at least I conceive that to be the objection. Four years ago, when I had the honour of being examined before the Committee upon watch and light duties, I then took the liberty of suggesting a similar preventive Police upon the land; for I feel confident, from the experience of this system, that it would be attended with the same success upon land, and particularly it would remove those two chief nuisances which are to be found upon the land, and to which the Police of the Metropolis is directed, namely, the removal of prostitutes and beggars. These nuisances would be removed if there was a moving Police upon the land day and night, as we have upon the River: that is my opinion of it; but at the same time, it is not for me to suggest what ought to be done.

Are you in possession of that plan; have you a copy of it?—I dare say I could find it; I gave it in to the Secretary of State, who has a copy of it, but I dare say I could find it.

Do the Clerks of your Office attend regularly?—Yes, they do. We have got two most excellent young men in the Office.

Do they hold any other situation besides that of clerk?—None, that I know of.

Do they practise as solicitors?—No; they are not in the law, nor do I want them.

How long have they filled their present situation?—I should suppose (but I am only speaking at a guess) that the one might have been there four or five years, and the other about twelve months before that.

Have you got with you any account of the expense of your establishment for the last year?—We are limited to 8,300 *l.* a year; I believe the penalties and forfeitures, and fees, upon the average of the last four years, which would go in part reduction of this expense, amount to 1500 *l.* per annum; so that the expense is so much short by that sum; and the average expense of the establishment to the public would be about 6,500 *l.* per annum.

Do the surveyors receive certain fixed salaries?—They receive a fixed salary, and they and the people under them are stimulated to exert themselves by a moiety of the different forfeitures and penalties.

Is that settled by Act of Parliament?—Yes; the other half goes towards reducing the expenses of the establishment; and the clerk who keeps these accounts,

and

and receives them, makes them out every quarter, and settles with the receiver, swearing him to his accounts.

John Harriott, Esq.

Do you consider that the fixed salaries paid to the surveyors, and officers under them, are sufficient to ensure the office proper persons to fill those situations?—That is, I confess, a doubtful question; I observed before, that we got the salaries very lately increased from the small sum of 65 *l.* per annum, according to the standing and merits of the men; so that the Magistrates might raise the common surveyors, in proportion to their merits, up to 100 *l.* per annum. Now it was with some difficulty that we got that; we are limited to 8,300 *l.* per annum. Now what they complain of is, that they are not on the same footing with people in a similar situation; for instance, as the officers of the revenue, in the excise and customs, who have nothing like the severity of duty to perform, as our men, although their allowances are much higher. There is a very tight duty to perform, and there is some difficulty in keeping them to it. It requires the active superintendence of one Magistrate to keep the system in a state of vigour; and I trust I may be allowed to say, after eighteen years experience, that I am the main key-stone of the plan. My superintendence of it is gratuitous. When I speak of the active superintendence of one magistrate, I mean that the superintendence must be performed by one, and one only; for if it was apportioned to three separately, they would be jarring, and counteracting each other.

Then the Committee are to understand, that of the three Magistrates of which your bench is composed, you are the person who may be considered as the principal superintendent?—Yes; the others who are there, are, comparatively speaking, but a few hours in attendance; the whole of the superintendence, to make the system effective, must necessarily be with one, and that one ought to be a person who has some nautical knowledge.

Do you not think that it would be a plan very much conducive to the public service, if the Magistrates had the power of giving specific rewards for the active services of the persons employed under them, though those services might not be attended with success in the detection of the particular crime for which they might have been employed?—There can be no doubt or question upon it, that that would be highly beneficial; and I can show it in this way: It frequently puts Magistrates to a very awkward and unpleasant strait, that when a person is brought forward, charged with an offence which subjects him to a penalty of some kind, there are circumstances which arise, of one description or another, that would make it more beneficial to the public to commit the person to prison for a week or a month, or whatever the time may be, instead of paying the penalty; then the officer gets nothing for his pains. That will at once show the advantage it would be, to give the officer some reward, notwithstanding the commitment. Now the Navy Board are so well aware of that, that in the number of convictions which take place for plundering the naval stores, indeed all the Government Offices, the Victualling, Ordnance, and all descriptions of Government Offices, but particularly the Navy Office, whenever that is the case, pay the moiety of the penalty themselves to the officer, when the Magistrates deem it more conducive to the public service to send such persons to prison. But we have no power to remunerate the officer in such case. There are cases where our officers have represented to us that they have been obliged, in cases where the most active police could not detect, to give informers some douceur; and although there may be no doubt of the guilt of the party accused, yet the case has failed, either for the want of some formality, or their not being able to make it out until it is too late. In such cases, the officers have been at an expense, and it has not been in our power to remunerate them.

Is the attendance of the different Magistrates regular in the Office?—That is a difficult question to answer in detail; but in general I can say, without difficulty, that the duties of the Office altogether are not exceeded by any other Office; I think I may venture to say that.

What are the office hours enjoined by the Act of Parliament?—The same as other Offices exactly.

Do you ever receive any assistance from the County Magistrates?—Never; I do not suppose I have seen a County Magistrate there these seven years. Formerly I used to have two or three to look in; indeed they cannot, for this reason, we are so locally situated, that we are more likely to want a Magistrate from Kent, Surrey, or Essex than from Middlesex, for the County Magistrates could not act with us in general, for the shores on both sides of the River are not within their

jurisdiction,

John Harriott,
Esq.

jurisdiction, so that they would be of no assistance whatever to us. I enter every thing down, myself, in a diary, of whatever comes into the Office, and every accidental occurrence that happens; I enter regularly the name of the culprit, the nature of the charge, the punishment, or whether he is discharged.

Have you found, within these late years past, that the offences committed on the River have been greater or less than in the years preceding?—This last winter, that I expected would be the worst, has been the calmest that I have ever known. They have been lessening gradually; indeed I may say for the last eighteen years they have been lessening. The River now, compared to what it has been, is as smooth as a millpond. No person can have any conception upon this subject, but those who are witnesses.

Do you keep up a correspondence with any of the different Police Establishments in the Metropolis?—Very little; if there is any thing that at all connects us with them, they communicate by sending their hand-bills to us.

But you have no other system of correspondence?—No; their system is so different from ours.

Do you not think that it would conduce very much to the detection and apprehension of offenders, if there was a species of Circular, that went round from your Office to all the different Offices in the Metropolis, and *vice versa*, stating therein some of the capital charges, or any of the particular occurences of the day, that might have been brought before the respective benches?—I believe that all which is necessary in that way is done; but it is little, and can be but little; I think that all that is necessary is really done; I never have occasion to send, at least very seldom. In short there has been a communication upon every thing necessary to communicate. Whether there may be any communication between the other Offices I do not know, we are so little connected with them.

Edward Markland, Esq. one of the Magistrates of Shadwell Police Office called in, and Examined.

Edward Markland,
Esq.

WHAT is the extent of your jurisdiction?—It takes from Poplar up to St. George's in the East. St. George's in the East is the first: then there is Shadwell: then comes the ambit of Ratcliff, which includes all Stepney, the parish of St. Anne Limehouse, and the ambit of Poplar and Blackwall. We have of late got Bow, which was formerly attached to Lambeth-street Office; but they favour us with a great deal of their custom now.

Is the duty performed by the Magistrates generally according to the provisions of the Act of Parliament?—I believe there has been no complaint at all; we have scarcely any *amateurs* come to see us; to be sure we are very distant, and therefore it may be too far to come to see us.

But it has never happened that a Magistrate has not been present in the hours, both of morning and evening, of business, regulated by the Act of Parliament?—I would not take upon myself to say *never*; but I should rather imagine the number of instances would not exceed twice in the course of the year.

No public inconvenience has occurred?—Never in the least; I have resided in the Office ever since I have been appointed; and as far as myself goes, I have never slept out of the house as long as I have been appointed.

Is the attendance of the Clerks regular?—Perfectly so; very commendably indeed.

Do they hold any other situations?—None in the least, that I know of.

Are they solicitors?—No.

They do not practise as solicitors?—Never, that I know of.

You have seven Officers?—We have eight constables: seven, and one who is called the gaoler; but he is a constable likewise, and an office-keeper.

Do you consider that number sufficient for the duty they have to perform?—I think, generally, the number is sufficient; I do not know that we would require any more.

Their pay is a guinea a-week?—Taking into consideration that pay, together with payment for extra trouble, it is calculated at 70 *l.* per annum to each man, that is, including service of warrants, and other things of that sort.

Have you any regulation in your Office in respect of any emoluments which they may derive, in the nature of perquisites or gifts, from persons coming to the Office to require their aid and assistance?—None in the least; whatever they have is gratuitous from the persons that employ them.

Do

Edward Markland, Esq.

Do you pay attention to the demands that are made by the officers for the extra services that they may be supposed to perform for individuals, to take care to secure that they shall not be exorbitant?—I never heard a complaint of that sort from any person in my life. Not having heard a complaint made, I never gave the subject any attention.

Do you know that they are in the habit of making these demands?—No, I have never heard of it; my answer would be, that I never heard of such a thing.

Then these eight officers perform their duty for the amount of the salary, which is 70*l.* per annum, and they do not receive gratuities from individuals?—I do not say that; if a person employs them to go and do any extraordinary business, or if they are called up at night, in consequence of any disturbance, to give their assistance, then I dare say they do give them something as a gratuity; but I do not know that they ever ask any thing out of the way, nor did I ever hear any complaint made that they did require any thing of the kind. There is another thing which they are authorized to receive, I mean what they receive upon convictions at the Old Bailey Sessions.

But that is taken into the account of the 70*l.* a-year?—Yes, it is.

Do you consider that the salary of one guinea per week, with the additional small allowances, raising it to 70*l.* per annum, is sufficient for their labour?—I do not; their attendance is very great.

What should you consider to be the proper salary?—I should think at least 100*l.* a-year.

Do you not think, therefore, that the salary being so small, it would have one of these two effects, either that the office would not obtain persons that were properly qualified to fill the situation, or that it would expose the public to the hazard of having the officers holding those situations tempted to a breach of their duty?—I should wish that they had better salaries; but I do not know that ever there has been any complaint of their doing wrong; I should much rather they had better salaries. But let me observe, that I have been there six years; I found them all there, but one; they are all old servants, and as respectable, indeed I may say the most respectable, of any Office in Town. I never heard a complaint against any one of them; I assure you I do not spare them; and certainly I understand to what your question alludes, namely, whether they might not let offenders escape for the time, that they might get hold of them after.

Do you not think that the smallness of the salary has a tendency to expose the officers to temptations?—Certainly it has, in the nature of things it may have that tendency; but I do not say it has had the tendency.

Do you not think that it would be a very good plan if the Magistrates had the power of rewarding the different officers in their department, for any specific duty that they might perform?—Do you mean rewards for the conviction of felons?

Yes?—I think that is better left as it stands by the law; the Magistrates would never satisfy them, if it was left to their discretion; indeed they would not be satisfied; there is a specific sum that they are to have, and they know that they are to have no more; probably the Magistrates might think it too much for the trouble they have had, and then they would cut them off, which would of course cause great disturbances and heartburnings: I hope the distribution of rewards will never be left to the Magistrates.

Do you not see that occasion may arise in which there may be the greatest exertions used, and yet there may be no detection?—Certainly.

Under these circumstances, do you not think that it would be very advantageous for the public service if the Magistrates had the power of specifically rewarding those officers who had meritoriously done their duty, though that duty might not have been successful?—We already have the power of remunerating services such as you refer to; for sometimes they have two or three pounds given to them when they have been very active and attentive, when they have been sent out of the county, down into Essex or elsewhere.

Then is not the payment of that money allowed as travelling expenses?—It is allowed as extra trouble, I think, for that it is put down; it is put down as payment for extra trouble, and a reward for apprehending offenders.

Do you think that the Magistrates have a sufficient power at the present moment of rewarding their different officers for any extra trouble they might have?—Whatever we have done has never been complained of; whatever we have done, we have sent the particulars to the receiver every month, with every particular and item,

which

Edward Markland, Esq.

which accounts, I dare say, are always laid before the Secretary of State for the Home Department, and we have never had any fault found; we have a very tight hand upon this subject; we are very cautious, for fear of being called over the coals.

You must observe this, that my question does not proceed upon the supposition that you have given too much; but I ask whether you think that you have sufficient power to reward your officers for the extra duty that they may perform?—Yes, I think we have; I think that upon the ground that I have stated; what we have done upon the subject has never been found fault with; probably if we gave more, it might have been passed over with the same silence.

Since you have filled the situation of a Magistrate of Shadwell, has it fallen under your observation that the offences which have been brought before you have increased, have been stationary, or have diminished?—Rather increased of late, within these two years.

Can you assign any reason for that?—The reason I assign is, that I think the world is growing more depraved every day, and the intoxication in liquor is the groundwork of it.

Do you think that the disposition to drinking amongst the lower orders of the people, is the cause of the increase of the number of offences?—I am decidedly of that opinion; I am perfectly satisfied that nine out of ten of the cases which come before me, the offender's excuse is, that he or she was in liquor, " I was intoxicated," is the expression; and the women are fully as bad as the men: in short, the gin-shops are filled.

Do you or either of your brother Magistrates attend to the licensing of public-houses in your district?—Sometimes.

Are the numbers of public-houses, gin-shops, &c. increased, within your knowledge?—In some divisions they are; in the division that is nearest us, namely, Shadwell, they increased three last year; I think there were 80 before, and there were 83 licensed last year.

Were you present at the licensing of those houses?—I was not, last year; the year before, I was. I have a list of the whole public-houses throughout the whole district, in which the number of inhabitants is taken out of Carlisle's Topographical Description, by which you will see the number of public-houses and inhabitants: This is the Account.

PARISHES, &c.	Number of Public Houses in each Parish	Population of each Parish, taken in 1801.
St. Mary Whitechapel - - - - -	114	23,606
St. George - - - - - - -	96	21,170
Bethnal - - - - - - -	90	22,310
St. Catherine's - - - - - -	26	2,652
Ratcliffe - - - - - - -	46	5,606
Christ Church - - - - - -	55	15,091
Poplar and Blackwall - - - - -	43	4,493
St. Botolph Aldgate - - - - -	38	6,153
Hackney - - - - - - -	50	12,730
Shadwell - - - - - - -	83	8,828
Mile-End Old Town - - - - -	45	9,848
———— New Town - - - - -	20	5,253
Shoreditch - - - - - - -	124	34,766
Wapping - - - - - - -	36	5,889
Norton Falgate - - - - - -	24	1,752
Bow - - - - - - - -	10	2,101
Bromley - - - - - - -	15	1,084
Limehouse - - - - - - -	36	4,678
Public Houses in 1815 - - -	951	188,730

Being about 198½ Inhabitants to a Public House.

Is

Is that Account correct?—Yes. There is one observation I would make in answer to the question put; the inhabitants of Shadwell, as the Committee will perceive by the Account, amount to 8,828 only, and yet the public-houses amount to 83; they will also observe, that in Norton Falgate the inhabitants are only 1,752, and yet the public-houses are 24; the public-houses are too many by one-third.

Edward Markland, Esq.

Can you explain to the Committee, whether there is any thing in the situation of the people of those two districts that you have named, which calls for an unusual or for a greater number of public-houses than in any of the other districts contained in that paper?—Certainly, Shadwell having such a number of sailors and ships, a greater number of public-houses is necessary; the whole shore of Shadwell is on the river Thames, and there are so many colliers and other ships, that a greater number is necessary than in other parishes; but Norton Falgate is a very long way from the Thames, and there are only 1,752 inhabitants, and 24 public-houses.

Is that in your district?—It is not, if I do not mistake; but with respect to the licensing business, it is in what they call the Tower Hamlet division, which belongs to Worship-street.

Is it your opinion that the number of public-houses is much greater than what the calls of the public require?—I think so; the increase this year is six, in the Tower Hamlet division.

Have you ever been present during the licensing of the public-houses?—Yes, I have been twice; I have been there two licensing days.

Were you there last year?—No, not this last September; I might drop in, but I did not go there for the purpose of business; I was engaged at the Office; that was one of my full days.

Do you know whether it is the custom in that division for any number of the Magistrates to meet before the licensing day, to settle what houses should or should not be licensed?—I believe it is usual throughout all England for the Magistrates to meet before the licensing day, for the purpose of receiving complaints from constables and officers, and inhabitants of the town, and likewise to receive proposals for new houses; that is done always every year, and I believe it is done at Whitechapel and Osborn-street, where the meeting is held for the purpose of fixing the days of meeting, likewise the days for hearing appeals and transfers of licenses for the whole year.

I dare say you have had better information upon the subject than we have; but certainly Sir Daniel Williams has informed the Committee in his evidence, that no such meetings are held?—Certainly he ought to know better than me; I never attended on the day, before, but I always understood there had been a day appointed for receiving complaints; I do not know that they do, but certainly it stands to reason that there must be some meeting of that kind, or how could the clerks have orders to issue summonses throughout the division, to attend upon particular days.

Do you recollect whether you were present in the year 1815, at the licensing day?—That was last year; I believe I dropped in for a little while.

You do not recollect any circumstance connected with the licensing the Marlborough Head public-house, Shoreditch, kept by a man named Charles Price, who was convicted five or six times of suffering tippling in his house?—I do not recollect any thing at all about that.

Are the number of public-houses that are within that district ever considered by the Magistrates as an excess, and that it would be a wise plan to diminish them?—No, I do not know that it has; I believe it is an opinion of my own, and I believe, contrary to the general opinion of my brother Magistrates, with whom I have conversed upon the subject, that the number ought to be diminished. They have a different opinion of public-houses than what I have; their opinion is, that a public-house once a public-house, should always be a public-house; I think differently. They think that a new tenant may come in, or an old one may be turned out, but that the house should continue a public-house always. That is a doctrine I do not concur in; and I think that when a landlord misconducts himself, he ought not only to be punished, but that the public-house should be put down.

In point of fact, have many complaints been brought before the Magistrates, of the conduct of the masters of public-houses in your Division?—I believe that the most that have ever been made, have been from my own township of Shadwell.

Were

Edward Markland,
Esq.

Were you present at the licensing days of 1813 and 1814, on which the licences were taken away from some of those public-houses?—I was.

According to your opinion, were any licences renewed, on those days, that ought to have been rejected?—Why certainly I thought that some ought not, because I voted against them.

Were there any strong cases laid before the Magistrates, sent by the church-wardens and the officers of the parish as well as by many respectable persons, setting forth the gross immoralities, indecencies, debaucheries, and vices of every description, that had taken place in those houses?—No doubt of it there were.

Was the subject discussed by the Magistrates?—As to discussing, I do not rightly understand in what sense the Committee means to use the expression; but the subject was taken into consideration.

Was it matter of discussion?—Certainly the churchwardens and parish officers and inhabitants attended and explained the matter very fully; I remember that very well.

Was there any considerable warmth upon the subject, between the different parties?—What parties?

The churchwardens and others on the one side, and the persons wishing to have their houses licensed, on the other; and did not the different Magistrates take different sides of the question?—I do not think the people were in the room who were complained against; but they were called in afterwards, and then told what the complaints were against them; I do not know whether they were in the room at the time; the Magistrates heard fully and deliberately every article of complaint, and formed their judgment afterwards.

But it was the subject of general canvass?—Yes; they cross-examined the parties, and entered fully into the subject.

According to your opinion, and the vote that you gave on that occasion in confirmation of that opinion, those houses ought not to have had their licences?—Certainly I voted against them.

Do you know whether those houses continue to be managed in the same way now?—I believe every house in the place is bad; I believe we have scarcely any but what are bad and immoral. What makes me think there are too many public-houses, is, that many of the publicans do not thrive in them; and one in particular that I could mention as an instance, namely, the Duke's Head in Old Gravel-lane, which belonged last year to Henry Pearce, who was licensed in September last year. Robert Dye succeeded him last year; afterwards Bean came in; and now one Morgan lives in it. Every one of these people, I believe, were selling ale and spirits without licence; for the transfer of licenses is only once in two months, therefore during the intermediate time the brewer gets hold of the house, and puts in a man till he can get another tenant to come in. So that we are entirely ignorant of the person who is actually the occupier; we do not know who are selling liquors, we do not know any thing about it; and, in short, it is a dead letter as to the idea of the Magistrates appointing tenants to public-houses. And no later than yesterday I was passing by a house which had been kept by a man named Peg, in Ratcliffe Highway, which had been licensed to him last year, and I found that he had disposed of the house, and upon looking over the door I saw the name of Williams painted upon it; I asked Williams, where he came from, and from whom he took the house; he said, he took it from Peg, and that he had come from St. Martin's in the West. Now this is a house that draws only five butts a month, therefore the man must inevitably stop. Why then the parish gets burthened with all these people. Therefore it is a grievance in two shapes; it takes it out of the management of the Magistrates, who cannot possibly know what people are put in; and secondly, the brewers may put in whom they think proper; in some cases they put a man into three houses as a *locum tenens.*

Do you not think that the system of the brewers connecting themselves, either by mortgage or by purchase, with the different public-houses in the Metropolis, is one highly injurious to the public?—I think so, decidedly.

Has any plan occurred to you, in which a change might take place beneficially, by legal enactment?—I cannot say that such a plan has occurred to me; the liberty of the subject would, I think, be infringed, if you were to say, you shall not have a public-house, or shall not be interested in such property. It is past my view,

and

Edward Markland, Esq.

and I must leave it to wiser heads. The Legislature will not let them act as Magistrates in the licensing of public-houses; and I wish that they had not so many public-houses as they have, for in some instances they act with great severity and cruelty.

Do you know whether there are in your own District a great number of public-houses under the control and management of particular brewers?—I do not, so as to particularize them.

Have you ever heard it to be the opinion entertained in the district in which you attend to license the public-houses, that if a victualler comes there with a recommendation from a particular brewer, he has a better chance of getting a licence, than if he comes without?—Why I don't see hardly how that can be known, for when I have been there, I have been satisfied that every man has been licensed as a publican, with reference to the number of houses in the district; and it is impossible to know where he got his licence. Such, however, is the opinion entertained in the district; but I do not know that it is well founded. I infer the reason why the question is asked. The opinion is so; but I do not know whether it is well founded, or not. I know that some houses are so recommended and supported, but I do not know that they have the greater share of favour on that account. It has been held out by the brewers to be so, for a particular purpose.

For the purpose of creating custom, and giving the house a name?—Yes.

Have the number of spirit-shops increased in your district within these few years?—There are very few spirit-shops; but there are a vast number of public-houses and alehouses, all of which must have spirit licences.

Are you aware that though by law dealers in spirits are obliged to have beer licences, yet in point of fact there are many of those houses that sell no beer?—I have been told that there is one or two; but I do not know it for a fact myself.

Have you any doubt that the multiplication of those spirit-shops is highly injurious to the morals of the public?—That is decidedly my opinion.

Is there any regulation in your Office, that the public-houses should be closed at particular hours of the night?—The orders are, eleven o'clock.

Do you believe that those orders are generally executed?—There are houses, which are called watering-houses, in which they claim some privileges; I do not know why, but because hackney coaches stand there, and I am afraid they are open all night. But the generality shut up by twelve o'clock; I believe they do.

Are there any houses in your district that are technically known by the name of flash-houses?—No, I do not know of any.

In which thieves assemble, and which are notorious receptacles for common thieves?—No, I do not know of such houses by that name: that was the most notorious, which I have already mentioned, that had four landlords; and it might not be amiss to mention, that whilst Mr. Dye was the landlord, in the course of a very short time I committed two persons out of that house, who are now under sentence of death, one for robbing a man of notes to the value of 200*l.* and the other to the value of 24 *l.* How Mr. Morgan conducts himself I do not know, but I shall make it my business to inquire.

Has that house long had a bad character?—No, I do not know that it had; at least it was not so notorious as to come under my cognizance till now.

Of course you would feel it to be your duty, in case a house was of notorious bad character for the reception and encouragement of abandoned people of both sexes, to resist the renewal of the licences on the licensing day?—Certainly; I make a minute, before the licensing day comes, on the list of the public-houses, when any thing comes before me which is matter of complaint against the publican; and before the licensing day arrives, I have the minute copied out, and sent to the chairman of the Magistrates who attend, and he takes cognizance of the complaint; this was the case with respect to the three public-houses alluded to.

Are these recommendations upon the subject of not renewing the licence, generally attended to?—Why they are, by giving the parties a reprimand, or something of that sort; but I do not think that that has much effect; I think a little more severity ought to be used; but that is matter of opinion amongst the Magistrates.

But is it not the practice of the Magistrates to attend to these reports of the different Magistrates of the Police within their jurisdiction, when these reports are unfavourable to the character of persons holding public-houses?—They always are attended to; and the men against whom the complaints are made, are put off

until

Edward Markland,
Esq.

until the last day of licensing, when the licence is suspended, the parties are reprimanded, or the licence is taken away, just as it happens.

Is it a frequent occurrence at the period for renewing licences, for the Magistrates to take away the licence?—Why, at the last licensing day there was not a single one taken away, at least I believe not; the year before, there were three renewed; and the year before that, these same three were taken away. But I believe in my district, that the greatest attention which the Magistrates might use, or the greatest severity which they could exercise, would not keep the public-houses free from some objection or other.

Should you consider that if you made a special report against a particular public-house, setting forth that it was the resort of thieves and persons of bad character, you would be secure that the Magistrates would deprive that person of his licence for keeping a house of such description?—No, I do not think I should, since I should have no more than my own vote.

Should you not think that as a Police Magistrate, reporting on the conduct of the publicans within your jurisdiction, that your reports, unless rebutted by positive contradictory evidence, should have such weight?—I think they would pay me the compliment to think so, but I do not think they would allow it.

Do you not think that the good of the public service would be much advanced if they did?—Certainly, if they thought upon the whole that the complaint was well founded.

I mean to ask you, if you do not think that a report from a Police Magistrate, whose peculiar province and duty it is to attend to such matters, in which he sets forth that such and such public-houses are the resort of thieves and persons of bad character, that that report ought to ensure, on the part of the Magistrates, that the persons holding such public-houses should lose their licences?—Certainly I do think so.

Did you find any complaints last year against any public-houses?—Nothing very serious; I believe I did make some observations upon some gambling; but nothing serious, nothing that required the severity of putting a stop to the licence, merely a reprimand.

I see in the paper before me, a person whose office is called that of a gaoler; have you a gaol?—The officer has always gone by that name; he is one of the constables, who has the care of the prisoners, and he is not one of those who serve the warrants; he is always in attendance to bring the prisoners from the great distance which our Office is from Clerkenwell and Coldbath Fields prisons, which is really one man's work.

What prison do you send persons to?—Generally, for petty crimes, to the New Prison Clerkenwell, and for felonies to Newgate.

Are you aware of the state of Clerkenwell prison?—I never was in it.

What is the distance between Clerkenwell prison and your Public Office?—It is all through the City; it must be three miles and an half; it is nearly two miles to the Mansion-house.

Do the prisoners walk from the Office to the gaol?—If they like to have a coach, and pay for it, they may have it; if not, they must walk; in case of their being infirm, we order a coach, and put it to the account of the Office.

Jovis, 6° *die Junii*, 1816.

The Honourable HENRY GREY BENNET, in The Chair.

William Fielding, Esq. one of the Magistrates of Queen's-square Police Office, Examined.

WHAT office do you belong to?—The Queen's-square Police Office.

What is the extent of your jurisdiction?—We comprise St. Margaret's and St. John's Westminster; and going on westward, it includes Chelsea, which comes within our particular district; Kensington and Hammersmith; then going on eastward, it includes St. Martin's-in-the-Fields and St. James's, which last parish is more immediately within our special district. We may go on to St. Clement Danes, to St. Paul's Covent-garden, and to Soho; but the greater part of these last parishes are taken up by the jurisdiction of Marlborough-street and Bow-street Offices. I have not mentioned Mary-le-bone, although within our special jurisdiction at our Quarter Sessions, therefore Mary-le-bone may stand for Soho.

Do you consider the number of persons that you have attached to your Office, as Police officers, as sufficient to keep the proper watch and ward for the Police of that extensive district?—I certainly cannot think the present establishment by any means sufficient to such purposes; but if I may be now permitted, as I was lately, by the Chairman of the Mendicity Committee, I will take the liberty to suggest a single and most simple alteration in the construction of the Police; by introducing a new character, between the high and the petty parish constable. If such a character were appointed, and if there were one in every parish within the Police districts, a new and vast efficiency would be introduced to the Police, and most especially with regard to the objects of the Mendicity Committee.

Be so good as to explain the nature of the appointment, and the duties that would belong to this new officer, whom you propose to be established?—I would call him the Superintendent Constable, to have power and authority over all the inferior constables; he should be immediately attached to the Police Office, appointed by the Magistrates, and to have his particular duties assigned by them; and by way of facilitating the thing, instead of waiting for them to be appointed, either by an Act of Parliament, by the Court Leet, or by the Sessions, I should suggest their immediate appointment, which I think might take place under the provisions of the Police Act, with the approbation of the Secretary of State for the Home Department. That noble Lord, if it should please him, might have the nomination and appointment of such officers; but if it were to please him, I should think it would be more efficacious to leave us, the Magistrates, to find out the proper individuals for such situations. I took the liberty of suggesting this proposal to the Chairman in the Mendicity Committee; this new character should be amply paid. He would not have any of the inferior duties of the Police constable to perform; such as serving warrants, or being obliged to go on the different messages of the Magistrates; but he would be called upon to exercise a constant surveying vigilance throughout the parish. With respect to the mendicity of the town, his services would be very important; for he would be employed frequently to inspect and regard, and clear away all public and bye places, thoroughfares, and of all nuisances; for instance, such as are to be found at the doors of pastry cooks shops, &c. &c. I would name (for example) *Farrance*'s, where the foot passenger may see a vast number of nuisances assembled in front of the door. Women with children begging, or pretending to carry baskets with some sorts of wares to sell. If such a character therefore as this were appointed, a part of his duty would be, to clear the streets and such public places, from this kind of nuisance.

Would you place under his controul the different watchmen of the parish?—I should think that should be a part of his duty, and which might be brought into very considerable advantages; I think that if he had the superintendence of the watch, and the superintendence of the constables, vast improvements would follow.

The appointment of watchmen is under the superintendence of the high constable for each district?—Not so; that business is chiefly under the immediate

management

William Fielding, Esq.

William Fielding,
Esq.

management of the parish officers, the vestrymen, as they are called; but the vestrymen are but too often apt to oppose the Magistrates in their business; they wish to have a degree of bashawship amongst themselves.

Do you not know that the different parishes of the Metropolis thought, when the Committee of the Police sat in 1812, and suggested the propriety of bringing in the bill into Parliament, commonly called the Bill for the Watch and Ward of the Metropolis, that there ought to be no interference on the part of the Legislature in the Police, with regard to the appointment of the constables?—I know that such a species of jealousy exists in every parish throughout all the town; but I would make this observation; that where the parishes have select vestries, where they have such a select vestry, as in the parish of St. George Hanover-square, where a vast number of educated people attend the vestry, nothing of that sort is to be feared; but in our immediate parishes, I have known myself, that there was the greatest degree of inclination to spurn, as it were, at the authority of the Justices; and they like to do all this business themselves, namely, to appoint every watchman, and have as much power as they can.

Have you any doubt that one of the causes of the deficient Police, touching the state of the streets of the Metropolis, is very much owing to the bad selection of watchmen by the different parishes in the Metropolis?—I have no doubt.

Have you any doubt that a better regulated establishment of watchmen would be one of the means of correcting this evil?—Most assuredly, I have none.

Then the Committee are to understand, that your proposal of appointing a Superintending Police Constable, and of placing under his management and control the different watchmen of his parish, would be one of the means by which those evils would be remedied?—Assuredly.

What would be the amount of the salary that you would consider sufficient for this Superintendent?—If I may take the liberty of suggesting an idea upon such a subject, it would be this:—our officers at present are paid 52 guineas a year, that is one guinea a week; they have, in addition to this, their profits arising from the service of warrants, summonses, and many other things that afford occasional emolument, which it is not necessary now to mention; if they were allowed, therefore, 52 guineas a year, and if they have the additional emolument arising from the service of warrants and other accidents that employ them, which altogether may not possibly produce them too large a reward for the duty they perform; I should think, that in order to make these new superintendent officers as serviceable as they ought to be, they should be paid higher; not much more than 2,000 *l.* would be required for the whole energy so proposed; for a salary to such officers, 80 *l.* 90 *l.* or 100 *l.* would hardly be thought too much. A very decent man, perhaps a shopkeeper, a person capable of doing every possible duty to be required, might be found, by the vigilance of the Magistrate.

What do you think the place of a Police officer in your establishment is annually worth?—It is very difficult for me to say exactly, but I should suppose that one, two, or three of them may, by accident, make perhaps, taking the whole year together, about 100 *l.*; several of them receive very much short of that; I should really think, that the average value of the place is not to be rated at more than 80 *l.* or 85 *l.* per annum.

You say the value of these places is made up of different ingredients; there is the standing salary, in the first place; there is the share of rewards and service of warrants, in the second; and there is, in addition to these two sources of emolument, the money which individuals may receive from private persons, for what may be termed extra duty; for of course the more intelligent officer will be more constantly employed, and will therefore make the greater annual emolument. Do you not then think that the most intelligent officer of your department makes more than 100 *l.* per annum?—I think, occasionally, that has certainly happened; I think that one, two, three, it may have happened that there have been four men, that have more than 100 *l.* certainly; and I think, that sometimes from accidents, as for instance, men of fortune who have occasion to employ an officer for particular business, will sometimes give him money.

Is it not the frequent practice of individuals coming to your Establishment for the assistance of Police officers, to fee the officers whom they employ?— I think they might do that, for I think the officers would neither be so active, diligent or earnest, if they were not. There is a limit with respect to fees received by the officers. There is a certain distance to be gone by a man serving a warrant for a shilling.

Those

Those fees that fall upon the general class of mankind, in particular cases, shall not be exceeded by the rules of the Office.

William Fielding, Esq.

Do you consider yourselves as Magistrates, as in duty bound to watch over and control the excessive payment of these gratuitous fees to the Police officer?—Most assuredly; and I would say, with regard to my brother Magistrates and myself, that instances have arisen, where expectation has been carried beyond our approbation; and we have constantly endeavoured to bring it within the most moderate and most allowable shape; we have frequently overruled and dissuaded officers in our Office, against all extravagant expectations of that sort.

Do you not generally consider that the salary of the Police officers is small?—Certainly, I do.

So that if it were not for these occasional resources, by which they receive additional emolument, you would find it difficult to obtain in your Office, proper persons for the price the Establishment pays?—Certainly so; and I will just enumerate a few instances, from which your mind must draw the same conclusion that I form. First of all, they are expected to be clean in their persons; in the next place, they are expected to live as near as they can to us; they have therefore their lodging to pay. They have to keep themselves in this cleanliness that I have mentioned, and there are several other circumstances, which made me take the liberty of saying, that I thought they were not over-paid with 52 guineas a year; and if I may take the liberty of breaking into your question, I would go on further, to add; I understand that the Committee that were assembled last year or the year before, had gone some length into an inquiry into the subject of the rewards paid upon the conviction of offenders, I mean Parliamentary rewards for the higher offences, such as burglary, highway robbery, and so forth. Sometimes, if such offenders are met with by the officers, they obtain rewards upon their conviction; but I understand it to be the opinion of the gentlemen of your House, that rewards ought to be given, especially to men who have deserved them from their activity, whether the event take place as to the conviction, or not;—that whatever may be the event, a reward ought to be given; and that the Magistrates should have the power of giving such reward. In my opinion, that would be a much better thing than the Parliamentary rewards, which are given only in the event of conviction.

Do you not think that it would be of much more advantage to the public service, if the Police officers were paid for special services, than by having any share in the different Parliamentary rewards which are settled by statute?—Certainly, I do think so; I am an old counsellor, and have practised a good deal in criminal courts, and I have uniformly found, that when it was necessary to call a Police officer to the establishment of a particular fact, or of any material part of the case, and the idea of reward struck the Jury, so misguided were they, that it was the means of the failure of justice in a great number of instances, under the silly idea of disappointing the officer of his reward, and therefore not giving to his evidence the weight that it ought to have received; and many times I have seen that, in opposition to the best direction of the Judge.

Do you think that the system of Parliamentary rewards has another effect; namely, that without supposing that Police officers of any one of the departments neglect their duty, yet that it might happen, that where emolument was to be got by the conviction of a person, a certain degree of carelessness towards offences where nothing was to be obtained, would be the natural consequence on the part of those officers?—First of all, if you would permit me to take occasion again to state the impression of my mind, as to the useful application of the new character or description of officer that I have mentioned:—Upon the subject of Mendicity, there is a reward, by the 17th of Geo. II. for a constable or other person that will bring before the Magistrates any person, so that he shall be convicted of being a vagrant, amounting to the sum of ten shillings. Sorry I am to say, that this stimulus has not the effect which the Legislature intended; for in many cases it has failed altogether, and has given way to an entirely new practice; for the constable had rather give up the expectation of receiving such a sum, than hazard the consequences of the indignation of the mob in prosecuting such a person, or bringing him before the Justice. In this and some other cases which may be alluded to, there is the very objection raised by the multitude that arises in the minds of Juries, namely, that the officer is an informer, and that he informs from the hope and expectation of obtaining the reward to be given by the statute. That opinion has gone abroad in the world, and will, I fear, continue to be the opinion of the world; but still we know of no other means by which

many

William Fielding, Esq.

many offences can be met or prevented, or the offender brought to justice, than through the medium of information, and the penalty upon conviction by information will be the general motive of the informer. In very many principal cases, informations form especially a part of the Magistrate's jurisdiction; but we take care, as much as we can, that the informer shall by no means become a witness. The reward has, indeed, in a great number of instances, a tendency to produce informations, in cases where the jurisdiction over certain offences is confined to the Magistrates. Certainly informations cannot be altogether done away with; but the more it was possible to do away with them, the better in general would it be, with a view to the interests of the poorer classes.

Of course then, it is your opinion, that the system of Parliamentary reward, would have this effect; (without meaning to say any thing against individual officers) that it would have a tendency to prevent officers from paying that due attention to the suppression of criminals in the commencement of their career, because till they had committed those crimes for which the Act of Parliament gave a reward upon conviction, the officers would not do their duty, until they were certain of obtaining the reward upon the conviction?—That possible consequence must naturally as well as logically be admitted. The general supposition that has gone very largely abroad in the world is, that the officer of the police who might have immediately the custody of the offender, until he has done something that will produce a reward upon his conviction, will not touch him; that is the prevalent idea amongst the people. I myself have no idea that such principle has ever been acted upon; at least, I do not know, of my own knowledge, that it has; but the prejudice of the world is to that effect. If that, therefore, was the case, it must have a tendency to the prejudice of the officer's character, who could be influenced by such considerations. Hence, and almost alone, the observable tendency to affect the minds of jurymen in the administration of justice. If the system of reward now suggested were adopted, it would operate to remove that prejudice against the character of officers, who would have more satisfaction in himself from the conscientious discharge of his duty, and would feel more caution in his conduct through life; and not being the subject of such prejudicial remark, he would act fairer and with more energy towards the public.

May you not add to that answer, that you have been a witness in a great many cases, where this feeling of the Jury has operated to the prejudice of public justice? —Many, many times; the law of the land that has precluded an interested person from being a witness, is a question of great delicacy; and in very many instances we are obliged in the administration of our duties, to admit the testimony under Acts of Parliament, of witnesses whose evidence could not be received in a Court of Justice in civil matters; such evidence would be rejected in civil matters. Undoubtedly, in some cases the Magistrate is called upon to exercise very unpleasant duties; and they often have to consider the powers given them as very unfortunate. Certainly, we are often obliged to admit evidence into the establishment of offences which come before us, that operates contrary to the fair exercise of our best powers and delicacy. We do all we can, however, to keep the officer as pure as we can.

Has any plan ever suggested itself to your mind, of establishing a better system of preventive Police, than what at present exists, independent of the one which you have mentioned, namely, a Superintendent Constable in each parish?—Principally, my thoughts have been turned upon the efficience of such a superintendent character, forming the most beneficial preventive imaginable of crimes, at once simple and most powerful. May I take the liberty of suggesting another thing, which I communicated to Mr. Perceval very shortly before his death; I likewise did so to a Captain Manby, who has been much noticed for his mathematical exertions, desiring him to make use of the idea, or avail himself of it as his own. The suggestion was this; there are upwards of 15 insurance offices against fire, in London; I suggested, that if two firemen from every one of those insurance offices, were to traverse up and down the streets of the Metropolis every night, they would cross one another often and often. Let every man be provided with his axe and his link or flambeaux; then this would be such effective means of security from fire, that the public would be highly pleased with such an establishment. It would be equally beneficial to the offices themselves, for it would be a vast provision against the accidents of fire; for these men, upon the discovery of a fire, might proceed with their axes, and with their lights, into the houses where the accident occurred. Another thing I should take the liberty of suggesting, is,

that

that these two men in their walks about the town, should have, under the authority of the Magistrates in the different districts, the office or power of constables.

William Fielding,
Esq.

Is there not an establishment already in existence in London, known by the name of the Fire Patrole?—I do not know that there is.

Can you give the Committee any general information upon the subject of Fire Police?—I cannot.

Is there not a reward paid at the different Police Offices to the firemen for the execution of their duty?—Yes; to the first engine, not comparing the time of the fireman's arrival with any knowledge that he derived of the time when the fire began, but only being the first engine, we have the power of giving 30 *s.* ; then we give also to the second and to the third, to which at least we give 10 *s.* ; but the man who is called the turncock for the water, is likewise entitled to a reward.   It sometime happens that a long space of time elapses before water is to be found.

Can you state any particular of any culpable delay on the part of the fire offices, in sending out engines in case of fire?—I know only, that at some times there has been a scarcity of water; I know that our parish engine of St. Margaret's has generally been very active, and generally acts with the greatest alacrity.

Has it ever occurred to you, that it would be advisable to re-model the different offices of Police that are at present established, making one as central Police Office in chief, and the other as subordinate?—It never has entered into my consideration, that there could be any real and important benefit resulting from such central situation; the ultimate utility would be trifling.

Do you not think, that one of the advantages to be derived from such an establishment, would be a more intimate correspondence, not only with the different provinces, but, what is more important, in the different parts of the Metropolis, so that one general system of watching might be established?—The more frequent the intercourse that existed amongst us would be all the better.

In the different parishes of the Metropolis, the office of constable is one of fatigue, and for which no payment is made.   Do you not think, that if payment somewhat of the same nature which takes place in respect of the constables which are employed by the Police, was made to the parish constables, that you would thereby collect a small army, if I may use such a phrase, that might be called out in case of any sudden tumult in each parish?—Most unquestionably; as without (looking upon the essential stimulus of payment) it would be in vain to expect activity, vigilance, or vigour, in the discharge of such duties.

The petty constables are not under the Police Magistrates?—No; no more than that they have the control and authority over them; they are obliged to execute the Magistrates warrants.

Do you know how many constables are appointed for the city and liberties of Westminster, that are sworn in by the High Steward?—I believe 18; that is 13 for St. Margaret's, and 5 for St. John's.

Do you not consider that number as much inferior to the wants of the public?— Indeed I do.

Have you any doubt, that a better arranged establishment of constables ready for public service on public emergencies, would be one of the means of doing away the necessity of calling in upon all occasions the assistance of military force?—It might have some operation most assuredly.   The delicacy of calling in military force ought at all times to be considered by the Magistrates; but if I, as a Magistrate, should think there was a necessity for calling for it, and that there was an appearance of danger to the public, I should think it necessary to do it.

Have you any doubt, that the system such as has been followed for many years past, of so small a civil power, so little suited as it is to the increasing population and wants of the Metropolis, has had a tendency to put the civil power out of this use; to make it little considered as an efficacious means of remedying public danger, and in a manner to compel the Magistrate, on the first symptom of public danger, to look alone to the military for protection?—I really conceive, according to my own experience all through my life, that upon the real existence of any tumult, and there was a probability of any neighbourhood contributing to that tumult, that all the Police which we now have, or could have, with the addition of every different officer, would be inadequate to the thing.   And I think that the whole Police power, supposing it were double, would be an inadequate body upon which to place full reliance.   I also think, that for the purpose of public peace, an early appearance of the military would be dreaded, and under that dread much benefit might

be

William Fielding,
Esq.

be expected; always supposing that the Police will first of all be tried to ascertain the point of safety; but if danger seemed to threaten beyond that point, I should think, as a Magistrate, I should best perform my duty by thinking of and immediately calling out the military energy.

Do you not see, that if cases should arise, and in your recollection many must have arisen, in which an active body of Police, to be drawn from that class of the community forming the householders, more particularly interested than any other class in the suppression of disorder or whatever may tend to the disturbance of the public peace; that an assemblage of those persons, for the purpose of early putting down a tumultuous concourse of even a few individuals, which is the origin of every disturbance that arises, would be a much better mode of putting down such disturbances, than instantaneously, as has been the custom for many years past, of calling in the assistance of the military?—No doubt can be entertained upon the question you ask. If a powerful Police could be collected more early, the effects you speak of would attend it. I recollect what passed in the riots of the year 1780. It happened to me to see a great deal of those riots; and I remember that when the house of my uncle, Sir John Fielding, was destroyed by the mob, if there had been only ten constables there at the time the riot commenced, it would have been most certainly saved. And I remember well, that when my Lord Mansfield's house in Bloomsbury-square was entered, that if there had been a band of constables stationed there at the origin, that would have had a very considerable power of preventing the accumulation of that species of mob which was soon collected; it having begun by an assemblage of the young and thoughtless only. First it began with ten, to that ten were added another ten, that produced forty, and so on to the immense number that were then collected.

Have you any doubt, that a domestic parish arrangement might take place in every parish of the Metropolis, by which the constable shall be placed under the Superintendent Constable that you have named; that Superintendent Constable should be under the Police, by which means a daily attendance of the constables would take place, preventing thereby the nuisances which at present infest the streets; and in case of public disturbance, the whole body might be called out, interposing, in the first instance, their strength to check any riotous disturbance?—I certainly think, that this very officer that I took the liberty of supposing would be the means of keeping, at all times, in the utmost readiness the whole force that could be called forth of the Police; that it would be the means (and it is perfectly new in the idea) of having his eye over all the additional constables that might be appointed; over all the special constables that we might appoint, to whom we pay 5 s.; and that he should be the man under whose authority we should place even our own immediate men appointed at the Office; and I think that that would be a species of officer who would produce the same sort of efficiency that is produced in the army by the serjeant and the corporal, for they are the people upon whom the military officers rely for the strict execution of their regulations; so with respect to the Police; for this class of officer would carry our orders into execution; he would be a kind of superior man, always kept in activity, to know the strength of his parish, how to muster them, and to call them forth.

How many years have you been in the Police?—My father, Henry Fielding, was an old Magistrate. God knows, I have seen a good deal of the Police of the Metropolis; I am a very old Magistrate for Westminster; I have been near fifty years standing in the commission; but I was not appointed to the place which I now hold in the Police until about eight years ago. I have been eight years this June appointed.

From your observation since you have been acting as a Magistrate, do you think that the morals of this Metropolis are in a state of improvement; that they are stationary, or are on the decline?—It must indeed be upon the merest conjecture that my answer will be built; but I really think, that from the increasing wickedness of the times, from the increasing gin-drinking, from the dirt, and the overpowering multitude of children that are in every part of the town, without our being able to clear the streets of the thousandth part of them, that there must be a vast increase of immorality, most assuredly.

Do you then consider that the increase of crime, which, according to the different returns that have been laid before Parliament, seems at present to be an established fact, proceeds from a positive diminution of public morals, or from an increase of population?—Most assuredly, from the increase of the profaneness of the times, and from the increase of a very profligate population, which has met with no impediment,

nothing

William Fielding, Esq.

nothing to correct it. It is going on now as it was before, notwithstanding all our vigilance and particular care, to prevent every youth from idling about the town who has the least likely appearance of being a dishonest lad; but having done that, and having all our views and exertions fail upon the subject, and knowing that this parish of St. Margaret's at this moment contains such a herd of these little vagabonds, and there being nothing in existence by which we can get rid of them, I therefore conclude, that the increase of immorality proceeds from the increase of population.

Do you think that that class of society, meaning the lower, the idlers of which may be considered as the profligate class, as they are in all other classes, that that class is more indigent than formerly?—I think that the town has now a body of people that must be more indigent than they were before such an increase of population, the poor children now being in such vast numbers, their parents have not the means, nor have the Magistrates the means, of providing them with work in the common way. With respect to apprenticing them, even if it was the wish of their parents to put them out as apprentices, there is not enough of that. To be sure, there is less of apprenticeship now, notwithstanding the increase of population, than there was only a few years ago.

Do you think that within your district, or your means of knowledge, that there has been a much greater supply of workmen within these few years, than there has been work for them to do; or that latterly work has been taken from them, in consequence of the badness of the times, which was given to them before?—I cannot think the work has been taken from the people immediately within our view: We have had a good many workmen upon the river Thames, particularly about Vauxhall Bridge. These public works have certainly employed many, nor has work ever been taken from them. Occasionally stoppages have taken place, but only at particular periods. We see however in our view, brought together here, a vast number of poor wretches, applying to us for passes; it is miserable to see them. We see amongst them a vast number of people, who having parishes, are still capable of work, and who rather want work than an inclination to go to work; the majority of them, I believe, would gladly work if they could be employed; and certainly at present there is a general complaint of the want of work. In our particular view, we see hundreds that would probably betake themselves to work, if there was work for them.

Is there a greater number of juvenile depredators brought before your office than formerly?—Certainly; oh, certainly.

Do you consider that number to be the result of a greater demoralization of the people, or that they themselves have become more indigent?—I think they have become worse in point of morals, from the increased associations of those profligate youth; and it has been worse, year after year. We have several times had all the vagabond boys that were to be found, perhaps, in the whole range of St. Martin's in the Fields, brought before us. We have not had them before us upon charges for any particular crimes, but only for such offences as probably attach to them, under the denomination of disorderly. To send them to prison would be cruel; and there is no way of providing for them; but if there was a mode of sending them either to America, to the Cape of Good Hope, or to the West India Islands, we have an opportunity of taking 500 amongst them; and I am sure the Magistrates could very speedily supply those places with inhabitants if they were wanted.

Do you know, within your district, of the establishment of that class of brothel which is devoted to children alone, and in which no grown-up person can obtain admittance?—I do not; I know we have a species of brothel of the very worst kind; and we often think the benefit it would be to society, if we could effect the suppression of them. The indictment of them by the parishes would be expensive; and the keepers of them are so miserable themselves, that it is hardly worth proceeding against them by such means. This parish being so immediately a station of the Guards, there will be always enough of such houses. I have heard of there being two or three places, but where they are situated I have not been able to learn, where the youngest creatures are the chief objects of frequenting those houses; but I have not been able to find out any of them yet.

You do not know, then, of houses in which they make up considerably more than a hundred small apartments, built round two courts, and which are entirely devoted to the use of children?—Certainly not.

510.   Are

William Fielding, Esq.

Are there not great difficulties in putting a stop to the establishment of houses of this description, and putting down bad nuisances of that sort?—Certainly there are; I do not know that you have ever seen the process of burning out the keepers of a brothel. When I was at the Temple this was established as a scheme for that purpose, and it took place in the little allies near Temple-bar. They set two men with lamps, before the door, they did not prevent the people going in, but the intention of this was to try the effects of shame, and the curiosity that this excited among the spectators, prevented persons, from a sense of shame, to enter the house; and even the most hardened and profligate did not go into them; and by these means the bad houses were knocked up. Some of them would not subsist longer than a week, some not above a fortnight. This was the practice which subsisted when I was a Templar, and certainly it appeared to have the effect; and from time to time men were appointed to visit those houses in the same way once in every six months. That expedient, probably, would have the same effect now; but by way of coming at the regular and respectable witness, who can command the credence of the Jury; it is very difficult to find such persons, such witnesses do not like to give away their time, and others do not like to be seen in such cases. Sometimes, a father who has a child, probably abused in such places, he will go through the whole prosecution, and not spare the expense of obtaining a conviction. But in general, amongst other people in this town, there is a great reluctance to come forward as witnesses in such cases.

Is it then your opinion, that unless in case of a private individual suffering, there is a difficulty in finding persons of respectable character as witnesses, whose evidence would be such, as to induce a Jury to find a verdict against these houses?—As to insure a verdict of conviction; I allow there may be a great number of cases in which verdicts have been given against such houses, and a great number of whores and bawds have been turned out of their seats of infamy; but certainly the witnesses in almost every case, have been of such a description, as to hazard the verdict.

Are many informations laid before your Office against houses of this description?—Very few.

Do you consider the abuse of houses of this description as coming under your control, as guardians of the public morals?—Most assuredly, upon information. In such cases we should proceed to the utmost of our exertions for the punishment of such offenders; we should use every exertion to come at, if possible, the necessary witnesses, and then call upon the overseers of the parish to establish the prosecution, and to look to the expense of the thing. We have called upon them at all times, to be instrumental as it were, in getting at the best kind of case to go before the Jury.

If any case was laid before your Office, such as I have before described, should you not feel it your duty to strain every nerve to bring the parties to justice?—Through thick and through thin, night and day: And I would answer for my worthy colleagues, that every power and means within the Police should be exerted to the abolition of it.

Can you state to the Committee at all, to what amount the expense would go of bringing to conviction a house of ill-fame in the Metropolis?—I should suppose first, the case of a prosecution brought by private persons, who are to bear the expense; I shall afterwards speak of the expense of a prosecution brought by the parish. Supposing that the private individuals are to bear the expense of the prosecution, and they were to go to work in the way to insure conviction, they must in the first place employ an attorney, and in the next place they should employ counsel, which would, I think, be absolutely necessary. They must then collect their witnesses, and probably, they would be attending the Court a day or two. Under all these circumstances, the expense could not be less than fourteen, fifteen, or sixteen pounds. If the proceeding is instituted by the parish, I think the charge ultimately to be made by the parish officers, which the parish would have to discharge, would not be less than 30 *l.*

Do you not think that the expense of attending these prosecutions constitutes the principal reason why so few of them are prosecuted?—I think that is a strong reason, a very strong one, perhaps the strongest. We have a place in our neighbourhood vulgarly called Duck-lane, and the Almonry, where these houses exist; we do all we can to put them down, but private interest too frequently interferes. We could yearly fill the gaol with its due proportion of persons of this description. No one can see this evil without lamenting it; but in some cases it is impossible to prevent it.   You

William Fielding, Esq.

You have stated, that you think the increase of depravity amongst the lower orders of society, is less a real increase of immorality than an attendant upon augmented population; do you not well recollect, that twenty or thirty years ago there were establishments in this Metropolis which the better morals of the present day would hardly tolerate; I mean establishments such as the Blue Lion, the Bull in the Pound, the Apollo Gardens, the Dog and Duck, the Temple of Flora, and the Shepherd and Shepherdess; you remember all these different establishments, do not you?—I think, pretty nearly the whole of them; the Shepherd and Shepherdess I do not now recollect; all the others I do. I remember the Apollo Gardens, the Dog and Duck, and the Temple of Flora, and a dreadful society of vagabonds were certainly collected together in those places. In that time of day the character of a highwayman on horseback was a more frequent character than it has been of late years. I think the horse patrole of the Office at Bow-street has been of a very considerable degree of service in putting down that class of depredators; the character of the highwayman is certainly less heard of since the putting down those two infernal places of meeting, the Dog and Duck and the Temple of Flora, which were certainly the most dreadful places in or about the Metropolis; they were the resorts of women, not only of the lowest species of prostitution, but even of the middle classes; they were the resorts, as well of apprentices as of every sort of dissolute, profligate, and abandoned young men.

Do you remember, that it was a general system in this Metropolis some years ago, for the lower orders to amuse themselves by what was called bullhanking, and driving the bulls about the streets?—I do not particularly remember that; but I have heard that there was a nuisance of that sort, much more frequent than of late years.

Of all these nuisances hardly a vestige remains?—I am happy to think so.

Then in these particulars there has been a great improvement in the public morals?—Certainly, a great improvement, from the vigilance of the Magistracy as to the curing of these nuisances.

Some years back, was it not a general system in the different streets of this Metropolis, for singers to go about singing most indecent songs?—Certainly.

That does not now exist?—It is partly, indeed I may say entirely, done away with. The new description of officer which I have suggested, would be particularly applicable in the suppression of this kind of nuisance; he should be continually on the watch, and have his eye on characters of this description; this sort of nuisance has frequently came to our knowledge, and as soon as I have heard of such things, I have sent out an officer and have had them brought in instantly before me. Most commonly I have sent them away without committing them, but I have threatened them with commitment in case they should be found again, and by this means I have got rid of them from the neighbourhood.

Do you remember any of those enormous associations in the Metropolis that went by the name of " Cutter Lads?"—No.

They were before your time?—Yes, before my time in the Police of the Metropolis. Do not understand me to mean that such associations have not existed; I have no doubt they have existed, but the practice has not existed in my time.

But you have notice of their name?—Yes.

They are altogether extinct?—Yes.

You know nothing of them now?—No.

Does it not appear to you, that upon taking an occasional walk on any Sunday in the year in fine weather, that there is a striking change for the better, within your own observation, in the manners, morals, behaviour and appearance of the lower orders in the different districts round about the Metropolis; suppose, for instance, a person chose to walk towards Pentonville, and see the beautiful fields in that neighbourhood, filled with thousands of people walking with their families, would he not find the manners and dress of those people very much improved, to what they formerly were?—I think it would be very difficult for a philosopher to form his conclusions of the manners and morals of the people from the appearances he observes in such places, for there are so many of the circumstances that contribute to make up such appearances, that alone engage the eye with a sort of captivation, without engaging the intellect as to the state of morality, or more than a superficiality of manners. The increased population will flock to those places where they may find fresh air and amusement; the multitude in the enjoyment of this air, will in their walks wear the pleasant characters of regularity

and

William Fielding,
Esq.

and order. For myself, being so very lame, I have not had much experience of late years, not being able to walk about; I have observed, however, that there is an increase of decency, in proportion to the attention we have been able to pay to the behaviour of the lower orders of the people in this neighbourhood. The journeymen tradesmen are not so frequently met with in their daily working habits; you do not see them with their dirty aprons on, and so forth; but I am persuaded, from what I have heard, although it has not come within my own observation, that there is a great deal more decency amongst the lowest orders of the people than there used to be, in their respect for churches and places of worship. The doors of places for sectary meetings used to be surrounded by the lowest blackguards; the conduct of the lower orders in this particular, is now very different to what it used to be; it used to be a habit of the lowest blackguards to attend about the doors of those places, and make the greatest disturbance and annoy the frequenters of them in their religious worship. That practice has not altogether yet ceased; but however, we have used every exertion within our power to suppress it, and we have suppressed it in a great many instances where complaints have been made. And here again, the utility of the appointment of the new description of officer I have mentioned, would be most conspicuous, for he would be required, as an easily discharged duty, to have his eye towards all the places of worship in his parish. The petty constables do not, and will not attend; but if the petty constables were under the control and command of the Superintendent during the time of Divine Service, decency and decorum would be effectually maintained.

Do you think that the Sabbath-day is better observed in the Metropolis now than it was ten years ago?—Much better.

You are now speaking of the sectaries no less than the Establishment?—No doubt; we have had prosecutions carried on in a spirit rather severer than we wish, against butchers for selling meat on a Sunday morning.

Do not you think that is pushing the matter rather too far?—Certainly it is pushing it too far; and if the same zeal was pursued in prosecuting thieves, more advantage would be derived to society. We have had our office loaded with miserable informations by a society of miserable sectaries, the penalty being only 5 s.; and we could do no otherwise than impose the fines; some of these persons do not appear to be actuated by any motive of advantaging the public. But this is a species of information not very apt to captivate the common informer.

Has it ever occurred to you, that considerable impediments are thrown in the way of the execution of public justice, from the want of a character who might be named a public accuser; individuals not having in many instances, either the time or the means of obtaining for themselves that justice which is their due?—I have had such an abhorrence of the very name of a public accuser, from its existence at the time of the French revolution, that I have taken no opportunity and have had no inclination to cogitate upon such a matter; but this I am sure of, that if there was a character in the nature of a solicitor or attorney, to watch the views of justice, as well as of the very interesting circumstances of particular parties often coming before us, and they could have their assured assistance, the benefit would be wonderful. But in the character of public accuser, as counsel, I have an abhorrence to such an appointment. But if there was a well-regulated institution, such as I have mentioned, it would be attended with considerable advantage; it would aid the parties having a strong title to justice. The want of such assistance it is frequently our misfortune to lament. Not having any jurisdiction over any thing that is like *trespass,* we have only to do with breaches of the peace and assaults. There is another little matter that occurs to me to mention to the Committee; I mean the unfortunate disputes that prevail amongst the lower orders of the people, with respect to their lodgings, as between landlords and tenants; disputes of that kind are altogether out of our jurisdiction. I have frequently thought, that although it would add vastly to the trouble of the Magistrates, yet it would be of great importance to these poor people, if there was authority given to the Magistrates, when the rent did not exceed 5 s. a week, that the Magistrates should have a power by summary jurisdiction to settle the disputes, under the power of fine and of imprisonment, if the fine is not paid in a day or two, as it should be found necessary. This power to the Magistrates would be a source of great comfort and of immense advantage to the lower orders of the people. We have no power of this description; and we have a hundred complaints of that sort in the course of the week; and we are obliged to say, " My poor fellow, I would do any thing for you, but I have no power."

And

And of course, the only remedy that the parties have in such cases is in action of *William Fielding,* *Esq.*
trespass?—They may go to the Court of Conscience for sums under forty shillings; but in many cases the only remedy is *trespass*, which it is not worth their while to bring; this happens in a thousand cases, and we are obliged to say we have no means of relieving them. There is another case, in which it would be beneficial to give the Magistrates a similar power; I mean, in case where the only remedy is for the party to bring what is called an action of *trover*, to recover goods that are in the hands of dishonest, designing, and crafty people; but where there is no actual theft or fraud, we frequently try, for the sake of the poor people, the experiment of sending a summons, perhaps to the people belonging to an inn, who have detained their goods; then, if the keepers of the inn were more knowing than they were some time ago, they would throw the Magistrate's summons into the fire. In such cases we cannot stir a step, and we hesitate shewing our teeth when we cannot bite.

Do you not think that it would be advantageous, if crimes against the public peace were attacked by some person who might be considered as a public prosecutor?— No doubt it would be attended with good effects; no doubt that all matters which are ultimately to go before a jury and a higher court, having the advantage of being under the care of a public prosecutor, who would get up and go through with it, would be an immense blessing to the people.

You then think it would be of great advantage to the public, if there was a person paid by the public, who would act in the nature of a public solicitor for individuals, who are not in a situation to pay themselves?—Most assuredly; there can be no doubt of it, if the appointment is made by the Magistrates.

Would not the ends of justice be answered by preventing what too often takes place, namely, those collusions between the prosecutor and the person accused?— No doubt about it.

Do you not think, that even if this plan should not be adopted, that bills of indictment ought to be prepared, and subpœnas and summonses issued, free of expenses, where the public interest is concerned, to persons wishing to have an indictment and other proceedings?—There can be no doubt of it; for though the expense of an indictment is no more than 2 s. 6 d. or 3 s., yet it turns aside the intentions of justice in even the most miserable cases, ninety-nine times out of an hundred.

I think it is the practice in the country, but I do not know that it is so in London, that for losses of time and expenses, allowances are paid by the different counties to prosecutors?—At the Old Bailey only; they give there a species of reward as well as indemnity for money laid out, and allowances to different witnesses; at the other Sessions they will not. I know not the reason why; but it is losing a vast benefit to the public. I think it should be in the option of the Justices at the Sessions. In many of the counties, for instance in Essex and Kent, they will do it at the Sessions, but they will not do it here; I do not know why. But the less expense that should be in every process to detect crime, certainly the better is it for the public. Such proceedings should be free of all the expense possible to the prosecutor. We have so many instances of poor wretches coming to us for relief of this sort, that we do not know what to do. God knows, we should have no peace in this town, without the system of warranting one another, as it is called, that is, coming to the Justice for a warrant; and I suppose that seven out of twelve of the cases that come before us, the poor people have no money. You must have warrants, or there will be no peace.

When bail is tendered before you, are you very particular in ascertaining the sufficiency of persons who offer themselves as bail?—According to the nature of the offence, we require the bail; it may be said to be more or less upon the nature of the offence, when the bail is offered; for persons who commit single assaults or minor crimes, then we wish to take the bail in as low a sum as possible; I myself, in cases of that description, do not require the security which is almost constantly required. For offences of that description, the Magistrates generally bind them over in the sum of 20 l.; but frequently I bind them only for 10 l. and that answers the same purpose; but whenever there is any case where the security of the public requires an appearance at the Sessions, as Magistrates, we are always bound to be particular. Sometimes we require twenty-four hours notice of bail, who are offered before we admit them; but in general it may be said, that these matters are constantly attended to.

William Fielding, Esq.

Is it not a common practice, that that sort of bail is tendered, which is known by the name of Jew bail?—Not very frequently; it is more frequently known at Westminster Hall in civil matters, than it is in criminal proceedings; but it will make its appearance sometimes, and in general, when they are known, we reject them or not, as we think proper; but that depends entirely upon the nature of the case; if it is satisfactorily made out, that they are of such a description as is mentioned, we reject them.

Do you happen to know, whether of the estreats that are directed to these bail, the money is looked after and paid into the Exchequer?—That is out of my power to say, I know nothing about it; I know this, that the securities, and the account of the recognizances that are taken by the different Police Offices are kept, and returned to the Sessions. Of that number there will, however, be a great many indeed; where the parties having done their duty, their recognizances are discharged. Some people will, ultimately, have their recognizances remaining before the Clerk of the Peace, who invariably, upon the appearance of the indictments, sends to the other parties to come and take them up, or else they will be estreated; and really, I believe, as to the doctrine of estreats and forfeitures, it is productive of great inconvenience to the public. There is a great deal to be said to you upon that subject, when you come to inquire into it; but I profess myself so ignorant, that I cannot give any information upon it.

Do you attend the licensing of the different public-houses within your district?— At present, Mr. Colquhoun having been in the Office long before I came there, and having to my certain knowledge taken great pains to enquire as to the propriety or impropriety of certain ale-houses having licences, and having undertaken himself to attend to that business, I have never yet appeared at the meetings, being perfectly persuaded, that he is a man not to be affected by any improper motives.

Have you many complaints laid before your Office, of the misconduct of victuallers and publicans?—Not a great many. We have this particular advantage, that as there is within our parish a military station, that is to say, of the Guards; it is the practice of the military officers or serjeants, by way of looking after their own men, to be called upon by one of our officers, who goes with them into all the public-houses, under the idea of searching for the soldiers who may happen to be there. By these means, the publicans get rid of the people at a reasonable hour, and consequently the public-houses are kept quiet and well ordered, and they are shut up at an early hour. This rule respecting the military, prevents a great degree of riot that might otherwise take place.

Have you any hour fixed within your district, within which the public-houses shall shut up?—We fix eleven o'clock, and we contrive to keep them pretty near to it. We scarcely omit a night without sending an officer round, with a patrole, to see that they are shut up at a proper time, and in the morning we generally ask, who went with the patrole last night, so that that is the means of preserving a particular degree of tranquillity here, and it keeps the publicans in order; and then they know that Mr. Colquhoun, who makes it his business to attend to these matters, would make a complaint against the person who misconducted himself on the general licensing day; and therefore I believe the publicans are very well managed amongst us. We are, however, subject to the obvious inconvenience of having within one district, other public-houses and gin-shops, which are licensed by the Board of Green Cloth.

Can you give us any information respecting those licences?—All those public-houses and gin-shops about Charing-Cross, and many other places, are licensed by the Board of Green Cloth. Sometimes representations are made, not particularly by me, but by other Magistrates, to the Board of Green Cloth, complaining of the conduct of those publicans and gin-shop keepers. The complaint comes from us, but they license them in spite of our recommendation to the contrary. In and about Charing-Cross, there are a great number of evils which we cannot control, only because the Board of Green Cloth license those houses.

What jurisdiction has the Board of Green Cloth?—Similar to the magistracy, they are the Magistrates of the parish; they have a jurisdiction according to certain privileges; not that I can suggest any kind of impropriety on the part of the Board of Green Cloth. The good nature of these gentlemen prompts them to do many things, which, if they knew the consequences, I am sure they would not do.

Should

William Fielding, Esq.

Should you consider that an opinion coming from your Office against any victualler, or holder of a public-house or gin-shop, within your jurisdiction, is likely to have weight with the licensing Magistrates, or with the Board of Green Cloth, in taking away those licenses for improper conduct?—I should, certainly suppose, they would do us the honour to attend to every representation of that sort; but simply for the benefit of the public in that part of the town, I should think it is much fitter that the power of licensing should be with the Magistrates, rather than with the Board of Green Cloth.

From your experience, have they paid much attention to those recommendations?—Not knowing where precisely to hit upon the fact, I cannot say; I rather think it has; but I think Mr. Colquhoun has named some, that have been mentioned to the Board of Green Cloth; I think that was about twelve months ago.

Do you think that it would be an improvement in the Act by which Magistrates license publicans, if an appeal against their decisions lay at the Quarter Sessions?—I must own, (and perhaps I may be blamed for the opinion) that I think there ought to be no appeal. I do not want to give Magistrates more power than they should have for the benefit of the public, but I look upon all appeals from the summary jurisdiction of the Magistrates to the Sessions, to be injurious to the public, and I could give some striking instances to justify that opinion. For instance now, in the case of pawnbrokers; we have a fair jurisdiction over pawnbrokers, and we are obliged to keep them in order; but as they are allowed an appeal to the Sessions from our decision, it is highly injurious to the public; for in a variety of cases they go immediately to the Sessions with an appeal, and then the poor person in whose favour perhaps we made the decision, would be unable to support the respondent's part for want of money; and in such case the intention of the Legislature is rendered perfectly nugatory. I might say the same thing with regard to an hundred other instances, where this principle has had this tendency. You will remember the Stage Coach Act, for preventing coach-owners from carrying more than a certain number of people on the outside of their coaches. When that Act first came out, we had not a final jurisdiction given to us, and I believe about eight out of ten of the convictions were quashed upon the appeal to the Sessions, for some trifling defect in form, when the fact of the offence having been committed was obvious, so that the Act was rendered a nullity; but I have not the least hesitation in saying, that so far as I have pointed out, the doctrine of an appeal to the Sessions, is faulty and injurious, to a considerable degree. I would mention another thing which I think would be of great service to the public; I mean some alteration in those laws which established the principle of limiting penalties within a maximum and a minimum. I would take the liberty of suggesting, that instead of having the penalties limited to a certain minimum, it would be advisable to leave it to the discretion of the Justices to apportion the penalty to the circumstances of the case. Let the penalty, if you please, be fixed at a certain maximum, beyond which the Justices shall not go; but do not let it be said, that the Justices shall not adjudge a penalty under a certain sum. I wish to God this was the principle running through all the Acts of Parliament; " the offender shall be fined in a sum not exceeding the maximum;" but do not limit the Justices to a minimum; that is to say, leave it to the Justices to exercise their own discretion, to reduce the penalty down even to a halfpenny, if you please, if they see that the case before them requires no heavier punishment. We have a very considerable Act of Parliament, that is often acted upon to the great oppression of the lower orders of the people; I mean the Act fixing penalties to those people who drive their carts without number or name. Upon informations against poor people offending against this Act, the Justices have no discretion in awarding the penalty, and the offender is liable to the penalty. The offence is a considerable one; and though I think it ought to be suppressed entirely, and when detected, ought to be punished; but the language of the Act of Parliament is this; " the party shall be fined 40 s." Now, in some cases, such a penalty as this is to the offender like the national debt; these poor devils could not pay twenty, ten, or even five shillings. This, I think, is in this respect a very oppressive Act; it is a more natural and just principle, with respect to penalties, that these Acts should run thus; " shall forfeit any sum not exceeding so much," so as not to prevent the Magistrate from putting a sum less than 40 s. upon the offender, according to the circumstances of the case; but in this very instance 40 s. is an immense sum for a poor man to pay.

Are

William Fielding,
Esq.

Are you aware, that within your district there are a great many public-houses that either belong to brewers, or are held as property, or rented by them, or on which they have mortgages ?—I believe the greatest part of them are under the thumb of the brewers. The object of the brewer is to employ his capital, and he will naturally purchase up all the public-houses he can, so that he might supply them with his own beer.

Have you ever heard that there is an opinion abroad, and prevalent in the community at large, that those houses that belong to brewers have a better chance of being licensed than those that are termed free houses ?—I am sure I cannot answer that question. That it is the brewer's interest to have his houses in proper situations is very obvious; and it is natural from the respectability of the houses he would be most likely to possess, that such respectability and fitness of situation would forward the brewer's claim to a licence.

Is it not the common practice of the Justices always to grant licences to the houses that have been once licensed, and to consider the licence as following the property, as a matter of course ?—You mean having a claim to the licence again, notwithstanding whose hands the house may be in. I do not think that my colleague, to whom I have entirely surrendered this duty, has ever been actually bound up by such an idea; and I know that there have been certain districts in which houses have been licensed for half a century, and in such cases very few licences have been taken away.

In point of fact, is there not a greater disposition to favour those houses, both in the granting of licences as well as in renewing them, that are held by opulent brewers, than those that are termed free houses ?—Upon my honour that is not a thing with respect to which I can speak from experience; but I should only consider, according to the events of human nature, that is likely to have some little weight; but upon my honour, I believe that the gentleman who does the business part of the licensing, is as pure as air from any improper feeling in the discharge of that duty.

Do you consider the public-houses of the Metropolis falling into the power and being under the control of the brewer, is very injurious to the public interest ?—There cannot be a doubt that every the least advance towards a monopoly, must be prejudicial to the public.

Do you think that it would be a bad change for the public interest, if the whole trade of the public-houses was left entirely open, that any person of any description might go and take out a licence, and open a public-house or spirit-house, at pleasure, subject, however, to certain regulations which might be established by law, for the better government and management of those houses ?—I think the present system of subjecting the licences to the discretion of the Justices is the best possible mode that can be established; and I do not see at present, any mode by which it could be improved for the better. There certainly should be some strict regulations in the business of licensing; but at present, having seen many instances where the apprehension that their licences would be affected, if the disorders complained of were repeated, has a good tendency; we have frequently had publicans brought before us, and we have made use of that admonition, that if such things were ever seen again, their licences would be taken away. It appears to me that the law as it at present subsists, which gives the Magistrates the power of licensing, ought to be left as it is.

Do you not think that a regulation might be devised and penalties levied for misconduct, that would answer all the purposes that are now gained by the power which the Magistrates possess, and which they can only execute once a year, leaving the trade of public-houses as open as the trade of butchers and bakers ?—I think there cannot be a doubt of that; the power only to be exercised once a year is too tardy and too unfrequent an opportunity of correcting many abuses that certainly are in public-houses; many abuses must occur which require immediate redress, and we are particularly earnest in preventing their repetition, and not unfrequently do we admonish them of the immediate interest they have of well-regulating their houses, for any repeated misconduct would certainly hazard the loss of their licences. But as a general answer to your question, certainly ingenuity and philanthropy may establish power, and that power may be established with penalties that may be productive of some advantage; but I believe it is a general opinion, that we cannot have a better system than what we have at present.

How

How many publicans are there in London?—Mr. Colquhoun has formed some *William Fielding, Esq.* calculation upon that subject; but I cannot say, myself, as to the accuracy of it. I should think they are rather more than the number he states it at, 6000.

Is it then your opinion, that it would be much for the public interest if Magistrates had a power or some means of control over the public-houses, beyond what they have now, once a year only, on the licensing day?—I can only answer that question as I have done before; I think that there should be a better security for the good behaviour of the publican, and that that security should come within the power of the Magistrate to enforce; I think that there being an intermediate power to correct some abuses, would perhaps be of advantage. I do not wish to increase penalties; but larger penalties might be more efficacious, no doubt; but as to the very thing itself, I mean the power of taking away the licence altogether, striking, as it essentially does, upon the very existence and interest of the man, I should not wish that the authority of the Magistrates were carried farther than it does at present exist; I should not wish that, by any means: the Magistrates have a great power. I think that great use may be made of the present power in keeping the publicans in order; for, having the terror of their licence being taken away, they will, for their own interest, keep their houses well regulated; and of all the other things that would come under my eye, if I were to live in a neighbourhood where there were any expedients of this kind to be used, by the interests that might be made upon the subject, I should think it a very great grievance; but at present I am out of all the objections to the thing that might arise in my district.

Are the number of spirit-shops much increased in your division?—I think they are. The spirit-shop is a thing of considerable profit; it is of very considerable value, most undoubtedly; and that they are in an over abundance, there cannot be a doubt.

Do you not think that the number of spirit-shops are very much diminished from what they were 30 years ago?—I cannot conceive that that can be the case; the increase of the town, and the increase of the population, would rather make me suppose that they were very considerably increased.

That is, a mere nominal increase; I mean a real increase in proportion to the population?—I really do not apprehend, from the opportunity I have had of forming a judgment, but it has not been very great, that there can be any doubt of the number being increased; but I may be mistaken; and I could not form a correct judgment without referring to books.

Do you not recollect that it was a complaint made in all the publications of the day, about 30 or 40 years ago, that in almost every eighth or tenth house in the Metropolis there were spirits found for sale?—I know, from my father's writings upon that particular subject, there did exist a vast number of spirituous liquor-houses.

Hogarth has attacked the subject in his drawings?—Yes, he has. In that treatise which my father wrote, namely, a consideration on the increase of robberies, which has been rather a popular little thing, though not so great a favourite as his Tom Jones, his idea of the gin-shop was terrible. He then acted as a Magistrate, and, I believe, was then the only Magistrate in London of any degree of consequence, and ought to know something of the subject.

Then is it your opinion that the gin-shops are increasing every day?—I should think so, and must increase, from the increased value of such property; for a man keeping a snug gin-shop has a much more profitable concern than if he kept a public-house, where he would only be selling his pints and quarts of beer, which is less profitable than selling glasses of gin.

Is it not a practice for persons to take out the beer licence as a cover, merely for the sale of spirits, never selling any beer at all?—Most assuredly; that practice has crept in; and in our particular division, if we have a suspicion of that sort, we send off immediately in order to ascertain the fact.

And you consider that as decidedly illegal, and a ground for shutting up that house?—I should think it would be pretty nearly so.

To what prison do you commit prisoners?—Principally to Tothill-fields, as to those matters that happen within the city and liberties of Westminster; as to those offences which are committed within the county, we send to the county prison, which is Cold-bath Fields.

510. Have

William Fielding, Esq.

Have you ever, as a Magistrate, visited the Cold-bath Fields Prison?—I have not, from my particular lameness. Since I have been a Magistrate, I have never been able to walk so far, and I cannot get into a carriage without difficulty.

Do you know, whether that is a prison at all suited for the number of persons that you send there?—I really do not know, never having visited the prison before I came down here, and never having had an opportunity of seeing it since. But I very frequently interrogate the gaoler of Tothillfields Bridewell, upon the conduct and care of his house; and I always receive the most satisfactory information, not from him only, but from the people calculated to give evidence of that sort; and as to the Cold-bath Fields Prison, I was of the number of Justices who voted for the appointment of the man who is there now; I mean *Atkins,* who I then thought the best suited man that could be for the purpose, being a man of great intrepidity, which is the greatest quality that can recommend such a man.

Have you any reason to think otherwise now?—Not the least; rather the contrary.

Are you in the habit of committing many perons under the 17th George II. commonly termed the Vagrant Act?—Certainly, we have our common share; and there is one thing that particularly contributes to operate as a reason why a great many people are brought before us. Grosvenor-place is the residence of the nobility and gentry, and being in the parish of St. George Hanover-square, the vestry have appointed two constables to keep double watch, and bring the vagrants found there before us. One of the men who has been lately appointed, is as deaf as a beetle, and he has continued to bring such miserable people before us, that it is impossible to look at them without feeling compassion, and before the constable can be entitled to the 10*s.* reward, under the Act, the Magistrate must convict and send to prison; therefore we are subject to many very disagreeable feelings, the necessity of that being put on us; on that account it operates with considerable injustice.

I am speaking of reputed thieves, not vagrants?—Bow-street and other Police offices, near places of entertainment, have most of those sorts of people. We have not many of them brought before us. The Opera House being particularly within our district, one should have thought that would have occasioned many to be brought before us; but certainly we have not had many.

Are not the Magistrates authorized, upon the oath of one person, to commit for six months?—They are authorized to commit till the next Sessions, and the party may appeal from the commitment. Then there is a case of appeal; and in many instances from their informality, and the great nicety required in drawing up such commitments, such commitments have been quashed. That has taken place in many cases. We have not many commitments of that sort; but that jurisdiction is with us, as it is with other Offices; but in fact we have not had a great many.

May I be permitted here again to say that the superintendent officer I have proposed, will be in every parochial advantage to the Police, what a serjeant-major is to the discipline of a regiment.

Veneris, 7° die Junii, 1816.

The Honourable HENRY GREY BENNET, in The Chair.

———————

John Townsend, called in, and Examined.

John Townsend.

YOU are one of the Police officers at Bow-street?—Yes.

How long have you held that situation?—I think somewhere about four-and-thirty years; rather better.

Do you hold that situation at present?—Yes.

Is your time employed at the Office alone, or do you attend at the Court at levees and drawing-rooms, and all public places?—Both, day and night.

What, in general, do you consider is the nature and extent of the duties of your office?—The duty of the office, as a matter of course, is to attend at the Office, and at other public things for the officers; but two of us have been more immediately placed about the Court. I think in the year 1792, when Mr. Dundas was Secretary of State, and Mr. Pitt was Minister, that appointment took place in consequence of the various depredations committed at Court, and in consequence of the King and the Royal Family being frequently teased with lunatics: that was the original occasion of that appointment taking place.

You speak now of your duty as it is connected with the Court; what is your duty as connected with the Public Office in Bow-street?—To attend when any of the Magistrates want my assistance within the jurisdiction of Middlesex, for I cannot go out of town on account of attending on the Court-days, and particularly if there is any thing wanted at Windsor; or supposing that the Prince goes out of town to Brighton, and so on, then we attend there.

How many officers of the Police consider themselves as particularly attached to the Court, following the Court where it goes?—When the Regent goes to Brighton, for instance, Sayers and I go. There are two officers appointed at Windsor, who are unconnected with the Office, Rivett and Dowsett.

Except when the Regent is at Brighton, your residence is constantly in London?—Yes.

Do you attend at the Office in Bow-street every day?—No, not every day; that would be impossible.

Is it considered as the duty of the Police officers all to attend at the Public Office daily, or to go turn and turn about, so many one day and so many another?—I never knew that to be the case; but it frequently happened in the early part of my life, that the public may want an officer, especially public bodies; for instance, the Excise-office, the Custom-house, the Stamp-office, the Bank, they all come there; and if they see an officer, whoever is in the way they instantly go, because if they were to wait for matter of form, perhaps the party they wanted to apprehend would be gone.

Is it customary to have an officer from Bow-street constantly in attendance at the Bank?—No, only ten days a quarter; that Sayers and I do every quarter, and have done for many years, these five-and-twenty years, I dare say. Depredations used to be committed there dreadfully at dividend-times; and when Mr. Giles and Mr. Thornton were governor and deputy-governor, the application was made, and we went.

Is that considered as part of your ordinary duty, or do the Directors of the Bank recompense you for that as a special service?—We have a guinea a day for it.

That is paid by the Bank?—Yes.

Independent of the salary which arises from the Office?—Independent of our salary.

When you attend at any of the other Offices—you have named the Custom-house, the Stamp-office, and so on, do they pay you for that attendance?—Certainly.

At the same rate?—At the same rate, provided there is no reward. In the instance where the officers so vigorously apprehended that banditti that murdered

510.

the

John Townsend.

the Revenue Officer; there, for the first time in my life, I find that the Government, or the Solicitors and Commissioners of Excise, have given 1,000 *l*. reward to whoever should give information, or cause the parties to be taken, together with the apprehenders, and so forth, to which I have no doubt they will be all entitled. The usual way in distributing the 40 *l*. on convictions is, that the Recorder gives the prosecutor from five to fifteen and twenty pounds, according to circumstances, and the apprehenders the remainder, that comes to, perhaps, only three or four pounds a-piece, though the world runs away with the ridiculous idea that the officers have 40 *l*. It is a singular circumstance, but in all cases of felony there are but two cases where there is any reward at all; those are a highway robbery and a burglary; all the others are mere bagatelles, for they are merely certificates, what the vulgar call Tyburn-tickets, to free from parish-offices.

Those are worth 20 *l*. a-piece, are they not?—I have sold them as low as 12 *l*. In such a parish as Saint George's, Hanover-square, the people are of so much consequence that they will serve themselves. The highest is in Covent Garden, where it is worth 25 *l*.; for the constable of the parish must sit up, I think, one night out of three; and whoever is hit upon as a parochial constable says, " This is a hard thing, and therefore I will buy myself off;" and a ticket in that parish, therefore, is worth more. If an officer gets a guinea a day, it is a chance whether he gets any reward; that must depend upon the liberality of those Public Offices who choose to pay it; I am very sorry to say, that sometimes they are rather mean upon that subject.

You mean the guinea a day is for your trouble in attending at the Public Offices for the prevention of crimes, and the apprehension of robbers?—The public bodies employ an officer to go to apprehend persons; the solicitor comes, if any body touches their office, to the Office in Bow-street, to get proper assistance to apprehend those persons; then, after the thing is finished, if there is no reward, of course the officer has his guinea a day for his trouble.

Is the time of the officers much taken up by the Public Offices?—That must depend materially upon public business; they may be very quiet this week; next week there may not be an officer to be had; so much so does it happen at Bow-street, that they are obliged to refer to minor officers—some of the patrole, and send them rather than the Public should be injured.

Do you then think, considering the demand that is made both from public bodies and from individuals upon Bow-street, that the establishment of the regular officers is sufficient?—I think, myself, that what there is wanting of the established officers is made up by the patrole, who step in directly; therefore I think, upon the whole, the establishment is large enough; for if once the establishment was made more than the officers could do, they would starve one another; it is like a rank of chairs, or of hackney coaches; if there are too many there is not employment for them; and when it does not so happen that they are all employed, what is the consequence? sometimes I have myself, in the early part of my life, when I was in the habit of going to do the business for Public Offices, been out of town for a week or a fortnight. I went to Dunkirk, in the year 1786, to fetch over four, that were hanged. I went for Mr. Taylor, a Hamburgh Merchant. There are certain cases in which we may be employed longer; there have been officers for eight or ten days on the poaching cases. Vicary was down for a fortnight in Gloucestershire, with Colonel Berkeley; frequently it takes a great deal of time to detect a banditti like that.

In those cases where the individual, in a case similar to that you have just mentioned, sends for a Bow-street officer, the expense of his journey, and the payment of his trouble, is defrayed by the individual?—Certainly.

Are the Police officers much sent out of the metropolis on the service of individuals?—A great deal; the great means of their living, in a measure, is that of their being employed, as I have always termed it, upon foreign service; that is out of their local jurisdiction, because the officer's salary is only a guinea a week.

If it was not for the rewards for the industry and services of the Police officers, which are paid for by individuals who employ them, should you think the salary which is paid them such as could procure proper officers for the purposes of the Public?—Impossible.

Have you any doubt that there is no officer at present employed at Bow-street, who could continue to maintain the situation which it is fit he should
hold,

hold, by the salary and regular allowances made him from the Office. — Im- *John Townsend.*
possible.

At how much should you estimate the ordinary profits which an officer of the Police makes, from what is called the 40 *l.* Parliamentary reward ?—That must entirely depend upon the quantity of persons that he convicts, together with the distribution of each of the rewards by the Recorder to the officer, whether the Recorder distributes liberally or not ; for it is upon the Judges on the Assize, and the Recorder in London, that the officer depends, as to that liberality, or not.

In point of fact, it does not amount to any great sum in the course of the year ?— A mere bagatelle ; a mere nothing.

Should you put it at 30 *l.* a year, upon the average ?—I have very great doubt whether there is an officer on the establishment who has ever made 30 *l.* a year by rewards. There are eight sessions in a year ; taking it for granted that the officer should convict two capital felons for a burglary, or a highway robbery, each session, which I am certain they do not, because in many cases the Jury will take off the burglary, and the officer is left in the lurch ; therefore it is a robbery, not burglariously breaking and entering, but stealing only ; then the officers apply to the Judge for what they term their expenses, which they are allowed, which is somewhere about four shillings a day for their time ; therefore I am perfectly satisfied they cannot get 30 *l.* a year.

Hardly ever 20 *l.* perhaps ?—I should think not one of them.

Should you not think that it would be a much better mode of rewarding the services of the officers of the Police, if it was left in the breast of the Police Magistrates to pay, for every special service that each officer did, the reward which those Magistrates thought fit to apportion ?—I have always thought so ; from the earliest part of my time I have thought it, and for the best of all reasons ; I have, with every attention that man could bestow, watched the conduct of various persons who have given evidence against their fellow-creatures for life or death, not only at the Old Bailey, but on the Circuits, and I have always been perfectly convinced that would be the best mode that possibly could be adopted to pay officers, particularly because they are dangerous creatures ; they have it frequently in their power (no question about it) to turn that scale, when the beam is level, on the other side ; I mean against the poor wretched man at the bar : why? this thing called nature says profit is in the scale ; and, melancholy to relate, but I cannot help being perfectly satisfied, that frequently that has been the means of convicting many and many a man ; and I told Sir Charles Bunbury my opinion upon that subject thirty years ago, when he wanted to get rid of rewards, it should be in the breast of the Judges on the Circuit, and the Judges at the Old Bailey, or the Judge who tries at the Old Bailey, whether they have convicted or not convicted the party, if they see the officer has done his duty towards the Public, and his duty fairly and uprightly towards all parties, they should have a discriminating power to pay that officer according to the nature of the case : then the officer does not stand up and look at this unfortunate creature, and swear to this or that thing, or the other thing, for what ? for the lucre—for nature is nature, do with us what you will ; and therefore I am convinced, that whenever A. is giving evidence against B. he should stand perfectly uninterested.

Do you not think that that feeling you have expressed governs the conduct of the Jurymen in finding the verdict, when the principal evidence is an officer of the Police ?—I have no doubt about it ; and indeed so it would to ourselves, provided we did not know the officer. I, for one, should naturally say, if placed upon the Jury, yes, it may be true these officers are speaking truth ; but it turns out by cross examination that there is 120 *l.* to be given if these three men are convicted, and therefore I cannot believe all these men have sworn ; but if there was no reward, the officer might be always paid liberally, provided the Judge had the power by Act of Parliament to pay it, and no doubt this has been the chatter ; there can be no question about it ; but the prosecutor says, " how am I to do? if this man is not convicted I shall not get my expenses. Here is going to Kingston, or somewhere else ; how much shall I have allowed to be paid by the county ? It will not half pay the expenses." " Yes, says the Officer, this is a pretty thing ; I will take care I will play no more at this game ;" because that game will not afford even the poor devil of an officer to appear decent on the Monday morning, or to acquit himself, perhaps, from being summoned before the Court of Conscience for some trifling debt ; for I have been always of opinion, that an officer is a dangerous subject to the com-

munity.

munity, if he is not so kept and so paid as to afford him the means of being honest; for in some cases, God knows, it has been frequently the case. I remember a case, which was proved, in the time of the trading Magistrates, where there was a fellow who was a public officer belonging to Justice Hyde, was hanged, and yet he was one of the officers; but I well remember what the man said at the time he was executed, for in those days, before the Police Bill took place at all it was a trading business; and there was Justice this and Justice that. Justice Welch in Litchfield-street was a great man in those days, and old Justice Hyde, and Justice Girdler, and Justice Blackborough, a trading Justice at Clerkenwell-green, and an old iron-monger. The plan used to be to issue out Warrants, and take up all the poor devils in the streets, and then there was the bailing them 2 *s.* 4 *d.* which the Magistrates had; and taking up a hundred girls, that would make, at 2 *s.* 4 *d.* 11 *l.* 13 *s.* 4 *d.* They sent none to gaol, for the bailing them was so much better. That was so glaring that it led to the Police Bill, and it was a great blessing to the Public to do away with those men, for they were nothing better than the encouragers of blackguards, vice, and plunderers; there is no doubt about it.

Having stated these different objections to the officers of the Police receiving rewards, do you not think there is another objection also, namely, where the officers hold in their hands the balance of life and death in any evidence that they may give, it is possible that a rich criminal may have an influence over a needy officer highly injurious to the public interest?—No question about it; I will give the Committee a case in point; supposing for instance, when I convicted Broughton, which, I believe, is now twenty-two years ago, and who was convicted for robbing the York Mail. I convicted, at the same assizes, the summer assizes, a celebrated old woman, Mrs. Usher, worth at least three thousand guineas, for she made over that property by her attorney. I was then in the habit of attending Vauxhall, for which I received half-a-guinea, and a half pint of wine, which I relinquished, and took the fifteen-pence: Mrs. Usher picked a lady's pocket; I was close by and secured her. She was tried before Baron Hotham. Mr. Ives, the gaoler in Surrey, before the trial came to me, and said, "Townsend, you know mother Usher very well," "yes," said I, "these ten years;" he said, "cannot this be stached?" meaning put an end to: I said no, it was impossible that it could be; because the case was very plain, and of all women upon earth she ought to be convicted; and in my opinion, if she is convicted capi-tally, nothing but her sex and her old age, ought to save her from being executed; and I shall think it my duty when she is convicted to state to the Judge, after convic-tion, my opinion upon her case, which I did. She was convicted, and Baron Hotham ordered me my expeness, which expenses, I believe, amounted to four guineas and a half. I set off immediately in a post-chaise to give evidence against Broughton. The present Attorney-General was her counsel. Baron Hotham said to me, "this woman you seem to be well acquainted with;" "Yes, my Lord," said I, "I am very sorry to say she is a very old offender; but her age, which your Lordship has heard her give, and her sex, are the only plea that ought to save her;" for the Jury found her guilty of stealing, but not privily, which took away the capital part; there-fore she was sentenced to two years imprisonment, in the New Goal in the Borough. I then lived in the Strand; two of her relations called upon me, trying to see what could be done, and they would have given me 200 *l.* not to have appeared against that woman. She was a very rich woman, and made over all her property before she was convicted; she got the best part of it by plunder. On Broughton, who was tried for robbing the Mail, I found 135 *l.* in bank-notes, a gold watch, and a guinea and a half. Mr. Parkin, the solicitor, paid me. Justice Buller staid till I got down there to give evidence against him; finding a letter which confirmed the evidence of Shaw the accomplice, who was the planner and plotter of that robbery, I traced poor Broughton, and another, who went afterwards to America. Broughton was convicted. Broughton was brother to one of the King's Messengers, and another brother kept the Red Lion in Barnet for years. There was another plan laid, so that if an officer had not been firm the consequence would have been, that temptations would be fre-quently thrown in officers way, and how is it possible to avoid those temptations, provided the officer so employed has not the means of barring off those temptations by being paid liberally for what he does; for however we may be, in whatsoever state we are placed, nothing can be so dangerous as a public officer, where he is liable to be tempted; for, God knows, nature is at all times frail, and money is a very tempting thing; and you see frequently, that much higher characters than Police officers and thief-takers, as they are called, have slipped on one side, and kicked over places; but I

have

John Townsend.

have been always but of one opinion; I am convinced it is so, and so I told Lord Melville, at the time he was Secretary of State, the Police Bill being framed, that the only thing, I, for one, objected to, was the paltry salaries they gave the officers. I, it is true, have steered clear, but I do not owe that to any merit myself. I have been lucky enough to have situations where I have been very very liberally paid; and whether it has been my own sobriety, or attention, it matters not; but I have had many gratuities, and from the first people in the nation, or I might have been as liable to temptation as any one in London; but I have a fellow-feeling for other officers, and I must say, that I think that some of the officers deserve every praise, though I do not change ten words with some of them in the course of a week, but for their attention and their sobriety; and I cannot help again repeating, that nothing but their industry would enable them to get through the piece; for what is so small a stipend as a guinea a-week?

Have you at all formed an opinion what would be an adequate salary that Government ought to pay to an officer in that situation?—I am not one of those that would give money to make them lazy, because there is a line to be drawn; but I think that a guinea is too little; because, taking the thing for granted that a man has been very lucky this week, the next week, and the other week, yet he may stand upon his oars for a month, then it takes all the cream off that milk entirely; and I am decidedly of opinion that he should be held up and made respectable. I would give them a hundred a year, or two guineas a week, and the effects of their industry.

Giving a power to the Magistrates to reward them according to their merit?—Yes; and to the Judges at the assizes.

Do you think that it is an advantageous plan for the Public Police offering the large rewards, which the Government and individuals occasionally do, for the apprehension of offenders?—Yes, I will state why I do: In case of those desperate affairs which have appeared before the eyes of the Public, such as the murder of the Revenue Officers, or the glaring outrages committed by poachers, if there was not a liberal reward, I do not speak of a thousand pounds, but a couple of hundred pounds; we should reckon, in the old school, that an hundred pounds was large; and we used all to fly about; but in the case of the Revenue Officers a thousand pounds was given. It gives an opportunity of those people belonging to the party impeaching. One of them says " damn it, I am made for ever; I will go and tell"; and it gives a large scope for a man to reflect—supposing I go with others and commit a depredation to night, and I afterwards give information, they are bound to pay me the reward; for the advertisement is, whoever shall give infortion, or cause the parties to be apprehended, and I have caused that by my information. It is not one time in twenty that there is any thing like 1,000 *l.* The largest sum ever given by the Bank was 200 *l.*, and that does not always come to the officer, for if there is a person who has been the means of giving the officer information, they must give that person. I remember a case of an intended robbery at the Post Office, where the Receiver General's Office was to be robbed; the very keys were all made, and nothing could stop it, and they only waited for a very large sum, for they were in the Office twice. I think there was too much said about it; the consequence was, the officer got a little blamed. Why? was not it a noble information for these men to go and convince the Solicitor and Secretary of the Post Office that a banditti was to have come in on such a night, and plundered the Office of from ten to 20,000 *l.*? There was a doubt as to the fact; but they went so far as to prove it. I said to Vickery, " prove your case; bring all the parties forward, face to face," for in most cases we never bring our informer forward; for, as I observed to Lord Loughborough, on a question by Sir William Garrow, " Ah! Townsend, you have been very lucky, who gave you information?" and I laughed at the question. It would not do for us to answer those questions.

In the case you allude to, Vickery was paid a large sum of money?—I do not know the amount of the sum exactly; I do not think he got much himself.

Do you not think that those large rewards being offered have a tendency to make the officers of the Police, to a certain degree, neglect where there is no reward offered?—I should hope not; because it has frequently occurred, and does frequently occur, that officers take up a variety of people, and convict them for transportation, and they get nothing. I have many times myself; and I recently saw it done by several of our own officers, who have not got a farthing. Sometimes they meet an old thief, and search him, and find something upon him that leads to discovery, and he is tried and convicted, and they get nothing but what the Court gives them, what is termed the expenses, of four shillings, or three and sixpence a day.

Are

John Townsend.

Are the officers of the Police much in the habit of frequenting that species of public-house, which is technically known by the name of a flash-house, where thieves and people of bad character resort, for the purpose of looking after those people?—I am not able to answer that, for I have not been with any one who is an officer of our Office at present, in a case of that description; but I should strongly suspect they do; but they will be much more able to answer that than I can.

Do you think the existence of those houses assists at all in the detection of thieves? —I am decidedly of opinion, and always was, that a flash-house, as they term it, which is a disorderly house, or a house to which those men must resort; for the fact is, a thief will never sit amongst honest men, it is not his province to do it, nor would he trust himself with those people; therefore there must be bad houses the same as there are brothels, because A. says to B. I will meet you at such a place to night. I know five-and-twenty, or six-and-twenty years ago, there were houses where we could pop in, and I have taken three or four, or five and six at a time, and three or four of them have been convicted, and yet the public-house was tolerably orderly too. I do not know whether they go and sit amongst them, and eat and drink, and so on, that is another part of speech; we did not formerly do much of that sort of traffic.

Did you consider the existence of those houses in that day as tending to facilitate the detection of offenders?—No question about it; for it has often turned out that when the information has come to the Office, as it might be this morning, of a foot-pad robbery done so and so, poor Jealous and another Officer, McManus, who was many years in the Office, and I, have slipt out and gone to some of the flash-houses and looked about—nobody there; and gone to another, and very likely hit upon the party going to it, or in it.

Do you believe the existence of similar houses at this day affords similar facility to that afforded at the time you speak of?—I cannot say how they are managed now; but I do not hear that they are any worse managed; I do not hear of any misconduct from any of the officers, I mean of their doing any thing imprudent, or I should be one of the first to take care that that came to the fountain head, for I have always been but of one opinion, if you are caught tripping, off you must go. The moment persons are disturbed meeting at such a house, and the license is taken away, they must distribute themselves somewhere, then it would be a length of time before the officer, however vigilant and attentive, will find them out again; though they frequently get at them through the women that they live with; very likely through the misconduct of this poor unhappy part of the community, will, after they have been living a long length of time with one wretch, give her a kick or a blow, and turn her out, and then comes the woman, out of revenge, and tells the officer where the parties use, or where they are to be found, so that in many cases the women are great assistants to the officers.

Is the flash-house an assistance to the officer?—Certainly the flash-house can do the officer no harm, if he does not make harm of it; if an officer goes there, and acts foolishly, and does any thing improper, the same as for me to go to-night to all the brothels, (I believe I know all of them, but was there ever any one who would say that I went and asked to have a glass of wine, and so on, there, and that no money should be asked;) what sort of a servant should I be? I ought to be turned out, and never employed in the department of the Police again. Who has been more in confidence than I have been with the youngest part of society of the highest rank. How often have I gone to brothels, there to talk over a little accident that might happen to A's son, or B's son, or my Lord this or the other's son? but the consequence was not a morsel of liberty, or how would Townsend act upon those functions of authority, and get what the parties asked me to do; no, he must go there full of power, with great distance towards the keeper of that brothel; and as to the poor wretches, in many cases, I have been employed to bring daughters home to their parents, persons of great respect and consequence; we have not found them at one place, but at another; we have taken them home, and there there has been an end to it; the respectable young men, however liberally educated, are often very great fools, for they often subject themselves to vast inconveniences through their own misconduct, by committing themselves ridiculously and absurdly, going to brothels and getting into scrapes, and what has been the consequence! the consequence is, " Townsend, what is to be done?" sometimes with the father, and sometimes with the party himself: but how would this thing be executed if I were to attempt any thing like what I stated before? No, I will take upon myself to say, I never drank a glass of wine with those sort of characters, because it will not do; in

order

John Townsend.

order to execute my duty properly I must keep them at a proper distance; and it is only a foolish man that would attempt it.

Do you think, from your long observation, that the morals and manners of the lower people in the metropolis are better or worse than formerly?—I am decidedly of opinion, that, with respect to the present time, and the early part of my time, such as 1781, 2, 3, 4, 5, 6, and 7, where there is one person convicted now, I may say, I am positively convinced there were five then; we never had an execution wherein we did not grace that unfortunate gibbet with ten, twelve, to thirteen, sixteen, and twenty; and forty I once saw at twice; I have them all down at home. I remember, in 1783, when Serjeant Adair was Recorder, there were forty hung at two executions: the unfortunate people themselves laugh at it now; they call it a bagatelle. I was conversing with an old offender some years ago, who has now quite changed his life; and he said, " Why, Sir, where there is one hung now, there were five when I was young;" and I said, " Yes, you are right in your calculation, and you are very lucky that you were spared so long, and have lived to be a better man." I agree with George Barrington, whom I brought from Newcastle; and however great Lord Chief Baron Eyre's speech was to him, after he had answered him, it came to this climax: " Now," says he, " Townsend, you heard what the Chief Baron said to me; a fine flowery speech, was it not?" " Yes:" " But he did not answer the question I put to him." Now how could he? Now after all that the Chief Baron said to him after he was acquitted, giving him advice, this word was every thing: says he, " My Lord, I have paid great attention to what you have been stating to me, after my acquittal: I return my sincere thanks to the Jury for their goodness: but your Lordship says, you lament very much that a man of my abilities should not turn my abilities to a better use. Now, my Lord, I have only this reply to make: I am ready to go into any service, to work for my labour, if your Lordship will but find me a master." Why, what was the reply to that?—" Gaoler, take the prisoner away." Why, who would employ him? that was the point. It is really farcical with me sometimes, when I have heard Magistrates say, " Young man, really I am very sorry for you; you are much to be pitied; you should turn your talents to a better account; and you should really leave off this bad course of life." Yes, that is better said than done; for where is there any body to take these wretches? I will take upon myself to say, that I have known this to be a clear case, which they have said to me; " Sir, we do not thieve from disposition; but we thieve because we cannot get employment: our character is damned, and nobody will have us:" and so it is; there is no question about it. Then again, upon the other hand, there are cases where men might do, but will not.

Do you think, that, taking the small number of executions, which is the modern practice, there is a less or greater number of crimes committed now than formerly? —I think myself there are less; and I am not alone in that. I am astonished, considering the times. Now, for instance, what was expected? that there would be knocking down, and this, and that, and t'other. What was the character of this Sessions, when the Committee are told, and for a confirmation they may send to the Secretary of State's Office, how many criminals were convicted? I have known 220 tried at one Sessions; I have convicted myself from thirteen to twenty-five for returning from transportation at one Sessions.

Is it your opinion, according to your observation, that the morals and manners of the lower people are better?—I really do not think they are worse; and with respect to cruelty in robbery, such desperate things as we had formerly, there is not a thing to be compared to. His Majesty was advised by Mr. Thomas Townsend, then Secretary of State in 1783, to punish with severity. Mr. Taylor's father was Sheriff at that time; in that very Sessions the enormity of the offences was thought so desperate, and plunder had got to such an alarming pitch, that a letter went down, by command of His Majesty, to the then Judges and Recorders sitting, that His Majesty would dispense with all the Recorders Reports, and that they should select the worst of the offenders out, and order them for execution, as the Court should think fit: they did so; I think it was either five or seven in the Sessions week, on the Friday were selected, called up on the Saturday, and sentenced, and ordered for execution on the following Friday.

Was not the punishment of death put into execution more frequently then than it is now; were not criminals then hung for the same species of offences for which they are now transported?—The number capitally convicted now is not so large, by any means.

510.

According to the returns laid before Parliament, at different periods, the number of persons committed for trial seems to have increased considerably of late years; should you consider that increase to arise from the augmentation of the population of the city, or from the increase of crimes amongst the lower orders?—The increase of the population must be taken into consideration, certainly.

Do not you attribute part of it to the increased activity of the Police?—Certainly it is not to be compared, for a moment; when I first knew it, there were three Justices at Bow-street, Sir John Fielding and two others; and the head Magistrate, for his remuneration, took fees on what they did—paltry fees; and the Act of the Legislature swept away all the Magistrates two-and-four-pences, and all the rest of their emoluments of that kind; Sir John Fielding was paid by those fees of Office.

Had Sir John Fielding any salary?—Very trifling, if any; the Chief Magistrate used every Monday morning to settle with the Clerk the account of those fees.

The activity of the officers of Bow-street has infinitely increased of late years?—No doubt about it; and there is one thing which appears to me most extraordinary, when I remember, in very likely a week, there should be from ten to fifteen highway robberies. We have not had a man committed for a highway robbery lately; I speak of persons on horseback; formerly there were two, three, or four highwaymen, some on Hounslow Heath, some on Wimbledon Common, some on Finchley Common, some on the Romford road. I have actually come to Bow-street in the morning, and while I have been leaning over the desk, had three or four people come in and say, I was robbed by two highwaymen in such a place; I was robbed by a single highwayman in such a place. People travel now safely by means of the horse-patrole that Sir Richard Ford planned. Where are there highway robberies now? as I was observing to the Chancellor at the time I was up at his house on the Corn Bill: he said, " Townsend, I knew you very well so many years ago." I said, " yes, my Lord; I remember your coming first to the bar, first in your plain gown, and then as king's counsel, and now Chancellor. Now your Lordship sits as Chancellor, and directs the executions on the Recorder's report; but where are the highway robberies now?" and his Lordship said, " Yes, I am astonished." There are no footpad robberies or road robberies now, but merely jostling you in the streets. They used to be ready to pop at a man as soon as he let down his glass; that was by banditties.

You remember the case of Abershaw?—Yes; I had him tucked up where he was; it was through me. I never left a court of justice without having discharged my own feeling as much in favour of the unhappy criminal as I did on the part of the prosecution; and I once applied to Mr. Justice Buller to save two men out of three who were convicted; and on my application we argued a good deal about it. I said, " My Lord, I have no motive but my duty; the Jury have pronounced them guilty. I have heard your Lordship pronounce sentence of death, and I have now informed you of the different dispositions of the three men. If you choose to execute them all I have nothing to say about it; but was I you, in the room of being the officer, and you were to tell me what Townsend has told you I should think it would be for a justification for you to respite those two unhappy men, and hang that one who has been convicted three times before." The other men never had been convicted before, and the other had been three times convicted; and he very properly did. And how are Judges or Justices to know how many times a man has been convicted but by the information of the officer in whose duty and department it is to keep a register of old offenders. The Magistrate sits up there, he knows nothing of it till the party is brought before him; he cannot.

Do you think any advantages arise from a man being put on a gibbet after his execution?—Yes, I was always of that opinion; and I recommended Sir William Scott to hang the two men that are hanging down the river. I will state my reason. We will take for granted, that those men were hanged as this morning, for the murder of those Revenue Officers—they are by law dissected; the sentence is, that afterwards the body is to go the surgeons for dissection; there is an end of it—it dies. But look at this: There are a couple of men now hanging near the Thames, where all the sailors must come up; and one says to the other, " Pray what are those two poor fellows there for?"—" Why," says another, " I will go and ask." They ask. " Why, those two men are hung and gibbetted for murdering His Majesty's Revenue Officers." And so the thing is kept alive. If it was not for this, people would die, and nobody would know any thing of it. In Abershaw's case I said to the sheriff, " The only difficulty in hanging this fellow upon this

place

place is its being so near Lord Spencer's house :" But we went down, and pointed out a particular place; he was hung at the particular pitch of the hill where he used to do the work. If there was a person ever went to see that man hanging, I am sure there was a hundred thousand. I received information that they meant to cut him down. I said to Sir Richard Ford, " I will counteract this ; in order to have it done right, I will go and sit up all night, and have eight or ten officers at a distance, for I shall nail these fellows ;" for I talked cant language to him. However we had the officers there, but nobody ever came, or else, being so close to Kent-street, they would have come down and sawed the gibbet, and taken it all away, for Kent-street was a very desperate place, though it is not so now. Lord Chief Justice Eyre once went the Home Circuit ; he began at Hertford, and finished at Kingston. Crimes were so desperate, that in his charge to the Grand Jury at Hertford, he finished : " Now, gentlemen of the Jury, you have heard my opinion as to the enormity of the offences committed ; be careful what bills you find, for whatever bills you find, if the parties are convicted before me, if they are convicted for a capital offence, I have made up my mind, as I go through the circuit, to execute every one." He did so : He never saved man or woman ; and a singular circumstance occurred, that stands upon record fresh in my mind ; there were seven people convicted for a robbery in Kent-street, for calling in a pedlar ; and after robbing the man, he jumped out of window. There were four men and three women concerned ; they were all convicted, and all hanged in Kent-street, opposite the door ; and, I think, on Kennington Common eight more, making fifteen ; all that were convicted were hung.

Do you think the milder execution of the law, which is at present practised, has had any bad effect in increasing the number of criminals ?—It is impossible, almost, to say ; one would hope not : but I really do not know what to say to that ; I do not know what the Penitentiary House may do, for I know very little of its regulations yet, but I will take upon myself to say, that the confining a person for five years will be more punishment than ten executions. Lock a man up for five years, it is any thing, and every thing. I do not know what its rules may be, but I know to an old thief it would be dreadful, day after day. I have always been decidedly of opinion, and have told the Judges so, nobody, in my opinion, ought to suffer death but those who commit murder, maim and cut ; and setting fire ; and offences against nature ; as to all the rest, if you sent them to the Penitentiary House I think it would be preferable.

State to the Committee what you think are the leading obstructions to the conviction of criminals against the public peace ?—In the first place, persons object to the expense ; we all know that the expense is not so much, provided the prosecution is not conducted by attorney and counsel ; but we cannot beat that into the public ; and if that is done there comes a bill of twenty or thirty pounds. Others do not like it because there is such a waste of time ; sometimes they must wait three, four or five days at the Old Bailey before their trial comes on, besides the examination at the Office, all of which are existing circumstances, that are daily occurring, and therefore a great many people will not prosecute ; and in some cases persons are deterred from an unwillingness to have their names brought in.

Do you think reasons such as you have given, operate very strongly on a great proportion of those individuals who suffer injury in one way and another, and prevent their appearance ?—I think there are a great number of offenders escape merely because persons will not go to the expense and trouble of prosecuting.

John Nelson Lavender, called in, and Examined.

WHAT Office do you belong to ?--Queen-square.

How long have you belonged to that Office ?—Six years, the nineteenth of last March.

Did you hold any situation in that Office, or any other, prior to your appointment there ?—Yes, I held a situation in Bow-street Office for five years.

Is the situation you hold now to be considered as one in the way of promotion ? —Not exactly so : I left Bow-street ; I was one of the Patrole ; I left on account of a quarrel with the late Mr. Bond.

What is the nature of the duties of your Office ?—We have to attend from eleven in the morning to three in the afternoon, and from seven to eight in the evening.

Do

John Nelson Lavender.

Do you all attend regularly, or is it only a proportion of you each day?—We all ought to attend, but if we are out on our duty that attendance is not required; it is understood that we should attend, but if there is any business comes into the Office, or any information of felony, we are dispatched.

It is a rule of the Office, that the individual wanting your assistance is sure to find some of you there at Office-hours?—Yes; and when the Office is shut there is a house of call for us.

Your salary is one guinea per week?—It is.

Are you accustomed to attend at any of the Public Offices?—No, I attend at the Opera House twice, and sometimes three times a week; I succeeded Mr. Townsend in that appointment.

Of course you receive from the Managers of the Opera an emolument for so doing?—Yes, I receive a guinea a night; and I am obliged to provide other assistance.

Are you accustomed to receive compensation from private individuals, who employ you on any specific service in which you are engaged?—Yes; and that is the only means by which we can exist.

If it were not for that reward which you receive for specific services performed, should you consider the salary paid by the Public as sufficient to induce you to keep the situation which you at present hold?—Certainly not; I could not do it, from the nature of my business; that salary would very frequently be spent in one half of the first day, we are obliged to spend a good deal of money in obtaining information of which the Government knows nothing.

Do you receive in cases of convictions or apprehension of offenders under the Statute, a share in that reward which is known by the name of the Parliamentary Reward?—I have received several shares; but that is a business which I always decline, if I can possibly avoid it; no Police Officer can go into the box at the Old Bailey with any comfort to himself, knowing that he will be asked the question by counsel, which is always extremely unpleasant.

You are then quite aware, when you are placed in that situation that it is one of suspicion to a Jury who are to receive your evidence, and to your own breast it is most painful?—I feel it so always.

Can you state to the Committee what is the amount which you should suppose any officer at your Office has made in any one year by the Parliamentary rewards? —I think that in our Office there has been less made than in any other Office. I should conceive no one of them has ever made 30 *l.* a year by those rewards. We have had very few convictions in our District for these four or five years; I do not think there have been more than four or five burglaries.

Should you not think the other officers, as well as yourself, would be much better satisfied with having rewards for specific services performed, paid either by the Magistrates, or ordered by the Judge, you then being a competent witness, than by the present mode?—I think I can answer, that with a great deal of truth, on the part of myself and my brother officers, that it is the feeling of every one of them that the Parliamentary reward should cease; that they would feel much better satisfied to be paid by the Magistrate for any extra services performed.

Even though the amount received might be less than they now receive?—Certainly. I have convicted two as notorious offenders as have troubled the town for many years, last Sessions; the celebrated Roberts, and White, Conkey Beau, as he is called; and the only reward I got for that was sixteen shillings.

Was that a share of the Parliamentary reward?—An allowance made by the county to prosecutors and witnesses attending.

In the nature of a compensation for loss of time?—Yes; but it was by no means a compensation; in the one case the parties are bankrupts, and the officers are left merely to that.

Have not the Magistrates at the different Police Offices a power to give something in the nature of rewards for extra services?—The Police Act mentions it; but I have always found our own Magistrates decline it; they scarcely pay the expenses of the officers. At the Bow-street Office I believe they are paid for every thing, and that very liberally; but they are under a different establishment from the other Police Offices. I do not think, since I have been at Queen-square Office, which is six years, that my payment for extra services has amounted to seven pounds, except where I have been out as an extra constable on public fetes, and on such occasions.

Supposing that the Parliamentary rewards were taken away, and that the officers

of

of the Police were to receive for their exertions the eward which individuals might think fit to pay them for their trouble, what should you think a sufficient salary on the part of the public?—As an officer is expected to keep himself, and to be above temptation, and to do nothing mean, I should not think the Government could think of giving him less than 120*l*. or 130*l*. a year.

Are you not of opinion, that if the present salary was doubled, and the Magistrates had power to reward their officers for extra services, and the Judges the same at the assizes, that that would be a sufficient remuneration to the officers for their services?—Yes; if the Magistrates and Judges would pay officers for their expenses in travelling, whether they succeed or not; for on many occasions we do not succeed, and then it is very hard for an officer to be out of pocket his expenses; I am sure I have spent more than half my salary in expenses, which are actually thrown away, and which I have no means of recovering; and if I did not do that I should perhaps get nothing at all.

Do you think that an increase of salary to the extent that you have mentioned, 120*l*. or 130*l*. a year, would be the means of causing a greater relaxation on the part of the officers than now exists?—No; I should not think it would; if their salaries were increased, there would be still the same thirst for gain, and for the Magistrate's reward; as for the Parliamentary rewards, it would increase their zeal for the public service, it would make a man more desirous of keeping his situation.

Is it your practice to frequent those public-houses which are called flash-houses, for the purpose of looking after thieves, and persons of bad character, whom you may want to find?—Certainly it is.

Do you consider the existence of those houses as facilitating that object?—They are certainly a necessary evil; if those houses were done away we should have the thieves resort to private houses and holes of their own, and we should never find them.

Is it your opinion that flash-houses are used by old offenders as places for the instruction of the juvenile offenders?—No; I do not think they are.

As you are in the habit of frequenting those houses, do you frequently meet with juvenile offenders associating with old offenders in those houses?—No; I have seen old offenders pick them out: the young offenders begin by seeing one another at the Theatre door, and in the Park; a great proportion of them are out-door apprentices.

You are of opinion that the flash-houses do not increase the number of offenders? —No, I think not; I believe there is more instruction given in the streets than in those houses; they come there as any other tradesmen will, and sometimes they come there to divide their spoil: there was an instance of a man being robbed in the street; the thieves got away, and we found them immediately in a house in Wild-street.

Do you know whether there are any houses for the exclusive reception of young offenders, boys and girls?—I do not believe there are any; I heard of one, and that we very completely put a stop to; that was not a public-house, but a coffee-house in Round-court in the Strand, and of a most miserable description; we found some young girls, and, in fact, boys there; that was about two years ago.

You have no reason to believe that any such houses now exist?—No.

That you considered as a rare instance?—Yes.

In point of fact, it is not so much in public-houses, as they are called, that those people assemble, as in houses of the nature of oyster-shops?—I do not know how that is.

Do you know of an oyster-shop in Carlisle-street, Soho-square?—I know there is an oyster-shop there.

There is also one in Brydges-street?—Yes; that is a receptacle for thieves, no doubt; it is kept by a bawdy-house-keeper; I think the woman's name is Benjamin, at least she is the owner of it, if she does not live there.

Do you not think that in houses of that description the boys and girls are trained up in such a system of vice as to lead afterwards to the perpetration of greater crimes?—There is no doubt at all about that; but the way in which girls are brought into this sort of mischief is by old bawds going about the town, and laying their hands on every girl who has a pretty face; and they actually seduce the boys before they think of such things.

Do you think that shutting the doors of houses of this description would be the

*John Nelson
Lavender:*

means of the prevention of crimes ?—Yes, it would be a most desirable thing ; there is a house in Bedford-court, which is a nest of the greatest evil; it is the business of the parish to remove them, but they do not interfere.

Is it not very difficult to prosecute those houses to conviction ?—I do not think it is, for it is done on the representation of two house-keepers to the constable of the ward, and then the parish indict.

Has it fallen within your knowledge, what has been the result of those prosecutions?—Yes, in one or two the parties have been convicted, and suffered six months imprisonment ; one case in Villiers-street in the Strand.

Do you know the expense of those prosecutions ?—That depends upon the lawyers bill.

Fifty or sixty pounds ?—Yes, it is generally as much as that ; it is generally the vestry-clerk of the parish, and he makes as good a thing as he can of it.

Do you not consider it as part of your duty to report the existence of those houses to the Magistrates of your Office ?—No, I do not ; I consider it the duty of the parish constable, or the constable of the ward.

The constable of the parish has no connection whatever with your Office ?—Not any. I think it would be a better thing if he had.

He is appointed by the High Constable ?—He is elected at the Court-Leet, and frequently receives a sum of money to be substitute for a respectable housekeeper; half the men who are constables take it for the ten or twelve pounds at Easter. There is an enmity between the parish constables and the police constables, and always has been ever since I knew it.

It is your opinion, that if their was a greater connection between the Police Offices and the different Boards of Police, it would tend to the prevention of crimes? —I am sure it would, if the Parish Officers were made dependent upon the Magistrates ; they set us at defiance, and say they do not belong to us, but to the parish, and then the persons for whom they serve stand by them, and there is no doing any thing with them.

Is it not a matter of common notoriety, that the watchman is generally a person, who supposing him to be awake, which he seldom is, is in the constant habit of receiving money from the women of the town who parade the streets in his district? —That is too true, for I have seen it ; I have absolutely seen the watchmen abused for not protecting the girls after they have given them money ; and I have seen the watchmen abuse the girls, and beat them for not giving them money ; I took a watchman off his duty in the Strand for doing that about a year and a half ago.

Do you know any thing about the way in which persons, when charges are made against them, are taken and lodged in the watch-house ?—I know the watchmen take them to the watch-house unless half a crown is given them, and then frequently not.

When you go to the flash-houses, is it your custom to associate with the persons there ?—Yes ; and a man must do that for a good while before he will be able to gain any information.

The Committee have been given to understand, that it frequently happens that offenders are suffered to frequent flash-houses, after it is known that they have committed an offence ; but the offence they have committed not being of such a nature as to hang out a large reward, those persons have been suffered to escape without apprehension ; is that the fact ?—I do not believe it ; I have passed almost the whole of my life in the Police, my father was in it, and I never heard of such a thing.

The Committee are to understand, that if you ever had any information against a person, and knew where to find him, you would take him into custody ?—I can lay my hand upon my heart and say I would immediately.

Whether the offence for which he was taken would be productive of great reward or small?—Certainly ; how can an Officer calculate upon what he would be worth if he was left ; I know there has been such an idea, as that a man would not be taken until he was worth so much, but it is not so ; there is very little difference in the rewards ; I would never associate with a man concerned in the Police if I knew such a thing of him. I believe the only reason why Police Officers frequent flash-houses is to obtain information for the good of the Public ; certainly for our own good as well ; for a man cannot be expected to attend merely for the good of the Public ; but it is not for the company.

James

James Bartlett, called in, and Examined.

WHAT situation do you hold?—Watch-house keeper of St. Paul, Covent-garden.

Who appoints you to that situation?—The Watch Committee of the parish.

Is it a permanent situation, held during good behaviour, or by annual election?—Elected once a-year.

How long have you held it?—Eight years.

Have you a charge-book?—Yes.

Are the names of all the persons, as well as for what they are charged, written in that book?—They are, except from the Police officers; when they bring them we do not enter the charge, only from the watchmen, beadles, and so forth.

Is it generally signed by the person who gives the charge?—Always.

Are the leaves of this book ever torn out, or is it otherwise defaced?—No.

Are charges ever written upon sheets of paper, and stuck upon the book afterwards?—No, it has never been the practice since I have been there.

Are you in possession of the book in the state in which it has been kept for the last twelve months?—I am, and farther back than that; four or five years back.

Then you state to the Committee that it is kept regularly?—Yes.

What is the average number of charges you have nightly?—Sometimes we have not had a charge for four or five weeks together, and sometimes eight or ten of a night.

When a person is given into your charge, what is your mode of securing him, where do you place him?—In the watch-house.

Have you more rooms than one?—Four; three strong-rooms and a bed-room.

Are the strong-rooms floored?—All boarded.

Are they damp?—One is a little damp, but the others are not; we have two up stairs and two down, one down stairs is a little damp, but the other is very dry; we seldom put any body there, if we can help it.

Does it often happen that many of those unfortunate boys and girls who frequent the booths of Covent Garden, which is their nightly resort and shelter, are brought to you by the constables for the night?—No; they are not brought by the constables of the night, they are often brought by the watchmen and beadles.

What do you do with them?—Take them before a Magistrate, and the Magistrates desire us to go for their friends, and some are delivered up to their friends; some have been sent to Tothill-fields for a time.

But, generally speaking, the number of boys and girls who sleep out under the booths and baskets of Covent Garden, have no friends, being without parents, and entirely destitute of friends?—Very few of them; not one out of one hundred of that description; their friends have generally sent them out begging, and if they do not bring home money as they ought to do, they flog them; that is the story we get from them.

Should you not consider that to the amount of thirty or forty persons sleep nightly in Covent Garden who have no home to go to?—No, not so many as that; perhaps eight or ten.

Are those persons known to the constables?—Yes.

How are the constables appointed?—By the court of Burgesses.

The constables that serve are those that are appointed; or are they those that are paid by others for taking the burthen of their situation?—There are about three that serve themselves, and three that find substitutes.

How many are there of them altogether?—Six.

Are there but six constables in your parish?—No, our parish is very small; it is only twenty acres of land altogether, we are quite surrounded by St. Martin's.

The Theatre and the Garden are part of your parish?—Yes, part of the Theatre, the Lobby.

Who appoints the watchmen?—They are appointed by the Committee.

How many are there?—Seventeen.

Are you aware that there is an understanding between the watchmen and the women of the town, that parade the streets in your parish?—That is a caution we strictly give, but I am afraid it is too much the practice.

510.   Have

James Bartlett.

Have you not seen, in your situation, that it has often happened that women of the town have been brought by the watchmen, and there is every reason to believe they would not have so brought them if the watchmen had been paid?—No, I do not believe that.

Do you not think then, that the watchmen receive money of the women of the town for permitting them to pursue their avocations unmolested?—No, I do not.

If they do not receive money, do you not think they receive spirits?—Yes, they do, I am afraid, drink with them, because I have often caught them drinking with them, and I have instantly discharged them, which I am empowered to do.

What is your attendance at the watch house?—I live there, my apartments are there; our hours of duty are from eight to seven in the winter, and from ten to five in the summer.

Is there a person always up in the house?—Yes.

What is the nature of the attendance of the watchmen in your parish, and how do they relieve each other?—They do not relieve each other, they go on at the usual hour of setting, and remain till the morning, and call the hour and the half-hour.

Is there any person that over-looks them?—The beadle.

Is it the duty of the beadle to go out at different hours of the night?—It is.

Does he do it?—Yes, he does, two or three times in the night; he is ordered to go out every hour.

Is it the duty of the watchmen to prevent disturbances in the streets, and to prevent the flocking together of women of the town, and idle persons?—Yes, it is; they are ordered to disperse them.

How do you account for it, that the streets in the neighbourhood of the Theatre are, during all hours of the night, in the state they are?—It is on account of the parish being so near the Theatres that the girls lodge round there: Drury-lane, and the parts adjoining, are quite full of them; it is quite handy for them to go on with their purposes.

If it is the duty of those watchmen to prevent idle and dissolute persons from remaining in the streets, how comes it to pass that they are permitted to remain there, and not turned to their own houses?—I think they do the best they can.

Is it not a matter of public notoriety, not only during the Theatre, but after the Theatre has closed, that those streets present but one scene of riot and debauchery?—No, it is not the case; it may happen now and then; but I have strictly ordered the men to clear the streets as soon as the Theatres are over; and if they will not go, to take them before a Magistrate immediately. We have had thirteen or fourteen at the watch-house in a night; after the Theatres are over I do not think you will find many persons in the street; there are one or two watering-houses in the neighbourhood, and they will flock there, from all parts, to obtain spirits.

What is the salary the watchmen receive for their nightly duty?—Twelve and sixpence a week in the summer, and 17 s. 6 d. in the winter.

Are the watchmen generally old or young?—They are middle-aged men.

Lunæ, 10° *die Junii,* 1816.

The Honourable HENRY GREY BENNET, in The Chair.

The Rev. *Joshua King,* called in, and Examined.

YOU are clergyman of the parish of Bethnal-green?—The rector of that parish.

How long have you held that situation?—About seven years.

Do you principally reside there?—Yes, I do, and discharge all the duties myself.

Is it a very large parish?—It consists of a population of about 40,000, generally the lowest description of people; the overflowing population out of Spitalfields have settled in that parish.

As clergyman of the parish, you have felt it your duty to make yourself acquainted, as far as lay in your power, with the state and condition of the Police?—Surely.

What is that?—I am sorry to say that it is most deplorable; every Sunday morning, during the time of Divine Service, several hundred persons assemble in a field adjoining the church-yard, where they fight dogs, hunt ducks, gamble, enter into subscriptions to fee drovers for a bullock; I have seen them drive the animal through the most populous parts of the parish, force sticks pointed with iron, up the body, put peas into the ears, and infuriate the beast, so as to endanger the lives of all persons passing along the streets.

This on the Sunday?—At all times, chiefly on the Sunday, Monday, and sometimes Tuesday; Monday is the principal day; one or two thousand men and boys will, on these occasions, leave their looms and join in the pursuit; pockets are frequently picked; persons are tossed and torn; one day in the last summer, I am informed, that one man was killed, and two so severely wounded, that their lives were despaired of.

Did you ever learn whether that information was correct?—I am persuaded, with respect to one of them who was tossed in St. John-street, near my house; the other two were in Hackney-parish; they drove the beast into Hackney, where the accidents happened; one was taken to the hospital, where I understood he died.

Do they ever drive the bullock across the church-yard?—Yes; about two months ago, during the time of Divine Service, to the great consternation of the congregation, a bullock was hunted in the church-yard; and although Mr. Merceron, a Magistrate for the county, the beadles, and Mr. Merceron's clerk, who is a constable, were present; I cannot learn, that they took any steps to put a stop to so wanton and disgraceful an outrage; on the contrary, I have reason to believe, that the officers of my parish frequently connive at and sanction such practices.

What reason have you to believe that?—I have sent for a constable to request that he would furnish me with the names of some of the ringleaders, and I never could yet obtain a single name, though most of them were resident in the neighbourhood, and must be known to him, and I have sometimes seen him actually join in the chace.

Did you ever speak to Mr. Merceron, or to any of the Magistrates, or lay any special complaints before the Bench of Magistrates?—I complained to Mr. Merceron, about five years ago, of the disgraceful practice of bullock-hunting, and expressed a wish to be in the commission of the peace, that I might more effectually prevent such practices. Upon that occasion, Mr. Merceron declared that there was no kind of amusement he was so fond of as bullock-hunting, and that in his younger days he was generally the first in the chase; he discouraged me at the same time from entertaining any hopes of getting into the commission, by saying, no person could be appointed unless he was recommended by the other Magistrates; and that if any other Magistrate was necessary for the district, he should take care to recommend his friend Mr. Timmings, and not me.

Did

The Rev.
Joshua King.

Did you ever make any complaint to any other Magistrate, or to the Bench?— I have made a complaint to the Police Office, Worship-street, twice; they have sent officers both times immediately.

Did the interference of the officers of Worship-street put a stop for that time to the evil you complained of?—Yes, certainly, immediately; the mob dispersed, and I believe they took the bullock from them; in fact, I have taken two bullocks from them which they had driven into the church-yard I opened a stable door in the church-yard, the bullocks took refuge there, and I put a lock on and locked them in.

Do those bullocks, according to your belief, belong to any butcher, or are they purchased for the purpose of hunting?—I believe they belong to large droves, which are coming to Smithfield market, and that the persons who assemble in this field, fee the drovers to let them select a bullock out of their herd.

In the way to market?—Yes, on the Sunday, and sometimes in their coming from the market on the Monday.

Are those scenes of riot and confusion more frequent on the Sunday or the Monday?—On both days; but bullocks are, I think, more frequently hunted on the Monday than the Sunday; but this mob, which assembles on the Sunday, assembles generally on the Sunday about eleven o'clock, or a little before.

Was two months ago the last period in which the bullock-hunting has taken place?—No, there has been bullock-hunting since that; and I apprehend, from the inquiries I have made within the last few days, that it has been discontinued within the last fortnight or three weeks; since this Committee has been sitting, an alarm has been produced, and more pains taken to prevent those outrages.

You have mentioned the name of Mr. Timmings, whom Mr. Merceron called his friend, and whom he wished to recommend to be a Magistrate; did you know him?—He was a person who had retired from keeping an ale-house; a man extremely ignorant.

Were you personally acquainted with him?—Yes, he is since dead.

Have you made any application to the Lord Lieutenant or to any one else, for the purpose of being in the commission?—I wrote soon after, I expressed my wish to Mr. Merceron, to the two members for the county; from the one I received a letter, saying that he never interfered, and from the other I received no answer.

Independent of the bullock-hunting, are the scenes of riot and disorder great during the Sunday in the fields adjoining the church?—Extremely so.

Crowds of disorderly people of both sexes?—Yes, but principally men and boys; and when I have spoken to some of the Police officers, they have told me that they durst not interfere, on account of their being so numerous and so desperate.

Are you at all acquainted with the condition in which the public-houses are in, in your parish, whether they are orderly or disorderly?—Some of them I apprehend are very disorderly, and I cannot but think that great blame is imputable to the acting Magistrates for the district, for not suppressing the licences of such houses.

Do you know any that have been in that disorderly condition for several years?—Some of them have been represented as being very disorderly; and I will take the liberty of mentioning those that have been particularly specified, if it is wished.

Did you ever lay any complaint against the conduct of those houses before the licensing Magistrates?—I never did.

Do you know whether such complaint has ever been made by the officers of the parish?—No, I do not.

If those houses are considered as so disorderly, can you assign any reason why you did not feel it your duty to lay such information?—It was not till lately that any particular houses were pointed out.

How long is it since you have learned that there are particular houses in your parish that come under that description?—Probably about a month or six weeks ago.

How long have you been resident in the parish?—Seven years.

It is only within this month or six weeks that you have heard of any of the houses being disorderly?—No, I have heard that some of them were disorderly, but none were pointed out specifically to me till lately.

You considered the houses as for the resort of the lower classes of people in that neighbourhood?—Yes.

What

What are the particular houses the names of which you have learnt?—There are three that have been particularly pointed out; the one is the Sun in Slater-street, the Three Sugar Loaves in St. John-street, and the Seven Stars in Fleet-street.

Have those houses been particularly named to you, as being the three worst in the parish?—I do not know that they have been named as the worst, but as very disorderly.

Do you know any others that are disorderly?—None that I can speak to, as so disorderly as those two or three; others have been named, but I have not had an opportunity of making minute inquiry respecting them.

Do you know whether any complaint has ever been laid before the Magistrates, in respect of those houses?—I do not,

Do you know any thing as to the mode in which those houses are held, or who is the proprietor, or with whom they deal, that would lead you to think that any protection would be given them against such complaints, if they had been made?—The three houses I have mentioned belong to property of which Mr. Merceron is rent-gatherer; he took a lease of the latter house, that is of the Seven Stars, in the year 1788, and afterwards underlet it to Messrs. Hanburys; that and the Three Sugar Loaves are in Messrs. Hanburys trade.

Are those facts within your own knowledge?—Yes, they are.

Is the manner in which those houses are conducted particularly disorderly?—I have reason to believe it is; the Seven Stars and Three Sugar Loaves are a receptable for suspicious characters, at hours when all other public-houses are closed; and at the Sun, a club significantly termed a cock and hen club, has been, and I believe still is held.

In which boys and girls meet?—Yes, and get drunk and debauch one another.

Do you know, whether Mr. Merceron has the management of, as rent gatherer, or is the proprietor of many public-houses in the parish?—I have been given to understand, that Mr. Hanbury holds ten or twelve public-houses under him.

You do not know that of your own knowledge?—No, I do not; but I know that he serves a great number of those houses upon that property where Mr. Merceron is agent and rent-gatherer, from the boards over their doors.

Is there any personal difference between you and Mr. Merceron?—Nothing, except what has arisen from a disapprobation of his official conduct; he is the treasurer of the parish, has amassed a large fortune without any ostensible means; takes care to elect the most ignorant and the lowest characters, on whom he can depend, to fill all parochial offices, and to audit his accounts; when I say elect, I mean that his influence is so extensive in the parish, that whoever he nominates, the vestry is sure to sanction and appoint.

Has there been a considerable opposition to that influence within your own memory, by the parishioners?—Yes, there has; and indeed I am told that previous to my coming into the parish, the same opposition was manifested; that for the last 25 years, the respectable part of the parish have been contending with him for a successful examination of his accounts, and have never succeeded; with the assistance of the Dissenters, with whom he has identified himself, and the publicans who dare not withhold their support, he bears down all opposition; a grant of upwards of 12,000 *l.* from Parliament, during a time of great distress in the parish, in the year 1800, passed through his hands for the relief of the out-door poor, which I have reason to believe was not applied to the purpose for which it was intended, nor is it satisfactorily accounted for.

What reason have you to believe that?—I have got an extract, which I have made from the parish register, in which it appears to have been audited, and I have been informed, that he pretended he had mislaid or lost his vouchers, and not a single voucher was produced; Mr. Mitford, jun. was, I believe, sent down by Government, to inquire how the money had been expended; I am not aware how far he was satisfied. I have brought with me an extract from the parish register, purporting to be an audit of the account; that 505 *l.* which appears at the bottom, remained in his hands about two years; there was then a little disturbance in the parish, and it was brought forward and paid to the Poor's Rate account.

[The

The Rev.
Joshua King.

[The Extract was read, as follows :]

Easter Monday, 1802.

Joseph Merceron, Esq. one of the Committee appointed on Easter Monday last, for the Management of the Money voted by Parliament, for the Relief of this Parish, reported that they had received from Government the sum of £.12,165. 4. 4.

	£.	s.	d.
Paid by Weekly Payments - - - -	6,894	4	6
Paid sundry Tradesmen's Bills - - -	518	9	1
Paid Stationery, Printing, and incidental Expenses	109	8	7½
Paid to Poor Rate Account - - - -	3,412	13	4
Paid to Building Account - - - -	724	16	7
Balance in hand - - - -	505	12	2½
	£.12,165	4	4

Can you explain that part of the account by which that 3,400*l.* was paid to the Poor Rates?—That was before I came into the parish, and I cannot; I inquired at Down, Thornton & Co.'s banking-house, as to the amount of the sum that had gone through Mr. Merceron's hands, and I have reason to believe that he received nearly 500*l.* more than appears in that account; I have received a letter from their clerk to that effect; Mr. Merceron denies having received the money, and says it was brought to him by the church-wardens; the church-wardens are since dead, and how the matter stands cannot be explained.

You cannot explain at all how it came to pass that 3,412*l.* was paid over to the head of the Poor's Rate?—Not at all.

Has this business ever been investigated by the parish since you have been Rector?—An attempt has been made to investigate, but unsuccessfully.

From what cause?—Mr. Merceron did not think proper to give any account of it.

Were you not strong enough in the vestry to force him to an account?—By no means; I will state what occurred a very short time ago :—In order to prevent investigation, I have seen him instigate his creatures to riot and clamour, even within the walls of the church; he has taken his stand on the church steps, and proposed three times three huzzas, taking his hat off and being the foremost in the shout; so successful was he on that occasion, that lately he has adjourned all public vestry meetings to the church-yard, where a mob has collected to support him. He instigated that mob, at a late meeting, to attack a person of the name of Shevill, who, had he not taken refuge in my house, would probably have fallen a sacrifice to their fury.

What was the cause of the supposed quarrel between Mr. Merceron and Mr. Shevill?—Mr. Shevill had addressed the parishioners, requiring that Mr. Merceron should publish an annual account of the monies passing through his hands; Mr. Shevill published two addresses, which appeared to me very candid, and those, I believe, were the reasons of Mr. Merceron attacking him.

Is it the practice for the vestry to assemble in the church-yard?—That is a thing never known till lately.

How long has the practice been adopted?—I think on two late occasions, when they expected a very full meeting that has taken place.

Has every householder a right to vote at vestry meetings?—Every one rated at 15*l.* and upwards.

Do you believe that all those who have assembled were rated at 15*l.*?—The great bulk of the mob were not rated at that sum.

Of course they had no means in the church-yard of keeping the vestry distinct from the others?—Certainly not.

Have any legal measures ever been taken to correct the abuses of which you complain?—About three years ago, I advocated the cause of the parishioners, and instituted two indictments against Mr. Merceron; the one for having fraudulently altered the Poor Rates, after they had been allowed, whereby he doubled and trebled the rates of some, and reduced the rates of others; the other was for perjury, founded upon a series of oaths he had taken before the Commons, the Court of Delegates, and the Chancellor, upon the authenticity of which it chiefly depended, whether he retained some property he had possessed himself of, belonging to a poor idiot and her orphan sisters, or no; contrary to the uniform tenor of which oaths, the three Courts unequivocally decided and compelled him to restore the property.

The

The property, in point of fact, was restored?—It was; the houses and the money were restored, in pursuance of a decree of Chancery, bearing date 23d November 1812.

The Rev. Joshua King.

By what means did you become acquainted with the fact, as to his altering the Poor's Rate?—From the information which I received from the vestry clerk himself, who furnished me with the Poor's Rate books, and pointed out the alterations that had been made.

Did you obtain a verdict against him?—I was dissuaded by the person whom I was so unfortunate as to employ as my solicitor on the occasion, from being in Court at the time of the trials; he contrived to instruct the leading counsel to declare, that I had consented to a verdict of acquittal being obtained for the defendant without trial, although I had given positive instructions to proceed with the trials; the counsel have declared, both before and subsequent to that mysterious transaction, that had the trials gone on, there was no doubt of his being convicted.

Is the vestry clerk now living?—He is; I have extracts by me which I think amount to about five hundred cases, where alterations took place in the rates pointed out by the vestry clerk, and who still holds that office.

What is his name?—James May.

Is Mr. Merceron popular among the lower classes of the inhabitants in your parish?—Universally abhorred; but having the collection of rents to a very considerable extent, and a number of houses of a small description in the parish, and as he can command the publicans by being a licensing Magistrate, and having been a commissioner of the property tax, and sitting on all appeals with respect to the assessed as well as parochial taxes, he has had an opportunity of most despotically tyrannizing over the parish.

Is it the prevailing opinion in the parish, that a victualler has a better chance of obtaining a licence from the licensing Magistrates, if he applies for that licence through the medium of one person more than another?—Unquestionably; a man is considered a fool who applies for a licence through the medium of any other person than Messrs. Hanbury; I know there is an intimacy and connection between Mr. Merceron and them, for I heard Mr. Merceron formerly declare, when I was on better terms with him than I am at present, that Hanbury was a devilish good fellow, that he was always sending him presents, that he supplied his house with beer gratis, and that the week before he had sent him half a barrel of porter.

What is the state of the poor at this moment in your parish?—It is truly wretched; the house is overflowing with poor; I believe they are at this time crowded together in beds, and that there are as many as six or seven in a bed; the men and women are in separate wards, that is the only distinction which can be made; the master of the workhouse has declared to me, that the house is not capable of containing more than 350, and I believe at the present time there are 700.

Do you know whether there is a great want of work among the weavers who inhabit your parish; are many looms out of employment?—Very many.

It has been stated that there are nearly 3,000 looms out of employ in that vicinity at the present moment; do you know whether that is correct?—I am not aware of the exact number.

Is the situation of the poor in your parish worse now than it was last year?—I should conceive much, and the great inhumanity of the parish officers consists in the very scanty pittance they allow the out-door poor; they compel them all in the very crowded state of the house to come into the house, or they do not allow them more than from one shilling to three shillings per family, according to their number.

What is the allowance paid by the parish for each person in the workhouse per head per week?—I have no means of knowing that at all, but believe they cost the parish about 5 *s.* 6 *d.* per head.

Do you know what is the amount of bread, meat, &c. received per week, in the workhouse, each person?—Ninety oz. of bread, 18 oz. of meat, ¼ lb. of butter, or 7 oz. of cheese; three pints of water gruel, and three pints of broth; three teaspoonfuls of salt, and ½ lb. of soap, per ward; also, seven pints of small beer, valued at about 5 *s.* 6 *d.* per barrel.

Do you know what is the amount of the poor rate that was levied last year, or is to be levied this year, in the parish?—I do not.

From

The Rev.
Joshua King.

From your observation, during a residence of seven years, can you state to the Committee, what is the moral condition of the inhabitants of your parish at present, contrasting it with what it was a few years back?—Not at all improved, or likely to be, in consequence of the want of education; for although we have such an enormous population, we are only educating an hundred and twenty children under the Establishment, and we have only one parish church, capable of containing about twelve hundred, for the accommodation of all. I am not aware what number are educating by the Methodists, but I believe a considerable number.

Are there any other schools established in your parish?—None, where they are educated free of expense, excepting those which the Dissenters may have established; they are principally Sunday schools.

Is there any school of the British and Foreign School Society?—Not immediately in my parish, but in the parish of Spitalfields adjoining, there is a very large one.

Do many of the children of your parish attend?—I do not know the number, but I should conceive a considerable number.

You consider the state of your parish as more indigent at present, and as ignorant as it was some years back?—Quite, or more so.

It is then to the joint operation of increased indigence, and not augmented knowledge, that you attribute most materially the depraved state of the lower orders?—Certainly.

Do you know, whether the parish officers pay a regular attention to keeping the streets orderly and quiet at night?—Considering the description of population, I think they are as orderly as can be expected.

By whom are the constables named?—Every officer in the parish is appointed by Mr. Merceron, and all obey his mandates.

Is he high constable?—No, he is not.

Who is the legal officer holding this office?—I do not know who is the constable for this year; the officers are elected on Easter Monday, and I think the list is not yet printed.

Whoever Mr. Merceron thinks proper to nominate, is chosen as a matter of course?—Quite so.

Martis, 11° *die Junii,* 1816.

The Honourable HENRY GREY BENNET, in The Chair.

The Reverend *Edward Robson*, called in, and Examined.

YOU are a Magistrate of the county of Middlesex?—Yes.

Do you act as a Magistrate in the district in which you live?—Yes.

Are you accustomed to sit upon the bench at either of the Police Offices, to aid and assist the Police Offices?—No, I never go to any but one, except once in two years perhaps; but as I happen to live within half a dozen doors of Whitechapel Office, I go in almost every day, and have done ever since I have been a Magistrate, which is eleven years.

You give your assistance to that Office almost daily?—If there be any necessity; I am there merely as a lounger more than any thing else; but if any one of the Magistrates happens to be out of the way, or any thing occurs in which I can be of use, I give my assistance.

Do you attend on the licensing day?—Yes.

Have you so done for some time past?—Yes, ever since I was a Magistrate; indeed for the last year I have been so ill I have not attended every transfer day; there is only one licensing day in the year, the others are transfer days.

Are the public houses within your district, orderly or disorderly, speaking generally?—I suppose they may generally be considered orderly; there are some less so than others, but in general I suppose very passable.

Since you have acted as a Magistrate, have you had many complaints laid before you as to the conduct of particular victuallers holding those houses?—Yes, there have been a good many, but the chief of them petty offences; there is one man that never will be licensed, there is a standing rule against him; he attempted last year to make application to the Secretary of State, and there was a letter came down to the Magistrates, or rather the Police Office, desiring to know the motive that swayed the Magistrates in refusing a license to that man.

From whom did that letter come?—From Mr. Becket.

What was the name of the person?—Hugh Parsons; he had been tried as a felon, and had been guilty of a variety of delinquencies; it would have been a most improper thing to have licensed him.

What answer did the Magistrates return to that letter?—A statement of the offences for which he had been tried, the felony and other things; he was a most unprincipled fellow.

Do you know much of the state of the public-houses in the neighbourhood of Whitechapel and Bethnal Green?—I know in the immediate neighbourhood of Whitechapel, as well as any body I believe, for I was for many years Curate of Whitechapel; that brought me into immediate contact with the publicans, for I had to sign their applications, and I never signed one without seeing him; they came to the Vestry, and I gave them a charge as it were.

Are not complaints made against many of those houses in that district, by their respective neighbours; and have not complaints been laid before the Office of the conduct of those houses?—I cannot say that there have been many; the complaints are chiefly made, I dare say three or four in a year, in an anonymous way; we cannot find out who sends them; the Magistrates employ their officers to go and ascertain the fact at some uncertain hours, and to look about them.

Have not complaints been made from Police Offices, relative to the conduct of persons holding public-houses, within your division?—No, I think not; I remember one complaint made, apparently from Worship-street.

Do you not recollect that Mr. Gifford, one of the Magistrates of Worship-street, made a complaint on five or six convictions before himself for tippling?—Yes; but it proved that Mr. Gifford was mistaken in point of law; it was not a conviction before the Sessions by a Jury, but by a Magistrate, and we had the opinion of the Common Serjeant upon it.

510.

Do

Rev. E. Robson.

Do you not think, that though the conviction, if it had been by a Jury, would have been imperative, and that the Magistrates could not legally have granted that licence; a conviction before a Police Magistrate of five different times in one year breaking the statute was a sufficient reason for the Magistrates withholding the licence?—I never knew that he was convicted so often as five different times; not more than once or twice perhaps.

Was not that given in evidence before the Magistrates?—Perhaps it might; but I really do not recollect that it was; it never struck me to have been more than once; I thought it was one conviction; Mr. Gifford is very warm, he is rather severe, and perhaps that might operate upon some minds, as it certainly did on mine, to make inquiry into the circumstances of the conviction, and I thought the man was rather hardly dealt with.

Should you have thought the man hardly dealt with, if evidence had been tendered to you of his having been four or five times convicted, within a twelvemonth, of the same offence?—If the circumstances were made out, I think it would have been very proper for the Magistrates to have refused the licence, but I suspected that Mr. Gifford had been very severe with him; we were all inclined to be of a different opinion from Mr. Gifford; I believe he was the only one of opinion the license should be withheld, and even then we would not proceed without advice.

The advice of the Common Serjeant was a mere technical advice, as to whether the conviction imperatively called upon you to refuse the licence, was it not?—In some measure it is; but he enters into it, if I recollect right, with a great deal of feeling, that there could be no other Magistrate found that could withhold the licence but Mr. Gifford; I think he said so, in the latter part of it.

Do you believe that the Common Serjeant had the five convictions before him, at the time he answered that case?—I am not certain.

Were you present in 1814, at the licensing of the houses in Shadwell, which had been suppressed the year before; namely, the White Hart, the Pavior's Arms, and the Duke of York?—I was.

Was it not stated to you by the Parish Officers, and other principal inhabitants, in their Memorial against the re-licensing of those houses, that there was such a profusion of public-houses, that every eighth or ninth house in the street was a public-house; and that the re-opening of those bad houses could be no accommodation to the neighbourhood, and neither more nor less than a public nuisance?—I have been long of opinion that there were far too many public-houses by the water-side in Wapping and Shadwell; but those houses that were complained of certainly were not worse than the majority of the rest; and there is one circumstance that staggered us all a good deal, and I remember that I took a very active part in it, for I asked individually every person that was present, whether he had himself personal knowledge of the enormities that were stated; I asked every body except Mr. Fletcher; I did not ask him, because I am persuaded that he being in office at that time, had; but in that parish there happens to be a good deal of dissension, and I conceived that Mr. Fletcher, and certain persons acting under his influence, were biassed very much in the opinion they gave, an opinion formed though upon certain facts; that parish has been in such a lamentable state, that at least for seven years the parish church has had no duty performed in it, because a repair of the church is necessary, or rebuilding it, and propose what they will, there is an opposition to it, so that things run so very high, if I may call them by that name parish party, it makes one pause and consider; we had a great number of people brought up; that is to say, they came before us on the other side, at the head of which was a Mr. George Fox, well known thereabouts, and almost as popular a man amongst his people as Fletcher amongst his; the evidence Mr. Fletcher gave was perfectly rebutted by them; but for a whole year the houses continued shut up; in one of the houses there had been a gallery erected for music, where they had, what they call in vulgar terms, a cock-and-hen club; but before the house was re-licensed, we were satisfied that the gallery was taken away, and the room no longer applied to such purposes; I cannot tell the sign. One of the houses was in a very particular predicament; they were obliged, before they could have a lease of the house, to take a lease of some miserable houses behind, which were originally bad houses, houses of ill fame; and at the time when the license was stopped, the man declared that he wished for nothing more than to get rid of those houses which had been imposed upon him; and before the licence was restored, he did get rid of those houses, and that nuisance was done away. Then as to Townsend's house,

which

which was one that was blamed too, we found that he did not always reside; he is a *Rev. E. Robson.* fruiterer, and resides in Aldgate; to my great astonishment, I found a man keeping a public-house in Shadwell, that was a fruiterer in Aldgate, and because he could not reside there always, he was refused a licence, and they were obliged, at a minute's warning, to find a person to be licensed.

Do you think that the mere taking away a gallery in which a few fiddlers could sit, was that sort of alteration in the house, with strong evidence before you of its being still continued to be the place of assemblage of licentious persons of both sexes, that could warrant the Magistrates restoring the licence one year after having taken it away the year preceding?—The gallery and the room were the things chiefly complained of; they seemed to make the body of the complaint, and they were never made use of as a dancing-room for a whole year.

Is it not notorious that all the houses, almost without exception, in that neighbourhood, have large rooms at the back part of the houses, or in the houses which have been for many years past used as dancing-rooms for sailors and their girls?—Far from large; they are generally very small houses in that quarter.

Are there not a great number of houses to which there are such rooms?—Certainly; and being so general we thought it very hard they should fall upon these houses in particular.

What induced the Magistrates to take way the licence?—It was taken away for one year till the nuisance was abated, and that being done it was restored. The principle on which the Magistrates act is, that it is a kind of mixed consideration; we conceive that the house is property belonging to some person or other not the landlord, the property of some individual: the house, therefore, being brick and mortar, cannot be guilty of any moral crime, it is the landlord who is the person who is guilty; and if we turn him out, and the house be licensed to another, and he a proper person, the guilt is put an end to.

In point of fact were they not licensed, in some instances, to the same person?—Oh, certainly; but the power of doing wrong was taken away by the alteration that took place.

Do you think that the mere taking away of a place where fiddlers sat was a sufficient correction of bad conduct to warrant you, with the strongest evidence before you, which was tendered in writing, and which was given *viva voce*, of licentious company being assembled there every hour of the day and night, in licensing the house next year, having refused it the year preceding?—We had evidence on the other side; we had evidence in defence of those people, and against the evidence which had been adduced by Mr. Fletcher; but then it was not the mere taking away and the mere loss of the room with the gallery, they had lost a great deal, for being shut up for a whole year, they lost all the advantage of their profit for the whole year. We went down to the spot and saw with our own eyes; they were so convinced they had acted improperly, that with every sign of contrition, they gave us every reason to hope that they were in earnest, and would do well in future.

Were the circumstances that induced Mr. Fletcher to represent the conduct of the three houses before mentioned, represented to be from those three houses being notoriously bad houses, much worse than other houses in the same neighbourhood; or did it arise out of an intention on the part of Mr. Fletcher, and those persons with whom he acted, to reform the public-houses generally in the parish, and therefore pitching upon those three for that purpose, rather than for any particular misconduct of those individual houses?—That perhaps might be his motive; one can hardly look into a man's breast to discern the motive from which he acts. We found fault with the constable, and I thought Mr. Fletcher might have certainly lodged informations against far more than three houses; the seeking out three seemed too invidious a thing, and knowing the fury and heat with which things were carried on in that parish, that made us call for proof, which we had, on the other side.

Then you are of opinion Mr. Fletcher might, with as much propriety, have made the same complaint against six or twelve houses, as against those three in particular?—Oh, yes, against twenty at least. I will mention one circumstance that may have influenced the mind of Mr. Fletcher; Mr. Fox is a coal-undertaker well known in that neighbourhood; if public-houses are wanted in any neighbourhood, and if they serve the public convenience, they are particularly necessary. At our end of the town, the eastern part, we are in a very increasing state, and on account of the East and West India Docks and the London Docks, many old

public-

Rev. E. Robson.

public-houses have been pulled down, and many not restored, so that it is not that they want to remove the license from such a house to such a house. Many of them have been pulled down and the docks placed over that situation. We have endeavoured to license the new houses very thinly and sparingly; for two reasons, first, that we reckoned there was quite sufficient for the neighbourhood; and secondly, that the men should be enabled to get a living profit, and not prey upon each other, and not be driven to an improper mode of obtaining a livelihood. We have had petitions for thirty, or more than thirty new houses; in September there are such petitions and counter petitions, it is troublesome beyond measure; there is such grumbling and grudging and heart-breaking; persons who think they can make any interest, are doing it; I have been astonished by the applications I have had made to me.

It is customary, prior to the licensing of public-houses, for any of the Magistrates to talk over the matter and settle what houses shall be licensed?—There is something like that, but it is nothing more than conversation at the Office; yesterday there were Mr. Flood, and Mr. Windle, and myself, three Non-Police Magistrates, and finding ourselves sitting in the Office and with perhaps nothing to do of public business, we naturally fell on business of that kind; I know of nothing else.

Is it not the custom prior to the day in September on which the licences are granted, for two or three of the Magistrates, such as Sir Daniel Williams, Mr. Merceron, and yourself, to meet and take into consideration what licences shall be granted?—No further than I have informed the Committee; perhaps there have been six or seven in the Office, or perhaps only one or two.

Do you recollect Mr. Beaumont applying to you in 1815, to license a Public-house belonging to him, within your district?—That I do indeed; and I was the person who brought within purview of the Magistrates, Mr. Beaumont's first beginning; it was an unpardonable thing; Mr. Beaumont having some houses amongst the new buildings, for he has been a speculator in buildings both at the Western end of the town and at the Eastern end of the town, made application for licences; there are three houses for which he wanted licences; there was a low kind of man he met with, who was a Surveyor under the property-tax, now done away, and that fellow talked over Mr. Beaumont in such a manner (it is astonishing how he could do it) that he absolutely lent that man a large sum of money, because he was given to understand, that perhaps there were some of the Magistrates that were needy men, in want of money, and who would be very glad if he had so much to lend them.

What is the man's name?—Smallwood; he is dead now, he killed himself by drinking; I heard of this, and thought it proper immediately to make it known to my brethren in the public room, and we sent for Smallwood, he lived hard-by, then we sent for Smallwood and Beaumont, and Beaumont only came; we made another attempt to have them face to face, and hear their complaints and defences, but then Mr. Smallwood said he had been advised, and that he certainly meant to proceed against Mr. Beaumont for usury, for that he had charged him a large sum of money; then Mr. Beaumont altered the whole complexion of the thing, which certainly did not take off the imputation; he said he had not lent him the money, but he had discounted him some bills, which came pretty much to the same thing; I was burning a great many papers and letters the other day, and I lighted upon a letter of Mr. Beaumont's, explaining things to us; it is written by his clerk, but signed by himself. Mr. Beaumont, we understood, was asking or making interest to be put into the Commission, and we knew of this mean transaction, and therefore we resolved to lay the matter before the Chancellor, that we would not have a man come amongst us that could suppose any of us guilty of so mean a thing as to borrow money of so miserable a wretch; and I wrote the letter, this is a copy of the letter I wrote to the Chancellor, but before we could have the meeting to determine that the letter was a proper one, he was in the Commission, and the letter was at an end; then we made an application to the Magistrates at Clerkenwell, but they said they had nothing to do with it; they could not interfere.

Mr. Beaumont applied to you to license a house he had built?—He did certainly.

Did you recommend him to give the trade of that house to Messrs. Hanbury?—No; indeed I have always blamed Messrs. Hanbury's house for having had any dealings with him at all.

When you heard that he had made an arrangement, which was then considered to be final, did you not, in the presence of Mr. Davies, one of the Magistrates, advocate the licensing of his house?—Never; I believe I was the principal person that stept

forward

Rev. E. Robson.

forward not to license any of them ; this last year one of them was licensed, because a neighbourhood was built up to the house; it was before without a neighbourhood, and therefore was not wanted.

In point of fact the house at that time was not licensed ?—No, not in 1814.

Do you recollect any treaty, or were you privy to any treaty, then held by Messrs. Hanbury prior to the licensing day with Mr. Beaumont ?—No, certainly not.

And you will state to the Committee that you did not support the licensing of that house, when the treaty was supposed to be entered into with the Hanburys', and oppose it the moment you found it was broken off?—Not till the year 1815; then I thought it would be very proper to license it.

Who was the proprietor of the house in the year 1815, when you thought proper to license it?—Beaumont, I conceived; I think he was upon the spot.

Is the house licensed at present ?—Yes, certainly, and it will continue, and must by Act of Parliament till next September.

Mr. Beaumont has another house in White-horse-lane at Mile-end, for which it is understood he has applied repeatedly during the last three or four years for a licence ; do you recollect any thing respecting that transaction?—Only generally, that it not being necessary for the public convenience, therefore was not licensed ; when I say so, I speak of my own opinion.

· Do you recollect a certificate being shown to you, or the other Magistrates, that there was no other public-house near White-horse-lane, which was three furlongs in length, that there were three hundred and fifty new houses near it; and that a public-house would be a great convenience ?—Yes, I know that Mr. Smallwood had a plan of the houses, but it did not appear that although there were that number of houses, they were tenanted and occupied.

The principle that governs your conduct in licensing houses is, that there shall be a sufficient neighbourhood, so that the keeper of the public-house shall be able to have his livelihood, and that the public shall have their wants supplied?—Certainly; that is the main principle that governs my conduct.

Supposing the facts to be as just stated, how could you refuse to license a house in White-horse-lane, while you re-opened the three houses in Shadwell?—I think I have answered that question, by stating, that the greater number of those houses were mere empty shells, and the former public-houses still existed, which though not just in White-horse-lane, might certainly serve for a considerable time, and not annoy the public very much.

Do you know any thing of the general management of the parish of Bethnal Green, as to the morals and manners of its inhabitants?—No; I cannot say that I can answer that.

Do you know any thing of the bullock-hunting there?—No; we have bullock-hunters in Whitechapel road sometimes, but the hunters are generally pursued and brought to justice; but there is a great difficulty in getting at the name of any man ; there is no means of punishing a drover; it can be done only by information; he says, " I will not tell you my name;" and then what are we to do? If the man at the Turnpike gate could demand the name of a person passing between such and such hours on the Sunday, it would be a very good thing. I have been annoyed by the barking of dogs and the driving of cattle to Smithfield on a Sunday morning in Whitechapel; and as I have said, " what meaneth that lowing of cattle in my ear?" it is a very great nuisance.

Can you take upon yourself to say, that, according to the best of your recollection, during the period when the licensing of Mr. Beaumont's house first mentioned was under discussion, you did not recommend Mr. Hanbury to him, and tell him they were very good people ?—So they are.

And that the Magistrates wished to serve them?—No, I never said that, or any thing that could be tortured into that.

Will you equally take upon yourself to say, that being afterwards informed by Mr. Beaumont that he had been to Messrs. Hanbury and offered them the trade or interest in his house, you did not turn to Mr. Rice Davies, then sitting with you, and represent how much obliged to Mr. Beaumont the public were for causing so good a house to be built in such a situation ; that he had pulled down an old house, the Marquis of Granby, on the same estate, where the public houses were too crowded, and that that public-house ought to have been licensed before?—Certainly I never said any such thing. I told him that he did a very foolish thing to pull down the Marquis of Granby prior to the building of those houses behind it; he would have done a far better thing to have come to remove the licence from the

510. Marquis

Marquis of Granby, about to be pulled down; but he pulled that down, and then built this among new houses, hit or miss, quite in the dark.

It has been stated in evidence before this Committee by many persons, by Magistrates no less than by others, that a general opinion is entertained in that neighbourhood, that a victualler who comes before the Magistrates as a dealer with Messrs. Hanbury, has almost a certainty of having his house licensed; do you believe that to be the opinion, or according to your experience, is it the fact?—I really believe that the people that do not obtain a licence will be very much inclined to fancy so, and to say so; for there is such trouble taken, and anxiety, and pushing of interests, and reflections after a thing is past, that one does not know what they may say or do; but I will speak to my own feeling, and Sir Daniel Williams's, whom I know perfectly well. We have before said, in answer to that application, " Look at the list of applications; there have been only so many out of so many granted to Hanbury;" and they are but a very small number, considering that Hanbury, living in the neighbourhood and being a great brewer, must have naturally a great interest, not with the magistrates, but in the well-being of his trade. Hanbury in that neighbourhood is the Whitbread of Whitechapel, or the Meux and Reid of the other side of the town. If two houses were to come before me, *cæteris paribus*, I should be inclined to license his house; he is a man of so much public spirit in the public charities, and the London Hospital in particular; he has been liberal in a very great degree: I do not know much of Mr. Hanbury himself.

You do not then deny that the opinion exists?—I dare say that the opinion is as it is supposed in the question, but I think it is unfounded.

The Committee have been furnished with a list of the new-licensed houses in the division in which you reside and act; it appears to them that that list is incorrect; it also appears that a very large proportion of the persons newly licensed have been licensed in one and the same trade, namely Mr. Hanbury; how do you reconcile that circumstance with the statement you have just made?—I do not conceive that that is the fact; I have no conception of it.

Mr. *James May*, called in, and Examined.

WHAT situation do you hold?—Vestry Clerk of St. Matthew, Bethnal Green.

How long have you held that situation?—On my own account from 1788.

Have you brought with you the rates of which you had notice yesterday?—I have.

In whose custody are those rates kept?—In the library of the church, when out of hand.

You as vestry clerk make the rate, do you not?—Yes, myself or my clerk.

After the rates are allowed by the Magistrates, they are lodged in the church?— They are then put into the hands of the collector, after they are allowed by the Magistrates.

Turn to the rate of 1807.—[*The Witness produces the books.*]

After these rate books are allowed by the Magistrates, are they ever altered, or have they ever been altered by any individual?—Yes, there is no doubt of it.

Who was that individual who altered them?—When any errors have been made in the rate, I have altered them.

After the rates are made and allowed by the Magistrates, have any alterations in those rates taken place?—It appears there have.

By whom have those alterations been made?—By various persons; some by me, when there has been an error crept in; perhaps my clerk has not copied them right, and then I have put them to rights; or when any other persons have come into the houses, the collectors have altered them.

Is it the practice in your parish for the rates, when signed by the Magistrates, not to be considered as final, but for the collector to increase or diminish as he thought fit?—No person ought to alter the sum after it has been signed by the Magistrates, unless it was a clerical error.

Such an alteration has taken place in the rates of this parish?—No doubt it appears so.

By whom have those alterations been made, besides the vestry clerk and the collector?—If the Committee will have the goodness to let me look at the books, I will state. [*The Witness referred to one of the books.*] There appears to have been a rate altered in the case of John Johnson, rated at 24 *l.*, paid 7 *l.* 10 *s.* altered to 40 *l.*

By

By whom was that altered?—It appears to me, but I am a very bad judge of *Mr. James May.* hand-writing, to be the hand-writing of Joseph Merceron, esquire, but that I cannot swear to.

There appears to be an alteration of the rate of George Titkins, from 16*l.* to 18*l.* in whose hand-writing is that?—The same.

There appears to be an alteration made, after the rate has been allowed by the Magistrates, in the names of John Marshal and John Robinson; in whose hand-writing do those alterations appear to be?—In the same hand-writing.

Whose hand-writing is that?—Joseph Merceron's, esquire.

Can you find the name of Charlotte Cowdry?—

[*The Witness referred to an entry, by which it appeared that she was rated at* 40*l.* paid 7 *l.* 10 *s. and changed into* 60*l., paid* 11 *l.* 5 *s.*]

In whose hand-writing is that?—It appears to me to be that of Joseph Merceron's, esquire.

Was not that alteration made after the rate was allowed by the Magistrates?—No doubt of it.

Cast your eyes over the Book, and inform the Committee whether there are not a great number of instances in which an alteration has taken place in the same hand-writing?—[*The Witness turned over the Book.*] I see as many as seven or eight.

Look at the book again, and say whether there are not nearer eighty or ninety?—I cannot say indeed.

Turn to Edward Hartley?—That is altered.

Is that altered by Joseph Merceron, esquire?—It is.

Turn to Edward Hughes, is that altered by Mr. Merceron?—Yes, there is no doubt of that.

Have you any doubt that the hand-writing of the alteration, in the case of Edward Hughes, is Mr. Merceron's?—Not the least.

You would swear to that, if you were upon your oath?—Certainly, I could not do otherwise.

Turn to George Steers in folio 4, and state whether that is not altered by Mr. Merceron?—I believe that is by the Collector.

Turn to the name of John Bryan, in the same page?—That I believe is by the Collector.

Do you recollect the case of William Blessed, and the history of that transaction?—I have no particular recollection of any particular circumstances of Mr. Blessed, respecting any alteration in the book.

Do you not remember that he appealed against his rate?—I recollect his appealing against a rate, but not against that rate, to my knowledge.

Do you not remember that he sustained considerable persecution on the part of Mr. Merceron, for that appeal; and that for the payment of the rate bailiffs were put into his house, and he expended a considerable sum of money in defending himself against it?—To the best of my belief that was not upon an altered rate; I sued him for payment of his rates, but to the best of my knowledge and belief that was not an altered rate.

Do you remember the case of Charlotte Cowdry, who was raised by a stroke of Mr. Merceron's pen from 40 *l.* paying 7*l.* 10*s.* to 60*l.* paying 11 *l.* 5*s.*; do you remember whether she was in a distressed situation?—I believe she was very distressed.

Do you recollect whether she was obliged to quit the parish almost in the situation of a pauper?—I am very sorry to say she was.

Can you give to the Committee any reason why, according to your judgment, the rise from 40*l.* to 60 *l.* took place?—No, I cannot, nor did not know it till after it took place.

There cannot be a doubt as to its illegality?—There cannot be a doubt of it.

Since the year 1807, has Mr. Merceron been in the habit of altering the rate?—There are some altered in 1808, I see.

Are there any altered in 1809?—I have never looked.

Have you ever been instructed by Mr. Merceron to alter the rate yourself?—Never; I should not have done it unless it had been a clerical error committed by myself or my clerks.

Have you ever seen him alter the rate?—No, never.

Do you not believe, that in the altering of the rate, raising some and lowering others, Mr. Merceron served his friends and punished his enemies?—I am sure that I cannot speak to that.

Have

Have you any doubt that Miss Charlotte Cowdry stood in the latter predicament when she was raised from 40 l. to 60 l.?—I never had.

What was Mr. Merceron's own house rated at, at the time Miss Cowdry's house was raised from 40 l. to 60l.; turn to the rate and inform the Committee?—Mr. Merceron was rated at 30 l. in the year 1807.

Was Mr. Merceron's house a better house, or as good a house as Miss Cowdry's? —Not the house he then lived in; the house he now lives in is much better.

Do you recollect at what his house at present is rated?—It is either 50 l. or 60 l. but I cannot speak positively; it is the same rate that his predecessor paid.

Do you recollect Mr. Wrightson's house?—Yes, I recollect that.

That house was rated at 80 l.; was it not until Mr. Wrightson appealed to Clerkenwell?—I cannot speak to that without the book; these books have been tied up with the very string which was round them at Westminster till they came here; I have not looked at them since they were at Westminster Hall. In 1807, Mr. Wrightson was in the assessment at 75 l.; Mr. Wrightson appealed to the Magistrates at the Petty Sessions in the vestry, and it was there altered by myself to 65 l. for the whole of his premises and tenants; his own house was rated at 75 l.; that is in my hand-writing.

Turn to Mr. Blessed's case in 1807.—[*The Witness referred to the entry.*]

Mr. Blessed's rate stands at 15 l., it is altered to 35 l. In whose hand-writing is that?—It appears to me to be Mr. Merceron's.

Was it upon this that Mr. Blessed appealed?—I believe not; to the best of my knowledge not.

Was it upon this he went into court?—Probably it was.

Upon that occasion, when the book was handed up to the jury, was not the leaf turned down, so as to conceal the alteration?—I cannot speak precisely to the fact, but it does appear so. The leaf had a turn in it in the middle, as if it had been turned back.

Did you turn down that leaf yourself, and if so, by whose direction?—I never had a direction to turn that leaf down from any persons whatever.

Can you speak positively as to the object of this leaf being turned down?—No, I cannot; I have not a recollection of it; it must have been for some particular thing, because it is particularly turned down. I think it was when Mr. Liptrap and the Reverend Mr. King were attending at my Office that I turned down those leaves; many leaves were turned down then.

Were you in Court when the book was handed up to the Judge?—I really think the book never was handed to the Judge; to the best of my recollection and belief, the book never was handed to the Judge.

Did that come out in evidence, which now appears in the book, that Mr. Merceron the Justice, had, after the rate was signed by the Magistrates, doubled it?—No; it is the first time I have heard of any thing of the kind.

The question refers not to the doubling of the leaf, but to the doubling of the rate?—No, it did not.

You have stated to the Committee, that you believe in that book there are about seven or eight alterations made in the rate?—There are a great many more; I have observed as many as that, so far as I have looked.

You have stated to the Committee, as far as you have looked over the book, you have observed seven or eight alterations made by Mr. Justice Merceron in the rate book, after it had been allowed by the Magistrates; it appears, having turned over a very few leaves of the book, that there are twenty alterations made in the same hand-writing, does it not?—Yes.

Refer to those names and tell the Committee by whom those alterations were made; Mary Allen, in page 17, by whom is that alteration made?—The alteration is from thirty to forty pounds; it appears to me to be by Mr. Merceron.

In folio 19, William Hillery; by whom is that alteration made in the rate?—It appears to be Mr. Merceron's.

In folio 20, Miller; by whom is that alteration made in the rate?—I have no doubt that that is by the Collector.

In page 24, Benjamin Burrows; by whom is that alteration made in the rate, from 24 l. to 30 l.?—It appears to be Mr. Merceron's.

In page 25, John Meakins; by whom is that alteration made in the rate, from 20 l. to 24 l.?—That appears to be the same.

In page 26, Sayer Myers; by whom is that alteration made in the rate?—That appears to be Mr. Merceron's.

In

In page 29, James Howsham; by whom is that alteration made in the rate?—It appears, by Mr. Merceron.

In page 32, John Simmonds; by whom is that made from 8*l.* to   ?—Mr. Merceron.

In page 33, Thomas Hammond?—I cannot speak to that.

In page 34, Joseph Young, from 18*l.* to 24*l.*?—Mr. Merceron altered that.

The same page, Thomas Mears?—By the same.

In page 35, John Johnson?—That appears to be Mr. Merceron's.

That appears to be altered from 24*l.* to 40*l.*?—It is from 4*l.* 10*s.* to 7*l.* 10*s.*

Page 35, John Marshall, the rate from 16*l.* to 18*l.* by whom is that altered?—Mr. Merceron.

And John Robinson, in the same page?—Mr. Merceron.

In page 36, Abraham Gartie, by whom is that altered?—By Mr. Merceron.

Turn over the leaves of the book, and see whether there are not many other alterations by the same person?—A great many.

And these alterations have been all made by Mr. Merceron, the Treasurer of the parish, after the rate had been allowed by the Magistrates?—Yes, they were.

Are there any alterations made in the rate-book by Mr. Merceron, reducing the amount of the original rate?—I do not know of any.

The Committee observe, that Daniel Daniel's rate has been altered from 45*l.* to 60*l.* and subsequently altered to 55*l.* by whom is that subsequent alteration made?—By Mr. Merceron.

Was that alteration made upon appeal?—I cannot speak to that; in general they are in my hand-writing, or the Collector's, when they are upon appeals.

But as this is in Mr. Merceron's hand-writing, you believe it to be not upon appeal?—I believe it may have been, notwithstanding that, on an appeal; when I have been very busy, Mr. Merceron has taken the book, and put it at what the rate ought to be.

Can you inform the Committee what the total of the several alterations made by Mr. Merceron in the rate, after it was allowed by the Magistrates, amounted to, in the year 1807?—I certainly cannot; the Reverend Mr. King took the amount out of the book at my Office; but what the amount was, I have not the least recollection.

It appears by the books you have produced, that Mr. Merceron began altering the rates in the year 1805; how long has Mr. Merceron continued to alter the rates?—I cannot tell any more than appears by the books; I have looked into the years 1806, 1807 and 1808.

It appears that alterations have been made in the years 1805, 1806, 1807, 1808 and 1809?—I do not know that they have in 1809; my order is for the production of the books for 1805, 1806, 1807 and 1808, which are here.

From your situation as vestry clerk, being conversant with these books, can you, from your recollection, say whether any alterations have been lately made by Mr. Merceron in the rate, after it has been allowed by the Magistrates?—No, not to my knowledge, any one.

It appears, by a list of between sixty and seventy houses produced to the Committee, and stated to be rented by Mr. Merceron up to the year 1807, that the houses were rated together at 96*l.* 9*s.* 2*d.*, and that upon Mr. Mitchell's becoming tenant of those houses, in the year 1808, the rate was increased to 227*l.* 9*s.* 7*d.* being an advance of 131*l.*; can you state to the Committee the reason of that advance?—No, I do not know of any such advance; I know that when Mr. Mitchell came into possession of the premises they were let at a very small rent, and shortly after Mr. Mitchell came into possession of them, I have invariably understood that he raised the rents double, and some more.

Mr. Mitchell raised the rents?—Yes. I have heard many persons say, that before Mr. Mitchell came into possession of the premises, they paid only 8*l.* a year, and that Mr. Mitchell had raised them to 16*l.*, 17*l.*, and 18*l.*

Are you acquainted with two houses in Acre-street, rented, in the year 1807, of Mr. Merceron, one occupied by Richard Davis and the other by Richard Pullen, the rates of which houses appear to have continued the same in 1808 as in 1807; can you give any reason why the rates of those two houses were not advanced at the same time that the other sixty odd were?—No, I cannot speak to those houses at all; I have less knowledge about that part of the parish than any other. It is very frequently the case that two houses appear to the eye on the outside to be of the same size, and when you go up stairs you find that one shop runs over the two

houses,

houses, which house, to which the shop belongs, would let for twice as much, and sometimes three times, on account of the length of the shop.

The Committee do not ask you with respect to the size of the houses, but with respect to two houses, out of sixty or seventy included in the list referred to, stated to belong to Mr. Merceron, the rates of which were not altered when the rates of all the others were more than doubled?—I cannot account for it; I have not the least knowledge of it.

The list above referred to begins with Norman alias Whitehead, and finishes with Cross; you tell the Committee that you cannot account for the reason of the alteration in the rate of the sixty odd houses?—I cannot.

Turn to folio thirty-one in the book in your hand, you will find the name of Norman alias Whitehead, rated at 9 *l.*; has any alteration been made in that rate after it was allowed by the Magistrates, and by whom?—The alteration is certainly not made by the Magistrate; it appears to me to be by the collector, but I cannot speak to that, those are not collected on; those alterations are merely memorandums to go into the next book, it does not appear that any of them have been collected on; but this is a memorandum which any man might make, to go into the next book.

Those alterations you state, are not made by Mr. Merceron?—Most certainly not.

That alteration was made after it was allowed by the Magistrates?—I cannot say when it was done; it appears to be a memorandum to put into the next rate, as it has not been collected on; as far as my belief goes, the houses there stated were not Mr. Merceron's.

Not in 1807?—Nor now; I think they belonged to the Reverend Mr. Natt, or Henry Busby, esq.

They are stated to belong to Mr. Natt, but rented by Mr. Merceron?—I do not believe they ever were rented by him; Mr. Merceron collected the rents of them, I believe, but he had no interest in the houses; I must have heard in some casual way or other if they were his.

Mr. Merceron was the agent for the estate?—I think he was.

And as such he had an interest for his employer in keeping the rate down as low as possible?—The same as every other agent, no doubt.

Then the moment that the rents of the houses ceased to be collected by Mr. Merceron, the rent is raised from 96 *l.* to 227 *l.*?—I cannot speak at all to that.

That appears from the book, does it not?—When the houses were parted with, they were sold by public auction, and when Mr. Mitchell came into the possession of them, I have always understood that he more than doubled his rents on the tenants; and if he did so it was a very natural thing to put him up in the payment of the taxes; but I do not believe they were Mr. Merceron's houses.

He gathered the rents?—He did.

Have you any later rate here than 1808?—No, I have not.

Are all the houses in the parish rated according to their real value?—As far as that could be ascertained; our rate states, it is according to the full rent or value thereof, but if a house is let at seven or eight-and-twenty pounds, and the others have been rated at twenty-five, I have considered the twenty-five as a proper rate, and have not put them up.

Do you know whether there is in the rates after the year 1809 any further alteration of names in the hand-writing of Mr. Merceron?—Not to my knowledge.

For how many years does it appear in the rate-books, going backwards from 1808, that Mr. Merceron has been in the habit of altering the rate?—As far as I have the books before me, 1808, 1807, 1806, and 1805.

It is part of your duty to be present at any of the meetings of the vestry?—Always.

Have those meetings latterly been very tumultuous?—Certainly.

Has it been the practice to adjourn the meetings of the vestry, from the church to the churchyard?—No.

Has that ever happened?—We have adjourned to the portico of the church, under the portico.

So that you had in front of you all the public that choose to assemble?—No, the vestry-men took care to keep away those that were not vestry-men, and they could be much better discerned there than in the vestry-room.

Of course, they could not keep those that were not vestry-men from being lookers-on, some few yards off?—Certainly, all who were in the churchyard were lookers-on.

For what reason was the meeting adjourned from the vestry-room to the churchyard?—Because the vestry-room was not large enough to hold half that attended.

Have

Mr. James May.

Have you ever seen Mr. Merceron wave his hat and give three cheers as a token of triumph, for having gained any particular object?—Never.

Will you take upon yourself to say, that as you have attended every time that the vestry has been so summoned, that circumstance has never happened?—Never in my presence, certainly.

Do you attend Divine Service regularly every Sunday in the parish church?—I do not.

Are you a dissenter?—Oh no; my whole family attend at the church.

Have you ever witnessed bullock-hunting, and that riotous assemblage of persons in the neighbourhood of the church and the churchyard, which have been detailed in evidence before this Committee?—Oh yes, many times, the most disgraceful thing in the country; I have often offered to turn out as a volunteer to prevent it; on Monday and Friday we have a bullock or a poor cow hunted; the butchers round Hackney and Bethnal-green have paid the Police Officers for having their bullocks brought home safe, and as soon as that pay ceased, their attention ceased.

Have you ever seen bullocks driven across the churchyard on a Sunday?—Never in my life.

Have you ever seen in the neighbourhood of the church or churchyard, duck-hunting and dog-fighting?—There is scarcely a Sunday that there is not; I have gone out with the greatest anxiety when my wife and family were going to church to pro-tect them.

Do you consider, as the master and father of a family, that such an assemblage of persons amounts in point of fact to an interruption of your family, attending Divine worship?—Most certainly, and the greatest disgrace I ever knew to a civilized country; I am sixty-four years of age, and we have now twenty times more than there was forty years ago.

Do you know whether any complaints have been made, upon that subject, to Mr. Merceron, the resident Magistrate, or to the bench?—I never made a personal one, but I understand many have been made to the Police Office.

How near does Mr. Merceron live as a Magistrate, to the place where these assemblages of licentious persons take place?—I should suppose about a quarter of a mile; it is close to the church and churchyard; the congregation must be frequently disturbed by it, and it is dangerous to persons to come; there is as public a road over the Hare-street fields as can be.

Do you not suppose it is the duty not only of the Police Officers, but of the Con-stables of the parish, to put a stop to such a meeting?—I have used every influence in my power, and I believe for the last five or six months it has been lessened some-what; being Clerk to the Trustees as well as Vestry Clerk, I have intreated the Trustees to double our number of Headboroughs; we have now twenty-eight instead of fourteen, in order to have Peace Officers in the parish; that they have done for three years, but they can do nothing; one Police Officer will do more than all our twenty-eight Headboroughs.

Do the Police Officers ever interfere?—I have not seen them more than once these three years.

By whom is the High Constable appointed?—By the Magistrates for the Tower Hamlets district.

How are the Officers of the Parish nominated?—By the Governors and Directors of the poor, and the choice goes to the Vestrymen in Vestry assembled.

Are they, in point of fact, most of them persons (as the parish is divided in its interest) in the interest of Mr. Merceron?—They are not; that in great part lies with me, and I can assure the Committee, that our eight-and-twenty Headboroughs are the most respectable men that there are in the Tower Hamlets.

The question relates to the Parish Officers, are they taken by rotation through the parish or indiscriminately?—Every one that has served three years, goes on the list regularly; Mr. Merceron has no more to do with it than any other person; it is my duty to put on every one that is ripe, as they call it; he goes on the list which I return; the Overseers are appointed under an Act of Parliament.

What is the number of poor now in the house?—Six hundred and thirty-nine.

What is the allowance paid by the parish for each of the in-door poor?—They have two-pence in a shilling on their earnings; the out-door poor are maintained according to the number of their families; some have 3s. some 4s. some 2s. some 1s.

What should you reckon the cost per head of the in-door poor?—I have under-stood from 5s. 3d. to 5s. 4d.

510.

Jovis, 13° *die Junii*, 1816.

The Honourable HENRY GREY BENNET, in The Chair.

Thomas Furly Forster, Esquire, called in, and Examined.

YOU are one of the Committee of the Society called " The Refuge for the Destitute?"—I am.

What is the nature of the establishment?—The nature of the establishment is exactly what the title imports, a refuge for the destitute. We have not funds at present to take in all; the general characters that are now taken in are from prisons, by the recommendation of the Secretary of State, or of the Recorder, and sometimes merely of the gaoler : if they are discharged, and the gaoler gives a good account of them, we take them in upon his recommendation.

How many are there at present in the house?—Forty-two men and boys, and sixty-two or sixty-three females.

Have you many applications beyond your means of reception?—On almost every committee-day we have had seven or eight that we have not taken in, merely from want of funds.

Has that circumstance been made public by any advertisement?—Yes; at our general dinner, and by the papers we have printed.

In what mode do you circulate those papers?—By sending them to subscribers; and any person may have them by application to the treasurer or the committee.

How long has this society been established?—Eight or nine years.

From your experience, since the institution has been established, can you state that in by far the greater number of instances the purposes of the institution have succeeded?—I think by much the greater; for in one single year out of three-and-twenty discharged, eighteen were doing well.

You state to the Committee positively, that in that object of the institution, namely, the reformation of offenders, and a provision for the destitute, your institution has succeeded?—Much beyond what I could ever have expected. I will give the Committee one instance : at the anniversary dinner we give the objects a dinner before we dine; and last year, at that dinner, the objects that had been in came to see their friends, and there were seven, most of whom were prostitutes of the lowest order, when we took them in, came there, showed us their certificates that they were married, and married well, and settled with families, and had children.

According to your observation, do you think that the increased number of applicants that come to your establishment, proceeds from the number of criminals in the country being increased, or from the population being considerably augmented?—We used to have, in the time of the war, hardly any men come, perhaps one or two, now we have every week three, four, or five : of females, I think there are much about the same number, always a great many more than we could possibly take in.

Do you think, according to your own observation, that the morals and manners of the lower orders are in a worse state than they were some years back?—I have had very few opportunities to make observations; I should think they are better in some things, and worse in others; where they have been educated, I think they are generally better.

Of course, education being infinitely more general than it was some years back, the manners of the lower orders of people, taken as a whole, must be improved?—I should think so.

Your charity is supported entirely by subscription?—Yes.

To what amount are the funds of your establishment?—The annual subscription last year was 850*l.* 5*s.*; donations during that time 1,954*l.* 17*s.*; legacies 230*l.*; dividends on 1,500*l.* three per cent. stock, and 200*l.* five per cent. navy annuities, 55*l.* a year; collections after sermons, 329*l.* 14*s.* 8*d.*; washing and needle-work, 878*l.* 4*s.* 3*d.*; pens, fire-wood, shoes, and flax-beating, 204*l.* 19*s.*; unmanufactured stock and goods unsold, 66*l.*; making all together, 4,568*l.* 19*s.* 11*d.*

To what amount are the expenses?—6,214*l.* 9*s.* 3*d.*

So

T. *Furly Forster*, *Esq.*

So that according to that statement the establishment is worse by nearly 2,000 *l.*?—Nearly so.

What means do you look to for supplying that deficiency?—Subscriptions; and I believe we shall have some of it from Government.

You expect to receive a portion of it from Government?—I hope so.

You have made an application to the Government to that effect?—We have.

In what are the objects principally employed?—The females in washing, needle-work, and all kinds of house-work; I mean, cleaning rooms, and those things which will make them good servants; the men in shoe-making, pen-cutting, twine-spinning, flax-dressing, cutting wood for fire, and carpenters work.

Do you find any difficulty in procuring work for the men?—We had very great difficulty at first; but it is getting less.

By exertion you have surmounted it?—Yes; and we think we shall very soon be able to pay the expenses of their living.

Is the number you have the greatest you can accommodate?—We could accommodate more men; the male establishment is separate, and will hold two or three hundred.

What is the expense of the establishment for men capable of holding two or three hundred?—I cannot answer that.

Were your houses built for the purpose?—No; one of them was a madhouse in the Hackney-road, and the other an old sugar-house at Hoxton.

How do they occupy their different apartments; are they one or two in a room, or have each a room to themselves?—There are two rooms for the men, and three for the women; they have separate beds.

If you had funds, could you put up 200 beds?—More for the men, I should think; they occupy only one floor of part of the sugar-house.

Do you adopt classification to separate the old offenders from the young beginners?—We have not had funds to fit up the rooms to accomplish that at present.

State the amount of the disbursements, and the nature of them?—Rent, taxes, and insurance, 287 *l.* 18 *s.* 6 *d.*; Salaries and wages, 496 *l.* 14 *s.* 9 *d.*; provisions, 1,440 *l.* 1 *s.* 4 *d.*; coals, candles, soap, &c. 609 *l.*; clothing, linen, and shoes, 640 *l.* 15 *s.* 4 *d.*; expenses of the sick, 35 *l.* 7 *s.* 10 *d.*; repairs, alterations, removing the male objects to Hoxton, furniture, implements of trade, &c. 2,240 *l.*; stationary, printing, advertising, &c. 176 *l.* 1 *s.* 2 *d.*; gratuities on dismission, expenses of sending objects to their friends, &c. 86 *l.* 19 *s.* 10 *d.*; cartage and incidental expenses, 88 *l.* 15 *s.* 2 *d.* poundage to collectors, 35 *l.* 17 *s.*; stock in trade, 77 *l.* 0 *s.* 8 *d.*; making a total of 6,214 *l.* 9 *s.* 5 *d.*

What is the rent of the female establishment?—210 *l.*: We have spent in repairs and alterations about 2,500 *l.*

What is the rent of the male establishment?—130 *l.*; with liberty to purchase within ten years, at a fixed price of 2,400 *l.*; the repairs and alterations of the part now used have cost about 1,000 *l.*

Can you furnish to the Committee a calculation of what each person costs per head?—The men cost about 5 *s.* 10 *d.* per week, per head, including the masters; the expense of the females I do not exactly know, but it is something more than that.

What is the nature of the diet?—The rule is meat three times a week, and the other times soup and puddings.

Do you allow malt liquor?—Yes, common beer; and to the women, who wash very hard, we allow a little porter.

How many hours a day do they work?—They always work from six to six, except when at dinner, but very often much longer. We have the whole washing of Christs Hospital, and of many private families. Sometimes they get up at two in the morning, and then we give them something more.

Mr. *James Miller*, called in, and Examined.

Mr. *James Miller.*

YOU belong to a committee for inquiring into the causes of juvenile delinquency?—I do.

Do you think, according to your observation, that juvenile delinquencies have very much augmented of late years?—I am inclined to think not so much as is generally supposed; I apprehend they are more known from being more investigated.

Do you think that the number of juvenile delinquents that appear upon the books of the different Offices, proceeds more from the activity of the Police in detecting

510.   them,

Mr. James Miller.

them, than from any real augmentation in the number of crimes?—I should hope so; and am inclined to think so; of course these things must be conjectural, in a great measure.

You have examined several hundred cases of juvenile delinquents within the last year have you not?—I think from seven to eight hundred in the course of the last year.

Can you give to the Committee any account of what you think is gained by those examinations, as to the principal causes of those delinquencies?—I take the first cause to be the want of education and instruction; the habit of gambling, particularly on Sundays, unrestrained; the neglect of the poor as to any care of their children: We have traced a considerable number of the cases to fairs.

Are there not above eighty days of fairs in the neighbourhood of the Metropolis annually?—We made out fully eighty, and thought there were rather more.

Within what distance of the metropolis?—Within ten miles of the metropolis.

Are those all held upon different days?—Some might be on the same day, but I should apprehend in general they varied; I did not notice whether any two might be on one day. They begin at Easter, and continue till Bartholomew fair, inclusive.

At what period of the year is Bartholomew fair held?—In September.

Those fairs are the resort of the idle and the profligate?—Generally.

And there are to be found assembled most of the worst characters in the Metropolis?—Certainly.

From your inquiry amongst the children themselves whom you have seen, did they state to you what they considered themselves as the principal causes of their being led into vice?—I think from their own statement generally, poverty has often been made an excuse, and getting into bad company; the major part of them say they were led by others, and probably that is the case; some by older thieves, who told them they would be excused on account of their youth; and they gave them little sums, sixpence or a shilling, or half-a-crown, to go and take an article, which they were afraid to take themselves.

Did you not obtain from some of those persons an account of the existence of a species of establishments in the nature of public-houses, and of brothels, that you did not know existed before?—Frequently; we have had a number of instances. I recollect one or two houses of a very remarkable kind, in the parish of Bloomsbury: I could not get into those houses, not being licensed public-houses; they were maintained as private houses, but had an opportunity of examining the roofs of a large court-yard which had been built in rows of little dwellings, two or three rooms; and I was informed they could make up two hundred beds on one person's premises; that it was not uncommon to answer at the window, that there were no beds, and in half an hour again that there were; their business sometimes was so extensive as that, and chiefly among younger persons. We were told by the father of a boy who is now ordered for execution, that his son came out of the Three Brewers public-house, in Wheeler-street, Spitalfields, which he considers as a house of resort for thieves and bad women, with seven or eight others, and two or three girls; they saw the prosecutor, whom they considered as a little in liquor, the girls attacked him first, and then left him to the young men or boys, who committed the robbery; and this boy has also frequented another house called the Magpie, in Skinner-street, Spitalfields, which we have likewise had reported to us several times; it is a house much resorted to by Jews. We have heard of a variety of others, though perhaps it is difficult to rely upon the testimony we get; they are sources of course doubtful at all times.

Do you not think that it would be no difficult matter to obtain a verdict of a jury, for the purpose of putting down such a nuisance as the house you first mentioned, in the parish of Bloomsbury?—I have applied for that purpose to a gentleman who is Vestry-clerk of the parish, and who informs me, that the parish will prosecute if we can find sufficient evidence; but persons who have other engagements in life cannot follow it up in that way: if we could obtain evidence we could follow it up.

Have you heard from several boys, to the full extent of enormity you have stated?—From two or three boys; the house is well known; the person's name is Cummins; she has a country-house, and keeps her carriage. All the buildings thereabouts are in the hands of Cummins and another person of the name of Linnett.

Do they receive their rent by the week, or by the night?—By the hour; they charge from half-a-crown to three and sixpence as the price of a room.

Have

Mr. James Miller.

Have you generally found the children you have visited in the different prisons, to be without education?—About two-thirds of them are without education; and as to those who state they have been in schools, when we come to investigate, we find they have not attended schools with any regularity, nor been enabled to read.

Of course without any idea of morals or religion?—In general. I have found some who could repeat the catechism and commandments; but in general we find they have spent their Sundays in the fields, and among disorderly young persons. The father of the young person now under sentence of death, acknowledged to me he had never given him any religious instruction.

Have you received any account from the person keeping the school in Newgate, in respect to complaints that were laid before him, and evidence given by the boys under his charge, as to vicious practices said to have taken place in the different Sunday and parish-schools in the metropolis?—I do not think the papers we have received, called a Report from the children in Newgate, was intended to be sent to our committee, but being anxious to get the names, another member of the committee, and myself, applied to Sir Thomas Bell for the names; he gave us the report, and we found it to contain so extraordinary a charge of profligacy, arising or resulting from various schools, that it was determined in our committee to send an extract to each school, containing so much as in the report applied to them, and we have received their answers, which we have endeavoured to combine together in a short report, which I think proves in a very satisfactory manner that there was little or no ground at all for the statement made in the report.

Mr. *Henry Newman*, called in, and Examined.

Mr. H. Newman.

HAVE you turned your attention to improvements in the Police of the Metropolis?—I have.

You hold in your hand a short paper which you have drawn up, which you think would considerably tend to that effect?—I do.

[*It was delivered in, and read, as follows :*]

Outlines of proposed Improvements in Police.

" In order to a proper arrangement or disposal of the numerous criminals now infesting the Metropolis, it is recommended to provide,

" 1st. An establishment for the safe and separate custody of persons before trial, who are committed on suspicion, so that they may not be injured by associating with experienced offenders.

" 2d. A classification of crimes and offences, together with a scale of restraints or punishments proportionate to the offences committed.

" 3d. A workhouse-prison (somewhat after the plan of the Philadelphia prisons) for vagrants and offenders not hardened in vice, in which the prisoners shall be employed in such manufactures as may hereafter be thought advisable.

" 4th. A prison or penitentiary for criminals more hardened.

" 5th. That these two prisons shall be under the superintendence and control of a disinterested committee, whose services shall be gratuitous, and that they shall be built as near London as may be convenient for the committee to attend, or for the convenience of attendance; both objects, perhaps, may be included in one prison.

" 6th. A very strict search after receivers of stolen goods, and liberal rewards to such officers as shall detect and assist in suppressing them. These officers to be under the control of,

" 7th. A central Board of Police, as recommended by Mr. Colquhoun, which Board shall have the licensing or superintendence of public-houses, in order to detect and suppress houses of resort for thieves and suspicious characters.

" 8th. The appointment of a public Prosecutor for the Crown, so that criminals may not escape punishment on account of the injured party being deterred by the expense from prosecuting to conviction."

John Henry Gell, Esquire, called in, and Examined.

J. Henry Gell, Esq.

YOU are a Coroner for the city and liberties of Westminster?—I am.

Do you consider it as your duty always personally to attend when the coroner is summoned?—There is a peculiar power in Westminster; ours is not an elective situation. The Dean and Chapter of Westminster have the gift of all the offices in Westminster;

J. Henry Gell, Esq.

Westminster; and, by the ancient custom of the Chapter, they have a right of allowing a deputy, named by the coroner, to assist him; I believe that is peculiar to the liberties of Westminster; I do not know whether it extends to counties or not.

The Committee are to understand that the Dean and Chapter of Westminster possess a peculiar privilege of dispensing with the personal attendance of the coroner, and giving the permission of appointing a deputy?—Yes; (the deputy being approved by them) in the case of illness or necessary absence.

Is that approbation specifically asked for every time when a deputy is appointed, or is it permanently given?—It is permanently given: for instance, when my father was coroner, and necessarily absent on Chapter business, he appointed me, which was many years ago, in the year 1795, and I was then approved by the Dean, and I have occasionally assisted him in that appointment.

Have you a deputy at present?—I have at present; he has never acted yet.

The Committee have in their possession two reports: one on the coroner's inquest on the body of Edward Wise, shot dead in March 1815; and another on the body of John Watson, who was shot on the same day; did you attend for your father?—I principally did; he may have shown himself occasionally, but I was there the whole of the times the inquests were held; the one was three days, and the other four.

You were there as deputy, not as principal?—As deputy.

Did your father's occupations take him so much out of town, that you, in point of fact, did more the duty of coroner than himself?—No; not so much absence as age and infirmity: he is between eighty and ninety, and his constitution is very much shaken.

What other situation do you hold under the Chapter besides that of coroner?—We are called receivers to the Dean and Chapter; we receive their reserved rents.

Does that duty take up much of your time, and carry you much out of town?—No: there is a sort of attendance in the cloisters, where the office is held, but it does not carry me out of town when they go to hold Courts; it is only once in three years.

Does it, in point of fact, much interfere with your duties as coroner?—No; I should not say that it does.

What is the number of inquests you have to hold?—Sometimes four or five in a week, and sometimes not one in four or five weeks: upon the average, taking the number twenty years past, I should think somewhere about thirty in a quarter.

Some of the cases take up a great length of time?—In some instances; and perhaps I have been obliged to go a second day on one inquisition, owing to the jury not attending, or evidence satisfactory to the jury not being produced.

Do you know whether the Dean and Chapter possess the privilege of appointing a coroner and deputy, by grant, or by custom?—I should think their right of appointment to all offices would be by statute, possibly by custom a deputy may be; but I cannot answer that; it seems to be more likely to have originated in custom.

How long have you nominated your deputy?—Not more than a week or ten days.

Will he not, in point of fact, do the principal duty of the office?—Not that I am aware; I have had four or five since my appointment, and have made a point of going to all of them, unless absolutely prevented. I have been this morning to one, and am going to another, in a case of murder, and I always go wherever I can; I have never called for him yet: there have been several inquisitions within that time.

Who is the person you have appointed?—Mr. Hugh Lewis; he is very respectably recommended to me.

To what amount are the emoluments of the coroner at present?—There is nothing more than the twenty shillings; there is no stipend.

Can you state to the Committee what is the reason, when the stipends are so small, that the office of coroner is so much sought after?—Upon my word I cannot; I can only say, that I would never myself put up for an elective one. I know of nothing but the stipend of the situation.

And the credit of the situation?—Yes, if that is to be taken as any thing.

Do you act as a solicitor?—No, I am not a solicitor; and therefore, in my case, it leads to no sort of profit whatever but the mere twenty shillings.

John Vickery, called in, and Examined.

IN what office are you?—In Bow-street.

How long have you held that office?—About five years at Bow-street, regularly appointed. I have been seventeen years in the police altogether.

Attached to the Bow-street Office?—Part of the time at Bow-street, and part at Worship-street; I began at Worship-street.

The Committee have been told by persons holding similar situations with yourself, that the mode by which your services are remunerated, is considered by them as objectionable in many points of view; first, the payment being very small, a guinea a week; and secondly, because the share that they have in what is technically called blood-money, is uncertain; and depends not so much upon their own labour, as upon the accident of conviction; and that they would be much better pleased if the fixed salary was increased; and that in lieu of the blood-money, the Magistrates or Judges were empowered to reward specific service with a specific payment; are you of that opinion?—I am clearly so.

From your experience, as a Police officer, do you think that Juries are apt to look upon the evidence of a Police officer in an unfavourable point of view because he is supposed to have a profit on the conviction of the person against whom he is appearing as an evidence?—I never felt that as regarding myself; but I certainly think there is a prejudice of that sort; and I have heard it named after trial, and by Juries.

Is it not customary for a counsel for the defendant to put the question to you, on your appearing in the box, whether you are not to gain something on the conviction? —It often has been so in the early part of my life-time, but not lately so to me.

Can you then have any doubt that that question is put for the purpose of decreasing the value of your evidence?—I am clearly of opinion that it is.

Have you any doubt that cases must constantly happen where public justice receives an injury from the evidence, which is sound and good, not being considered as such, the parties being supposed to have a private interest in the conviction?—In some instances I know it is so. I know the public opinion is against the officers entirely, in consequence of that reward by Act of Parliament; and the officers are not considered by the public as so respectable as they would be if those rewards were done away.

Do you think, from your observation, that the morals and manners of the lower orders of people are better or worse than they were when first you were engaged as a Police officer?—I do not think there is an increase of offences since the peace, as far as comes within my knowledge; but the thieves are seeking out for larger stakes, as they term it; greater property is to be obtained by their mode of plunder, and they take care as well at the same time, to evade the Act of Parliament, where they are liable to suffer death. There is a species of offence which has grown up entirely in my time, for the offence was never committed at the early part of my being in the Police, I mean the stealing of bankers parcels, in their way from the country to the town-houses; there the offence is only transportable, and the men who have been convicted, and returned from transportation, know that they are known to the coachmen, and that if they were to commit offences that subjected them to death, they should be ordered for execution, and therefore to evade this, this offence has been studied, and some of them have got fortunes, and have almost disappeared from the Police.

The heavier offences, robberies attended with cruelty, have considerably diminished, have they not within these few years?—Highway robberies nearly completely so; there is nothing like the old practice of highway robbery there used to be; it was not at all an uncommon thing to be informed of men meeting at certain public-houses, in the middle of the day, and setting out to commit offences of that sort; but that is not the case now; and that has been prevented by the vigilance of the Police; the Police get no assistance from the public, for if we go to a public-house to get information, it is with the greatest possible care we dare intrust what we want with the publican.

They are more the friends of the thief than the thief-takers?—They are so; and they are so from interested motives; they are better customers.

Do you think the juvenile depredations are much increased?—I do; very much so indeed.

For

John Vickery.

For small offences, generally?—Certainly; and there have been capital offences, offences made capital by statute, but not of that daring nature perhaps; a boy cutting panes of glass after dark, that is a burglary by law; that is not a daring offence, like meeting a man in the dark; but it is considered, for the protection of property, necessary to make that a burglary; a number of boys have been convicted of these offences, and I fear that those boys were not aware when they committed those offences that they were putting themselves in that situation to forfeit their lives to the laws of their country.

Are there not at the present moment a considerably less number of executions than formerly?—Certainly, than when I began. It was not an uncommon thing for eight or ten to suffer at a time, but now it is rare to hear of more than three or four.

Do you think the milder character which crimes have taken for some years past has not considerably arisen from the executions being much less than formerly, and the general administration of the law being more merciful?—I do not exactly know how to answer that; I have not considered the thing sufficiently to give an answer. I am well aware that, as far as regarded the officer, the officer has been much protected by the leniency of the Prince Regent in the execution of his office, in the apprehension of offenders.

You do not mean to say that fewer persons are capitally convicted than formerly, but fewer punished with death?—No; but the offences are of much less consequence that they are convicted of, than they were, for burglaries were much more frequent. Seven or eight years ago I took an account of the number of informations for burglaries at Worship-street; I calculated that within one month there was property stolen in the city of London, and particularly about Basinghall-street, to the amount of 15,000 *l.*; and I do not think any one of those parties was even known or apprehended, though they were sought after night and day. There was a man at that time who was vigilant, and he was a beadle of Coleman-street ward; he made an attack upon this man, and he got his eye knocked out, it was supposed, with an iron crow; I went to get the description of the parties, but he gave no account that could warrant us in apprehending any body.

It is then your opinion, that although there may be an augmentation of the number of crimes, the nature of the crimes are much less atrocious than formerly; and that the augmentation consists in the smaller offences?—I do; privately stealing from dwelling-houses, shop-lifting, and stealing, as in many instances where parties have been indicted for burglaries, where they have found them guilty of stealing above forty shillings in a dwelling-house, which gets rid of the reward, the parties are equally liable to the punishment of death, but the county does not pay the reward.

How much, taking one year with another, do you, or any man in the Office, to your knowledge, receive from the Parliamentary rewards?—I can speak for myself, I do not think I have received, during the five years I have been at Bow-street, 20 *l.* and I am not so much connected with men in a minor situation to myself, to know what they receive; but out of the six or seven principal officers at Bow-street I should not think there is one man who has received 40 *l.* in the year for it; I speak of the rewards under the Act of Parliament, I do not include those offered by advertisements by parties injured. I have considered the business of the Police has been a business of mine, as it were, that I have been a servant of the Police, and it was part of my business to give it my best studies, and I certainly have seen great inconveniences arise from the rewards by Acts of Parliament, and in one particular instance I got myself very much ill-treated in consequence of it, and that was in apprehending a man of the name of Asker, seven years ago, for robbing the house of the clerk of Mr. Wesley's chapel in the City-road. He lived in a little house in Windmill-street, Finsbury-square; he had to go in the evening of Sunday to perform his office in chapel; before he went there he sat down to read by a candle, and it was suspected that the parties who robbed his house must have seen into his house by means of his candle, the windows not being shut. He left his house to go to his duties, when he returned, he found his house stripped of a considerable quantity of wearing apparel and other things. When I come to hear a statement of the party, I am well aware whether it comes within the meaning of a burglary or not. The parties, after two or three days, were apprehended, and the property found upon them, and the man identified the property. It went to the Court to be tried, and the parties were convicted capitally, but the burglary was taken off; he was convicted of stealing above forty shillings in the dwelling-house. Mr. Shelton, the clerk of Arraigns, made out a bill in the usual way, a trifling sum to the prosecutor, and included in the same

bill

bill something for the witnesses; it is never more than a few shillings. I had received it from the hands of Mr. Shelton, and handed it over to the prosecutor; he said, "Mr. Vickery, there is a reward attached to this, as well as this, I suppose?"—"No, Sir, there is not, for the Jury have got rid of the burglary, and there is no reward for this man's conviction;" "Why he is convicted capitally?" "So he is." "God bless me! what can be the reason?"—"Why, Sir, that you have neglected to state before the Jury, that you had been reading by candle-light, prior to your going out to evening service, and on that account we did not prove the burglary." "God bless my soul! you ought to have told me that," was his reply, "for this will not half pay my expenses for attending here." There was a good deal more said; he was in full expectation of the reward. If I had said, you must mention the circumstance of your candle's being lit before you went out to chapel, I have no doubt the Jury would have convicted him of burglary, but I never suggest these things to witnesses, nor ever join in any thing of the kind. There is another thing attached to rewards, called the Tyburn-ticket; I believe the Act of Parliament gives the Tyburn-ticket solely to the apprehender, but it is the custom of the Courts, both in London and on the Circuit, to give that to the prosecutor.

Do you recollect under what Act it is?—I do not. The Tyburn-tickets in some parishes are at present of some trifling value, in others they are of no value whatever: I think they might be made of very great value, and great benefit to the public, and without any sort of expense to the Government. The plan that I should propose regarding Tyburn-tickets is this: in the generality of parishes at present it is of no value; for instead of the officers wishing to be out of office, they are all trying, for some reason or other, to get into office, and that makes them of no value; but I should submit, whether that would meet with the opinion of the Committee is another question; if the Tyburn-ticket were appointed, by this Act of Parliament to come solely to the apprehender, and to add to it another little privilege, which might be granted, independent of exempting them from parochial duties, to exempt any person holding that ticket from serving as a soldier or a sailor at sea, I am persuaded that would make any person, when there was a cry of "stop thief," run out; but the Police have all the public duty upon themselves, and nine times out of ten they cannot get an honest answer; if there were an inducement held out upon the cry of "stop thief," or a burglary, or a murder, or some capital offence, I am satisfied that the thing would then be valuable, and the lower order of people would all lend a hand to get hold of the thief when he was running, and that would attach not only to London but to England; I do not think that would at all injure the service in any way; for in the whole metropolis of London, at one time, there are not outstanding more than five hundred Tyburn-tickets, for it is only transferable once: I should suggest that it should be put out of the power of the holder of the ticket ever to make use of it himself, and then transfer it.

That where a person once availed himself of the ticket it should be at an end?—Yes, whether it was the man who received it of the Court, or in the hands of another; and to guard against a fraud of that sort, before the ticket is used it ought to be registered by the clerk of the peace. There is a situation in which I have myself laboured under great difficulty, and that is in the way of travelling, in following delinquents through the different counties: It is a thing that frequently happens, that robberies or burglaries are committed in London, and the parties apply to Bow-street; not having sufficient time, or sufficient evidence, to get warrants against the parties, they give such an account as warrants the Magistrates in granting them an officer to follow the person, and we follow him with a warrant, perhaps, and if we find him at an inn, and we have to get a warrant, he will get on twenty or thirty miles a-head of us again, and I have been in this way troubled several times, because out of the county of Middlesex we are not officers; whether it would be considered at all a trespass upon the liberties of the subject, to make a certain number of officers constables for England, is a consideration I would submit. I have been called upon by the Public Boards, at the time of so many French prisoners being in this country; I have been obliged to wait and call in the assistance of a constable to execute a warrant. In felonies we are not constables to execute a warrant out of the county; and I have been put to great expense, where it would have been avoided, if we could have seized the party without waiting to apply for the assistance of a constable of the district. I should certainly advise that the power should not be put into too many hands, and that the Judges should be the

parties

parties to swear the men in, whom they would intrust with such an authority, for that is not an authority of a minor nature, and should be intrusted only to persons who can be depended upon. To prevent offences is a great deal better than punishment. I have never waited to see a party commit an offence; but that I would take him in the act of doing it, rather than when the act was done; and I know that within twenty miles round the metropolis the nobility and public have been very much annoyed by persons travelling out of London with horses and carts; this description of thieves are the most difficult of detection; they get eight or ten miles out of town, or even farther, and commit their burglaries without ever being seen by the persons whose houses they attack, or any persons on the road; they get into London by three or four o'clock in the morning, and then there is the greatest difficulty in the world to find them. It is well known, that there are persons living in London, who live by letting horses and carts to this description of fellows, for the express purpose of committing this sort of offence; now if it was thought in the wisdom of the Legislature to make a forfeiture of the horse and cart where any stolen goods should be found, or any implements being conveyed at night by persons, unless they can give an account of themselves, or give sufficient reason for the possession of the implements, and that the men should be liable to the punishments they now are as vagrants, I think it would be productive of much good.

For whose benefit should it be forfeited?—I had rather it should be for the benefit of the Crown, or the poor, than of the apprehender.

Do not you conceive that if certain instructions, or certain obligations were laid upon the collectors of tolls, to take the numbers or the names on carts passing through at such hours of the night or day, or the numbers of hackney-coaches, that might lead to the detection of offences committed in this way?—I think it would, if the collectors themselves were honest men; if there was any little sort of remuneration attached to the keeper of the toll-gate for that sort of service, imposing the services on him, I have no doubt it would then be faithfully done; but interest is so much the concern of every working man in the country, I cannot myself go to a public-house to ask a question of a publican, but I must call for something to drink before I can ask the question; I do not taste it, but I must pay something, or I cannot get information; and I think the proposal made would be of essential service, provided there was some benefit attached to it for the collectors; but their taking the number of the cart would do no service, unless they were to come forward, and swear before the magistrates, to the best of their belief, of the persons that were in the cart.

Might not there be a reward held out to the collector of the tolls to make a return of the number of hackney-coaches or carts, in the event of the information he might give, in consequence of that registry leading to the detection of offenders receiving a part of the reward, or a part of the amount for which the cart and horse were sold?—I think that might benefit the thing. There is another thing at which I would take the liberty of hinting: there is an old observation, and a very true one, that if there was no receiver there would be no thief; and I am well persuaded, that there are immense fortunes made in this town by receivers of stolen goods. It would be proper, I think, to exempt officers from the liability to an action of trespass, in case it should be necessary to enter such houses where they suspect there are stolen goods, with or without warrant. It is very certain, that there are a great many articles of merchandize, the marks of which are so completely obliterated, that it is utterly impossible for the owners of such goods to swear to their property; and I have found a considerable number of cases, in my experience, where the parties cannot be convicted in consequence of the marks being obliterated; and this observation is particularly applicable to woollen cloths, cotton, and all articles of linen-drapery goods. I would suggest, for the consideration of the Committee, and the wisdom of Parliament, whether it would not be expedient to enact some law for this purpose, if it should not be considered as trespassing too much upon the liberty of the subject, which ought at all times to be attended to. The suggestion is this: whether it is not desirable that, where persons are reputed to be, and are, notorious receivers of stolen goods, and have often been found out connected in transactions of this kind—whether it is not desirable, I say, to compel persons of this description, in whose houses stolen goods are found, to account for the possession of them, in some satisfactory way or other. With respect to the receiver, the Committee very well know that he cannot be prosecuted for a felony, unless

the

John Vickery.

the thief himself is caught; and the practice is not now as it used to be, as to the mode of committing this species of offence; for we find now that the thieves do not take the goods immediately to the receiver, but takes them home, and sort them out for the purpose of making the best market; and, if we can believe our information, in nine cases out of ten the goods are bargained for before they have got into the possession of the thief; and such secrecy is preserved between the receiver and thief, that one can scarcely ever discover where the goods are concealed. When we know that a robbery has taken place, the consequence of this, and of the difficulty of tracing the goods, is, that when the thief is brought before the Magistrate upon the charge of the robbery, he declines then to go into his defence, but reserves himself till he comes to trial; and then he proves a complete alibi, which he is enabled more effectually to do, because the receiver holds the goods back, and in consequence of which the thief gets an acquittal.

Then the remedy you propose is, that when a person is notoriously in connexion with thieves, as a receiver of stolen goods, and goods found upon his premises, suspected to have been stolen, he shall account for them before the Magistrate?—What I mean is, that in cases where the owner of goods is not able to swear to the property found in the possession of a receiver of stolen goods, by reason of which the thief escapes conviction, the receiver should be made answerable to account for the manner in which he became possessed of the property, and produce bills of parcels to show that he had purchased them, and had come honestly by them. A law of this description would, I think, prevent a great deal of mischief of this sort; and I am well satisfied it would be the means of detecting the receiver.

Would you add any thing to your evidence upon any other head of information? —With respect to the subject of rewarding officers for extraordinary services, to which the Committee has alluded, I think that the power of rewarding the officers should be in the hands of the Magistrates, rather than of the Judges; for nobody can tell who are most deserving of reward for activity and exertions so well as the Magistrates themselves; and I am persuaded, that if this power was left in the hands of the Magistrates it would excite an emulation amongst the officers to obtain the good opinion of the Magistrates: But as this matter stands at present the officers are careless of the Magistrates; for they know that however active their exertions may be, they will never receive an extra sixpence from the Office. I do not speak merely of Bow-street, for there the Magistrates do exercise a power of rewarding the officers for extraordinary exertions; but I speak of the Offices connected with the Police in the different parts of the metropolis. I held a situation in one of those offices for twelve years; and I may venture to say, that with all the exertions I could make, and all the industry I could use, I never had the means of saving a single sixpence for my family in case any accident might happen to myself. There is another thing I would mention to the Committee; I am not speaking for myself, for perhaps I may never want it, but I am speaking on behalf of men who will want it; for it is to be observed, that many of the officers hardly receive more reward for their services than is just enough to enable them to live without becoming thieves; and therefore I should suggest that a provision should be made for such men as are wounded, or receive severe bodily injuries in the performance of their duty; or who are worn out in the service; it is a weary life, and wears men out very fast; and without praising those men too much, I think something should be done for those men who have done their duty to the utmost of their power through a long life, in protecting the lives and property of the Public. I hope the Committee do not think I am saying too much when I suggest that some trifling provision should be made, in the nature of superannuation-money, for those men who have attained the age of fifty, sixty, or seventy years, or who otherwise may be incapacitated from age or infirmity, to do their duty. I got myself cut all to pieces two years ago, and that was in an attempt to take two men who had committed a murder; but I did not expect to live: I was laid up for six months, and I was in that situation at the time, that I should not have left my wife and family a farthing if I had died.

Did not the Office make you any allowance for your wounds?—Never a farthing. They paid my doctor's bill: but in fact they had it not in their power. I know they would willingly have done it; and Sir Nathaniel Conant said he would have done all in his power for me, if he could.

There is no allowance made for old age or infirmities?—None whatever. There is to the Magistrates and clerks, but the officers are considered nothing in the thing.

Have you any other suggestion to make?—There is another thing I would venture

to

John Vickery.

to suggest: I do not know whether the House has it in contemplation to extend the Police to the country as well as to town; but if they should, there is one or two things in which a great deal of good may be done at a little expense: That is, instead of having officers appointed by the parish in rotation for a certain twelve months, without any pecuniary reward for their services, that constables should be appointed for those parishes at small salaries; for it is very well known that a tradesman who happens to be chosen constable for the year will never think of exerting himself, nor indeed has he time, for the benefit of his neighbours. For if he hears that one of his neighbours is robbed, he won't wag out of his own shop till the Magistrate sends for him, and obliges him to do his duty. Therefore I think that if you had parish constables appointed, to be paid small salaries out of certain parish rates, it would be attended with considerable advantage.

You mean, to be appointed by the Magistrates?—Yes, from time to time as they may be entitled to their favour; for if you give a small salary to the officer, and appoint a certain number of officers according to the number of inhabitants, you give him an interest in looking after the property and lives of his neighbours, which he has not now, by reason of which a great deal of injury is done to the public service. There is a great deal of injury arising from the present system; for if a decent tradesman, or respectable inhabitant, is called upon to serve the office of parish-constable, he is indifferent to the performance of its duties, and he considers the office in some respects as an office of disgrace, and to avoid it he will give a man two or three guineas to perform the duties: the man to whom he pays the money is careless in the discharge of the duty, for it is not worth his while to give up all his time and attention to the Public for so small a sum. There is another disadvantage arising from the present system; that there is no regular communication between the Police of the metropolis and the Police of the country: there is no Office in the country to which we can write a letter upon the subject of any offence that may happen to be committed in town; for there is no constable regularly appointed to whom we can write, or who is bound to give any official communication. At Liverpool there is a Police establishment; and if we have occasion to write down there, our letter is attended to, and we get a regular answer. The same observation applies to Birmingham and Manchester; but it is not so at Canterbury and other large towns: and if I should write to a Magistrate, probably he would treat my letter as a matter of indifference, and as out of the ordinary course of things; and indeed it is not intended that a Magistrate should have the trouble of these things: but if you give a constable of a village, or a hundred, twelve or fifteen pounds a year, you make him an active and useful man; and I should propose that the Magistrates should pay his extra charges or expenses; by this means we could keep up a communication with each other, and if a man's horse was stolen, we might get at it through the means of such constable; but if I were to write down into the country to a common parish-constable, desiring that he would stop any property that might have been stolen here, the property would be gone before he would stir a step: probably the man would answer my letter by return of post, and say, " Mr. Vickery, I have received your letter; I would be glad to do any thing in my power; but pray who is to pay me my expenses?" in the mean time the property is gone, and the parties too.

You are aware of the existence of certain houses called flash-houses?—Perfectly.

Are you of opinion that these flash-houses tend to facilitate the detection of offenders, or otherwise?—I am sure they do; I am well aware they do; but these houses are not now as they were, because they are visited by the officers from time to time, whenever they think fit, without the least molestation or inconvenience; they may go into these houses, look round, and see what company there are there, and what they are doing, without any interruption: formerly we could not go into these houses without a Magistrate's warrant; and probably if we went to make any inquiries, we should not come off without some insult or molestation; but now it is quite otherwise. I hold myself much above this kind of gentry, and I am always treated with great civility.

But there are a number of houses of that sort frequented by particular bands of thieves?—I am aware of that; they are attended with this advantage, for they often furnish the means of detecting great offenders; they afford an opportunity to the officers of going round, and knowing the suspicious characters, or of apprehending persons described in advertisements. It is desirable that the officers should know there are such houses, for there is a regular correspondence carried

on

on between the thieves of Birmingham, Liverpool and Manchester, and other places, and the thieves of London; and probably by going to those houses the officers may learn a good deal of useful information respecting desperate characters in all parts of the country. There is another advantage, that they are able to find out the haunts of those men who have returned from Botany Bay, and the nature of their connexions; they materially help in the detection of offenders, and if the officers did not go round where these men frequent, we should never know how to proceed after those parties that are connected together in gangs, and bring them to conviction: I think, however, it would be much better if these houses were done away with altogether, but it is not in the power of the Magistrates to do it altogether. I will tell you where there is an evil in existence: I have known instances where men have been transported for seven years, and have come back to this country, and have got licences for public-houses.

Was that lately?—I have not been in the way to know of that within the last six or seven years, but I have known instances of that kind: I knew one man who had been fourteen years at Botany Bay, and got a licence on his return; that was Tom Bray, of the Black Horse in Golden-lane, near Barbican. He is now dead. He was licensed there only for a short time: he was transported for fourteen years. Now I have an objection to transportation for seven years; I think seven years transportation does a great deal of harm, for a young man who is transported at the age of 17 or 18 years, or is sent on board the hulks for seven years, and at the end of that time comes home, and returns to his old connexions, becomes much worse than he was before; and it most frequently happens that a man's habits are much worse upon his return than when he went out. I think it is much better that the transportation should be for fourteen years, for then there is no prospect of returning again, whereas, when they only go for seven years, they do not forget their old connexions and companions at home, and as soon as they come back to England, what do they do—they return again to their old connexions, and are as bad as ever.

From your own experience, do you find that persons who are discharged from the hulks, or return from Botany Bay, are altered for the better in their habits and manners, or are become worse, and return to their old pursuits?—After they are returned, in nine cases out of ten they return to the same sort of habits, and become as bad as ever. I will tell you an instance: The man who injured me was prosecuted when he was taken; he was taken the next day but one after he injured me, by some of my companions: I had wounded him in the arm, and therefore he was more easily apprehended. He was convicted for the assault, but not of the capital offence, as the Judge held that the poker was not an instrument to cut, and therefore the capital part of the offence was got rid of. Mr. Gurney prosecuted on that occasion. He was then indicted by the desire of the Court for the assault. The man was named Evans. He was convicted, and sentenced to two years imprisonment; he was likewise ordered to find security for his good behaviour for two years from the expiration of his imprisonment; himself in 100 *l.* and two sureties in 50 *l.* each. He has now put in bail. I was asked whether I had any objection to his being bailed; I said I had none whatever, provided I was satisfied with the sufficiency of bail; but I said I should like to see him before he was bailed. I said, I would make some inquiries as to the bail: I do not like to keep this man in prison a moment longer than the law keeps him there, but I should like to see him and speak to him. I accordingly saw him, and I thought proper to give him some admonition as to the conduct and habits of life he should pursue when he should be liberated. I had heard a very excellent character of him in gaol for his conduct there, and that made me lean a little more towards him, and I had hoped that his conduct would be much for the better. He is a shoemaker by trade. He has got into all his old habits again, though it is not above three weeks since he was liberated.

Where was he confined?—In the House of Correction, Cold-bath-fields, under Atkins, where I understood he conducted himself with great propriety; and on that account I was not disposed to deal hard with him.

Did I understand you to give a decided opinion respecting the flash-houses, as giving greater facilities in apprehending offenders?—Why all that depends upon the keepers of the houses. I have received great assistance from the keepers of the houses, but that is not general.

Do you think they do more harm than good; that is to say, do you think they

do

do more harm by assembling together the more vicious persons, by which those who are less vicious are made as bad as the worst; or that they do good by enabling the Police officers to find those people who would meet together somewhere or other, and that it is for that reason the good they do, you think, is greater than the bad?—I do. It is impossible to prevent these men having their meetings: and suppose they were to meet at each man's private lodging at different times, we should have no sort of admission to the private lodging, where they might mature their crimes better than at a public-house. The thing that would make it more desirable for us would be, if the landlords of these houses would co-operate with us in detecting the offenders, but so much depends upon the men who are the land-lords of those houses, that they have it in a great measure in their power to prevent the advantage that might arise from it. Great advantage would arise if the con-duct of the publican was watched with respect to the renewal of his licence. I do not think it is possible or prudent to take away his licence altogether; but I think the Magistrate may take care to be strict with him in the conduct and management of his house. If the Magistrates are particular, a great deal of the mischief may be prevented.

Are they so particular?—I think they are, as far as the law will justify them. I think it is a pity that the power of controlling the licenses is taken out of the hands of the Magistrates, for it makes the publicans more independent; they have a great deal more power than when they were licensed by the Magistrates: I have often been totally foiled by being deceived by the publicans; in such cases I have thought it my duty, in the Public Office to which I belong, to make a complaint before the Magistrates, who have always thought proper to have the case heard, and have en-deavoured to stop the licences of the publicans.

You mean in those cases where publicans have supported thieves?—Certainly so ; if they were disposed to assist the officers, which their public duty requires they should do, it would be of great assistance to us in detecting thieves.

Mr. *William Morgan*, Examined.

WHAT are you?—A shoemaker.

Where do you reside?—At Ross, in Herefordshire.

Were you once the proprietor of a public-house in Gill-street?—Yes.

How long is that ago?—It is seven years last licensing day since the house was licensed.

How long were you in possession of that house before it was licensed?—I tried two years without success.

Whom did you apply to?—I did not apply to any body in particular; but I was two or three years applying in the usual way, but without success, for the two first years.

Was it by getting a petition of all the inhabitants and churchwardens of the parish?—Yes, I applied in that way.

What happened to you in the third year?—I think I lived in Orange-street, Bloomsbury, and a person named Smith, clerk to Messrs. Trueman and Hanbury, called upon me, and asked me if I had not lived in Gill-street, and had been trying for a licence; I said, Yes; and he asked me whose trade I thought of going into; I answered, Messrs. Meux and Company, the brewers in Liquorpond-street; he said, that unless I should agree to deal with Messrs. Trueman and Hanbury, the house never should be licensed; " And," says he, " if there was a coal-shed in that street I would license it;" and then after that, he put me rather to the alarm; and I said to several of my friends, " I think the best way is to promise them the trade;" and afterwards the house was licensed; but I thought it no sin to disappoint them; and then we had some beer from Meux and Company, but after that twenty drays came down from them, and filled the street and the house; and then fearing further damage, and that the licence might be taken away, I granted a lease to Messrs. Meux and Co. and Messrs. Meux and Co. are now in possession.

Had you any remonstrance made to you for the breach of your promise, or did any thing take place in consequence?—Nothing; only a little spite; but I did not take notice of all that passed, as it is so long ago.

Soon after this, was there another public-house opened in the neighbourhood?— There was another public-house built immediately behind mine, where another

public-

public-house had formerly existed; they have got a licence for that since; it is situated in Rich-street.

How far from the house you had occupied?—I cannot tell the precise distance.

Was it about fifty yards?—I cannot tell as to yards; it was immediately behind.

But a short distance from your house?—Yes.

Were there many public-houses in that neighbourhood at the time your house was licensed?—There was not one at that time, and the inhabitants begged for one.

Do you apprehend that house would have been licensed if you had parted with your house to Messrs. Truman and Hanbury?—I think that house in the back never would have been licensed, in my opinion; that is my opinion upon it.

Is it not the general opinion of all the victuallers in that neighbourhood, that if they wished to have a licence they must apply to Messrs. Truman and Hanbury's house?—Yes, that is the case, I think.

Mr. *James May*, again called in, and Examined.

HAVE you now got the rate-books of your parish?—Yes.

Turn to the rate-books of 1809, and see whether you find any alterations in the rates in the hand-writing of Mr. Merceron?—I have turned down every leaf.

Have you looked through the books generally?—Yes. [*Witness produced the books.*]

How lately have you looked through them?—I have looked through the whole of these books; about four others were returned to me this morning. In 1809 the Rev. Mr. King, the rector of the parish, desired me to send him the books for 1809 and 1810, which I accordingly did, and from that time to this moment I have never got back the book for 1809; I was the whole of last year looking for the book of 1809 and 1810, and I took down every book from the year 1627, when the parish became a parish, and I find I have totally lost the book for 1809; I have no doubt they were in the possession of the Rev. Mr. King, or under his protection, for he returned the other books afterwards; he had 50 books from me at the time I have spoken of; but I have never been able to find, or get possession of, the 1809-10 books.

You have then examined the books you hold in your hand; have you found in those rate-books many entries in which the rate is altered in Mr. Merceron's hand-writing?—Many.

How many should you say, in rate-cases?—From 12 to 20.

As there are many entries in which the rate has been increased; are there any instances in which the rate has been diminished?—None, to my knowledge.

Turn to 1809, folio 18, " Solomon Mendo, 2*l.* 16*s.* 3*d.* relieved to 2*l.*?"—I cannot find that without the reference to the division.

Turn to the 2d division, folio 4, "Moses Messiah, relieved to 2*l.* from 2*l.* 16*s.* 3*d.*"; is that entered?—It is not Mr. Merceron's hand-writing; I do not think it is.

Is that rate lower?—It is lower.

Is that done before appeal?—I think it was; I do not know that the collector did any thing but what was on appeal.

Is it the custom, when a rate is reduced upon the regular appeal, to enter in the books a memorandum that such a thing was done?—Yes.

And am I to take it for granted, that when such memorandum is not entered the rate was not reduced by an appeal?—It may frequently be not put down when there is an appeal. It frequently happens that there are 3 or 400 persons in the room, and 8 or 9 books to attend to; and when any entries are made in the books by me, my hand-writing appears to them. I sign *J. M.*

Now turn to folio 8, in which it appears that Thomas Tyler has been relieved from 14*l.* to 8*l.*?—That was on appeal; that is perfectly right.

In folio 10, Richard Vandrum; the rate there appears to have been raised from 8*l.* to 14*l.* and it does not say on appeal?—The collector collected that; it is in his hand-writing.

Is that rate raised on appeal?—I have no doubt it was on appeal.

Then how comes it that that is not stated in the book to be collected on appeal, the same as Thomas Tyler?—When they come into the large room, there are four other persons, each of whom name the books in which the rates are collected; I hand over the books to them, and I desire them to make entries, and put down a note in all cases where there is an appeal, and it very frequently happens in the hurry in which the business is obliged to be done that such remarks are not made.

510. Turn

Turn to the third division, folio 58, and inform the Committee whether you find the names of Abraham Angle, Solomon Divine, and explain the nature of the entry opposite to them?—The entry is Mr. Atkins's tenements Hoxton, farmed at 6 *l.*

Is that the hand-writing of Merceron?—No, the collector's.

Solomon Divine was reduced from nine to six pounds; was Mr. Merceron instrumental to that, and was that upon appeal?—I think it was.

It appearing, by your own statement, that Mr. Merceron altered the rate in the former entries without an appeal, do you believe that wherever there is a reduction of the rate in his name, as found, that it was done on appeal?—It may be done on appeal sometimes; I cannot speak positively as to that; sometimes it is otherwise.

Do you believe it has been done otherwise?—I never saw him sign a book in my life.

Did you ever remonstrate with Mr. Merceron upon the alterations which he took upon himself to make in the rates?—Until the indictment in the Court of King's Bench, I did not know that there was any alteration in the books; they were not known until the accounts were audited. I did not know of the alterations until just before the indictment took place, and I said it was a very wrong thing.

What were the words you used to Mr. Merceron?—I can only speak generally; I thought it a very improper thing for any person to alter the rate; it ought to be altered at the vestry, or on appeal, or except there was a clerical error; and even then I thought it should be done at a vestry meeting.

What did Mr. Merceron say in justification of his conduct?—Generally that he did not know it was wrong.

Did you apply to Mr. Pulley for legal advice to know how to act, when you discovered that Mr. Merceron had so misconducted himself, under an apprehension that you might be involved in such misconduct?—I think not; certainly not.

Did you apply to any one for legal advice?—No; I knew it was wrong myself; I had been in the habit of attending for my father and myself for forty-five or forty-six years, and there is not any book in print upon the Poor Laws that I have not provided myself with. I knew the law myself very well upon the subject, and therefore I did not apply to Mr. Pulley, or any body else; I knew it was wrong.

Did you make any public statement of it to the vestry; or at any time express your abhorrence at so scandalous a transaction having taken place?—I do not know that I did; I said that Mr. Merceron had improperly altered the rates; I do not know that I ever made use of any such expression.

And when did you make use of that observation?—I think in 1812.

He had continued to alter the rates as late as 1812?—That does not appear to me; I have looked through all the books from 1810, 11, 12, down to the present time, and after having looked through all of them for that period, I do not see any alteration since that time; not since the prosecution was taken up.

That is from the latter end of 1811, or beginning of 1812?—Yes.

Then the alterations appear to have existed for ten years, from 1802, or from 1801 to 1811?—I have not the 1809-10 books. In 1811 there do not appear to be any.

Then during the whole of that period, meaning a period of nine or ten years, Mr. Merceron has been in the habit of altering the rates, raising some, and reducing others at is own pleasure?—It appears so by the books.

Does he sign the rates?—Yes, I believe every rate.

Who is Mr. Flood, the other Magistrate?—A Magistrate of Whitechapel.

What is his profession?—I do not know; he has no profession; I think he is a gentleman.

These rate-books are signed by Mr. Merceron, as a Magistrate?—Yes.

Every rate has been signed a great many years?—Yes.

You will no doubt feel it your duty, from the questions which the Committee have put to you, to provide yourself with further information, in case the Committee should summon you next year, to speak more positively as to the alterations of the books, respecting the relief being given upon appeal, or not?—I will endeavour to take every step for that purpose.

Veneris, 14° die Junii, 1816.

The Honourable HENRY GREY BENNET, in The Chair.

———————

Mr. *Samuel Yardly*, called in, and Examined.

YOU are chief clerk at Worship-street office?—I am.

Have you brought with you the late warrants of appointment of constables?—I have brought with me all the appointments of constables since the last Police Act.

How many are there?—We have nine constables.

How many new appointments have there been since the last Police Act?—There appear to have been four.

What were the names of the parties, and by whom appointed.

[The Witness delivered in the Appointments, which were read, as follows:]

Gentlemen,   Whitehall, 1st May 1815.

I AM directed by Lord Sidmouth, to acquaint you, that his Lordship has appointed Thomas Garton to be one of the Constables at the Public Office Worship-street, in the room of the late William Armstrong,

I am, Gentlemen,

The Magistrates,   Your most obedient humble Servant,
Public Office Worship-street.   *J. Becket.*

Gentlemen,   Whitehall, 22d February 1816.

I AM directed by Lord Sidmouth, to acquaint you, that his Lordship considers William Hill is a fit and proper person to be appointed a constable at the Public Office Worship-street, in the room of the late Anthony Cavalier; and his Lordship desires that you will swear him in to act as such accordingly. I am also to acquaint you, that William Hill has received directions to attend you for that purpose.

I am, Gentlemen,

The Magistrates,   Your most obedient humble Servant,
Public Office Worship-street.   *J. Becket.*

Gentlemen,   Whitehall, 28th May 1816.

I AM directed by Lord Sidmouth, to acquaint you, that his Lordship considers William Foy to be a fit and proper person to act as a constable at the Public Office Worship-street, in the room of William Hill; and I am to desire that you will appoint William Foy to be a constable at that Office accordingly.

I am, Gentlemen,

The Magistrates,   Your most obedient humble Servant,
Public Office Worship-street.   *J. Becket.*

Was William Foy appointed a constable in consequence of that order?—No, he was not appointed; I believe he did not accept the office; there is the subsequent appointment of a person instead of him.

Were the other two persons appointed?—Yes, Garton and Hill; Hill was afterwards discharged in consequence of being absent from the Office, and Foy was directed to be sworn in, but did not accept the office; the last, William Attfield, has been sworn in, in consequence of Foy declining to accept the office. This is the appointment under which Attfield was sworn in.

Gentlemen,   Whitehall, 7th June 1816.

With reference to my letter to you of the 28th ultimo, directing the appointment of William Foy, to be a constable at the Public Office Worship-street, in the room of William Hill, I am now directed by Lord Sidmouth, to acquaint you, that William Foy has declined being appointed; and that his Lordship desires you will appoint William Attfield, whom his Lordship considers to be a fit and proper person, instead of William Foy.

I am, Gentlemen,

The Magistrates,   Your most obedient humble Servant,
Public Office Worship-street.   *J. Becket.*

All these appointments of Police officers were made in consequence of directions to that effect coming from the Secretary of State?—They were, except that of William Foy, who, it appears by a subsequent letter, had declined accepting the office.

Mr.
Samuel Yardly.

Have you any knowledge of the Act of Parliament, by which that authority is given to the Secretary of State?— I have a knowledge of the Act of Parliament.

Within your knowledge, has any remonstrance on the part of the Police Magistrates taken place, in consequence of what evidently appears to be a new construction of that Act?—I believe there has been in one instance, on the part of one Magistrate.

Do you know what was the result?—No, I cannot say.

What Magistrate was that?—I believe, Mr. Gifford.

Do you know whether in any instance any person has been appointed by the Secretary of State, who afterwards turned out to be an improper person to fill that office?—Yes, one of those four, William Hill.

Was it he who turned out to be what is known technically by the name of a Jew Bail, and is now in the King's Bench prison?—I have heard he is a sham bail, but I never knew him till he came to the Office.

For what was he turned out?—Because he was not present to discharge his duty; he was in custody several weeks.

On inquiry, did he turn out to be a person of bad character?—He turned out to be a sort of hired bail, a man who had formerly been in the habit of being hired as bail; I never knew the man till he came down to be sworn in.

Do you believe that he was a person who carried on the trade formerly of what is termed Jew bail?—I certainly have reason to believe it.

Are you of opinion that the Police Office in Worship-street can be as well supplied with efficient officers, under the present mode of appointment, as it would be were those appointments made, as the Act appears to point out, by the Police Magistrates themselves?—I think the Magistrates would be able to select proper persons who knew the district and were acquainted with the various parts of that district, equally so with the Secretary of State.

Are you not of opinion that the Magistrates would be able to select the more proper officers of the two?—I do not know the more proper, I do not know the source the Secretary of State has for the selection; I know the Magistrates would have as much opportunity as the Secretary of State, of selecting proper persons, men residing in the district.

You do know, that out of the four last persons selected by the Secretary of State, one declined to accept the office, and another turned out to be an improper person soon after he was appointed?—Certainly.

Are you not then of opinion the Magistrates would make a better choice than the Secretary of State?—I should certainly think that the Magistrates could make quite as good a selection.

Have you any doubt that that is the proper interpretation of the Statute of 54 George III, cap. 37, section 16, which is in the following terms: " And be it " further Enacted, That the Justices appointed as aforesaid, shall in their respective " offices, retain and employ a sufficient number of fit and able men, subject to the " approbation of His Majesty's Secretary of State for the Home Department, " whom they are hereby authorized and empowered to swear in, to act as constables, " for preserving the peace, and preventing robberies and other felonies, and ap- " prehending offenders against the peace, within the said counties of Middlesex " and Surrey respectively, as well by night as by day; which said constables so " appointed and sworn as aforesaid shall have all such powers and authorities, " privileges and advantages, as any constable duly appointed now has, or here- " after may have, by virtue of any law or statute now made or hereafter to be " made, and shall obey all such lawful commands as they shall from time to time " receive from the said Justices, for the apprehending offenders, or otherwise " conducting themselves in the execution of their said office or employment; and " such Justices or any two of them, shall and may at any time dismiss from his said " employment every such constable belonging to their respective offices, whom " they shall think remiss or negligent in the execution of his duty, or otherwise " unfit for the same, and appoint, subject to such approbation as aforesaid, others " in their stead : Provided always, that no greater number than twelve shall at " one and the same time be so retained as aforesaid, at any one of the said public " offices: Provided also, that if any person so appointed constable as aforesaid, " shall be dismissed from his said employment as aforesaid, all powers and autho- " rities vested in him as a constable, under and by virtue of this Act, shall " immediately cease and determine, to all intents and purposes whatever"?—I have

no

no doubt it was the intention of the Legislature, that the Magistrates should appoint, subject to the approval of the Secretary of State.

How long have you filled the situation of a clerk at the Police Office?—I have been a clerk at the office ever since the first establishmect of the Police in August 1792, and I have been chief clerk about thirteen years.

Have you any other situation under Government, besides that of chief clerk?—None.

Do you practise as a solicitor?—I do.

Do you practise as a solicitor in the office?—Never.

Do you attend daily your situation as chief clerk?—Constantly.

And are there during the hours at which the Magistrates sit?—Always, except prevented by illness.

Then your situation as solicitor, is no obstruction at all to your attendance at that office?—Never; I never found it to be; my common law business is generally done by agency, so that it is never an obstruction.

From your observation since you have filled that situation, do you think that the number of criminals brought before the Magistrates, has considerably increased within the few last years?—I think they have within the few last years.

What is the general character of the crimes for which persons are brought before the Magistrates?—We have not had any very atrocious crimes of late; simple larcenys, burglaries and so on, nothing very enormous.

Do you think that is a real increase, owing to the morals of the people being more corrupted, or that it proceeds from the great increase of the population, which has of late years taken place?—I think it applies more to the population than to increase of crime.

Is it attributable to an increased vigilance of the Police?—I can hardly form a judgment upon that; our officers have been vigilant of late.

You are not aware that they have been more vigilant than they were in former years?—No, I am not.

Do you think the general system is better understood and conducted, and that there is a more extensive watch and ward, if that term may be used, kept by the officers of the Police over the conduct of individuals in the Metropolis, than there was some years ago?—I think in regard to our own Office, there is.

Do you think that the same is going on in other parts of the town?—I have reason to believe it.

So that the increase of crimes which appears to have taken place, may be attributed to two causes: first, the augmentation of the population; and secondly, the increased vigilance of the Police?—I think so.

Juvenile depredations have very much increased?—Very much lately.

Can you give to the Committee an opinion, what are the principal reasons that have increased juvenile depredators of late years?—I think a great deal the profligacy of their parents, and the neglect of parents. There are so many children selling matches, and leading an idle life; and if they have not the means of supporting themselves, they will pilfer from shops and stalls of every description. I think it is owing in a great measure to the profligacy and neglect of their parents, who spend more in public-houses than they can afford, and ought to spend.

Do you think drunkenness has considerably increased among the lower orders, of late years?—I think it has.

Do you speak of the middling classes, or the lower orders of society?—I speak of the lower classes, itinerants and costermongers, persons driving jack asses, and so on.

Has there not been of late years a great influx of Irish into the Metropolis?—I do not think at our end of the town there has.

There has in the neighbourhood of St. Giles's?—They associate more there than they do at our end of the town.

Joseph Merceron, Esq. called in, and Examined.

YOU are a Magistrate of the county of Middlesex?—I am.

How long have you filled that situation?—I should think one or two-and twenty years.

Have you, during the whole of that time, resided in the parish in which you now live?—I have.

510.

Then

Mr.
Samuel Yardly.

Joseph Merceron,
Esq.

Then of course you can speak as to the state of the morals and manners of its inhabitants, having acted as a Magistrate there during the course of one-and-twenty years?—Certainly.

Do you think their morals and manners are in a better or worse, or in a stationary state, as compared with what they were when first you knew the neighbourhood?—As far as it relates to drunkenness I think there are not so many drunken people, but as far as relates to swearing and profane talking, particularly among the younger part of the lower orders, there is much more; I speak of boys of ten, twelve, and fourteen; I think that is very much increased.

What is the present state of the parish; are the people indigent or comfortable?—They are extremely indigent; the parish of Bethnal Green is what may be called Spitalfields, principally weavers, and the weaving business is extremely bad at present.

It has been stated to a Committee now sitting, that there are nearly three thousand looms out of employ; taking seven men to a loom would make twenty-one thousand persons, should you think that was near the mark?—I should think it was too much, if it was taken as applying to Bethnal Green alone, but perhaps that may be correct as applying to Spitalfields in general; including the whole district, I should think it may be a fair calculation.

You have stated to the Committee, that according to your opinion and observation, the vice of drunkenness is on the decline in your neighbourhood; the Committee have been informed that there is a practice which, though perhaps now less than what took place sometime ago, still exists, namely, the practice of bullock-hunting; does that exist in your parish much in the present time?—It does exist, but I think not to the extent that it did some two or three years ago.

In point of fact, is there not very often bullock-hunting on a Sunday, or has not that circumstance occurred?—I believe it has; but I believe in general it is on a Monday, when the cattle come into Smithfield; I think there has been an instance of its being on a Sunday, but I cannot speak to a certainty of that.

Has it not happened, within your own knowledge, that a bullock has been driven across the church-yard during Divine Service?—I have heard so.

Were not you in church?—I was in the church, I recollect, but I knew nothing of it till I went out, and then I understood a bullock had been driven across the church-yard.

Is it not the custom for idle and profligate youth of both sexes to assemble in a field adjoining the church-yard, and during the whole Sunday amuse themselves by baiting animals, fighting dogs, and other riotous amusements, unrestrained and uncorrected by the Police?—There is no question but that a great number of disorderly people assemble on a Sunday as mentioned, but when it is said unrestrained, I believe every step has been taken to restrain them that can be.

How then does it come to pass that these assemblages take place every Sunday, and that they take place with impunity; if they were punished, you must be quite aware they would not be repeated the following Sunday?—I do not know that they take place every Sunday; I should think not; I believe they are mostly in the summer time; I have repeatedly sent to the Police Office in Worship-street for their headboroughs to come and disperse them; not above six weeks ago I sent, and Mr. Moser attended with some of the officers: but I believe it is principally on a Sunday that they assemble there, in consequence of some ponds into which they put some dogs and ducks.

How long is it since the last bullock-hunting took place?—I cannot say.

When was the last you saw?—I believe about six months ago, and I began to feel great personal risk, and rescued the bullock from a man in Bethnal Green Road; two lads were taken up and sent to the Worship-street Office, in consequence of my interference.

Can you take upon yourself to say, that every exertion has been used by the Magistrates, to put down these riotous assemblages of persons which take place on the Sabbath-day in your district?—I can only speak for myself; I have repeatedly on a Sunday sent to the constable, and ordered him and the headboroughs to go round the parish during the time of Divine Service; and I believe the same has been done by the Magistrates of the Worship-street Office, in whose district Bethnal Green is.

Do you attend the licensing of public-houses in your district?—I generally do.

Have you so attended for a number of years?—I have.

State

Joseph Merceron,
Esq.

State to the Committee in how many public-houses in that quarter you are interested, either as proprietor, or as agent for other persons?—I should suppose I have ten or twelve public-houses of my own, and I should think much about the same number as trustee and agent for some families; I cannot speak with precision at the moment.

Can you state to the Committee the names of the different Signs, beginning with those belonging to yourself, and those that belong to others for whom you act?—I cannot at present.

[The witness was directed to furnish the Committee with this information.]

Does the house called The Sun, in Slater-street, belong to you?—It does not.

Is it one of those that belongs to an estate of which you are the manager?—It is not; it did formerly belong to a large estate of the family of Busby, but it has been sold some years.

Does The Seven Stars in Fleet-street, belong to you?—It does.

To whom have you let that?—To Messrs. Hanbury and Company.

Does a house in St. John-street, called The Three Sugar Loaves, belong to you?—It does not.

Does it belong to an estate to which you are a rent-gatherer?—It belongs to an estate of the family of Petley; I receive the rent for them as a friend.

Is that house underlet also to Messrs. Hanbury?—I do not know; I do not know who the brewer is.

Of whom do you receive the rent?—I think a person of the name of Butler pays the rent.

The tenant in possession?—I believe he is.

How many houses belonging to yourself, and houses belonging to others, do you underlet to Messrs. Hanbury and Truman?—I think I receive from Hanbury for two houses that he pays me for.

Belonging to yourself?—Yes; I do not know who my other tenants let them to; Mr. Hanbury pays me for two.

It may happen that your undertenant may sub-let the house to Mr. Hanbury, without your knowing it?—I have no doubt that many of those I let to other people they let to Hanbury; they have the greatest number of houses in that district by far.

Can you state to the Committee the number of houses they have in that district?—No.

Have any complaints ever been made to your knowledge, before the Magistrates, of the conduct of persons holding those public-houses just mentioned, namely, the Three Sugar Loaves and the Seven Stars?—Upon my word I cannot take upon myself to say; probably they might, at our general annual licensing, and at the two months licensing; I think the Sun was a very bad house, it has been shut up and opened and shut up again; I think there have been heavy complaints against the Sun.

Can you state to the Committee why, if the successive landlords of the Sun have so conducted themselves, their licence has been continued?—I cannot.

Were you, as a Magistrate, present when those complaints were made against that house on the licensing day?—I know of none; I dare say there were complaints, but I do not recollect.

Should you, as a Magistrate, knowing that this house was as bad as you have just now stated, not have felt it your duty to oppose the licensing of this house, on the licensing day?—Certainly.

Did you so oppose it?—I do not know that there were any charges made.

You have stated to the Committee, that you know many complaints have been made as to the bad conduct of the house, and that it was a very bad house?—It was frequently shut up; and I believe there have been complaints.

Knowing it has been repeatedly shut up, and that it was a bad house, did you on the licensing day resist the licensing of it?—I do not know that there were any complaints on the licensing day.

Did you not, as a Magistrate, knowing of these complaints which you before stated you did, feel it your duty to state your knowledge of the facts to the other Magistrates?—The complaints might be probably, the house being shut up, which it had been a considerable time; the house being shut up, and a new person coming in, I did not feel that to be any ground of complaint; I mean by being shut up, if a tenant cannot live in a house, and there are two or three tenants in the course of the

Joseph Merceron,
Esq.

year, that is a ground of complaint for the house not being continued; but I do not know of my own knowledge; I knew the house had frequently changed hands.

You have stated, not only that it frequently changed hands, but that the conduct and management of the house was particularly bad?—I beg leave to say, I did not know that of my own knowledge; the ground of complaint, as I conceived, against the house, was, that there was no trade to it, and nobody could live in it.

Have you heard any complaints of that house being the resort of idle and profligate persons?—No, I have not.

Never of drunkenness and gambling, and that species of club known among the lower orders, by the name of a Cock and Hen Club assembling there?—Never any thing of the kind, to my knowledge.

Did you then believe it was an orderly house?—I should suppose it was not an orderly house.

Were you not present the last licensing day; and did you not give your sanction to the licensing of that house?—I do not know that I was present.

You stated, that you were always present at the licensing?—I should think I was there, but cannot say.

Then thinking you were present, and knowing it was a disorderly house changing tenants three or four times in a year, how can you reconcile to your conscience the consenting to the re-licensing of that house?—I do not know that I gave my consent to it; it was perhaps done as a matter of course.

Do you know that you opposed it?—I do not know that I did.

But you know the house has changed tenants three or four times in a year, and is a disorderly house?—I do not know that it is a disorderly house; I know a house among poor people in that district where they cannot get business, will have improper persons come to it; but the great objection to the house, I conceive, was its changing tenants, and their not being able to live.

Any minor objection of its changing tenants, and their not being able to live, was not considered by you as sufficient to authorize the shutting up of the house?—I do not know that any complaint was made, of course I made none myself.

Is it your custom, when you know of facts against a house, to suppress the knowledge of those facts, and to consent to the house being re-licensed, as a matter of course?—Certainly not; I never consent to any thing being suppressed.

What is the character of the house which you state to be your own, called The Seven Stars, in Fleet-street?—I know of no complaint against it.

Do you believe it to be an orderly house?—I have heard nothing to the contrary.

Do you say the same of the Three Sugar Loaves in St. John-street?—The Three Sugar Loaves has lately been rebuilt; I have heard no complaints against that house.

Do you think, you being a Magistrate residing in that neighbourhood, that any of the houses named could be disorderly, without your knowing something of the matter?—Certainly they might.

Do you think there could be assembled in those houses a nightly resort of thieves, and boys and girls meeting in what are termed Cock and Hen Clubs, with the different varieties of low debauchery in which bad people indulge, without its coming to the knowledge of the Magistrates?—I should think it was impossible but it would be known at the Police Office in Worship-street.

Is it not as much or more the province of the constable of the parish to attend to the conduct of the victuallers, than of the Police officers in Worship-street?—I should think it was, but I believe it is not done.

Have you then, as an active Magistrate which you are in that district, interfered that the constable should do his duty?—I have frequently sent to him to do his duty.

When you have known that that duty is not done, what has been your process to enforce it?—I have frequently desired him to go out on a Sunday morning to see that the houses were regularly shut up during Divine Service, taking his headboroughs with him, which he has always informed me was done.

You have stated to the Committee, that he has not done his duty; what have you done as a Magistrate, in consequence?—I believe the constable of the parish does not do his duty as he ought to do.

What steps have you taken to make the constable of the parish do that duty, which belongs to him as much as to the Police Magistrates?—I have certainly never made any complaint of that kind; because, whenever I have sent for him, he has promised to go round to the different houses and do that duty; and I have considered that he did do it.

At

At what hour are the public-houses ordered to be shut up?—Before Divine Service on Sundays, and before eleven o'clock every night.

Joseph Merceron,
Esq.

Do you know whether the constable goes round, or that any one goes round, to see whether that regulation is enforced?—I believe they do, at times.

Do you believe that it is enforced?—Occasionally.

Do you think the practice of the public-houses is to shut up at eleven at night, or to keep open?—I believe the great majority shut up at eleven o'clock.

Have any complaints ever been made to you against those who do not shut up by eleven o'clock at night?—No.

Do you know that any complaints have been made against them elsewhere?—I believe there have been, at Worship-street Office.

Do you mean to state, that the general conduct of the public-houses in your district is good and orderly?—I do; their general conduct, I believe, is orderly.

Have you never had any complaints brought before you, or do you, of your own knowledge, know that they have been brought before the Police Magistrates, with respect to particular houses in your district?—No, I do not; complaints are brought at our licensing.

When those complaints are brought, what course is taken?—The chairman, whoever may happen to be in the chair—

Who is the permanent chairman?—Sir Daniel Williams. The chairman hears the complaint; the constables generally make their return of complaints, and of course the matter is submitted to the Magistrates present.

Has it often happened that licences have been taken away in your district, for the misconduct of the victualler?—Yes, they have been taken away.

Lately?—Yes, I believe almost every year, more or less.

Have those houses been in your own parish, against which the complaints were laid, and the tenants of which were punished by losing their licences?—I do not recollect immediately, whether in my parish or in the district we act for, the Tower division, which is a very large district.

There are nearly a thousand public-houses in it?—I believe there are.

Are any of the houses which have lost their licences, among those which are your own, or for which you collect the rents?—I do not recollect at present; a reference to the books will ascertain that.

You cannot recollect whether any house of your own, or belonging to a person for whom you collect the rents, have been among those which, through the misconduct of tenants, have lost their licence?—I should think there are among them, but I do not recollect any.

Were you present at the licensing of the last year, 1815, when a house was licensed near St. George's in the East, which had been refused being licensed the year preceding; or do you recollect any thing of that circumstance?—I believe there have been several applications for St. George's in the East.

Do you recollect that there was one house, which the Magistrates visited the year before, and which they determined not to license, but the year after, which was last year, it was licensed; the reason for its being refused being, a conviction of its being perfectly unnecessary to the neighbourhood?—No, I do not recollect the circumstance.

Were you present the year in which the licences were taken away, in Shadwell parish, from the Duke of York, the White Hart, and the Pavior's Arms?—Yes, I was.

For what were they taken away?—They were taken away for disorderly and improper conduct.

In what respect?—I believe encouraging improper people and apprentices, and late hours; I believe there was a complaint made by the parish officers of Shadwell; but that complaint came principally through the Shadwell Office.

The offences for which they lost their licences were, encouraging drunkenness, disorderly meetings, receiving apprentices, and general disorderly conduct?—I think those were the complaints made by the parishes.

In consequence of the complaints of the parish officers, the Magistrates thought fit to take away their licences?—Yes.

That was in the year 1813?—Yes; the houses were re-licensed the next year.

Were you present when they were licensed in 1814?—I think I was; we had a very full meeting of the Magistrates.

Can you state to the Committee what was the reason which induced the Magistrates to re-license houses, against which such complaints were made the year

preceding,

preceding, as to induce them to shut them up, two of which were then held by the same landlords who lost the licences the year before?—I do not know who the landlords were; I believe the parish of Shadwell had been in hot water for some years, and I believe the representation which was made to the Magistrates was, that a great number of the charges made against those houses were ill founded; and I believe that some back room, or some back premises, were removed and taken away where these people used to associate; to the best of my recollection, that was the fact.

It has been given in evidence before the Committee, that all the change which had taken place was the removal of a music gallery in those back rooms, but that there was no material change as to the management of the house; and the defence which has been set up is, that these were no worse than the other houses in the street; it has also been proved to the Committee, that every seventh or eighth house in the street is a public-house?—I know there are a great number of public-houses, but to what extent I cannot say; I know very little of Shadwell division.

Do you not recollect that the churchwardens and other parish officers, as well as many principal inhabitants, opposed the re-opening of those houses, not because they were so much worse than others, but because they were desirous to punish some, and because it had been proved before you, and was offered to be proved on oath, that the masters of those houses were the same who had held them the preceding year?—I cannot speak with precision upon that, there was a great deal of business took place on that head; Sir Daniel Williams was chairman; there was evidence on both sides; there were persons who supported those houses being re-licensed, but I cannot, with certainty, state the reason.

What is the general character of the public-houses in Shadwell district?—I have always understood that they were very noisy, that that was their general character, and they generally are where they are amongst sailors.

Do you believe as to the three houses the licences of which were stopped, they were stopped because that they were so much worse than other houses, generally speaking, in that district, or for the purpose of being an example, in the hope that an amendment would take place in the conduct of the publicans?—It strikes me it was, because they were more riotous than the other houses.

And yet the Magistrates thought fit to re-open those houses, under the same people?—That is a circumstance I did not call to mind.

Was any evidence tendered to the Magistrates, that at least one of the parties, namely the party that kept the Duke of York, was the same person that then held one of the houses about to be licensed?—I do not know; I cannot speak to that.

You cannot say whether such evidence was refused or not?—Certainly I cannot; this took place at the general licensing, when fourteen or fifteen Magistrates were present.

Did you support the re-licensing of those houses, or did you oppose it?—I believe we were unanimous in the re-licensing of them, to the best of my recollection; we went upon the spot I believe, twelve or fourteen Magistrates, and I believe there was no difference of opinion.

Do you recollect whether Mr. Fletcher the churchwarden, and others who took a part against those houses, tendered themselves to be sworn, to prove all the facts which they had alleged in the memorial which they presented, and other facts connected with the bad conduct of those houses and of the persons who proposed to keep them, and that the Magistrates at Shadwell refused to hear them?—There was no meeting at Shadwell.

Was there not a meeting at Shadwell on the 12th of September?—The meeting at Shadwell was only in the street.

On the 19th of September was there not a meeting of Magistrates?—That I suppose was the general re-licensing day; I was there.

On that day was not evidence tendered by the churchwardens themselves, proposing to be put to the oath to substantiate the facts of their memorial, and did not the Magistrates, one of whom was yourself, refuse to hear them?—Mr. Fletcher the churchwarden, and some other gentlemen were at Osborn-street, previous to the Magistrates going to Shadwell to view the houses; I recollect Mr. Fletcher being there, and some other officer with him.

Do you recollect the fact of their tendering themselves to be sworn, and that the Magistrates refused to hear them?—No, I do not recollect their tendering themselves to be sworn; they were there to answer any questions, I suppose.

Will

Joseph Merceron,
Esq.

Will you take upon yourself to say, they did not tender themselves to be sworn to give that evidence?—I do not recollect the circumstance, but I will not say it did not take place.

Was it not stated to the Magistrates, by the parish officers and other principal inhabitants, in their memorial, and offered to be substantiated upon oath, that there was such a profusion of public-houses, that every eighth or ninth house in the street where those houses were situate, was a public-house, and that the re-opening those houses instead of being an accommodation would be a great nuisance to it?—I should think there might be, but I cannot recollect the circumstances; the minutes of the Magistrates would, of course, inform the Committee.

In point of fact, why were the houses re-opened, it being clear they could not be wanted, from the number of houses in the street; and it being also clear, that the same parties, at least one of the same parties, was to hold one of the houses for which a licence was asked?—I cannot recollect sufficiently to state.

The question the Committee wish to have answered is, what, to the best of your recollection, was the reason given by the Magistrates, and what was the reason you yourself gave as a Magistrate, for re-opening those houses?—I can give no further answer but that the parish had been in hot water a great while; and that a gentleman of the name of Fox, and others, said, this was a complete party business, and that the houses ought to be re-licensed, inasmuch as those houses were not worse than the others, and that they had suffered severely, and that it would—I remember that a great deal was said, but I believe all the Magistrates present were unanimous in re-licensing them.

What is the principle upon which you open a public-house, or keep a public-house when it has been once licensed; is it not the wants of the neighbourhood?—That I conceive to be the first cause, public accommodation.

Did you think, or was it before you when you came to a decision to re-open them, that the public convenience required those houses to be re-licensed?—I cannot speak to that.

Some little time ago this question was put to you, whether the three houses, the licences of which were taken away, were notoriously worse than other houses in the neighbourhood, and whether the licences were taken away on that account, or whether for the purpose of an example to others, they not being worse than the generality of houses; to which your answer was, that you thought they must be worse than other houses?—I did.

You now state, that Mr. Fox appeared at this meeting, that there he delivered in a statement of a high party spirit existing in the parish, that those houses were not worse than the other houses and therefore ought to be re-licensed, and upon that you acted; at the same time that you say, you believe the licences were taken away because they were notoriously worse?—I should presume so.

What is your real opinion, do you believe those houses were notoriously worse than other houses in the same neighbourhood; or do you believe Mr. Fox's statement, upon which you acted, is true, that they were not notoriously worse, but that they were taken away on account of party spirit?—I believe there was a great deal of party spirit in it, but I should suppose they might be worse.

What part did you take the year before, when there was this party spirit; were the Magistrates affected by the party spirit?—I was not.

What part did you take the year before; did you oppose the granting of the licences, or support their being taken away?—I cannot speak to that.

Do you think it was the party spirit that affected the Magistrates, when they took away the licences?—No, I do not.

Then what do you mean, by stating it to be party spirit which had caused those licences to be taken away?—I believe it was the representation of the constables to the Magistrates, who stated that those houses were worse than the others.

Did not the Magistrates hear the parties, before they took away the licences?—I believe they did.

Do you believe that the Magistrates came to an unjust decision?—I should think not; I believe they did what they thought right; I can only speak for myself. The houses, in general, in that district are bad and noisy; there is a great deal of noise and fiddling, and we should, as compared with those in Spitalfields, call them very noisy and bad.

Is it customary for the Magistrates, or any number of the Magistrates, to meet prior to the licensing day, to discuss what houses shall or shall not have licences?—Not that I know of.

510.

Is

Joseph Merceron, Esq.

Is there not a view day?—Formerly we used to have a view day, but not of late years; there are regular days fixed : two licensing days and an adjournment. I know of no private meeting; there is none to my knowledge.

Do not you believe Sir Daniel Williams, and Mr. Robson, and other Magistrates, generally meet previous to the day for re-licensing public-houses, and agree what houses shall or shall not be licensed?—Certainly not.

Then the Committee are to believe that that statement, if made to them, is a statement that is not true?—As far as relates to myself.

Do not the Magistrates go round and view the houses where new licences are applied for, previous to the re-licensing day?—Formerly we used to do it.

Did they not do it last year?—Not to my knowledge; they determined on the spot.

Were there any fresh licences last year?—I believe there were.

And there was no previous meeting, for the purpose of forming an opinion as to the propriety of re-licensing them or not?—I do not recollect; I should think not.

Formerly it used to take place?—Some years back, I think it did.

How many years?—I believe it has been discontinued these ten or twelve years.

Then at present there is no meeting of the Magistrates at all, previously to examine the houses for which licences are to be asked on the licensing day?—The Magistrates go round in a body to examine the houses for which licences are applied for, not individual Magistrates.

A day is appointed for the Magistrates to go round and examine those houses for which licences are applied for, prior to the licensing day?—No doubt of it.

At that meeting of the Magistrates, do they decide amongst themselves which are the houses fit for, and which they intend to license, and which not?—It is decided upon the spot, by the whole body of Magistrates; the whole body goes round, looks to the houses; the clerk attends with the memorial; and the Magistrates, in the open street, decide upon the spot, Aye or No.

You have stated, that though there is a public meeting of the Magistrates to examine the houses for which licences are to be granted, there is no previous meeting of two or three of the active Magistrates, to settle among themselves what houses they will agree to support the licences for?—Not to my knowledge.

You yourself never attended any such meeting, and do not believe that such meeting has ever been held?—I never attended, and there are not such meetings, to my knowledge.

Have you ever been spoken to by the Rector of your parish, upon the disorderly state of the lower orders of the parish in general, and upon those riots and disturbances which take place in the neighbourhood of the church?—No; I have had no communication with the Rector for a long time.

Did he never make any complaint to you, of the indecencies of the system of bullock-hunting, and riotous assemblages of persons in the neighbourhood of the church, during Divine Service?—Never.

He has never talked to you officially, he as Rector of the parish, and you as Magistrate, upon this subject?—He never has.

The Committee have had in evidence before them, on the part of Mr. King, the rector of the parish, that a prosecution was commenced by him against you, some short time back, for having altered the parish rates after they had been made and allowed; they have also examined the Vestry Clerk, and inspected the different rate-books, in which they find several alterations, which are stated by the clerk to be in your hand-writing, and to have been made subsequent to the rates being allowed, and that the rates so altered, increased, or diminished, have been collected on; the Committee think it right to communicate this evidence to you, and wish to know whether you have any remarks to make, or any explanation to give?—No further than that business has been, I believe, satisfactorily explained; it was the cause of an action in the Court of King's Bench, and there the parish was satisfied it was all through a mistake, and that whatever alterations were made, and whatever money was received, had been regularly brought to the parish account.

Are the Committee to understand, that you admit you made the alterations?—Certainly not.

Do you deny then, that those different entries in the rate book are in your hand-writing?—I should wish to see them.

Are you aware that you ever did make any alterations in the rate books?—Certainly.

After

After the rate had been allowed?—O no, but not since our late Act of Parliament. What Act of Parliament was that?—The 53d of the present King.

Casten Rohde, Esquire, called in, and Examined.

DO you act as a Magistrate?—I have done so, but not lately.

What was the district in which you acted?—Sometimes I used to attend at Lambeth-street occasionally, but very seldom indeed; but now I live in Spring-gardens, and have been used to attend at Queen-square occasionally.

How long is it since you have acted in the Whitechapel district?—I have left that part of the town these eleven years; I have not been there, except attending the licensing.

Do you attend on the licensing of the public-houses?—Yes.

Have you attended on the licensing day, for a number of years?—I have.

Do you think that the Magistrates who attend there, pay particular attention to the character and claims of every individual soliciting a licence, and that they are in no degree influenced by the name and protection that any particular person, brewer or otherwise, may give to the individual soliciting?—I can hardly answer that question; I can only answer it generally, that from some observations I have heard made, I think that there has been some influence somewhere, but I cannot tell where nor how.

Do you think that in point of fact, on the licensing day, a victualler coming to request a licence for a new house, with the protection and countenance of Messrs. Hanbury and Truman, would have more chance of obtaining a licence, than if he came there for a free house?—I rather think that he would have more attention paid him than otherwise; it appears so to me, that there has been more particular attention paid to people soliciting public-houses, when it has been in the firm of Truman and Co. than otherwise. I think in the distribution of licences to new houses, it is very difficult, almost amounting to impossibility, to get a licence to a new house, except a hint has been given, or it is understood, the owner of it or the tenant means to deal with that house: I speak from the number of houses I have seen licensed in their trade.

And refused in others?—Yes.

Is there not a difficulty in any person's obtaining a licence in that district, who has not the interest of Messrs. Hanbury and Co.?—It appears to me that there is.

Have you not known instances of persons applying for a licence to a new public house, which in point of neighbourhood and situation you thought ought to be licensed, but which was not licensed; and could you trace the cause of its not being licensed to any other circumstance than its not being in Mr. Hanbury's interest?—No; I have seen houses where I thought they might have been licensed, and where there were public-houses wanting; but at the same time they did not get their licence, but I cannot tell why they were refused.

To what did you attribute that refusal?—I could not tell that; it was so general a thing among the Magistrates, I cannot speak to it.

Do you think the number of public-houses has very much increased of late years?—No, I think the contrary, that they are decreased, from a calculation that was produced before us, where it was observed, the last year and the year before, that they had considerably decreased, as many as 20 or 30 in the division.

It is stated to this Committee, in evidence by Magistrates as well as by Victuallers, that unless a person applying for a licence to a new house in the district in which you act, promised to deal with Messrs. Hanbury and Company, he stood no chance of being licensed; do you believe that to be the fact?—No, I cannot say that he stood no chance of being licensed; but at the same time I think, by what means I cannot tell, but by some means or other, Messrs. Hanbury appeared to be in favour with the Magistrates, and to get houses in preference to any body else.

Mr. *William Day*, called in, and Examined.

ARE you the principal conductor of the horse patrole?—I am.

How long have you held that situation?—As conductor above two years; I was inspector before that.

[The Witness delivered in a Card, the contents of which were read, as follow:]

POLICE HORSE PATROLE.

A STATEMENT, showing, the several Roads round London on which the HORSE PATROLE are nightly on duty, and the several Places at which the Men and Horses are stationed.

Roads Patrolled.	Places at which the Men and Horses are stationed.	
Dartford - - -	Walworth - - -	New Cross.
Maidstone - - -	Blackheath - -	Welling.
Bromley - - -	Bexley Heath -	Dartford.
Croydon - - -	Sidcup - - -	Bromley Common.
Sutton - - -	Kennington - -	Croydon.
Epsom - - -	Clapham - -	Tooting.
Wimbledon } Kingston } - -	Sutton - - -	Ewell.
Richmond - - -	Westminster - -	Pimlico.
Hounslow - - -	Putney Heath -	Kingston.
Staines - - -	Wimbledon - -	East-sheen.
Colnbrook } Windsor } - -	Turnham Green -	Hounslow.
By Staines and Colnbrook {	Bedfont - -	Staines.
	Colnbrook.	
Uxbridge - - -	Bayswater - -	Hanwell.
Edgware - - -	Uxbridge - -	Paddington.
Hampstead - - -	Kilburn - -	Edgware.
Highgate - - -	Somers Town -	Highgate.
Barnet - - -	Hampstead - -	Whetstone.
Enfield - - -	Barnet - - -	Stoke Newington.
Edmonton - - -	Newington-green -	Enfield.
Epping - - -	Enfield Highway -	Stratford.
Chigwell - - -	Woodford - -	Woodford Bridge.
Romford - - -	Loughton - -	Romford.

What is the cost of your establishment?—About 8,000 l. a year, commencing from January last.

How long has your system been established?—From January 1805.

What was the cost of it then?—8,000 l. a year, intended to have been, but the number was not completed till it was reduced to 6,000 l. a year.

Who is at the head of the establishment?—I presume, with respect to the conduct of it, I am, under Sir Nathaniel Conant's direction, and that of the Secretary of State for the Home Department.

As conductor?—Yes.

What is the salary and what are the allowances you receive, as conductor?—One hundred pounds per annum, with a guinea a week for the keep of my horse.

What do the patrole receive?—Four shillings a night, twenty-eight shillings a week.

And allowance for the keep of a horse?—Yes; the horses are foraged of late, by a plan which Mr. Read adopted, and which we have found far better than the men keeping their own horses.

Is that all they receive?—Yes, exclusive of the expenses for shoeing their horses and turnpikes, which they pay.

Have they no other perquisites?—None whatever; not being employed in the day further than taking care of their horses, they may do any thing they can.

Is their nightly attendance constant and regular?—Yes, according to the season of the year; at a certain time they go out, and at a certain time they are dismissed from their duty.

Has the plan, such as it is, answered the expectations of those who designed it?—I presume it has, inasmuch as we have had scarcely any highway or footpad robbery since the establishment; and in those which have happened, the parties have been apprehended, with a very few exceptions.

How many highway and footpad robberies had you, within the circumference of your jurisdiction, last year?—I am not prepared to answer that question exactly, but there were last year more than for any year during the establishment; but not so many as we might have expected.

It

It is a notorious fact that there have been few, if any, highway and footpad robberies, since the period of the establishment of your system?—Very few indeed ; a greater number last year of any we have had since the establishment.

Do the persons who act as the patrole, share at all in the Parliamentary rewards for the apprehension of offenders?—Yes, in common as other officers of Police.

Can you state to the Committee, what has been the value, to the most successful individual in your establishment, of those Parliamentary rewards in any one year?—I should think it has never exceeded 10 *l*. for any one man.

Do you think that it averages 5 *l*. to each, annually?—No ; there can be no average made of it, it so rarely occurs.

Do you think the salaries they receive are sufficient?—I do ; for the description of men of which they are composed; I think it is not more than they ought to have, but that it is amply sufficient.

In point of fact, there is on all the roads named on the card you have delivered in, a patrole during the hours of night?—Several patrole on each road.

Do they receive any instruction to stop and examine suspicious carts and conveyances travelling the road in the night?—No; it has not been considered as part of their duty to do that; the establishment was intended to protect persons travelling the road on horseback or in carriages.

If they saw persons whom they knew to be notorious offenders, coming from or returning to London, in the course of the night, would they not feel it their duty to stop them, and inquire into their proceedings?—They do that according to their own judgment and discretion, without our giving them any instructions.

Do they, in point of fact, stop persons of that description?—I cannot say that they do ; they would do it if they had a strong suspicion ; some of the men have been employed many years before in the Police, and what is termed known characters ; if they knew persons to be reputed thieves they would stop them certainly, without any special directions.

[The Witness delivered in the following Papers, which were read.]

ORDERS for the government of the POLICE HORSE PATROLE, under the direction of Sir *Nathaniel Conant*, Chief Magistrate at the Public Office Bow-street; Mr. Day, conductor :—London ; printed by J. Downes, 240, Strand, 1813.

POLICE HORSE PATROLE.

ORDERS for the government of the POLICE HORSE PATROLE, under the direction of Sir *Nathaniel Conant*, Chief Magistrate at the Public Office Bow-street, November 1813; Mr. Day, conductor.

1. ALL orders given by Mr. Day, to the patrole, or to the inspectors, and delivered by them to the patrole, are to be strictly obeyed.

2. The patrole are to obey with the strictest punctuality, all orders they shall receive as to the time of their going and continuing on duty; and they are to proceed on the road at such a pace as will bring them to the extreme end of their journey at the time they are directed ; they are there to halt ten minutes, before they begin their journey back.

3. The patrole stationed on the same road, are to meet and communicate together, both going and returning, halting for each other at some given spot half way on the journey. They are to be attentive to any informations they may receive of any robbery having been committed or attempted, or of any suspicious persons having been seen on the road, and to endeavour to get a description of them and the road they have taken ; and if any robbery be committed or attempted, the patrole first receiving information of it, is to join his companion if he can conveniently do it, and use every exertion to take the offenders ; or if he cannot conveniently join his companion, he is to make an immediate pursuit with such other assistance as he can get, and if the party should be apprehended, to lodge them in some place of security until he can bring them to Bow-street, which he is to do by eleven o'clock the following morning, and to warn the witnesses against them, to appear there at the same time.

4. Every patrole when on duty, is to have all his appointments with him in proper condition, his pistols loaded, and his sword worn on the outside of his coat ; and no patrole under any pretence whatsoever, is to go into any public or other house during the time of his duty ; and they are to make themselves known to all persons, as well in carriages as on horseback, by calling out to them as they pass, in a loud and distinct tone of voice " Bow-street Patrole."

Mr.
William Day.

5. If any patrole shall lose any part of his appointments, it is to be replaced at his expense.

6. No patrole whilst he is on duty, is to deliver his horse to the care of any other person, or suffer him to be out of his sight, for the purpose of being put into a stable, or otherwise.

7. If any patrole shall be taken ill, or his horse shall become lame or unfit for duty, he is to report it immediately to Mr. Day; and in the case of his horse being unfit for duty, he is to do duty on foot (taking his pistols with him) and to go not less than half the distance that he would on horseback.

8. If any patrole shall not be met by his companion, on the road, in the manner directed, he is to report the same on the following morning to Mr. Day; and not any excuse will be admitted for neglecting to make such report.

9. No patrole is to use his horse for any other purpose than his regular duty, nor keep his horse at grass without leave for that purpose; nor is he, except in case of illness, to intrust his horse to the care of any other person.

10. Each patrole will be allowed for his horse per week, a bushel and a half of oats, three bushels of chaff, a truss and a half of hay, and a truss of straw.

11. Every patrole is to feed his horse regularly three times a day; namely, at eight o'clock in the morning, one o'clock in the afternoon, and when he gets home from his duty at night: he is to remain at his stable one hour at least from eight o'clock in the morning, to dress his horse and clean his appointments; from one o'clock in the afternoon he is also to remain there half an hour at least, to dress his horse; and when he returns at night from his duty, he is to be sure to let his horse be clean and dry before he leaves the stable.

12. No patrole is to be absent at any time, more than two miles from the place he is stationed at, except on duty, without leave for that purpose; nor is he to change his lodgings without first giving notice of it to Mr. Day.

13. Mr. Day, with the inspectors, will inspect the patrole once every month, in the several districts appointed for that purpose, when the men are to appear in the uniform of the establishment, with their arms and all their appointments, which with their horses will be expected to be found in perfect order, and fit for service.

14. The inspectors in their respective districts, are to visit the patrole on their night-duty, and to report to Mr. Day any particular occurrence or neglect of their duty, on the following morning. The inspectors are also to report their own duty to him in writing every week, and specify in such report what has been the general conduct and behaviour of the patrole during that period.

15. The inspectors are also frequently to visit the stables of the patrole, at the hours they are directed by the 11th order to be there, and report to Mr. Day any neglect or disobedience of such order.

———————

List of APPOINTMENTS used by each HORSE PATROLE.

Headstall with chain-rein, bridle complete, saddle, with holsters and flounces, girths, stirrup leathers and irons, surcingle, crupper, cloak, pad and straps, and breast-plate, horsecloth, cloak, sabre and belt, pair of pistols, turnscrew, picker and worm, pair of handcuffs and key, book of orders and warrant.

The above appointments, excepting the headstall, chain-rein and horsecloth, to be brought by each man, with his horse, at every monthly inspection; and the whole of the appointments to be brought at the quarterly inspection in January, April, July, and October.

———————

ORDERS for the government of the POLICE HORSE PATROLE Dismounted, under the direction of Sir *Nathaniel Conant*, Chief Magistrate at the Public Office Bow-street; Mr. Day, conductor:—London; printed by J. Downes, 240, Strand, 1816.

———————

POLICE HORSE PATROLE DISMOUNTED.

ORDERS for the government of the POLICE HORSE PATROLE Dismounted, under the direction of Sir *Nathaniel Conant*, Chief Magistrate at the Public Office Bow-street; Mr. Day, conductor.

1. All orders given by Mr. Day, to the patrole or to the inspectors, and delivered by them to the patrole, are to be strictly obeyed.

2. The patrole stationed on the same road, dismounted and mounted, are to meet and communicate together, both going and returning. They are to take notice of any suspicious persons they may see on the road, and to attend to any information they may receive of any highway or footpad robbery having been committed or attempted; and if any such robbery has been committed or attempted, they are to use every exertion to take the offenders; and if the party should be apprehended, to lodge them in some place of security, until they can bring them to Bow-street Office, which they are to do by eleven o'clock the following morning, and to warn the witnesses against them, to appear there at the same time, and to apprize Mr. Day thereof.

3. Every

3. Every patrole, when on duty, is to have his warrant, truncheon, and cutlass with him, and he is not to go into any public or other house during the time of his duty.

4. If any patrole shall lose either his truncheon or cutlass, they are to be replaced at his expense.

5. If any patrole shall be taken ill, or become lame, or unfit for duty, he is to report it immediately to Mr. Day.

6. If any patrole shall not be met by his companions, on the road, either mounted or dismounted, in the manner directed, he is to report the same on the following morning to Mr. Day; and not any excuse will be admitted for neglecting to make such report.

7. No patrole is to be absent at any time more than two miles from the place he is stationed at, except on duty, without leave for that purpose; nor is he to change his lodgings without first giving notice of it to Mr. Day.

8. Mr. Day, with the inspectors, will inspect the patrole once every month, in the several districts appointed for that purpose; when the patrole are to appear in the uniform of the establishment, with their truncheon and cutlass.

9. The inspectors in their respective districts, are to visit the patrole on their night-duty, and to report to Mr. Day any particular occurrence or neglect of their duty, on the following morning. The inspectors are also to report their own duty to him in writing every week, and specify in such report what has been the general conduct and behaviour of the patrole during that period.

––––––––––––

Do the horses belong to the horse patrole themselves, or are they the property of Government?—They are the property of Government.

In case any of the officers of the patrole are wounded in the execution of their duty, is a compensation made to them?—No; we have lamented that we have not been able to do it, for one or two have suffered; they are told in fact, that when they are no longer able to do their duty there is no resource for them.

They are told that, when they are first employed?—Yes; to prevent any mistake or misconception.

Do you not think it would be advisable, after many years service, or after wounds received in the public service, that some provision should be made for the parties?—I think it would be very humane.

Do you not think it would make a man active in the discharge of his duty, if he knew that if he suffered, the public would compensate him as far as was in their power?—No, I do not think it would operate in that way.

Do you not think that, putting the case of a man who goes into action with a conviction that if he is wounded he will be taken care of for life, and of another man who goes into the service, with a certainty of being turned adrift without provision for existence, the first would go much more readily into action than the other?—As a matter of opinion, I do not think that would operate at all; if a man does not possess natural courage, I do not think that would produce it.

What office do you hold in the Home Department?—I am keeper of the Criminal Register, and have been so from the year 1800.

Do you not find your two offices interfere with each other?—Not the least, the one being at night and the other at day.

How many officers are there for the regulation of the patrole?—Two inspectors and one conductor (myself.)

What is the salary of the inspectors?—It is double that of the patrole, it is 8*s.* a d

And horses found them?—Yes.

Lunæ, 17° *die Junii*, 1816.

The Hon. HENRY GREY BENNET, in The Chair.

———————

Mr. *James May*, again called in, and Examined.

YOU have stated to the Committee in your former examination, that consider-able alterations had been made in the rates of the parish of Bethnal Green, for many years past, from the year 1802 to the year 1809; and you have also stated, that those alterations took place after the rates had been allowed?—I said that I could never speak positively as to that; I said I had never seen them altered. The rates regularly go out of my hands without alteration; and then there is the addition; the sum comes to more money than is put into the rate. When the rate is made by me, I deliver it out.

To whom?—To the collectors.

Not before it is allowed?—Not till it is allowed.

State to the Committee clearly what you do?—I make out the rate.

After that, what is done?—After the rate is made out, it is signed by the church-wardens and overseers of the parish, and then it has also the signature of the magistrate; the rates are then delivered to the collectors; they are taken out of my hands; they take the books, and the books never come back into my hands, nor do I see them, until after they are audited.

According to the best of your belief, do you think that these alterations would appear in the book, if the rate were made before the rate was allowed, or after?—I think they could not be before.

Do you not think that if they had been before, there would be a difference in the summing up in each page, from what appears there at present?—Most certainly.

The Committee wish Mr. May to understand, that the answer he has given to the question just now put, is in direct contradiction to the answer he gave to the same question the last time he was examined before the Committee?—I never meant it to be understood that I myself saw the rate altered; I said most decidedly that I never saw any person alter the rate, and for this plain reason, that when the rate was signed, it amounted to a certain sum of money, and was then given out of my possession into the hands of the collectors. I never again see the books until they are sent back, and then they are audited, and signed as an audited account; and then if there is any deficiency, the amount of the deficiency appears. [*Here the Witness took one of the books into his hand.*] I wish to explain to the Committee what I mean. The appearance of the book does exhibit a difference, and that is the only answer I can give to it. In point of fact, I make out a sum total for the assess-ment, which is delivered into the hands of the collectors; for instance, here is a sum total of 2,796*l.* 8*s.* 11*d.* which is the amount of the assessment.

Is that the original assessment?—That is the original assessment. Take this original assessment, and I think the Committee will see that an alteration is made; the assessment is 2,796*l.* 8*s.* 11*d.* the sum collected by the collectors is 1,745*l.* the difference is 947*l.* and there remains in the hands of the collectors 114*l.* 0*s.* 2*d.* I never look to the original assessment.

Turning to the rate of 1807, the original assessment appears to be 2,796*l.* 8*s.* 11*d.*; that is also signed by the magistrates, with the same sums?—This is the audit [*pointing to an account in Witness's hand.*]

The same sum is allowed by the magistrates, Mr. Merceron and Mr. Williams is not that so?—That is the fact.

It then appears upon the face of the rate, that in many instances a greater sum was collected than what was originally rated in the original rate book; and admitting that, can you have any doubt that the alteration must have taken place after the rate was allowed?—No, I cannot; I never saw it; I never saw Mr. Merceron alter the audit; I never took notice of any alteration even, in the audit book. If the assessment had not been altered, it remains in the same sum, and I know nothing of it; I take no notice of any altered rate, upon the audit of the accounts; I turn generally to my book, and I find what the amount of the assessment comes to, and

I alter

I alter the book by the original assessment; and the thing appearing, and the objection being on it, it would make a greater increase than what appeared in the original assessment. When we come to find a sum of money which would have increased the assessment, we know it; we could not call the amount of the assessment 2,796 *l.* when it would be 2,800 *l.*

And that is proof to you that the alteration has been made after the rate allowed by the magistrate?—That is my reason for thinking so; but I cannot say that I ever saw it altered; that is my only reason for thinking so.

Turn to the name of Thomas Nichols; what is his original assessment?—At 16 *l.*

He paid upon that, what?—Three quarters of a year's assessment.

He paid for the half year, what?—The sum of 1 *l.* 10 *s.*

He paid upon the rate of 16 *l.* the first half year?—Yes.

According to the assessment, what rate did he pay subsequent to that?—According to the book, he appears to have paid for the half year 1 *l.* 2 *s.* 6 *d.*

He pays nothing for the next quarter?—He does not pay his original rate on this. I see the collector has put it down; he does not even make up the three pounds; instead of an increase, it appears a decrease.

In whose handwriting is his rate changed from a rate of 16 *l.* to 24 *l.*?—In Mr. Merceron's handwriting.

Turn to folio 35, Second Division; whose handwriting is that?—These are the collector's; all of them.

Turn to folio 95; whose handwriting is that?—Mr. Merceron's.

I see there the name of Samuel Burder; what is his house rated at?—At 45 *l.*

And what does he pay rate?—He pays 7 *l.* 14 *s.* 7 *d.* for three quarters; he was originally rated at 8 *l.* 8 *s.* 9 *d.* for 45 *l.*; that does not pay the whole of it.

If he had paid the other quarter, he would have paid at the rate of 55 *l.*?—Yes.

In whose handwriting is the alteration of Mr. Burder's assessment from 45 *l.* to 55 *l.*?—Mr. Merceron's.

I observe that is an alteration at Midsummer; what is meant by "Midsummer 55 *l.*"?—That is when a person comes in at Lady-day; that is put in as explanation, and proves that he does not come in until after Lady-day, which shows that he was assessed from Midsummer.

Then according to this, he pays no more than is mentioned here for the three quarters?—I should think so, but I cannot speak positively to it.

If he is audited for three quarters, he pays no more?—I cannot speak to the fact.

Who can speak to the fact?—I cannot say.

Do you not think, from the appearance of the entry in the book, that he was resident in the house only three quarters of a year; that the rate having been altered to 55 *l.* a year from 45 *l.* he had paid according to the increased rate of 55 *l.*?—Yes.

Look to folio 39; Peter Hilliard; is there an alteration there?—Yes; it appears to me to be Mr. Merceron's handwriting.

What is the rate entered?—7 *l.*

What is the rate paid upon the house?—On the first quarter there is nothing paid on that 7 *l.*

Is there any alteration in the rate?—There is an alteration.

To what amount?—The alteration is to 10 *l.*

The original rate is 11 *s.* 8 *d.* and the altered rate is 1 *l.* 13 *s.* 4 *d.*; and the half of 1 *l.* 13 *s.* 4 *d.* is 16 *s.* 8 *d.* which is the sum collected?—Yes, it appears so.

The money is collected on the altered rate?—Yes.

Have you any doubt that the altered rate is after the rate is allowed?—No.

When does this book begin?—Lady-day 1807.

And the house is rated to Lady-day at 7 *l.* and is altered to 10 *l.* and the last half-year is collected upon the 10 *l.*; and that therefore is proof that the collection is made after the rate is made?—Yes.

Do not you understand, as a vestry clerk, that it is equally criminal to alter a rate after as before it is made, or before as after?—I should think so.

If any person presumes to make an alteration in the rate, he not being the person that made the original rate, do you think he has any right whatever to interfere or meddle with the effect of a rate?—I cannot say.

The house which is situated in Back-lane near the Green, occupied by John Brown the prior part of the year; I would ask you who paid the original rate for John Brown's house?—William Henry Drewit.

510.   I observe

*Mr.
James May.*

I observe here it is " John Browne 18 *l.*—3 *l.* 7 *s.* 6 *d.* ;" is there any alteration in that rate?—Yes; "Henry Drewit, 24 *l.*"

Whose handwriting is that?—The 24 *l.* is Mr. Merceron's.

The first half-year, John Brown appears to be rated at 18 *l.* ; the rate amounts to 3 *l.* 7 *s.* 6 *d.* ; he paid half a year's demand, being 1 *l.* 13 *s.* 9 *d.* ; he was succeeded by Henry Drewit, who is rated at 24 *l?*—Yes.

And pays upon that rate 2 *l.* 5 *s.* ?—Yes.

Do you know the handwriting of the collector that signed that receipt?—[*Receipt put into Witness's hand.*] Yes.

That is a receipt given to Mr. Drewit for the payment of the half-year's rate at 24 *l.* ?—Yes; I have no doubt about it.

Is it possible that the alterations made in the rate-book, which appear in Mr. Merceron's handwriting, could have been made before the rate was allowed, without your knowledge?—My answer to that question is, that the rate being allowed on the 7th of August, and the person not coming in at or about Michaelmas, such alteration must have been made after the rate was allowed.

Joseph Merceron, Esq. again called in, and Examined.

*Joseph Merceron,
Esq.*

IN your examination the other day, you were asked whether there were any alterations in your hand writing in the rate-book ; you answered, that you would wish to see them ; you added also, that though you had made alterations of the rate before it had been allowed, you had never made any alterations after that event ; is that the answer you chuse to abide by?—I would wish to see the particular items, to speak to it with precision.

Is that your handwriting, " Thomas Nichols," [*Book put into Witness's hand*]?—That " 24 *l.* from Michaelmas," is my handwriting ; I think it is my handwriting.

Was that written before, or after the rate was allowed?—That I cannot say.

You have stated, *that you never made any alterations after the rate was made?*—When I say *never*, I would speak to it if I was to see the particular sums and the particular names ; *I should think I never did.*

There is a particular name before you, " Thomas Nichols, from Michaelmas :" was that laid before the rate was signed, or not?—I cannot say ; I have no remembrance of it.

It appears that Thomas Nichols paid that smaller rate of assessment the first half year?—Yes.

And the subsequent quarter he has paid at a greater rate of assessment?—Yes.

It is then quite clear it must have been made afterwards?—That does not follow, because when the signature of the magistrates was put to the book, it might have been done before; the book was signed on the 3d September; he pays the last quarter.

The first half year is from Lady-day to Michaelmas, and the next quarter is from Michaelmas to Christmas ; how is it possible that the alteration of that rate could be made before it was allowed, if the rate was allowed on the 3d of September, this being the quarter from Michaelmas to Christmas?—I beg to state, that I am not going to justify any of these things, because I candidly state to you, that the whole of this has been the subject of a prosecution by the Rector of the parish ; and if you will give me leave, I will read to you the whole of this business as it came before the Court of King's Bench, which, I think, is the best answer that I can give.

It appears to the Committee that the best answer you can give, is to state to them clearly and explicitly the facts, leaving them to draw their own inference from those facts ; have you not in any one of the rates of the year 1807, and in the course of 1808 (limiting the question to these two years) altered the assessment after the rate was allowed?—*Exactly* so ; and I must beg leave to state, that from the peculiarity of the Act of Parliament under which we have acted, that has been so for many many years, and even frequently so in the course of the year.

How came you, then, to state to the Committee the other day, that you never had made any alterations after the rate had been allowed?—*Really you must have misunderstood me.*

In your evidence the other day, the questions were put to you as follows: " Are you aware that you every day make alterations in the rate book?" the answer is, 'Certainly.' " After the rate had been allowed?" answer, 'O no.'—But not since our late Act of Parliament.

What Act of Parliament was that?—The 53d of the present King.

It

Joseph Merceron,
Esq.

It then appears, that in this as well as your last examination, you have stated, that you never did make any alteration of the rate, and now you unequivocally state, that it was your repeated practice; explain that inconsistency?—*It has been the practice of the parish ever since I have known it.* Those irregularities, which I certainly call them, were occasioned by the peculiarity of the late Act of Parliament, which requires rates by classes; and even if that Act of Parliament did not exist, the practice would have been the same. The rates were made annually once a year; and if an *empty* was put at the time the rate was made, which was frequently the case when the collectors went out, and if upon going out at Lady-day or Michaelmas they found a new tenant in such houses to which an *empty* had been put, they set down the tenant's name in the books, and the rent of the house, so that the rate may be collected upon it. The rates and the money were regularly brought to account, whether it was from Lady-day to Midsummer, or Michaelmas to Christmas. There were irregularities, there is no question about it; but the whole of the money was regularly brought forward to the account, and Mr. May the vestry clerk knew that very well, and was there for that purpose; there were columns down for that purpose.

In the case before you, of Thomas Nichols, there is no tenant that goes out; how do you account for the rise of the rate in that instance?—The collectors of the poor rates, of the land-tax, or of the watch or lamp duties, go round three or four times a year, make their survey, and if it came to their knowledge that there was an increase or rise of the rent, it was mentioned to the vestry. Wherever a tenant's rent was increased, that of course was brought forward before the vestry, and the rate increased.

Then, according to the practice of the parish, it was a perfectly useless transaction the magistrates allowing the rate, when it appears that you had the power which you have exercised; that the collector has the power which he has exercised (for we have it in evidence) to raise or diminish the rate of any individual, according as he or you thought fit?—*That certainly was so done,* and was known to be the practice for years, and would have continued perhaps till now, if this indictment had not taken place.

Were there not constant and repeated appeals and discussions in the parish upon that subject, upon this power which you and other individuals assumed, of raising and of lowering the rate at your pleasure?—By whom?

By the complaining individuals so rated?—No, I believe you will find that not one of these are rated at more than at what they had a right to be rated. We called them by the name of surcharges at that time.

Take that book in your hand [*Witness took the book;*] Mr. Blesset's original rate stands at 15 *l.* it is altered to 35 *l.*; is that alteration in your handwriting?—The 35 *l.* is my writing.

Was it upon that that Mr. Blesset appealed?—I cannot say.

You remember Mr. Blesset's appealing against the rate?—Indeed I do not.

Do you not remember that Mr. Blesset's case was one that created a considerable noise?—There was an action brought against him.

And do you not remember that it was upon that rate he appealed, or not?—I do not indeed.

Is that your handwriting?—I know nothing of it; it is not.

Look at it again [*Book put into the Witness's hand.*]—The " Michaelmas," I think, is; the " 24 *l.*" I should think was also my hand-writing.

I can tell you, it is stated to be your hand-writing?—This column was made to take in the money of the intermediate surcharges [*Witness here pointed out a column in the book;*] all this money was received after the book had been signed by the magistrate. The parish went upon this idea, that the whole would be lost when the tenant came in at Midsummer, and that if they continued to the Lady-day following the three quarters would be lost. The name of the person that came in was put down on this side, and the money was brought forward to account in that column, which is called the surcharge column. That irregularity was the subject of the prosecution carried on by the Rector, and which my lord Ellenborough said—

That is not the question; the question is, whether that is your handwriting?—To the best of my knowledge, " 24 *l.* for Michaelmas," is my handwriting. Lord Ellenborough said, that the offence proceeded from irregularity, without corrupt motives.

There was, in point of fact, no trial?—O yes, there was.

510.

Joseph Merceron, Esq.

There was no trial, for the cause was given up, was it not?—They brought no evidence. With the permission of the Committee, for my own satisfaction, in order to show what the proceeding was upon the trial, I would wish to place upon the Minutes an extract from the *Times* newspaper of Monday, June 14th, 1813, containing an account of what passed at the trial, as taken from the short-hand writer's notes.

[Here the Witness put in the Newspaper; and, with the consent of the Committee, the following extract was desired to be put upon the Minutes.]

(Advertisement.)

The KING and JOS. MERCERON and another.

THE Attorney General.—My Lord, there are two indictments against Merceron, with others set down for trial; viz. Merceron with Billington, and Merceron with William Cone; the last of which, we think, it will be best to take first, if your Lordship has no objection to our doing so.

Lord *Ellenborough.*—Very good.

The Attorney General.—May it please your Lordship; Gentlemen of the Jury; This is a prosecution by indictment against Joseph Merceron and William Cone, for a misdemeanor. The first defendant upon record, I mean the gentleman of the name of Merceron, is probably well known to some of you as having been long a magistrate, and engaged in the collection of the public rates in the neighbourhood of Bethnal-green, he himself having a large estate there: and this prosecution was instituted upon an inspection of the parish books, as to which I shall only say a word: By the Act of Parliament, the payments of these rates are to be made quarterly, but alterations have been made by Mr. Merceron, in regard to the mode of payment thereof, which led to the raising of a larger collection than would have been otherwise necessary, in a parish where there had been considerable warmth and discussion and agitation upon parochial subjects; that warmth and agitation led to a suspicion, that that which was incorrect from its nature, was incorrect from a corrupt motive, and that the collector had received sums of money which he should not have received, such conduct being for corrupt purposes. Whilst gentlemen of the profession are discharging a duty to the public or individuals, I believe that well-informed persons have no objection to our receiving information from those who are concerned on the other side: my learned friends who are with me, have with me looked into this case, and we have found that there is much complexity in the proof; and also we have come to the conclusion, that the conduct of these defendants might have been with a view to prospective alterations and improvements in the rate. I am informed by my learned friends, that they are in a condition to show that every shilling that was drawn by the defendants was so drawn from no corrupt motive, but that the whole of the monies so received can be satisfactorily accounted for; and therefore I have only to say upon this occasion, that if his Lordship judges it proper, we shall decline calling evidence upon this prosecution.

Mr. *Topping.*—May it please your Lordship; Gentlemen of the Jury; My learned friend has stated but a small part of this case, and I have only to add on behalf of my client, that I have no doubt those who prosecuted this indictment, grounded it upon a mere inspection of the rate books, the accounts of which may be audited every year, or oftener if required; and if that had been done in the present instance by those who prosecute, they would have found that every shilling collected by Mr. Merceron, the treasurer, has been accounted for to the parish, and that not one farthing of the money received has come into his hands, nor into the hands of Cone the collector. It is sufficient for me, that my learned friend, who appears for the prosecution, has in this case most handsomely said, that there is nothing that has been found in the discussions and investigations that have taken place between him and the other learned gentlemen concerned, that has tended to cast the slightest imputation upon the fair character or honourable conduct of my client: I shall therefore only say, that from the communications made by the gentlemen now sitting before me, I am convinced that there is not a man of a more peaceable temper than Mr. Merceron, nor a man more disposed to promote harmony in the parish, which I am sure could never have been interrupted by him; and not only that, but he is a gentleman of a most honourable mind. I shall only further add, that I hope the proceedings that have taken place towards this prosecution, have cast no imputation upon my client.

Lord *Ellenborough.*—Gentlemen of the Jury; From the statement which has just now been made by the learned counsel, it appears that the offence charged in this case, has proceeded from an irregularity, without any corrupt motives. The prosecutors do not bring the case before you in proof; and therefore it is your duty to acquit the defendants, by finding them not guilty.

The Jury, in pursuance of his Lordship's directions, found a verdict of Acquittal.
Similar Verdicts were given in two other Indictments which stood for trial this day, and in which Mr. Merceron was also defendant.

Was

Was this advertisement, as it is so styled at the head, put in by your authority?—
I think it was put in by Mr. Dann, my solicitor.

Joseph Merceron,
Esq.

In point of fact, was any evidence tendered by the other side, to support the
charge, that this was not done carelessly but corruptly?—There was no evidence
of that sort.

Was not the case given up by the solicitor for the prosecution?—I believe not;
I never understood it was; I was ready to meet the charges.

In point of fact, did not the counsel for the prosecution decline going into any
evidence upon the subject?—Yes, but not by my desire; there was no compromise
on my part, nor any wish to decline meeting the case; I was quite ready to have
gone into it, and I am sure I should have met it satisfactorily.

When these alterations took place in the rate, did they take place openly at the
vestry, or do they take place in your own office secretly and covertly?—I never
made any alterations in the poor rates in my life, but either at the vestry-room or at
the governors' room in the workhouse; never in my life.

Were the alterations made in the presence of the vestry clerk?—In the presence
of the vestry clerk; I can show you in the book, for year and year, the same thing
made by him.

Made by the vestry clerk?—Yes.

Are the alterations made by the vestry clerk, mere clerical errors which he has
corrected, or substantial alterations in the rate?—For instance, here is a rate collected
at Michaelmas, [*the Witness exhibiting the book*] and you observe there is an
alteration; that is done by the collector, of course: they take the half year.

But show us some made by the vestry clerk?—I may venture to speak for years
and years back, such alterations have been made by him.

The vestry clerk has stated to the Committee, not only that he never made the
smallest alterations himself, except as to mere clerical errors, but that he never saw
you or any one else make any alterations any where in the rate; that he and his
father had been vestry clerks forty odd years, that he knew his duty too well to
make such alterations, and that he told you of the impropriety of so altering them
yourself; is that statement founded in fact?—It cannot be; I will state to you
this, as a fact, to prove it: *with respect to the alterations made in Mr. Blesset's rate,*
Mr. May was well acquainted with that alteration; of course he must have known
it, as he carried on the action against Mr. Blesset; he saw that it was my hand-
writing; of course then, if he did not know it was my handwriting, how came he
to proceed with that action; that is clear conviction that he knew of it; it was
not done in secret, but openly and publicly, either at the vestry-room or in the
governors' room at the workhouse.

Do you believe that that was the rate against which Mr. Blesset appealed; the
alteration, I see, is from 15 *l.* to 35 *l.*; was that the rate upon which he appealed?—
I recollect his appealing; if he only appealed once, it could be only upon that rate;
I cannot be positive, but I should think it was; and if it was, Mr. May must have
been present, and he must have seen it was an alteration, either by me or the
collector, and of course he must have seen it; why should he have carried on the
action against this man, if he had not known and seen it; if he had told me it was
illegal or irregular, I should have stopped directly; he never told me it was illegal;
Mr. May never did, never.

I should like to see any of the alterations of the rates in Mr. May's hand-
writing?—That is Mr. May's writing " Caslon" [*pointing to the book.*]

That does not appear to be an alteration of the rate by Mr. May; it may be his
handwriting, but it is not an alteration of the rate; whose handwriting is that 40 *l.*?—
It is mine.

Here, then, is a positive alteration of the rate from 24 *l.* to 40 *l.* in your hand-
writing?—I do not deny it.

Can you show any instance of any kind, of an alteration of the rate in Mr. May's
handwriting?—No, I think not. The way that I understand he altered the book
is this, he inserted the names of persons that came into the houses, with the rents,
for new tenants, in the book, which I was told was as irregular as the rest, I mean
as the alteration of the rate.

But do you not see that there is a great difference between the alterations, such
as you have named, and any alteration in which there is a new charge to the
tenant, which you have made at your own will and pleasure, as in the instance you
have admitted, where the rate was raised from 24 *l.* to 40 *l.*?—Certainly not at my

will

will and pleasure; it is never done privately by myself, but by the collectors of the assessed taxes, by whom it is usually done, who go round and make their surcharges; they then attend at their different meetings, and they give the numbers and the amounts, and then they put, into the column I have pointed out, the amount of the rate collected upon it.

It appears in the rate book, that a person of the name of Charlotte Cowdery, who held a house which was rated at 40 *l.* pays 7 *l.* 10 *s.* which is raised by a stroke of your pen to 60 *l.* thereby making her pay 11 *l.* 5 *s.*; do you remember any thing concerning that transaction, and how her rate came to be so altered?—I knew Miss Cowdery very well, and her rent was raised from 40 *l.* to 60 *l.* as I understood from the representation of the collectors; and as her rent was 60 *l.* she was rated accordingly. I wish you to understand that all these increases were upon actual rents paid by the tenants; they were not overrated; and the rates from which the alterations took place were for rents which they had been accustomed to pay for years back; the alterations never took place except when the rents were raised.

Do you remember whether, at the time that you raised that rate, any representation was made by her, as to her being in a state of poverty, and being unable to pay that rate?—No.

Do you remember whether she was in a distressed situation at that time?—I believe at the latter part of her time her school fell off; she was in low circumstances.

Did she not in point of fact about that time, or shortly after, go out of the parish in a state very little better than a pauper?—I cannot say.

Do you not know she was poor?—I know she was in low circumstances.

At the time the rate was advanced?—I do not know at what time she quitted the parish; whether it was immediately after that, or not, I cannot speak with certainty.

At the time she was paying that rate, will you take upon yourself to say that every house in the parish that ought to have been raised in the same proportion, had been raised?—That I cannot say.

Do you believe that it was so?—I think not.

Why then Charlotte Cowdery was singled out as a person to have her rate raised by two thirds more, when other peoples houses were not raised at all?—I do not think she was singled out; there were many others put in at the same time, I have no doubt, from the survey of the parish officers and collectors, who frequently went round the parish.

Had you ever any personal contest or misunderstanding with Miss Charlotte Cowdery?—Never, to my knowledge; but on the contrary, I had a regard for her, and to show it, my youngest daughter went to school there.

Was she at school with her then?—I do not know; I had no words with her, I assure you; but when that sum was mentioned, it was not for me to say that it was too much.

You entered that sum yourself; it is in your handwriting?—Yes; then of course I did alter it. I take it that that was one of those that was fixed upon in the prosecution: I admit it.

Do you believe that at the time you signed that rate, she was in a condition and state to pay it; to pay that increased tax?—I never thought she was in such distressed circumstances as those in which she appeared to be, until the time she quitted the parish; I did not know that things were so bad with her.

Do you know how soon she quitted the parish after that rate was increased?—I do not.

Will you take upon yourself to assure the Committee, speaking decidedly, that those alterations were always done in the face of day, and that before witnesses at the vestry, or in the workhouse before witnesses, and that they were never done secretly and covertly in your own office?—Never covertly in my own office in my life, but they were done either at the vestry or at the committee room in the workhouse, and in the presence of witnesses, and also in the presence of the vestry clerk.

I put it to you again; have you ever done it in the presence of the vestry clerk?—I have no doubt of it, over and over again; I have no doubt of it.

Does not the vestry clerk usually attend when vestries are held?—Yes.

Does he not always?—Not always; he has had frequently a clerk attending, but he frequently attends himself.

Then you mean to say, that these alterations that have been made at a vestry, have

have either been made in his presence or in the presence of his clerk?—No; *Joseph Merceron, Esq.* frequently he might not be there, he might not come till late.

Is it the practice of the parish of Bethnal Green, to hold the vestries with the attendance of the vestry clerk, or the vestry clerk's clerk?—There are vestries or public meetings, for we have frequently vestries and public meetings of the governors, and the principal part of the business of the parish is transacted by the governors, and many of these alterations were no doubt made by the governors or vestry-men, and perhaps Mr. May or his clerk might not have been there at the time; but that Mr. May knew of it is clear, particularly so, for Mr. May kept all the books, and these columns were made with his knowledge; he had them for the express purpose of looking at those alterations which we have been told since is irregular. [*Here the Witness took one of the books into his hand, and pointed out to the Committee several alterations*] " Mr. Dunbar has eight houses," this is my writing; this name of " Thomas Cooper," is the collector's; " Mr. Dunbar has eight houses, to pay from Midsummer, 6 *l.* 2 *l.* 6 *s.* 8 *d.*"

Where is he rated?—Here [*pointing out the place;*] each house is rated at 6 *l.* which makes 2 *l.* 6 *s.* 8 *d.*; the collector takes the money, and this was brought forward.

Whereabouts is that 2 *l.* 6 *s.* 8 *d.*?—Here [*pointing to the book.*] Here is " John Patters," these were two houses, afterwards advanced to 16 *l.*; this is done by the collector; he takes 16 *l.* as the rent; the next is " Henry Slater, 2 *l.* 6 *s.* 8 *d.*;" you will then see the sum-total cast up. This is my rate, " new advanced houses." If we had not done this, we should go on six or nine months longer, and the money would be lost; and in order to do justice to the parish, we have put them in. [*Here the Witness pointed out several other instances where alterations were made.*] When the indictment was preferred, it was the supposition of the Reverend Mr. King, that this money, which was collected and paid by the collector, was kept by me; but I have the satisfaction to say, that upon an examination of my accounts for seven years, there was only a mistake in 11 *s.* 3 *d.*; I therefore say this, in order to do away the impression that I have had any corrupt motives in this transaction. As to there being irregularities in the mode of doing this, there is no doubt that irregularities have existed, but those irregularities have arisen from the nature of the Act of Parliament; the Act of Parliament was so very inconsistent, that we did it in order that the parish might keep pace in its receipts with the increase of rents; it was entirely owing to the peculiarity of the Act of Parliament; owing to persons coming frequently into new houses, or new tenants coming into old houses; and, owing to the general fluctuation and the nature of the rents, we were obliged to make these alterations, for if we did not, the system required by the Act of Parliament would be productive of great loss to the parish; the parish would have lost a great deal of money if we had not done what we did.

It has been shown to you, that in one case in which there had been no new tenant coming in, yet there was clearly a rise in the rate?—There was.

How do you account for that?—From the survey that has been made four or five times in a year by the parish officers and collectors of the taxes, and from circumstances which may have arisen in the course of time, particularly relating to the increase of rents; and in such cases the rates have been increased. In the case alluded to, the house was only rated at 40 *l.*; but the officers having discovered that the rent was increased to 60 *l.* they made a representation of it to the governors, and then that rent was put down and rated accordingly with an increased rate, and the money was afterwards brought forward to the parish account.

Then you will take upon yourself to say that this survey takes place two or three times in the course of the year, and after such surveys are brought to you, that no person's house whatever was left unsurcharged, where the rent had been risen upon the old tenants, or upon the new?—Certainly not; at least what were brought by the persons who surveyed were not left out; some of them however were not introduced, unless it appeared quite clear that they were increased in rent.

My question is, whether any of them were left out?—Certainly not; I never knew a survey which was made by the parish officers, from which it appeared that rents had been increased, but what those rents were regularly put in, and that without favour or affection: and what I wish to mention is, that these surcharges are not put upon any particular set of people, but even upon my own tenants, and upon other people in the same way: no difference whatever is made, it was

a general

Joseph Merceron, Esq.

a general rule. If you will take it for granted, that this was very irregular, I will explain every thing else satisfactorily to the Committee.

Mr. James May.

Mr. *James May*, again called in, and, in the presence of Mr. *Merceron*, Examined.

LOOK at that book [*book put into the Witness's hand*] and tell me whether the audit of that account was ever stuck in where those wafers are seen?—I have no doubt about it; I have not the least doubt in the world.

In that account, was the difference between the money collected according to the original rate, and all the money collected by the surcharge, entered down?—Every farthing, I have no doubt; and I never had a rate-book, but what the surcharge was entered down.

Produce any book to the Committee in which the surcharge is included in the audit?—There is an audit where it is included [*the Witness produced a book, and explained the point in question to the satisfaction of the Committee.*]

It has been stated by Mr. Merceron to the Committee, that in the different alterations that he made in the rate after the rate was laid, were made in the open vestry-room or in the committee-room of the workhouse, and he has no manner of doubt that those alterations were made and entered down in your presence; what do you say to that, is the fact so?—*I never saw him alter a rate in my life.*

Do you constantly attend the vestries?—I attend nineteen times out of twenty.

And you never saw Mr. Merceron alter a rate in the rate-book after the rate was laid?—Not to my knowledge.

Do you believe the rate could be altered in your presence, without your seeing it?—No, certainly not.

Have you ever stated to Mr. Merceron your opinion, as to the propriety of altering the rate?—There have been conversations of that kind.

When?—The time I cannot recollect, it is some years ago.

Prior to the indictment preferred by Mr. King against Mr. Merceron, or subsequent to that?—It was about that very time.

Prior or subsequent to the indictment brought?—At the very time.

Does the audit account bear the signatures of the persons who were present, generally speaking?—The audit account in question, and all of them, are always signed by nine, churchwardens or vestrymen.

What is the date of the one you are now speaking of?—The 11th of August 1809, and it is signed by the churchwardens, overseers, and vestrymen.

Do they all sign the audit?—Only nine are required by the Act of the 3d of George III.

How comes it that the account you have put into my hand has no reference to the one you before spoke of; refer to the book Bethnal Green No. 1, 2d Division, 1808?—That was never audited, it goes on for twelve months; it never was audited in that year.

Mr. *Merceron's* Examination resumed.

Joseph Merceron, Esq.

THE Committee have felt it to be their duty to show you the evidence that was given by the Reverend Joshua King, upon part of your conduct as a Magistrate in your district; they wish to know whether you have any explanation to give upon that subject? [*The Reverend Joshua King's evidence put into the Witness's hand.*]—I have; I wish to state, that with respect to that part of the evidence detailing bullock-driving through the church-yard on Sunday, I was not acquainted with the fact till I came out of church.

What did you do in consequence?—There was nothing to be done, the bullock was gone; I inquired of the sexton, and he told me the bullock was gone; I knew nothing of it. With respect to that part where Mr. King says, " I have reason to believe that the officers of my parish frequently connive at and sanction the practices of bullock-hunting," I believe it to be totally unfounded, as far as relates to the officers. With respect to where the Witness states that I declared that " I was fond of bullock-hunting, and that in my younger days I was generally the first in the chace," such conversation never did take place, and the fact is totally false. A conversation did take place respecting his getting into the commission; he wished to know what expense it would be, which I told him. I never mentioned to him my idea of recommending Mr. Timmings as a magistrate.

You were called upon by the Committee to produce a list of the public-houses belonging to you, and the names of the tenants; do you produce it?—Here it is. [*Witness produced the following*]

LIST

LIST of Public-Houses belonging to me, and Names of Tenants.

Joseph Merceron,
Esq.

SIGNS.	SITUATIONS.	TENANTS.
White Swan - - -	Swan-street - - -	Messrs. Hanbury.
Seven Stars - - -	Fleet-street - - -	Ditto.
Black Bull - - -	Thomas-street - -	Adams.
Ship - - -	Brick-lane - - -	Smith.
Two Brewers - - -	Ditto - - - -	Mackay.
King's Arms - - -	George-street - - -	Castoldi.
Red Cross - - -	Hare-street - - -	Whitling.
Queen's Head - - -	Fleet-street - - -	Lewis.
Bricklayers Arms - -	Narrow-street - - -	Bradshaw.
Clay Hall - - -	Old Ford - - -	Taylor.
Duke of Argyle - -	Laystall-street - -	Chipman.

LIST of Public-Houses belonging to Others (Rents received by me.)

SIGNS.	SITUATIONS.	TENANTS.
King's Arms - - -	Sclater-street - - -	Hall.
Half Moon - - -	Bacon-street - - -	Fox.
Adam and Eve - - -	Brick-lane - - -	Battall.
Turkey Slave - - -	Ditto - - - -	Pruvo.
Buck's Head - - -	James-street - - -	Green.
Fox and Hounds - -	Hare-street - - -	Burchall.
White Horse - - -	Hare-street - - -	Butler.
Hare - - - -	Brick-lane - - -	Burchall.
Fighting Cocks - -	St. John-street - -	Butler.
Ram and Magpye - -	Fleet-street - - -	Whitting.
Three Sugar Loaves - -	St. John-street - -	Butler.

Would you say any thing else respecting the evidence given by the Reverend Mr. King?—In answer to the question put to Mr. King, whether there was any personal difference between himself and me, I have to say that there is very great personal difference between Mr. King and myself, I having been indicted for a misdemeanor and perjury by the Rector, and which proceedings were the subject of an action and a trial. And I further add, that whatever fortune I have, has been procured in an honourable way. I deny electing the most ignorant and the lowest characters to fill parochial offices and audit my accounts. As to the account of monies received from Government, I refer to the vestry books for a just appropriation of those sums; and I say that every farthing received on that account was fairly and justly brought forward to the parish account, and of which the parish is well satisfied. I deny having instigated the mob to attack a person of the name of Shevill; two hundred vestrymen present will speak to that. I am quite satisfied with the opinion the parish have of me; it has not altered for thirty years, and I will endeavour to keep it.

In point of fact, are not those meetings of the vestry very tumultuous?—The two last have been noisy; but in general they are extraordinary quiet.

Do the vestries adjourn to the church-yard?—In two instances they have, the vestry-room not being sufficiently large.

Is that statement, of your having given three cheers, standing on the steps of the church-porch, correct?—I do not recollect such a circumstance; some years ago it might have been so, but I cannot speak with certainty as to the time; I do not deny it, it was in consequence of some national rejoicing.

Were you then acting as a Magistrate?—No, I was acting as a vestryman.

But were you then acting as a Magistrate, and at the same time as a vestryman, when you stood upon the steps of the church cheering?—Certainly not.

Were you then in the commission of the peace, that is what I mean?—At the time that took place, I think not; I do not recollect the time; but it might have been whilst I was in the commission, as I was one-and-twenty or two-and-twenty years in the commission.

It might have been since you were in the commission of the peace?—Yes. I now refer to the charge exhibited against me by the Rector, founded upon a series of

oaths

Joseph Merceron,
Esq.

oaths taken before the Commons, the Court of Delegates, and the Chancellor ; and I refer for the whole proceedings in that case to Messrs. Aldridge & Smith, my solicitors on that occasion. I deny that I committed any perjury in the business ; the charge is wicked, malicious, and untrue.

The property, in point of fact, there spoken of, was it ever restored to the parties ?—In consequence of the decision of the will of this poor woman, who was declared an idiot, a lease, that was part of the property, I had ; and that lease (her will being set aside) went back to the heirs at law ; but the lawsuit was against her executors, the Rev. Mr. Natt and the Rev. John Moore.

It has been stated to the Committee, that there is a close intimacy and connexion between Mr. Hanbury and you ; and one of the evidences of that, which the Rev. Joshua King has named, is, that he heard you declare, when you were on better terms with him than you are on at present, that Hanbury was " a devilish good fellow, that he was always sending you presents ; that he supplied your house with beer *gratis*, and that the week before he had sent you half a barrel of porter :" is that statement true ?—I believe the only part of the statement that is true, is, that I might have said that Hanbury was a devilish good fellow, for I have a very great regard for him. The presents that Mr. Hanbury sends me, are no more than now and then he sends me a hare and a brace of pheasants ; and as for supplying my house with beer gratis, I deny it. I requested, myself, that he would send me half a barrel of porter at a time, for which I pay him ; it is a favour he does me ; I am very fond of his porter ; I pay him for it, and take the receipts for what I have paid him ; and I have done that two or three years ago. I never had a pint of porter from Mr. Hanbury but what I paid for.

Do you not know that it is a received opinion in the district where you are residing, or have you not often heard of it, that victuallers who come with any other recommendation than that of Messrs. Hanbury & Trueman, have but little chance of obtaining a licence ?—I have heard that so mentioned.

In point of fact, do not nearly two thirds of the public-houses in that district deal with Messrs. Hanbury & Truman?—I cannot speak with certainty as to that ; but I should suppose that a great many of them do deal with them.

In going along any of the streets in that district, is it not written on the sign of very nearly every public-house, that they deal for their beer with Messrs. Hanbury and Truman ?—Certainly, on that account, from the locality and the influence they possess, Mr. Hanbury being a respectable, charitable man, and doing a great deal of good. Another thing, the weavers prefer Hanbury's porter.

Of that list that you have given in of your own houses, and the houses for which you receive the rents, do not the greater proportion of them deal with Messrs. Hanbury and Trueman?—There appear to be eleven houses belonging to me ; two of them Messrs. Hanbury and Trueman occupy as my tenants ; the others are let to those different people mentioned in the list.

In point of fact, do not the others sublet to Messrs. Hanbury?—Many of them are ; the greater proportion of them are ; I have nothing to do with the other people to whom the houses are let ; I have no control over my own tenants, as to whom they may let the houses to.

The whole of them deal with Messrs. Hanbury and Truman?—A great proportion of them do ; there are three or four of them I cannot speak to. I beg leave to state, that they are all old public-houses, of upwards of 50 years standing, and that I never applied for a new licence since I have been in the commission of the peace, which is upwards of twenty years.

You have stated to the Committee yesterday, that you never recollect any complaints made against any of these houses ; do you continue of the same opinion to-day ?—That is not quite so ; with the exception of the one house called The Seven Stars, with that exception, I have no occasion to alter that opinion. They were never made to me.

Have they been made to other Magistrates, that the houses are or have been considered in bad repute ?—I cannot speak to what complaints have been made to the different Police Offices, those complaints being made generally at the general licensing day in September.

Do you make it a part of your duty to ascertain that your tenants conduct themselves with propriety, and manage their houses with decorum ?—Not more than for the publicans in general, I make no distinction ; and I believe the public-houses in Bethnal Green are as orderly as any other public-houses in the division.

Martis, 18° *die Junii,* 1816.

The Honourable HENRY GREY BENNET, in The Chair.

Mr. *Jenkin Jones,* called in, and Examined.

WHAT situation do you hold in the Phœnix Fire Office?—Secretary.

What number of firemen have you in your office?—Twenty firemen and five supernumerary men. They may be called twenty-five firemen.

How many porters have you got?—I think we have five, in both establishments: we have in fact six, but one is superannuated.

How many engines have you?—Four, at present.

What are their stations?—One in Wellclose-square, another in Tooley-street, another in Carter-lane, and another at Charing-cross.

How many horses are there to each engine?—Two horses draw them; but we do not keep the horses, we contract for them.

Where are the horses kept?—In general they belong to some carman that lives near.

Are the horses always ready?—They ought to be; but they are not exactly devoted to the purpose of the engine, as their owner employs them for other objects.

So that it might happen there might be no horses ready, in case of an alarm of fire?—I never knew of a case of that kind happening, for the contractor is bound to supply them.

How much time does it require to get the engine out, in case of alarm of fire?—I cannot answer that question: it depends very much upon the presence of the firemen, and of the carman having the horses ready.

Can you speak as to an average for the last six months?—That is a thing that comes so little under my observation, that I cannot answer the question. When the engine and firemen and horses are ready, it takes about five minutes.

Who has the care of the engine?—The fireman.

Where does he reside?—He is resident upon the establishment.

There is one resides at each engine establishment?—Yes.

What are the privileges of the firemen?—As to privilege they have only that given by the statute of the 14th of the king, the privilege of being free from impressment: they are all watermen.

Is that the constant practice, that they should be all watermen?—It is the constant practice; it is a practice that has prevailed ever since the institution of firemen in different offices.

What is the quantity of water thrown by your largest engine?—I cannot answer that question without referring to the documents. The engine-makers give printed cards, stating the precise quantity, and the height and the distance the engine carries water: there are certain rules.

How are the firemen paid?—They are paid by the job; at sixpence an hour for their time.

So that if they are out 24 hours, they get twelve shillings?—Yes; they are also paid for chimney alarms, and things of that sort.

The firemen live in different parts of the Metropolis?—They keep their dwelling or lodging along the water side in general.

Do you know whether the firemen have any regulation among themselves, or what is the mode of communicating the alarm of fire among each other?—The man of each corps who has the call, gives the alarm; they agree to call each other at any time there is an alarm; and it is their interest to do that, for they do not get paid if they do not attend within two hours after the alarm is given.

How long is it, generally speaking, after an alarm of fire is given, that a sufficient number of firemen is assembled at each engine to work it?—That must depend very much upon the place where the accident is; and if it is near an engine station, or near their residence, the supply of firemen is rapid; but if it is at a remote corner of the Metropolis, where the firemen do not reside, and where there is less likelihood for an accident to happen, the time must be greater before the firemen are on the spot.

Suppose,

Mr.
Jenkin Jones.

Suppose, for instance, a fire to take place at Portman-square; what time would it be before the engine could start from the engine station?—That depends upon the alarm given at the engine-house; supposing the alarm to be given immediately, I should think the engine would be there in half an hour, probably less. I think, in most cases, if the alarm is given immediately at the engine-house, an engine would be at any part of the Metropolis in half an hour; I should suppose so. In general, the parish engines get first to the spot; but they are of very little use.

Are there engines in each parish?—Each parish is compelled to keep an engine.

Have you not men always on the watch?—No: formerly there was a fire police kept up by the Sun Fire Office and the Phœnix Fire Office, jointly, to attend in particular parts of the Metropolis; but the expense was so considerable, and as the other Offices did not chuse to contribute towards it, we dropped the establishment, not chusing that they should enjoy the benefit, when they did not contribute towards the expense.

There were in point of fact offices lighted up at night?—At the different engine-houses there were lights, and the firemen used to assemble there, and station themselves as patroles in the streets and neighbourhood during the night. I am not sure that it was of very great utility.

It has been stated by Mr. Fielding, one of the Magistrates of Westminster, as a useful suggestion for the benefit of the public, that if two firemen from every one of the Insurance Offices were to traverse up and down the streets of the Metropolis every night, they would cross one another often and often. Let every man be provided with his axe, and his link or flambeaux. Then this would be such effective means of security from fire, that the public would be highly pleased with such an establishment. It would be equally beneficial to the officers themselves, for it would be a vast provision against the accidents of fire; for these men, upon the discovery of a fire, might proceed with their axes and with their lights into the houses where the accident occurred. Should you think that an advisable plan?—We should have no objection to it, if the public would defray the expense. We should beg leave to decline it on our part, as we have done already a great deal for the security of the public, and are at an enormous expense; indeed at present the whole expense incurred by other offices and ours, for the increased security of the public, amounts to fifteen or twenty thousand pounds, which sum alone is spent upon the firemen.

In point of fact, the protection of the Metropolis from fire depends solely upon the private companies?—Certainly. The Act of Parliament requires the provision of the engines in each parish; sometimes it is of use, sometimes not. They are compelled to keep two, but they are small ones; one is much smaller than the other; the larger one is almost useless; the small one is useful to take into chambers or small apartments, but the other engine is so out of sorts that nobody makes any use of it; it is almost useless. We think these parish engines to be of little or no effect, and we find them so, generally speaking.

Generally speaking, except during the season of hard frost, is water always ready?—The engines are always at the spot before they can get a supply of water, and that is the worst part of the situation of the Metropolis in that respect. There are some parishes that are very ill supplied with water; for instance, the parish of Soho; and, generally speaking, the Eastern districts, where, if a fire happens, sometimes there is a great difficulty in getting water.

When the Water Companies were established, or more properly projected, was it not an argument that was used to recommend them to the favour of the public, that their steam engine would be always ready, day and night?—Some of them so promised.

Has that promise been fulfilled?—I should think not, certainly; it may be ready, but the engine has not sufficient power; I know that in the Eastern district the supply of water has been very precarious, and there has been great want of water to set the engine at work. I have made it my business to inquire at the Shadwell Water Company upon the subject; there was some explanation given, but I forget whether it was satisfactory.

Is it not true that engines are often unable to get to the fire until three quarters of an hour after it has happened?—I cannot answer that, but a fireman may be able to say; but, as I said before, that must depend so much upon the proximity of the fire to the engine I should say it was a much shorter time, in those places in the neighbourhood of which the engines are stationed; for instance, Wapping, the
Tower,

Tower, and the neighbourhood of the River, where accidents are likely to happen, and where our engines are mostly stationed, the engine would be on the spot immediately in case of accident; there is also a greater supply of water in the neighbourhood of the River.

How soon after a fire breaks out can water be got, in consequence of the steam engine that is now used by some of the Water Companies?—I cannot answer; but I should suppose it could be got in about half an hour.

I have been told twenty minutes?—I should think from twenty minutes to half an hour; we sometimes cannot get a sufficient quantity even by the steam engine.

There are several steam engines used by the water-works?—I do not know whether the Middlesex water-works have one; there is an immense steam engine at Paddington; indeed I believe they all work now by steam.

Do you mean that the water is not to be had unless the steam engine is working?—In some cases, in large fires, the supply of water is not so great as is desirable; the first difficulty is to turn on the water from the service pipes; there is a difficulty about that, and I am not sure that the key is kept as it ought to be, in the houses upon which the directions are placed, referring to where the service pipe is; I am not sure that they comply with the Act of Parliament in that respect. Unquestionably fires would be stopt much sooner if we were sure of an adequate supply of water; but the engines have to wait, and are known frequently to wait a considerable time before they can get a sufficient supply of water to keep them acting. Our business is to take the risk of the fire as it happens, and we do not wish to mislead the public upon that subject; our own interest will induce us to do as much as we possibly can to prevent accidents happening in the Metropolis.

It has been stated, that if posts were placed at certain distances in the streets, and an iron pipe of four inches diameter, with a hose secured to them, and they were supplied by the steam engine with water, that, in case of accident, fires might be put out without the use of engines; is that a practicable expedient?—The Water Companies would answer that question much better than I; but if that was the case, there would be a greater quantity of apparatus wanted to render it applicable to the service required. The supply at present of water is something of the same nature; there is not a pipe used in the way suggested, but the water is projected into the service pipes, and there is an opening, which they call the screw cock, and then the water is laid on from the service pipe to the engine, and then it plays upon the fire.

A fire must be constantly kept alive to keep the steam engine working?—If the steam engine is a machine to be kept constantly going, and a constant supply of fuel, I should think the expense would be so great that it would never answer; beside, another thing, the steam engines now in use have hardly a sufficient power to supply our wants; and consequently to make the system suggested effective, it would require steam engines of an immense power, and the expense of this would be so great, if indeed the system was practicable, that it would never answer the purposes of the projectors. I think it would be impossible for any steam engine to extend its powers so greatly as to be able to ply the water with sufficient strength for the purpose of extinguishing a fire at the extreme ends of the town; for instance I should take it, that the engine at Paddington would have very little power to project water into Holborn. Suppose the steam engine had the power of sending water to a certain height through several pipes, as may be done to 20 or 30 feet higher than in the ordinary case; but when you come to make the angles and detours of common pipes in bye places, it would be almost impossible to make it answer the purpose, without an enormous expense, as I said before.

What are the regulations at your office respecting the duties of firemen?—We have no printed regulations; there is a code of practices that have grown out of orders of the board, and orders from the secretary, which regulate our course of proceeding; I do not know that they could be very usefully collected for the information of the Committee; of course it is our object to make them as useful to the public as we can, for our own sake.

There is no fire patrole at present?—None; and I wish it to be understood that it would be attended with almost an useless expense; the Sun Fire Office kept one, for ostentation; the Sun Fire Office had a patrole met at Snowhill. The truth is, that the alarm of fire goes very rapidly; and unless, for the purpose of immediate extinction, you had a very large patrole indeed, it would be useless; and then the immense expense of such an establishment would be so great, that it would never answer the purpose.

510.   Have

Have the firemen any particular power given them by law?—None.

Not as to pulling down houses?—None. If they have any power of that sort, it rests upon the common law, and it is a disputable point; however they do act in that way, whether it is legal or not. I know it is a disputable point, whether they have a right to pull down houses. For my own part, I should always venture to do it, and would order it to be done, upon the principle of safety; but certainly I have not been able to find any decision upon the subject. It is thrown out incidentally by Lord Coke, in one of his cases, which justifies the reasoning upon which the practice might be supported. That great lawyer says, that it may be done upon the same principle that a man in a sinking boat has the power of throwing a cask of wine overboard. It is, however, better to leave the law undefined, for you might have it too much strained or too little. With respect to fire patroles, we have no objection to establish them, if the public will pay the expense of them.

Have you not a fire patrole now?—No; there was one established, as I said before, established between the Royal Exchange and Sun Fire Office, which cost 3,000 l. a year; but there are now so many fire offices established, and as they have refused to contribute towards the expense, we determined to suppress it; and we have reduced the expense of our Office from 3,000 l. to 700 l.

You hold yourselves liable to make good any damage done to a house by the explosion of gunpowder in a house adjoining, where there is no fire?—Certainly not, we are answerable only for damage by fire; but where a fire arises in an adjoining house by the explosion of gunpowder, then we pay for the damage done by that fire; but we do not hold ourselves liable for any other sort of accident occasioned to an adjoining house in consequence of the explosion of gunpowder.

But supposing the damage to be done in consequence of a fire where gunpowder is deposited, and then damage is done to the adjoining house; do you not then pay?—Certainly not; no more than we pay for the windows broken at Hounslow, by the blowing up of the powder mills.

I always thought you did?—No, certainly not. There can be no question about it, that where a fire arises in another house in consequence of the combustion of gunpowder, we hold ourselves liable for the damage; as in the instance of the Custom-house, where there was a fire on the opposite side of the street in consequence of the explosion of gunpowder at the Custom-house, and there we paid without hesitation to the opposite side; but we should not think of paying the damage by the mere explosion of the gunpowder itself at that time.

John Sayer, called in, and Examined.

YOU are a Bow-street Officer?—Yes.

How long have you been in the Bow-street Office?—I think about twenty-eight or thirty years; I was there in the time of the riots; I was there I know at the time of the riots in 1780.

Holding the situation which you fill now in that Office?—Yes; I was an officer first at Litchfield-street, and from Litchfield-street I went to Tothill-fields Bridewell, where I was seven or fourteen years as a turnkey; then I went from there to Bow-street. I was there I know at the time when there were a great many robberies committed in Westminster by a gang of desperate men, about thirteen or fourteen in number.

How long ago is it since that gang existed?—Sixteen, eighteen, or twenty years.

That description of gang of persons does not exist at the present moment?—No; in that time of day an officer could not walk in Duck-lane, Gravel-lane, or Cock-lane, without a party of five or six men along with him, they would have cut him to pieces if he was alone. There was a robbery committed in Mr. Tomkins's, at Islington, and they throttled Mr. Tomkins's wife; the thieves were two in number, a man of the name of Gamby, and one Wilkinson, and I took them in St. Giles's; they belonged to a gang of about six or seven; of that gang were convicted and hanged.

How do you account for that change in the manners and conduct of the people of the Metropolis?—I do not wish to take particular merit to myself. I left this place that I was at, in consequence of being solicited to come to Bow-street; I was solicited to come there, and I got rid of most of the highwaymen and footpads in a very short space of time; I may say that in six, eight, or ten years, there was no such thing heard of.

Then this change for the better that has taken place, you consider as arising from the

John Sayer.

the increased activity of the Police, as well as to the improved state of the morals of the public?—I have no doubt of it.

Do you remember the existence of the Apollo Gardens, the Dog and Duck, the Shepherd and Shepherdess, and the Bull and Pound?—All, well; I have been at them all.

Were not those places the resort of the criminal and profligate of both sexes?—Clearly so.

Are not their suppressions of great advantage to the manners of the Metropolis?—No doubt.

Do you think that at this present moment they would be tolerated?—To the Dog and Duck, and the Apollo Gardens, more young men fell victims than to any other places in the Metropolis. These places are not heard of now.

Do you remember the system of bull-hanking through the Metropolis, on Sundays and other days, by the lower orders of the population?—That practice has ceased; there is not so much of it as there used to be. Bull-hanking is bull-baiting. What the Committee speak of is bull-hunting. Hanking is baiting them at a stake; hanking is where they tied the bull to a stake, and baited him with dogs. Bull-hunting is where they take a beast from a drover, worry him till he gets mad, and then drive him through the streets, merely to break windows and create confusion; and in some of these cases many people were killed.

Do you remember the manner in which the Bridewell boys used to follow the bulls throughout the streets in the greatest state of fret, form themselves into associations, and appoint some one as their foreman?—I have a recollection of it; I remember hearing of it; I do not recollect seeing it myself, but I believe it is very correct.

The whole of that practice is now at an end?—Clearly so.

Do you not think that, generally speaking, the manners of the lower and middling classes of the people in this Metropolis are more decorous, more sober, and more domestic, than they were thirty years ago?—I cannot answer that: as to their sobriety, I cannot say.

You doubt as to their sobriety?—Yes.

But do you not think that their manners in general are more regular and domestic?—I think they are.

The very non-existence of these places of resort in those parts, for instance, is a proof?—Clearly so. Another thing I must suggest to you, that would be a very good thing if such measures were done away, that is, that which is the ruin of hundreds of young men; I mean the hiring of boats of a Sunday; there are more young men fall victims from that thing, than any one thing I know.

Explain what you mean?—For instance, I am an apprentice; and it is customary for many apprentices to raise money enough to buy a cutter; with this cutter they go up the River, to Richmond or Kew, and they spend their two shillings or their crown-piece, or perhaps half-a-guinea. Those who cannot buy a boat, they go to Godfrey's, and hire a boat at so much. Forty or fifty of these boats go up in this way, of a Sunday. These young men cannot support this expense, and from that they commence thieves. It is this that hangs a number of young men; and so far it is the same as bull-baiting; for if, by chance, there should be a bull-baiting, they are sure to go to it; and, if for no other reason, I should also go to a bull-bait, because I should be certain of seeing a set of thieves that I should not see at any other places. The thieves will meet together at all these places.

It has been given in evidence before this Committee, both by the Magistrates of the different Offices, as well as by the Police Officers, that they consider the system of Parliamentary reward, commonly known by the name of "Blood money," by which prosecutors, informers, and witnesses are paid, is one very injurious to the public interests; is that your opinion?—It is clearly my opinion; and I think that the system of paying reward in that way is very bad. In my humble judgment, if Government gave the Judges a power of rewarding every man according to his merit, and according to the service he has performed, it would be attended with advantage. The system, at present, I think very mischievous; whereas if the power of rewarding was left with the Judges, it would be the best way of rewarding them, because the Judges would be able to form a judgment as to who deserved the most. There have been many guilty men acquitted through the ingenuity of counsel, and the way they have of abusing an officer, is asking him whether he did not expect the reward that had been offered: many of them say they do not expect it, and

probably

probably the man on his trial is acquitted in consequence. But if I were to be asked by any of the gentlemen of the jury, whether I expected the reward, I should say yes; for if there is a reward, I expect it. But it is not the case that the officer gets it; all rewards are distributed to the different persons attending upon the trial, and the greater part of it goes to the witnesses and the evidence; but the officer is held out as the person alone who receives it, and the public think so, and will constantly oppose him.

The officer only gets a share of the reward?—He only gets a part.

How much money did you ever get in any one year, in the nature of Parliamentary reward?—I cannot say exactly; I had Clarke, Haynes, Eversham, and other persons convicted, and probably I might have had 50 l. or 100 l. from the parties who employed me.

I speak of Parliamentary reward; have you ever made 20 l. a year?—Yes.

From 20 to 40 l.?—Very likely more than that; I might have had perhaps 100 l. being part of perhaps twenty rewards, in a year, but I cannot say what the amount is exactly: I have sometimes made five, sometimes ten pounds a piece, for each conviction, according to what it was. Sometimes, when there are many men taken together, for instance, when three or four are taken for one offence, and then these four men being convicted, there are four rewards. The first thing done is to reward the prosecutors, then the witnesses, and then the officers, whatever the Recorder chuses to give them.

Do they reward the prosecutors and witnesses, besides their expenses?—Yes, and they give them the best part of the reward. I have known a man go down to Kingston, and get three guineas and a half out of 80 l. and come home money out of pocket. It is one of the worst things to reward the parties in this way, and I am against it, for it does a great deal of mischief.

Do you not, as an individual, find that, when you are placed in the box as a witness against a criminal or a person accused, that you are in an unpleasant situation, when you are aware that for the evidence you are about to give, you are to receive the payment of a sum of money, supposing that you convict the person that is accused?—I have always considered it in this way, that I should be much more pleasantly paid by any thing that the court should allow, than having it held out to me and to the jury, that I am giving evidence against a criminal in the expectation of getting a reward of 40 l.

Without meaning to make the observation either to yourself, or to any other of the Police Officers, who, as far as we have heard of them, conduct themselves extremely well, do you think that it is but too likely that this species of rewards may have a tendency to induce an Officer to speak more positively against an individual, than he might otherwise be disposed to do, if there was no reward by which he expected to gain personal profit?—I think so; I have often hoped not, but I think it may be fact in some cases.

From the long experience that you have had, have you not in point of fact seen cases in which you could not but think that something of that sort has happened?—Clearly so.

Do you not think, then, that it would be a much better plan if those officers were rewarded according to the specific services performed; because you must be well aware that an officer will take the greatest possible pains, and yet not be able to succeed in any conviction at all, either from want of evidence, or from the humanity of the jury, or from any other causes, and yet the services may be performed; do you not therefore think that the officer who has so done his duty should have some share in the reward, even though his services have not obtained the conviction of the offender?—I have no doubt of it. I am perfectly satisfied of the excellence of such a plan; and I am satisfied it is a thing that has been long wished for by every respectable officer, I may say for years past, who have always expressed their opinion against the present mode of rewarding. It is a very bad thing, in my opinion, and that is the opinion of the rest of the Officers; and Townsend and myself have always talked about it, and wished it to be done away with. It is one of the worst things that was ever done; for even if a man is stating the plain truth, and when he is brought into the box, then there is this reward always stands in question; it is always in every body's mouth, and the jury say, " The officer will never meddle with a thief until he weighs his weight; the thief-catchers will not take him till they are sure of getting 40 l. by him."

Whereas they may not get above 3 l. or 4 l.?—Yes, whatever the Recorder chuses

John Sayer.

chuses to give ; and if it is in the country, the Sheriff takes so much for paying it ; there is 5 *l*. or 6 *l*. for some fees taken out of it, in the country. The last man that I took, I brought out of Oxfordshire.

How long is that ago ?—His name was Campbell, and I brought him out of Oxfordshire for horse-stealing.

How long ago is that?—Eight, nine, or ten years ago.

But that is not so now?—I believe not. Then there is so much for the bill to be sworn, so much is taken from each officer; then there is for the witnesses 6 *d*. a-piece; the blame is upon the officer; he has all the odium of it; it is said that he has all the reward ; he bears the weight of it.

Do you consider your salaries at the present moment as sufficient to maintain you in your present situation ?—If it was not for the assistance that we receive from private individuals, we could not ; it is impossible.

You have your bills for expenses paid ?—I believe that, taking Townsend and myself, we get more money than the other officers ; we attend the nobility and gentry, and if any accident might happen to them, we might get five or six guineas, whilst another man might be at the Office the whole day, and not get any thing; this is from our being publicly known.

What bills of expenses have you, besides a guinea a week ?—We have no expenses from the Office ; if we do any thing for any gentleman, or any body in town, or if you were to send to the Office, or come to me for my assistance, you pay me ; the Office will not pay me ; you may pay me what you think fit.

Are there any cases in which the Office pays your expenses ?—Yes, if we go into the country for the Office, the Office would allow us a guinea a day, and fourteen shillings for expenses. If a gentleman writes up to town, who has had his house broken open, and desires that an officer may be sent down, a man is immediately sent down, and he gets the expenses from the gentleman.

Suppose a gentleman has his house robbed in the country, and he was to write to the Office to send you and Townsend down to assist him, would you be paid by the gentleman or by the Office?—By the gentleman, unless the Magistrate sends. If the Magistrate was to send down, the Office would pay the officer ; but if the gentleman writes, the gentleman pays.

Then for what duties do the Magistrates pay your expenses ?—We attend at Carlton House, and follow all the movements of the Royal Family ; therefore wherever the Royal Family go, we go ; on public occasions we attend them. We are not suffered to go into the country ; we must not go into the country; we never go into the country at all, without it is when the Royal Family go. To fetes or balls Townsend and myself go, but nothing out of town ; Lavender, Vickery, and those Officers, are those that travel out of town.

Then their expenses, when they travel out of town, are paid by the individual who sends for them, and not by the Office, unless they are sent upon public matters ?—I believe that is the case. You know there is a number of other Officers belonging to other Offices ; but they never have so much of that sort of business as our Officers. Wherever there is a very bad character, our Office generally receives the information against him, and we send after him. In the other Offices, the men may never go out of town three times in a year.

You are acquainted with a great number of the dangerous characters or suspected persons who are constantly about London?—Yes.

Do you happen to know amongst them persons who have been on board the Hulks?—A great many. There are a great many men about the town that have been on board the Hulks, or returned from Botany Bay. I always make a rule, when any thing occurs to these men, if they are in custody or under conviction, of acquainting Mr. Capper, at the Secretary of State's Office, or the Recorder, of the circumstance of their having so returned.

In 1812, by the Return before the Committee, there were above 400 persons pardoned from the Hulks ; should you think that made a difference in the number of thieves about London?—I should think it did ; but most of these men go for sailors into the navy, or into the army. Certainly I should think it made a difference.

I see that in 1812, 1813, and 1814, there were between two and three hundred convicts free pardoned from the Hulks ; now, from your observation, what opinion should you form of the manner in which these persons employed themselves, after leaving the Hulks ?—Why I am of opinion that many many men that are there, that have committed themselves in the younger part of life, may become very good members of society; but as for men who were convicted once before, I am of

510.   opinion

opinion that nothing ever will alter them. I mean men who have committed the first offence perhaps from distress; many a man who is distressed, may be as well-disposed as any man in the world; may either from accident, from error, or from distress, commit an offence which subjects him to seven years transportation, and yet he may afterwards become a good member of society.

In point of fact, are there not many young men who have been on board the Hulks, have committed offences again?—Frequently.

Do you not think that when there is a great discharge of men from the Hulks, that there is a great access of thieves upon the town?—No doubt. If the Officers had power, there could not be a thief walk the streets. At Ascott Heath, the other day I was there, and I saw several known thieves together; I cannot meddle with them, I have no power to meddle with them.

What power could be given you to meddle with them?—That is out of my judgment to say; if I lay hold of them, they would say, "I am a gentleman;" I say he is not, I can prove him otherwise; "Have you seen him do any thing?" I have not; the law therefore will acquit him immediately.

Generally speaking, do you not consider that persons who have been discharged from the Hulks are made worse by their confinement there, instead of being made better?—I should think that if it is a man that is not an old offender, there cannot be a doubt of it; for instance, if you had a servant, and that servant was convicted of robbing you, when he goes to these Hulks he sits down and hears the tales told, and the adventures of old offenders; he then tells the situation of his master's house and property, and if three or four men go out from the Hulks, they know where to go and commit a robbery.

In point of fact, has it ever come to your knowledge that robberies have been committed, the plans of which were laid on board the Hulks?—No doubt of it.

Is it then your opinion that if a young man for his first offence, little used to bad company, except that association in which he is found, is sent to the Hulks, there living with people who have passed the best part of their lives in the perpetration of crimes, listening to their stories, and depraved by their manners and conversation, that he comes out of the Hulks a worse member of society than he had been?—I have no doubt of it.

And have you any doubt then that the Hulks may be considered as amongst the causes of the number of thefts that are committed upon the town?—I cannot answer to that; it is out of my line to answer it.

You have stated, that people are made worse by confinement on board the Hulks; can you have any doubt then that, when they are discharged, the town would suffer?—It would be the same in every place of confinement. The only way, in my own opinion, of remedying the evil would be, if it were possible, to keep the young and the old offenders separate; that is the only thing that could prevent it. The Hulks or Newgate would be just the same. The mischief is, that the moment a boy comes to the gaol or place of confinement, there being no power of putting him any where else, he sits down and hears the old housebreakers describe the way in which they committed their offence, and he listens to them with devouring ears; and if he is acquitted upon trial, he goes out qualified with all the necessary knowledge to perpetrate greater crimes, and probably at length comes to an untimely end. My opinion therefore is, that if all the old offenders were classed together, and the young ones kept separate and apart from them, it would be much better: however, this is for the Committee to consider. I am sure of it, that from my experience and all that I have seen in my lifetime, that whenever the boys or young men come into gaol and get amongst these old offenders, they are infallibly ruined.

Do you know of the existence of what are called "Flash-houses?"—Perfectly well; I very often go to those flash-houses, and find many thieves in most of them.

Whom you know to be reputed thieves?—There is no doubt of it.

From different parts of the town?—Yes.

Are you of opinion that the flash-houses assist in the detection of offenders?—I think so; it being flash-houses that collect them together. In Sir John Fielding's time there was the Blakeney in Bow-street, next door to the Office; that was a house that men and women used to drink in. We would find a great deal of difficulty, when informations were brought to Bow-street, in being able to apprehend the offenders, unless there were such houses; but when this sort of people use the house in Covent-garden or St. Martin's-lane, we should have him at once by merely going there.

John

John Henry Capper, Esq. (from the Secretary of State's Office) called in, and Examined.

WHAT situation do you hold?—Clerk in the Secretary of State's Office, for the management of the criminal business.

What salary have you?—The salary is 270 *l.* a year, and I have 400 *l.* a year for my length of service, having been 22 years in that Office.

Is that the salary allowed you for being superintendent to the department of the Hulks?—No.

Have you any thing at all for that?—I have a salary under the Act of Parliament, of 400 *l.*

That is not the salary specified in the Act of Parliament?—No; the salary is not specified, only in general terms, " such as His Majesty may be pleased to appoint." Mr. Graham the late Inspector, had 350 *l.* Lord Sidmouth has made an addition to that sum, of 50 *l.* a year to my salary, for this service.

Do you periodically visit the Hulks?—Yes; I have visited them more than is directed by the Act of Parliament.

How often do you visit them?—I visit them, generally speaking, about five times in the year; I have inspected at Woolwich, I think, nine or ten times in the last year.

Can you state to the Committee the number of persons who were present at the last time you visited them?—As near as I can say at this moment, about 2100 at the different stations. They were reduced till lately; but the numbers have been increased, owing to the great addition of transportable offenders at the last Lent Assizes.

You have lately sent a great number of persons to New South Wales?—There were 300 male convicts sent within the last six weeks.

Were those part of the 2100 you have mentioned?—No; that is the number since the embarkation. The removal of the transports to the Hulks from the different gaols since then, have brought them up to 2100.

I see, by the Return laid before Parliament last year, there were 273 persons pardoned free; in 1813, 246; in 1814, 252: can you state to the Committee how many were pardoned in 1815?—Not exactly at this moment; but I should take it for granted, 320; I would say 300 certainly.

In 1812 there were pardoned conditionally, 135; in 1813, 9; in 1814, none: were those conditional pardons for persons entering into the army and navy?—Yes.

State to the Committee how there comes to be the disproportion between the first and second year and the last?—In consequence of the refusal to receive them into the army and navy.

Was that refusal from their having turned out ill?—There were prejudices in consequence of what took place in the House of Commons, upon a statement made by General Ferguson, which induced the Commander in Chief to refuse receiving any more transports into the army. As a distinct regiment they have behaved very well, I understand; but otherwise, when mixed with other corps.

Upon what principle are the free pardons granted?—They are granted to those men who have served six years with order and regularity out of the seven on board the Hulks; which is invariably granted.

If a man serves six years with propriety, he receives a free pardon, without serving the seventh year?—Yes; that forms a great part of the number I am alluding to; I mean the 300 persons free pardoned.

Do people receive pardons under other circumstances, besides serving the six years?—In certain cases; selections are made by the captains, of two out of every hundred, in each quarter, as the best behaved on board: these are submitted by me to the Secretary of State, and if the nature of the offence is such as will admit of it, the recommendations are generally attended to by the Secretary of State. Every exertion is made to induce the friends of such men to receive them, and provide them employment upon their discharge.

But what means have the captains of becoming acquainted with the characters of these men?—They have means brought by the gaolers, which is registered in books kept on board; a counterpart of which I have also by me, deposited in the Secretary of State's Office, furnished under the Act of Parliament which recently passed; and also other private information I have from the different counties from which the convicts were sent; added to which, are the recommendations of the gaolers from the different counties where they have been confined. I have an

account

J. H. Capper. Esq.

J. H. Capper,
Esq.

account of their offences, and their former characters, for by the Act of Parliament, the gaolers are compelled to inquire into their character: they have conformed strictly to what is required. By this means, we find out who are the bad, and who are the good characters. I have found this system answer uncommonly well.

In point of fact, when the people are sent up from the counties, are there any pains taken to give you a distinct account of the character of the persons, and of what is known of them; whether they are old or young offenders?—Yes, I have a regular registry which contains the whole of it.

And you have, since that Act of Parliament, a general registry of the different Hulks, and the persons there in confinement, and of the character that belongs to them?—Yes, I have complete books kept on board each particular hulk to which each individual is sent, and a counterpart of which I keep in town, and as to the particular offence that he has committed; generally speaking, it is now furnished tolerably correct: their removal to any particular hulk must depend entirely upon the convenience and to where the Secretary of State may think proper to send them.

The extent of the hulk; and something must depend upon the fulness of the hulk at the time?—Yes.

When a man is sent to the Hulks, does the part of the ship in which he is to be placed, depend upon the pleasure of the captain?—No; he must be placed in a class purposely for new prisoners; if there are any circumstances very favourable to the man, from his former habits of life, there is a difference made, under my authority; I have written down this very day, to desire that three men, convicted of offences of a different description to the usual class of offenders, may be placed among those of better behaviour.

What divisions are there in the ship at Portsmouth?—There are seven divisions in the Captivity. There is no plan that will answer better than the one fitted at Sheerness, under the suggestion of the Committee of The House of Commons.

You are fitting up another ship on the same plan?—Yes; that is with only varying the carrying out the privies without the ship, instead of within board.

Do you keep the same number of divisions?—Yes.

Do you think it will be an advisable plan, if it were possible, to have the hulks so divided (I do not mean each individual hulk) but, taking one hulk for old offenders, another for persons of less bad character, a third for lesser offences, and a fourth for boys?—Boys I am decided about, and I think it practicable; but with regard to the others, I have my doubts about it, and I will tell you how the necessity of it is obviated: when we have very bad characters, we ship them off the first opportunity, so that the worst of offenders will not accumulate in the way they have done, having the means of ascertaining their characters as before stated; those for life and fourteen years are first selected, then those that are for seven years, of very bad characters.

Is it customary now to send persons to New South Wales, who are only sentenced to seven years transportation?—A great many are sent; for many of the worst offenders are only transported for seven years.

What rule is observed, with respect to clearing the Hulks, by sending off offenders to New South Wales?—Just as was observed before; it depends upon the number of life and fourteen years convicts, and those of bad characters, as well as the boys; not having the means at present of employing them satisfactorily.

By "bad character" do you mean those whom the captain reports?—No, I have a return from the different counties. I would not depend upon the captain's report, except as to cases of bad conduct on board, which is always minuted in the ship's books; but this does not now often occur, of bad behaviour on board. There are many instances where a man, being sentenced to transportation for seven years, behaves very well; and if that man comes recommended with a tolerably good character, there is every encouragement held out to him to reform; indeed so there is with those of bad character. But if a prisoner comes with a bad character, I should doubt very much of his being reformed; after a second conviction, I consider it completely hopeless: it is such a certificate of bad character, that he cannot, unless from illness, be kept back from being sent to New South Wales. It has been done, formerly, but it will not be done again. When a man comes with a tolerably fair character, our first object is to attend to his morals, every example being set him to induce him to reform; he soon sees that those who behave well are removed from one class to another, and he in his turn looks forward for the like indulgence, which he is sure to meet with, if he behaves well;

and

J. H. Capper.
Esq.

and in this way they are removed, until they stand in a situation to be selected for recommendation to the Secretary of State as objects of mercy.

These selections are out of men who have served six years?—No; many of these men are selected who have been only three years and a half. All the prisoners under seven years sentence, who have served six years with a fair character, would be pardoned under the general regulations which Lord Sidmouth has authorized.

In point of fact, does it come to your knowledge to what extent and in what number the men who return either from Botany Bay or the Hulks, resume their old practices in London?—I may hope that the number is very considerably decreased, and I really think so. It does happen that some of the worst return to their old habits. I am sorry to say that it is a new and a younger class of persons that are committing depredations at this moment. There are very few of the old offenders now about, and the number will be lessened every day, for the reason I have given, by the shipment of that class of offenders for New South Wales as soon after their conviction as possible; and by the Governor of New South Wales conforming to the instructions which have been given him, not to allow these persons to return before the expiration of their sentences, I look forward to a considerable reduction in this town of what are called old offenders.

How many persons were sent last year, can you state to the Committee, to Botany Bay, whose sentence was only for seven years?—I cannot say at this moment.

Was it a very considerable number?—I should think there was 300, I will venture to assert that; but I am not at this moment able to say precisely what the number was.

In the four last years, I see by the Return which I hold in my hand, that there were 2,348 males sent, above 21 years of age, and females above 21 years of age; and 386 males under 21 years of age, and 100 females; can you give to the Committee any account of how many of those you suppose were under sentence for seven years transportation; there were near two thousand seven hundred persons; out of that number, what is the proportion sentenced to seven years?—Certainly 800.

Do you know whether any provision is made in New South Wales for the return of those persons, particularly for the women, after the period of their transportation is expired?—I understand a communication upon this subject was made to the Governor of New South Wales, by the Secretary of State for the Colonial Department, soon after the Report of a Committee of the House of Commons upon Transportation, in 1812; but whether it has been acted upon further, I do not know.

Do the convicts in general prefer remaining in the Hulks, or being transported to Botany Bay?—They give the preference to transportation, generally speaking; the young men in particular; the boys are almost all anxious to go, with very few exceptions.

At least for the voyage?—Yes.

Do you attend in general to these applications?—Yes; to all the applications made from the youths, attention is paid.

Have you many young people of both sexes lately committed to the Hulks?—Males only are sent to the Hulks; within these six months there have been 100, of 20 years of age and under.

Is there any place for women whom it is intended to send to Botany Bay, previous to leaving this country?—There is none whatever.

Is not their presence in many gaols, very much complained of?—Very much; particularly at Bristol, Lancaster, and the gaol of Newgate, which I need hardly mention to the Committee.

Would it not be worth while to fit up a hulk for their reception?—I think a ship could be fitted for their reception, as a temporary place of confinement; but I am of opinion, that however short the time might be of their remaining on board, it would be absolutely necessary to adopt some plan for their constant occupation; without which, I am fearful, no good would result from their removal. It would be of great advantage to shut out the access of children and other young persons, who frequent the gaols to see the women.

Are they not in many gaols, at this moment, associated with persons of a different description?—Yes. At this time there are 95 women under sentence of transportation in Newgate; and in the different gaols in England and Scotland there are about 140. A ship has just been taken up for the purpose of conveying 100 to New South Wales, after a selection has been made for the Penitentiary.

Have many of these persons been under sentence of transportation for a con-

510.   siderable

J. H. Capper.
Esq.

siderable length of time?—Yes; but they are those whose state of health will not permit them to go abroad. There are not many longer than from September or October last. That is too long, but there are great difficulties in disposing of these persons. Of course the Penitentiary will be of considerable utility in relieving, particularly the gaol of Newgate.

They all go by Portsmouth?—No, from the River. I always have them embarked at Deptford, as I find that place most convenient in many respects, particularly as to my going on board during the time of their embarkation, and seeing into their state and condition before their sailing.

Would it not very much conduce to the better management of the Hulks, if the present hulks could be laid aside, and new ones built upon the approved principle of that one at Sheerness?—Certainly.

What obstacle is there to that improvement?—The expense.

Have you any idea of the expense of fitting up a hulk upon the principle of that at Sheerness?—I am now employed in fitting up one in the same way. I should think the Navy Board would not charge more than 6,000l. for it; it is a 74-gun ship. I feel confident that it is the best plan.

Do you not think that if the plan was generally carried into effect, you would be able to introduce on board each ship different species of domestic work?—I think it possible.

Do you not think that the question of work is one of the greatest importance?—Certainly occupation with persons in confinement ought to be a leading consideration.

An ACCOUNT of the Number of Persons who have been Discharged from the Hulks since 1 January 1815; also the number of Persons received on board the Hulks since that time, of 21 years of age and under; and also the number of Persons removed from the Hulks for Transportation to New South Wales since 1st January 1815, of the age of 21 years and under.

	1815.	To 1st June 1816.
Free Pardoned - - - - - - -	362.	163.
Pardoned Conditional - - - - - -	- -	3.
Sentence Expired - - - - - - -	19.	12.
Number of Persons of 21 years and under, received on board the Hulks - - - - - -	319.	194.
Number of Persons removed from the Hulks for Transportation, of 21 years of age and under -	251.	97.

John Henry Capper,
Superintendent.

Mercurii, 19° *die Junii*, 1816.

The Honourable HENRY GREY BENNET, in The Chair.

John Gifford, Esquire, again called in, and Examined.

HAVE you any thing to add or explain in the former evidence that you gave before the Committee?—I wish to correct one unintentional misrepresentation in my former evidence, relating to the prescribed hours of attendance by the Act of Parliament; on looking into the last Police Act, of the 54th of His present Majesty, I found that the constant attendance of one Magistrate was required at the Office from ten in the morning till eight in the evening. I do not suppose that the Legislature could mean that a Magistrate should sit ten hours upon the bench transacting magisterial business, because, with the business of our Office, if it were to continue ten hours, no human constitution could support it. But in point of fact, as far as concerns myself, my attendance under the roof of the Office, which I apprehend is all that the spirit of the Act could require, has been from ten o'clock in the morning till eight, and much longer.

Do you know any thing concerning a public-house which was kept by Mr. William Simpson, in Hackney Fields, in the parish of Shoreditch?—That house was the sign of the Duke of Wellington, and is kept by Thomas Field; it is the freehold property of Messrs. Simpson and Day, the former a haberdasher, the latter a bricklayer in Shoreditch. Field paid them a thousand pounds for a lease of twenty-three years, subject to an annual rent of 60*l.*; the house was in an unfinished state, and Field agreed to finish it: it cost him 500*l.* to make it habitable. There is a clause in the lease compelling him to buy his beer of Messrs. Truman & Hanbury for fourteen years. The fact is, that this licence was granted to Simpson, who was not occupant of the house at the time when the house was unfinished, but was carrying on the trade of a haberdasher in Shoreditch, as he is at this moment, which I take to be illegal. I was asked how many public-houses there were in Norton Falgate; I have looked to it, and on the West side of Norton Falgate, from the corner of Worship-street to the place where the county ends, a space of about one hundred and ten yards, there are four public-houses, three of which are liquor-shops; in five houses here, the first, the third, and the fifth, are public-houses; there is also a liquor-shop on the opposite side of the way, the Blue Coat Boy, which is converted into a liquor-shop, there being no tap-room. One of the above liquor-shops, the Cossack, was formerly called the Blakeney's Head, and was much resorted to by thieves; the licence was stopped in consequence of complaints from the Office in Worship-street, but was afterwards granted again.

To the same person?—I believe it was afterwards granted to the same woman, on condition that she should transfer it to another person; I have been so told by my own officers, but I am not quite sure that that is the fact. In Shoreditch, there are twelve liquor-shops from Union-street to Kingsland-road, little more than half a mile, besides fourteen other public-houses. There are three or four Acts of Parliament, which are connected with objects of police, which require amendment, being in their present state inoperative. The Act of Charles II. known by the name of the Lord's Day Act, requires alteration and amendment; in its present state it is perfectly inefficient. A man has been held, not to be responsible for the act of his servant; when the penalty is not paid, and there is return of nulla bona to a distress warrant, imprisonment ensues; therefore as criminal punishment is the penalty of the Act, it is held the master cannot be responsible for the conduct of his servant.

That can only take place when there is a return of nulla bona?—Yes; by that Act, the 29 Charles II. c. 7, goods exposed to sale on the Lord's Day are declared to be confiscated, but no power is given to seize them, so that the Act is nugatory as far as that goes; if that power could be given, it would be useful, and put a stop to a great deal of profanation of the Sabbath. There is another Act which is of some consequence in matters of police, which is the Act of the 9th and 10th of William III. Chapter 7, on which we are called on to act very frequently, where persons who sell fireworks are liable to a penalty; if the penalty is not paid a distress warrant is issued; and there, upon the return of nulla bona, which is the general return, you can proceed no further. If it is an offence deemed worthy of punishment, something further should be done, because any person at present can evade the penalty.

John Gifford, Esq.

Sir *John Silvester*, Bart. F.R.S. Recorder of the City of London,
called in, and Examined.

HOW long have you been Recorder of the City of London?—Thirteen years; I was chosen in 1803.

From your observations, since you have filled that situation, do you think that the progress of crime in the Metropolis is considerably on the increase?—In numbers certainly, but in depravity not by any means; we have less depravity now than ever we had.

You mean by that, less serious offences?—Less serious offences.

Have offences considerably increased amongst the juvenile part?—They have; but when you consider the proportion of children, I do not think they have increased in proportion. I was lately looking to a return of the parish schools in the parish I live in, and found 300 at one school and 400 at another, and 500 at another; and last Thursday there were 12,000 children at Saint Paul's; which shows what an immense number of children there are.

You think the increase, according to the returns laid before Parliament, of the number of offences, is more from the augmented population than from the augmentation of crime?—Yes, certainly. There are several things which tend to increase felonies, certainly, not only the population, but many other things.

Will you be so good as to state to the Committee what, in your opinion, added to the increased population, are the causes that have a tendency to augment crime?—There are several: first, the post-office hour being changed from eleven or twelve o'clock at night, which we all remember, to seven o'clock and eight o'clock, by which numberless young men in all situations, merchants clerks, bankers clerks, attornies clerks, in short, every young man is dismissed at an earlier hour; by eight o'clock, when the post goes out, they are at complete liberty, which was not in my younger days the case.

Do not you think that the system of out-door apprentices, which has much increased, has a bad effect on the morals of youth?—Certainly, I think so most undoubtedly that the out-door apprentice system is a great evil; and I am very sorry to see that the Statute of Elizabeth is not enforced, where a man was compelled to take apprentices.

Will you proceed to state any other causes, besides that you have mentioned?—The very easy access to London. The moment a man commits depredations in the country, and is known, his access to London is the easiest thing in the world, and that brings London as a point, where he is almost sure to meet with a more easy mode of committing depredations; not only the population is greater, but the objects of depredation are increased.

And he is better concealed?—Yes. And the number of persons out of employ is another cause.

Do you think that the indigence of the lower orders of the Metropolis has considerably increased within these few years?—I do not know that it has. But you see not only people come to town, but many debtors are brought to the Metropolis, who are guilty of frauds; and the line between fraud and felony is so very narrow, it is easily broken: a man begins with fraud, and frequently ends in felony. I am afraid that the number of felonies always increase after insolvent acts. Another cause of increase, I am very free to say, is owing to the capital part being taken off from the privately stealing from the person; that offence has increased beyond conception, in large gangs.

Do you not think that the readiness with which individuals are now induced to prosecute for that offence, in consequence of the capital punishment being taken off, and the result of that prosecution being generally transportation, which is milder than that of death, has a tendency to check it?—No; I think that is a fallacy.

Has it not increased the number of prosecutions?—I do not believe that any man was ever deterred from prosecuting; a man need not to have laid it as privately stealing from his person, he might have laid it as a common larceny.

In point of fact, are there not now many more prosecutions for that offence than formerly?—There are many more prosecutions, certainly, because there are many more offenders; but there are many more escape prosecution, it is an offence so easily done, and so difficult of detection.

Do you think that all persons receiving the sentence of transportation, consider such a sentence as a punishment?—I cannot well answer that question.

Do you not think that the extended system of education, which is making much progress about the Metropolis, has also been one of the causes which has a tendency

at

Sir John Silvester,
Bart.

at least to diminish the increase of crime among the younger classes?—I think it has, and will diminish them; but at this moment I think the increased number of juvenile offenders arises, first of all, from the great number of children of convicts that are let loose on the public, and children of soldiers who have been killed, and who are left unprotected, and who therefore take to wrong courses. I hope this course of education will be beneficial if they instil into them good principles, because mere education without principle I hold to be of no use.

Have you ever at all been able to obtain any thing in the nature of a calculation, of the average number of persons in London and the Metropolis, who may be considered as living by a system of fraud?—I hold it to be impossible; calculations may be loosely made, but persons have no data upon which they can proceed to make a correct calculation.

You have stated to the Committee, that you think that taking away the capital part of the punishment for privately stealing from the person, in point of fact, has a tendency to increase the number of offences; do you think that the lenity with which the capital punishments of this country have been executed, has had equally that tendency?—Yes, I do: it is a melancholy thing to say.

Do you not think that there has this effect been produced by the lenient execution of the law, that it has a tendency to make offenders against the law content themselves, with simple robbery, and not add murder to it, when the punishment of death is almost confined entirely to the last offence, unless circumstances of cruelty accompany those of robbery?—I do think it has that effect, for we have now no cruel offenders, no extraordinary violence against the person, as we have had formerly; and therefore that was what made me say that the crimes are attended with fewer instances of depravity than they were; they are more in number.

Therefore the result of your observation is, that though the sum total of the crimes is increased, the gravamen of the crimes is considerably less?—Most certainly.

The Committee have had before them many of the Magistrates of the Metropolis, and have been solicitous to examine into the state of the Police, and into the apparent causes of the accumulation of offenders, as well as the condition of the Police itself; they would wish to ask from you, whether you have any thing to suggest in the administration of the Police, which has come under your observation, to remedy any of the evils which at present exist?—Upon my word I have not; I know so little of their mode of carrying on business, that I cannot suggest an opinion. There is only one thing I should like to suggest, if it could be done, which is, that there should be some reward given for the detection and conviction of receivers, because that is another mode of increasing crime, by the ease with which people part with stolen goods; if that could be prevented, and a greater difficuty thrown in the way of disposing of the property, the better it would be.

Has any plan suggested itself to your mind, in addition to the laws which at present exist upon the subject?—I have thought of many things; but the difficulty of suggesting an alteration of the laws is the greatest of any I know; and above all, the danger of trenching on the liberty of the subject.

It has been stated to the Committee by different Magistrates, no less than by the Police Officers themselves, that they consider the mode of rewarding the detection of offenders, known by the name of Parliamentary rewards, as one which they look upon as prejudicial to the public interest, and which they would wish to have changed; have you any opinion upon that subject?—Yes; I think very differently; I think that rewards do not tend to any improper ends. I thought I might be asked that question, and I have brought with me a List of Rewards. On the first day of every session, after conviction, I distribute them at the Old Bailey; but I do not make a distribution till I have considered every individual case, and the merits of every witness, upon the back of the indictment; I then apportion the rewards according to the best of my judgment.

Do you know whether that is the practice at the different Assizes in the country?—I do not know that.

Can you state to the Committee what is the amount of rewards that you ordinarily annually divide?—I cannot.

Nor any thing like it?—No; it would be all guess work.

Is there any account kept?—Yes, there is an account kept; the Sheriff pays it within a month, and therefore he has an account; I sign the certificate as to how it is disposed of; but it is impossible to say the amount, it varies so much.

The evidence before the Committee has not gone so far as to say that no rewards should be given, but it has been proposed, not only by various Magistrates, but also

by

by the Police Officers themselves, that they would be better pleased that the rewards should be paid at the discretion of the Judge, of the Recorder, or of the Police Magistrate, for services performed, than settled by Act of Parliament in that manner which is generally known by the name of Blood-money, because all the different parties have stated that they consider themselves as coming into court with a stain upon their evidence; and that it has been distinctly avowed by more Officers than one, that they themselves have witnessed evidence given against an offender, apparently for the sole purpose of getting the reward; the Committee wish to learn from you, whether in that view of it you consider the Parliamentary rewards as the best mode?—I can only speak for myself; and can say, that I consider the present mode as the best mode. I see great inconvenience in the Police Magistrates distributing it, because they may be considered as liable to partiality to their own Officers, it seems to me. I divide it now, and no Act of Parliament could give me more power than I have at present. They talk of blood-money as applied to Officers; low and ignorant people will do that; but I do not find that the Police Officers outstrip the truth, and it is perhaps because they know that I watch them; I find the country constables much more anxious for the reward than the town constables.

Do not you see that the consequence of a settled reward, to be paid only upon conviction, must at all times have a tendency to induce people to go very far in their oaths, for the sake of what they are to gain by that conviction?—I really have not seen that; I have seen it go so far as for juries to acquit; the Officers know if I saw they went too far, when I distribute I should say, You gave your evidence improperly, and therefore I must give less. But I never saw it.

If juries are induced to acquit, public justice is thereby stopped?—That so seldom happens, that it has become scarce a question; I do not say it never happens.

Do not you see that the present system of rewards has also this objection, that unless there is conviction, the greatest possible exertion on the part of the Constable or Police Officer goes unrewarded?—I do not know how they are to be considered as unrewarded, because they have their expenses allowed; whenever there is no reward upon a conviction, the Officers have their expenses; whenever there is a conviction, and there is a reward, they have no expenses paid.

The Committee have had it in evidence, that the allowance for expenses is but small, and, even where there is conviction, it repeatedly happens that the division is so small as not in any degree to cover the expense of the Officers?—To that I cannot answer, because I do not know what expense they are at; if there are a great number of persons to divide the reward, they must each have a smaller part of it. As to the expense of witnesses, it is always allowed by the court, where there is no reward. The expense of witnesses during the last year at the Old Bailey, for the county of Middlesex, was 3,728*l.* which is no small sum.

The rewards are paid by the county?—I believe the Treasury pay the rewards.

Do you consider the amount of Parliamentary rewards as sufficient, or their limitation to particular crimes as proper; or would it be advisable to give rewards to the same extent, or to a smaller, for the detection of other offences?—In regard to the receivers of stolen goods generally, I think it would be an advantage, because you would excite people to watch them, and do something; now, nothing is done. As to the other offences, I do not know what to say; my opinion is that the rewards, with regard to the receivers, would be very proper. I want to induce people to detect receivers, because that is the chief foundation of all the crimes.

Have you heard that portions of the Metropolis are divided into a species of walk for different gangs of pickpockets?—Yes, I have been informed that the town is divided into different walks for gangs of pickpockets.

The ordinary punishment now awarded for confirmed pickpockets, is transportation for life?—Yes, that has always been my rule; seldom or never for the first offence, but whenever I have found them to belong to a gang, or are confirmed bad characters, I transport them for life. I hold in my hand an Account of the Acts of Parliament under which the Rewards are claimed.

[It was delivered in, and read, as follows:]

A LIST of REWARDS given by Acts of Parliament on the Conviction of Offenders.

4 Wm. & Mary, cap. 8, intituled, " An Act for encouraging the apprehending of Highwaymen."—Forty Pounds upon conviction of every Highwayman.

6 & 7 Wm. III. cap. 17, intituled, " An Act to prevent counterfeiting and clipping the Coin of this Kingdom."—Forty Pounds upon conviction of every person who

have

have counterfeited the Coin, or clipping, &c. the same, or shall bring into the king- *Sir John Silvester,* dom any clipt or counterfeit Coin. *Bart.*

5 ANNE, cap. 31, intituled, " An Act for the encouraging the Discovery and Apprehension of Housebreakers."—Forty Pounds upon the conviction of every Burglar or Housebreaker.

14 GEO. II. cap. 6, intituled, " An Act to render the Laws more effectual for the preventing the stealing and destroying of Sheep and other Cattle."—Ten Pounds upon the conviction of every Sheepstealer, &c.

15 GEO. II. cap. 28, intituled, " An Act for the more effectual preventing the counterfeiting the current Coin of this Kingdom, and the uttering or paying false or counterfeit Coin."—Forty Pounds upon the conviction of any person of Treason or Felony relating to the Coin, upon this Act; and Ten Pounds upon conviction for counterfeiting Copper Money.

16 GEO. II. cap. 15, intituled, " An Act for the more easy and effectual conviction of Offenders found at large within the Kingdom of Great Britain, after they have been ordered for Transportation."—Twenty Pounds upon the conviction of a person returning from Transportation before the expiration of the term for which they were ordered to be transported.

Has the number of offenders that have been brought lately before you, to be tried at the Sessions, been unusually great?—Yes.

How many had you last Sessions?—I think we had nearly three hundred.

Do you recollect the number the Sessions before?—No, I do not.

What should you consider as the average number of cases, in times less weighed down by criminal offences than the present?—That I cannot say, because they fluctuate; they have been gradually increasing of late years.

Do you recollect the proportion of the number of cases of offenders that were brought before you at the last Sessions for privately stealing?—I cannot tell.

Was it very considerable?—Yes, there was a great many. Many of these pickpockets are indicted for stealing from the person; some of them are indicted for highway robbery, because they used force; so that there is no saying exactly how many there were.

The offences however were not heavy, in general?—No.

Do you recollect how many were sentenced to capital punishment?—Two and thirty, and I have each man's case to draw up.

Joseph Merceron, Esquire, again called in, and Examined.

I HAVE seen an extract from the Poors Rates of 1813, of the parish of Bethnal *Joseph Merceron,* Green, and I see inserted in it a charge made by Messrs. Dann & Crossland for *Esq.* 925*l.* 1*s.* 3*d.*; was that your attorney's bill for the prosecution brought against you by the Rector of the parish?—It was the attorney's bill for the prosecution brought against me and the collectors; there were two or three, against Cone and myself and Billington.

Was that paid by a vote of the vestry?—A vestry was expressly called for that purpose, I think.

I see also, an account, of the 2d of July 1813, 142*l.* 12*s.* 7*d.* paid to May, and on the 9th of October 192*l.* 4*s.* 7*d.* paid to May; do you know on what account those payments were made?—I do not.

Also, on the 17th of May, 200*l.* paid to May; can you state on what accounts those sums were paid?—I cannot answer what they were for.

The whole sum that appears to be paid to May, is 534*l.* in one year?—Yes.

Do you not know what that was for?—I do not know the particulars.

Have you any notion for what those payments were made?—I should suppose it was for parochial business; it must be of course for parochial business; but it will appear by the accounts: You will find much larger sums than these, I believe, afterwards.

What is the salary of May?—He receives 200 *l.* per annum as vestry clerk.

Jovis, 20° *die Junii,* 1816.

The Honourable HENRY GREY BENNET, in the Chair.

John Gifford, Esq. again called in, and Examined.

John Gifford,
Esq.

HAS the business of your Office of late much increased?—Very much indeed; the commitments in December last were double what they were in the preceding December.

Have they gone on increasing for four years past?—They have gone on increasing within the last twelve months.

Can you contrast the number of committals of your Office with the committals of any other of the Police Offices?—The only mode of doing it is by a reference to the Newgate Calendar. I have not compared the number of commitments from our own Office with the number of commitments from other Offices, except at Bow-street. I find the commitments for trial at the Old Bailey at the last Sessions, from our Office, were fifty-five, comprising seventy-two individuals; from Bow-street, they were only twenty-six, comprehending twenty-nine individuals.

Then the difference between these two sums, together with the whole of the number of persons put upon their trial, must be divided among the other Offices?—Yes, and the other Magistrates residing out of the Metropolis: The whole number of the commitments, as it appears by the Newgate Calendar, the last Sessions, were one hundred and seventy.

Is your district more populous than any of the other districts?—Our district is certainly populous; but I have not compared it with the estimated population of other districts, so as to be able to speak with accuracy.

Do you consider that the mass of your population consists of that class of persons who ordinarily commit crimes, meaning the poor and indigent?—It certainly does contain a vast number of poor persons; but the largest number of poor persons of any particular class in our district, is the journeymen weavers, and persons connected with the weaving trade; and I believe, generally speaking, they are as honest a race of people as any in existence, although labouring under very great distress.

Their distress at present is very severe?—It is extremely severe; so much so, that I have reason to believe twelve thousand looms are out of employ.

Do you know how many men are estimated as working either at each loom, or connected with it?—Men, women, and children, I should suppose not less than twenty thousand; perhaps thirty thousand. When I say twelve thousand looms are out of employ, some of those looms are partially employed; but if you estimate the work usually done in those looms, and then deduct the deficiency, it would make a total of twelve thousand looms unoccupied.

In those commitments from your Office, were there many for privately stealing from the person?—I think not for privately stealing; some for open street robberies; indeed one at three o'clock in the afternoon, in the presence of a number of people.

Do you think that the crime of picking of pockets has of late very much increased?—I cannot say that the crime of picking pockets, as far as my observation goes, has increased; but the crime of street robberies, which are properly speaking highway robberies, has very much increased.

You mean by that, picking pockets, attended with violence?—Yes.

Do you think that the desire of persons robbed in the streets to recover their property by offering a reward, rather than by prosecution, tends to encourage or increase the number of street robberies?—If such practice prevailed, of which I am not aware to any extent, it would be productive of that effect.

You have stated, that according to your observation the number of committals for privately stealing from the person has not increased of late years; do you think that
the

the change of the law upon that subject, taking away the capital part of it, has had any effect in diminishing it?—I am not competent to say that; I am not aware of it at all.

Do you think that it would be a considerable furtherance to public justice, if there was a person in the situation of a public prosecutor?—I certainly think it would materially promote the ends of justice, by bringing forward many more prosecutions than are at present brought forward, owing to the dread of the parties at incurring the expense and trouble of a prosecution.

Do you think it would also prevent that of which every day furnishes fresh examples, namely, collusions between parties?—I do think so.

In what way do you think that person ought to be appointed and paid?—I should think the appointment should be vested in the Crown, and he should be paid by the public as the Judges are paid.

He would of course be somewhat in the situation of the Attorney General, who would constantly act for individuals?—Yes, as far as criminal prosecutions are concerned.

He would have the arranging of the evidence, and the leading and conducting the prosecution?—Yes.

Acting in joint capacity of solicitor and counsel?—Yes.

Have you ever heard it to be the opinion entertained in the district in which you attend to license the public-houses, that if a victualler comes there with a recommendation from a particular brewer, he has a better chance of getting a licence than if he comes without?—Unquestionably.

Do you think that the system of brewers connecting themselves, either by mortgage or by purchase, with the different public-houses in the Metropolis, is one greatly injurious to the Metropolis?—I am of opinion that it would be highly desirable that neither brewers nor distillers should be proprietors of public-houses. But I should think that any law that tended to disqualify them from holding such property, in the present state of the trade, would be such an invasion of private property as the British Parliament would be loth to encourage; at the same time I think that if a law were passed having only a prospective operation to prevent Magistrates from granting licences to any houses which shall, after the enactment of such law, become the property of such brewers or distillers, it would have a very beneficial effect, and would, I should think, be equally satisfactory to the brewers and to the public.

In what way do you think the public are prejudiced by the victualling-houses being the property of the brewers?—I think they are prejudiced in this way: that in some instances, brewers of a certain description, I mean men in a little way, who have property in public-houses, can make the publicans take whatever liquor they please to impose on them; and in that way it appears to me the public are injured.

But where the competition is so great as it is in London, would not the consequence of a supply of bad liquor, in the way you speak of, be the means of destroying the property of the brewer who should give such a supply?—In some situations it might, in others it would not.

Do you know whether it is the general practice in the country for the public-houses to belong to the brewers in the neighbourhood?—Pretty generally so.

You say that you think a prospective enactment to prevent the houses that should hereafter become the property of brewers and distillers from being licensed, would have a beneficial effect; but do you not think at the same time it would be an act of injustice towards the brewers, who are called upon to advance money to persons taking the public-houses, the only security they could receive for which was the lease of that house?—I do not think so, because I think it would prevent persons, who have not sufficient property, from carrying on the business of a publican, and from taking public-houses, and that therefore it would secure a better description of landlords.

Do you think that any material objection could be urged, beyond the objection of affecting the property at present vested, to the change of the existing system, by giving to every individual a right, as matter of course, to apply for a licence to set up such spirit-shop or ale-house, subjecting them however to control by a legal enactment, so that, in the case of misconduct, punishment might immediately follow?—I think that the increase of public-houses and of spirit-shops, which would be produced by such a permission, would be a very great evil.

Do you think that such increase would take place; for why should there be more ale-houses and spirit-shops established, than butchers or bakers, or any of the other

trades

John Gifford, Esq.

trades which are necessary to the public?—Because I think that the temptation to consume spirits, by persons who have contracted the habit, is much greater than the temptation to consume meat, or any other necessary article of life, for in proportion as the stomach is accustomed to use ardent spirits, it becomes debilitated, and can with difficulty digest, and is averse to the reception of common food.

Do you not think it also would be the means of lessening the respectable part of the victuallers, and increasing those of the lower description?—I should think it would certainly increase those of a lower description.

Do you think that any alteration in the practice of the entire independence that exists at the present moment between the Police Magistrate and the Constable of the parish, would be an advantage to the police?—I think that if the parish constables were placed more immediately under the control of the Police Magistrates, that if the Police Magistrates were empowered to direct the church-wardens or officers to reward them out of the parochial fund, for extra services and loss of time, very beneficial consequences to the public would ensue. I think also, if Magistrates had the power of dismissing, if not of punishing watchmen, for misconduct, and had a negative at least on the appointment of watchmen, that would be beneficial also to the public. I see constant robberies committed under the very eye of the watchman; I have known frequent instances of thieves passing with stolen property by the stations of watchmen, and consequently when they ought to be in view of them, and of houses being robbed very near those stations, that I am convinced they must have connived at the escape of such thieves and the commission of such robberies.

Do you not think that great public inconvenience is experienced by the refusal of watchmen to assist in the apprehension of offenders because it happens not to be immediately within the district he is ordered to act?—If such is the case, certainly; but I am not aware of it; there can be no doubt that a watchman is bound to quit his district at the cry of Stop thief! and to assist in the pursuit.

John Armstrong, called in, and Examined.

John Armstrong.

YOU are one of the Officers of Worship-street?—I am.

How long have you filled that office?—Since the latter end of 1778.

How long have you filled the situation of a Police Officer?—Ever since the establishment: I was one of those appointed by Mr. Justice Flood, Major Gascoigne, and Mr. Colquhoun, who were the first that came to our Office.

From your observation, do you think there are more offences committed against the public peace and property, than when you first belonged to the Office?—Some offences, such as street robberies, are become very prevalent now.

You mean by street robberies, the taking property by force from the person or by hustling?—Yes, such as men going out to different avenues to watch an old gentleman, meeting at corners, and, as if by accident, running against him, and then he is robbed; and it is impossible, under those circumstances, for their persons to be distinguished.

Do you think the offence of picking of pockets, or stealing privately from persons, has increased of late?—In our neighbourhood there has not been so much of late; ours is a poor district.

But generally speaking, do you think it has increased in other parts of the Metropolis?—From what I have heard reported, and what I have seen attending the Sessions, I think it has.

Do you think that taking away the punishment of death from the offence, has contributed to increase the offence?—I really cannot answer that, from my own knowledge.

Your salary is a guinea a week?—That is the allowance from the Secretary of State.

Independent of other profits that you make from serving individuals?—Yes. When Mr. Justice Nares was at our Office, he was good enough to wait on some gentlemen, and then he gave me to understand that I might put down 5*l.* per quarter for extra duty, which would always be given me while the Magistrates approved of my conduct; which I have done ever since that.

Do

John Armstrong.

Do you receive much from private individuals, either for going out of town, or for attending to their complaints when made at your Office?—When a gentleman applies to our Office, the Sitting Magistrate gives me, or any other person, an order to go; if that gentleman does not remunerate us, we have no allowance from our Office, except supposing we pay coach-hire, 1 s. 6 d.; 2 s. 6 d.; 3 s. or so on; that is repaid us.

In point of fact, are you always, or generally, remunerated by the individual who makes the complaint at your Office?—Mostly.

Do you in general share much in those rewards which are called Parliamentary rewards, for the apprehension and conviction of offenders?—I have in my practice been always dealt with by the Recorder, who has been at the sharing of the rewards, in a very liberal manner.

How much, taking it upon the average of the last few years, do you suppose that you have received a year of those Parliamentary rewards distributed by the Recorder? —The last reward I was paid, was for a man I apprehended in Rose-lane; not knowing of the house being broke open, but stopping him with the property.

The Committee do not ask you what was the last reward you got, but how much you got last year, or the year before that, or the year before that?—I should suppose I might in the course of a year sometimes to my share get 20 l. or sometimes more; three of us generally working together.

Are you satisfied with that mode of payment for your trouble, or should you prefer, that for every specific service the Magistrates should make you a specific payment?—Certainly; leave it with the Magistrate, who would know the merit of his Officer, and what he had done.

John Nelson Lavender, again called in, and Examined.

J. N. Lavender.

YOU have stated in your evidence, that you have seen the watchmen abuse the women of the town, and beat them, for not giving them money?—Yes.

Do you not think that this conduct of the watchmen, in levying a tax upon those unfortunate persons, and of course tolerating and winking at their riotous and disorderly conduct in the streets, is a great public nuisance?—No doubt of it. I think many prostitutes upon the town are servant girls, who have been driven there through the caprice of their masters or mistresses, who frequently discharge them, and refuse to give them any character. I have had many complaints from female servants personally to me upon that subject; I may say, two or three hundred.

Are many of the lower servants in the Metropolis to be considered as belonging to that class?—No, not while they are servants; but I am afraid there are many servants driven to that course of life by the reason I have stated; and the Magistrates have lamented that they have not had it in their power to compel masters or mistresses to give a reason why they dismiss their servants.

Do you think, from your knowledge, that there has been a very great increase of the women of the town in the streets of late years?—I have not made that observation; I have always seen the streets full of them.

Do you think that their conduct has been more disorderly and riotous in the streets than formerly?—I think it has; that they have certainly got more depraved.

Do you not attribute that to the connexion and interest that subsists between them and those whose duty it is to keep the streets orderly?—I think, in some measure, it may.

Do you think that the persons themselves are more depraved, and given to drinking, than formerly?—I think pretty much the same in that way, except in their general habits and conduct there is more horrid language made use of; and I think they are more hardened, and have got to a greater pitch.

From your observation, do you think that the crime of stealing privately from the person, better known by the name of picking pockets, has increased latterly?—No doubt of it; it has a great deal increased, there are so many young thieves now; some of them are quite children, and can scarcely crawl.

To what cause should you attribute this increase of the number of pick-pockets?— I am hardly competent to answer that question.

Should you think that the taking away the capital part of the punishment has had any effect that way?—No, I do not; I think even before they become dexterous pick-pockets, the gallows is not enough to deter them from it.

Do you not think that the taking away the capital part of the punishment has had this effect; that it would induce more persons to prosecute, where death would not be

J. N. Lavender.

the consequence of conviction, than if it was so?—I have no doubt of it; I have heard objections made to prosecutions for that reason, that they do not wish to hang the person.

Do you think that practice which is stated to be prevalent, of offering rewards for the recovery of property, and not by prosecuting the person who stole it, must have a considerable effect in increasing the number of criminals of that description?—Yes; and I think it has an injurious tendency.

Is it not a practice at this moment prevalent?—I rather think it is.

So that an individual who has lost his watch, for instance, will advertise a reward for the watch, and which when he recovers, he pursues the business no further?—That is frequently the case, I have no doubt.

The result of that, of course, is the encouragement of the delinquent?—No doubt.

Do you think that if the collectors of the tolls at the different gates in the environs of the town were obliged by law to register the numbers of coaches, and the names and numbers of carts, that passed through their gates after dusk, and to search such as came through at very unseasonable times with a suspicious appearance, would be the means of facilitating the ends of justice?—I think it would, but I do not know whether you could give them that power.

Do you think that the offences which are committed are of considerable less atrocity of character than formerly?—Yes, I think they are.

Can you give any reason for that?—No, I cannot; there are not so many highway robberies or footpad robberies as there used to be, nor is there so much cruelty as there used to be.

It has been stated to the Committee, that it would considerably augment the value of what is generally termed a Tyburn ticket, if annexed to it was an exemption from military and naval service, superadded to the parochial service which belongs to it now?—It certainly would increase the value of it.

Do you think it would make the possession of it much more valuable in the eyes of the person who was to receive it?—I should think it would; it would depend a great deal upon the person whose hands it got into.

Do you think that if it was generally known that the possession of a Tyburn ticket did protect persons from those two services, it would operate as a greater inducement upon the apprehension of offenders?—No, I do not think it would; it would not add to any thing of that sort.

Do you not think it might induce people to assist in the apprehension of offenders?—It might induce them to assist in the apprehension of offenders, but it would be placing them in the situation that has all along been complained of.

What is the value of a Tyburn ticket of Saint George Hanover Square?—From twenty to twenty-five guineas.

Do you think the value is as much as that, when you consider all the parochial offices are filled by persons of a better description in that parish?—I should think it is worth twenty guineas certainly.

What do you think would be the value of it if it exempted persons from serving in the army and navy?—I hardly know; some persons will give twenty thirty or forty guineas for a substitute, and of course then it would be of considerable value.

The Reverend *Horace Salisbury Cotton*, called in, and Examined.

The Rev. H. S. Cotton.

YOU are Ordinary of Newgate?—Yes.

How many prisoners are there at present in Newgate?—Thirty-one men under sentence of death, and two women, that is including one who has just received a respite; and 397 convicts, males, and 131 females.

Amongst the women, are there any that are advanced in age?—There are two women about 70 years old, but not above two; and about twelve of 60 years old.

Are there any that are particularly young?—There are about six girls who are under sixteen.

Are the two women that are above 70 years of age capitally convicted?—Yes.

How long have they been detained in prison since their conviction?—They have not been above two years.

They were both of them convicted upon the second offence, of passing bad money?—Yes, I think they were.

They

They were the persons, one of them at least whom you mentioned in your evidence last year before the Gaol Committee, whose detention was considered as so burthensome?—I think both of them.

The Rev.
H. S. Cotton.

Considerable alteration has taken place since last year in the prison?—Considerable.

Are the women separated now into classes?—No; there is a feeble attempt to do it, but we have not the means of doing it.

The six girls under sixteen, are they convicted, or for trial?—Some of them are convicted; I can speak to that.

Do you know whether any of them are for trial?—I do not at this moment.

You cannot state whether they may not all be convicted?—I cannot.

But whether they be all convicted or not, they are mixed up with female transports and felons?—Yes.

How many boys have you in the school?—Twenty-six.

What is the greatest number you have ever had?—Thirty-three.

What is the smallest number?—Five.

What are the average ages of the boys you have now in your school?—About twelve years.

When was the school first established?—The 25th of August 1814.

How many have passed through it since its establishment?—One hundred and sixty.

Out of that number, how many have been convicted?—One hundred and ten.

How many capitally convicted of the 110?—Eighteen.

Have any, and how many, been transported for life?—Two.

How many have been transported for fourteen years?—One.

How many for seven years?—Thirty-three.

In how many instances have the judgments been respited, and the boys sent to their friends, or to institutions?—Twenty-three.

What are those institutions?—The Philanthropic, The Refuge for the Destitute, and The Marine Society.

What becomes of the remaining number?—Thirty-three fined or imprisoned in the houses of correction, or whipped, or so on.

Have any of the number before alluded to, been admitted at the school?—Sixteen.

Have you found children benefited by attending the schools, in point of conduct and morals?—Very much indeed.

Are there many of those boys who have repeatedly been in custody?—Four have been repeatedly in custody; upwards of seventy times between them.

Can you state their names?—Burnet, aged nine; Harper, aged twelve; Morn, eleven; and Sweeny, thirteen.

Burnet was capitally convicted, was he not?—He was.

If the Committee mistake not, he was the boy who had been three years on the town, and who was without father or mother?—I think he has a mother.

The two boys Harper and Morn were those boys that travelled down to Portsmouth for the purpose of attending the fair at the head of a gang of boys like themselves?—Yes.

About what time was this?—In the summer-time, when Portsdown fair was held.

Have you had a boy there of the name of Wilson?—Yes.

What age was he?—Fourteen.

Has he been in Newgate lately?—Yes; he was acquitted there, and brought in again on the very same day, convicted, sent to the Refuge, got out from there, and is now in Tothill Fields Bridewell.

Is there a boy in Newgate of the name of Leary?—Yes.

Do you know any thing uncommon concerning that boy, as to the number of times he has been convicted?—He was a very extraordinary boy; I should suppose that he has been in every prison in London, I have had him two or three times in Newgate; he has been under sentence of death with us.

What age is he?—About fourteen.

Is he an intelligent boy?—Very much so; we sent him to the Philanthropic, and from there he has broken out; he has since come in a prisoner, and is now transported for life.

He was in the school, but would not stay there, not approving the discipline?—Yes; he insisted upon going into the yard.

Have you the means of making that separation and assortment in the school which you would think proper, keeping those boys separate from each other who may be

considered

The Rev.
H. S. Cotton.

considered in the first class as young beginners, and in the second as old offenders?—No.

Are they not all stationed together in one long room, in which they eat, drink, and sleep?—At present they are.

Is there a place providing of a different description?—Yes, where we are to have four rooms, and a yard, and a pump.

Shall you then be able to make that separation and classification which is so essentially necessary?—In some measure.

Do you not think that it would be very essential to have some place for the confinement alone of particular individuals?—Certainly.

You must of course be aware that it is quite impossible for a boy of a better class of life than those ordinarily confined under suspicion of crimes, or under conviction of crimes, should be sent there; and at present there is no means of separating them? -No, there is not.

At present have you a lad coming under the description just named?—I have.

Have you no means at present of employing those boys?—I began yesterday to set them to shoe-making, two or three of them.

Have you any doubt that it would be highly advantageous if such employment was furnished?—No doubt whatever, highly advantageous, if it was furnished throughout the prison to men and women as well as boys.

Is it want of room, which is one of the principal reasons why no employment of work is given in the prison?—I believe so.

Have you ever been able to learn from those juvenile depredators, what have been the principal causes and inducements to their committal of the crimes for which they are imprisoned?—I think generally they state, that playing in the streets at buttons is one cause; they begin with that, and then go on to halfpence and money.

Do you not think that want of moral and religious instruction, and the entire want of education, is one of the principal causes?—I do.

Amongst the boys that have passed through your school, have many of them been unable to read, when you first had them?—Many.

Should you think any thing like one half of the number?—I should think about one half.

Have they generally stated to you (those who have been able to read) any thing concerning the schools which they attended?—Yes; they have said that they had companions in those schools, who had gone out with them on an evening.

There was a Report drawn up on that subject, which was submitted to one of the Sheriffs, was there not?—There was.

Did you ever have any answer that was sent from the schools against which complaints were made, to the charges which were alleged against them upon the evidence of those boys?—I had, in one or two instances.

Did you consider those charges as answered in their defence?—Not any one, that I saw.

Do you not think that the practice which prevails in many of those schools, of boys and girls going and coming at the same hour to the evening schools, as likely to lead to those results which you had in evidence from the boys?—To every evil result.

Do you know whether, in any of those schools, there is a want of distinction kept between the sexes of the children, so that they are taught in the same room?—I have understood so, but I do not know it of my own knowledge.

Of the boys that you have in your school, did they not many of them, even of a very early age, profess to keep what are termed flash-girls, which they supported out of their thefts?—All of them. Burnet, who is only nine years of age, has also a person whom he terms his girl.

Has it not often happened, that persons have presented themselves at Newgate, calling themselves sisters and relations of the boys, who had been prevented afterwards from coming, from its being found out that they were common prostitutes, and kept by the boys?—Repeatedly.

From your information that you have obtained, do you not consider the facility of disposing of stolen property, even to the smallest amount, is one of the principal causes of theft?—Yes.

Has it not come to your knowledge that pawnbrokers will take any thing of children, even of six and seven years of age?—It has; there was an instance only last Sessions, of a pawnbroker being obliged to confess that he took a pledge from

a child

The Rev.
H. S. Cotton.

a child very young, when he had before stated he had taken it from a young man of nineteen, for which he received a severe lecture from the Judge.

Amongst boys that are committed to Newgate, is the crime of picking pockets one of the most prevalent?—Yes.

What next in the order of crimes?—Shoplifting.

And occasionally housebreaking?—Yes.

Do you not think that though you have taken away boys at an early age from associating with the felons and convicts in the other yards, that the number of boys that are still left above the age that are admitted to your school, mixed indiscriminately with classes of the worst description, old offenders, convicts, transports, and known thieves, to be the means of corrupting the morals, and taking away even the little good that may be left in the dispositions of those boys?—Undoubtedly.

Do you think in the present state of the gaol, for want of room, that there is any possibility of making that classification and separation of offenders which would tend to prevent this?—There is no possibility at present.

When the new plan is carried into execution, will there then be room sufficient?—There will be some sort of attempt at classification.

What is the new plan of alteration of the prison?—The debtors are removed to another gaol, and the space is now taken for convicts.

How many debtors were removed to the new gaol?—I should think about 400; but I am speaking at random.

Are you of opinion that the gaol of Newgate, now the debtors are removed, is sufficiently large for the convenient classification and accommodation of the convicts?—No; I would not allow more than ten together.

Is the punishment of transportation much dreaded by those who are sentenced to it?—By some, but not at all by others.

More by women than men, or *vice versa*?—I cannot say.

Have there not been instances on the women's side, of persons who wished to be transported?—Yes, volunteers.

Did you ever know an instance of a person committing a crime for the express purpose of being conveyed to New Holland?—I recollect a man of the name of Warren Carr, who robbed Mr. Thornton.

Had he no other reason, that you know of, besides the mere wish of getting out of the country, to induce him to commit the crime?—Yes, his wife had been transported three or four Sessions before, and he wished to join her; he had repeatedly applied at the Secretary of State's for leave to go out to her, and when he found he could not go out to her, he determined to commit a crime for which he would be transported.

In general it is a punishment much more dreaded by the old than by the young?—It is very little dreaded by the young.

Amongst the boys, the punishment is dreaded but little?—Very little.

They consider it more a party of pleasure or an expedition, than any thing else?—Yes, often that is the case; they hear tales told in the gaol of what a fine country it is, and how well they shall be off there.

Of course the more it becomes popular, the less it answers the purpose of a punishment?—I should think so.

Do you know whether many persons return to Newgate, who have been transported to Botany Bay, their time being over, or who have been discharged from the hulks?—Yes, many have.

So that it is a common thing that persons who have come from the one place or the other, should commit a fresh crime and be brought back to Newgate?—It is not an uncommon thing.

Is there not an expression which is common in Newgate, describing a person of that description, calling him a " family man?"—Yes.

Are there any instances of persons who have been transported a second time?—Yes, I think there are.

Robert

Robert Owen, Esq. called in, and Examined.

HAVE you had much experience in directing and superintending the conduct of the lower orders among the working class?—Yes.

For how many years?—Upwards of twenty-five years; during the whole of which period I have had from five hundred to upwards of two thousand persons under my immediate direction.

What particular description of persons were they?—Men, women and children, who were employed chiefly in cotton factories; mechanics, belonging to almost all trades; and many others, engaged in the usual occupations of common life.

From whence were the men, women, and children taken, whom you have employed in cotton mills?—Very often from amongst the most ignorant, wretched, and helpless in society.

Were they principally Scotch, or mixed with Irish and English?—Chiefly Scotch; many from the North Highlands of Scotland, with some Irish, and very few English.

Have these persons, by your direction of their labour and partial expenditure, been able to maintain themselves?—Yes; upwards of two thousand, on an average of seventeen years, have been placed under such arrangements as to support themselves during that period without any one of them receiving, up to the time I left them in March last, one shilling relief from the parish; and they support themselves in sickness and in old age as well as in health.

In what manner do they support themselves in sickness and in old age?—By a fund which they raise among themselves, by contributing one-sixtieth part of their wages.

Is it in the nature of a Saving Bank?—Not precisely so.

Is the money vested in your hands, or vested according to their own discretion, as they think fit?—It is distributed according to the rules which the most respectable of them formed themselves several years ago; and those individuals now superintend the distribution of this money, according to their own rules: they have it entirely under their own direction.

Then it is in the nature of a benefit club?—Yes; but still different in many respects from that.

Have those persons had regular employment during the whole period of seventeen years?—Except for four months in 1808, when, in consequence of an embargo in the American ports, it became imprudent in us to manufacture cotton at the high price to which it advanced.

What became of the population during that period?—The proprietors gave them subsistence.

In what manner?—They paid them their full wages during the whole time.

What was the amount you expended?—As near to 7,000 *l.* as I can calculate.

Upon what principle did you recommend this measure?—On the principle of preventing crime, and its consequent misery; because if the poor cannot procure employment, and are not supported, they must commit crimes, or starve; and I have always considered that 7,000 *l.* to have been more advantageously expended than any other part of our capital.

What do you consider the chief immediate cause of temptation to intemperance, idleness, vice, and misery, among the poor and working classes?—The spirit-shops and small pot-houses; the former I consider to be a great national evil, and therefore a scandal to the Government that permits their continuance; and the latter appear to me to be injurious, though in a less degree, and to be wholly unnecessary.

Do you not think that, taking into consideration the coarse food which the lower orders of people live upon, that spirits, or something like spirits, or malt liquor, is essential to enable the stomach to digest that food?—I consider malt liquor to be absolutely necessary for them under many circumstances; but it has always appeared to me much better that some arrangement should be made by which the poor could obtain it at home, rather than be subject to associate in public-houses.

What in your experience have you found to be the next temptation leading to evil among the lower orders?—The Poor Laws, as they are now put into practice.

In what respects have you found them so great an evil?—By affording direct encouragement to idleness and profligacy of every description.

Of

Robert Owen, Esq.

Of course when you are speaking of the effect of the Poor Laws, you are not speaking of your own experience at Lanark, but the result of your experience in England?—The result of my experience in Manchester.

Can you explain by individual cases, in what way the Poor Laws operate so much against the public good?—In my own experience I have known workmen who in the years 1791 and 1792 could and often did earn from three to four pounds per week, and in 1793 were upon the parish, and themselves and families supported regularly from the funds raised under the name of the poor rate, in the town of Manchester; and similar proceedings, though not perhaps of so marked a nature, have occurred from that time to the present.

Do you think that that circumstance arose from any particular improvidence of the individual, or from the great commercial distress which fell upon that district which you have last mentioned, by which thousands were thrown out of employment?—It arose from a combination; but if those individuals had not been led to depend upon the support from this adventitious fund when they were in the practice of earning from three to four pounds per week, they would have made a different domestic arrangement, and expended twenty or twenty-five shillings a week, and put by the remainder, against a time of difficulty.

Have you any other cause of evil and temptation to mention?—Yes, though it is less extensive in its effects; I mean the State Lotteries, as they are calculated to deceive the ignorant and the unwary, and to legalize the principle of gambling; no government who really wishes to encourage morals among its subjects, ought to resort to such means for revenue.

From your long experience and attention to the subject, what general measure have you found to be the best aid to your system of domestic police?—The most efficacious, and that which I am now satisfied from experience will be certain in its beneficial effects, is a well-devised system of training and instruction for the poor and working classes, I mean one that shall directly apply to form the habits and dispositions of children from their infancy.

Do you know much of your neighbouring town of Glasgow?—I know it partially.

From your observation there, do you think that the morals of the lower orders of that populous town have improved within these late years?—I think they have.

Are the children better educated?—Yes.

Will you state generally, whether you think that the population of that district is on the advance in point of moral influence, or on the decline?—Until within these last two or three years I think the population of Glasgow did not improve in morals; but since the general introduction of Sunday-schools and a system of education, there has been a material apparent improvement in the general appearance of the children.

Martis, 25° die Junii, 1816.

The Honourable HENRY GREY BENNET, in The Chair.

Mr. *William Tooke,* called in, and Examined.

WHAT is the situation you hold?—Deputy Bailiff of Westminster.

Have you turned your attention to the improvement of the Police in that great district of the Metropolis known by the name of the City of Westminster?—I have.

Will you state to the Committee what is the present constitution of the city of Westminster, the form of it, and the mode of its government?—In point of fact, there are two distinct systems in Westminster; there is what is called the Court of Westminster, constituted by Act of Elizabeth, of which the Lord High Steward is the chief, who acts by deputy; and a court of Burgesses and assistants appointed by him, who preside over twelve different wards, into which Westminster is divided. The Act of Elizabeth, and the regulations made by Lord Burleigh, the first High Steward, are stated in the printed Report of a Committee of this House, made in 1812; the privileges and powers of the Court of Burgesses have been by various Acts of Parliament very much reduced, and in point of fact amount at present to little more than the appointment of eighty constables for the preservation of the peace, and of a leet jury for presenting nuisances.

Have they not the management of the sewers and highways?—No; those two departments have been taken away by Act of Parliament, and vested in distinct commissioners for each district; the assize of bread has also recently been taken away from them.

Who appoints the burgesses?—The Lord High Steward.

He has the power of selecting them amongst the principal householders in each ward?—Yes.

Is any emolument or privilege attached to the situation of burgess?—None whatever.

Is any emolument or privilege attached to that of High Steward?—No emolument, certainly; I am not aware of any privilege.

Who is the next officer?—The Lord High Steward ranks first, then his deputy.

What is the situation of the deputy?—He is in the nature of a recorder; he presides at the court.

Who is the deputy?—Mr. Robson, a solicitor; he charges the jury, used to fix the assize of bread; and the situation, when the court was in full operation, was filled by a serjeant at law, or other eminent dignitary of the law.

What causes are brought before the court?—Nothing but presentments of nuisances.

Is there any appeal from the decisions of the court to any other court?—I apprehend not; they amerce upon the presentment of the jury, without appeal. The next persons in the court, after the Lord High Steward and his deputy, are the High Bailiff and his deputy.

Who appoints the High Bailiff?—The Dean alone.

It is a situation that is put up to sale?—It is in the patronage of the Dean, who takes 2000 *l.* for it when it is vacant.

Is that a fixed sum, or does he raise it?—It has not been raised, it has been a fixed sum; but of late it has been transferred and sold by licence, where the life is equal, otherwise the dean has had 2000*l.* On the last appointment he made, he had that sum.

Mr. Morris is now High Bailiff?—He is.

Do you know what are the emoluments of the High Bailiff?—The emoluments and duties of the High Bailiff appear by a Report of a Committee of this House appointed to inquire into that specific subject; by that Report, the sum paid by Mr. Morris for his office appears to be considerably more than the 2000*l.* but that was owing to its being a transaction between him and his predecessor, with the sanction of the Dean.

Who appoints you?—The High Bailiff, with the sanction of the Dean, who approves.

Is

Is your situation one of free gift, or do you purchase it?—One of perfectly free gift, from the friendship of Mr. Morris.

Mr.
William Tooke.

Are the emoluments of your situation settled by salary, or do they arise from fees?—The emoluments of my situation are altogether salary.

Paid by Mr. Morris out of the proceeds of his own office, or from any other source?—Retained by me out of fines received for the High Bailiff, amounting, as stated in the Report to which I have alluded, to 100 guineas a year.

Having given to the Committee the outline of the constitution of Westminster as at present existing, do you think that the establishment so detailed possesses within itself means of being brought into active operation for the better aid of the Police of the City?—Before I answer that, I should notice one other efficient officer of the court, the High Constable, under whose immediate control the eighty constables appointed by the Court of Burgesses are placed.

Do you think those eighty constables sufficient for the duty of Westminster?—By no means.

Is that the whole power which the High Constable possesses, in case he should want the aid and assistance of the householders of Westminster?—That is the whole.

He has not any means of summoning more than eighty?—He has not. And in answer to the question just put, whether the court, as constituted, contains powers of improvement for the general purposes of the Police of Westminster; I apprehend, by some enlargement of the number of constables, and the power of the Court of Burgesses, it might be rendered available for an advantageous improvement in the Police of Westminster.

Can you state to the Committee any particulars upon this subject?—I should conceive that if the court could be assimilated to the system adopted in London, under the Act of 10 George II, that the Court of Burgesses would then be rendered available for the purpose of controlling and giving regulations for the watch of Westminster in its different parishes and wards.

It has been stated to the Committee by a magistrate, that in his opinion a superintendent constable in each parish in the Metropolis would further very much the general interest of the public safety, the other constables of the parish being under his control; would you consider the burgess, whom according to your plan you would constitute the efficient officer, to be placed in a situation similar to that which has been described?—I think it would be more desirable that the High Constable should have three deputies or assistants, dividing Westminster into three districts, that the Court of Burgesses should sit frequently, and those burgesses would be representatives of each ward or parish, and there would be a greater unity of proceeding than by independent constables acting under the authority of the Secretary of State.

In that case you would do away with those different Offices of public Police that have Westminster under their charge?—I should conceive that the most desirable part of the plan; and after having stated the constitution of the court of Westminster, having set out with stating that there were two distinct bodies in Westminster, I have described the court of Westminster; the other body to which I alluded consists of the Police officers and magistrates acting independently of that court.

Then you would think that the burgesses whom you propose to raise into active duty, would be in a similar situation to the aldermen of the city of London, who act as magistrates, and who sit on the bench as such?—Exactly so.

Should you think it advisable that those different burgesses should act gratuitously, or should receive a salary?—It would be desirable that they should act gratuitously.

Do you think that in the different parishes of Westminster a person could be found in each parish who would be qualified by experience to fill the situation you describe necessary there?—I apprehend there could.

Do you apprehend there would be any difficulty in finding persons who would be ready to accept those situations?—I apprehend no difficulty.

Of course the whole internal arrangement of Westminster, its Police in all its details, would be under their charge?—It would.

Who should you propose to preside at the head of the establishment?—The deputy High Steward.

What are the principal objections in the present mode of carrying on the Police in the city of Westminster, that you think your new plan would be calculated to remedy?—The total want of cohesion and union between the several officers and magistrates; the two orders of constables that exist, the eighty appointed by the

510.   court,

Mr.
William Tooke.

court, and the indefinite number sworn in by the Police Offices, and paid by them at the rate of five shillings a day.

Out of what funds does that payment come?—I am not aware from what fund.

No tax levied upon the householders of Westminster?—Not that I am aware of: but it is the source of much disunion on public occasions between the two sets of constables, who more frequently wrangle among themselves, than unite to keep the peace.

Without specifying any particular instance, have you ever seen, of late years, much inconvenience arise to the Public from that disunion you have named?—Not of my own knowledge; it has been reported to me by the inferior officers.

At present, as Westminster is constituted, there is no power in the High Bailiff to put down any disturbance, the extent and character of which is greater than what could be resisted by the force of eighty constables?—There is not.

Have you any doubt that, taking for instance the disturbance of last year upon the Corn Bill, if the High Bailiff had had that power, those assemblages of riotous people about the Houses of Parliament might have been speedily dispersed?— Under the direction of one responsible officer, with power to call out all housekeepers, I conceive it would.

Of course the High Bailiff, finding himself weak in the civil power, is of necessity obliged to look to the military upon every occasion?—He is obliged to look to the military or the magistrates in the first instance, being himself too weak to provide for the security of Westminster.

Is the High Bailiff a magistrate?—No, he is not.

Of course then he must act by the orders of the Magistrates in those cases of disturbance?—By the order of the magistrates, and of his own authority, in the nature of a sheriff for preserving the King's peace. He cannot commit.

Has he not the power, in the character of sheriff, to call out what may be considered as the posse comitatus of Westminster, namely, every housekeeper in it?—I apprehend in extreme cases he might; but I never heard of that measure having been resorted to.

Those eighty constables carry with them a staff that denotes them?—They do.

Do the sworn-in constables by the Magistrates do the same?—Some of them do, smaller ones generally; they carry some ensign of their office.

Is it customary for the Magistrates to select different people in the different parishes, whom upon all occasions, when they want them, they swear in as constables? —I do not know in detail the mode they adopt.

Do you know whether the selection falls upon persons fitted for the situation; should you say that the paid constables are respectable persons?—I am informed they are not equal in respectability to those nominated by the Court of Burgesses, who are housekeepers.

Is there any other evil of Police besides those you have mentioned, that you think would be remedied by a change in the system?—I think that a considerable change in the mode of licensing public-houses in Westminster, would have a very beneficial effect.

Are there not two modes by which they are now licensed, one by the Magistrates on the licensing day, and the other by the Board of Green Cloth?—I believe so.

Can you state to the Committee in what way you think the new system in that respect would be better than the old?—It would contribute, in my opinion, materially to the improvement and the regularity of those houses, if they were licensed by commissioners appointed for that purpose, and not by the magistrates, there being instances in many cases of their being made the subject of considerable difficulty, unless they happen to be in particular connexion with a brewhouse: and great abuses have existed and do exist in the licensing of public houses, particularly down the River, which would be entirely obviated, and the character of the Magistrates much improved, by the licensing being removed altogether out of their control.

Who do you think should nominate those commissioners, and of what class of men should they be composed?—With submission, I should suppose it should be the Secretary of State for the Home Department, and gentlemen with independent salaries appointed, altogether out of trade, or connexion with trade.

Why do you think that the commissioners would be less under any improper influence which the brewers and distillers are now suspected to have over some of the magistrates, than the magistrates themselves?—From the pledge and responsibility of their character, and their being immediately removeable in the event of any mis-

conduct

conduct on their part; if regulated in the way the Commissioners of Hackney Coaches are, I should apprehend the evil would not exist of any undue collusion with the brewers or distillers; at present they are much too near in contact.

Is it not a matter of general public notoriety, of course one that is very difficult to be distinctly proved, namely, that there are, in almost all the licensing districts, brewers who have obtained that species of influence, that a victualler coming under the protection of one of them, has a better chance of obtaining a licence than if he stood in a situation claiming it as a free house?—I have always understood that to be the case.

It is of course known to the victuallers themselves, that it is better to have a friend such as has been described, than to stand on their own bottom?—Undoubtedly.

Can you state to the Committee any cases that have fallen under your own observation, that have led you to form the opinion you entertain, beyond mere ordinary report?—I could particularly specify the hamlet of Poplar, Blackwall, and Limehouse, as being particularly under the influence alluded to.

You have, then, in that division no doubt that the brewers have an influence over the Magistrates, in keeping what houses they choose licensed, and in licensing as many as it is their interest to license?—No doubt, and excluding all others who are not within that connexion.

Can you state to the Committee an outline of a plan of Police for the better government of the Metropolis, of which you consider Westminster to be a principal member?—I have considered that, if practicable, it would be desirable that Westminster, being assimilated in its government to the city of London, and the Middlesex parishes, which are perhaps equal in proportion to Westminster, being also governed in a similar manner, their constituted authority assembling at Hicks's Hall, there would be then an unity of design; and those three co-ordinate powers, consisting of the Lord Mayor of London, the deputy High Steward of Westminster, and whatever name might be given, Chairman, or otherwise, of the Chief Magistrate of Middlesex, with an immediate reference and constant communication with the Secretary of State for the Home Department, or his under Secretary, specially appointed for that sole purpose, might give such prompt information of irregularities, and would operate so much as a check upon offences in the nature of prevention, and afterwards of prompt punishment in case of commission, as would very much tend to improve the security of the whole Metropolis.

Of course then you have in contemplation the putting down the different Police establishments in the Metropolis?—I think they would be rendered useless by the execution of such a plan.

Are you aware that there is any superiority in the Police of the city of London, managed as it is after a plan somewhat similar to the plan you propose to adopt in Westminster, over this part of the town, which is under the Police Offices?—Unquestionably there is an unity of design, and a general superintending control and responsibility on the part of the head officer of London, which does not exist in Westminster or Middlesex, and therefore evasion is rendered much easier on the part of the offender.

Do you think that there are a greater number of offences committed in this end of the town, and that, when committed, go unpunished, than in the city of London?—There are more brothels and more irregular public-houses in Westminster than in London; I believe that is an ascertained fact.

In point of fact are there many houses in the city of Westminster that are known to be of the very worst description?—Many.

Do you consider those houses as tolerated by the Magistrates as places where the thieves can resort, and where so resorting they can be found, or as existing in the state that they are unknown to them?—I consider them as an evil resulting from the loose state of the Police, without any imputation on the Magistrates: But the great advantage that I should propose by the plan above suggested would be, that the court of burgesses would have some efficient officer in the nature of a city solicitor, who then might, upon public grounds, prosecute what is now left to individuals to present as nuisances. It is a source of great protection to the city of London that the chief magistrate, upon his own information and from his own knowledge on facts stated before him, can direct the officer of that corporation to prosecute, at the city charge, houses of that description.

Do not you know that upon any two individuals giving security of 20*l.* to the parish, that parish is bound to prosecute any house of ill fame, against which an indictment should be found?—I was not aware of that.

Are

Mr.
William Tooke.

Are you not aware that the difficulty is not in the prosecution, but in the means of obtaining conviction?—I am not particularly acquainted with the detail of these matters, but I apprehend that the establishment of such an officer would check and prevent the existence of such nuisances.

You must be aware that the difficulty is in getting that species of evidence of the nature of those houses that the jury will credit; how do you think that the appointment of another officer to prosecute would remedy that inconvenience?—I am not so immediately aware of the difficulty in the evidence, I should more fear an indisposition to prosecute.

But if according to the law as it now stands, parishes are bound to prosecute upon two individuals becoming security for the expense, in what way do you think that the appointment of a public prosecutor, and the charges of the prosecution being paid in another manner, would further the object you have in view?—Because I should conceive that it would be an invidious and almost a dangerous task on the part of any two individual housekeepers in a parish to originate a prosecution of that sort, independently of their being deterred by the very circumstance of the trouble and risk of entering into that security.

Then it is your opinion that the reason that it is not done, is made up of two causes; first, the expense, and secondly, the odium of the character of an informer?—Exactly so.

So that if there was a legal officer, whose duty it was to do it, upon proper information being laid before him, much of the present bad system upon those subjects would be remedied?—I conceive it would.

Do you know whether the office of coroner is appointed by the Dean and Chapter, by charter, or by prescription?—That I do not know; Mr. Vincent, their chapter clerk, might be referred to upon such a point.

They claim the power of appointing also a deputy; are you aware of it?—I have observed it; I did not know it till lately. To recapitulate the three distinct branches which I have before endeavoured to state, as the means of improving the state of the police of Westminster, I would notice, first, the assimilating the court of burgesses to the court of aldermen, by giving them powers similar to those given to the aldermen by the Act of 10 George II.; secondly, the increasing the number of constables to at least 200, and placing them under the control of one responsible officer; thirdly, the new modelling the system of licensing public-houses, by the appointing of special commissioners for that purpose solely; and lastly, by constituting a similar jurisdiction to that of the court of aldermen and burgesses, in that remaining part of the Metropolis which lies in the county of Middlesex.

How many householders are there in Westminster?—I have always known them computed at 14,000; and upwards of 12,000 have voted as such, paying scot and lot in Westminster. I should not be afraid to estimate the gross population of Westminster at 200,000. The plan of Police suggested by me must be considered as altogether prospective, and as merely implying an efficient deputy high steward at an adequate salary, a court of burgesses and assistants properly qualified by property and ability, and an able high constable with three assistants to be also adequately paid; the court so constituted, to have the power of levying money by rate. And incidentally a considerable benefit might accrue to the good government of Westminster, by enabling the court of burgesses to levy a rate for defraying the proper and necessary expenses of elections of members of Parliament to serve for the city of Westminster.

John Thomas Barber Beaumont, Esq. again called in, and Examined.

J. T. B. Beaumont,
Esq.

IN your former evidence, you gave an opinion in favour of establishing asylums for deserted children; if such asylums were formed, what legal powers would you think necessary for the separation of such children from their bad connexions?—I assume as a principle, that where the authority with which parents are naturally invested for the well-being of their children, is grossly neglected or perverted to their harm and that of society, the good of both requires that it should cease; and that society to which those children are to become an aid or a disturbance, in self-defence ought to stand in the parents place, and put the children in the way of becoming useful members of society. I should therefore propose that any peace or parish officer should be empowered to take children begging or wandering in indigence, before a magistrate; the magistrate in his discretion to commit provisionally. If in a certain time the parents do not claim the children, and give satisfactory assurance

of

of their capacity and disposition to take care of them, that two magistrates may *J. T. B. Beaumont, Esq.* then make an order for the settlement of the children permanently; all right of the parent over the child then to cease, all access to be denied, and a new surname to be given to the child in the place of its paternal one; provided that the children may be restored to their parents upon proof of subsequent ability and inclination to bring them up in the right way.

Do you not see that in a great population, which is one of the causes of the distress arising among the lower orders of people, and the consequent crime which follows upon such distress, you would by this means give a bounty to parents to desert their children, as well as a bounty to early marriages, without having the means of supporting the offspring, the result of them?—I think not. I think that the disgrace of having their children separated from them, upon the grounds and in the manner I have stated, could never be anticipated as a motive of encouragement to early marriages; and I think further, that no parents, excepting the extremely profligate, would be induced to abandon their children in consequence of the asylum which I advocate.

You have also observed, that you thought much of the waste of time in attending prosecutions at the Sessions might be saved, by exhibiting lists showing the order of trials; have you ever proposed any thing of the kind at the Sessions?—Yes; I have in my pocket a copy of the resolutions which I have prepared, and they stand for decision at the next Sessions.

[It was delivered in, and read, as follows:]

" THAT the bills of indictment be numbered; that the grand jury be requested to take them up in numerical order; and that a list of the bills be made up as referred, and hung in the hall.

" That as bills of indictment are found, the cases intended for hearing at Clerkenwell in the same session, be entered in a list in numerical order, and hung in the hall.

" That bills 'for trial at the Old Bailey,' be entered in another list, and hung in the hall.

" That bills ' not found' be entered in another list, and hung in the hall.

" That the cases be taken up according to their numbers, excepting when very special reasons appear to the contrary; and that as they are disposed of, they be marked off in the list."

I would observe, that as it is, witnesses crowd about the door of the grand jury room, watching every motion of it, in expectation of being called, for many days oftentimes before their bill is taken up. When the bills are brought into court, the crier declares upon each, whether it is found or not; but as few of the witnesses can be in court, and of an evening seldom any persons besides the officers of the court are present, the notice then given is merely nominal; parties, whose bills are thrown out, remain ignorant of the fact, and continue in attendance until the end of the Sessions; and those whose bills are found, have to wait constantly upon the listen for the calling of their names. They may be kept in this state of suspense for a week; but as they cannot be on the watch, nor witnesses kept together without intermission so long, it not unfrequently happens that when called on they are not within hearing; the evidence is thus lost, and offenders escape.

How is the table of fees settled at the Middlesex Sessions?—I do not know. We have no table of fees, that I ever saw; I have often inquired about them, but could never learn how they were fixed, or what became of them.

Do you know the reason why there is no table of fees settled for Middlesex, as for the county of Surrey and other neighbouring counties?—I believe the law ordains that the fees of Quarter Sessions should be fixed by the Judges of the Assizes; but as there are no Assizes in Middlesex, the fees cannot be fixed in that manner, or table of fees ought certainly to be settled and exhibited.

In point of fact, are not the fees in Middlesex much less than those in Surrey?— I do not know.

In your former evidence, you spoke of some serious difference that had subsisted between you and the Tower Hamlet Magistrates; were those differences of a public nature, and referrable to the Police?—I think they were; they arose from complaints of extortion on the part of their agents. I will describe one or two of them, and the Committee may then judge. A large common sewer runs through the fields at Mile End, I wished to make a covered drain leading into it; I was told I ought to apply to the Justices and local Commissioners of Sewers for leave. I did so in 1812. Their clerk called on me, and said, there were two ways of having

J. T. B. Beaumont,
Esq.

permission, the one would answer my purpose, the other would not; for the first mode, and to have it directly, a fee of 50*l.* would be expected. I refused this, and preferred a complaint at the Police Office, before Sir Daniel Williams; he referred me to Mr. Merceron, as the person who managed the sewer business. Mr. Merceron said, it must be a mistake; I then desired an audience at the next meeting of the Commissioners of Sewers, when I might confront the person who called on me. I attended, and sent in my card three or four times to Mr. Merceron, when, after waiting an hour, the clerk came out to me, regretted I should have made the complaint, and said, that what was asked was not in the way of a demand, but an appeal to my liberality, that if I thought 50*l.* too much, perhaps I might not object to 5*l.* as there would be some expenses on the survey; I said I should be willing to pay for whatever trouble I gave, and went away, as I found it was uncertain whether I should be admitted. In the end, a permission was withheld for six months, and then was made out in a way that was of no use to me; and until this day I have not been able to make the drain. Another and a more serious difference arose out of my making a complaint against a person holding an office of trust, and much in communication with those Justices, who, as he said, on their behalf applied to me for 400*l.* for the licence of a public-house. This person is now dead, and I therefore did not mean to have adduced the case; but as I found that Mr. Robson has made gross misrepresentations of it, I may be permitted to narrate the facts. In August 1814, a Mr. Smallwood, surveyor of property tax in White-chapel, called upon me with an offer to secure the licensing of my public-house; he said that two of the Justices were in want of four or five hundred pounds, and if I would advance a loan to them, the thing would be done. I rejected the offer with indignation. I said, that I had heard of many similar applications being made to others; that I should soon be a magistrate myself, when I would look into the business, and if I found any of the Justices so mean as to traffic with their licences, I would do my best to unseat them. I then mentioned the application to Mr. Rogers, belonging to the Police Office Whitechapel, observing, that an investigation ought to take place, in order to discover who were Smallwood's employers, if he had any, or to put a stop to his levies on the public in their name, if he had none. I also mentioned, that about a year before, Smallwood had called on me, and asked me to discount a bill of 200*l.* for him, at which time he offered to instruct me in the forms of application for a licence, and spoke of his intimacy with some of the Justices. As the bill had only two or three weeks to run, as Smallwood had just waved an assumed right of way from his garden into my fields, and as I apprehended he might prevent the licensing of my house if I refused so common a civility, I complied, and gave him a check on my bankers for the amount. The bill was paid as soon as due. I also mentioned the complaint to Major Forsteen, a magistrate, and a particular friend of Sir Daniel Williams, telling him, that I had put the case into the hands of Mr. Rogers. Mr. Rogers, I understand, stated my complaint to Sir Daniel Williams in writing, and to Mr. Robson verbally, and pressed for an investigation. This call was answered in a curious way; unknown to Mr. Rogers or myself, Sir Daniel Williams, Mr. Robson, and some other of the magistrates, held a conference with Smallwood, upon which it was entered in their minute book, with much affected formality, that he denied that he had applied to me as I had stated, or that any thing had been said about licensing on either side, but that I called on him, when, *without his asking*, I offered him 200*l.* charging him five pounds for a fortnight's use of it, and that I said " I should soon be a magistrate myself, when I would upset those fellows." It will tire the Committee, I am afraid, to detail only a few of the tricks and evasions employed on this occasion to prevent a full and fair investigation. The first I heard of the recrimination thus got up was on the licensing day. A few days afterwards there was a meeting of Magistrates at Whitechapel, when I attended as one of their body. I had previously written two letters to Sir Daniel Williams, as chairman, urging an immediate inquiry. As soon as Sir Daniel took the chair, I addressed him on the subject of my complaint, but was instantly stopped, I was " out of order;" the first thing was to read the minutes of the last Board; the moment this was done, Mr. Robson rose, and said he had something to say in a matter wherein I was concerned, but had some difficulty as I was in the room; the chairman begged of me to withdraw; I claimed the right of being first heard, but I was again " out of order," as Mr. Robson was on his legs. To avoid noise and rudeness I withdrew. When I returned, I was preparing to revive the subject, upon which the chairman again stopped me, as being again " out of order;" they had determined not to go

further

J. T. B. Beaumont, Esq.

further into the complaint, but had referred their minutes to the Session. At the end of six weeks, a copy of their minutes, but artfully varied so as to suppress the fact that I had originated the complaint, and to make it appear that it was a discovery of their own, was read in the Justices' room at the Sessions. There was a general exclamation, that such a paper ought not to have been sent, and should not be received, in which cry Mr. Merecron and others who had sent it were loudest, upon my warmly entreating the Bench to go into the inquiry. I afterwards endeavoured to revive the inquiry at Whitechapel, without success. I then attempted to commence a suit in law against Smallwood and his friends; but I was stopped, as I was refused all access to their minute book, until it was found that I was on the eve of compelling its production by way of mandamus. In the end I found, upon the best legal and equity advice, that, bad as was the conduct of the parties, the law did not reach them; and as regarded my public-house, unless I made my peace with them in some way, they might keep it shut up for ever, for any relief I could gain from the laws.

Why did you think Smallwood could prevent the licence being granted to your public-house?—From the representation he made of his intimacy with the Magistrates.

What were the reputed circumstances of Smallwood, when he made the application to you for the 200 *l*.; and what was his situation?—I had only seen him once before, and that was upon my requesting him to stop up a garden gate which opened into my fields; and at that time I knew nothing more of his character, than that he was a surveyor of property tax.

Are you in the habit of discounting bills for persons of whom you know so little as you did of Mr. Smallwood?—No, nor of any other person; excepting sometimes as a favour, and that very seldom indeed.

When you discounted the bill, what did you deduct for the interest?—I deducted nothing; I gave him a check for 200 *l*. and here is an entry, in my bankers book, of its being paid [*producing it;*] and here is the check itself.

[*It was delivered in, and read, as follows :*]

Messrs Hankey & Co.

56 Pall Mall.   London, Sep. 6, 1813.

Messrs Morland, Ransom & Co. Pay Thos Smallwood, Esq. or Bearer, Two hundred pounds.

J. T. Barber Beaumont.

£. 200.

What did he pay you for the loan of the money?—Nothing. In respect to the circumstances of Mr. Smallwood, as I learned afterwards, I have heard some of the Magistrates, who were commissioners of property tax, I think Mr. Flood or Mr. Windle, say that his gains on surcharges had amounted to some thousand guineas a year; he was a man who lived in an expensive way, and had somewhat the exterior of a gentleman; he had been in the army.

Who were Messrs. Flood and Windle?—Mr. Flood is a painter and glazier in Whitechapel; Mr. Windle has been unfortunate in trade, I do not know what he is doing now.

Are they magistrates?—Yes.

Both of them Middlesex magistrates?—Both of them.

Is there any other public-house on your land at the East end of the town, besides the one which in your former evidence was described?—Yes, there is one on my Limehouse estate; I have between forty and fifty new houses on that property; I applied in vain to get it licensed, and as the Justices licensed a house very near to it in the interest of Messrs. Hanbury, I gave up all expectations of seeing mine licensed, and had it let in tenements. It however happened that the owner of the other house crept out of his agreement with Hanburys, and sold the lease of the house to another interest. Mr. Aveling, the manager of Messrs. Hanburys' brewhouse, then wrote to me, to know on what terms I would grant them a lease of my house; I agreed to grant them a lease for sixty-one years; and the house was licensed. I beg to add, that I have never expressed a wish for the licensing any other house in the Tower Hamlet division, and that I never had any interest in any public-houses, excepting the two I have stated, and one on my land at Shepherd's Bush, which is at the opposite extremity of the Metropolis; I have upwards of fifty houses on my land there. On each

J. T. B. Beaumont, Esq. estate, my own tenants were sufficient to maintain the public-house which I provided for them, but I could not get one licensed. A brewer taking one of those houses, succeeded differently. They cost me between five and six thousand pounds, and the greater part of that sum I have in a manner lost in the attempt to have a respectable and free public-house on each of my estates.

What do you mean by saying you have lost between five and six thousand pounds in attempting to get your public-houses licensed?—Because houses built expressly for public-houses, and best adapted for that use, are oftentimes and generally very ill suited for any other local purpose. Such is the case with mine; and the two houses at Mile End and at Shepherd's Bush, have both continued empty from the time they were built until now.

Did those two houses cost you between five and six thousand pounds?—Those two cost me about four thousand pounds; they are very capital houses.

It has been stated, that the greater part of the three hundred and fifty new houses in and near White Horse Lane, were mere empty shells on the last licensing day, which is the excuse given by one of the Magistrates for not having himself assented to the licence being granted; do you admit that fact?—There were only eight houses that were unfinished, and only about six others uninhabited; by far the greater part of those houses have been tenanted about three years.

It has been stated by Mr. Robson, that that conversation which you in your former evidence informed the Committee had taken place between you, relative to his recommending Mr. Hanbury to you, as a person to supply your public-house, and that as such you would have his Mr. Robson's support at the licensing day, never in point of fact did take place, and that the whole of it is a false statement on your part; do you still maintain before the Committee, that the conversation stated in your former evidence took place?—The evidence I gave before the Committee, was upon a full and careful recollection of the facts, and is strictly true; part of it may be cleared up, I should conceive, by the Committee calling before them Mr. Davis, in whose presence Mr. Robson decidedly advocated at that time the licensing of the house.

The statement, if the Committee recollect right, is this, that when you had agreed with Mr. Hanbury for the taking of your house, you had Mr. Robson's support for the licensing; the moment that that agreement broke off, Mr. Robson ceased to give you that support?—Yes; that is the substance of it.

Do you still stand to that statement?—Decidedly.

It has been stated to the Committee, that you are what is termed a speculator in houses; is that the case?—By no means, I conceive; I never bought a house or sold one. I am an owner of land, at each end of the town, which, in the growth of the Metropolis, has been taken for building purposes; I have employed a large capital in assisting those who have built on it, and in building thereon myself; in doing this, I have done no more than has been done by Mr. Portman, the Duke of Portland, and other owners of land in the neighbourhood of London, on a larger scale.

Mr. *Thomas Single*, called in, and Examined.

Mr. Thomas Single. WHAT are you?—A builder.

Do you live near White Horse Lane?—I live in White Horse Lane.

Do you know whether the greater part of the new houses near White Horse Lane were, on the first of September last, mere empty shells?—I am sure there were not more than eight or nine that stood in the carcass.

Were the greater part inhabited at that time?—Yes; there was about that quantity uninhabited, to the best of my recollection.

Is there any public-house in that neighbourhood?—Not very near.

How near is the public-house to where the greater number of houses are?—There is not one very near.

How near?—Perhaps two or three hundred yards.

Has a public-house been wished for in that neighbourhood?—Very much, I believe, by all the inhabitants.

Has any petition been signed by them, praying for a public-house?—Yes.

How long ago was the petition sent?—Before last September.

But no public-house was licensed in consequence?—No.

Sir *Samuel Romilly*, a Member of the Committee, was Examined.

DO you know whether the repeal of the Act of Queen Elizabeth, which punished the crime of privately stealing from the person with death, has caused an increase or a diminution of the crime?—I do not believe that the repeal of the Act has caused any increase of the crime, and on the contrary, I believe that as far as it has had any operation, it has prevented the commission of the crime. Having myself brought into Parliament the Bill for making that alteration in the law, I have taken great pains to ascertain, as far as I have been able, what effects it has produced. Upon examining the returns which have been made to the House of Commons, of the trials and convictions of prisoners at the Old Bailey, I find that a much larger proportion of persons charged with picking pockets have been convicted since the capital punishment was taken away, and that their sentences have been much more severe than they were before, and consequently that both the certainty and the severity of the punishment have, since this alteration has taken place, been very greatly increased. If it should appear that soon after the alteration of the law, the crime of picking pockets had increased considerably, it would not necessarily follow that that alteration was the cause of the increase. Offenders of this description were very rapidly increasing in number before the alteration took place; and the subsequent increase, if there has been any, may fairly be ascribed to those causes, whatever they were, which operated before the capital punishment was abolished. In 1805 (and the returns do not go further back) there were only 23 persons indicted at the Old Bailey for privately stealing from the person; in 1806, there were 35; in 1807, 37; and in the first six months of 1808 (the Act which repealed the Statute of Elizabeth having received the Royal Assent on the 30th of June) there were no fewer than 31 persons indicted for that offence, being at the rate of 62 in the year. It appears that within the same period, and since the passing of the Act, the whole number of criminals in the Metropolis, charged with different offences, have greatly increased. The number of persons committed for trial at the Old Bailey in 1806, was 899; the number in 1807 had increased to 1017; in 1808 to 1110; in 1809 to 1242; in 1810 it was 1214; in 1811, 1252; in 1812 it had increased to 1397; in 1813 it was 1478; and in 1814, 1413; being a gradual increase, upon 899 persons, of 499, or more than one half; and the same causes which have produced the increase of other larcenies must have operated with respect to the crime of stealing from the person. As a proof that it is not to the repeal of the capital punishment, that the increase of the crime of picking pockets, if it has taken place, is fairly to be ascribed, I may refer to what has taken place with respect to the crime of stealing privately in a shop property to the value of 5 *s*. It appears from the returns which I mentioned before, and from which I have had a Table extracted, which I will produce, that in the Metropolis that crime has gone on increasing in a regular progression during the last 9 years, till the number tried in the last of those years at the Old Bailey is three times as many as were tried in the first of them. If the capital punishment had been taken away, with respect to that crime, it would have been confidently stated that that abolition had been the cause of this increase of criminals; but as the crime of shop-lifting still remains punishable with death, we know with certainty that it is to other causes that this effect must be ascribed. If therefore the crime of picking pockets had increased since the law was altered, it would not follow that that increase was the effect of the alteration. But I entertain great doubt whether there has been in fact any increase of the crime within the period during which it can be imagined that the alteration of the law operated. The mode in which it has been attempted to prove the fact, is by showing that there have been a greater number of prosecutions for the offence since than there were before the capital punishment was abolished. An increase however of prosecutions does not of itself prove an increase of crimes. One of the strongest grounds relied on by those who proposed the abolition of the capital punishment was, that the extraordinary severity of the law prevented persons, whose property was stolen, from prosecuting; and it was insisted that when the punishment of death was taken away, that unwillingness to prosecute would be removed, and consequently prosecutions would multiply. It appears somewhat a strange mode of proving that any measure has failed of success, to show that it has produced the very effects which were expected from it. If of 100 offences committed before the repeal, only 10 were the subject of prosecution, an increase of the crime would not be proved by showing that prosecutions have increased from 10 to 90. The truth however is, that there are no means of comparing even the number of prosecutions before, with those which have taken place since the repealing Act

510.
was

was passed, because that Act abolished the aggravated offence which had existed from the time of passing the Statute of Elizabeth, namely, stealing privately from the person, and substituted in its place a new aggravated offence, one of a much wider description, and which was intended to comprehend a much greater number of cases, namely, that of stealing from the person, whether privately or not. The reason for thus altering the description of the offence, was, that the privacy of the stealing, requisite to bring the act within the Statute, though it did not in truth constitute the heinousness of the crime, had the effect of greatly confining the operation of the law. If the person robbed perceived the theft while it was committed, the Judges held that it was not done privately; and in many instances the very effrontery with which the crime was committed, protected the delinquent from the more severe punishment which the law had appointed. The difficulty of bringing a case within the Statute was such, that though the crime of picking pockets was frequent, prosecutions, or at least convictions upon the Statute, even if there had been no reluctance in prosecutors or juries to do their duty, never could be very numerous. To remove these defects in the law, the Statute was framed at the suggestion of Sir Thomas Plumer, then Solicitor General, in its present form; and at the suggestion of the same gentleman, the offence by this its larger description was made punishable, not indeed with death, but yet with much greater severity than simple larceny, with transportation for fourteen years, or even for life. The consequence of this alteration of the law has been, not only to remove the unwillingness of prosecutors to indict, but to bring within the aggravated crime described in the new Statute, a very great number of offences, which even the most willing prosecutors never could before have charged as a capital crime, or any otherwise than a simple larceny. Nothing therefore can be more calculated to deceive, than to compare the number of persons indicted since the Act of 1808, for stealing from the person, with those indicted before the passing of that Act, for stealing *privately* from the person. They are quite different offences. I have had a Table extracted from the returns before-mentioned, which I will also produce; and from this it will be seen, that in the half year which elapsed immediately after the Act passed, only 28 persons were indicted for the new offence of stealing from the person, fewer than in the preceding half year had been indicted for stealing *privately* from the person. In the two next years, when, if ever, it should seem that this alteration in the law would have its greatest operation (that being the time when the supposed benefit to offenders, of having the sentence of transportation for life, which would be often executed, substituted in the place of a sentence for death, which never was executed, would make the strongest impression on their minds) it appears that the whole number of persons indicted for stealing from the person was in one of them 99, and in the other only 98. In the following years, indeed, these indictments have greatly increased; in 1811, they were 151; in 1812, 149; in 1813, 189; and in 1814, (which is the last year for which any return has been made) 191. I have already observed, that this increase I ascribe to the same causes, whatever they are, which have of late years occasioned crimes to be so greatly multiplied in the Metropolis. To judge of the probability of the offence having increased in consequence of the alteration of the law, it would be necessary to ascertain whether since the alteration has taken place the offence has not met with more or less impunity than it did before. Now we find, that of 126 persons, the whole number indicted for stealing privately from the person in 1805, 1806, 1807 and 1808, the bills were thrown out by the grand jury as to 49, and consequently only 77 were tried, and of these only 6 were convicted of the aggravated offence charged in the indictment; 35 were convicted of simple larceny, and 36 were acquitted. In 1809, the first year after the law was altered, 99 persons were indicted of larceny from the person; as to 34 of these, the bills were thrown out by the grand jury, and consequently, 65 were tried; and of these, no fewer than 43 were convicted of the whole aggravated crime charged in the indictment; of only 1 was the offence reduced to simple larceny, and only 21 were acquitted. In the next year, 1810, the number of persons indicted at the Old Bailey for larceny from the person, was 98; the bills thrown out were 33; consequently, 65 were tried. Of these, 40 were convicted of the whole charge in the indictment, 1 of simple larceny, and 24 were acquitted. In 1811, there were indicted at the Old Bailey for this offence, 151 persons, of whom 103 were tried, and of these 58 were convicted; of only 2 the offence was reduced to simple larceny, and 43 were acquitted. The alteration which thus took place in the administration of the law, recently after the law had been altered, appears to be very striking, and was not, it

should

should seem, much calculated to encourage men to commit the crime. Before the law was altered, only 6 out of 77 persons, that is about one-thirteenth of the whole number tried, were found guilty of the whole crime of which they were accused ; but after the law was altered, nearly two-thirds were convicted of the crime they stood charged with. In one year, out of 65 tried, 45 were convicted ; in the next, out of 65, forty were convicted. It ought, however, to be observed, that of the 77 persons tried in the three years and a half immediately preceding the repeal of the Act of Elizabeth, although only 6 were capitally convicted, yet of the rest, 35 were convicted of simple larceny, and 36 were acquitted : but from hence it appears that only about half the number tried suffered any punishment, and near half enjoyed complete impunity ; whereas after the law had been altered, two thirds were punished, and only one third escaped all punishment. Of those too, who since the law was altered, have suffered punishment, the punishment has been much more severe than could before be inflicted ; the offenders convicted of simple larceny could not be transported for more than 7 years ; but all the persons convicted of larceny from the person, under the law as it is now altered, may be sent into transportation for 14 years, or for life ; and accordingly, of the 43 persons convicted of larceny from the person in 1809, 6 were actually transported for life, 5 were transported for 14 years, and 23 for 7 years. So in the year 1810, of 45 persons convicted of the whole aggravated charge (for, besides the 40 mentioned before, there were 5 others, who, having been indicted of robbery, were convicted of stealing from the person) 9 were transported for life, 2 for 14 years, and 23 for 7 years. In the last years, the sentences have been still more severe. In 1811, 25 of those who were convicted of stealing from the person were transported for life ; in 1812, 22 ; in 1813, 30 ; and in 1814, 48. That this great diminution of the chance of escape, and this great increase of the severity of punishment, have really operated to allure men to the commission of the crime, it is surely impossible for any one to believe. Among the facts which the returns made to the House of Commons furnishes us with, there is none which, with respect to the crime of stealing from the person, seems more worthy of observation than the very large proportion of bills of indictment preferred for this crime in London and Middlesex, which are thrown out by the grand jury. It seems to be of this crime alone that so great a number of unfounded charges are preferred. In 1809, of 99 bills of indictment for stealing from the person, no fewer than 34 were rejected, being about one-third ; while the bills preferred for all other offences in the same year were 1098, and of those only 120 were rejected, being one-ninth. In 1810, of 98 bills of indictment for stealing from the person, 33 were thrown out by the grand jury ; while the bills preferred for all other offences were 1073 in number, and those rejected amounted only to 119. In 1811, of 151 indictments for stealing from the person, 48 were rejected by the grand jury ; while of 1061 indictments for all other offences, only 124 were rejected. And in the following years, as will appear by a Table which I will also produce, the proportions have not been materially different. When it is recollected that the suspicion of this crime generally falls upon boys or very young persons, and that the consequence of an unfounded charge against them is to compel them to pass some weeks or months in prison in the very worst society they could be thrown into, and that which is best calculated to convert the suspicions entertained against them into reality ; it must, I think, appear very important to ascertain, if it be possible, to what cause is to be ascribed the much greater frequency of these mistakes in the administration of the police, with respect to this offence than to any other.

Sir
Samuel Romilly.

The

Sir
Samuel Romilly.

[The following Tables were delivered in, and read.]

N° 1.

TABLE of the Number of Persons committed for Trial at the Old Bailey, for the crime of Stealing privately from the Person, in the following Years; and of the Number indicted, convicted, acquitted, &c.

	Committed for Trial for Stealing Privately from the Person.	Indicted of Stealing Privately from the Person.	Convicted of the whole Charge.	Convicted of Simple Larceny.	Acquitted.	No Bill found.	
1805.	11	5	1	2	2	—	*Those marked, in the columns of persons indicted, with the Letter L, though indicted for Stealing privately from the Person, had been committed for Simple Larceny; those to which the letter R is added, had been committed for Robbery; and those to which are added RSG, had been committed for Receiving Stolen Goods.
		16 L*	- -	8	4	4	
		2 R	- -	- -	1	1	
	Total - -	23	1	10	7	5	
1806.	24	14	1	- -	6	7	
		20 L	- -	9	3	8	
		1 RSG	- -	- -	1	—	
	Total - -	35	1	9	10	15	
1807.	21†	14	2	3	4	5	† Of these 21, three were discharged by proclamation, there being no prosecution.
		23 L	1	7	7	8	
	Total - -	37	3	10	11	13	
1808. to June 30, when the Act 48 G. 3. passed.	21	16	1	3	3	9	
		15 L	- -	3	5	7	
		31	1	6	8	16	
Grand Total - -		126	6	35	36	49	

In this period, from 1 January 1805, to 30 June 1808, comprising three years and a half, 6 persons were capitally convicted of this offence, but none were executed. From the 30 June 1808, the crime of privately stealing from the person did not exist; but the crime of stealing from the person was an aggravated species of felony, punishable by transportation for life, while the severest punishment that can be inflicted for simple larceny is transportation for 7 years. The following Table therefore relates only to the crime of stealing from the person.

N° 2.

Sir Samuel Romilly.

N° 2.

TABLE of the Number of Persons committed for Trial at the Old Bailey, for the crime of Stealing from the Person; and of the Number indicted, convicted, &c.

	Committed for Stealing from the Person.	Indicted of Stealing from the Person.	Convicted of the whole aggravated Charge.	Convicted of Simple Larceny.	Acquitted.	No Bill found.
1808. from June 30.	17	12	6	2	4	—
		16 L*	5	1	10	—
		28	11ᵃ	3	14	—
1809.	65	57	30	1	9	17
		36 L	10	--	11	15
		4 DH	2	--	--	2
		2 R	1	--	1	—
		99	43ᵇ	1	21	34
1810. 4 of these were discharged by Proclamation.	66	44	19	--	13	12
		50 L	18	1	10	21
		1 DH	1	—	—	—
		1 NR	1	—	—	—
		1 R	1	—	—	—
		1 RSG	--	--	1	—
		98	40ᶜ	1	24	33
1811. 2 of these were discharged by Proclamation.	86	76	34	--	23	19
		70 L	22	2	18	28
		3 DH	--	--	2	1
		2 R	2	—	—	—
		151	58ᵈ	2	43	48
1812.	90	79	37	1	18	23
		62 L	23	2	17	20
		5 DH	3	--	--	2
		1 NR	1	—	—	—
		2 R	1	--	--	1
		149	65ᵉ	3	35	46

ᵃ Of the 11 convicted of the whole aggravated charge, 3 were transported for life, 2 for 14 years, 4 for 7 years; 1 imprisoned a year, 1 imprisoned 6 months.

ᵇ Of these 43, 6 were transported for life, 5 for 14 years, 23 for 7 years; 1 imprisoned for 2 years, 2 imprisoned for 1 year, and 6 for 6 months and under.

ᶜ 5 Persons indicted in this year of Robbery, were convicted of Larceny from the Person; making in all 45 Persons convicted of this offence. Their sentences were, 9 transported for life, 2 for 14 years, 23 for 7 years; 1 imprisoned for 2 years, 5 for 6 months; 1 whipped, 5 fined.

ᵈ 8 Persons indicted of Robbery, were convicted of Larceny from the Person, in all 66. Of these, 25 transported for life, 27 for 7 years; 1 imprisoned 2 years, 2 imprisoned for 1 year, 7 for 6 months; 4 fined.

ᵉ 4 indicted of Robbery, making in all 69. Of these, 22 transported for life, 1 for 14 years, 14 for 7 years; 2 imprisoned for 2 years, 6 for 1 year, 10 for 6 months; 1 whipped, 13 fined.

(continued)

* Those marked in this column with L, were committed for Simple Larceny; those with DH, for Larceny in a Dwelling-house; those with R, for Robbery; those with NR, for Larceny on a Navigable River; and those with RSG, for Receiving Stolen Goods.

Sir Samuel Romilly.

N° 2—*continued.*

	Committed for Stealing from the Person.	Indicted of Stealing from the Person.	Convicted of the whole aggravated Charge.	Convicted of Simple Larceny.	Acquitted.	No Bill found.	
1813.	106	90	47	- -	28	15	[a] 13 indicted of Robbery, making in all 106 convicted of Larceny from the Person. Of these, 30 were transported for life, 2 for 14 years, and 19 for 7 years; 3 were imprisoned for 2 years, 16 for 1 year, 16 for 6 months and under; 1 whipped, and 19 fined.
		89 L	42	2	25	20	
		2 B	- -	- -	- -	2	
		3 DH	1	- -	- -	2	
		4 R	3	- -	1	—	
		1 RSG	- -	- -	- -	1	
		189	93[a]	2	54	40	
1814.	127	110	62	2	28	20	[b] 13 indicted of Robbery, making in all 104 convicted of Larceny from the Person. Of these, 48 were transported for life, 3 for 14 years, 18 for 7 years; 2 were imprisoned for 2 years, 6 for 1 year, 21 for 6 months and under; and 6 were fined.
		74 L	24	1	23	26	
		3 DH	2	- -	1	—	
		3 R	3	—	—	—	
		1 RSG	- -	- -	- -	1	
		191	91[b]	3	52	47	

N° 3.

TABLE of the Number of Persons committed for Trial at the Old Bailey since the Year 1804, for Larceny privately in a Shop; and of the Number indicted, convicted, acquitted, &c.

	Committed.	Indicted.	Convicted of the Capital Felony.	Convicted of Simple Larceny.	Acquitted.	No Bill found.
1805.	19	16	- -	12	4	—
		17 L*	- -	12	4	1
		33	- -	24	8	1
1806.	21	19	3	10	5	1
		5 L	1	2	2	—
		24	4	12	7	1
1807.	21	17	1	11	4	1
		18 L	1	15	2	—
		35	2	26	6	1
1808.	31	26	1	17	8	—
		16 L	3	8	4	—
		42	4	25	12	—

(continued)

* Those marked with L, though indicted Capitally, were committed for Simple Larceny; those marked with DH, were committed for Larceny in a Dwelling-house; and those with LP, for Larceny from the Person.

N° 3—continued.

	Committed.	Indicted.	Convicted of the Capital Felony.	Convicted of Simple Larceny.	Acquitted.	No Bill found.
1809.	39	27	7	8	9	3
		22 L	1	15	4	2
		2 DH	- -	- -	1	1
		51	8	23	14	6
1810.	29	20	7	11	2	—
		21 L	- -	12	9	—
		1 DH	- -	1	—	—
		1 LP	- -	1	—	—
		43	7	25	11	—
1811.	39	24	6	12	5	1
		19 L	3	8	4	4
		6 DH	1	4	1	—
		1 LP	- -	1	—	—
		50	10	25	10	5
1812.	49	39	15	15	8	1
		45 L	2	30	13	—
		1 DH	- -	1	—	—
		85	17	46	21	1
1813.	46	32	9	13	8	2
		38 L	7	20	7	4
		7 DH	2	4	1	—
		77	18	37	16	6
1814.	43	31	6	14	9	2
		44 L	4	27	8	5
		1 DH	- -	1	—	—
		76	10	42	17	7
Grand Total -		516	80	285	122	28

In the course of ten years, from 1805 to 1814 inclusive, 516 persons were indicted Capitally for this offence. Of these, only 80 were Capitally convicted, and not one was executed. Of 285, the Jury, either finding the property not to be of the value of 5 s. or that it was not stolen privately, acquitted the prisoners of the Capital part of the charge, but found them guilty of Simple Larceny.

N° 4.

TABLE of the Number of Bills of Indictment preferred to the Grand Juries of *London* and *Middlesex,* in the following Years; and of the Number of Bills thrown out by them.

	Bills of Indictment for Stealing from the Person.		Bills of Indictment for all other Offences.		TOTAL.	
	Bills preferred to the Grand Jury.	Bills thrown out by the Grand Jury.	Bills preferred.	Bills thrown out.	Bills preferred.	Bills thrown out.
1809 - -	99	34	1098	120	1197	154
1810 - -	98	33	1073	119	1171	152
1811 - -	151	48	1061	124	1212	172
1812 - -	149	46	1198	136	1347	182
1813 - -	189	40	1244	167	1433	207
1814 - -	191	47	1197	93	1388	140

Mercurii, 26° die Junii, 1816.

The Honourable HENRY GREY BENNET, in The Chair.

———————————

Mr. *Alexander Russell,* called in, and Examined.

WHERE do you live?—No. 6, Dean's-court, St. Martin's-le-Grand.

Were you ever concerned in the prosecution of disorderly houses?—Yes.

State to the Committee what passed?—I think there were four houses that we prosecuted, and they were all found guilty; it cost the liberty, I think, between two and three hundred pounds to indict them.

Were you one of the jury who found them guilty?—No, I was one of those that prosecuted; the jury at Hicks's Hall found them guilty.

When you prosecuted those houses, did you enter into a recognizance with the parish to pay the expenses?—The parish paid a part.

In what portion did the parish pay, and in what portion did you pay?—I think we paid about half.

How many of the parishioners joined together for that purpose?—It was made a general thing of. From the liberty a certain number of men were elected; eight commissioners of the pavement; and those commissioners were deputed by the body at large of the liberty to proceed against those houses.

You call Saint Martin's-le-Grand a liberty?—It was a liberty within the city of Westminster; but since the Act for the Post-office, it is joined to the ward of Aldersgate.

Did you find any difficulty upon the subject?—We found a great difficulty in waiting at Hicks's Hall before our case came on; we were there nearly eight days, though the name was at the top of the list.

What was the occasion of that delay?—I believe it was owing to the attorney we employed, and their attorney, wishing to tire us out.

Did you find any difficulty in getting evidence to prove that these were disorderly houses?—No, we had no difficulty, because we brought forward inhabitants living in the same spot, who wished to get rid of the houses.

What was the nature of the evidence they adduced?—The evidence they gave was, that there were continually girls standing at the door enticing young people in, and at all times of the night fighting and quarrelling, giving charge, and sometimes men taken out.

Having got a verdict against those houses, what followed?—The whole of them went away, except one; one stood trial.

Did you gain a verdict against that single house that stood trial?—Yes; the woman was sentenced to the pillory, and three months imprisonment, I think; but Doctor Lettsom came forward, and affirmed she was pregnant, and the pillory was set aside.

Did you in point of fact suppress all the houses?—The whole went, but the whole returned, although there was some process of law hanging over their heads that they were liable to be punished. The expense was so great, the liberty would not enter into it again.

Do they continue the same still?—They do; in fact, they have increased since that.

Do you mean increased in number beyond the four in that street, or in bad conduct?—They are increased in number. They are small houses, and they offer such a rent, that middling tradesmen cannot give it.

But the proprietors are very glad to take it from people of this description?—They have been hitherto.

Do the neighbours complain of the same scenes of riot, and drunkenness, and fighting, as heretofore?—Just the same. There are two houses have come since, of a different description, for they may be called day houses; they are only houses of accommodation; if a girl picks up any person in the street, there are rooms at all hours for them.

Are there any houses there peculiarly adapted and appropriated to the reception of children of both sexes?—Not that I know of.

The

The existence of these houses is, then, considered by the neighbours as the same nuisance as formerly, and that nuisance is not abated, solely on account of the expense?—That is the thing; the expense prevented their prosecuting the second time; but it is entirely in the hands of the City now.

Mr.
Alexander Russell.

Mr. *John Grant*, called in, and Examined.

WHERE do you live?—At 26, Saint Martin's-le-Grand.

Are you an officer of the parish?—No.

Have you been an officer?—I have gone through all the offices of the parish.

Mr.
John Grant.

During the time in which you filled any of those situations, were you concerned in the indictment of disorderly houses?—Yes, no less than ten of them; I was the only person that they fixed upon to do that.

Were those prosecutions conducted at the expense of the parish, or at that of individuals?—At the expense of the parish, but a good deal of it at the expense of those who took it up.

Did you make an engagement with the parish that you would be answerable for so much money?—No.

In point of fact what did those prosecutions cost?—About 300*l.* I think.

In all?—Yes.

Did you succeed in those prosecutions?—All of them, with a great deal of difficulty.

Of what nature were those difficulties?—There was one case, of a person of the name of Waters, who I suppose had been there very nearly two years before we got rid of her.

Did she stand trial?—She stood trial, and was convicted.

Is she gone?—Yes, she has been gone some time, but there were others returned in her place.

Are any of the persons against whom verdicts were found, or who, fearing a verdict, quitted their houses, returned to them again?—There have been some of them; one of the name of Cohen in particular, a Jew.

Why have not the parish followed up their prosecution, and abated the nuisance of those houses?—There is a great deal of demur with the parishioners, on account of the expense.

You would then have the Committee to understand, that it is the expense alone that deters the parish from pursuing the prosecutions of those houses?—Yes.

Some of the same people have come back, and continue to keep houses of the same description?—Yes.

Is the nuisance very great in the neighbourhood of those houses?—Very great.

Assemblages of riotous and disorderly persons?—Yes.

Fighting and drunkenness?—Yes, every thing that is bad.

Indecent exhibitions?—Yes; I have the misfortune of being more troubled with them than any other person, on account of part of the watch-house being under my premises behind, and they are continually bringing them into that watch-house at all hours of the night.

Of course in the neighbourhood of those houses you would be unwilling that your wives or daughters, or even your sons, should pass?—No doubt of it.

Nothing then but the expense prevents your further prosecution of those houses?—Nothing else; it is the expense that deters us from doing it, and the parish are very poor indeed.

Are any of those houses that are disorderly houses, public-houses?—They do not actually keep beds for them in those places, but they encourage them by drinking drams and sitting in the places, and other things that they ought not to do.

Have any complaints been made against those houses, on the licensing day, by the parish?—Against some of them; some of them abused the parish officers, and were very insolent.

To whom were those complaints made?—They have been made to the headboroughs and the commissioners; that place was ruled by six headboroughs and eight commissioners, according to Act of Parliament.

Were any complaints made to the Magistrates in order to prevent the licences being granted?—I do not know that they applied to them about the licences; but they applied several times to the Magistrates to know how they should get rid of them, and they were told there was no other way than to indict them.

The

Mr.
John Grant.

The question applies to public-houses?—I do not recollect an instance of having any of them before the Magistrates.

But in point of fact, the conduct of some of the public-houses is so notoriously bad, that you will state to the Committee that the officers of the parish have repeatedly made complaints of it?—No doubt of it, we frequently have.

In what district of the Police was your parish, when those evils took place?—Hatton Garden was the place we used to take them to.

Did you ever make any complaints, or do you know that any complaints ever were made, to the Magistrates at Hatton Garden, with regard to the conduct of the different publicans in your parish?—I do not recollect, but I believe there have been.

Do you recollect any instance in which they lost their licence, and the house was shut up in consequence?—No; but several went away in consequence of being fearful of the licence being taken from them, and let their houses to others; they shifted in that manner.

Their houses still continuing as bad as before?—There are not so many of them, but there are a great many now.

The houses still continuing as bad in conduct as they were before?—Yes, very bad.

Is your parish principally the residence of the poorer class of persons?—Our parish is united to Christ's parish: the name of the parish is Saint Leonard's: the church was burnt down in the fire of London, and was never after rebuilt.

If you had money in your parish, or amongst yourselves were able to afford it, should you have the least hesitation in prosecuting those houses?—A number of the people together would do it, I have no doubt; we have been at a great deal of expense.

Nothing, then, but the cost deters you from pursuing them to conviction?—Yes.

What office do you hold in the parish?—I am the oldest commissioner.

Mr. *George Lee*, called in, and Examined.

Mr.
George Lee.

YOU are one of the headboroughs of St. Martin's-le-Grand?—I was; but it is all done away with now.

Did you hold that situation when the prosecutions took place with regard to these disorderly houses?—I did.

How long is that ago?—I suppose it must be four years ago; I think somewhere about that time.

You succeeded on those prosecutions?—Yes, we got one verdict.

And the other persons, fearing a verdict, fled?—Yes.

Are any of those persons who fled, come back again?—They are.

They keep houses of the same kind and description as before?—They do.

Were the expenses great attending those prosecutions?—I think they were nearly 300 *l.*; 202 *l.* our parish paid.

Were those expenses paid by the parish, or paid by individuals?—Paid by the parish; and part of it by some individuals.

What prevents your prosecuting at the present moment those persons who returned?—After they returned, we were placed under the control of the City of London. I believe our finances will not allow it.

In point of fact, it was the expense alone that deterred you from proceeding with the prosecution?—Yes.

Were any other impediments thrown in the way of putting down those houses, except the expense?—Nothing else.

The proofs of the guilt of the parties, and the disorderly character of the houses, were notorious?—They are. One woman was sentenced to the pillory.

Is the conduct of the persons keeping those houses, and is the general character of the houses, as bad now as before the conviction?—I do not think they are. The present Lord Mayor has in a great measure improved them; for as soon as we came under the City jurisdiction, he attended in person; he was at the watch-house the very night that that part of the ward came into the City of London, and sent several of his officers to parade the streets till twelve or one o'clock, to see that every house was shut up, and there was no disorder. We had no constables then, and now we have.

Since you have been under the Police of the City, the houses and the parish in general have been more orderly than heretofore?—They have.

Are

Are there many public-houses in your division, that countenance and support those disorderly houses?—I cannot say; there are several liquor-shops, where they go in and out to the bar; I do not frequent any house.

When you were headborough, did you ever make any complaint to any Magistrate, of the conduct of any victualler?—Yes, and their licences have been suspended; there was one man's licence suspended for twelve months.

At present, then, you state, that the houses are better conducted than they were before?—Yes, I think they are. Next door to Mr. Grant was the watch-house, and there have been charges in the middle of the day, and a great many at a late hour of the night; but we have had none of that since we have been under the Police of the City.

At present what is the process that you would pursue, if you wished to put down one of those houses?—If I was foreman of the inquest or the annoyance jury, I should make a presentment, on Plough Monday at Guildhall, of any house of ill fame, and then there is an order for the City solicitor to prosecute, which is paid for by the City.

The expense, instead of falling on the parish of St. Martin's-le-Grand, as formerly, and on a few individuals, would be paid out of the general City fund?—Yes.

And the prosecution be conducted by the City solicitor?—Yes.

[*Joseph Butterworth*, Esq. a Member of the Committee, delivered in the Proceedings of a Common Council of the City of London, holden on the 19th of May 1814; also, the Proceedings of a Common Council, holden on the 17th of January 1816.]

Mr.
George Lee.

Joseph Butterworth,
Esq.

John Nares, Esq. called in, and Examined.

YOU are a Magistrate of Bow-street?—Yes.

How long have you been there?—Between nine and ten years at Bow-street, ten years at Worship-street, and two years at Shadwell.

Having been so many years in the situation of Police Magistrate, the Committee would wish to have your opinion, whether you think crimes, speaking in general, have considerably augmented since you first filled the situation which you now hold?—I think not.

The Committee have had in evidence, and indeed the observation of every one must have given him the information without that evidence, that atrocious crimes have of late years considerably diminished?—I have no doubt of that.

Can you say the same of crimes of a less bad character, such as swindling, picking of pockets, highway robbery, and offences of a milder nature?—As to swindling, there is no manner of doubt that that has increased considerably, if you mean by swindling obtaining goods under false pretences; with respect to pickpockets, I think they have increased.

Do you think that that increase of the number of pickpockets is the result of the crime itself having increased, or that, the capital punishment having been taken away from the crime, more persons are brought before the Office for having committed it, because individuals are more ready to prosecute now than formerly?—I think that the dread of punishment has had an effect there, and that now they are more bold than they were before, because they go in such gangs now.

Do you think the number of juvenile depredators considerably increased?—Considerably, in my opinion.

The Committee have been told by different Magistrates whom they have summoned before them, as well as by many of the Officers of the Police, that they would much rather prefer that the system of Parliamentary rewards should be done away with, and that the Magistrates or the Judges should have the power of apportioning to each individual Officer the reward for any specific service which he might have performed; are you of that opinion?—I am decidedly of that opinion, and have been for many years; and I will state another circumstance, that it was the opinion of my father, who was a judge, that it would be an essential service to the public to take away those rewards. And I will tell my reason, which is this: an officer goes into court with a prejudice against him, because the people conceive that he is giving his evidence in order to obtain the reward; and so the jury very often consider, most certainly. An officer would go into court with much more satisfaction to himself, I am certain, and there could be then no prejudice against him in any way whatever. And

John Nares,
Esq.

as

John Nares,
Esq.

as to the small sum that an officer receives as a part of the reward, it is no sort of encouragement to him, in my opinion.

The truth is, that if the Officers do not get rewarded for their exertions by private individuals, neither their share of the Parliamentary reward, nor the salary that they receive, would be sufficient to secure to the Public those good Officers which it now possesses?—I have been convinced, ever since I belonged to the Police, that the great object was, that the Officers should be handsomely paid, to keep them honest; or, depend upon it, they might get five times as much as they do now, if they chose to be dishonest.

Do you think that the number of known brothels and gaming-houses has very much increased in the Metropolis of late years?—I should think they have; of the lowest order, I should think, very much so.

Are there not more brothels and gaming-houses in the district which you now have under your care, than any other part of the Metropolis?—I do not know as to gaming-houses; as to brothels I have very little doubt.

What means have been adopted for the suppression of those houses?—Several of them have been indicted by the parish. There is a house now, not a brothel, but a notorious bad house, a public-house, where, according to my advice, the Officers had a warrant, and a vast number of persons were taken on a Sunday morning; the warrant was not executed till two or three o'clock on the Sunday morning, and it was amazing the number of persons that were there; and I understood, as soon as it was light in the morning, women were opening their windows, exposing themselves to the persons in that house. They took up a great number; and, added to that, the parish are prosecuting the man on his recognizance, which is, in my opinion, the best way of going to work on those occasions.

Since you have sat at Bow-street, have keepers of gaming-houses ever been brought before you?—Of keepers of gaming-houses about there, none that I know of; there have been some from St. James's-street and Pall Mall, but it is a wonderful difficult thing to get into a gaming-house.

Have any person at any time been brought before you for having been found gaming at such houses?—None, that I recollect.

Do you recollect no one having been brought before you for having been found gaming at any of the houses in St. James's-street and Pall Mall?—Yes, where they went with warrants to apprehend them.

What description of persons were they?—Officers. There was one very curious case, that the Secretary of State and myself had a dispute about.

Had they been playing for large or small sums?—They certainly had been playing for large sums. We could not ascertain what had been taken away. Our Officers did not take above six or seven pounds, I think. But the fact is, we always order the Officers, when they go on that business, to bring the money that is upon the table away, and produce it when they come to give their evidence, to show that gaming has been going forward.

What was the largest sum that ever was seized upon those occasions?—It is reported to me that two people who got off, and I never could get them, or if I could have got them, I should not have scrupled committing them, got 400*l.* which they run off with.

What people were those?—It was only mentioned to me who they were. It was a warrant of Mr. Graham's, and they were brought afterwards before me. The warrant, I am sorry to say, was put into the hands of a Foreigner belonging to the Alien Office, but our Officers went with him. That man, with two more men, rushed in before the Officers, and plundered the table at first. Then our Officers came, and found but very little; and then this person, who had no authority whatever, searched all the gentlemen who remained in the room, and took the money out of their pockets, and kept a list of that money; and I never could get that man, he was off.

Out of the kingdom?—I do not know where he went to; he never came to account for the money.

By whose warrant were the parties apprehended?—The warrant of Mr. Graham.

What was he, then?—A Magistrate of Bow-street.

Did Mr. Graham give the warrant into the hand of a foreigner, who conducted himself after the manner you have so described?—I believe he did, but I am not positive. Adkins was the officer who went with the warrant.

The warrant was of course served by your constables?—It was. These men said they had orders to act upon it.

What

What men?—This foreigner, and Mr. Capper, belonging to the Alien Office, who went in a uniform, and with a drawn sword.

Is that a usual mode of proceeding?—I never heard of such a thing in my life.

Do you think that a legal mode of proceeding?—Certainly not; I never was so angry about any thing in my life, and I went to complain to Mr. Becket about it.

What were the names of the parties?—I think the name of one was Dr. Senate.

Was he a foreigner?—I do not know that he was; the other was, that went first. This foreigner that took down the list, which was very correct, no doubt, never brought the money forward. I did tell Mr. Becket, that if he did not come, I should not scruple to send a warrant after him. I did not scruple to say, that if he had come, and the gentlemen swore to this, I should commit him for a robbery.

In point of fact, you never saw either the parties or the money?—All the parties were brought before me, that were gambling.

But you never saw the parties who seized the money, or the money itself?—No. There is a circumstance which now occurs to my recollection; I sent Adkins repeatedly after this man; I could not find him; what did he do, but leave a twenty pound note for Adkins, and I told Adkins to keep that money till it was called for.

How was it left, at Adkins's house?—I believe at Adkins's house.

By whom?—Supposed to be left by the foreigner. I think the amount of the money was an hundred and odd pounds.

Did you make a complaint of the whole of this conduct to Mr. Becket as well as to Mr. Graham?—I do not know that I ever had much conversation with Mr. Graham on the subject; he was exceedingly ill at the time; but I can perfectly recollect what Mr. Becket said. When I was extremely angry about it, he said, " There! we have got into a gambling-house, and you are jealous that we have found it out."

What was the final result of the whole?—The final result was, that the gentlemen were held to bail that were gambling, and I never could get at this foreigner in any way. Mr. Capper told me he tried to get at him, and could not.

Or the money either?—Or the money.

How long is this ago?—Three or four years ago.

Do you believe the foreigner is in England now?—No, I do not; I do not know the least in the world what became of him. I told Mr. Alley, who was counsel for the gentlemen, Do you find him out, and I will grant a warrant.

By whom, then, was the money seized?—The money was seized by Mr. Capper and by this foreigner. We never search the pockets of people for their money, but they were made to pull all their money out of their pockets, and then there was a list taken of the money each party gave up, and this list was sent to me in the morning; and, as far I recollect, Mr. Graham said, this person would come with the money, but I never could get him.

In whose hands was the money deposited?—In the hands of this foreigner.

What became of it?—He spent it, I suppose, except this twenty pounds, which Adkins is to account for.

Adkins has the twenty pounds now?—Adkins has the twenty pounds now.

Had you any conversation, and if you had, state the whole of it, with Mr. Becket, upon that subject?—I certainly had a conversation with Mr. Becket, part of which I have related, and I told him that I must insist upon that foreigner coming forward.

Did Mr. Becket tell you why the foreigner was at all employed in the transaction, or how Mr. Capper of the Alien Office could be concerned in that transaction, and enter the house in uniform with a drawn sword?—I went to Mr. Becket, when I discovered all this, to say I thought this a very simple transaction as could possibly be, and I said that it was a disgrace to the office, and that I was sure neither Mr. Reid nor myself would have granted such a warrant upon the evidence of such a man as that. But I fancy they did not know that Mr. Capper was to go in this uniform; he belonged to some corps. The Officer very properly came, and gave the account of it to me directly.

This was not Mr. Capper of the Secretary of State's Office?—No, his brother, of the Alien Office.

Did Mr. Becket give you any explanation why the foreigner was concerned at all in it?—No, I do not know that he did; he had given information of this gambling-house, and he said, as I have mentioned before, that we were jealous of the Alien Office finding out this house.

510.

Had

John Nares,
Esq.

Had Mr. Capper any part of the money?—I believe not, at least I think he told me he had never had any of the money; my recollection upon the subject may be incorrect, but I think he said not.

Is it not an unusual proceeding for the Alien Office to employ itself in forcibly entering gambling-houses?—I never knew it before.

Has such a circumstance to your knowledge transpired since?—Certainly not.

Where was the house?—I think the house was in Pall-Mall, as well as I recollect; I think Adkins and Perry executed the warrant.

Did Mr. Becket express himself to you as satisfied with the conduct of the Alien Office, or as dissatisfied?—He appeared to me to justify the Alien Office, at least justified the proceedings that took place; whether it proceeded from the Alien Office, or who it proceeded from, I do not know.

You never were able to obtain any account of the foreigner who robbed the persons after the manner you have described, or any account of what became of the money which he so stole?—Certainly not; and I remember one expression of Mr. Becket's perfectly well, and that was, he said, " Why you are bullied by Alley;" I said, I would not be bullied by Mr. Alley, or Mr. anybody.

Should you not, on an information laid, have felt it your duty to commit Mr. Capper, as having been concerned in the robbery?—I do not know what to say on that, because we cannot tell what the evidence might have been, exactly: I should have run the risk of an action, most undoubtedly, I think.——There is a thing that has struck me many years, and I am convinced it would be of the utmost importance to prevent robberies of waggons and robberies out of town; and that is this, These people go out with a horse and cart, that horse and cart they hire; now if it could be done, the same as under our Police Act, to authorize officers, where they see these reputed thieves, to stop those carts, and if they found implements of house-breaking, which most probably they would in going out, then that they should be brought before a Magistrate, and committed, under Mr. Selwyn's Act, for having picklock-keys and implements of house-breaking upon them; or when they return, a million to one but they would be seen coming back with the stolen property: what I wish to have done into the bargain is, that the horse and cart shall be forfeited, the same as in the Excise and Customs laws, then it would be extremely difficult for these men to get a horse and cart.

Are you not also of opinion, that if the collectors of tolls were empowered to examine horses and carts having a suspicious appearance, and hackney coaches, going out of town or returning at unseasonable hours, with a view to the detection of property that may have been stolen, it would tend to the conviction of offenders of that sort?—I think that toll-collectors are the worst set of people in London; and you will get nothing from them: The great object would be, if what I propose took place, that many of our patrole certainly would employ themselves upon this business; and they would take care to watch the turnpikes.

Would it not be better to make that law obligatory on the patroles, to attend at each gate in the environs of the Metropolis?—If they were to attend at each gate, as far as it appears to me, they would not catch the thieves, because they would in all probability know where the officers were stationary exactly, and therefore they would take care and avoid that place if possible.

Is there any possibility of getting to the Metropolis without coming through some toll-gate?—I do not know. There is another thing I may mention: At present our conductors of the patrole always meet at the same place; now that is known to thieves a good deal. When poor Mr. Reid was ill, and I had the management of the patrole, I used to change their time of going, which had a very good effect.

The time of entering upon their duty?—Yes. Many robberies, particularly robberies in houses when people are out of town, are committed just in the early part of the morning when the watch is gone off; now it is a very material thing, in my opinion, to have officers go about at that time. There have been several such robberies committed, and it happened to me this winter; a man got into the area, and got the plate that was in use, and put into a basket; but he was alarmed, and the plate was left in the area in the basket, with a string to pull it up.

Robert

Robert Hayward, called in, and Examined.

WHERE do you live ?—At No. 2, Queen's-row, Walworth.

What is your profession ?—A carpenter.

Did you build a house in that street, now named The Pilgrim public-house ?—Yes.

Was it for the purpose of carrying on the trade of a public-house ?—Yes.

How long ago is that ?—Five years.

In the year 1810, or thereabouts?—Somewhere thereabouts.

Had you any difficulties in getting it licensed ?—No, none.

Did you obtain a licence for it the year it was finished ?—Yes, I did.

Did you give the trade of that house to the house of Messrs. Meux & Co.?—Yes, I did.

Had you any interview with any of the partners of that house upon that subject ?—Yes, I had.

Who were the parties with whom you had that interview ?—Mr. Benson.

Any body else ?—I think Mr. Young was there.

Who is Mr. Benson ?—One of the firm of Messrs. Meux & Trail.

Is he a Magistrate of the county of Surrey ?—I believe he is, but I am not able to say ; I think I have seen him sit on the bench.

Where did you meet and make this agreement ?—They called on me, and I went to their house at Camberwell.

Did you breakfast there ?—No, I did not.

Who wrote the agreement?—There were but three in the room ; I will not swear which wrote it.

Did Mr. Benson write the agreement ?—I will not swear it.

Do you think he did ?—I think he did ; I am not sure.

You think it was Mr. Benson?—Yes.

You signed it ?—I did.

What was the nature of that agreement ?—The nature of the agreement was, that I was to deal with them for a certain time.

That is to say, you were to deal for all beer and stout sold by you at the above house for a certain term ?—Yes.

What was that term?—Seven years.

What was the penalty ?—None.

Was there no penalty of granting that firm a lease of the premises for an equal term of seven years?—No.

What was the use of the agreement unless there was a penalty ?—The use of the agreement was for the loan of some money that I had of them.

Was any promise made of their interest in obtaining you a licence ?—No further than they said they would do all they could.

Was a licence obtained ?—It was.

And the house was opened ?—Yes.

Afterwards you were unfortunate ?—Afterwards I was unfortunate.

The Pilgrim house was submitted to public sale ?—Yes.

For what term ?—For the whole term; fifty-one years, I think.

At a rent of 30*l.* per annum ?—No; at the rent of 28*l.* per annum.

Is the present tenant, David Bonner, subject to your agreement ?—Yes.

When does it expire ?—I should suppose in about two years.

About 1817 ?—Yes.

· Mr. *Philip Holdsworth*, called in, and Examined.

WHAT situation do you hold ?—Not any; I have lately resigned my situation of Upper Marshal of the City of London.

How long did you fill that situation ?—Between eighteen and nineteen years.

What are the principal duties of the City Marshal ?—To regulate the Police of the City ; to know that they do their duty; to inquire where nuisances exist, to put men on duty to attend to them and correct them; to report to the Lord Mayor every morning the state of the City's internal quiet on the preceding day and night; to attend the Lord Mayor every day in the Justice room ; to attend him on all occasions of pageantry, and wherever the sword of state goes.

150.

State

Mr.
Philip Holdsworth.

State to the Committee the strength of the Police of the City of London ?—An Upper and Under Marshal.

How paid ?—By salary and gratuities.

What are the salaries ?—The Upper Marshal has 400 *l.* a year, and 100 *l.* a year the Court of Aldermen make him a present of as a gratuity.

Have you nothing else in the nature of allowance for house ?—No, not any thing.

Or fees ?—The fees are such as these; the Commissioners of the Lottery give each marshal 40 *l.* a year to give an eye towards the place where the wheels are, by directing the patrole for the night, if fire happens, to get the wheels away, and to assist at the drawing, to keep the peace. There are other fees to the amount of 50 *l.* a piece to each of the Marshals, but we do not take a fee for any thing without we have the Lord Mayor's consent.

Then the Committee are to understand that the whole of your salary, perquisites, gratuities, allowances, &c. amount to 600 *l.* per annum ?—Yes, within ten pounds more or less.

State the salary of the Under Marshal ?—The Under Marshal has a less income by 50 *l.* a year; every thing else is equally divided between us. Then there are eight marshalmen, six for the City and two for Southwark; there are always two in attendance at each Justice room; and then there are two called outwaiters, whose duty it is, two or three times in the night to attend the patrole on the patrole, and to report their state to the marshal in the morning.

What is their salary ?—I understand their situations are each worth 140 *l.*; they are clothed; and I should have stated that the City Marshals have their uniforms, and a chair at the sword-bearer's table daily; and the marshals men, when in waiting, dine at the Mansion-house.

What is the number of the patrole?—There are twelve day patrole.

At what salary ?—At a guinea and a half a week each : they have an opportunity of getting money, because where they are employed, whether it is where burglaries are committed, or where they are put on particular duty, the gentlemen employing them give them something for their trouble, but of that they must tell the Lord Mayor; they run a risk of losing their situation if they accept a present without informing him.

In point of fact do you believe that report is constantly made to the Lord Mayor ?—I really do believe it is.

Are there any night patroles ?—Yes; the City is divided into four divisions, and there are three day patroles to each division; their duty is to patrole the street to prevent thieving of every description, particularly to watch the pickpockets, to remove nuisances, prevent begging; and they have warrants also to apprehend felons; that is their duty, and a very active body of men they are.   Then there are eight night patroles, two to each division; they come upon duty at this time of year at nine o'clock, and in the winter time they come on duty at six, and their business is, twice during the night at least, but as much oftener as they possibly can, to visit each watch-house, to see that the constable of the night is in the watch-house attending his duty; they sign their names each time they come, in a book that is there for the purpose. When the Marshals go round to see the state of the ward, they see that book, and if the patroles' names are not signed, they must give a reason for it; then they come to the Marshal's office the next morning, and the clerk receives in a book any report they have to make, which is laid before the Lord Mayor daily.

These regulations, which appear to be so good, you take upon yourself to say are constantly executed ?—I do; it is impossible for it to be otherwise, because the Lord Mayor must daily see the account, and that book is signed by the Lord Mayor daily; and the Marshals are upon oath; they are annually sworn that they screen no man from favour or affection.   Then there is another description of force, which is called the ward constables; they consist of about 314, either men serving in their own right as housekeepers, or hired constables; if housekeepers do not serve when chosen, they pay something to the deputy of the ward, and he finds a substitute : their duty is to take their turns nightly in the watch-house.   The Marshals are commanded by the Lord Mayor to summon the constables upon any occasion to attend them; such as executions, pillories, common halls, during the Sessions at the Old Bailey, and upon any emergency the Lord Mayor may think necessary.

Such as riots and disturbances?—Yes; or upon any suspicion of a disturbance the Lord Mayor directs the Marshals to order them out.

Is

Is this service one of fatigue, and not paid for ; or do these constables of the night receive for their daily and nightly duty a sum of money?—The ward constables, if they are serving in their own right, have no remuneration ; if it is a substitute, he is paid, and they seem amply satisfied with what their principal gives them ; they have no opportunity of making any more than the sum given for their services.

Mr.
Philip Holdsworth.

In point of fact are a great number of these constables hired constables?—Nineteen out of twenty are hired ; there is the pity.

Does it fall, then, upon each parish or each ward to furnish a certain number of constables ; and if so, how are they furnished, by ballot or by rotation?—By rotation ; they are returned at the ward motes.

Do you consider that number of constables as sufficient to keep the peace of the City?—Yes, amply ; because we very seldom have occasion to have more than the ward constables, with the addition of that part of the police which is paid by the court of aldermen. We have not had occasion to have any additional hired constables since the trial of Bellingham ; there were then a great many hired, and placed in different parts of the City, out of sight, to be ready in case of necessity, and also on the day of his execution ; but we have not hired a constable since.

You consider then, from your own experience as Marshal, that the strength of the Police of the City is in point of fact fully sufficient for keeping the peace, and performing the different offices of Police in that part of the Metropolis?—I do.

Do you consider the Police of the City of London as better than that of other parts of the Metropolis?—Certainly ; we have temptations in the City for the marauder beyond what there are in any other part of the Metropolis, particularly during the Stock Exchange time, and during the business hours of bankers. In clearing checks, the clerks of the bankers in Cornhill and Lombard-street are passing with their bill-cases with a vast deal of property in them, and it is a very unusual thing for them to be robbed, or for a robbery to be committed about the Stock Exchange or the Bank. I always kept two men at the clearing-house, and two others in Lombard-street, just before four o'clock, and we have hardly heard of a pickpocket daring to look at the house ; and it is very seldom you meet one in Lombard-street or Cornhill, they go the back ways.

Do you consider the crime of picking pockets to be much increased of late years? —It has much increased within the last eight or nine months. It was considerably better for the three or four years preceding ; there had been fewer pockets picked in the city of London than in the previous ten or eleven years. Within the last nine or ten months they have increased ; but it seems to be checked again by the Lord Mayor's strictness and assiduity, and by his severity on the Officers of Police. He is so active, that every officer is on the alert ; and I think that has corrected picking pockets within the last two or three months very much. They are decreased very much.

Do you consider the increase of the pickpockets to have arisen from the neglect of the officers in doing their duty, and the diminution to have arisen from their increased exertion?—I must confess I think the officers were not so much on the alert for the three or four months before this Lord Mayor came into the office, as they were for the preceding four or five years. I find now a very increased assiduity ; and I consider, and am satisfied in my own mind, that the correction has arisen from their activity, and the Lord Mayor's strict commands.

Do you think, from your observation, that, generally speaking, crimes have multiplied of late years to what they were some years preceding?—Great crimes are fewer. Daring, desperate things, seem to be worn out, except daring forgeries. The principal part of the crimes now are domestic robberies. If an honest man comes from the country, where he goes to get his dinner, whatever it may be, there is generally some fellow lurking about, who learns what tradesman he is ; if he is a grocer, for instance, he says, Cannot you bring me a few nutmegs or spices, and sell them, your wages are not a great deal. There is a description of people who go about tempting and persuading young men to rob their places, to get some luxuries more than their wages will allow.

Are those offences, which you term domestic robberies, common in the City?— That is a thing that wants very much looking into ; the easy mode servant girls have of turning any thing they can bring away into money. There is scarcely what is called a chandler's shop in any part of the Metropolis, which sells every thing, whether

brick-

brick-dust, or emery, or small beer, or sand, but buys old bottles or linen, or any thing that a servant girl, when she goes there to purchase things, can take with her. The green-stalls will purchase things of them, and they find a facility in raising money upon any thing they take to these kinds of shops; and many girls lose their reputation by the encouragement women keeping these shops give them. This is not a suspicion, it is a thing proved and known.

Has any remedy ever suggested itself to your mind for that evil?—No, I have many times turned over in my mind what can be done, and I do not find any thing can, more than going with a search warrant; then persons must come and swear to it, and name the things they go to search for beforehand. When people have said, I think our servant robs us, and we do not know where she gets rid of the things, I have said, If you will give me leave I will place a man at such a place, and if your servant comes there, we will search the place. Many things have been found in chandlers' shops or green shops.

Do you think this species of domestic robbery has much increased of late years?— It is increasing still greatly.

So that you would state servants are less trustworthy?—They have become vile in the extreme; servant girls in particular; they are infamous.

Is the practice common in the City, to have out-door apprentices?—No, it is not.

Wherever it is, you consider it as a leading cause of the corruption of young people?—Always, invariably so. I have heard the Chamberlain of London observe, that seven apprentices out of ten who are unruly and bad, are out-door apprentices; but it is not so common in the City as out of it; it is not civic at all, or very little so.

Do you consider the number of juvenile depredators as very much increased of late?—Yes, within the last twelve months, beyond any thing I ever remember.

What are the offences that are principally committed by the children?—Picking pockets; taking things, on their hands and knees, from shops, such as haberdashers and linen-drapers; in the winter time, with a knife at the corner of the glass starring it, and taking things out, which has occasioned the tradespeople having so many guard irons; but still there are shops not so guarded, and they can find opportunities of continually robbing: Boys upon all occasions, when there is any thing which excites a crowd, are very active, and many of them extremely clever; they are short and active, and are generally attended by men.

Do you consider these boys as acting together in gangs, and trained by thieves grown old in the practice?—No question; they are trained by thieves who are adepts; these boys are generally apprehended three and four together, but they go in larger gangs than that.

Are they of very tender age?—Many of them from six years old to ten. The present Lord Mayor, seeing that description of thieves so much, would be able to convince the Committee that they are very young.

When children of this description are apprehended, to what prison are they sent?— Bridewell, where they are whipped.

Are some committed to Newgate?—If the Lord Mayor can find any body that will answer for them, and give them employment, he is very unwilling to commit them to Newgate, for it is a very bad school, unless they are kept separate; and I believe there has been something attempted lately to keep the early offenders from the ripe old thief; but the Lord Mayor generally sends them to Bridewell, and has them slightly whipped, and passed to their parish.

When they are sent to Bridewell, are any means taken to give them employment as well as moral instruction?—Yes, there are several kinds of employment.

Are they kept separate?—Yes, every one has a separate apartment, and they work in their rooms: They have different employments, but I cannot say what the employments are; one of those employments is the picking of oakum.

Are there many houses in the district of the city of London, that are known by the name of flash houses?—Not one; whenever there is, it is stopped immediately, and upon a very different opinion from what prevails in the county: In the county, they conceive them to be very useful to the officers, that they meet there whoever they want: In the city, as soon as a house of that sort is attempted to be established, the man has notice; and if he persists, he loses his licence.

At

At the next licensing day ?—No, immediately; we do not let it go on.

What authority has the Mayor and Court of Aldermen to take a licence away from a victualler, on proof of this conduct, before the next licensing day?—They enter into security for keeping good order, and they are called on by the inquest, and the alderman of the ward stops the licence; by what authority I do not know, but he does it.

You mean by that, that they call upon the securities to be answerable for the money for which they are securities?—Yes.

Who of course call on the person for whom they are security, to repay that money to them; and in that way the person gives up the house instead of paying the money?—Yes, that is it.

And by that process the house is shut up?—Yes.

You do not mean to say that an alderman of any ward has power to stop a licence between the periods of its being granted, and the re-granting of it for the preceding year?—I do not mean to say he has; by calling on the securities, they withdraw themselves, and he cannot keep the house open, because they refuse to be security any longer; then the house is shut up or re-let, for want of securities.

How many instances of such a circumstance as you have related, have happened within your knowledge, in the last seven years?—I think I can safely say from ten to a dozen; I think I could enumerate the houses.

Enumerate some of the houses, the licences of which have been so lost?—The Barley Mow in Field-lane, the Red Lion in Fleet-market, the Magpie and Stump in Skinner-street Bishopsgate; I can speak safely of those three, but I cannot speak with safety to any other. We never allow a flash house in the City.

Do you not find considerable inconvenience in not knowing where to look for those persons who have the character of reputed thieves?—The officers sometimes go out of the City, they know where to look for them, and see them together, and know new ones by seeing them in the company of old ones; but in the City we do not allow them a place of rest if we can help it; the officers go out of the City, and are always well treated.

With the exception of Field-lane, there is hardly any place of resort for theives ?—There are none in Field-lane; the only fault we have to find with that place is the riots of the Irish on Saturday night and all day on Sunday.

Is Petticoat-lane in the City?—One side of the way.

Are there not reputed thieves living there?—They frequent the houses in the county.

You consider that by the vigilance of the Magistrates and the Police, you have in point of fact nearly driven out of the City those nests of thieves which the Committee have in evidence exist in other parts of the town?—Yes; they never come into the City for the purpose of depredations, but they walk about as if they were afraid of going into the City. Soames just came through Temple-bar to take a peep in the City, and just beyond the Temple-gate he picked a pocket, and was returning with the pocket-book he had taken, when he was seized; one of our patrole saw him do it, and immediately took him by the collar, and found the gentleman whose pocket he saw picked; the case was as plain and clear as possible. But they all seem to go through the City as if they suspected somebody was after them; they do not make any pause; and if they do any thing there, they must do it very quick.

What have been the leading improvements in the Police, that the present Lord Mayor has put in execution since he has been in that office?—The leading improvement, I think, was mustering all the watchmen: I attended him four mornings; we started as early as four in the morning in December last, and during those four mornings he visited each watch-house, and desired I would inform the ward-beadle, that the watchmen were to be summoned at this watch-house and that watch-house at different hours, and he examined every man as to his health and his age, and he had all those discharged that were unfit, notwithstanding any length of service; if they were to be remunerated, he said, the ward must do it, and he would have more efficient men. I consider that to be one of the best things ever done; and I consider that the internal quiet of the City, and the security of the City, is mainly owing to that idea of the Lord Mayor's.

By whom are the watchmen appointed?—By the deputy and common council of the ward.

The

Mr.
Philip Holdsworth.

The deputy and common council of the ward have the management of the watchmen?—Yes, they are paid by the ward, and not by the chamberlain. I consider that the Lord Mayor having the old decrepid men discharged, and having their places filled up by proper men, I consider to have been of great utility. Men discharged from the army, who are wounded, make very good watchmen; they are employed; and the watchmen of the City are now able men, and have strength and activity. We have experienced the great utility of that, all through the City; there have not been more than eight or nine burglaries, the whole winter, in the City. Then again the Lord Mayor himself continues, when he is not expected, to take so many wards of a night, and look in at the watchhouse himself, and takes a marshalman or two with him, and catches them, they not expecting him; which has made the constables on the alert; and he is so punctual in business and so active, that every body is on the alert, and every body is expecting him. I think he has put a spirit of activity into the Police, which I do not remember in so eminent a degree before.

Were you acquainted with a person of the name of McCoul?—Yes.

You well recollect all the circumstances of his case?—I do generally.

Have you any doubt that he was entirely innocent of the accusations that were brought against him, and for which he was tried for his life?—I have no doubt of his being wholly ignorant of the transactions.

In point of fact, was he not employed by you in London, on the very day on which the charge against him was laid that he was uttering false notes in the country?—On two or three of those days he came to report to me what information he had gained on the business I employed him on.

He was a very useful person to you as giving you information on questions concerning the Police of London?—He was; he made me acquainted with people the characters of whom I wanted to know something of, he found means to discover what they were doing, and enabled me several times to prevent burglaries.

It is by means such as these, that you are enabled to apply the principle of a preventive police in the first instance to stop the commission of crimes, and if they are committed to discover the perpetrators?—Yes: It was by his advice in the first instance, that I prevented flash-houses in the City; he said he would never allow one; he said, Never believe they will assist you in finding men, but on the contrary, as soon as you find them forming, stop them. And he used to tell me where they were forming, and he said, Do not allow them to settle.

You consider those houses as furnishing resort to thieves, to be more prejudicial to the public in making thieves, than beneficial to the public by affording means of discovering them?—It is injurious to the public to allow them.

Do the Officers of the City obtain much money from those rewards which are called Parliamentary rewards?—No, very seldom; whenever they are entitled to it, they have it, but it is divided amongst the whole of them.

Do you consider those Parliamentary rewards as a good or bad mode of paying the Officers of the Police?—Infamously bad. I wish McCoul was here, he would name the men, and tell you the supposed crimes for which they suffered, and would give you proofs they were not guilty of the things they suffered for, but he would tell you the confessions of men who afterwards suffered; particularly I remember a man of the name of Arthur Connolly, who committed a highway robbery, and another man was executed for doing it.

Then have you any doubt that in this instance which you have just cited, and do you know of any other instances that lead you to believe, that persons have suffered the sentence of the law, evidence having been produced against them for the purpose of obtaining the reward settled by Act of Parliament?—I only of my own knowledge know of that instance; but I have been told, and I believe that there have been some two or three other instances, and I believe they could be proved, where people have suffered for crimes they did not do; and I am afraid sometimes men have sworn rather too hard.

Do not you consider it as furnishing a temptation to Officers to swear hard against a prisoner, when they are to receive money on his conviction?—I have frequently felt it, and often thought it; I have heard them give their evidence, and been in jeopardy for them.

Is it not within your own experience that juries, seeing an Officer in the box giving evidence against a prisoner, and it being within their knowledge that he is to have a reward upon the conviction of a prisoner, such evidence is often not believed by

them,

Mr.
Philip Holdsworth.

them, though it may be true, to the great impediment of public justice?—I have frequently heard some of the jury ask a witness that question, whether he does not expect, if the prisoner is convicted, to receive a portion or the whole of the money allowed by Act of Parliament, and whether that has not operated upon him at the time; and I have heard that question asked by counsel a hundred times, but I have frequently heard it from the jury.

Have you any doubt that the answers, when given by the witness in the affirmative, must have had that effect upon the jury, such as have been described?—I have often times been convinced that the jury have suspected that the man has been giving a very severe evidence, and too severe against the prisoner, that he has said more than is strictly the fact, and the jury have thought so themselves; the counsel frequently ask that question of him.

Has it ever fallen within your duty to inspect houses of ill fame?—Frequently.

What measures have been taken to suppress them?—By the Officers being about the neighbourhood of an evening, and preventing persons retiring there for those purposes that are suspected to be going on there.

Stopping them in the street?—They have prevented them going in.

Have you ever, in the discharge of the duties of your office, entered and examined any of those houses?—Yes, frequently.

Where?—Principally in Silver-street, at the back of Fleet-street; and in Lombard-street, which joins Fleet-street; in Fleur-de-lis-court; in Black Horse-court; and in a most infamous neighbourhood near Bishopsgate-street, Angel-alley.

Is the house in Silver-street continued in the same business at present?—Yes; it never has been shut up an hour within my recollection; it changes owners, and goes on again.

Is it not found extremely difficult to suppress houses of that kind, under the present existing laws?—There are few things more difficult.

Mr. *William Vale*, called in, and Examined.

Mr.
William Vale.

ARE you one of the common councilmen of the ward of Farringdon Without, for the City of London?—Yes.

In what parish do you live?—Saint Dunstan's and White Friars; my house is in both parishes.

Where do you live?—In Fleet-street.

What is the present state of the Police in your ward?—I think the present state of the Police, particularly in the parish where I reside, is improved of late; I do not think there are so many bad women about our neighbourhood as there were some years ago: I think there are as many houses of ill fame, but I think they are conducted in a different way to what they were; there is a great terror held over them.

Are there as many thieves?—I think not.

How many houses of ill fame are there in your parish of Saint Dunstan's?—About eight.

What measures have been taken to suppress them?—They have been presented by the inquisition repeatedly to the court of aldermen, and sometimes the court of aldermen have directed a prosecution by the City.

Have the tenants ever been convicted?—Yes; I remember one instance, of a house, in Silver-street, I think: I only recollect one instance of their being convicted, because in other instances they have pleaded guilty, and promised to quit the houses.

What penalty was inflicted upon the person convicted?—They were sent to the Giltspur-street Compter for a certain time, but I forget how long, it is some years ago; I think not more than a month, it might be more. I know of no conviction since that period. They have been presented by the inquest, and have been prosecuted by the City since.

And have they removed in consequence?—Two coffee-houses that have been open all night have removed; I do not know of any of the houses of ill fame being prosecuted since that.

Have

Have the houses that have been presented, continued in the same occupation?—Yes.

And where conviction has taken place, have not other persons carried on the same practices in those houses?—Yes; and I believe put in by those parties, according to my own idea.

So that it has been found extremely difficult to suppress houses of that description? —I think it is totally impossible, so long as men will let their houses to persons of that description.

Is it your opinion that a more summary mode of proceeding should be adopted to remove those evils?—Certainly I think there should be, if it is practicable.

From what cause has the state of your Police been improved of late?—I think the constables and the watchmen have been looked after better than they formerly were, by the common council, and those persons under whose directions they are, and by a selection of proper persons for the situations, and by seeing they do their duty.

Have you endeavoured to select patroles of good moral characters, whom you have reason to believe would not receive bribes from bad characters?—Yes; and I think we have succeeded in that respect.

Is it your opinion that many watchmen, and other civil officers, are in the habit of receiving bribes?—I can only speak from hearsay respecting that; I have not been able to satisfy myself on that point.

Is it your opinion?—It is my opinion they do, all, throughout the city of London; I have no doubt of it in my own mind.

APPENDIX.

LIST OF THE APPENDIX.

Appendix,

A P P E N D I X.

Appendix, N° 1ª.

ESTABLISHMENT of the PUBLIC OFFICE, BOW STREET.

Appendix, N° 1.—An ACCOUNT of the ESTABLISHMENT of the Public Office,

RANK of OFFICER.	HIS NAME.	By whom Appointed.	How Appointed.	When Appointed.	Duration of Interest.	RECEIPT: - - - - -			
						Salary.	By whom Paid.	Fees.	By whom Paid.
Chief Magistrate -	Sir Nathaniel Conant,	The Secretary of State for the Home Department - - -	By Letter under the hand of the Secretary of State -	Oct. 1813.	Not expressed.	£. 600 per Annum	John Baldwin, Esq. Receiver of the Seven Police Offices.	- -	- -
Magistrates - -	John Nares, Esq. - -	- - D° - -	- - D° - -	— 1807.	- - -	£. 600 per Ann. -	D° -	- -	- -
	Richard Birnie, Esq.	- - D° - -	- - D° - -	Sept. 1814.	- - -	£. 600 per Ann. -	D° -	- -	- -
Chief Clerk - - -	John Stafford - - -	- - D° - -	- - D° - -	Feb. 1803.	- - -	£. 214 per Ann. -	D° -	- -	- -
Second Clerk - -	Francis Thomas - -	The Magistrates with the approbation and direction of the Secretary of State - -	Verbally	July 1800.	- - -	£. 174 per Ann. -	D° -	- -	- -
Third Clerk - -	Samuel Keene - -	- - D° - -	- - D° - -	— 1799.	- - -	£. 134 per Ann. -	D° -	- -	- -
Extra Clerk - -	William Woods - -	- - D° - -	- - D° - -	Dec. 1808.	- - -	£. 54. 12. per Ann. -	D° -	- -	- -
Eight Officers -	Patrick McManus John Townsend John Sayer John Pearks Stephen Lavender John Vickery Harry Adkins Samuel Taunton	- D° - -	- - D° - -	- - -	- - -	£.1. 1. per Week each	- D° -	- -	- -
Patrole - - -	13 Conductors, or Captains - - - -	The Chief Magistrate, with the approbation and direction of the Secretary of State - - -	- D° -	- - -	- - -	5 s. per Night each	D°		
	87 Men - - -		- D° -	- - -	- - -	2 s. 6 d. per Night each - -			
Superannuated Patrole.	Christopher Codlan	- - D° - -	- - D° - -	- - -	- - -	3 s. 4 d. per Day -	D°		
	William Black Archibald Ruthven	- D° -	- - D° - -	- - -	- - -	2 s. 6 d. per Day each - -	D°		
	11 Men - - -	- D° -	- - D° - -	- - -	- - -	1 s. 3 d. per Day each - -	D°		
Office Keeper - -	Samuel Taunton - -	- D° - -	- - D° - -	- - -	- - -	£. 35 per Ann. - -	D°		
Messenger - -	John Sayer - - -	- D° - -	- - D° - -	- - -	- - -	£. 35 per Ann. - -	D°		
Housekeeper - -	Sarah Stafford - -	- - D° - -	- - D° - -	- - -	- - -	£. 35 per Ann. - -	D°		
Late Chief Magistrate's Widow -	Lady Ford - - -	By Order of the Secretary of State - -			- - -	Pension of £. 200 per Ann. - -	D°		
Officers Widows -	Mary Barnett Ann Mayner Rebecca Jeallous Elizabeth Fugion	By Order of the Secretary of State - -			- - -	Pension of £. 20 per Ann. each -	D°		
Two Door-keepers	William Brooks Thomas Jones	The Magistrates	Verbally -	- - -	- - -	15 s. per Week each	D°		
Two Gaolers - -	John Roguin Smith -	- - D° - -	- - D° - -	- - -	- - -	14 s. per Week -	- D° -		
	Samuel Lack - - -	- - D° - -	- - D° - -	- - -	- - -	7 s. per Week -	- D° -		
Assistant Messenger	Thomas Limbrick - -	- - D° - -	- - D° - -	- - -	- - -	7 s. per Week - -	D° -		
Constable of the Avenues to the Offices at Whitehall -	John Woodlands - -	By Order of the Secretary of State - -			- - -	£. 35 per Ann. - -	D° -	- -	- -
Surgeon - - - -	John Andrews -	By Order of the Secretary of State, for Medical and Surgical Advice and Attendance, including Medicines, &c. for the Officers and Patrole - - -				£. 140 per Ann. -	- D° -	- -	- -

ATTENDANCE:

THIS Office is open at all times, both night and day, with an attendance of Peace Officers therein, and a general attendance of Magistrates and Clerks, from ten in the morning till nine at night, and at such other times and places as the Public Service may require.

DUTIES:

ALL matters and things that relate to the Office of a Justice of the Peace, and especially as it respects the prevention and detection of felonies and atrocious offences in and near the Metropolis, and, when expedient, in distant parts of the kingdom.

Bow-Street, for the Years 1814 and 1815; both Years being alike.

RECEIPT:		TOTAL RECEIPT.	DEDUCTIONS.			Total Disbursements.	Net Annual Receipt.	Net Receipt Annual, upon an Average of the last Three Years.	Other Employments, Places, or Pensions, under Government.	Their Annual Value.
Other Emoluments.	From Whence.		Taxes.	Deputies and Clerks.	Contingencies.					
£.600 per annum for Daily Attendance at the Office of the Secretary of State for the Home Department, in order to assist at Examinations taken at that Office, and to receive directions in matters arising out of the Correspondence with Country Magistrates respecting the Public Peace, and also all matters relating to the Police of the Metropolis, &c. &c.		£.1,200 per Ann.	Income Tax £.120 per Ann.	- -	- -	£.120. per Ann.	£.1,080	- - -	For superintending the Horse Patrole Establishment	£.100.
-	-	£.600 per Ann.	Income Tax £.60 per Ann.	- -	- -	£.60. per Ann.	£.540	£.510, being £.450 for 1813, and £.540 per Ann. for 1814 and 1815.		
-	-	£.600 per Ann.	Income Tax £.60 per Ann.	- -	- -	£.60. per Ann.	£.540			
£.60 per Ann. as Editor of the Hue and Cry, and 10s. per week from the Patrole Establishment	The Receiver	£.300 per Ann.	Income Tax £.30 per Ann.	- -	- -	£.30. per Ann.	£.270	£.265. 10. being £.256. 10. for 1813, and £.270 per Ann. for 1814 & 1815.		
10s. per Week from the Patrole Establishment	- Do -	£.200 per Ann.	Income Tax £.20 per Ann.	- -	- -	£.20. per Ann.	£.180	£.180.	—	—
6s. per Week from same	- Do -	£.149 12. per Ann.	Income Tax £.15. per Ann.	- -	- -	£.15. per Ann.	£.134. 12.	£.134. 12.	—	—
		£.54. 12. per Ann.	- -	- -	- -		£.54. 12.	£.54. 12.	—	—
When sent on Journies, or employed on Public Business, the Magistrates allow them for their trouble and travelling expenses, which Allowance is charged in the Accounts of the Office, and paid by the Receiver.—When they are employed by private persons, such persons pay them for their trouble and expenses		Uncertain; depending wholly upon the business done	Income Tax -	- -	- -	Income Tax	Uncertain	Uncertain	McManus, Townsend and Sayer, have each an Allowance of £.200 per Ann. for attending Their Majesties, The Prince Regent, &c. on public occasions in Town.	
When employed at other times than their hours of duty, they are paid extra, according to their services		- - Do - -	- - Do - -	- -	- -	- Do -	- Do -	- Do.	—	—
-	-	£.61. 16. 8. per Ann.		- -	- -		£.61. 16 8	£.61. 16. 8.	—	—
-	-	£.45. 12. 6. per Ann. each		- -	- -		£.45. 12 6 each	£.45. 12. 6. each.	—	—
-	-	£.22. 16. 3. per Ann. each		- -	- -		£.22. 16 3 each	£.22. 16. 3. each.	—	—
Salary as Officer, inserted above	The Receiver	Uncertain -	Income Tax -	- -	- -	Income Tax	Uncertain	Uncertain.	—	—
Salary as Officer, &c. inserted above	- Do -	- - Do - -	- - Do - -	- -	- -	- Do -	- Do -	- Do.	—	—
Resident in the House	- -	£.35 per Ann.	- -	- -	- -		£.35	£.35.	—	—
-	-	£.200 per Ann.	Income and Pension Tax £.33. 10. per Annum	- -	- -	£.33. 10. per Ann.	£.166. 10.	£.166. 10.	—	—
-	-	£.20 per Ann. each	- -	- -	- -		£.20 each	£.20. each.	—	—
Pay as Patrole, above stated	-	£.84. 12. 6. per Ann. each	Income Tax £.5. 4. per Annum each	- -	- -	£.5. 4. per Ann. each	£.79. 8. 6. each	£.79. 8. 6. each.		
- - Do -	- Do -	£.82. 0. 6. per Ann.	Income Tax £.4. 16. per Annum	- -	- -	£.4 16. per Ann.	£.77. 4. 6.	£.77. 4. 6.	—	—
- - Do -	- Do -	£.63. 16. 6. per Ann.	- -	- -	- -		£.63. 16. 6.	£.63. 16. 6.	—	—
- - Do -	- Do -	£.63. 16. 6. per Ann.	- -	- -	- -		£.63. 16. 6.	£.63. 16. 6.	—	—
-	-	£.35. per Ann.	- -	- -	- -		£.35.	£.35.	Assistant Porter at the Home Department.	
-	-	£.140 per Ann.	- -	- -	- -		£.140.	£.140.	—	—

CONTINGENCIES AND INCIDENTS:
John Baldwin, Esq. Receiver of the Seven Police Offices, also performs the same duty in this Establishment.

NATH. CONANT.

J. NARES.

R. BIRNIE.

Appendix, N° 1ᵇ.

PUBLIC OFFICE, BOW-STREET.—CHARGES of the ESTABLISHMENT, payable for the Quarter ending 5th April 1814.

		£.	s.	d.
1.	To Sir Nathaniel Conant, for One Quarter's Salary - - - -	150	—	—
2.	To Sir Nathaniel Conant, for his Attendance and Services at the Secretary of State's Office, for one Quarter - - - - - -	125	—	—
3.	To Aaron Graham, Esq. for One Quarter's Salary - - -	150	—	—
4.	To John Nares, Esq. for - - - Dᵒ - - - - -	150	—	—
5.	To John Stafford, Chief Clerk, for Dᵒ - - - - -	53	10	—
6.	To Francis Thomas, 2d Clerk, for Dᵒ - - - - -	43	10	—
7.	To Samuel Keene, 3d Clerk, for - Dᵒ - - - - -	33	10	—
8.	To John Stafford, Chief Clerk, for One Quarter's extra Allowance to the three Clerks, for their Trouble arising from the Patrole Establishment -	16	18	—
9.	To John Stafford, Chief Clerk, for One Quarter's Salary to Patrick McManus, John Townsend, John Sayer, John Pearks, Stephen Lavender, John Vickery, Harry Adkins, and Samuel Taunton, the eight Officers, at £.1. 1. per week each - - - - - - - - -	109	4	—
10.	To the Patrole, One Quarter's Wages - - - - - -	1,237	15	—
11.	To John Stafford, Chief Clerk, for One Quarter's Allowance, consisting of 90 days, to the superannuated and infirm Patrole, namely ; Christopher Cridland, at 3s. 4d. per day ; William Black and Archibald Ruthven, at 2s. 6d. per day each ; and Henry Crocker, Samuel Gyde, Donald McGillivreay, John McGregor, Ephraim Wood, John Holloway, Anthony Browne, William Edwards, Alexander Stewart, William Williams, and Thomas Edwards, at 1s. 3d. per day each - - - -	99	7	6
12.	To Samuel Taunton, Office Keeper, for One Quarter's Salary - - -	8	15	—
13.	To John Sayer, Messenger, for - - - - Dᵒ - - - -	8	15	—
14.	To Sarah Dawbiney, Housekeeper, for - - Dᵒ, and Expenses - -	14	4	9
15.	To John Stafford, Editor of the Hue and Cry (£.110 of which he is to pay over to Joseph Downes for printing and publishing, and to retain the remaining £.15 himself for editing the same) as directed by Letter from the Secretary of State, dated 29th April 1813 - - - - -	125	—	—
16.	To One Quarter's Annuity to the Widow of Sir Richard Ford, late Chief Magistrate at this Office, by order of the Secretary of State - -	50	—	—
17.	To One Quarter's Annuity to the Widow of William Barnett, late one of the Officers at this Office, by order of the Secretary of State - - -	5	—	—
18.	To One Quarter's Dᵒ to the Widow of Samuel Mayner - - -	5	—	—
19.	To One Quarter's Dᵒ to the Widow of Charles Jeallous - - -	5	—	—
20.	To One Quarter's Dᵒ to the Widow of Edward Fugion - - -	5	—	—
21.	Two Quarters Parish Rates, due at Lady-day last - - - - -	27	—	—
22	Two Quarters King's Taxes, due at - Dᵒ - - - - -	23	4	—
23.	Two Quarters Rent of the Office, due at Dᵒ, deducting Half a Year's Property Tax - - - - - - - - - -	31	10	—
24.	Two Quarters Rent of the House late adjoining, and now part of this Office, due at Dᵒ, deducting Half a Year's Property Tax - - -	40	10	—
	£	2,517	13	3

EXTRAORDINARY CHARGES;

Being Money allowed by the Magistrates, for Expenses and Trouble incurred by the different Officers and Patrole, in the execution of their Public Duty.

		£.	s.	d.
25.	Pearks	27	16	6
26.	Adkins	8	10	6
27.	Taunton	17	16	5
28.	Bacon	13	10	—
29.	William Smith	21	5	6
30.	Mayhew	2	7	—
31.	Nichols	21	—	6
32.	Taylor and Brooks	19	10	—
33.	Woodlands	8	15	—
34.	John Roguin Smith	9	2	—
35.	Westbrook	6	12	—
	£.	156	5	5

INCIDENTAL CHARGES;

Consisting of Tradesmen's Bills and Accounts, allowed by the Magistrates.

		£.	s.	d.
36.	Mr. Andrews, Surgeon, one Quarter's Allowance for Medical and Surgical Advice and Attendance, including Medicines, &c. for the Officers and Patrole	35	—	—
37.	Downes, for Printing, Stationery, &c.	39	7	5
38.	Harrington, for Oil, Lamps, &c.	21	10	6
39.	Brecknell and Turner, for Candles, &c.	7	6	6
40.	Kennedy, for Newspapers, &c.	8	9	—
41.	Hawkes, for Ironmongery	23	8	6
42.	Mayhew, for Belts for Cutlasses and Pistols	8	—	—
43.	Brynnan, for Glazier's work	2	12	—
44.	Stafford, for the Prosecution of Florence McCarthy, for Sedition	20	18	8
45.	Mr. Warton, Surveyor, for making Plans, Estimates, &c. and surveying the Alterations and Repairs to the House adjoining the Office	63	3	2
46.	Day, for Annual Statement of the number of Offenders	2	2	—
	£.	231	17	9
		156	5	5
		2,517	13	3
	£.	2,905	16	5

Disbursements made at the Office during the Quarter - £. 99   1   10

By Fees and Fines received at the Office during the Quarter   83   7   —

£. 15   14   10

47.	Add Balance due to the Clerks	15	14	10
	£.	2,921	11	3
	Deduct the Amount of the Estimate added to the last Quarter's Account, for paying the Patrole the then current Quarter, from 6th January to 5th April 1814	1,650	—	—
	£.	1,271	11	3
	Add the Amount of the Estimate for paying the Patrole, from 6th April to 5th July 1814	1,650	—	—
	£.	2,921	11	3

WE, the Magistrates of the above Office, having seen and examined the above Account, do allow and approve thereof,

N. CONANT.   J. NARES.   R. BIRNIE.

Appendix, N° 1ᵇ.

PUBLIC OFFICE, BOW-STREET.—CHARGES of the ESTABLISHMENT, payable for the Quarter ending 5th July 1814.

		£.	s.	d.
1.	To Sir Nathaniel Conant, for one Quarter's Salary - - - -	150	—	—
2.	To Sir Nathaniel Conant, for his Attendance and Services at the Secretary of State's Office, for one Quarter - - - - - - -	150	—	—
3.	To Sir Nathaniel Conant, for his Attendance and Services at the Secretary of State's Office, from 5th January to 5th April, omitted in the last Quarterly Account, £.125 only having been charged instead of £.150	25	—	—
4.	To Aaron Graham, Esquire, for one Quarter's Salary - - - -	150	—	—
5.	To John Nares, Esquire, for - - - Dᵒ - - - - - -	150	—	—
6.	To John Stafford, Chief Clerk, for - Dᵒ - - - - - -	53	10	—
7.	To Francis Thomas, Second Clerk, for Dᵒ - - - - - -	43	10	—
8.	To Samuel Keene, Third Clerk, for - Dᵒ - - - - - -	33	10	—
9.	To John Stafford, Chief Clerk, for one Quarter's extra Allowance to the three Clerks, for their Trouble arising from the Patrole Establishment -	16	18	—
10.	To John Stafford, Chief Clerk, for one Quarter's Salary to Patrick Mᶜ Manus, John Townsend, John Sayer, John Pearks, Stephen Lavender, John Vickery, Harry Adkins, and Samuel Taunton, the eight Officers, at £.1. 1. per Week, each - - - - - - - -	109	4	—
11.	To the Patrole, one Quarter's Wages - - - - - - -	1,269	17	6
12.	To John Stafford, Chief Clerk, for one Quarter's Allowance to the Superannuated and infirm Patrole, namely; Christopher Cridland, at 3s. 4d. per day; William Black and Archibald Ruthven, at 2s. 6d. per day, each; and Henry Crocker, Samuel Gyde, Donald Mᶜ Gillivreay, John Mᶜ Gregor, Ephraim Wood, John Holloway, Anthony Browne, William Edwards, Alexander Stuart, William Williams, and Thomas Edwards, at 1s. 3d. per day, each - - - - - -	100	9	7
13.	To Samuel Taunton, Office Keeper, for one Quarter's Salary - - -	8	15	—
14.	To John Sayer, Messenger, for - - - - Dᵒ - - - - -	8	15	—
15.	To Sarah Stafford, Housekeeper, for - - - Dᵒ and Expenses - -	15	—	9
16.	To John Stafford, Editor of the Hue and Cry (£.110, of which he is to pay over to Joseph Downes, for printing and publishing, and to retain the remaining £.15 himself, for editing the same) as directed by Letter from the Secretary of State, dated 29th April 1813 - - - - -	125	—	—
17.	To one Quarter's Annuity to the Widow of Sir Richard Ford, late Chief Magistrate at this Office, by order of the Secretary of State - -	50	—	—
18.	To one Quarter's Annuity to the Widow of William Barnett, late one of the Officers at this Office, by order of the Secretary of State - -	5	—	—
19.	To one Quarter's Dᵒ - - - to the Widow of Samuel Mayner - - -	5	—	—
20.	To one Quarter's Dᵒ - - - to the Widow of Charles Jeallous - - -	5	—	—
21.	To one Quarter's Dᵒ - - - to the Widow of Edward Fugion - - -	5	—	—
22.	Sewer Rate, for the adjoining House - - - - - - - -	2	10	—
	£.	2,481	19	10

EXTRAORDINARY CHARGES;

Being Money allowed by the Magistrates, for Expenses and Trouble incurred by the different Officers and Patrole, in the execution of their Public Duty.

		£.	s.	d.
23.	Townsend - - - - - - - - - - - -	38	—	6
24.	Vickery - - - - - - - - - - - -	94	12	9
25.	Adkins - - - - - - - - - - - -	22	18	6
26.	Taunton - - - - - - - - - - - -	29	6	—
27.	Rivett - - - - - - - - - - - -	7	8	—
28.	Lavender - - - - - - - - - - - -	10	19	6
29.	Limbrick - - - - - - - - - - - -	23	15	—
30.	Bacon - - - - - - - - - - - -	21	18	—
31.	Lewis - - - - - - - - - - - -	19	15	—
32.	Jones - - - - - - - - - - - -	14	7	6
33.	W. Smith - - - - - - - - - - - -	16	17	6
34.	Perry - - - - - - - - - - - -	28	15	—
35.	Gibbs - - - - - - - - - - - -	13	10	—
36.	Mayhew - - - - - - - - - - - -	14	15	—
37.	Cox - - - - - - - - - - - -	14	17	6
38.	Nichols - - - - - - - - - - - -	6	5	6
39.	J. Smith - - - - - - - - - - - -	8	5	—
40.	Salmon - - - - - - - - - - - -	25	9	1
41.	Bishop - - - - - - - - - - - -	7	17	6
42.	Taylor and Brooks - - - - - - - - - -	19	10	—
43.	J. R. Smith - - - - - - - - - - - -	9	2	—
44.	Woodlands - - - - - - - - - - - -	8	15	—
45.	Westbrook - - - - - - - - - - - -	2	16	—
46.	G. Ruthven - - - - - - - - - - - -	4	4	—
47.	Nixon - - - - - - - - - - - -	3	18	10
48.	Westcott - - - - - - - - - - - -	2	8	—
	£.	470	6	8

N. B.—Sundry Extraordinary Expenses have been incurred during this Quarter, by the attendance of the Officers and Patrole in London and other Places, occasioned by the Visit of the Emperor of Russia, the King of Prussia, and other illustrious Strangers to this Country, which are intended to be made out, and charged in a separate Account.

INCIDENTAL CHARGES;

Consisting of Tradesmen's Bills and Accounts, allowed by the Magistrates.

		£.	s.	d.
49.	Mr. Andrews, Surgeon, one Quarter's Allowance for Medical and Surgical Advice and Attendance, including Medicine, &c. for the Officers and Patrole - - - - - - - - - - -	35	—	—
50.	Downes, for Printing, Stationary, &c. - - - - - - -	41	6	10
51.	Harrington, for Oil, Lamps, &c. - - - - - - -	14	19	—
52.	Bricknell and Turner, for Candles, &c. - - - - - -	9	19	9
53.	Kennedy, for Newspapers, &c. - - - - - - -	8	9	—
54.	Hawkes, for Ironmongery - - - - - - - -	47	1	—
55.	Soulsby, Allison and Co. for Coals - - - - - - -	41	5	6
56.	Brynnan, for Glazier's Work - - - - - - -	2	16	—
57.	Reed and Hunter, for Law Books - - - - - - -	3	17	6
58.	Stafford, for the Prosecution of James King, William Mansfield Evans, and Edward Sadler, for maliciously cutting Vickery, one of the Officers, in the execution of his Duty, with intent to murder him - - -	36	18	8
59.	Owen, for Illuminating the front of the Office six nights - - -	41	17	4
		283	10	7
		470	6	8
		2,481	19	10
		3,235	17	1

Disbursements made at the Office during the Quarter - £. 135 5 4
By Fees and Fines received at the Office during the Quarter, 115 14 —

		£. 19	11	4
60.	Add Balance due to the Clerks - - - - - - - -	19	11	4
		3,255	8	5

Deduct the Amount of the Estimate added to the last Quarter's Account, for paying the Patrole the then current Quarter, from 6th April to 5th July 1814 - - - - - - - - 1,650 — —

		1,005	8	5

Add the Amount of the Estimate for paying the Patrole, from 6th July to 5th October 1814 - - - - - - - - 1,650 — —

	£.	3,255	8	5

WE, the Magistrates of the above Office, having seen and examined the above Account, do allow and approve thereof.

          N. CONANT.   J. NARES.   R. BIRNIE.

Appendix, N° 1ᶜ.

PUBLIC OFFICE, BOW STREET.—CHARGES of the ESTABLISHMENT, payable for the
Quarter ending 5th October 1814.

		£.	s.	d.
1.	To Sir Nathaniel Conant, for one Quarter's Salary - - - -	150	—	—
2.	To Sir Nathaniel Conant, for his Attendance and Services at the Secretary of State's Office, for one Quarter - - - - - - -	150	—	—
3.	To John Nares, Esq. for one Quarter's Salary - - - -	150	—	—
4.	To Aaron Graham, Esq. late one of the Magistrates of this Office, for his Salary to the 16th day of September last, inclusive, 73 days - -	112	17	9
5.	To Richard Birnie, Esq. one of the Magistrates of this Office, for his Salary from the 16th day of September last, 24 days - - - -	37	2	3
6.	To John Stafford, Chief Clerk, for one Quarter's Salary - - -	53	10	—
7.	To Francis Thomas, Second Clerk, for D° - - - - -	43	10	—
8.	To Samuel Keene, Third Clerk, for - D° - - - - - -	33	10	—
9.	To John Stafford, Chief Clerk, for one Quarter's extra Allowance to the three Clerks, for their Trouble arising from the Patrole Establishment -	16	18	—
10.	To John Stafford, Chief Clerk, for one Quarter's Salary to Patrick Mᶜ Manus, John Townsend, John Sayer, John Pearks, Stephen Lavender, John Vickery, Harry Adkins, and Samuel Taunton, the eight Officers, at £. 1. 1. per Week each - - - - - - - -	109	4	—
11.	To the Patrole, one Quarter's Wages - - - - - -	1,287	2	6
12.	To John Stafford, Chief Clerk, for one Quarter's Allowance, consisting of 92 days, to the superannuated and infirm Patrole, namely ; Christopher Cridland, at 3s.4d. per day ; William Black and Archibald Ruthven, at 2s.6d. per day, each ; Henry Crocker, Samuel Gyde, Donald Mᶜ Gillivreay, John Mᶜ Gregor, Ephraim Wood, John Holloway, Anthony Browne, William Edwards, Alexander Stuart, William Williams, and Thomas Edwards, at 1s. 3d. per day, each - - - - - - -	101	11	8
13.	To Samuel Taunton, Office Keeper, for one Quarter's Salary - - -	8	15	—
4.	To John Sayer, Messenger, for - - - - D° - - - -	8	15	—
5.	To Sarah Stafford, Housekeeper, for - - - D° - and Expenses -	12	15	3
16.	To John Stafford, Editor of the Hue and Cry (£. 110 of which he is to pay over to Joseph Downes, for printing and publishing, and to retain the remaining £. 15 himself, for editing the same) as directed by Letter from the Secretary of State, dated 29th April 1813 - - - -	125	—	—
17.	To one Quarter's Annuity to the Widow of Sir Richard Ford, late Chief Magistrate at this Office, by order of the Secretary of State - -	50	—	—
18.	To one Quarter's Annuity to the Widow of William Barnett, late one of the Officers at this Office, by order of the Secretary of State - -	5	—	—
19.	To one Quarter's D° - - - to the Widow of Samuel Mayner - - -	5	—	—
20.	To one Quarter's D° - - - to the Widow of Charles Jeallous - - -	5	—	—
21.	To one Quarter's D° - - - to the Widow of Edward Fugion - - -	5	—	—
22.	Two Quarters Parish Rates, due at Michaelmas-day last - - -	31	11	8
23.	Two Quarters King's Taxes, due at D° - - - - - - - -	21	14	—
24.	Two Quarters Rent of the Office due at D°, deducting half-a-year's Property Tax - - - - - - - - - -	31	10	—
25.	Two Quarters Rent of the House late adjoining, and now part of this Office, due at Michaelmas-day last, deducting Half-a-Year's Property Tax - - - - - - - - - - - -	40	10	—
	£.	2,595	17	1

EXTRAORDINARY CHARGES;

Being Money allowed by the Magistrates, for Expenses and Trouble incurred by the different Officers and Patrole, in the execution of their Public Duty.

		£.	s.	d.
26.	Townsend -	85	18	—
27.	Pearks	2	17	—
28.	Adkins	42	14	4
29.	Taunton	2	3	--
30.	Limbrick	7	15	—
31.	Bacon	124	13	6
32.	Lewis	4	5	—
33.	Gibbs	45	12	6
34.	Mayhew	2	5	—
35.	Cox	6	7	6
36.	Nichols	55	2	6
37.	Bishop	7	12	6
38.	Taylor and Brooks	19	10	—
39.	Woodlands	8	15	—
40.	John Roguin Smith	9	2	—
41.	Edwards -	3	—	—
	£.	427	12	10

INCIDENTAL CHARGES;

Consisting of Tradesmen's Bills and Accounts, allowed by the Magistrates.

		£.	s.	d.
42.	Mr. Andrews, Surgeon, one Quarter's Allowance for Medical and Surgical Advice and Attendance, including Medicines, &c. for the Officers and Patrole	35	—	—
43.	Downes, for Printing, Stationary, &c.	40	19	—
44.	Harrington, for Oil, Lamps, &c.	20	11	—
45.	Soulsby, Allison & Co. for Coals	18	14	—
46.	Brecknell and Turner, for Candles, &c.	15	15	11
47.	Kennedy, for Newspapers, &c. -	8	9	—
48.	Lucas and Hodgson, for lighting Lamps at the Office Door	4	10	—
49.	Drury and Son, for Carpeting	17	10	6
50.	Parker, for Cutlasses, repairing Fire Arms, &c. -	23	8	6
51.	Lewis, for Constables Truncheons	12	8	—
52.	Brynnan, for Glazier's Work	2	—	—
		199	5	11
		427	12	10
		2,595	17	1
		3,222	15	10

Disbursements made at the Office during the Quarter   £. 168   3   1

By Fees and Fines received at the Office during the Quarter,   142 16 —

£. 25   7   1

53.	Add Balance due to the Clerks	25	7	1
		3,248	2	11
	Deduct the Amount of the Estimate added to the last Quarter's Account, for paying the Patrole the then current Quarter, from 6th July to 5th October 1814 -	1,650	—	—
		1,598	2	11
	Add the Amount of the Estimate for paying the Patrole, from 6th October 1814 to 5th January 1815 -	1,650	—	—
	£.	3,248	2	11

WE, the Magistrates of the above Office, having seen and examined the above Account, do allow and approve thereof.

N. CONANT.
J. NARES.
R. BIRNIE.

Appendix, N° 1ᵈ.

Public Office, Bow-Street.—CHARGES of the ESTABLISHMENT, payable for the Quarter ending 5th January 1815.

		£.	s.	d.
1.	To Sir Nathaniel Conant, for one Quarter's Salary - - - -	150	—	—
2.	To Sir Nathaniel Conant, for his Attendance and Services at the Secretary of State's Office, for one Quarter - - - - - - -	150	—	—
3.	To John Nares, Esq. for one Quarter's Salary - - - - -	150	—	—
4.	To Richard Birnie, Esq. for - - - Dº - - - - - -	150	—	—
5.	To John Stafford, Chief Clerk, for - Dº - - - - - -	53	10	—
6.	To Francis Thomas, Second Clerk, for Dº - - - - - -	43	10	—
7.	To Samuel Keene, Third Clerk, for Dº - - - - - -	33	10	—
8.	To John Stafford, Chief Clerk, for one Quarter's extra Allowance to the three Clerks, for their Trouble arising from the Patrole Establishment -	16	18	—
9.	To John Stafford, Chief Clerk, for one Quarter's Salary; to Patrick McManus, John Townsend, John Sayer, John Pearks, Stephen Lavender, John Vickery, Harry Adkins, and Samuel Taunton, the eight Officers at 1 l. 1 s. per Week, each - - - - - - - -	109	4	—
10.	To the Patrole, one Quarter's Wages - - - - - - -	1,292	10	—
11.	To John Stafford, Chief Clerk, for one Quarter's Allowance, consisting of 92 days; to the superannuated and infirm Patrole, namely; Christopher Cridland, at 3 s. 4 d. per day; William Black and Archibald Ruthven, at 2 s. 6 d. per day each; and Henry Crocker, Samuel Gyde, Donald McGillivreay, John McGregor, Ephraim Wood, John Holloway, Anthony Browne, William Edwards, Alexander Stuart, William Williams, and Thomas Edwards, at 1 s. 3 d. per day, each - - - - -	101	11	8
12.	To Samuel Taunton, Office Keeper, for one Quarter's Salary - - -	8	15	—
13.	To John Sayer, Messenger for - - - Dº - - - - -	8	15	—
14.	To Sarah Stafford, Housekeeper for - - Dº and Expences - -	12	8	—
15.	To John Stafford, Editor of the Hue and Cry, (£. 110 of which he is to pay over to Joseph Downes, for printing and publishing, and to retain the remaining £. 15 himself for editing the same) as directed by Letter from the Secretary of State, dated 29th April 1813 - - - - -	125	—	—
16.	To one Quarter's Annuity to the Widow of Sir Richard Ford, late Chief Magistrate at this Office, by order of the Secretary of State - -	50	—	—
17.	To one Quarter's Annuity to the Widow of William Barnett, late one of the Officers at this Office, by order of the Secretary of State - - -	5	—	—
18.	To one Quarter's Dº - - - to the Widow of Samuel Mayner - - -	5	—	—
19.	To one Quarter's Dº - - - to the Widow of Charles Jeallous - - -	5	—	—
20.	To one Quarter's Dº - - - to the Widow of Edward Fugion - - -	5	—	—
	£.	2,475	11	8

EXTRAORDINARY CHARGES;

Being Money allowed by the Magistrates, for Expenses and Trouble incurred by the different Officers and Patrole, in the execution of their Public Duty.

		£.	s.	d.
21.	Townsend - - - - - - - - - - - -	66	18	—
22.	Pearks - - - - - - - - - - - -	32	16	—
23.	Vickery - - - - - - - - - - - -	39	2	—
24.	Adkins - - - - - - - - - - - -	3	16	—
25.	Joseph Beckett - - - - - - - - - - -	20	5	6
26.	Richard Limbrick - - - - - - - - - - -	2	12	6
27.	Bacon - - - - - - - - - - - -	13	16	—
28.	Perry - - - - - - - - - - - -	2	13	—
29.	Nichols - - - - - - - - - - - -	2	16	6
30.	Salmon - - - - - - - - - - - -	2	2	—
31.	Bishop - - - - - - - - - - - -	10	19	—
32.	Taylor and Brooks - - - - - - - - - -	19	10	—
33.	John Rogum Smith - - - - - - - - - -	9	2	—
34.	Woodlands - - - - - - - - - - - -	8	15	—
35.	George Ruthven - - - - - - - - - - -	4	—	—
36.	Mance - - - - - - - - - - - -	3	13	6
37.	Wilson - - - - - - - - - - - -	2	1	—
	£.	244	18	—

INCIDENTAL CHARGES;

Consisting of Tradesmen's Bills and Accounts, allowed by the Magistrates.

		£.	s.	d.
38.	Mr. Andrews, Surgeon, One Quarter's Allowance for Medical and Surgical Advice and Attendance, including Medicines, &c. for the Officers and Patroles - - - - - - - - - - -	35	—	—
39.	Downes, for Printing, Stationary, &c. - - - - - - -	44	1	8
40.	Harrington, for Oil, Lamps, &c. - - - - - - - -	19	12	—
41.	Brecknell and Turner, for Candles, &c. - - - - - - -	7	16	6
42.	Hawkes, for Smith's Work, Ironmongery, &c. - - - - -	10	11	7
43.	Kennedy, for Newspapers, &c. - - - - - - - -	8	9	—
44.	Brynman, for Glazier's work - - - - - - - -	3	7	6
45.	Mr. John Cadogan, Builder, in further part, for Work done pursuant to his Contracts for repairing the adjoining House and Office - - -	750	—	—
	£.	878	18	3
		244	18	—
		2,475	11	8
		3,599	7	11

By Fees and Fines received at the Office during the Quarter £.126 2 —
Deduct Disbursements made at the Office during the Quarter - 121 6 6

	£.	4	15	6

Deduct Balance in the Clerk's hands - - - - - - -	4	15	6

| | | 3,594 | 12 | 5 |

| Deduct the Amount of the Estimate added to the last Quarter's Account, for paying the Patrole the then current Quarter, from 6th October 1814 to 5th January 1815 - - - - - - - - - - | 1,650 | — | — |

| | | 1,944 | 12 | 5 |

| Add the Amount of the Estimate for paying the Patrole, from 6th January to 5th April 1815 - - - - - - - - - - - | 1,650 | — | — |

| | £. | 3,594 | 12 | 5 |

WE, the Magistrates of the above Office, having seen and examined the above Accounts, do allow and approve thereof.

N. CONANT.
J. NARES.
R. BIRNIE.

Appendix, N° 1ᵉ.

PUBLIC OFFICE, BOW-STREET.—CHARGES of the ESTABLISHMENT, payable for the Quarter ending 5th April 1815.

		£.	s.	d.
1.	To Sir Nathaniel Conant, for one Quarter's Salary - - - -	150	—	—
2.	To Sir Nathaniel Conant, for his Attendance and Services at the Secretary of State's Office, for one Quarter - - - - - - -	150	—	—
3.	To John Nares, Esq. for one Quarter's Salary - - - - -	150	—	—
4.	To Richard Birnie, Esq. for - - Dᵒ - - - - -	150	—	—
5.	To John Stafford, Chief Clerk, for - Dᵒ - - - - - -	53	10	—
6.	To Francis Thomas, Second Clerk, for Dᵒ - - - - -	43	10	—
7.	To Samuel Keene, Third Clerk, for - Dᵒ - - - - -	33	10	—
8.	To John Stafford, Chief Clerk, for one Quarter's extra Allowance to the three Clerks, for their Trouble arising from the Patrole Establishment -	16	18	—
9.	To John Stafford, Chief Clerk, for one Quarter's Salary to Patrick Mᶜ Manus, John Townsend, John Sayer, John Pearks, Stephen Lavender, John Vickery, Harry Adkins, and Samuel Taunton, the eight Officers, at £.1. 1. per Week each - - - - - - - -	109	4	—
10.	To the Patrole, one Quarter's Wages - - - - - - -	1,262	6	3
11.	To John Stafford, Chief Clerk, for one Quarter's Allowance, consisting of ninety days, to the superannuated and infirm Patrole, namely ; Christopher Cridland, at 3s. 4d. per day; William Black and Archibald Ruthven, at 2s. 6d. per day, each ; and Henry Crocker, Samuel Gyde, Donald Mᶜ Gillivreay, John Mᶜ Gregor, Ephraim Wood, John Holloway, Anthony Browne, William Edwards, Alexander Stuart, William Williams, and Thomas Edwards, at 1s. 3d. per day, each - -	99	7	6
12.	To Samuel Taunton, Office Keeper, for one Quarter's Salary - - -	8	15	—
13.	To John Sayer, Messenger, for - - - - - Dᵒ - - - -	8	15	—
14.	To Sarah Stafford, Housekeeper, for - - - Dᵒ and Expenses - -	13	15	10
15.	To John Stafford, Editor of the Hue and Cry (£.110 of which he is to pay over to Joseph Downes for printing and publishing, and to retain the remaining £.15 himself for editing the same) as directed by Letter from the Secretary of State, dated 29th April 1813 - - - -	125	—	—
16.	To one Quarter's Annuity to the Widow of Sir Richard Ford, late Chief Magistrate at this Office, by order of the Secretary of State - -	50	—	—
17.	To one Quarter's Annuity to the Widow of William Barnett, late one of the Officers at this Office, by order of the Secretary of State - -	5	—	—
18.	To one Quarter's Dᵒ to the Widow of Samuel Mayner - - - -	5	—	—
19.	To one Quarter's Dᵒ to the Widow of Charles Jeallous - - - -	5	—	—
20.	To one Quarter's Dᵒ to the Widow of Edward Fugion - - - -	5	—	—
21.	Two Quarters Parish Rates, due at Lady-day last - - - -	30	16	8
22.	Two Quarters King's Taxes, due at - Dᵒ - - - - - -	21	14	—
23.	Two Quarters Rent of the Office, due at Dᵒ, deducting Half a Year's Property Tax - - - - - - - - - - -	31	10	—
24.	Two Quarters Rent of the House late adjoining, and now part of this Office, due at Dᵒ, deducting Half a Year's Property Tax - - - -	40	10	—
	£	2,569	2	3

EXTRAORDINARY CHARGES;

Being Money allowed by the Magistrates, for Expenses and Trouble incurred by the different Officers and Patrole, in the execution of their Public Duty.

		£.	s.	d.
25.	Townsend	61	2	—
26.	Sayer	61	2	—
27.	Pearks	2	2	—
28.	Taunton	11	5	6
29.	Adkins	2	2	—
30.	Limbrick	10	17	6
31.	Bacon	44	14	—
32.	Perry	10	—	—
33.	Gibbs	2	12	—
34.	Cox	2	2	6
35.	Nichols	6	15	—
36.	Salmon	3	19	10
37.	Bishop	11	10	—
38.	Taylor and Brooks	19	10	—
39.	John Roguin Smith	9	2	—
40.	Woodlands	8	15	—
41.	Murry	5	—	—
42.	Upton	5	15	—
43.	James John Smith	13	4	—
44.	Westbrook	18	10	6
45.	Ruthven	6	8	—
46.	Lines	4	—	—
47.	Dickens	2	4	—
	£.	322	12	10

INCIDENTAL CHARGES;

Consisting of Tradesmen's Bills and Accounts, allowed by the Magistrates.

		£.	s.	d.
48.	Mr. Andrews, Surgeon, one Quarter's Allowance for Medical and Surgical Advice and Attendance, including Medicines, &c. for the Officers and Patrole	35	—	—
49.	Downes, for Printing, Stationary, &c.	30	9	4
50.	Harrington, for Oil, Lamps, &c.	19	13	—
51.	Brecknell and Turner, for Candles, &c.	17	10	8
52.	Kennedy, for Newspapers, &c.	8	9	—
53.	Brynnan, for Glazier's Work	4	3	—
54.	Soulsby, Allison and Co. for Coals	36	13	—
55.	Reed and Hunter, for Law Books	2	11	—
56.	Day, for Annual Statement of the Number of Offenders	2	2	—
		156	11	—
		322	12	10
		2,569	2	3
		3,048	6	1

Disbursements made at the Office during the Quarter - £. 113 11 4
Fees and Fines received at the Office during the Quarter - 113 — 6

£. — 10 10

		£.	s.	d.
57.	Add Balance due to the Clerks	—	10	10
		3,048	16	11
	Deduct £.1,386. 1. 3. the Sum of £.263. 18. 9. being paid short of the Estimate of £.1,650, added to the last Quarter's Account for paying the Patrole the then current Quarter, from 6th January to 5th April 1815	1,386	1	3
		1,662	15	8
	Add the Amount of the Estimate for paying the Patrole, from 6th April to 5th July 1815	1,650	—	—
	£.	3,312	15	8

WE, the Magistrates of the above Office, having seen and examined the above Account, do allow and approve thereof.

N. CONANT.
J. NARES.
R. BIRNIE.

Appendix, N° 1^f.

PUBLIC OFFICE, BOW-STREET.—CHARGES of the ESTABLISHMENT, payable for the Quarter ending 5th July 1815.

		£.	s.	d.
1.	To Sir Nathaniel Conant, for one Quarter's Salary - - - -	150	—	—
2.	To Sir Nathaniel Conant, for his Attendance and Services at the Secretary of State's Office, for one Quarter - - - - - - -	150	—	—
3.	To John Nares, Esq. for one Quarter's Salary - - - - -	150	—	—
4.	To Richard Birnie, Esq. for - - - D° - - - - -	150	—	—
5.	To John Stafford, Chief Clerk, for - D° - - - - - -	53	10	—
6.	To Francis Thomas, Second Clerk, for D° - - - - - -	43	10	—
7.	To Samuel Keene, Third Clerk, for - D° - - - - - -	33	10	—
8.	To John Stafford, Chief Clerk, for one Quarter's extra Allowance to the three Clerks, for their Trouble arising from the Patrole Establishment -	16	18	—
9.	To John Stafford, Chief Clerk, for one Quarter's Salary to Patrick McManus, John Townsend, John Sayer, John Pearks, Stephen Lavender, John Vickery, Harry Adkins, and Samuel Taunton, the eight Officers at 1 l. 1 s. per Week, each - - - - - - - - -	109	4	—
10.	To the Patrole, one Quarter's Wages - - - - - - -	1,277	11	—
11.	To John Stafford, Chief Clerk, for one Quarter's Allowance, consisting of 91 days, to the superannuated and infirm Patrole, viz. Christopher Cridland, at 3 s. 4 d. per day; William Black and Archibald Ruthven, at 2 s. 6 d. per day, each; and Henry Crocker, Samuel Gyde, Donald McGillivreay, John McGregor, Ephraim Wood, John Holloway, Anthony Browne, William Edwards, Alexander Stuart, William Williams, and Thomas Edwards, at 1 s. 3 d. per day, each - - - - -	100	9	7
12.	To Samuel Taunton, Office Keeper, for one Quarter's Salary - - -	8	15	—
13.	To John Sayer, Messenger, for - - - - D° - - - -	8	15	—
14.	To Sarah Stafford, Housekeeper, for - - D° and Expenses - -	13	10	4
15.	To John Stafford, Editor of the Hue' and Cry (110 l. of which he is to pay over to Joseph Downes, for printing and publishing, and to retain the remaining 15 l. himself, for editing the same) as directed by Letter from the Secretary of State - - - - - - - - -	125	—	—
16.	To one Quarter's Annuity to the Widow of Sir Richard Ford, late Chief Magistrate at this Office, by order of the Secretary of State - -	50	—	—
17.	To one Quarter's Annuity to the Widow of William Barnett, late one of the Officers at this Office, by order of the Secretary of State - - -	5	—	—
18.	To one Quarter's D° - - - to the Widow of Samuel Mayner - - -	5	—	—
19.	To one Quarter's D° - - - to the Widow of Charles Jeallous - - -	5	—	—
20.	To one Quarter's D° - - - to the Widow of Edward Fugion - - -	5	—	—
	£.	2,460	13	2

EXTRAORDINARY CHARGES;

Being Money allowed by the Magistrates, for Expenses and Trouble incurred by the different Officers and Patrole, in the execution of their Public Duty.

		£.	s.	d.
21.	Townsend	87	—	—
22.	Sayer	87	—	—
23.	Pearks	11	12	6
24.	Vickery	39	19	—
25.	Adkins	12	6	—
26.	Taunton	8	4	6
27.	R. Limbrick	2	12	6
28.	Bacon	13	13	—
29.	Lewis	2	4	6
30.	C. Jones	17	—	—
31.	W. Smith	2	4	6
32.	Perry	4	17	6
33.	Mayhew	5	5	—
34.	Nichols	5	—	—
35.	Salmon	5	—	—
36.	Bishop	3	10	—
37.	Brooks and Jones	19	10	—
38.	J. R. Smith	9	2	—
39.	Woodlands	8	15	—
40.	G. Ruthven	3	15	—
41.	Godfrey	2	10	—
42.	Lines	2	6	—
43.	Vaughan	2	1	4
	£.	355	8	4

INCIDENTAL CHARGES;

Consisting of Tradesmen's Bills and Accounts, allowed by the Magistrates.

		£.	s.	d.
44.	Mr. Andrews, Surgeon, one Quarter's Allowance for Medical and Surgical Advice and Attendance, including Medicines, &c. for the Officers and Patrole	35	—	—
45.	Downes, for Printing, Stationary, &c.	30	10	—
46.	Harrington, for Oil for Lamps	15	6	6
47.	Brecknell and Turner, for Candles, &c.	9	17	9
48.	Kennedy, for Newspapers, &c.	8	9	—
49.	Brynnan, for Glazier's Work	5	15	—
50.	Soulsby, Allison and Co. for Coals	16	14	—
51.	Owen, for new Lamps, repairing, &c.	18	15	8
52.	Lucas and Hodgson, for lighting Lamps at Office Door, for One Year	4	10	—
53.	Mr. John Cadogan, Builder, the remainder of his Bill for Work done pursuant to his Contracts for repairing the adjoining House and Office	235	11	9
54.	Mr. Shearman's Bill of Costs, for defending an Action brought against George Oddy, one of the Patrole of this Office, in the due execution of his duty	7	—	4
55.	Payne, Constable of Birmingham, for Reward advertised by the Office, for the apprehension of Joseph King for Burglary	20	—	—
		407	10	—
		355	8	4
		2,460	13	2
		3,223	11	6

Disbursements made at the Office during the Quarter   £.126 19 2
Fees and Fines received at the Office during the Quarter   113 17 —
                                £.13 2 2

		£.	s.	d.
56.	Add Balance due to the Clerks	13	2	2
		3,236	13	8
	Deduct the Amount of the Estimate added to the last Quarter's Account, for paying the Patrole the then current Quarter from 6th April to 5th July 1815	1,650	—	—
		1,586	13	8
	Add the Amount of the Estimate for paying the Patrole from the 6th July to the 5th October 1815	1,650	—	—
	£.	3,236	13	8

WE, the Magistrates of the above Office, having seen and examined the above Account, do allow and approve thereof.

N. CONANT.   J. NARES,   R. BIRNIE.

Appendix, No. 1ˢ.

PUBLIC OFFICE, BOW STREET.—CHARGES of the ESTABLISHMENT, payable for the Quarter ending 5th October 1815.

		£.	s.	d.
1.	To Sir Nathaniel Conant, for one Quarter's Salary - - - -	150	—	—
2.	To Sir Nathaniel Conant, for his Attendance and Services at the Secretary of State's Office, for one Quarter - - - - - -	150	—	—
3.	To John Nares, Esq. for one Quarter's Salary - - - -	150	—	—
4.	To Richard Birnie, Esq. for - - D° - - - - - -	150	—	—
5.	To John Stafford, Chief Clerk, for - D° - - - - -	53	10	—
6.	To Francis Thomas, Second Clerk, for D° - - - - -	43	10	—
7.	To Samuel Keene, Third Clerk, for - D° - - - - -	33	10	—
8.	To John Stafford, Chief Clerk, for one Quarter's Allowance to the three Clerks, for their Trouble arising from the Patrole Establishment - -	16	18	—
9.	To John Stafford, Chief Clerk, for one Quarter's Salary to Patrick M°Manus, John Townsend, John Sayer, John Pearks, Stephen Lavender, John Vickery, Harry Adkins, and Samuel Taunton, the eight Officers, at £.1.1. per Week each - - - - - - - -	109	4	—
10.	To the Patrole, one Quarter's Wages - - - - - -	1,265	12	6
11.	To John Stafford, Chief Clerk, for one Quarter's Allowance, consisting of 92 days, to the superannuated and infirm Patrole, namely ; Christopher Cridland, at 3s. 4d. per day ; William Black and Archibald Ruthven, at 2s. 6d. per day, each ; and Henry Crocker, Samuel Gyde, Donald M°Gillivreay, John M°Gregor, Ephraim Wood, John Holloway, Anthony Browne, William Edwards, Alexander Stuart, William Williams, and Thomas Edwards, at 1s. 3d. per day, each - - - - -	101	11	8
12.	To Samuel Taunton, Office Keeper, for one Quarter's Salary - - -	8	15	—
13.	To John Sayer, Messenger, for - - - - Ditto - - - -	8	15	—
14.	To Sarah Stafford, Housekeeper, for - - Ditto and Expenses - -	13	11	3
15.	To John Stafford, Editor of the Hue and Cry (£.110 of which he is to pay over to Joseph Downes, for printing and publishing, and to retain the remaining £.15 himself, for editing the same) as directed by Letter from the Secretary of State, dated 29th April 1813 - - - - -	125	—	—
16.	To one Quarter's Annuity to the widow of Sir Richard Ford, late Chief Magistrate at this Office, by order of the Secretary of State - -	50	—	—
17.	To one Quarter's Annuity to the Widow of William Barnett, late one of the Officers at this Office, by order of the Secretary of State - -	5	—	—
18.	To one Quarter's - - D° - - to the Widow of Samuel Mayner - -	5	—	—
19.	To one Quarter's - - D° - - to the Widow of Charles Jeallous -	5	—	—
20.	To one Quarter's - - D° - - to the Widow of Edward Fugion -	5	—	—
21.	Two Quarters Parish Rates, due at Michaelmas-day last - - -,	28	15	—
22.	Two Quarters King's Taxes, due at - - D° - - - - - -	21	14	—
23.	Two Quarters Rent of the Office, due at - D° - deducting Half a Year's Property Tax - - - - - - - - - -	31	10	—
24.	Two Quarters Rent of the House late adjoining, and now part of this Office, due at D°, deducting Half a Year's Property Tax - - - -	40	10	—
	£.	2,572	6	5

EXTRAORDINARY CHARGES;
Being Money allowed by the Magistrates, for Expenses and Trouble incurred by the different Officers and Patrole, in the execution of their Public Duty.

		£.	s.	d.
25.	Townsend	68	5	—
26.	Pearks	43	3	6
27.	Lavender	6	19	—
28.	Vickery	32	6	6
29.	Taunton	4	13	6
30.	Dowsett	5	2	—
31.	R. Limbrick	11	—	—
32.	Bacon	17	16	—
33.	Lewis	4	15	—
34.	Wm Smith	4	15	—
35.	Perry	5	8	5
36.	Gibbs	3	15	—
37.	Mayhew	9	9	4
38.	Cox	14	—	—
39.	Nichols	23	4	6
40.	J. Smith	3	—	—
41.	Salmon	8	—	—
42.	Bishop	4	17	6
43.	Nixon	36	15	—
44.	Bond	16	19	—
45.	Brooks and Jones	19	10	—
46.	Woodlands	8	15	—
47.	J. R. Smith	9	2	—
48.	G. Ruthven	7	3	6
49.	A. Ruthven	2	11	—
50.	Upton	2	5	—
	£.	273	10	9

INCIDENTAL CHARGES;
Consisting of Tradesmen's Bills and Accounts, allowed by the Magistrates.

		£.	s.	d.
51.	Mr. Andrews, Surgeon, one Quarter's Allowance for Medical and Surgical Advice and Attendance, including Medicines, &c. for the Officers and Patrole	35	—	—
52.	Scrivener, for Plumber's Work	23	15	—
53.	Downes, for Printing, Stationary, &c.	34	7	—
54.	Harrington, for Oil, Lamps, &c.	20	11	—
55.	Brecknell and Turner, for Candles, &c.	9	9	—
56.	Kennedy, for Newspapers, &c.	8	14	—
57.	Brynnan, for Glazier's Work	4	13	3
58.	Buckley, for Floor Cloth	15	9	10
59.	Stafford, for sundry Disbursements made by Order of the Magistrates	22	—	6
60.	Gibson, for Window Blinds	12	11	—
61.	Cadogan, for Carpenter's Work	13	4	3
	£.	199	14	10
		273	10	9
		2,572	6	5
	£.	3,045	12	—

By Fees and Fines received at the Office during the Quarter - - - - - - - £. 153 7 —

Deduct Disbursements made at the Office during the Quarter - - - - - - - 121 18 6

Deduct Balance in the Clerk's hands - - - - - - 31 8 6

£. 3,014 3 6

Deduct the Amount of the Estimate added to the last Quarter's Account, for paying the Patrole the then current Quarter, from 6th July to 5th October 1815 - - - - - - 1,650 — —

£. 1,364 3 6

Add the Amount of the Estimate for paying the Patrole from 6th October 1815 to 5th January 1816 - - - - - 1,650 — —

£. 3,014 3 6

WE, the Magistrates of the above Office, having seen and examined the above Statement, do allow and approve thereof,

N. CONANT.   J. NARES.   R. BIRNIE.

Appendix, N° 1ʰ.

PUBLIC OFFICE BOW STREET.—CHARGES of the ESTABLISHMENT, payable for the Quarter
ending 5th January 1816.

		£.	s.	d.
1.	To Sir Nathaniel Conant, for one Quarter's Salary - - - -	150	—	—
2.	To Sir Nathaniel Conant, for his Attendance and Services at the Secretary of State's Office, for one Quarter - - - - - -	150	—	—
3.	To John Nares, Esq. for one Quarter's Salary - - - -	150	—	—
4.	To Richard Birnie, Esq. for D° - - - - - - - -	150	—	—
5.	To John Stafford, Chief Clerk, for D°, including an increase at the rate of £.50 per annum, having served ten years and upwards, such increase being pursuant to the Secretary of State's Letter of the 13th September 1815 -	66	—	—
6.	To Francis Thomas, Second Clerk, for D°, including a like increase, having also served ten years and upwards - - - - - - -	56	—	—
7.	To Samuel Keene, Third Clerk, for one Quarter's Salary - - -	33	10	—
8.	To John Stafford, Chief Clerk, for one Quarter's extra Allowance to the three Clerks, for their Trouble arising from the Patrole Establishment -	16	18	—
9.	To John Stafford, Chief Clerk, for one Quarter's Salary to Patrick Mᶜ Manus, John Townsend, John Sayer, John Pearks, Stephen Lavender, John Vickery, Harry Adkins, and Samuel Taunton, the eight Officers, at £.1. 1. per Week, each - - - - - - -	109	4	—
10.	To the Patrole, one Quarter's Wages - - - - - - -	1,251	10	—
11.	To John Stafford, Chief Clerk, for one Quarter's Allowance to the superannuated and infirm Patrole, namely; Christopher Cridland, 92 days, at 3 s. 4 d. per day ; William Black, 92 days, at 2 s. 6 d. per day; Archibald Ruthven, 54 days, at 2 s. 6 d. per day; Henry Crocker, Samuel Gyde, Donald McGillivreay, John McGregor, Ephraim Wood, John Holloway, Anthony Browne, William Edwards, Alexander Stuart, and Thomas Edwards, 92 days, at 1 d. 3 s. per day, each ; and William Williams, 57 days, at 1 s. 3 d. per day - - - - - - -	94	12	11
12.	To Samuel Taunton, Office Keeper, for one Quarter's Salary - - -	8	15	—
13.	To John Sayer, Messenger, for - - - D° - - - - -	8	15	—
14.	To Sarah Stafford, Housekeeper, for - - D° and Expenses - - -	13	9	8
15.	To John Stafford, Editor of the Hue and Cry (£.110 of which he is to pay over to Joseph Downes for printing and publishing, and to retain the remaining £.15 himself, for editing the same) as directed by Letter from the Secretary of State, dated 29th April 1813 - - - - -	125	—	—
16.	To one Quarter's Annuity to the Widow of Sir Richard Ford, late Chief Magistrate at this Office, by order of the Secretary of State - -	50	—	—
17.	To one Quarter's Annuity to the Widow of William Barnett, late one of the Officers at this Office, by order of the Secretary of State - - -	5	—	—
18.	To one Quarter's D° - - - to the Widow of Samuel Mayner - -	5	—	—
19.	To one Quarter's D° - - - to the Widow of Charles Jeallous - -	5	—	—
20.	To one Quarter's D° - - - to the Widow of Edward Fugion - -	5	—	—
	£.	2,453	14	7

EXTRAORDINARY CHARGES;

Being Money allowed by the Magistrates, for Expenses and Trouble incurred by the different Officers and Patrole, in the execution of their public Duty.

		£.	s.	d.
21.	Vickery	20	9	—
22.	Bacon	13	16	—
23.	Richard Limbrick	8	5	6
24.	John Smith	26	14	—
25.	Mayhew	5	10	—
26.	Nichols	7	7	6
27.	Salmon	3	18	—
28.	Brooks and Jones	19	10	—
29.	John Roguin Smith	9	2	—
30.	Woodlands	8	15	—
31.	Thomas Jones	2	5	—
32.	Upton	3	15	—
33.	A. Ruthven	5	8	—
		£. 134	15	—
34.	Add, One hundred Pounds, omitted by mistake in casting up the amount of the second column of the last Quarterly Account, due to Mr. Stafford, he having advanced the same	100	—	—
		£. 234	15	—

INCIDENTAL CHARGES;

Consisting of Tradesmen's Bills and Accounts, allowed by the Magistrates.

		£.	s.	d.
35.	Mr. Andrews, Surgeon, One Quarter's Allowance for Medical and Surgical Advice and Attendance, including Medicines, &c. for the Officers and Patrole	35	—	—
36.	Downes, for Printing, Stationary, &c.	37	5	8
37.	Harrington, for Oil, Lamps, &c.	19	—	6
38.	Brecknell and Turner, for Candles, &c.	10	12	6
39.	Kennedy, for Newspapers, &c.	9	2	6
40.	Parker, for repairing Fire Arms, Cutlasses, &c.	10	3	6
41.	Hawkes, for Ironmongery	14	11	1
42.	Soulsby, Ward, Holmes & Co. for Coals	35	7	6
43.	Brynnan, for Glazier's Work	6	2	—
44.	Cadogan, for Carpenter's Work	48	14	9
45.	To John Stafford, Editor of the Hue and Cry, for the additional Stamp Duty paid for that Paper from the 9th day of September last	15	12	6
		241	12	6
		234	15	—
		2,453	14	7
		2,930	2	1

	£.	s.	d.
Disbursements made at the Office during the Quarter	120	14	11
By Fees and Fines received at the Office during the Quarter	113	2	—
	£. 7	12	11

46.	Add Balance due to the Clerks	7	12	11
		2,937	15	—
	Deduct the Amount of the Estimate added to the last Quarter's Account, for paying the Patrole the then current Quarter, from 6th October 1815 to 5th January 1816	1,650	—	—
		1,287	15	—
	Add the Amount of the Estimate for paying the Patrole from 6th January to 5th April 1816	1,650	—	—
		£. 2,937	15	—

WE, the Magistrates of the above Office, having seen and examined the above Account, do allow and approve thereof.

N. CONANT.
J. NARES.
R. BIRNIE.

N° 1ᶦ.—1816.

. RULES, ORDERS, AND REGULATIONS,

For the Government and Observance of the FOOT PATROLE ESTABLISHMENT, at the POLICE OFFICE, Bow-street.—London, printed by J. Downes, 240, Strand, 1816.

1.—THE FOOT PATROLE ESTABLISHMENT is under the direction of Sir Nathaniel Conant, the Chief Magistrate, whose orders, when not personally given, will be communicated by Mr. Stafford, Chief Clerk, to the respective conductors of parties, who are strictly to obey all such orders and directions, and be responsible for carrying them into effect : the men are to be attentive and obedient to their conductors, and if they are not so, or commit any irregularity, or in any way neglect their duty, the conductors are to report them with the particulars of their misconduct; and they will be punished by suspension from pay or be discharged. Any neglect of duty or improper conduct on the part of the conductors, will be punished in like manner.

2.—[*Contains the names of the 13 conductors, with their respective places of meeting.*]

3.—The time of meeting, and the duration of duty, will be regulated by circumstances and the seasons of the year; and will be given out, and entered weekly in the Orderly Book, at Bow-street.

4. When each party assemble at the appointed place of meeting, the conductor, pursuant to his instructions, will divide them into two or more divisions, according to the effective strength of the party; and before he proceeds on his duty with the first division, he will select and place proper and experienced men at the head of the other division, and give them directions as to the particular part of the district they are to patrole, and when and where to meet again or communicate with each other; and the whole party will assemble together at the usual place of meeting when the time of duty shall expire, and then, if nothing shall have happened to require their further services, they shall be discharged by the conductor.

5.—Should the conductor be prevented by sickness or any other cause, from meeting the party at the appointed time, the senior man present is to take the direction of the party for the evening, and report the occurrence in writing, the next morning, at the office.

6.—Should the party hear of any murder, burglary, robbery, or other atrocious offence being committed, they are to procure every particular they can relative to the same, and the number of the offenders, and their description, and use every exertion in their power to apprehend them; and the conductor to report the circumstances at the office the next morning.

7.—The conductors are to attend every Monday morning, at Bow-street, at ten o'clock, and each to produce an Occurrence Book, to be kept by the conductor, in which he shall enter a journal of the duty of the party during the week, and report every particular occurrence that may have taken place; the conductors shall, at the same time, deliver in a printed report with the blanks filled up, of the effective strength of the party, the names of any that may be sick or absent without leave, and of such as may have had leave of absence, or been employed on office-duty; the number of pistols, cutlasses, belts, truncheons, &c. in the use of the party, and whether fit for service; the conductors will also peruse the Orderly Book, and any fresh orders they may find; they are to communicate to the men at the meeting place in the evening, or sooner if requisite; they are also to take from the book, the names of the men who shall be entered for the night duty at the office during the ensuing week, and for the orderly duty in the day-time, and they are to acquaint the men therewith, and will be considered responsible for their attendance accordingly : the conductors will also receive every Monday morning, the amount of the pay of the party for the preceding week, and are to pay the men in the course of the same day.

8.—Two of the parties of patrole in rotation to attend every Monday morning, at half past nine o'clock, with their pistols, cutlasses, belts, and truncheons, which will be inspected, and, if found in any way damaged or injured from the negligence or carelessness of the persons intrusted with them, the necessary repair shall be done, and the expense stopped from the pay of the person by whose default the damage shall be occasioned.

9.—Two men for the nightly watch at the office, are to be taken from the respective parties of patrole in succession, according to their number; but only one man is to be taken from the same party on the same night; they are to come on duty at nine o'clock in the evening, and to remain until nine o'clock in the morning; one of them to be always up and on the watch; they are to keep themselves within the watch-room, and remain perfectly quiet; and are not to suffer any person to come in, or remain with them, nor are they to leave the office, except on duty, until relieved by the door-keeper, in the morning; and in case of any particular occurrence taking place during the night, one of them is to call the officer in waiting for the week, whose name will be hung up in the watch-room, who will act according to the best of his judgment, and if he thinks it necessary, he is to acquaint the Chief Clerk or one of the Magistrates thereof, as the exigency may require.

10.—Any

10.—Any misconduct on the night duty, arising from drunkenness, negligence, or any other cause, will be attended with the immediate discharge of the person who shall be found to have offended; and no man whose turn it is for the night duty, will be suffered to send another to do the duty for him, without leave first obtained.

11.—The parties of patrole in rotation, will be excused from the road duty one night in thirteen, but on that night they are to be on duty at the office, in Bow-street, at a quarter before seven; and at seven, the conductor is to report to the Sitting Magistrate, whether the whole of his party are present; and they are to attend from seven o'clock until nine, when they will be dismissed, if their further attendance is not required; but if both or either of the men for the night duty should not be in attendance at the time, the conductor is to order one or two of his men, as the case may be, to take the night duty, and remain until relieved; and the conductor is to report the absence of the men who ought to have attended. The two men on the night duty will be relieved at nine in the morning by the door-keeper and the orderly man. An orderly man is to be furnished daily from the parties in rotation, and is to attend at the office from nine in the morning until nine in the evening, unless otherwise directed by the Sitting Magistrate.

12.—One of the conductors in rotation shall attend at the office, in Bow-street, every Sunday, from nine in the morning until one in the afternoon; and another conductor also in rotation, from one in the afternoon until five in the afternoon; and at five, one of the conductors, with his party, is to come on duty at the office, and not depart until nine, nor until the night duty is provided for, in the manner directed by the last regulation (No. 11.)

13.—When any party of the foot patrole meet any of the horse patrole, attached to the office, on duty on the roads, the conductor of the party of foot is to communicate to the horse patrole, any matters that may have occurred concerning their mutual duty, and receive his communications in return, and at all times to aid and assist the horse patrole in furtherance of his duty, when occasion may require.

14.—A printed Copy of the Rules and Regulations will be delivered to each of the conductors, who are to read them over to their men on the first day of every month, and on the Saturday preceding their inspections.

15.—All persons belonging to the Establishment, when on duty at the office, are strictly to obey the orders of the Sitting Magistrate.

Appendix, N° 2.ᵃ—An ACCOUNT of the ESTABLISHMENT of the PUBLIC OFFICE in

RANK of OFFICER.	HIS NAME.	By whom Appointed.	How Appointed.	When appointed.	Duration of Interest.	RECEIPT:					
						Salary.	By whom paid.	Fees.	By whom paid.	Other Emoluments.	From Whence.
Three Magistrates	Philip Neve, Esq. - Robert Baker, Esq. - George Hicks, Esq. -	The Secretary of State.	Sign Manual.	1792 1812 1813	During Pleasure.	£.600. per Ann. each by Act of Parliament.	The Receiver.				
Chief Clerk -	Alexander Bisson - - -	- D° - -	By Letter	1814	Good Behaviour	£.200. per Annum.	- D° -				
Second Clerk	John Fletcher - - - -	- D° - -	- D° - -	1814	- D° -	£.100. for the Year. £.134 for all Succeeding Years.	- D° -				
Seven Officers.	William Jackson - - John Foy - - - - William Craig - - - Thomas Foy - - - - Charles Jefferies - - - Samuel Plank - - - *George Bennett - 1814 Thoˢ Macintosh - 1815	The Magistrates The Secretary of State	Verbally. By Letter.	1795 1806 1808 1812 1813 1814 1814 1815	D° - -	21s. per Week.	- D° -	One Shilling for serving a Warrant or Summons.	The party Prosecuting.	- - -	- -
Three Superannuated Officers.	James Kennedy - - - Richard Burton - - - William Mason - - -	- D° - -	- D° - -	1792 1805 1807	D° - -	14s. per Week.	D°	—	—		
Messenger -	John Tapper - - - - -	- D° - -	- D° - -	1813	- D° - -	21s. per Week.	- D° -	One Shilling for serving a Summons.	- D° -	Resident in the House.	-
Housekeeper	Mary Sexton - - -	The Magistrates	Verbally.	1794	- D° - -	£.35. per Ann	- D° - -	- - -	- - -	Resident in the House.	-

* George Bennett officiated as Constable during the year 1814, when he died—and was immediately succeeded by Thomas Macintosh.

ATTENDANCE and DUTIES.

The Magistrates, Clerks and Officers, attend in the Office daily, pursuant to the directions of the 54th Geo. III. cap. xxxvii. and at such other times and places as the Public Service may require.

The general Business is to perform the duties of Justices of the Peace, attended by their Clerks and Constables, in the District attached to this Office, consisting of the Parishes of Saint James, Westminster—Saint George, Hanover Square—Paddington—Saint Mary-le-bone—Saint Pancras—Saint Giles in the Fields, and Saint George Bloomsbury (United)—and Saint Anne, Westminster;—and occasionally in the Out-Parishes of Pinner—Harrow—Willesden—Acton—and Fulham. On the enrolment of Aliens, great recourse of Foreigners has been had to this Office to make their Declarations. All Offices are executed in person. A Monthly Report of the number of Informations received, and of Persons committed or discharged, is made and presented to the Secretary of State for the Home Department, by one of the Magistrates.

GREAT MARLBOROUGH STREET; for the Years 1814 and 1815; distinguishing each Year.

TOTAL RECEIPT.	DEDUCTIONS: Taxes, Per Property.	Deputies and Clerks.	Contingencies.	Total Disbursements.	Net Receipt in 1814 and 1815.	Net Receipt Annual, upon an Average of the last Two Years.	Other Employments, Places or Pensions, under Government.	Their Annual Value.	SINCE 1813. Increase. Salaries, &c.	Officers.	Diminution. Salaries, &c.	Officers.
£.600. per Ann. each	£.60. per Ann. each	- -	-	£. 60. each.	£.540. each.	—	—	—				
£.200. Anno 1814 / £.225. Anno 1815	£.20. - - 1814 / £.22. 10. - 1815		-	£.20. - - 1814 / £.22. 10. 1815	£.180. - 1814 / £.202. 10. 1815	- -	—	—				
£.100. — 1814 / £.134. — 1815	£.10. - - 1814 / £.13. 8. - 1815		-	£.10. - - 1814 / £.13. 8. - 1815	£.90. - 1814 / £.120. 12. 1815	—	—	—	The Salary of the Chief Clerk continues £.200. per Annum.—An Increase has been granted by the Secretary of State, by Letter dated 16th September 1815, for length of Service—viz. For 10 Years, £.50.—For 15 Years, £.70.—and for 20 Years, £.100.—Which Increase has been claimed by the Chief Clerk, and allowed for 20 Years Service.			
Uncertain, depending wholly upon Business done; but, on an Average, the Officers returned their Income £.75. per Annum -	£.4. 10. per Ann.	- -	-	£. 4. 10. each.	£. 70. 10. each.	—	—	—	—	—	—	—
—	—	—	—	—	—	—	—	—	—	—	—	—
On an Average / £.60. per Annum	£. 3. per Annum -	- -	-	- £. 3. - -	£. 57. per Annum.	—	—	—	—	—	—	—
£. 35. per Annum -	- -	- -	-	- - - -	£. 35. per Annum.	—	—	—	—	—	—	—

R E M A R K.

John Baldwin, Esq. is the Receiver of this Office in common with the other Six Public Offices.

Public Office, Great Marlborough Street,
16th April 1816.

ALEXANDER BISSON,
Chief Clerk.

Appendix, N° 2.ᵇ

PUBLIC OFFICE, GREAT MARLBOROUGH STREET.

CHARGES of the ESTABLISHMENT, payable for the Quarter ending 5th April 1814.

	£. s. d.	£. s. d.
SALARIES.		
To PHILIP NEVE, Esq. ⎫		
To ROBERT BAKER, Esq. ⎬ the Three Magistrates - - -	450 — —	
To GEORGE HICKS, Esq. ⎭		
To Mr. Butler, Chief Clerk, to 3d February 1814 - - -	12 11 9½	
To Mr. Bisson, Second Clerk, to 14th February 1814 - -	14 13 8½	
To Mr. Bisson, Chief Clerk, from 15th February to the end of the quarter - - - - - - - - - -	27 7 11½	
To Mr. John Fletcher, Second Clerk, from 18th February, at £. 100. per annum - - - - - - - - -	12 17 6¼	
To James Kennedy, Richard Burton, and Willᵐ Mason, Constables, at 21 s. per week, 24 days - - - - £. 10 16 —		
To the said Three Constables, Superannuated, at 14 s. per week - - - - - - - £. 20 2 —	30 18 —	
To William Jackson, Jnᵒ Foy, Willᵐ Craig, Thoˢ Foy, and Charles Jefferies, Constables, at 21 s. per week - - - -	68 5 —	
To Samˡ Plank, Constable, from 12th February, at 21 s. per week	7 19 —	
To George Bennett, Constable, from 19th February, at 21 s. per week - - - - - - - - - -	6 18 —	
To Mrs. Mary Sexton, Housekeeper, at £. 35. per annum - -	8 15 —	
To Mr. Jnᵒ Tapper, Messenger, at 21 s. per week - -	13 13 —	653 18 11¼
INCIDENTAL EXPENSES.		
To Jnᵒ Marsden, for taking 194 Prisoners to Gaol - - -	12 2 6	
To the Housekeeper, for a Charwoman, Wood, Soap, and sweeping Chimnies - - - - - - - - -	2 16 6	
To the Messenger, for General Post Letters - - -	5 17 4	
To Dᵒ - - — 2d. Post Letters - - - -	2 17 6	
To Dᵒ - - — Sundries - - - - -	7 7 8	
	31 1 6	
To Messrs. Soulsby, for Coals - - - - - - -	21 — —	
To Mr. Bentley - — Stationary last year - - -	37 3 —	
To Mr. Wrangham — Newspapers, &c. - - - -	4 12 4	
To Mr. Fernall - — Chandlery - - - - -	7 9 5	
To Mr. Bilson - - — Turnery - - - - -	1 11 10	
To Mr. Row - - — Stationary - - - - -	12 18 2	
To Messrs. Reed - — Law Books - - - -	1 1 —	
To Messrs. Spencer — Oil, &c. - - - - -	3 — 4	
To Mr. Downes - — Printing - - - - -	16 2 —	
To Mr. Parker - — Repairing Arms - - - -	1 19 —	
To Mr. Thoˢ Foy, for apprehending a Felon in Cambridgeshire -	4 2 —	
To Mr. Richᵈ Staples, as Extra Clerk, 2 weeks in February last -	2 2 —	
To Mr. B. Johnson, prosecuting a Felon on the Black Act, in Surrey	13 12 1	157 15 2
NECESSARY DISBURSEMENTS, Rent, Taxes, and Repairs of the House.		
To Rent - - - - - - - - - - -	50 — —	
To Window and House Tax - - - - - - -	27 4 1	
To Poor Rate - - - - - - - - - -	11 7 6	
To Watch and Church Rate - - - - - -	2 12 6	
To Paving Rate - - - - - - - - -	1 16 10	
To Water Rate - - - - - - - - -	2 12 6	
To Mr. Hill - - for Carpenters Work - - - -	8 7 11¼	
To Mr. Jefferies — Glaziers - Dᵒ - - - -	5 3 —	
To Mr. Rogers - — Ironmongers Dᵒ - - - -	4 3 3	
To Mr. Burton - — Upholstery Dᵒ - - - -	6 — —	
To Mr. Roberts — Ironmongers Dᵒ - - - -	— 18 —	120 5 7¼
TOTAL - - - - £.		931 19 8½

Appendix, N° 2°.

PUBLIC OFFICE, GREAT MARLBOROUGH STREET.

CHARGES of the ESTABLISHMENT, payable for the Quarter ending 5th July 1814.

	£. s. d.	£. s. d.
SALARIES.		
To the Three Magistrates - - - - - - -	450 — —	
To the Chief Clerk - - - - - - -	50 — —	
To the Second Clerk - - - - - - -	25 — —	
To the Seven Constables, at 21 s. per week - - -	95 11 —	
To the Three Superannuated Constables, at 14 s. per week -	27 6 —	
To the Housekeeper - - - - - - -	8 15 —	
To the Messenger - - - - - - -	13 13 —	
		670 5 —
INCIDENTAL EXPENSES.		
To John Marsden, for taking 195 Prisoners to Gaol - - -	12 4 —	
To the Housekeeper, for Charwoman, &c. - - - -	2 12 6	
To the Messenger, — General Post Letters - - -	4 18 7	
To D° - - - - — Twopenny Post D° - - -	2 18 8	
To D° - - - - — Sundries - - - - -	5 12 2	
	28 5 11	
To Mr. Bentley - for Stationary, &c. - - - -	32 — —	
To Mr. Wrangham - — Newspapers, &c. - - -	5 — —	
To Mr. Furnell - — Chandlery - - - -	9 14 —	
To Mr. Bilson - — Turnery - - - -	1 6 —	
To Mr. Row - - — Stationary - - - -	7 11 9	
To Mr. Downes - — Printing - - - -	15 2 —	
To Messrs. Reed - — Law Books - - - -	4 9 6	
To Mr. Hardy - — 4 Sessions Newgate Calendars -	4 4 —	
To Mr. Day - - — Statements of Criminal Offenders -	2 2 —	
To Extra Constables, by Order of the Secretary of State -	5 5 —	
		115 — 2
NECESSARY DISBURSEMENTS, Rent, Taxes, and Repairs of the House.		
To Rent - - for one Quarter - - - -	50 — —	
To Land Tax - — four Quarters - - - -	11 3 1	
To Mr. Jefferies - — Glaziers Work - - -	2 1 6	
To Mr. Burton - — Carpenters Work - - -	1 9 9	
To Mr. Rogers - — Ironmongery - - - -	3 2 9	
		67 17 1
TOTAL - - £.		855 2 3

Appendix, N° 2 ᵈ.

PUBLIC OFFICE, GREAT MARLBOROUGH STREET.

CHARGES of the ESTABLISHMENT, payable for the Quarter ending 10th October 1814.

	£.	s.	d.	£.	s.	d.
SALARIES.						
To the Three Magistrates - - - - - - - -	450	—	—			
To the Chief Clerk - - - - - - - - -	50	—	—			
To the Second Clerk - - - - - - - -	25	—	—			
To the Seven Constables, at 21 s. per week - - - -	95	11	—			
To the Three Superannuated Constables, at 14 s. per week - -	27	6	—			
To the Housekeeper - - - - - - - - -	8	15	—			
To the Messenger - - - - - - - - -	13	13	—	670	5	—
INCIDENTAL EXPENSES.						
To John Marsden, for taking 256 Prisoners to Gaol - - -	13	7	6			
To the Housekeeper, for Charwoman, &c. - - - - -	2	16	6			
To the Messenger - — General Post Letters - - - -	5	4	3			
To Dᵒ — Twopenny Post Dᵒ - - - -	2	17	9			
To Dᵒ — Sundries - - - - - -	9	6	—			
	33	12	—			
To Messrs. Soulsby - for Coals - - - - - - -	18	—	—			
To Mr. Wrangham - — Newspapers, &c. - - - -	5	7	8			
To Mr. Furnell - — Chandlery - - - - -	3	16	7			
To Mr. Bilson - - - — Turnery - - - - -	1	—	1			
To Mr. Row - - - — Stationary - - - - -	12	8	6			
To Mr. Downes - - — Printing - - - - -	8	18	6			
To Messrs. Reed - - — Law Books - - - - -	—	16	6			
To Messrs. Spencer - — Oil, &c. - - - - -	3	—	11			
To Mr. Parker - - - — Repairing Arms - - - -	4	18	—			
To Mr. Bisson - - - — Extra Constables on 7th July 1814 -	3	11	—			
To Dᵒ - - - - - - — Dᵒ - - - - - on 1st Aug. 1814 -	5	8	—	100	17	9
NECESSARY DISBURSEMENTS, Rent, Taxes, and Repairs of the House.						
To Rent - - - - - - - - - - -	50	—	—			
To Window, &c. Tax - - - - - - - -	27	4	1			
To Poor Rate - - - - - - - - - -	16	7	2			
To Watch Rate - - - - - - - - -	1	19	—			
To Water Rate - - - - - - - - -	1	15	—			
To Mr. Jefferies - - - for Glaziers Work - - - -	—	6	6			
To Mr. Rogers - - - — Ironmongers Dᵒ - - - -	—	11	9	98	3	6
TOTAL - - - £.				869	6	3

Appendix, Nº 2 c.

PUBLIC OFFICE, GREAT MARLBOROUGH STREET.

CHARGES of the ESTABLISHMENT, payable for the Quarter ending 5th January 1815.

	£.	s.	d	£.	s.	d.
SALARIES.						
To the Three Magistrates - - - - - - - -	450	—	—			
To the Chief Clerk - - - - - - - - -	50	—	—			
To the Second Clerk - - - - - - - -	25	—	—			
To the Seven Constables, at 21 s. per week. - - - -	95	11	—			
To the Three Superannuated Constables, at 14 s. per week - -	27	6	—			
To the Housekeeper - - - - - - - - -	8	15	—			
To the Messenger - - - - - - - - -	13	13	—			
				670	5	—
INCIDENTAL EXPENSES.						
To John Marsden, for taking 235 Prisoners to Gaol - - -	13	12	6			
To the Housekeeper, for a Charwoman, &c. - - - -	2	16	6			
To the Messenger - — paying Christmas Boxes - - -	3	2	6			
To Do - - - - - — Sundries - - - - -	7	10	8			
To Do - - - - - — General Post Letters - - - -	5	16	4			
To Do - - - - - — Twopenny Post Do - - - -	3	2	4			
	36	—	10			
To Messrs. Soulsby - for Coals - - - - - - -	20	15	—			
To Messrs, Reed - - — Law Books - - - - - -	2	16	6			
To Messrs. Spencer - — Oil, &c. - - - - - -	2	19	—			
To Mr. Downes - - — Printing - - - - - -	7	15	—			
To Mr. Wrangham - — Newspapers, &c. - - - - -	5	1	2			
To Mr. Furnell - - — Chandlery - - - - - -	6	16	4			
To Mr. Row - - - — Stationary - - - - - -	6	7	1			
To Mr. Bilson - - — Turnery - - - - - -	2	—	6			
To Two Constables, for apprehending two notorious Swindlers -	4	9	6			
To Mr. Bisson, for paying the Expenses of the Prosecution against Bryan Helps, for Dog Stealing, moved into the King's Bench -	16	3	8			
To Mr. Bisson, for paying the Expenses of the Prosecution against Joseph Powell, for Fortune-telling, at the Old Bailey - -	13	3	—			
				124	7	7
NECESSARY DISBURSEMENTS, Rent, Taxes, and Repairs of the House.						
To Rent - - - - - - - - - - - -	50	—	—			
To Mr. Hill - - - for House Repairs - - - - -	856	14	1			
To Mr. Rogers - - — Ironmongery - - - - -	3	9	10			
				910	3	11
TOTAL - - - £.				1,704	16	6

ALEXANDER BISSON,

Chief Clerk.

Appendix, N° 2 f.

PUBLIC OFFICE, GREAT MARLBOROUGH STREET.

CHARGES of the ESTABLISHMENT, payable for the Quarter ending 5th April 1815.

SALARIES.

	£.	s.	d.	£.	s.	d.
To Philip Neve, Esq. ⎫						
To Robert Baker, Esq. ⎬ the Three Magistrates - - -	450	---	—			
To George Hicks, Esq. ⎭						
To Mr. Alexander Bisson, Chief Clerk - - - - -	50	—	---			
To Mr. John Fletcher, Second Clerk, to 17th Feb. 1815, at £. 100. per annum - - - - - - - - -	12	2	5			
To D° - - Residue of the Quarter, at £. 134. per annum -	17	5	1			
To Willm Jackson, Jn° Foy, Willm Craig, Thos Foy, Chas Jefferies, and Saml Plank, Constables, at 21 s. per week - - -	81	18	—			
To Ja^s Kennedy, Richd Burton, and Willm Mason, three Superannuated Constables, at 14 s. per week - - - - -	27	6	—			
To George Bennett, Constable, till his death, 26 days at 3 s. per day	3	18	—			
To James Macintosh, Constable, from 3d February to the end of the Quarter - - - - - - - - -	9	6	—			
To Mrs. Mary Sexton, Housekeeper - - - - - -	8	15	—			
To Mr. John Tapper, Messenger - - - - - -	13	13	—	674	3	6

INCIDENTAL EXPENSES.

	£.	s.	d.	£.	s.	d.
To John Marsden - - - for taking 282 Prisoners to Gaol -	10	16	---			
To the Housekeeper - - — a Charwoman, Wood, Soap, and sweeping Chimnies - - -	2	12	6			
To the Messenger - - - — Sundries - - - - -	6	11	4			
To D° - - - — General Post Letters - - -	5	7	7			
To D° - - - — Twopenny Post D° - - -	2	19	8			
	28	7	1			
To Messrs. Soulsby - - — Coals - - - - - -	16	10	---			
To Messrs. Reed - - - — Law Books - - - -	4	15	—			
To Messrs. Spencer - - — Oil - - - - - -	2	13	9			
To Messrs. Russell - - — Chandlery - - - -	5	11	5			
To Mr. Downes - - - — Printing - - - -	11	17	—			
To Mr. Wrangham - - - — Newspapers - - - -	5	1	10			
To Mr. Row - - - - — Stationary - - - -	11	16	7			
To Mr. Bilson - - - - — Turnery - - - -	1	2	6			
To Mr. Payne - - - - — Mending and winding Office Clock	3	7	—			
To Mr. Day - - - - — Copies of Summary Statements of Criminals - - - - -	2	2	—	93	4	2

NECESSARY DISBURSEMENTS,
Rent, Taxes, and Repairs of the House.

	£.	s.	d.	£.	s.	d.
To Rent - - - - - - - - - - -	50	—	—			
To Land Tax - - - - - - - - - -	9	4	2			
To Poor Rate - - - - - - - - - -	13	17	4			
To Paving Rate - - - - - - - - -	9	4	8			
To Mr. Hill - - - - for Carpenters Work - - -	25	1	5			
To Mr. Jefferies - - - — Glaziers D° - - -	4	1	6			
To Mr. Rogers - - - - — Ironmongers D° - - -	2	19	—	114	8	1
TOTAL - - - - £.				881	15	9

Appendix, N° 2°.

PUBLIC OFFICE, GREAT MARLBOROUGH STREET.

CHARGES of the ESTABLISHMENT, payable for the Quarter ending 5th July 1815.

SALARIES.	£. s. d.	£. s. d
To the three Magistrates - - - - - - - -	450 — —	
To the Chief Clerk - - - - - - - - -	50 — —	
To the Second Clerk - - - - - - - -	33 10 —	
To the Seven Constables, at 21 s. per week - - - -	95 11 —	
To the three Superannuated Constables, at 14 s. per week - -	27 6 —	
To the Housekeeper - - - - - - - - -	8 15 —	
To the Messenger - - - - - - - - -	13 13 —	678 15 —

INCIDENTAL EXPENSES.

	£. s. d.	£. s. d
To John Marsden - - - for taking 256 Prisoners to Gaol -	10 10 —	
To the Housekeeper - - — Charwoman, &c. &c. - -	2 16 6	
To the Messenger - - - — Sundries - - - - -	4 14 3	
To D° - - - - — General Post Letters - - -	4 11 9	
To D° - - - - — Twopenny D° - - -	3 2 8	
	25 15 2	
To Messrs. Reed - - - — Law Books - - - -	5 12 —	
To Messrs. Spencer - - - — Oil, &c. - - - - -	1 16 —	
To Messrs. Russell - - — Chandlery - - - - -	5 3 1½	
To Mr. Bentley - - - — Stationary - - - -	20 12 —	
To Mr. Downes - - - — Printing - - - - -	3 1 —	
To Mr. Wrangham - - — Newspapers, &c. - - - -	4 19 6	
To Mr. Row - - - - — Stationary - - - -	9 11 —	
To Mr. Bilson - - - - — Turnery - - - - -	1 7 —	77 16 9½

NECESSARY DISBURSEMENTS,
Rent, Taxes, and Repairs of the House.

	£. s. d.	£. s. d
To Rent - - - - - - - - - - -	50 — —	
To Window, &c. Tax - - - - - - - -	27 4 1	
To Watch Rate - - - - - - - - -	1 8 3	
To Mr. Hill - - - - for House Repairs - - - -	3 9 4	
To Mr. Jefferies - - - — Glaziers Work - - - -	3 3 10	85 5 6
	Total - - - - £.	841 17 3½

510.

Appendix, N° 2ʰ.

PUBLIC OFFICE, GREAT MARLBOROUGH STREET.

CHARGES of the ESTABLISHMENT, payable for the Quarter ending 10th October 1815.

	£. s. d.	£. s. d.
SALARIES.		
To the Three Magistrates - - - - - - - -	450 — —	
To the Chief Clerk - - - - - - - -	50 — —	
To the Second Clerk - - - - - - - -	33 10 —	
To the Seven Constables, at 21 s. per week - - -	95 11 —	
To the Three Superannuated Constables, at 14 s. per week - -	27 6 —	
To the Housekeeper - - - - - - - - -	8 15 —	
To the Messenger - - - - - - - - -	13 13 ---	678 15 —
INCIDENTAL EXPENSES.		
To John Marsden, for taking 270 Prisoners to Gaol - - -	10 17 —	
To the Housekeeper, for Charwoman, &c. - - - - -	2 12 6	
To the Messenger - — Sundries - - - - -	7 18 4	
To Dᵒ - - - - — General Post Letters - - - -	6 9 8	
To Dᵒ - - - - - — Twopenny Post Dᵒ - - - -	2 19 10	
	30 17 4	
To Messrs. Spencer, for Oil - - - - - - -	2 8 9	
To Messrs. Russell - — Chandlery - - - - - -	4 7 6	
To Mr. Downes - - — Printing - - - - -	4 10 —	
To Mr. Wrangham - — Newspapers, &c. - - - - -	6 3 8	
To Mr. Row - - - — Stationary - - - - - -	5 17 8	
To Mr. B.lson - - — Turnery - - - - - -	- - 16 —	
To Mr. Hardy - - — Six marked Newgate Calendars - -	6 6 —	
To Mr. Butler - - — Prosecuting Three notorious Swindlers -	15 17 11	77 4 10
NECESSARY DISBURSEMENTS, Rent, Taxes, and Repairs of the House.		
To Rent - - - - - - - - - - - -	50 — —	
To Poor Rate - - - - - - - - - -	7 9 5	
To Water Rate - - - - - - - - - -	3 10 —	
To Mr. Jefferies, for Glaziers Work - - - - - -	3 4 9	64 4 2
Total - - - £.		820 4 —

Appendix, Nº 2¹.

PUBLIC OFFICE, GREAT MARLBOROUH STREET.

CHARGES of the ESTABLISHMENT, payable for the Quarter ending 5th January 1816.

SALARIES.	£.	s.	d.	£.	s.	d.
To the Three Magistrates - - - - - - - -	450	—	—			
To Mr. Alexander Bisson, Chief Clerk, including an increase of £.100. per annum, for 20 years service and upwards - -	75	—	—			
To the Second Clerk - - - - - - -	33	10	—			
To the Seven Constables, at 21 s. per week - - - -	95	11	—			
To the Three Superannuated Constables, at 14 s. per week - -	27	6	—			
To the Housekeeper - - - - - - - - -	8	15	—			
To the Messenger - - - - - - - - -	13	13	—			
				703	15	—
INCIDENTAL EXPENSES.						
To John Marsden - - - for taking 241 Prisoners to Gaol - -	11	—	—			
To the Housekeeper - — a Charwoman, &c. - - - -	2	15	6			
To the Messenger - - — Sundries - - - - -	9	11	1			
To - - Dº - - - - — General Post Letters - - -	6	12	5			
To - - Dº - - - - — Twopenny Post Dº - - - -	2	17	10			
	32	16	10			
To Messrs. Soulsby - — Coals - - - - - -	18	1	—			
To Messrs. Reed - - — Law Books - - - - -	1	3	—			
To Messrs. Spencer - — Oil, &c. - - - - - -	4	6	3			
To Messrs. Russell - - — Chandlery - - - - -	4	1	—			
To Mr. Downes - - - — Printing - - - - -	13	6	—			
To Mr. Wrangham - - — Newspapers, &c. - - - -	5	17	10			
To Mr. Row - - - - — Stationary - - - - -	9	1	—			
To Mr. Bilson - - - — Turnery - - - - - -	1	18	2			
To Mr. Parker - - - — Repairing Arms - - - -	9	8	—			
To Mr. Hardy - - - — Six marked Newgate Calendars - -	6	6	—			
To Mr. Bisson - - - — Paying Christmas Boxes - - -	3	4	6			
				109	9	7
NECESSARY DISBURSEMENTS, Rent, Taxes, and Repairs of the House.						
To Rent - - - - - - - - - - -	50	—	—			
To Window, &c. Tax - - - - - - - -	27	4	5			
To Land Tax - - - - - - - - - -	4	12	—			
To Watch Rate - - - - - - - - -	1	14	6			
To Poor Rate - - - - - - - - -	7	4	7½			
To Paving Rate - - - - - - - - -	6	18	4½			
To Mr. Hill - - - - for House Repairs - - - -	1	5	4			
To Mr. Jefferies - - - — Glaziers Work - - - -	2	9	9			
To Mr. Rogers - - - — Ironmongers Dº - - - -	5	—	6			
				106	9	6
TOTAL - - - £.				919	14	1

ALEXANDER BISSON,
Chief Clerk.

Appendix, N° 2ᵏ.

PUBLIC OFFICE, GREAT MARLBOROUGH STREET.

AN ACCOUNT of the Quarterly and Annual Amount of FEES and PENALTIES,
for the Years 1814 and 1815.

	FEES AND PENALTIES 1814.	£. s. d.	£. s. d.
1814. April 5.	To Fees - - - - - - - - -	112 4 —	
—	To Penalties - - - - - - - -	19 12 6	
			131 16 6
July 5,	To Fees - - - - - - - - -	132 17 6	
—	To Penalties - - - - - - - -	36 7 —	
			169 4 6
Oct. 10.	To Fees - - - - - - - - -	172 17 —	
—	To Penalties - - - - - - - -	52 2 6	
			224 19 6
1815. Jan. 5.	To Fees - - - - - - - - -	138 6 —	
—	To Penalties - - - - - - - -	39 4 —	
			177 10 —
	Anno 1814, TOTAL - - - - £.		703 10 6
	FEES AND PENALTIES, 1815.		
1815. April 5.	To Fees - - - - - - - - -	152 19 —	
—	To Penalties - - - - - - - -	51 7 6	
			204 6 6
July 5.	To Fees - - - - - - - - -	167 — —	
—	To Penalties - - - - - - - -	40 5 1	
			207 5 1
Oct. 10.	To Fees - - - - - - - - -	186 5 —	
—	To Penalties - - - - - - - -	41 15 3	
			228 — 3
1816. Jan. 5.	To Fees - - - - - - - - -	173 7 —	
—	To Penalties - - - - - - - -	36 11 —	
			209 18 —
	Anno 1815, TOTAL - - - - £.		849 9 10

Public Office in Great Marlborough Street.

I, Alexander Bisson, Chief Clerk of the above Office, did make Oath before two Magistrates, that the above Accounts of Fees and Penalties, received at the said Office at the Periods above named, were correct and just Quarterly Accounts, to the best of my knowledge and belief.

ALEXANDER BISSON,
Chief Clerk.

Appendix, N° 2¹.

RECAPITULATION of the CHARGES of the ESTABLISHMENT of the PUBLIC OFFICE in GREAT MARLBOROUGH STREET, for the Years 1814 and 1815.

	ANNUAL CHARGES 1814.	£. s. d,	£. s. d.
1814. April 5.	Charges Payable - - - - - - -	931 19 8½	
July 5.	D° - - - - - - -	853 2 3	
Oct. 10.	D° - - - - - - -	869 6 3	
1815. Jan. 5.	D° - - - - - - -	1,704 16 6	
	Anno 1814, TOTAL - - - - £.		4,359 4 8½
	ANNUAL CHARGES 1815.		
1815. April 5.	Charges Payable - - - - - - -	881 15 9	
July 5.	D° - - - - - - -	841 17 3½	
Oct. 10.	D° - - - - - - -	820 4 —	
1816. Jan. 5.	D° - - - - - - -	919 4 1	
	Anno 1815, TOTAL - - - - £.		3,463 11 1¼

Public Office in Great Marlborough Street.

Two Magistrates of this Office did testify, that they had examined the above Quarterly Accounts, at the Periods above named, and the divers Bills thereto belonging; and that the different Articles therein charged were necessary for the Public Service at this Office, to which they had been applied, to the best of their knowledge and belief.

ALEXANDER BISSON,
Chief Clerk.

Appendix, N° 3ª.—An ACCOUNT of the ESTABLISHMENT of the

RANK of OFFICER.	HIS NAME.	By whom appointed.	How appointed.	When appointed.	Duration of Interest.	RECEIPT: — — — —		
						Salary.	By whom paid.	Fees.
Magistrates — —	John Turton — —	The King —	Sign Manual	31st Jan. 1801	— —	£. 600 per Ann. each	The Receiver	— — —
	Thomas Leach — —			13th Sept. 1803	— —			
	Robert Raynsford			12th March 1812				
Chief Clerk — — —	Robert Ford — — —	— — —	— — —	7th April 1807	— — —	£. 200 per Ann. —	D°	— — —
Second Clerk — —	John Rodd (to the 4 Feb. 1814) — —	The Secretary of State.	By Letter to the Magistrates.	14 Feb. 1811	Good behaviour.	£. 134 per Ann. —		— — —
	John Shearman, from 4th Feb. 1814 — —			4 Feb. 1814		£. 100 per Ann. for the first year, and £. 134 per Annum afterwards — — —		— — —
Officers — — —	James Hancock — —	Formerly by the Magistrates only, and now by the Magistrates with the approbation of the Secretary of State.	Verbally	— — — —	D° — —	21 s. per Week —	— D° —	One Shilling for serving a Warrant or Summons.
	George Wood — —							
	William Read, sen. —							
	John Hutt — — — —							
	Charles Brown — —							
	William Read, jun. —							
	John Limbrick — —							
Note —The two last-mentioned Officers were discharged on the 21st of January 1815, and no others have been appointed in their room.	Willm Thiselton — —							
	John Mathews — —							
	Charles Cooke — —							
Housekeeper — —	Cathe Marchant — —	Secretary of State — —	— — —	18 Nov. 1802	— D° —	£. 30 per Ann. —	— D° —	— — —
Messenger — — —	Charles Virgin — —	Magistrates —	Verbally —	30 Sept. 1813	— D° — —	21 s. per Week —	— D° —	— — —

Public Office, Hatton Garden,
24 April 1816.

POLICE OFFICE, HATTON GARDEN; for the Years 1814 and 1815.

RECEIPT:				DEDUCTIONS.			Total Disburse-ments.	Net Receipt in the said Two Years.	Other Employments, Places, or Pensions, under Government.	Their Annual Value.
By whom paid.	Other Emoluments.	From whence.	TOTAL Receipt in the said Two Years.	Taxes.	Depu-ties and Clerks.	Con-tingen-cies.				
			£. s. d.				£. s. d.	£. s. d.		
-	-	-	1,200 — —	Property Tax at £. 10 per Cent.	-	-	120 — —	1,080 — —	—	—
-	-	-	1,200 — —		-	-	120 — —	1,080 — —	—	—
-	-	-	1,200 — —	-	-	-	120 — —	1,080 — —	—	—
-	-	-	400 — —	- Dº -	-	-	40 — —	360 — —	—	—
-	-	-	11 3 4	- Dº -	-	-	1 2 4	10 1 —	—	—
-	-	-	225 13 4	- Dº -	-	-	25 14 —	199 19 4	—	—
The Party prosecuting	Payment for extra trou-ble in serving War-rants and Summonses, and Rewards for ap-prehending Offenders.	Payment of ex-tra trouble, &c. from the Party prosecuting; and Rewards for apprehend-ing Felons, from the Sheriff.	Uncertain, depending wholly on the Business done.	- Dº - at £. 30 per Ann. each, up to the 10th Oct. 1815; and at 90 s. per Ann. each from that period.	—	—	—	—	—	—
-	Resident in the House -	-	60 — —	-	-	-	-	60 — —	—	—
-	-	-	109 4 —	- Dº - at 18 s. per Ann.	-	-	-	107 8 —	—	—

JOHN TURTON.

THOMAS LEACH.

ROBᵀ RAYNSFORD.

Appendix, N° 3ᵇ.

PUBLIC OFFICE, HATTON GARDEN.

An ACCOUNT of the SALARIES of the Magistrates, Clerks, Constables, and others, belonging to the said Office; of the Incidental Expenses, and of the necessary Disbursements for the Rent, Taxes, and Repairs of the House, wherein the said Office is held;—for the Quarter ending the 5th day of April 1814.

	SALARIES.	£.	s.	d.	£.	s.	d.
1.	To JOHN TURTON, Esq. - - - - - - -	150	—	—			
2.	To THOMAS LEACH, Esq. - - - - - -	150	—	—			
3.	To ROBERT CAPPER, Esq. - - - - - -	150	—	—			
4.	To Robert Ford, Chief Clerk - - - - - -	50	—	—			
5.	To John Rodd, Second Clerk, to 4th February - - -	11	3	4			
6.	To John Shearman, D° from 5th Feb. at £.100. per annum	16	13	4			
7.	To Ten Constables, at 21 s. per week each - - -	136	10	—			
8.	To Catherine Marchant, Housekeeper - - - -	7	10	—			
9.	To Charles Virgin, Messenger - - - - -	13	13	—	685	9	8
	INCIDENTAL EXPENSES.						
10.	Mr. Downes, Printer - - - - - -	15	—	—			
11.	Messrs Staunton, Stationers - - - - - -	10	8	—			
12.	Mr. Hanwell, Tallow Chandler - - - - -	14	4	1			
13.	Mr. Kennedy, Newsman - - - - - - -	4	4	6			
14.	Messrs. Soulsby & Allison, Coal Merchants - - -	53	3	—			
15.	Messrs. Mullins & Free, Lamplighters - - - -	7	13	—			
16.	Mr. Armstrong, Oilman - - - - - - -	7	8	—			
17.	Mr. Parker, Gunsmith - - - - - - -	10	1	6			
18.	Messrs. Reed & Hunter, Booksellers - - - -	4	17	—			
19.	Mr. Day, for his Annual Account of Criminal Offenders -	2	2	—			
20.	Officers' Account of Extra Expenses - - - -	34	2	6			
21.	Housekeeper's Account of Incidents - - - -	4	14	8			
22.	Allowance to Alexander Tod, late Chief Clerk - - -	25	—	—			
23.	Alexander Mᶜ Killigan's Allowance - - - - -	3	18	—			
24.	R. Ford, the younger, for making out Recognizances, and assisting in the general Business of the Office - -	5	10	—			
25.	Messenger's Account of Petty Disbursements - - -	11	9	3			
26.	John Limbrick, Officer, for his Expenses of a Journey to Hayes in Kent, in consequence of a Burglary committed in the House of Sir Vicary Gibbs there - - -	5	—	—			
27.	Mr. Butterworth, Bookseller - - - - - -	2	3	—			
28.	Charles Brown, Officer, for his Expenses of a Journey to the Assizes for Suffolk, to give Evidence against Mary Gibbs, for Murder - - - - - - -	7	8	—			
29.	The like to ——— Miller, Keeper of the Gaol at Barking in Essex - - - - - - - - -	7	8	—			
30.	John Matthews, Officer, for his Expenses of a Journey into Hertfordshire, respecting a Felony - - - -	4	—	6	239	15	—
	NECESSARY DISBURSEMENTS, For the Rent, Taxes, and Repairs of the House.						
31.	House Rent - - - - - - - - -	30	—	—			
32.	Mr. Raddon, Glazier - - - - - - -	1	12	7			
33.	Mr. Hill, Carpenter - - - - - - -	5	9	—			
34.	Mr. Parker, D° - - - - - - - -	2	2	6			
35.	Mr. Harrow, Bricklayer - - - - - - -	1	7	—			
36.	Mr. Coates, Smith - - - - - - - -	4	4	10			
37.	Mr. Lawless, Chimney Sweeper - - - - -	—	15	—			
38.	Poor Rates, one Quarter, to Christmas - - - -	4	7	6			
39.	Watch Rate, one Quarter, to - D° - - - -	—	8	9			
40.	Water Rate, two Quarters, to - D° - - - -	1	5	—	51	12	5
				£.	976	17	1

THOMAS LEACH,
ROBᵀ RAYNSFORD.

Appendix, N° 3 ᶜ.

PUBLIC OFFICE, HATTON GARDEN.

SALARIES, INCIDENTAL EXPENSES, &c. for the Quarter ending 5th July 1814.

	SALARIES.	£.	s.	d.	£.	s.	d.
1.	To John Turton, Esq. - - - - - - -	150	—	—			
2.	To Thomas Leach, Esq. - - - - - - -	150	—	—			
3.	To Robert Capper, Esq. - - - - - - -	150	—	—			
4.	To Robert Ford, Chief Clerk - - - - -	50	—	—			
5.	To John Shearman, Second Clerk - - - -	25	—	—			
6.	To Ten Constables, at £. 1. 1s. per week each - - -	136	10	—			
7.	To Catherine Marchant, Housekeeper - - -	7	10	—			
8.	To Charles Virgin, Messenger - - - - - -	13	13	—			
					682	13	—
	INCIDENTAL EXPENSES.						
9.	Mr. Downes, Printer and Stationer - - - -	29	6	6			
10.	Mr. Hanwell, Tallow Chandler - - - -	12	2	—			
11.	Mr. Kennedy, Newsman - - - - - -	4	4	6			
12.	Messrs. Soulsby & Allison, Coal Merchants - - -	22	10	—			
13.	Mr. Armstrong, Oilman - - - - - -	5	14	1			
14.	Messrs. Desbois & Wheeler, Clockmakers - - -	1	18	—			
15.	Messrs. Reed & Hunter, Booksellers - - -	1	6	6			
16.	Messrs. Mullins & Free, Lamplighters - - - -	7	13	—			
17.	Housekeeper's Account of Incidents - - - -	5	8	8			
18.	Officers' Account of Extra Expenses - - -	35	1	—			
19.	Mr. Hiatt, Scalemaker - - - - - -	—	8	—			
20.	Mr. Alderson, for Illuminations in front of the Office -	80	—	—			
21.	Allowance to Alexander Todd, late Chief Clerk -	25	—	—			
22.	Alexander McKilligan's Allowance - - - -	3	18	—			
23.	R. Ford, the younger, for making out Recognizances, and assisting in the general Business of the Office - -	5	10	—			
24.	Messenger's Account of Petty Disbursements - -	8	5	9			
					248	6	—
	NECESSARY DISBURSEMENTS, For the Rent, Taxes, and Repairs of the House.						
25.	House Rent - - - - - - - - -	30	—	—			
26.	Mr. Coates, Smith - - - - - - -	3	14	10			
27.	Mr. Parker, Carpenter - - - - - - -	2	14	4			
28.	Mr. Raddon, Glazier - - - - - - -	—	13	—			
29.	Mr. Lawless, Chimney Sweeper - - - -	—	15	—			
30.	Paving Rate, one Year to Lady-day last - - - -	4	—	—			
31.	Church Rate - - - - - - - - -	—	11	8			
32.	Poors' Rate, one year to Lady-day - - - -	4	7	6			
					46	16	
	£.				977	15	4

THOMAS LEACH.

ROBᵀ RAYNSFORD.

510.

Appendix, N° 3 ᵈ.

PUBLIC OFFICE, HATTON GARDEN.

SALARIES, INCIDENTAL EXPENSES, &c. for the Quarter ending 10th October 1814.

	S A L A R I E S.	£. s. d.	£. s. d.
1.	To John Turton, Esq. - - - - - - -	150 — —	
2.	To Thomas Leach, Esq. - - - - - - -	150 — —	
3.	To Robert Capper, Esq. up to 23d September } 123 14 5 } inclusive - - - - - - - }		
	To R. Raynsford, Esq. from 24th September } 26 5 7 } to 10th of October exclusive - - }	150 — —	
4.	To Robert Ford, Chief Clerk - - - - - -	50 — —	
5.	To John Shearman, Second Clerk - - - - -	25 — —	
6.	To Ten Constables, at 21 s. per week each - - -	136 10 —	
7.	To Catherine Marchant, Housekeeper - - - -	7 10 —	
8.	To Charles Virgin, Messenger - - - - -	13 13 —	682 13 —

	INCIDENTAL EXPENSES.		
9.	Mr. Downes, Printer - - - - - - -	12 16 —	
10.	Messrs. Staunton, Stationers - - - - - -	3 18 —	
11.	Mr. Kennedy, Newsman - - - - - -	4 4 6	
12.	Messrs. Soulsby & Allison, Coal Merchants - - -	18 0 6	
13.	Mr. Armstrong, Oilman - - - - - - -	4 8 6	
14.	Messrs. Reed & Hunter, Booksellers - - - -	9 12 —	
15.	Messrs. Butterworth, Dᵒ - - - - - - -	2 8 6	
16.	Messrs. Walkden & Darby, for Pens and Ink - - -	2 6 —	
17.	Mr. Hanwell, Tallow Chandler - - - - -	7 5 7	
18.	Mr. Hiatt, Scalemaker - - - - - - -	— 4 —	
19.	Mr. Short, for Tin Plates, japanned, with the names of the Officers painted thereon - - - - - -	1 4 —	
20.	Housekeeper's Account of Incidents - - - -	4 13 8	
21.	Ten Officers' Account of Extra Expenses and Charges -	44 2 6	
22.	John Hutt, one of the Officers, Dᵒ - - - -	— 18 9	
23.	Allowance to Alexander Ford, late Chief Clerk - -	25 — —	
24.	Alexander McKilligan's Allowance - - - - -	3 18 —	
25.	Robert Ford the younger, for making out Recognizances, and assisting in the general Business of the Office -	5 10 —	
26.	Disbursements by Robert Capper, Esq. - - - -	18 4 —	
27.	Messenger's Account of Petty Disbursements - - -	6 6 8	175 1 2

	NECESSARY DISBURSEMENTS, For the Rent, Taxes, and Repairs of the House.		
28.	House Rent - - - - - - - - -	30 — —	
29.	Mr Raddon, Glazier - - - - - - -	1 5 —	
30.	Mr. Parker, Carpenter - - - - - - -	2 6 1	
31.	Mr. Berry, Chimney Sweeper - - - - - -	— 15 —	
32.	Two Quarters Watch Rate, to Midsummer-day last past -	— 17 6	
33.	Water Rate, Half a Year, to Dᵒ - - - - -	1 5 —	
34.	Land Tax, one Year, to Lady-day last - - - -	4 17 10	
35.	Poor Rate, one Quarter, to Midsummer-day last past -	4 7 6	45 13 11
		£.	903 8 1

THOMAS LEACH,

ROBᵀ RAYNSFORD.

Appendix, N° 3 ᶜ.

PUBLIC OFFICE, HATTON GARDEN.

SALARIES, INCIDENTAL EXPENSES, &c. for the Quarter ending 5th January 1815.

	SALARIES.	£. s. d.	£. s. d.
1.	To John Turton, Esq. - - - - - - -	150 — —	
2.	To Thomas Leach, Esq. - - - - - -	150 — —	
3.	To Robert Raynsford, Esq. - - - - - -	150 — —	
4.	To Robert Ford, Chief Clerk - - - - - -	50 —	
5.	To John Shearman, Second Clerk - - - - -	25 — —	
6.	To Ten Constables, at £. 1. 1. per week each - -	136 10 —	
7.	To Catherine Marchant, Housekeeper - - - -	7 10 —	
8.	To Charles Virgin, Messenger - - - - -	13 13 —	682 13 —
	INCIDENTAL EXPENSES.		
9.	Mr. Downes, Printer - - - - - - -	16 4 6	
10.	Messrs. Staunton, Stationers - - - - - -	11 7 9	
11.	Messrs. Soulsby & Allison, Coal Merchants - -	19 15 —	
12.	Mr. Hanwell, Tallow Chandler - - - - -	12 12 2	
13.	Messrs. Mullins & Free, Lamplighters - - - -	15 6 —	
14.	Mr. Armstrong, Oilman - - - - - -	5 14 2	
15.	Messrs. Walkden & Darby, for Pens, &c. - - -	3 — —	
16.	Mr. Hiatt, Scale maker - - - - - -	1 6 —	
17.	Desbois & Wheeler, for one year's care of the Office Dial	1 1 —	
18.	Messrs. Reed & Hunter, Booksellers - - - -	3 14 6	
19.	Housekeeper's Account of Incidents - - - -	4 14 8	
20.	Officers' Account of Extra Expenses - - - -	34 2 6	
21.	Alexander Mᶜ Killigan's Allowance - - - -	3 18 —	
22.	Allowance to Alexander Todd, late Chief Clerk - -	25 — —	
23.	R. Ford, jun. for making out Recognizances, and assisting in the general business of the Office - - - -	5 10 —	
24.	Messenger's Account of Petty Disbursements - - -	9 2 8	
25.	Mr. Furley, for furnishing the Office with the weekly Account of the Assize of Bread for Westminster - -	1 1 —	173 9 11
	NECESSARY DISBURSEMENTS, For the Rent, Taxes, and Repairs of the House.		
26.	House Rent - - - - - - - - -	30 — —	
27.	Mr. Hill, Carpenter - - - - - - -	26 12 5	
28.	Mr. Parker, Carpenter - - - - - - -	3 11 7	
29.	Mr. Raddon, Glazier - - - - - - -	2 12 9	
30.	Mr. Coates, Smith - - - - - - - -	4 7 8	
31.	Mr. Berry, Chimney Sweeper - - - - -	— 15 —	
32.	One Quarter's Watch Rate, to Michaelmas 1814 - -	— 8 9	
33.	One Quarter's Tithe to the Bishop of Hereford - -	— 10 —	68 18 2
		£.	925 1 1

THOMAS LEACH,
ROBᵀ RAYNSFORD.

Appendix, Nº 3 ᶠ.

PUBLIC OFFICE, HATTON GARDEN.

SALARIES, INCIDENTAL EXPENSES, &c. for the Quarter ending 5th April 1815.

	SALARIES.	£. s. d.	£. s. d.
1.	To John Turton, Esq. - - - - - - -	150 — —	
2.	To Thomas Leach, Esq. - - - - - - -	150 — —	
3.	To Robert Raynsford, Esq. - - - - - -	150 — —	
4.	To Robert Ford, Chief Clerk - - - - - -	50 — —	
5.	To John Shearman, Second Clerk, at £.100. per annum from 5th January to 4th February, and £.134. per annum from the 4th February to 5th April - - - - -	30 13 4	
6.	To Eight Constables, at 21 s. per week each - - -	109 4 —	
7.	To John Matthews, Constable, to 21st January, the day he was discharged - - - - - - - -	2 8 6	
8.	To Charles Cooke, the like - - - - - -	2 8 6	
9.	To Catherine Marchant, Housekeeper - - - -	7 10 —	
10.	To Charles Virgin, Messenger - - - - -	13 13 —	665 17 4
	INCIDENTAL EXPENSES.		
11.	Messrs. Staunton, Stationers - - - - - -	6 6 —	
12.	Mr. Downes, Printer - - - - - - -	20 2 9	
13.	Messrs. Soulsby & Allison, Coal Merchants - - -	54 — —	
14.	Mr. Hanwell, Tallow Chandler - - - - -	14 13 10	
15.	Messrs. Mullins & Free, Lamplighters - - - -	7 13 —	
16.	Messrs. Reed & Hunter, Booksellers - - - -	3 7 6	
17.	Housekeeper's Account of Incidents - - - -	4 13 8	
18.	Mr. Parker, Gunsmith - - - - - - -	8 1 —	
19.	Mr. Armstrong, Oilman - - - - - - -	7 8 10	
20.	Messrs. Desbois & Wheeler, Clockmakers - - -	— 16 6	
21.	Eight Officers' Account of Extra Expenses - - -	27 16 —	
22.	John Hutt and John Limbrick, Officers, Dº - - -	1 16 9	
23.	Alexander McKilligan's Allowance - - - - -	3 18 —	
24.	Allowance to Alexander Todd, late Chief Clerk - -	25 — —	
25.	R. Ford, jun. for making out Recognizances, and assisting in the general business of the Office - - - -	5 10 —	
26.	Messenger's Account of Petty Disbursements - - -	6 9 9	197 13 7
	NECESSARY DISBURSEMENTS, For the Rent, Taxes, and Repairs of the House.		
27.	House Rent - - - - - - - - -	30 — —	
28.	Water Rate, Half Year, to Michaelmas 1814 - - -	1 5 —	
29	Paving Rate, to Dº - - - - - - - -	2 — —	
30.	Poors' Rate to Dº - - - - - - - -	8 15 —	
31.	Church Rate - - - - - - - - -	— 14 7	
32.	Mr. Parker, Carpenter - - - - - - -	3 16 11	
33.	Mr. Coates, Smith - - - - - - - -	5 13 5	
34.	Mr. Raddon, Glazier - - - - - - -	1 15 6	
35.	Mr. Berry, Chimney Sweeper - - - - - -	— 15 —	54 15 5
		£.	918 6 4

THOMAS LEACH,
ROBᵀ RAYNSFORD.

Appendix, N° 3ᶠ.

PUBLIC OFFICE, HATTON GARDEN.

SALARIES, INCIDENTAL EXPENSES, &c. for the Quarter ending 5th July 1815.

	SALARIES.	£. s. d.	£. s. d.
1.	To John Turton, Esq. - - - - - - -	150 — —	
2.	To Thomas Leach, Esq. - - - - - - -	150 — —	
3.	To Robert Raynsford, Esq. - - - - - -	150 — —	
4.	To Robert Ford, Chief Clerk - - - - - -	50 — —	
5.	To John Shearman, Second Clerk - - - - -	33 10 —	
6.	To Eight Constables, at 21 s. per week each - - -	109 4 —	
7.	To Catherine Marchant, Housekeeper - - - -	7 10 —	
8.	To Charles Virgin, Messenger - - - - - -	13 13 —	663 17 —
	INCIDENTAL EXPENSES.		
9.	Mr. Downes, Printer - - - - - - -	19 3 6	
10.	Messrs. Staunton, Stationers - - - - - -	4 5 —	
11.	Mr. Hanwell, Tallow Chandler - - - - -	8 18 —	
12.	Messrs. Mullins & Free, Lamplighters - - - -	7 13 —	
13.	Mr. Armstrong, Oilman - - - - - -	5 18 1	
14.	Messrs. Walkden & Darby, for Pens and Ink - - -	2 6 —	
15.	Mr. Kennedy, Newsman, Three Quarters - - -	12 13 6	
16.	Messrs. Reed & Hunter, Booksellers - - - -	3 15 —	
17.	Mr. Hiatt, Scalemaker - - - - - - -	1 13 —	
18.	Housekeeper's Account of Incidents - - - -	5 — 4	
19.	Officers' Account of Extra Expenses - - - -	27 6 —	
20.	Alexander McKilligan's Allowance - - - - -	3 18 —	
21.	Allowance to Alexander Todd, late Chief Clerk - -	25 — —	
22.	R. Ford, jun. for making out Recognizances, and assisting in the general Business of the Office - - - -	5 10 —	
23.	Messenger's Account of Petty Disbursements - - -	6 16 7	
24.	Mr. Day, for his Annual Account of the number of Criminal Offenders, &c. - - - - - - - -	2 2 —	
25.	William Read, the elder (one of the Officers) for Advertisements, &c. - - - - - - - -	— 19 —	142 17 —
26.	Joseph Beckett's Expense in attending to, at and from London, and the Assizes at Bury St. Edmund's, the trial of Mary Gibbs for Murder - - - - -	- - -	7 11 —
	NECESSARY DISBURSEMENTS, For the Rent, Taxes, and Repairs of the House.		
27.	House Rent - - - - - - - - -	30 — —	
28.	Mr. Parker, Carpenter - - - - - - -	2 4 9	
29.	Mr. Harrow, Bricklayer - - - - - - -	3 — 9	
30.	Mr. Coates, Smith - - - - - - - -	1 14 9	
31.	Mr. Berry, Chimney Sweeper - - - - - -	— 15 —	
32.	Poor's Rate, one Quarter, to Lady-day - - - -	3 10 —	
33.	Rector's Tithe, two Quarters, to Dᵒ - - - -	— 5 —	
34.	Easter Offering - - - - - - - -	— 5 —	
35.	Land Tax, one Year, to Lady-day - - - - -	4 17 10	
36.	Paving Rate, one Quarter, to Midsummer - - -	1 — —	
37.	Watch Rate, two Quarters, to Lady-day - - - -	— 17 6	48 10 7
		£.	862 15 7

THOMAS LEACH.

ROBᵀ RAYNSFORD.

Appendix, N° 3 ʰ.

PUBLIC OFFICE, HATTON GARDEN.

SALARIES, INCIDENTAL EXPENSES, &c. for the Quarter ending 10th October 1815.

	SALARIES.	£. s. d.	£. s. d.
1.	To John Turton, Esq. - - - - - - -	150 — —	
2.	To Thomas Leach, Esq. - - - - - - -	150 — —	
3.	To Robert Raynsford, Esq. - - - - - -	150 — —	
4.	To Robert Ford, Chief Clerk - - - - - -	50 — —	
5.	To John Shearman, Second Clerk - - - - -	33 10 —	
6.	To Eight Constables, at 21 s. per week each - - -	109 4 —	
7.	To Catherine Marchant, Housekeeper - - - -	7 10 —	
8.	To Charles Virgin, Messenger - - - - -	13 13 —	663 17 —
	INCIDENTAL EXPENSES.		
9.	Mr. Downes, Printer - - - - - - -	22 9 9	
10.	Messrs. Staunton, Stationers - - - - - -	8 9 6	
11.	Mr. Hanwell, Tallow Chandler - - - - -	7 18 8	
12.	Messrs. Mullins & Free, Lamplighters - - - -	7 13 —	
13.	Mr. Armstrong, Oilman - - - - - - -	5 12 5	
14.	Mr. Kennedy, Newsman - - - - - - -	4 4 6	
15.	Messrs. Soulsby & Allison, Coal Merchants - - -	16 5 —	
16.	Housekeeper's Account of Incidents - - - -		
17.	Eight Officers' Account of Extra Expences - - -	27 6 —	
18.	William Read the elder (one of the Officers) the like - -	1 8 —	
19.	John Hutt, (one of the Officers) the like - - - -	— 14 6	
20.	Alexander McKilligan's Allowance - - - - -	3 18 —	
21.	Allowance to Alexander Todd, late Chief Clerk - - -	25 — —	
22.	R. Ford, jun. for making out Recognizances, and assisting in the general business of the Office - - - -	5 10 —	
23.	Messenger's Account of Petty Disbursements - - -	5 6 2	146 9 4
	NECESSARY DISBURSEMENTS, For the Rent, Taxes, and Repairs of the House.		
24.	House Rent - - - - - - - - -	30 — —	
25.	C. Virgin, for Carpenter's Work - - - - -	2 — —	
26.	Mr. Raddon, Glazier and Plumber - - - - -	3 9 5	
27.	Mr. Coates, Smith - - - - - - - -	2 1 11	
28.	Mr. Berry, Chimney Sweeper - - - - - -	— 15 —	
29.	Watch Rate, Half a Year, to Midsummer - - - -	1 5 —	
30.	Watch Rate, one Quarter, to D° - - - - -	— 8 9	
31.	Poor Rate, the like - - - - - - -	3 10 —	
32.	Paving Rate, Half Year, to D° - - - - - -	2 3 4	45 13 5
		£.	855 19 9

THOMAS LEACH,
ROBᵀ RAYNSFORD.

Appendix, Nº 3ⁱ.

PUBLIC OFFICE, HATTON GARDEN.

SALARIES, INCIDENTAL EXPENSES, &c. for the Quarter ending 5th January 1816.

	SALARIES.	£. s. d.	£. s. d.
1.	To John Turton, Esq. - - - - - - -	150 — —	
2.	To Thomas Leach, Esq. - - - - - - -	150 — —	
3.	To Robert Raynsford, Esq. - - - - - -	150 — —	
4.	To Robert, Ford, Chief Clerk - - - - - -	50 — —	
5.	To John Shearman, Second Clerk - - - - -	33 10 —	
6.	To Eight Constables, at 21 s. per Week each - - -	109 4 —	
7.	To Catherine Marchant, Housekeeper - - - -	7 10 —	
8.	To Charles Virgin, Messenger - - - - - -	13 13 —	663 17 —
	INCIDENTAL EXPENSES.		
9.	Mr. Downes, Printer - - - - - - -	20 1 6	
10.	Mr. Staunton, Stationer - - - - - - -	7 19 6	
11.	Mr. Hanwell, Tallow Chandler - - - - -	9 9 6	
12.	Messrs. Soulsby & Co. Coal Merchants - - - -	16 11 —	
13.	Mr. Armstrong, Oilman - - - - - - -	5 1 7	
14.	Messrs. Mullins & Free, Lamplighters - - - -	7 13 —	
15.	Housekeeper's Account of Incidents - - - -	5 2 —	
16.	Messrs. Johnson & Co. for Lamps, &c. - - - -	13 6 —	
17.	Messrs. Reed & Hunter, Booksellers - - - -	3 3 6	
18.	Officers' Account of Extra Expenses - - - -	29 4 —	
19.	Alexander Mᶜ Killigan's Allowance - - - - -	3 18 —	
20.	Allowance to Alexander Todd, late Chief Clerk - - -	25 — —	
21.	R. Ford, jun. for making out Recognizances, and assisting in the general Business of the Office - - - -	5 10 —	
22.	To the Officers, for extra Duty performed by them in attending several nights in Chancery-lane, Eagle-street, &c. to prevent a disturbance of the Public Peace by Crowds of Persons assembled at those places in consequence of the Execution of Eliza Fenning - - - - -	11 — —	
23.	Account of Petty Disbursements - - - - -	10 7 6	
24.	To William Read, jun. for Expenses incurred by him in apprehending John Farren for Felony - - - -	3 10 —	176 17 1
	NECESSARY DISBURSEMENTS, For the Rent, Taxes, and Repairs of the House.		
25.	House Rent - - - - - - - - -	30 — —	
26.	Sewers Rate - - - - - - - - -	1 15 —	
27.	Poor Rate, one Quarter, to Michaelmas - - - -	3 10 —	
28.	Mr. Coates, for Smith's Work - - - - - -	4 19 8	
29.	Mr. Harrow, for Bricklayers Work - - - - -	5 9 8	
30.	Mr. Berry, Chimney Sweeper - - - - - -	— 15 —	
31.	C. Virgin, for Carpenter's Work - - - - -	— 12 10	
32.	Mr. Parker, for the like - - - - - - -	— 14 6	
33.	Mr. Raddon, Painter - - - - - - -	3 5 3	51 1 11
		£.	891 16 —

THOMAS LEACH,
ROBᵀ RAYNSFORD.

Appendix, Nᵒ 4.²—An ACCOUNT of the ESTABLISHMENT of the PUBLIC OFFICE,

For the - - - -

RANK of OFFICER.	HIS NAME.	By whom appointed.	How Appointed.	When Appointed.	Duration of Interest.	RECEIPT: Salary.	By whom Paid.	Fees.	By whom Paid.	Other Emoluments.
Three Magistrates	John Gifford	The King	By Sign Manual	May 1800	— —	£.600 per Ann. each by Act of Parliament.	The Police Receiver	— —	— —	Three Rooms on the Attic Story
	Joseph Moser		Ditto	31 Jan. 1801	— —			— —		
	Sir William Parsons		Ditto	28 May 1807	— —			— —		
Chief Clerk -	Samuel Yardley	The Secretary of State	As Extra Clerk by the Magistrates, As 2d Clerk, As Chief Clerk	In Aug. 1792, In Oct. 1800, In Jan. 1803	— —	£.200.	Ditto			
Second Clerk	William Heritage		— — —	13 Oct. 1813	— —	£.134. 10.				
Ten Constables	John Armstrong	The Magistrates	Verbally	21 Aug. 1792	Good behaviour	1 Guinea per Week each, by Act of Parliament	Ditto	Generally 2s. for serving a Warrant or Summons; but the Amount beyond that depends upon distance	The Party Prosecuting, or the Defendant according to circumstances.	Rewards granted by Law on the Apprehension or Conviction of Offenders - - - Rewards occasionally offered and paid by Prosecutors - - Small Payments for Expenses on Journies and extra Services - John Crosswell who acted as Assistant Goaler, received 7s. per Week for bringing up Prisoners from New Prison for further Examination, and 1s. for every Prisoner admitted to Bail at this Office. And for taking Prisoners to Gaol One Shilling each.
	Samuel Harper	- Ditto -	- Ditto -	- Ditto -	Ditto					
	James Kennedy	- Ditto -	- Ditto -	25 May 1803	Ditto					
	Joshua Armstrong	- Ditto -	- Ditto -	24 Jan. 1806	Ditto					
	John Crosswell	- Ditto -	- Ditto -	23 Aug. 1810	Ditto					
	William Armstrong	- Ditto -	- Ditto -	31 Aug. 1811	Ditto					
	Anthony Cavalier	- Ditto -	- Ditto -	2 March 1812	Ditto					
	William Turner	- Ditto -	- Ditto -	25 Jan. 1812	Ditto					
	Daniel Bishop	- Ditto -	- Ditto -	31 Aug. 1803	Ditto					
	Barnard Gleed	- Ditto -	By Letter from the Secretary of State.	29 Jan. 1814	Ditto					
Office Keeper	Edward Balderson	The Secretary of State	By Letter -	Sept. 1814	Ditto	£.54. 12. per Ann.	Ditto	— —	— —	One Room each in the House, Coal and Candle
Housekeeper	Magdalen Bottom	- Ditto -	- Ditto -	3 Oct. 1808	Ditto	£.25 per Annum	Ditto	— —	— —	
Messenger -	Thomas Mance	- Ditto -	- Ditto -	5 July 1813	Ditto	£.54. 12. per Ann.	Ditto			

FOR THE YEAR 1815.

RANK of OFFICER.	HIS NAME.	By whom appointed.	How Appointed.	When Appointed.	Duration of Interest.	Salary.	By whom Paid.	Fees.	By whom Paid.	Other Emoluments.
Three Magistrates	The same as above -	—	—	—	—			—	—	—
Chief Clerk -	The same - - - -	—	—	—	—	£.225. In October 1815 increased to £.300 per Ann. having served as a Clerk in the Office 20 Years and upwards - -	—	—	—	—
Second Clerk	The same - - - -	—	—	—	—			—	—	—
Nine Constables	John Armstrong	Same as in 1814 -	Ditto -	- Ditto -	Ditto -	- Ditto -	Ditto -	- Ditto -	Ditto	- - Ditto - -
	Samuel Harper									
	James Kennedy									
	Joshua Armstrong									
	John Crosswell									
	William Turner									
	Barnard Gleed									
	Anthony Cavalier									
	Thomas Garton	By Secretary of State	By Letter from John Beckett, Esq.	1 May 1815						
Office Keeper	John Othen - - -	- Ditto -	- Ditto -	1 Dec. 1815	The same as in 1814.	—	—	—	—	—
Housekeeper	Magdalen Bottom -	— —	— —	— —						
Messenger -	Thomas Mance - -	— —	— —	— — —						

20th April 1816.

WORSHIP-STREET, for the Years 1814 and 1815; distinguishing each Year.

- - - - Year 1814.

RECEIPT: From Whence.	TOTAL Receipt.	DEDUCTIONS.			TOTAL Disbursements.	Net Receipt 1814.	Net Receipt Annual upon an Average of the last Three Years.	Other Employments, Places, or Pensions, under Government	Their Annual Value.	Since 1792, when the Office was established.			
		Taxes.	Deputies and Clerks.	Contingencies						Increase.		Diminution.	
										Salaries, &c.	Officers.	Salaries, &c.	Officers.
- - -	£. 600. per Ann. each	Property Tax, £. 60. each.	- -	- -	- -	£. 540. each.	£. 480. each	Master and Conductor of the King's Band.	£. 300 per Ann.	£. 200. per Ann. each by Act of Parliament.	—	—	—
- - -	£. 200.	Property Tax, £. 20.	- -	- -	- -	£. 180.	£. 180.	- - -	- -	£ 50. per Ann. in October 1811.	—	- -	An Extra Clerk.
- - -	£. 134. 10.	Do £. 12.	- -	- -	- -	£. 122. 10.	£. 122. 10.	—	—		—		
The Sheriff; Party Prosecuting; The Police Receiver when approved of by the Magistrates. The Keeper of the New Prison at Clerkenwell; Prosecutors at their option.	Uncertain, depending wholly on the Business done.	Property Tax, £. 1. 10. each per Annum.	-	- -	- -	Uncertain.	Uncertain.	- - -	- -	9 s. per Week each.	Four Constables.	—	—
- - -	£. 54. 12.	Property Tax £. 1. 10.	-	- -	- -	£. 53. 2.	£. 53. 2.	- - -	- -	£. 19. 12. per Ann.	—	—	—
- - -	£. 25.	- - -	-	- -	- -	£. 25.	£. 25.	- - -	- -	£. 12. per Annum.	—	—	—
- - -	£. 54. 12.	Property Tax £. 1. 10.	-	- -	- -	£. 53. 2.	£. 53. 7. 2.	- - -	- -	£. 23. 16. per Ann.	—	—	—
- - -	- - -	- - -	-	- -	- -	- - -	£. 510. each.	—	—		—		—
- - -	£. 225.	Property Tax £. 22. 10.	-	- -	- -	£. 202. 10.	£. 187. 10.	- - -	- -	£. 100 per Ann. In October 1815 having served as before stated 20 Years and upwards as a Clerk in the Office.			—
- - -	- - -	Property Tax £. 3. per Ann.	—	—	—	—	—	- - -	- -		—		—
- Ditto -	- Ditto -	£. 4. 10. each per Annum.	-	- -	- -	- -	- -	- -	- -		—		1 Constable since 1814.
—	—	—	—	—	—	—	—	—	—	—	—	—	—

SAMUEL YARDLEY,

Chief Clerk.

Appendix, N° 4ᵇ.

PUBLIC OFFICE, WORSHIP-STREET, SHOREDITCH.

An ACCOUNT of the Salaries of the Magistrates, Clerks, Constables, and others, belonging to the said Office; of the incidental Expenses, and of the necessary Disbursements for the Rent, Taxes, and Repairs of the House wherein the said Office is held;—for the Quarter ending the 1st Day of April 1814.

	SALARIES.	£. s. d.	£. s. d.
1.	To John Gifford, Esquire - - - - - -	150 — —	
2.	To Joseph Moser, Esquire - - - - - -	150 — —	
3.	To Sir William Parsons - - - - - -	150 — —	
4.	To Samuel Yardley, Chief Clerk - - - -	50 — —	
5.	To William Heritage, Second Clerk - - - -	25 — —	
6.	To Eight Constables - - - - - -	109 4 —	
7.ᵃ	To Richard Wilson, Constable, ten weeks - -	10 10 —	
7.ᵇ	To Daniel Bishop, - - Dᵒ - ten days - -	1 10 —	
7.ᶜ	To Barnard Gleed, - - Dᵒ - nine weeks and five days -	10 4 —	
8.	To Thomas Garner, office keeper, one week and four days -	1 15 —	
9.	To Bolton Todd, - Dᵒ - - - eleven weeks and two days	11 18 —	
10.	To Magdalen Bottom, Housekeeper - - -	6 5 —	
11.	To Thomas Mance, Messenger - - - - - -	13 13 —	618 19 —
	INCIDENTAL EXPENSES.		
12.	To Joseph Downes, for Printing - - - -	8 10 —	
13.	To Isaac Joel, for Newspapers and Sessions Papers - -	5 — 9½	
14.	To Messrs. Witherby, Stationer's Bill - - -	6 11 10	
15.	To petty Disbursements by Chief Clerk - - -	5 18 1	
16.	To John Armstrong, for Constables expenses and petty disbursements - - - - - - -	11 11 2	
17.	To George Armstrong, Tallow Chandler, for Candles -	13 9 6	
18.	To Office Keeper's petty disbursements - - -	4 4 9	
19.	To Messrs. Soulsby and Company, Coal Merchants Bill -	27 8 —	
20.	To Thomas Clack, Oilman, Bill - - - -	2 17 —	
21.	To Samuel Yardley, Bill of expenses in the prosecution against James King and Edward Harris, for felony, by order of the Secretary of State - - - - -	9 19 8	
22.	To William Turner, Cabinet-maker, Bill for a mahogany writing table, and repairing chairs, &c. - - -	8 3 —	103 13 9½
	NECESSARY DISBURSEMENTS For the Rent, Taxes, and Repairs of the House.		
23.	To One Quarter's Rent due at Lady Day 1814 - - -	29 10 —	
24.	To Taxes - - - - - - - - -	6 3 —	35 13 —
	£.		829 5 9½

WE, the Magistrates of the Police Office, Worship-street, Shoreditch, do hereby certify, that we have examined the above Account, and the different Bills, and find them correct; and that the different articles therein charged were necessary for the Public Service at this Office (to which only they have been applied) to the best of our knowledge and belief.

(Signed)   JOHN GIFFORD, ⎰ Magistrates of the Police Office,
            W. PARSONS,   ⎱   Worship-street.

Appendix, Nº 4ᶜ.

PUBLIC OFFICE, WORSHIP-STREET, SHOREDITCH.

SALARIES, INCIDENTAL EXPENSES, &c. for the Quarter ending 1st July 1814.

		£. s. d.	£. s. d.
	SALARIES.		
1.	To JOHN GIFFORD, Esquire - - - - - -	150 — —	
2.	To JOSEPH MOSER, Esquire - - - - - -	150 — —	
3.	To Sir WILLIAM PARSONS - - - - - -	150 — —	
4.	To Samuel Yardley, Chief Clerk - - - - -	50 — —	
5.	To William Heritage, Second Clerk - - - - -	25 — —	
6.	To Nine Constables - - - - - - -	122 17 —	
7.	To Bolton Todd, Office-keeper, four weeks - - -	4 4 —	
8.	To Magdalen Bottom, Housekeeper - - - - -	6 5 —	
9.	To Thomas Mance, Messenger - - - - -	13 13 —	
			671 19 —
	INCIDENTAL EXPENSES.		
10.	To Joseph Downes, for Printing - - - - -	6 6 6	
11.	To John Davis, for Newspapers - - - - -	4 4 —	
12.	To Messrs. Witherby, Stationers Bill - - - -	4 8 10	
13.	To Petty Disbursements by Chief Clerk - - - -	2 3 5	
14.	To John Armstrong, for Constables expenses and petty disbursements - - - - - - - -	6 19 8	
15.	To George Armstrong, Tallow Chandler, for Candles -	4 12 —	
16.	To Thomas Mance, Messenger, acting as office-keeper, for petty disbursements - - - - - - -	3 3 8	
17.	To Messrs. Soulsby and Co. Coal Merchants Bill - -	17 6 —	
18.	To Thomas Clack, Oilman, Bill - - - - -	1 18 —	
19.	To J. D. Ruffey, Lamp Contractor, Bill for illuminations -	13 — —	
20.	To William Day, for annual statement of the number of Criminal Offenders, &c. - - - - - -	2 2 —	
			66 4 1
	NECESSARY DISBURSEMENTS For the Rent, Taxes, and Repairs of the House.		
21.	To One Quarter's Rent due at Midsummer Day 1814 -	29 10 —	
22.	To Taxes - - - - - - - - -	5 10 —	
			35 — —
	£.		773 3 1

WE, the Magistrates of the Public Office, Worship-street, Shoreditch, do hereby certify, that we have examined the above Account, and the different Bills, and find them correct; and that the different articles therein charged, were necessary for the Public Service at this Office (to which only they have been applied) to the best of our knowledge and belief.

(Signed)   JOHN GIFFORD, } Magistrates of the Police Office,
              JOSEPH MOSER, }   Worship-street.

Appendix, N° 4. ᵈ

PUBLIC OFFICE, WORSHIP-STREET, SHOREDITCH.

SALARIES, INCIDENTAL EXPENSES, &c. for the Quarter ending 1st October 1814.

	SALARIES.	£.	s.	d.	£.	s.	d.
1.	To JOHN GIFFORD, Esquire - - - - - -	150	—	—			
2.	To JOSEPH MOSER, Esquire - - - - - -	150	—	—			
3.	To Sir WILLIAM PARSONS - - - - - -	150	—	—			
4.	To Samuel Yardley, Chief Clerk - - - - -	50	—	—			
5.	To William Heritage, Second Clerk - - - -	25	—	—			
6.	To Nine Coustables - - - - - - -	122	17	—			
7.	To Edw. Balderson, Office-keeper, four weeks and four days - - - - - - - - -	4	16	—			
8.	To Magdalen Bottom, Housekeeper - - - -	6	5	—			
9.	To Thomas Mance, Messenger - - - - -	13	13	—	672	11	—
	INCIDENTAL EXPENSES.						
10.	To Joseph Downes, for Printing - - - - -	13	13	—			
11.	To John Davis, for Newspapers - - - - -	4	7	—			
12.	To Messrs. Witherby, Stationers Bill - - - -	5	4	6			
13.	To Petty Disbursements by Chief Clerk - - - -	7	2	11			
14.	To John Armstrong, for Constables expenses and petty disbursements - - - - - - - -	22	14	5			
15.	To George Armstrong, Tallow Chandler, for Candles -	4	11	—			
16.	To J. D. Ruffy, Lamp Contractor, Bill - - - -	79	9	4			
17.	To Office-keepers Petty Disbursements - - - -	2	12	11¾			
18.	To William Turner, Cabinet-makers Bill - - - -	2	13	—			
19.	To W. E. Hardy, for five Newgate Calendars - - -	5	5	—	147	13	1¾
	NECESSARY DISBURSEMENTS For the Rent, Taxes, and Repairs of the House.						
20.	To One Quarter's Rent due at Michaelmas 1814 - -	29	10	—			
21.	To Taxes - - - - - - - - -	4	10	6			
22.	To Thomas Lewing, Carpenter's Bill - - - -	1	—	—	35	—	6
				£.	855	4	7½

WE, the Magistrates of the Police Office, Worship-street, Shoreditch, do hereby certify, that we have examined the above Account, and the different Bills, and find them correct; and that the different articles therein charged, were necessary for the Public Service at this Office (to which only they have been applied) to the best of our knowledge and belief.

(Signed)   JOHN GIFFORD,   ⎫   Magistrates of the Police Office,
               JOSEPH MOSER,   ⎬   Worship-street.
               W. PARSONS,   ⎭

Appendix, N° 4.ᵉ

PUBLIC OFFICE, WORSHIP-STREET, SHOREDITCH.

SALARIES, INCIDENTAL EXPENSES, &c. for the Quarter ending 1st January 1815.

	SALARIES.	£. s. d.	£. s. d.
1.	To JOHN GIFFORD, Esquire - - - - - -	150 — —	
2.	To JOSEPH MOSER, Esquire - - - - - -	150 — —	
3.	To Sir WILLIAM PARSONS - - - - - -	150 — —	
4.	To Samuel Yardley, Chief Clerk - - - -	50 — —	
5.	To William Heritage, Second Clerk - - -	33 10 —	
6.	To Nine Constables - - - - - - -	122 17 —	
7.	To Edward Balderson, Office-keeper - - -	13 13 —	
8.	To Magdalen Bottom, Housekeeper - - - -	6 5 —	
9.	To Thomas Mance, Messenger - - - - -	13 13 —	689 18 —
	INCIDENTAL EXPENSES.		
10.	To Joseph Downes, for Printing - - - - -	14 3 6	
11.	To John Davis, - for Newspapers - - - -	4 7 —	
12.	To Messrs. Witherby, Stationer's Bill - - - -	3 4 4	
13.	To Petty Disbursements, by Chief Clerk - - - -	2 — 4	
14.	To John Armstrong, for Constables expenses and petty disbursements - - - - - - - -	12 13 7	
15.	To George Armstrong, Tallow Chandler, for Candles - -	6 8 —	
16.	To Office Keeper's petty disbursements - - - -	2 12 1	
17.	To Allowance to Thomas Mance, for 18 weeks duty, as Office Keeper, to 1st September last - - - -	10 — —	
18.	To J. D. Ruffy, Lamplighter's Bill, for lighting the Office Lamps, one year, to Michaelmas last - - - -	5 3 —	
19.	To Thomas Clack, Oilman's Bill - - - - -	1 14 —	
20.	To Messrs. Soulsby & Co. Coal Merchant's Bill - -	16 10 —	78 15 10
	NECESSARY DISBURSEMENTS For the Rent, Taxes, and Repairs of the House.		
21.	To One Quarter's Rent due Christmas 1814 - - -	29 10 —	
22.	To Taxes - - - - - - - - -	5 15 5	35 5 5
		£.	803 19 3

WE, the Magistrates of the Police Office, Worship-street, Shoreditch, do hereby certify, that we have examined the above Account, and the different Bills, and find them correct; and that the different Articles therein charged were necessary for the Public Service at this Office (to which only they have been applied) to the best of our knowledge and belief.

(Signed)   JOSEPH MOSER, ⎫ Magistrates of the Police Office,
                   W. PARSONS, ⎭   Worship-street.

510.

Appendix, N° 4. f.

PUBLIC OFFICE, WORSHIP STREET, SHOREDITCH.

[SALARIES, INCIDENTAL EXPENSES, &c. for the Quarter ending 1st April, 1815.

	SALARIES.	£. s. d.	£. s. d.
1.	To JOHN GIFFORD, Esq. - - - - - -	150 — —	
2.	To JOSEPH MOSER, Esq. - - - - - - -	150 — —	
3.	To Sir WILLIAM PARSONS - - - - - -	150 — —	
4.	To Samuel Yardley, Chief Clerk - - - - -	50 — —	
5.	To William Heritage, Second Clerk - - - - -	33 10 —	
6.	To Nine Constables - - - - - - -	122 17 —	
7.	To Edward Balderson, Office-keeper - - - -	13 13 —	
8.	To Magdalen Bottom, Housekeeper - - - - -	6 5 —	
9.	To Thomas Mance, Messenger - - - - -	13 13 —	689 18 —
	INCIDENTAL EXPENSES.		
10.	To Joseph Downes, for Printing - - - - -	10 19 6	
11.	To John Davis, for Newspapers - - - - -	4 7 —	
12.	To Messrs. Witherby, for Stationary - - - -	3 12 —	
13.	To Petty Disbursements by Chief Clerk - - - -	3 12 —	
14.	To John Armstrong, for Constables expenses and petty disbursements - - - - - - - -	31 5 8½	
15.	To George Armstrong, Tallow Chandler, for Candles -	4 4 —	
16.	To Office Keeper's Petty Disbursements : - - -	5 12 4	
17.	To Messrs. Soulsby & Co. Coal Merchants Bill - -	14 6 —	
18.	To Messrs. Allen & Sons, Bill for repairing Pump - -	2 18 9	
19.	To Messrs. Reed & Hunter, Law Booksellers - - -	2 — —	82 17 3½
	NECESSARY DISBURSEMENTS For the Rent, Taxes, and Repairs of the House.		
20.	To one Quarter's Rent, due Lady Day 1815 - - -	29 10 —	
21.	To Taxes - - - - - - - - -	3 17 6	
22.	To Robert Stuckey, Bricklayer, Bill for Repairs - -	1 11 11	34 19 5
	£.		807 14 8½

WE, the Magistrates of the Police Office, Worship-street, Shoreditch, do hereby certify, that we have examined the above Account, and the different Bills, and find them correct; and that the different Articles therein charged, were necessary for the Public Service at this Office (to which only they have been applied) to the best of our knowledge and belief.

(Signed)   JOSEPH MOSER, ⎱ Magistrates of the Police Office,
                W. PARSONS,   ⎰   Worship-street.

Appendix, N° 4.ᵍ.

PUBLIC OFFICE, WORSHIP-STREET, SHOREDITCH.

SALARIES, INCIDENTAL EXPENSES, &c. for the Quarter ending 1st July 1815.

	SALARIES.	£. s. d.	£. s. d.
1.	To JOHN GIFFORD, Esquire - - - - - -	150 — —	
2.	To JOSEPH MOSER, Esquire - - - - - -	150 — —	
3.	To Sir WILLIAM PARSONS - - - - -	150 — —	
4.	To Samuel Yardley, Chief Clerk - - - -	50 — —	
5.	To William Heritage, Second Clerk - - -	33 10 —	
6.	To Eight Constables, 13 Weeks - - - -	109 4 —	
6.	To Wᵐ Armstrong, Constable, 13 Days - - -	1 19 —	
6.	To Thomas Garton, D° - - 9 Weeks and 3 Days -	9 18 —	
7.	To Edward Balderson, Office-keeper - - -	13 13 —	
8.	To Magdalen Bottom, Housekeeper - - -	6 5 —	
9.	To Thomas Mance, Messenger - - - -	13 13 —	
			688 2 —
	INCIDENTAL EXPENSES.		
10.	To Joseph Downes, for Printing - - - -	6 14 6	
11.	To John Davis, for Newspapers - - - -	4 7 —	
12.	To Messrs. Witherby, for Stationary - - -	9 13 4	
13.	To Petty Disbursements, by Chief Clerk - - -	1 11 6	
14.	To John Armstrong, for Constables expenses and petty disbursements - - - - - - -	19 2 9½	
15.	To George Armstrong, Tallow Chandler, for Candles -	3 18 —	
16.	To Office Keeper's Petty Disbursements - - -	2 3 5½	
17.	To Mr. William Day, for Copies of the Number, &c. of Criminal Offenders committed to the several Gaols in England and Wales, during the Year 1814 - - -	2 2 —	
18.	To J. D. Ruffy, Lamplighter, Bill for Illuminating the Office	16 1 6	
			65 14 1
	NECESSARY DISBURSEMENTS For the Rent, Taxes, and Repairs of the House.		
19.	To One Quarter's Rent, due Midsummer Day 1815 - -	29 10 —	
20.	To Taxes - - - - - - - -	5 — 2	
			34 10 2
	£.		788 6 3

WE, the Magistrates of the Police Office, Worship-street, Shoreditch, do hereby certify, that we have examined the above Account, and the different Bills, and find them correct; and that the different Articles therein charged, were necessary to the Public Service at this Office (to which only they have been applied) to the best of our knowledge and belief.

(Signed)   JOSEPH MOSER, ⎫ Magistrates of the Police Office,
           W. PARSONS,   ⎭   Worship-street.

Appendix, N° 4.ʰ

PUBLIC OFFICE, WORSHIP-STREET, SHOREDITCH.

SALARIES, INCIDENTAL EXPENSES, &c. for the Quarter ending 1st October 1815.

	SALARIES.	£. s. d.	£. s. d.
1.	To JOHN GIFFORD, Esquire - - - - - -	150 — —	
2.	To JOSEPH MOSER, Esquire - - - - - -	150 — —	
3.	To Sir WILLIAM PARSONS - - - - - -	150 — —	
4.	To Samuel Yardley, Chief Clerk - - - -	50 — —	
5.	To William Heritage, Second Clerk - - - -	33 10 —	
6.	To Nine Constables - - - - - - -	122 17 —	
7.	To Edw. Balderson, Office-keeper - - - -	13 13 —	
8.	To Magdalen Bottom, Housekeeper - - - -	6 5 —	
9.	To Thomas Mance, Messenger - - - - -	13 13 —	689 18 —
	INCIDENTAL EXPENSES.		
10.	To Joseph Downes, for Printing - - - - -	16 16 6	
11.	To J. B. Reeve, for Newspapers - - - -	4 8 —	
12.	To Messrs. Witherby, for Stationary - - - -	3 8 10	
13.	To Petty Disbursements by Chief Clerk - - - -	3 9 2	
14.	To John Armstrong, for Constables expenses and petty disbursements - - - - - - - -	23 9 4	
15.	To George Armstrong, Tallow Chandler, for Candles -	2 10 —	
16.	To Office-keeper's Petty Disbursements - - - -	2 5 3	
17.	To Messrs. Reed & Hunter, Law Booksellers - - -	1 3 —	
18.	To William Turner, Cabinet-maker, Bill - - - -	3 4 4	
19.	To Messrs. Soulsby & Co. Coal Merchants Bill - -	6 16 —	67 10 5
	NECESSARY DISBURSEMENTS For the Rent, Taxes, and Repairs of the House.		
20.	To One Quarter's Rent to Michaelmas 1815 - - -	29 10 —	
21.	To Taxes - - - - - - - - -	6 5 2	
	£.		793 3 7

WE, the Magistrates of the Police Office, Worship-street, Shoreditch, do hereby certify, that we have examined the above Account, and the different Bills, and find them correct; and that the different Articles therein charged, were necessary for the Public Service at this Office (to which only they have been applied) to the best of our knowledge and belief.

(Signed)   JOHN GIFFORD,   } Magistrates of the Police Office,
             JOSEPH MOSER,   }   Worship-street.

Appendix, N° 4.[i]

PUBLIC OFFICE, WORSHIP STREET, SHOREDITCH.

SALARIES, INCIDENTAL EXPENSES, &c. for the Quarter ending 1st January 1816.

	SALARIES.	£. s. d.	£. s. d.
1.	To JOHN GIFFORD, Esquire - - - - - -	150 — —	
2.	To JOSEPH MOSER, Esquire - - - - - -	150 — —	
3.	To Sir WILLIAM PARSONS - - - - - -	150 — —	
4.	To Samuel Yardley, Chief Clerk, including an Increase at the rate of £.100 per Ann. having served 20 years and upwards, such Increase being pursuant to the Secretary of State's Letter, of 13 September last - - - -	75 — —	
5.	To William Heritage, Second Clerk - - - - -	33 10 —	
6.	To Eight Constables - - - - - - -	109 4 —	
	To William Turner, Constable, 10 Weeks Salary - -	10 10 —	
7.	To Edward Balderson, late Office Keeper, 8 Weeks - -	8 8 —	
	To John Othen, Office Keeper, 5 Weeks - - - -	5 5 —	
8.	To Magdalen Bottom, Housekeeper - - - -	6 5 —	
9.	To Thomas Mance, Messenger - - - - -	13 13 —	711 15 —
	INCIDENTAL EXPENSES.		
10.	To Joseph Downes, for Printing - - - - -	14 18 6	
11.	To J. Reeve, - - for Newspapers - - - -	4 17 2	
12.	To Messrs. Witherby, for Stationary - - - -	8 9 11	
13.	To Petty Disbursements by Chief Clerk - - - -	5 4 7	
14.	To John Armstrong, for Constables Expenses, and Petty Disbursements - - - - - - - -	23 12 8	
15.	To George Armstrong, Tallow Chandler, for Candles -	4 2 —	
16.	To Thomas Clack, Tallow Chandler's Bill - - -	4 8 9	
17.	To Edw.d Balderson, late Office Keeper's Petty Disbursements	1 9 3	
18.	To John Othen, Office Keeper's Petty Disbursements -	1 19 11	
19.	To J. D. Ruffy, Lamplighter, Bill for lighting the Office Lamps for one Year, to Michaelmas last - - -	5 — —	
20.	To Messrs. Soulsby & Co. Coal Merchants Bill - -	14 — —	88 2 9
	NECESSARY DISBURSEMENTS For the Rent, Taxes, and Repairs of the House.		
21.	To One Quarter's Rent, to Christmas 1815 - - -	29 10 —	
22.	To Taxes - - - - - - - - -	5 4 7	34 14 7
		£.	834 12 4

WE, the Magistrates of the Police Office, Worship-street, Shoreditch, do hereby certify, that we have examined the above Account, and the different Bills, and find them correct; and that the different Articles therein charged, were necessary for the Public Service, at this Office (to which only they have been applied) to the best of our knowledge and belief.

(Signed) JOHN GIFFORD, } Magistrates of the Police Office,
JOSEPH MOSER, } Worship-street.

Appendix, N° 5.ᵃ

Appendix, N° 5.ᵃ—An ACCOUNT of the ESTABLISHMENT of the PUBLIC OFFICE,

RANK of OFFICER.	HIS NAME.	By whom Appointed.	How Appointed.	When Appointed.	Duration of Interest.	RECEIPT.							
						Salary.		By whom paid.	Fees.	By whom paid.	Other Emoluments.	From whence.	
						1814.	1815.						
						£. s.	£. s.						
Justices {	Rice Davies, Esq;	The King. { Sign Manual.		Aug. 1792.		600 —	600 —	{ The Receiver }	- - -	- - -	{ Resides in the House. Coal. }	- - - -	
	Sir Danl Williams		Sign Manual.	Nov. 1795.		Dᵒ	Dᵒ	Dᵒ - -	- - -	- - -	- - -	- - - -	
	Wm L. Rogers, Esq.			Oct. 1813.	Not expressed, either in the Act of Parliament or in the Appointments.	Dᵒ	Dᵒ	Dᵒ - -	- - -	- - -	- - -	- - - -	
Chief Clerk -	John Thompson -	{ The Secretary of State.	Verbally. {	April 1808.		200 — increased to £. 300 per annum, in October 1815, having served as a Clerk in the Office twenty years and upwards.	200 —	Dᵒ - -	- - -	- - -	- - -	- - - -	
Second Clerk	Wm Osman - -	- Dᵒ - -	- Dᵒ -	Dᵒ		134 —	134 —	{ The Receiver }	- - -	- - -	- - -	- - - -	
Constables {	John Griffiths - Robert Combes - Thoˢ Griffiths - Francis Freeman Samuel Miller - Ebenezer Dalton	The Justices.	Verbally.	- -		54 12 each	54 12 each.	Dᵒ -	One Shilling for serving a Warrant.	By the Party prosecuting.	Payment for extra trouble in serving Warrants, Shares of Rewards and Penalties, and for attending the Sessions.	For extra trouble from the Party prosecuting; Rewards for apprehending Felons, from the Sheriff; Penalties from the Party convicted : attending Sessions, from the Receiver, and the Treasurer of the County.	
	Moses Fortune - William Foster -	{ The Secretary of State.	By Letter.										
Housekeeper	Susan Sterne - -	{ Mr. Davies, the resident Magistrate.	Verbally.	- -		22 2	22 2	Dᵒ - -	- - -	- - -	{ Resides in the House, }	- - - -	
Messenger and Office Keeper	Charles Vine - -	{ The Secretary of State.	By Letter.	- -		54 12	54 12	Dᵒ -	{ One Shilling for serving a Summons.	From the Informer.	{ Dᵒ Coal and Candle. }	- - -	

WHITECHAPEL, for the Years 1814 and 1815; distinguishing each Year.

TOTAL RECEIPT.		DEDUCTIONS.				Total Disbursements.		NET RECEIPT.		Other Employments, Places, or Pensions under Government.	Their Annual Value.
		Taxes.		Deputies and Clerks.	Contingencies.						
1814.	1815.	1814.	1815.			1814.	1815.	1814.	1815.		
£. s.	£. s.	£. s. d.	£. s. d.			£. s. d.	£. s. d.	£. s. d.	£. s. d.		
600 —	600 —	60 — —	60 — —	- - -	- - -	60 — —	60 — —	540 — —	540 — —	...	- -
D°	D°	D°	D°	- - -	- - -	D°	D°	D°	D°	Colonel of the 1st Tower Hamlet Militia, now disembodied.	Colonel's Pay when the Regiment is embodied.
D°	D°	D°	D°	- - -	- - -	D°	D°	D°	D°	—	—
200 —	225 —	20 — —	22 10 —	- - -	- - -	20 — —	22 10 —	180 — —	202 10 —	—	—
134 —	134 —	12 12 —	12 12 —	- - -	- - -	12 12 —	12 12 —	121 8 —	121 8 —	—	—
Uncertain, wholly depending on the business done.		3 3 1 each.	3 18 9 each.	- - -	- - -	3 3 1 each.	3 18 9 each.	Uncertain, wholly depending on the business done.		—	—
22 2	22 2	- - -	1 5 -	- - 5	- - -	- - -	- - -	22 2 —	22 2 —	—	—
About 60 —	About 60 0	— 13 —	1 5 9	- - -	- - -	— 13 —	1 5 9	About 59 — —	About 58 — —	—	—

16th April 1816.

DAN¹. WILLIAMS.
R. DAVIES.

Appendix, N° 5.

PUBLIC OFFICE, LAMBETH STREET, WHITECHAPEL.

AN ACCOUNT of the CHARGES of the ESTABLISHMENT of the PUBLIC OFFICE, Lambeth-Street, Whitechapel; for the Quarter ending the 5th day of April 1814.

	£.	s.	d.
SALARIES.			
To Three Magistrates - - - - - - - - - - -	450	—	—
To Chief Clerk - - - - - - - - - - - -	50	—	—
To Second D° - - - - - - - - - - - -	33	10	—
To eight Constables, 13 weeks - - - - - - - -	109	4	—
To Housekeeper - - - - - - - - - - -	5	10	6
To the Messenger and Office Keeper, 13 weeks - - - - - -	13	13	—
INCIDENTALS.			
To the Constables, their extra expenses and disbursements, allowed them pursuant to the Act of Parliament - - - - - - - -	22	7	—
To sundry Expenses and Disbursements paid by order of the Magistrates, on account of the Office - - - - - - - - - -	10	—	2
To Coals - - - - - - - - - - - - -	20	10	—
To Candles and Soap - - - - - - - - - - -	6	14	6
To Stationary and Printing - - - - - - - - -	10	12	6
To Newspapers - - - - - - - - - - - -	4	16	3
To a summary Account of Prisoners, 1813 - - - - - - -	2	2	—
To illuminating the Office and lighting the Lamps, from Michaelmas 1813 to Lady-day 1814 - - - - - - - - - - -	22	17	6
To Rent and Land Tax - - - - - - - - - -	22	—	—
To Poor Rate - - - - - - - - - - - -	4	10	—
To Watch Rate - - - - - - - - - - - -	1	—	—
To Pavement Rate - - - - - - - - - - -	—	17	6
To the Lecturers of Whitechapel - - - - - - - -	—	12	—
To Water Rate - - - - - - - - - - - -	—	15	—
To Carpenters Work, &c. - - - - - - - - - -	10	5	4
£.	801	17	3

JN° THOMPSON,
Chief Clerk.

20th June 1816.

Appendix, N° 5. c

PUBLIC OFFICE, LAMBETH-STREET, WHITECHAPEL.

CHARGES of the Establishment, for the Quarter ending the 5th day of July 1814.

SALARIES.	£.	s.	d.
To Three Magistrates - - - - - - - - - -	450	—	—
To Chief Clerk - - - - - - - - - - -	50	—	—
To Second D° - - - - - - - - - - -	33	10	—
To eight Constables, 13 weeks - - - - - -	109	4	—
To Housekeeper - - - - - - - - - -	5	10	6
To the Messenger and Office Keeper, 13 Weeks - - - - -	13	13	—

INCIDENTALS.	£.	s.	d.
To the Constables, their extra expenses and disbursements allowed them pursuant to the Act of Parliament - - - - - - -	23	—	6
To sundry Expenses and Disbursements, paid by order of the Magistrates on account of the Office - - - - - - - - -	3	10	6
To Expenses of the Magistrates and Officers, during their attendance at Bow Fair - - - - - - - - - - - -	22	—	—
To Stationary and Printing - - - - - - - - -	5	17	6
To News and Session Papers - - - - - - - - -	2	5	—
To Cabinet Maker for Desks - - - - - - - - -	3	7	—
To Coals - - - - - - - - - - - - -	17	5	—
To illuminating the Office, lighting the out-door Lamps, and two new Lanthorns - - - - - - - - - - -	43	14	—
To Rent and Land Tax - - - - - - - - - -	22	—	—
To Poor Rate - - - - - - - - - - -	6	—	—
To Watch Rate - - - - - - - - - - -	1	—	—
To Pavement Rate - - - - - - - - - - -	—	17	6
£.	812	14	6

JN° THOMPSON,
Chief Clerk.

20th June 1816.

Appendix, N° 5.ᵈ

PUBLIC OFFICE, LAMBETH-STREET, WHITECHAPEL.

CHARGES of the Establishment, for the Quarter ending 10th October 1814.

SALARIES.	£.	s.	d.
To Three Magistrates	450	—	—
To Chief Clerk	50	—	—
To Second Dᵒ	33	10	—
To eight Constables, 13 weeks	109	4	—
To Housekeeper	5	10	6
To the Messenger and Office Keeper, 13 Weeks	13	13	—
INCIDENTALS.			
To paid Expenses of extra Constables on the Jubilee day and following night in the Parks	7	16	—
To the Constables, their extra expenses and disbursements, allowed them pursuant to the Act of Parliament	28	19	6
To sundry Expenses and Disbursements paid by order of the Magistrates on account of the Office	3	14	5
To Stationary and Printing	19	1	6
To Newspapers	4	7	2
To Candles and Soap	6	3	—
To Rent and Land Tax	22	—	—
To Insurance	3	12	—
To Poor Rate	6	—	—
To Watch Rate	1	—	—
To Pavement Rate	—	17	6
To Water Rate	—	15	—
£.	766	3	7

JNᵒ THOMPSON,
Chief Clerk.

20th June 1816.

Appendix, N° 5. *

PUBLIC OFFICE, LAMBETH-STREET, WHITECHAPEL.

CHARGES of the Establishment, for the Quarter ending the 5th of January 1815.

SALARIES.	£.	s.	d.
To Three Magistrates - - - - - - - - - - -	450	—	—
To Chief Clerk - - - - - - - - - - - -	50	—	—
To Second D° - - - - - - - - - - - -	33	10	—
To eight Constables, 13 weeks - - - - - - - -	109	4	—
To Housekeeper - - - - - - - - - - -	5	10	6
To the Messenger and Office Keeper, 13 weeks - - - - - - -	13	13	—
INCIDENTALS.			
To the Constables, their extra expenses and disbursements allowed them, pursuant to the Act of Parliament - - - - - - -	20	10	—
To sundry Expenses and Disbursements paid by order of the Magistrates, on account of the Office - - - - - - - - -	6	14	11
To Stationary and Printing - - - - - - - - -	6	3	—
To Coals - - - - - - - - - - - - -	19	5	—
To Candles - - - - - - - - - - - -	4	10	—
To Butterworth, for Books - - - - - - - - -	5	—	6
To News and Session Papers - - - - - - - - -	4	16	6
To Lighting the out-door Lamps - - - - - - - -	4	4	—
To Rent and Land Tax - - - - - - - - - -	22	—	—
To Poor Rate - - - - - - - - - - - -	6	—	—
To Watch Rate - - - - - - - - - - - -	1	—	—
To Pavement Rate - - - - - - - - - -	—	17	6
To Church Rate - - - - - - - - - - -	1	2	6
To Smiths Work - - - - - - - - - - -	1	15	3
£.	765	16	8

JN° THOMPSON,
Chief Clerk.

20th June 1816.

Appendix, N° 5. ᶠ

PUBLIC OFFICE, LAMBETH-STREET, WHITECHAPEL.

CHARGES of the Establishment, for the Quarter ending the 5th day of April 1815.

SALARIES.	£.	s.	d.
To Three Magistrates	450	—	—
To Chief Clerk	50	—	—
To Second D°	33	10	—
To eight Constables, 13 weeks	109	4	—
To Housekeeper	5	10	6
To the Messenger and Office Keeper, 13 weeks	13	13	—

INCIDENTALS.	£.	s.	d.
To the Constables, their extra expenses and disbursements, allowed them pursuant to the Act of Parliament	24	11	6
To sundry Expenses and Disbursements, paid by order of the Magistrates, on account of the Office	8	10	11
To Printing	6	16	—
To Coals	35	19	—
To Candles and Soap	10	6	—
To News and Session Papers	7	1	6
To summary Account of Prisoners, 1814	2	2	—
To lighting the out-door Lamps, and repairing Lamp Irons	3	12	—
To Rent and Land Tax	22	—	—
To Poor Rate	6	—	—
To Watch Rate	1	—	—
To Pavement Rate	—	17	6
To Lecturers of Whitechapel	—	12	—
To Water Rate	—	15	—
To Plumbers Work	3	13	10
£.	795	14	9

JN° THOMPSON,
Chief Clerk.

20th June 1816

Appendix, N° 5. *

PUBLIC OFFICE, LAMBETH-STREET, WHITECHAPEL.

CHARGES of the Establishment, for the Quarter ending the 5th day of July 1815.

SALARIES.	£.	s.	d.
To Three Magistrates	450	—	—
To Chief Clerk	50	—	—
To Second D°	33	10	—
To seven Constables, 13 weeks	95	11	—
To one D°, three weeks and three days	3	12	—
To Housekeeper	5	10	6
To the Messenger and Office Keeper, 13 weeks	13	13	—

INCIDENTALS.	£.	s.	d.
To the Constables, their extra expenses and disbursements, allowed them pursuant to Act of Parliament	20	19	—
To sundry Expenses and Disbursements, paid by order of the Magistrates on account of the office	8	9	6
To Expenses of the Magistrates and Officers attending Bow Fair	22	17	11
To illuminating the Office two nights, and lighting the out-door Lamps	23	11	—
To News and Session Papers	4	11	9
To Coals	16	5	—
To Rent and Land Tax	22	—	—
To Poor Rate	4	10	—
To Watch Rate	1	—	—
To Pavement Rate	—	17	6
To Bricklayer and Plasterer's work	1	19	9
To Stationary and Printing	7	8	—
£.	786	5	11

JN° THOMPSON,
Chief Clerk.

20th June 1816.

510.

Appendix, N° 5. [h]

PUBLIC OFFICE, LAMBETH-STREET, WHITECHAPEL.

CHARGES of the Establishment, for the Quarter ending the 10th day of October 1815.

SALARIES.	£.	s.	d.
To Three Magistrates - - - - - - - - - -	450	—	—
To Chief Clerk - - - - - - - - - -	50	—	—
To Second D° - - - - - - - - - -	33	10	—
To eight Constables, 13 weeks - - - - - - - -	109	4	—
To Housekeeper - - - - - - - - - -	5	10	6
To the Messenger and Office Keeper, 13 weeks - - - - - -	13	13	—

INCIDENTALS.	£.	s.	d.
To the Constables, their extra expenses and disbursements, allowed them pursuant to Act of Parliament - - - - - - - -	21	18	6
To sundry Expenses and Disbursements, paid by order of the Magistrates on account of the Office - - - - - - - - -	7	5	1
To Floor Cloth - - - - - - - - - -	2	18	3
To Stationary and Printing - - - - - - - -	16	7	—
To News and Session Papers - - - - - - - -	4	12	9
To lighting the out-door Lamps - - - - - - -	2	2	—
To Candles and Soap - - - - - - - - -	5	7	6
To Rent and Land Tax - - - - - - - - -	22	—	—
To Insurance - - - - - - - - - - -	3	12	—
To Poor Rate - - - - - - - - - -	4	10	—
To Watch Rate - - - - - - - - - -	1	—	—
To Church Rate - - - - - - - - -	1	16	—
£.	755	6	7

JN° THOMPSON,
Chief Clerk.

20th June 1816.

Appendix, N° 5. i

PUBLIC OFFICE, LAMBETH-STREET, WHITECHAPEL.

CHARGES of the Establishment, for the Quarter ending the 5th day of January 1816.

SALARIES.	£.	s.	d.
To Three Magistrates	450	—	—
To Chief Clerk	75	—	—
To Second D°	33	10	—
To eight Constables, 13 weeks	109	4	—
To Housekeeper	5	10	6
To the Messenger and Office Keeper, 13 Weeks	13	13	—
INCIDENTALS.			
To the Constables, their extra expenses and disbursements, allowed them pursuant to Act of Parliament	22	19	—
To sundry Expenses and Disbursements, paid by order of the Magistrates on account of the Office	8	3	3
To Coals	17	9	6
To Candles and Soap	5	—	6
To Stationary and Printing	6	14	—
To Newspapers	2	5	9
To Rent and Land Tax	22	—	—
To Poor Rate	4	10	—
To Watch Rate	1	—	—
To Water Rate	1	2	6
To Pavement Rate	1	15	—
To Glaziers Work	2	14	10
£.	782	11	10

JN° THOMPSON,
Chief Clerk.

20th June 1816.

Appendix, N° 6. ª—AN

Appendix, Nº 6.ª—An ACCOUNT of the ESTABLISHMENT

RANK of OFFICER.	HIS NAME.	By whom Appointed.	How Appointed.	When Appointed.	Duration of Interest.	RECEIPT.					
						Salary.	By whom paid.	Fees.	By whom paid.	Other Emoluments.	From whence.
Three Magistrates.	GEORGE STORY	The King	Sign Manual.	2 Aug. 1792.	- -	£.600. per Annum.	The Receiver of the Police.	- -	- -	- -	- -
	EDWARD MARKLAND	The King	Sign Manual.	27 Feb. 1811.	- -	£.600. per Annum.	Ditto.			Resides at the Office.	- -
	ROBERT RAYNSFORD Removed to the Public Office Hatton Garden, 23d September 1814, succeeded by	The King	Sign Manual.	See Return of Hatton Garden Office.	- -	£.600. per Annum.	Ditto.	- -		- -	- -
	HENRY GREGG	The King	Sign Manual.	23 Sept. 1814.	- -	£.600. per Annum.	Ditto.	- -		- -	- -
Chief-Clerk	John Jas Mallett	The Secretary of State.	Letter to the Magistrates.	16 Mar. 1810.	Good Behaviour.	£.200. per Annum.	Ditto.	- -		- -	- -
Second Clerk	Thomas Mallett	Ditto - -	Ditto - -	8 Nov. 1810.	Ditto.	£.134. per Annum.	Ditto.	- -		- -	- -
Seven Officers.	Joseph Holbrook William Hewitt George Partridge Robert Willans Ralph Hope - John Butler - John Brown -	The Justices.	Verbally	- -	Ditto.	£.1. 1. per Week each Man.	Ditto.	The Officers receive one Shilling per Mile for the service of Warrants, &c.	From the Prosecutor.	Payment for extra trouble in serving Warrants, shares of Fines in some cases, Travelling Expenses and Rewards for apprehending Felons, &c.	Payment for extra trouble from the party prosecuting, Shares out of Fines, Travelling Expenses sometimes allowed by the Magistrates, Rewards for apprehending Felons, from the Sheriff.
Gaoler - -	Michael Morris	Ditto - -	Ditto - -	- -	Ditto.	£.1. 1. per Week.	Ditto.	One Shilling, in some cases, for conveying Prisoners to Gaol.	The Prosecutor.	7 s per Week allowed out of the County Rate, paid at the New Prison, Clerkenwell.	By the Keeper of New Prison, Clerkenwell.
Officekeeper & Messenger	William Drummond	Ditto - -	Ditto - -	- -	Ditto.	£.1. 1. per Week	Ditto.	One Shilling per Mile for the service of Summonses.	The Prosecutor.	- -	- -
Housekeeper	Martha Brown	Ditto - -	Ditto - -	- -	Ditto.	£.30. per Annum.	Ditto.	- -		- -	- -

ATTENDANCE:

THE Justices are required by the Act of Parliament 54 G. III. Cap. 37. Sec. 3. to attend at the Office during certain hours in every day, with the exception of a few holidays. They are also called upon for various extra attendances, sometimes by the circumstances of their ordinary business, and sometimes by the directions of the Secretary of State, to take measures for preserving the peace on particular occasions.

The attendance of the Clerks is, during the time of business, appointed by the Police Act before-mentioned.

The attendance of the Officers and others is directed by the magistrates as may seem best for the dispatch of business.

of the Public Office, SHADWELL, for the Year 1814.

TOTAL RECEIPT.	DEDUCTIONS.			Total Disbursements.	Net Receipt, 1814.	Net Receipt Annual upon an Average of the last Three Years.	Other Employments, Places, or Pensions under Government.	Their Annual Value.	SINCE 1792.			
	Taxes.	Deputies and Clerks.	Contingencies.						Increase.		Diminutions.	
									Salaries, &c.	Officers.	Salaries, &c.	Officers.
£.600. per Annum.	£.60.	- -	- -	£.60.	£.540.	£.480.	- -	- -	£.200. per Annum.	At two separate advances of £.100. each, by Acts of Parliament.		
£.600. per Annum.	£.60.	- -	- -	£.60.	£.540.	£.480.	- -	- -	£.200. per Annum.	—	—	
£.600. per Annum	£.60.	- -	- -	£.60.	£.540.	£.480.	- -	- -	£.200. per Annum.			
£.200. per Annum	£.20.	- -	- -	£.20.	£.180.	£.180.	- -	- -	£.50. per Annum.	—	—	—
£.134. per Annum	£.12. 12.	- -	- -	£.12. 12.	£.121. 8.	£.121. 8.	- -	- -	£.34. per Annum.	- -	£.50. per Annum.	Extra Clerk.
About £.70. per Annum.	About £.4. 10. each.	- -	- -	About £.4. 10. each.	About £.65. 10. each.	About £.65. 10. each.	- -	- -	9s. per Week each Man.	One Officer.	—	—
About £.76. per Annum	About £.6.	- -	- -	About £.6.	About £.70.	About £.70.	- -	- -	9 s. per Week.	—	—	—
About £.60.	£.3.	- -	- -	£.3.	£.57.	£.57.	- -	- -	8 s. per Week.	—	—	—
£.30. per Annum.	- -	- -	- -	- -	£.30.	£.30.	- -	- -	£.2. 14. per Annum	—	—	—

DUTIES:

THE Business of the Justices consists in transacting such matters as come within the jurisdiction of a Justice of the Peace. The Clerks are attendant upon them in the discharge of these duties. The Officers duties are those of a Constable under the directions of the Magistrates. All Offices are executed in person.

The above is a correct Account according to the best of our knowledge and belief.

GEO. STORY.
23d April 1816. ED. MARKLAND.
HENRY GREGG.

Appendix, N° 6.ᵇ—An ACCOUNT of the ESTABLISHMENT

RANK of OFFICER.	HIS NAME.	By whom Appointed.	How Appointed.	When Appointed.	Duration of Interest.	RECEIPT.					
						Salary.	By whom paid.	Fees.	By whom paid.	Other Emoluments.	From whence.
Three Magistrates	George Story	The King.	Sign Manual.	2 Aug. 1792.	-	£.600. per Annum.	The Receiver of the Police.	-	-	-	-
	Edward Markland	The King.	Sign Manual.	27 Feb. 1811.	-	£.600. per Annum.	Ditto.	-	-	Resides at the Office.	-
	Henry Gregg	The King.	Sign Manual.	23 Sept. 1814.	-	£.600. per Annum.	Ditto.	-	-	-	-
Chief Clerk -	John Jaˢ Mallett	The Secretary of State.	Letter to the Magistrates.	16 Mar. 1810.	Good Behaviour.	£.200. per Annum, with an increase of £.12.10. for the Quarter commencing the 10th October 1815 (being an increase of £.50. per Annum from that time) having served as a Clerk in the Office Ten Years and upwards.	Ditto.	-	-	-	-
Second Clerk	Thomas Mallett -	Ditto - -	Ditto -	8 Nov. 1810.	Ditto.	£.134. per Annum.	Ditto.	-	-	-	-
Seven Officers.	Joseph Holbrook, William Hewitt -, George Partridge, Robert Willans -, Ralph Hope -, John Butler - -, John Brown - -	The Justices.	Verbally.	-	Ditto.	£.1.1. per Week.	Ditto.	The Officers receive a Shilling per Mile for the service of Warrants, &c.	The Prosecutor.	Payment for extra trouble in serving Warrants, shares of Fines in some cases, Travelling Expenses, and Rewards for apprehending Felons, &c.	Payment for extra trouble from the party prosecuting, Shares out of Fines, Travelling Expenses sometimes allowed by the Magistrates, Rewards for apprehending Felons, from the Sheriff.
Jaoler - -	Michael Morris -	Ditto - -	Ditto - -	-	Ditto.	£.1.1. per Week.	Ditto.	One Shilling, in some cases, for conveying Prisoners to Gaol.	The Prosecutor.	7 s per Week allowed out of the County Rate, paid at the New Prison, Clerkenwell.	Paid by the Keeper of New Prison, Clerkenwell.
Officekeeper & Messenger	William Drummond	Ditto - -	Ditto - -	-	Ditto.	£.1.1. per Week.	Ditto.	One Shilling per Mile for the service of Summonses.	The Prosecutor.	-	-
Housekeeper	Martha Brown -	Ditto - -	Ditto - -	-	Ditto.	£.30. per Annum.	Ditto.	-	-	-	-

ATTENDANCE and DUTIES similar to the Return made for 1814.

of the PUBLIC OFFICE, S H A D W E L L, for the Year 1815.

TOTAL RECEIPT.	DEDUCTIONS.			Total Disbursements.	Net Receipt, 1815.	Net Receipt Annual, upon an Average of the last Three Years.	Other Employments, Places, or Pensions, under Government.	Their Annual Value.	SINCE 1782.			
	Taxes.	Deputies and Clerks.	Contingencies.						Increase.		Diminution.	
									Salaries, &c.	Officers.	Salaries, &c.	Officers.
£.600. per Annum.	£.60.	- -	- -	£.60.	£.540.	£.510.	- -	- -	£.200. per Annum.			
£.600. per Annum.	£.60.	- -	- -	£.60.	£.540.	£.510.	- -	- -	£.200. per Annum.	At two separate advances of £.100. each, by Acts of Parliament.	—	—
£.600. per Annum.	£.60.	- -	- -	£.60.	£.540.	{ Not appointed Three Years. }	- -	- -	£.200. per Annum.			
£.212. 10.	£.21. 5.	- -	- -	£.21. 5.	£.191. 5.	£.183. 15.	- -	- -	{ For 1815 £.62. 10. the Increase for length of Service of £.50. per Annum, commencing only 10th October in that Year; see Column "Salary." }	—	—	—
£.134. per Annum.	£.12. 12.	- -	- -	£.12. 12.	£.121. 8.	£.121. 8.	- -	- -	£.34. per Annum.	- -	£.50.	{ Extra Clerk.
About £.70.each.	{ About £.4. 10. each }	- -	- -	{ About £.4. 10. each }	About £.65. 10. each.	{ About £.65. 10. each. }	-	- -	9 s. per Week each.	One.	—	—
About £.76.	About £.6.	- -	- -	About £.6.	About £.70.	About £.70.	- -	- -	9 s. per Week.	—	—	—
About £.60.	£.3.	- -	- -	£.3.	£.57.	£.57.	- -	- -	8 s. per Week.	—	—	—
£.30. per Annum.	- -	- -	- -	- -	£.30.	£.30.	- -	- -	£.2. 14. per Annum.	—	—	—

The above is a correct Account, according to the best of our knowledge and belief.

GEO. STORY.

23d April 1816.

ED. MARKLAND.

HENRY GREGG.

Appendix, N° 6ᶜ.

PUBLIC OFFICE, SHADWELL.

CHARGES of the ESTABLISHMENT, for the Quarter ending the 5th April 1814.

	£.	s.	d.	£.	s.	d.
To the Three Magistrates, Mr. Story, Mr. Markland, and Mr. Raynsford, one Quarter's Salary at £.600. per annum each -	450	—	—			
To Mr. J. J. Mallett, the Chief Clerk, at £.200. per annum - -	50	—	—			
To Mr. T. Mallett, the Second Clerk, at £.134. per annum - -	33	10	—			
To eight Officers, at £1. 1s. per week each - - - - -	109	4	—			
To William Drummond, Messenger, at £.1. 1s. per week - -	13	13	—			
To Mrs. Ramsden, Housekeeper, at £30. per annum - - -	7	10	—			
				663	17	—
INCIDENTAL EXPENSES.						
To Mr. Downes, for Printing and Stationary - - - -	18	14	—			
To Mrs. Ramsden, the Housekeeper, for Necessaries - - -	2	15	2			
To Mr. Farmer, for Newspapers, Sessions Papers, &c. - - -	6	17	6			
To Mr. Williams, for Oil and other articles - - - -	5	—	—			
To Mr. Kain, for Coals - - - - - - - -	20	7	—			
To Mr. Homan, for Candles - - - - - - -	4	15	6			
To Messrs. Griffin and Co. for six best box engraved Handcuffs	4	1	—			
To May and Amess, for Ink - - - - - - -	1	6	—			
To the Police Constables, for their extraordinary expenses in apprehending and prosecuting Offenders - - - -	14	11	9			
To Coach-hire, Porters, Postage of Letters, Posting up Bills, and other petty expenses - - - - - - - -	8	1	3			
				86	9	2
NECESSARY DISBURSEMENTS, Rent, Taxes, and Repairs of the House.						
To Mr. Burt, for one Quarter's House Rent, Ground Rent, and Land Tax, due at Lady-day last - - - - - -	22	2	—			
To Mr. Cook, for three Quarters Poor Rate, due at Lady-day last	11	—	—			
To Mr. Punderson, for four Quarters Pavement Rate, due Christmas last - - - - - - - - - -	3	12	—			
To Mr. Henfree, for a Pantheon Stove - - - - -	1	10	—			
To the East London Water Works - - - - - -	1	12	—			
To Mr. Richard West, Surveyor, for making an Estimate of Repairs necessary to be done to the Office, and drawing Particulars of same, per order of Mr. Dean and Mr. Clarke, which Estimate was transmitted to the Secretary of State - - -	3	3	—			
To Mr. James, for Smiths work - - - - - - -	4	4	2			
To Mr. Hopper, for Carpenters work - - - - - -	4	12	7			
To Mr. Hampsheir, for Bricklayers work - - - - -	4	10	8			
To Mrs. Gray, for Plumbers and Glaziers work - - - -	4	18	—			
To Mr. Miller, for repairing the Water Butts - - - -	—	12	6			
				61	16	11
				812	3	1
Deduct Fees and Fines received this Quarter - - - - - -				96	14	8
TOTAL CHARGE - - - - - £.				715	8	5

Appendix, Nº 6ᵈ.

PUBLIC OFFICE, SHADWELL.

ESTABLISHMENT, for the Quarter ending the 5th July 1814.

	£. s. d.	£. s. d.
To the Three Magistrates, Mr. Story, Mr. Markland, and Mr. Raynsford, one Quarter's Salary, at £.600. per annum each	450 — —	
To Mr. J. J. Mallett, the Chief Clerk, at £.200. per annum - -	50 — —	
To Mr. T. Mallett, the Second Clerk, at £.134. per annum - -	33 10 —	
To eight Officers, at £.1. 1. per week each - - - -	109 4 —	
To William Drummond, Messenger, at £.1. 1. per week - -	13 13 —	
To Mrs. Ramsden, Housekeeper, at £.30 per annum - - -	7 10 —	663 17 —

INCIDENTAL EXPENSES.

	£. s. d.	£. s. d.
To Mr. Downes, for Printing and Stationary - - - -	10 2 —	
To Mrs. Ramsden, the Housekeeper, for Necessaries - - -	2 9 5	
To Mr. Farmer, for Newspapers, Sessions Papers, &c. - - -	5 6 —	
To Mr. Williams, for illuminating the Office, &c. - - -	33 6 —	
To Mr. Kain, for Coals - - - - - - - -	17 7 —	
To Mr. Homan, for Candles - - - - - - -	4 9 6	
To Messrs. Reed and Hunter, for Law Books - - - -	3 17 6	
To the Constables of the Office, for their attendance to keep the Peace during the late Royal Processions, the holding of the Queen's Drawing Room, and at Bow Fair - - - -	12 12 —	
To the Constables of the Office, being their extraordinary expenses in apprehending and prosecuting Offenders - -	9 11 10	
To Coach-hire, Porters, Posting up Bills, Postage of Letters, and other petty expenses - - - - - - -	9 — 3	108 1 6

NECESSARY DISBURSEMENTS,

Rent, Taxes, and Repairs of the House.

	£. s. d.	£. s. d.
To Mr. Burt, for one Quarter's House Rent, Ground Rent, and Land Tax, due at Midsummer last - - - - -	22 2 —	
To Mr. Cook, for four Quarters Conjunct Rate, due at Lady-day last - - - - - - - - - -	5 — 10	
To the East London Water Works, due at Lady-day last - -	1 12 —	
To Mr. John Needs, for lighting the Office Lamps for two Quarters ending Lady-day, and a new Lamp - - - -	2 12 6	
To Mrs. Gray, for Painters and Glaziers Work - - - -	1 17 6	
To Mr. Miller, for a new Water Butt - - - - -	2 10 —	
To Mr. James, for Smiths Work - - - - - -	4 5 6	40 — 4
		811 18 10
Deduct Fees and Fines received this Quarter - - - - - -		89 19 10¼
TOTAL CHARGE - - - - - - - £.		721 18 11¼

Appendix, Nº 6ᵉ.

PUBLIC OFFICE, SHADWELL.

ESTABLISHMENT, for the Quarter ending the 10th October 1814.

	£. s. d.	£. s. d.
To Three Magistrates, Mr. Story, Mr. Markland, and Mr. Raynsford, succeeded by Mr. Gregg, one Quarters Salary, at £.600. per annum each	450 — —	
To Mr. J. J. Mallett, the Chief Clerk, at £.200. per annum	50 — —	
To Mr. T. Mallett, the Second Clerk, at £.134. per annum	33 10 —	
To eight Officers, at £.1. 1s. per week each	109 4 —	
To William Drummond, Messenger, at £.1. 1s. per week	13 13 —	
To Mrs. Ramsden, Housekeeper, at £.30. per annum	7 10 —	
		603 17 —

INCIDENTAL EXPENSES.

	£. s. d.	£. s. d.
To Mr. Downes, for Printing and Stationary	16 — 9	
To Mrs. Ramsden, the Housekeeper, for Necessaries	2 2 11	
To Mr. Farmer, for Newspapers, Sessions Papers, &c.	5 6 —	
To Messrs. Reed & Hunter, for Law Books	— 17 —	
To Mr. Williams, for Oil and other articles	2 3 6	
To Mr. Johnson, for Candles	4 10 —	
To the Constables of the Office, for their attendance and expenses to keep the Peace during the Procession to and from Saint Paul's Cathedral, on the day of Thanksgiving	2 15 —	
To the same, for their attendance and expenses at Whitehall, during the Royal Procession to and from the House of Peers on the 30th July last	2 10 —	
To the Constables of the Office, and twelve Special Constables, for their attendance and expenses during the Exhibitions in the Parks, on the 1st August last	10 — —	
To the Constables of the Office, being their extraordinary expenses in apprehending and prosecuting Felons and other Offenders	9 15 2	
To Coach-hire, Porters, Postage of Letters, Posting up Bills, and other petty expenses	5 5 2	
		61 5 6

NECESSARY DISBURSEMENTS,

Rent, Taxes, and Repairs of the House.

	£. s. d.	£. s. d.
To Mr. Burt, for one Quarter's House Rent, Ground Rent and Land Tax, due at Michaelmas last	22 2 —	
To Mr. Cook, for Poor Rate, due Midsummer last	4 10 —	
To the Globe Fire Office, for Insurance up to Midsummer next	2 4 —	
To Mrs. Gray, for cleaning the Office Windows, &c.	1 4 6	
To Mr. James, for Smiths work to the Lock-up Rooms	2 12 10	
To Mrs. Rothon, for sweeping the Office Chimnies for two years, up to Midsummer last	4 4 —	
To Mr. Needs, for lighting the Office Lamps, for two Quarters ending Michaelmas last	2 2 —	
		38 19 4
		764 1 10
Deduct Fees and Fines received this Quarter		84 2 8
TOTAL CHARGE £.		679 19 2

Appendix, N° 6 f.

PUBLIC OFFICE, SHADWELL.

ESTABLISHMENT, for the Quarter ending the 5th January 1815.

	£. s. d.	£. s. d.
To the Three Magistrates, Mr. Story, Mr. Markland, and Mr. Gregg, one Quarter's Salary, at £. 600. per annum each	450 — —	
To Mr. J. J. Mallett, the Chief Clerk, at £. 200. per annum	50 — —	
To Mr. T. Mallett, the Second Clerk, at £. 134. per annum	33 10 —	
To eight Officers, at £. 1. 1s. per week each	109 4 —	
To William Drummond, Messenger, at £. 1. 1s. per week	13 13 —	
To Mrs. Ramsden, Housekeeper, at £. 30. per annum	7 10 3	663 17 —

INCIDENTAL EXPENSES.

	£. s. d.	£. s. d.
To Mr. Downes, for Printing and Stationary	19 16 —	
To Mrs. Ramsden, for Housekeeper's Necessaries	3 10 11	
To Mr. Farmer, for Newspapers, Sessions Papers, &c.	5 11 —	
To Mr. Williams, for Oil and other articles	3 15 6	
To Mr. Kain, for Coals	23 17 —	
To Mr. Appleton, for Candles	3 8 —	
To Messrs. Reed & Hunter, for Law Books	5 2 —	
To the Constables of the Office, for their attendance and expenses at Whitehall during the Royal Procession to and from the House of Peers on the 8th of November last	2 5 —	
To the Constables of the Office, being their extraordinary expenses in apprehending and prosecuting Felons and other Offenders	12 18 5	
To Coach-hire, Porters posting up Bills, Postage of Letters, and other petty expenses	7 4 8	87 8 9

NECESSARY DISBURSEMENTS,

Rent, Taxes, and Repairs of the House.

	£. s. d.	£. s. d.
To Mr. Burt, for one Quarter's House Rent, Ground Rent, and Land Tax, due at Christmas last	22 2 —	
To Mr. Hill, Builder, for Repairs done to the House	31 15 —	
To Mr. Cook, for one Quarter's Poor Rate, due at Michaelmas last	4 10 —	
To Mr. Punderson, for three Quarter's Pavement Rate, due at Michaelmas last	2 14 —	
To Mr. James, for Smiths work done to the Lock-up Rooms, &c.	4 16 5	
To Messrs. Urquhart & Todd, Coopers Bill	— 15 —	
To Mr. Cole, for a Matt	— 18 —	67 10 5
		818 16 2
Deduct Fees and Fines received this Quarter		132 17 1
TOTAL CHARGE — — — — — £		685 19 1

Appendix, N° 6 ᵍ.

PUBLIC OFFICE, SHADWELL.

ESTABLISHMENT, for the Quarter ending the 5th April 1815.

	£. s. d.	£. s. d.
To the Three Magistrates, Mr. Story, Mr. Markland, and Mr. Gregg, one Quarter's Salary, at £.600. per annum each	450 — —	
To Mr. J. J. Mallett, the Chief Clerk, at £.200. per annum - -	50 — —	
To Mr. T. Mallett, the Second Clerk, at £.134. per annum - -	33 10 —	
To eight Officers, at £.1. 1. per week, each - - - -	109 4 —	
To William Drummond, Messenger, at £.1. 1. per week - -	13 13 —	
To Mrs. Myers, Housekeeper, seven weeks, ending 13th February	4 — 6	
To Mrs. Brown, Housekeeper, six weeks, ending 5th April last -	3 9 6	663 17 —

INCIDENTAL EXPENSES.

	£. s. d.	£. s. d.
To Mr. Downes, for Printing and Stationary - - - -	19 10 —	
To Mr. Farmer, for News-papers, Sessions Papers, &c. - - -	4 14 6	
To Messrs. Reed & Hunter, for Law Books - - - -	2 7 6	
To Mr. Kain, for Coals - - - - - - - -	17 7 —	
To Mr. Appleton, for Oil, Candles, &c. - - - - -	5 8 7	
To Mr. Day, for the Statement of Criminal Offenders, for two years	4 4 —	
To Messrs. May & Amess, for Ink - - - - - -	1 4 —	
To Mrs. Myers, for Housekeeper's Necessaries, up to the 13th February last - - - - - - - -	1 14 10	
To the Police Constables, their extraordinary expenses in apprehending and prosecuting Felons and other Offenders -	21 12 9	
To Coach-hire, Porters, Postage of Letters, and other petty expenses - - - - - - - - -	8 6 5	
To Mrs. Brown, for Necessaries, from 13th February to 5th of April last - - - - - - - - -	4 6 1	90 15 8

NECESSARY DISBURSEMENTS,
Rent, Taxes, and Repairs of the House.

	£. s. d.	£. s. d.
To Mr. Burt, for one Quarter's House Rent, Ground Rent, and Land Tax, due at Lady-day last - - - - -	22 2 —	
To Mr. Poole, for two years and a quarter's Property Tax for the Office, due Christmas last - - - - - -	14 17 4	
To Mr. Cook, for four Quarters Conjunct Rate, due Lady-day last	6 10 —	
To the East London Water-works, due Michaelmas last - -	1 12 —	
To Messrs. Gray & Son, for cleaning the Office Windows, &c. -	2 1 —	
To Mr. James, for Smiths work - - - - - - -	3 10 —	
To Mr. Hopper, for Carpenters work - - - - - -	3 18 3	54 10 7
		809 3 3
Deduct Fees and Fines received this Quarter - - - - - -		123 10 7
TOTAL CHARGE - - - - - £.		685 12 8

Appendix, N° 6.ª

PUBLIC OFFICE, SHADWELL.

ESTABLISHMENT, for the Quarter ending the 5th July 1815.

	£. s. d.	£. s. d.
To the Three Magistrates, Mr. Story, Mr. Markland, and Mr. Gregg, one Quarter's Salary at £. 600. per annum each - - -	450 — —	
To Mr. J. J. Mallett, the Chief Clerk, at £. 200. per annum - -	50 — —	
To Mr. T. Mallett, the Second Clerk, at £. 134. per annum - -	33 10 —	
To eight Officers, at £. 1. 1 s. per week each - - - -	109 4 —	
To William Drummond, Messenger, at £. 1. 1 s. per week - -	13 13 —	
To Mrs. Brown, Housekeeper, at £. 30. per annum - - -	7 10 —	663 17 —

INCIDENTAL EXPENSES.

	£. s. d.	£. s. d.
To Mr. Downes, for Printing and Stationary - - - - -	11 10 —	
To Messrs. Reed & Hunter, for Law Books - - - - -	— 9 6	
To Mr. Farmer, for Newspapers - - - - - - -	4 5 —	
To Mr. Williams, for illuminating the Office - - - - -	10 14 —	
To Mr. Appleton, for Candles, Oil, &c. - - - - -	5 9 —	
To Mrs. Brown, the Housekeeper, for Necessaries - - - -	1 16 1	
To Mr. Miller, for a Tub for the Lock-up Rooms - - - -	2 2 —	
To the Police Constables, their extraordinary expenses in apprehending and prosecuting Offenders, and for their extra attendance and expenses during Bow Fair in keeping the peace -	15 9 4	
To Coach-hire, Porters, Postage of Letters, Sticking up Bills, and other petty expenses - - - - - - - -	6 2 —	57 16 11

NECESSARY DISBURSEMENTS,
Rent, Taxes, and Repairs of the House.

	£. s. d.	£. s. d.
To Mr. Burt, for one Quarter's House Rent, Ground Rent, and Land Tax, due Midsummer-day last - - - - -	22 2 —	
To Mr. Cook, for two Quarters Poor Rate, due Lady-day last -	9 — —	
To Mr. Bryan, for four Quarters Rector's Rate, due Lady-day last -	1 7 —	
To Mr. Hullock, for two Quarters Water Rate, due Lady-day last -	1 12 —	
To the Globe Insurance Company, for one Year's Insurance from Fire	2 4 —	
To Mr. James, for Smiths work - - - - - - -	1 8 6	
To Mr. Hopper, for Carpenters work - - - - - -	3 11 2	
To Mrs. Gray, for cleaning the Office Windows, Glazing and Plumbers work - - - - - - - -	3 3 6	44 8 2
		766 2 1
Deduct Fees and Fines received this Quarter - -	- - -	162 16 3
TOTAL CHARGE - - - - - - £		603 5 10

Appendix, N° 6.ⁱ

PUBLIC OFFICE, SHADWELL.

ESTABLISHMENT, for the Quarter ending the 10th October 1815.

	£. s. d.	£. s. d.
To the Three Magistrates, Mr. Story, Mr. Markland, and Mr. Gregg, one Quarter's Salary, at £. 600. per annum each - -	450 — —	
To Mr. J. J. Mallett, the Chief Clerk, at £. 200. per annum - -	50 — —	
To Mr. T. Mallett, the Second Clerk, at £. 134. per annum - -	33 10 —	
To eight Officers, at £. 1. 1s. per week each - - - - -	109 4 —	
To William Drummond, Messenger, at £. 1. 1s. per week - -	13 13 —	
To Mrs. Brown, Housekeeper, at £. 30. per annum - - -	7 10 —	663 17 —

INCIDENTAL EXPENSES.

To Mr. Downes, for Printing and Stationary - - - - -	16 18 2	
To Mr. Farmer, for Newspapers - - - - - - -	4 7 —	
To Messrs. Kain & Son, for Coals - - - - - -	30 14 —	
To Mr. Johnson, for Candles - - - - - - -	3 5 —	
To Mr. Williams, for Oil and repairing the Lamps - - -	2 1 —	
To Mrs. Brown, the Housekeeper, for Necessaries - - -	1 10 2	
To the Police Constables, their extraordinary expenses in apprehending and prosecuting Offenders - - - - -	9 11 6	
To Coach-hire, Porters, Postage of Letters, Posting up Bills, and other petty expenses - - - - - - -	6 19 6	75 6 4

NECESSARY DISBURSEMENTS,
Rent, Taxes, and Repairs of the House.

To Mr. Burt, for one Quarter's House Rent, Ground Rent, and Land Tax, due at Michaelmas last - - - - -	22 2 —	
To Mr. Cook, the Collector, for two Quarters Poor Rates, due at Michaelmas-day last - - - - - - -	9 — —	
To ditto - - - - - - for two Quarters Conjunct Rate, due at the same time - - - - - - - -	4 — —	
To Mr. Hullock, for two Quarters Water Rate, due same time -	1 12 —	
To Mr. Deason, for Sewer Rate - - - - - - -	1 5 —	
To Mrs. Rothon, for sweeping the Office Chimnies - - -	1 1 —	
To Mr. James, for Smiths work, &c. - - - - - -	3 18 9	
To Mr. Needs, for lighting the Office Lamps for three Quarters up to Midsummer - - - - - - - - -	3 3 —	46 1 9
		785 5 1
Deduct Fees and Fines received this Quarter - - - - - -		110 10 —
TOTAL CHARGE - - - - - £.		674 15 1

Appendix, N° 6.ᵏ

PUBLIC OFFICE, SHADWELL.

ESTABLISHMENT, for the Quarter ending the 5th January 1816.

	£.	s.	d.	£.	s.	d.
To the Three Magistrates, Mr. Story, Mr. Markland, and Mr. Gregg, one Quarter's Salary, at £. 600. per annum each - -	450	—	—			
To Mr. J. J. Mallett, the Chief Clerk, including an increase at the rate of Fifty Pounds per annum, having served ten years and upwards - - - - - - - - - - .	62	10	—			
To Mr. T. Mallett, the Second Clerk, at £. 134. per annum - -	33	10	—			
To eight Officers, at £. 1. 1 s. per week each - - - -	109	4	—			
To William Drummond, Messenger, at £. 1. 1 s. per week - -	13	13	—			
To Mrs. Brown, Housekeeper, at £. 30. per annum - - -	7	10	—	676	7	0

INCIDENTAL EXPENSES.

	£.	s.	d.	£.	s.	d.
To Mr. Downes, for Printing and Stationary - - - -	19	4	—			
To Mr. Farmer, for Newspapers - - - - - -	4	11	—			
To Messrs. Reed & Hunter, for Law Books, &c. - - - -	8	3	—			
To Mr. Williams, his account for Oil, &c. - - - - -	4	—	6			
To Mr. Appleton, his account for Candles - - - - -	5	17	—			
To Mrs. Brown, the Housekeeper, for Necessaries - - - -	4	—	3			
To the Constables of the Office, for their attendance and expenses at Whitehall during the Royal Procession to and from the House of Peers, on the 12th day of July last - - - -	2	5	—			
To the same, their extraordinary expenses, in apprehending and prosecuting Offenders - - - - - - -	10	9	1			
To Coach-hire, Porters, Postage of Letters, Posting up Bills, and other petty expenses - - - - - - -	9	1	2	67	11	0

NECESSARY DISBURSEMENTS,
Rent, Taxes, and Repairs of the House.

	£.	s.	d.	£.	s.	d.
To Mr. Burt, for one Quarter's House Rent, Ground Rent, and Land Tax due at Christmas last - - - - -	22	2	—			
To Mr. Cook, the Collector, for one Quarter's Poor Rate, due same time - - - - - - - - -	4	10	—			
To Ditto, for one Quarter's Conjunct Rate, due same time - -	2	—	—			
To Mr. Punderson, for four Quarters Pavement Rate, due same time	3	12	6			
To Mr. Hopper, for Blinds, &c. - - - - - - -	2	9	3			
To Mr. Hill, Builder, his Bill for sundry works done at the Office -	871	5	7			
To Mr. Hampshire, his Bill, for Bricklayers work - - -	4	9	2			
To Mr. James, for Smiths work - - - - - - -	3	19	2	914	7	8
				1,658	5	8
Deduct Fees and Fines received this Quarter - - - - - -				75	9	10
TOTAL CHARGE - - - - - - £.				1,582	15	10

WE do hereby Certify, That the foregoing is a correct Account of the Charges of the Establishment of the Public Office, Shadwell, for the Years 1814 and 1815, which Charges have been respectively approved and certified by us to the Secretary of State, for each Quarter of such period, as being necessary for the Public Service at this Office, to which only they have been applied, according to the best of our knowledge and belief.—Dated this Fifth day of June 1816.

GEO. STORY.
ED. MARKLAND.

Appendix, N° 7.ᵃ

Appendix, N° 7.ª—An ACCOUNT of the ESTABLISHMENT of the

RANK of OFFICER.	HIS NAME.	By whom Appointed.	How Appointed.	When Appointed.	Duration of Interest.	RECEIPT.		
						Salary.	By whom paid.	Fees.
Three Magistrates.	P. Colquhoun,	His Majesty	Sign Manual	Aug. 1792.	- - -	£ 500 per Ann. each.	The Receiver	- - -
	Wm Fielding,	- - Dº - -	- - Dº - -	2d Aug. 1808	- - -			- - -
	T. B. Plestow,	- - Dº - -	- - Dº - -	4th May 1806.	- - -		- - -	
					Not expressed.			
Chief Clerk	R. Blakiston	Secretary of State.	Letter to the Magistrates	27th Dec. 1803.	- - -	£. 200 per Ann.	Dº	- - -
Second Dº	Wm Miller	- - Dº - -	- - Dº - -	10th Mar. 1812.	- - -	£. 134 per Ann.	Dº	- - -
Eight Officers.	James Bly	Magistrates		23d Nov. 1801.				One Shilling for serving a Summons or Warrant; or more, according to distance.
	James Gillmor	- - Dº -		5th Sept. 1803				
	J. Nelson Lavender	- - Dº - -		19th Mar. 1810.				
	Edward Green	- - Dº - -	Verbally	27th April 1810.	Good Behaviour.	One Guinea per week each.	Dº	
	George Pople	- - Dº - -		30th Mar. 1812.				
	Thomas Pace	- - Dº - -		13th May 1812.				
	Thomas Garner	Secretary of State.	Letter to the Magistrates	5th Feb. 1814, on the death of Wm Geary.				
	John Cobham	- - Dº - -		17th Aug. 1814, on the discharge of Josh Cooper.				
Housekeeper	Elizabeth Reeves	The Receiver	Verbally	1792.	- - -	£. 35 per Ann.	- - -	- - -
Messenger	Robert Dale	Magistrates	- - Dº - -	12th Feb. 1806.	- - -	One Guinea per week.	- - -	- - -

An ACCOUNT of the ESTABLISHMENT,

RANK of OFFICER.	HIS NAME.	By whom Appointed.	How Appointed.	When Appointed.	Duration of Interest.	RECEIPT.		
						Salary.	By whom paid.	Fees.
Three Magistrates.	P. Colquhoun Wm Fielding T. B. Plestow	- - -	- - -	- - -	- - -	£.500 per Ann. each.	- - -	- - -
Chief Clerk	R. Blakiston					£. 200 per Ann, except as to the last Quarter, when it was increased at the rate of £.50 per annum, having served 10 years and upwards.		- - -
Second Dº	Wm Miller	- - -	- - -	- - -	- - -	- -	- - -	- - -
Eight Officers	James Bly James Gillmor Jnº N. Lavender Edward Green George Pople Thomas Pace Thomas Garner Jnº Cobham	Vide Account or Return for 1814.	Ditto.	Ditto.	Ditto.	Same as 1814.	Same as 1814.	Same as 1814.
Housekeeper	Ezh Reeves		- - -	- - -	- - -	- - -	- - -	- - -
Messenger	Robert Dale		- - -	- - -	- - -	- - -	- - -	- - -

PUBLIC OFFICE, QUEEN-SQUARE; for the Year 1814.

By whom paid.	Other Emoluments.	From whence.	TOTAL RECEIPT.	DEDUCTIONS.	Net Receipt, 1814.	Other Employments, Places, or Pensions under Government.	Their Annual Value.
- - -	{ Resident in the House. }	- - -	} £.500 per Ann. each. }	- - -	} £.450 each.	{ Receiver of the Thames Police. }	£.400.
- - -		- - -		- - -			
- - -	- - -			} Property Tax.			
			£.200.	- - -	£.180.	—	—
- - -	- - -	- - -	£.134.	} - - -	£.121. 8.	—	—
The Party prosecuting or complaining.	{ Payment for extra trouble in serving Warrants and Summonses, going Journies after Offenders, and Rewards for apprehending them.	{ From the Party prosecuting in general, or when allowed for Rewards from the Sheriff or County.	} Uncertain, depending wholly on the business. }	D°	—	—	—
- - -	- - -	- - -	£.35.	- - -	£.35.	—	—
- - -	- - -	- - -	£.54. 12.	Property Tax.	£.53. 19.	—	—

for the Year 1815.

By whom paid.	Other Emoluments.	From whence.	TOTAL RECEIPT.	DEDUCTIONS.	Net Receipt, 1815.	Other Employments, Places, or Pensions under Government.	Their Annual Value:
- - -	- - -	- - -	{ £ 500 per Ann. each. }	- - -	£.450 each.	—	—
				} Property Tax.			
- - -	- - -	- - -	£.212. 10.	- - -	£.191. 5.	—	—
- - -	- - -	- - -	£ 134.	} - - -	£.121. 8.	—	—
Same as 1814.	Same as 1814.	Same as 1814.	Same as 1814.			Same as 1814.	Same as 1814.
- - -	- - -	- - -	- - -	} D°	—	—	—
- - -	- - -	- - -	£.35.	D°	£.32. 7. 6.	—	—
- - -	- - -	- - -	£.54. 12.	Do	£.53. 19.		

WE certify the above to be true, to the best of our knowledge and belief,

23d April 1816.

P. COLQUHOUN.
Wᵐ FIELDING.
T. BORNEW PLESTOW.

Appendix, N° 7. [b]

PUBLIC OFFICE, QUEEN-SQUARE.

A QUARTERLY ACCOUNT of the various Expenses incurred for the different Quarters of the Years 1814 and 1815.

ESTABLISHMENT, &c. for the Quarter ending 5th April 1814.

SALARIES.	£.	s.	d.
To P. Colquhoun, ⎫ - - - - - - - -	150	—	—
Wm. Fielding, ⎬ Esquires, Magistrates - - - - -	150	—	—
T. B. Plestow, ⎭ - - - - - - - -	150	—	—
To Mr. R. Blakiston, Chief Clerk - - - - - - -	50	—	—
Mr. Wm Miller, 2d D° - - - - - - - - -	35	10	—
Seven Constables, 13 weeks, at £.1. 1s. per week - - - -	95	11	—
The Representatives of William Geary, deceased, late one of the Constables ⎫ who died 11th January, say one week - - - - - - ⎭	1	1	—
Thomas Garner, his Successor, appointed 15th January, say 11 weeks and ⎫ 3 days - - - - - - - - - - - ⎭	12	—	—
Miss Reeves, Housekeeper, 3 months - - - - - -	8	15	—
Robert Dale, Messenger, 13 weeks, at £.1. 1s. - - - - -	13	13	—
INCIDENTAL EXPENSES.			
Mr. Staunton, Stationer - - - - - - - -	5	11	10
Mr. Downes, Printer - - - - - - - - -	6	6	6
Mr. Bain, for Newspapers - - - - - - - -	4	9	11
Messrs. Sculaby & Allison, for Coals - - - - - -	47	10	6
Messrs. Reed & Hunter, Law Booksellers - - - - -	—	5	6
T. Stone, for Coopers work - - - - - - -	—	10	—
Wm Beach, for Green Baize, &c. for Magistrates Room - - -	1	3	9
City Assize of Bread, one year - - - - - - -	—	7	—
Westminster, D° - - - - - - - - -	—	5	—
Mr. Dale, Messenger for petty expenses of Postage, &c. - - -	3	—	8
Mr. Blakiston, for what he has paid Constables and others on public service ⎫ (per order of Magistrates) - - - - - - - - ⎭	9	10	—
George Neave, for Candles - - - - - - - -	1	15	5
Joseph Cooper, for a Constable Staff - - - - - -	1	14	—
Richard Lewis, for D° for Thomas Garner - - - - -	1	15	—
William Booth, for Turnery Goods - - - - - -	—	2	—
NECESSARY DISBURSEMENTS:			
Rent, Taxes, and Repairs of the House.			
One Quarter's Rent due Lady-day - - - - - - -	16	—	—
Mary Johnson (an old bill) for Carpenters work - - - -	1	17	6
James Porter, for one year's Land Tax due Lady-day 1813 - -	3	17	3
Matthew Burt, for Smiths work - - - - - - -	1	4	9
William Tarte, Glaziers D° - - - - - - - -	—	15	9
John Hill, Carpenters work - - - - - - - -	—	12	—
£.	773	4	4

Appendix, Nº 7. c

PUBLIC OFFICE, QUEEN-SQUARE.

ESTABLISHMENT, &c. for the Quarter ending 5th July 1814.

SALARIES.

	£.	s.	d.
To P. COLQUHOUN, ⎫	150	—	—
WM. FIELDING, ⎬ Esquires, Magistrates	150	—	—
T. B. PLESTOW, ⎭	150	—	—
To Mr. R. Blakiston, Chief Clerk	50	—	—
Mr. Wm Miller, Second Dº	33	10	—
Eight Constables, 13 weeks, at one guinea per week	109	4	—
Miss Reeves, Housekeeper, 3 months	8	15	—
Robert Dale, Messenger, 13 weeks, at one guinea	13	13	—

INCIDENTAL EXPENSES.

	£.	s.	d.
Mr. Staunton, Stationer	6	18	5
Mr. Downes, Printer	4	17	—
Mr. Bain, for Newspapers	4	11	6
John Prosser, for two Cutlasses for Pople and Garner, per order of Magistrates	3	14	—
Anne Allen, (Wood account) to May 1st 1814	1	11	—
Mr. Dale, Messenger, for petty expenses of Postage, &c.	2	8	10
Mr. Blakiston, for what he has paid Constables and others on Public Service (per order of Magistrates)	1	7	—
Thomas Bentley, for illumination Lamps, &c.	2	2	—
Messrs. Reed & Hunter, Law Booksellers	3	13	—
Messrs. Soulsby & Allison, for Coals	17	14	—
Mr. Day, for Statements of the number of criminal Offenders	2	2	—
George Neave, for Candles	2	3	2

NECESSARY DISBURSEMENTS :
Rent, Taxes, and Repairs of the House.

	£.	s.	d.
One Quarter's Rent, due Midsummer last	16	—	—
Robert Southby, for sweeping Chimnies	—	8	6
Mr. Hutchins, for Sewer Rate, made 20th November 1812	3	10	—
William Knowles, one year's Water Rent to Lady-day 1814	2	6	—
Mr. Burton, for paving and lighting to Dº	1	2	6
Wm Cuthbertson, for half a year's Poor and Watch Rates to Lady-day 1814	8	16	5
Dº for half a year's assessed Taxes to Dº	15	17	11
John Hill, for Carpenters Work	1	—	9
£.	767	6	—

Appendix, N° 7.ᵈ

PUBLIC OFFICE, QUEEN-SQUARE.

ESTABLISHMENT, &c. for the Quarter ending 5th October 1814.

	£.	s.	d.
SALARIES.			
To P. COLQUHOUN, ⎫	150	—	—
WM. FIELDING, ⎬ Esquires, Magistrates	150	—	—
T. B. PLESTOW, ⎭	150	—	—
To Mr. R. Blakiston, Chief Clerk	50	—	—
Mr. W. Miller, 2d Dᵒ	33	10	—
Eight Constables, 13 weeks, at one guinea per week; Joseph Cooper was ⎫ discharged 16th, and his successor appointed 17th August ⎭	109	4	—
Miss Reeves, Housekeeper, 3 months	8	15	—
Robert Dale, Messenger, 13 weeks, at one guinea	13	13	—
INCIDENTAL EXPENSES.			
Mr. Staunton, Stationer	3	15	—
Mr. Downes, Printer	9	11	6
Mr. Bain, for Newspapers	4	6	7
George Medhurst, for Bread Scales for use of Office	2	7	—
Mr. Dale, Messenger, for petty expenses of Postage, &c.	2	10	6
Mr. Blakiston, for what he has paid Constables and others on Public Service, ⎫ (per order of Magistrates) ⎭	12	13	6
Messrs. Reed & Hunter, Law Booksellers	4	12	6
George Neave, for Candles	—	15	6
William Booth, for Turnery Goods	—	9	9
Messrs. Soulsby & Allison, for Coals	17	14	—
NECESSARY DISBURSEMENTS: Rent, Taxes, and Repairs of the House.			
One Quarter's Rent, due Michaelmas	16	—	—
Willᵐ Tarte, Glazier	1	14	6
Mattʷ Burt, for Smiths Work	1	2	—
£.	742	14	4

Appendix, N° 7.ᵉ

PUBLIC OFFICE, QUEEN-SQUARE.

ESTABLISHMENT, &c. for the Quarter ending 5th January 1815.

	£.	s.	d.
SALARIES.			
To P. COLQUHOUN, ⎫	150	—	—
WM. FIELDING, ⎬ Esquires, Magistrates	150	—	—
T. B. PLESTOW, ⎭	150	—	—
To Mr. R. Blakiston, Chief Clerk	50	—	—
Mr. W. Miller, Second D°	33	10	—
Eight Constables, 13 weeks, at one guinea per week	109	4	—
Miss Reeves, Housekeeper, 3 months	8	15	—
Robert Dale, Messenger, 13 weeks, at one guinea	13	13	—
INCIDENTAL EXPENSES.			
Mr. Staunton, Stationer	4	3	6
Mr. Downes, Printer	16	16	6
Mr. Bain, for Newspapers	4	10	7
Mr. Dale, Messenger, for petty expenses of Postage, &c.	3	18	2
Mr. Blakiston, for what he has paid Constables and others on Public Service, ⎫ (per order of Magistrates) ⎬	4	16	—
Messrs. Reed & Hunter, Law Booksellers	1	4	—
George Neave, for Candles	2	19	—
Anne Allen, Wood account to December 1814	—	11	—
NECESSARY DISBURSEMENTS: Rent, Taxes, and Repairs of the House.			
One Quarter's Rent, due Christmas	16	—	—
Insurance of Premises one year, from Michaelmas 1814 to Michaelmas 1815	2	15	—
Robert Southby, for sweeping Chimnies	—	10	6
Henry Burton, for two quarters Paving Rate to Michaelmas 1814	1	2	6
James Porter, one year's Land Tax to Lady-day 1814	4	2	8
Jn° Hill, for Carpenters Work, &c.	4	15	2
Wm Tarte, Glazier	—	17	6
£.	734	4	1

Appendix, N° 7.

PUBLIC OFFICE, QUEEN-SQUARE.

ESTABLISHMENT, &c. for the Quarter ending 5th April 1815.

SALARIES.	£.	s.	d.
To P. COLQUHOUN, ⎫ - - - - - - - - -	150	—	—
W. FIELDING, ⎬ Esquires, Magistrates - - - - - -	150	—	—
T. B. PLESTOW, ⎭ - - - - - - - -	150	—	—
To Mr. R. Blakiston, Chief Clerk - - - - - - - -	50	—	—
Mr. Wm Miller, Second D° - - - - - - - -	33	10	—
Eight Constables, 13 weeks, at one guinea per week - - - - -	109	4	—
Miss Reeves, Housekeeper, three months - - - - - -	8	15	—
Robert Dale, Messenger, 13 weeks, at one guinea - - - - -	13	13	—

INCIDENTAL EXPENSES.

	£.	s.	d.
Mr. Staunton, Stationer - - - - - - - - - -	6	13	8
Mr. Downes, Printer - - - - - - - - - -	6	15	—
Mr. Bain, for Newspapers - - - - - - - - -	4	9	5
Mr. Dale, Messenger for petty expenses of Postage, &c. - - - -	3	4	3
Mr. Blakiston, for what he has paid Constables and others on Public Service (per order of Magistrates) - - - - - - - -	2	14	6
Mr. Hardy, for nine marked Calendars, to January 1815 - - - -	9	9	—
Richard Lewis, for a Constable's Staff for Lavender, one of the Constables, (per order of Magistrates) - - - - - - - -	1	15	—
John Patrick, Bill for Lamp Oil, &c. (one year's) - - - - -	15	16	—
M. Booth, for Floor Cloth and Turnery - - - - - - -	3	14	3
Messrs. Reed & Hunter, Law Booksellers - - - - - -	2	13	—
Messrs. Soulsby and Allison, for Coals - - - - - - -	34	18	—
George Neave, for Candles - - - - - - - - -	2	4	6

NECESSARY DISBURSEMENTS:
Rent, Taxes, and Repairs of the House.

	£.	s.	d.
One Quarter's Rent, due Lady-day last - - - - - - -	16	—	—
Mr. Cuthbertson, for Poor, Highway, and Watch Rate, three Quarters to Christmas last - - - - - - - - - -	13	4	7
D° for two Quarters Assessed Taxes to Michaelmas 1814 - - -	15	17	11
John Hill, for Carpenters Work - - - - - - - -	1	16	2
£.	806	7	3

Appendix, N° 7.ᵉ

PUBLIC OFFICE, QUEEN-SQUARE.

ESTABLISHMENT, &c. for the Quarter ending 5th July 1815.

SALARIES.

	£.	s.	d.
To P. COLQUHOUN, ⎫	150	—	—
WM. FIELDING, ⎬ Esquires, Magistrates	150	—	—
T. B. PLESTOW, ⎭	150	—	—
To Mr. R. Blakiston, Chief Clerk	50	—	—
Mr. Wᵐ Miller, Second Dᵒ	33	10	—
Eight Constables, 13 weeks, at one guinea per week	109	4	—
Miss Reeves, Housekeeper, 3 months	8	15	—
Robert Dale, Messenger, 13 weeks, at one guinea	13	13	—

INCIDENTAL EXPENSES.

	£.	s.	d.
Mr. Staunton, Stationer	3	11	11
Mr. Downes, Printer	8	2	—
Mr. Bain, for Newspapers	4	14	6
Mr. Dale, Messenger, for petty expenses of Postage, &c.	2	19	9
Mr. Blakiston, for what he has paid Constables and others on Public Service (per order of Magistrates)	—	13	6
Mr. Day, for Statements of the number of Criminal Offenders	2	2	—
Richard Lewis, for a Constable's Staff for John Cobham (per order of Magistrates)	1	15	—
Messrs. Reed & Hunter, Law Booksellers	—	10	6
George Neave, for Candles	—	14	—
M. Booth, Turnery Goods	—	11	9
S. Burgess for posting Bills about Aliens	1	10	—

NECESSARY DISBURSEMENTS:
Rent, Taxes, and Repairs of the House.

	£.	s.	d.
One Quarter's Rent, due Midsummer last	16	—	—
To Property Tax, to be returned to Mr. Vernon the Landlord, which he has overpaid or allowed to Lady-day last	3	4	—
Robert Southby, for sweeping Chimnies	—	7	—
Henry Burton, for paving and lighting, half a year, to Lady-day 1815	1	2	6
William Knowles, for one year's Water Rent to Dᵒ	2	6	—
Mr. Cuthbertson, for half a year's Assessed Taxes to Dᵒ	15	17	11
The like, for Poor, Highway, and Watch Rates, to dᵒ	4	8	2
Wᵐ Tarte, Glazier	—	11	6
Mrs. Burt, Smiths work	1	6	—
£.	737	10	—

Appendix, N° 7.[h]

PUBLIC OFFICE, QUEEN-SQUARE.

ESTABLISHMENT, &c. for the Quarter ending 5th October 1815.

SALARIES.	£.	s.	d.
To P. COLQUHOUN, ⎫	150	—	—
WM. FIELDING, ⎬ Esquires, Magistrates	150	—	—
T. B. PLESTOW, ⎭	150	—	—
To Mr. R. Blakiston, Chief Clerk	50	—	—
Mr. Wm Miller, Second D°	33	10	—
Eight Constables, 13 weeks, at one guinea per week	109	4	—
Miss Reeves, Housekeeper, 3 months	8	15	—
Robert Dale, Messenger, 13 weeks, at one guinea	13	13	—

INCIDENTAL EXPENSES.	£.	s.	d.
Mr. Staunton, Stationer	5	2	1
Mr. Downes, Printer	7	12	6
Mr. Bain, for Newspapers	4	18	3
Messrs. Soulsby & Allison, for Coals	15	14	—
Mr. Dale, Messenger, for petty expenses of Postage, &c.	3	15	2
Mr. Blakiston, for what he has paid Constables and others, on Public Service, (per order of Magistrates)	—	18	-
Mr. Hardy, for corrected Newgate Calendars, for February, April, May, and June Sessions last	4	4	—
George Neave, for Candles	—	11	10
M. Booth, for Turnery Goods, &c.	—	9	6

NECESSARY DISBURSEMENTS:
Rent, Taxes, and Repairs of the House.

	£.	s.	d.
One Quarter's Rent, due Michaelmas last	16	—	—
Insurance of Premises, one year, from Michaelmas 1815, to Michaelmas 1816	3	—	—
£.	727	7	4

Appendix, N° 7ᶦ.

PUBLIC OFFICE, QUEEN-SQUARE.

ESTABLISHMENT, &c. for the Quarter ending 5th January 1816.

SALARIES.	£.	s.	d.
To P. COLQUHOUN, ⎫ - - - - - - - - -	150	—	—
WM. FIELDING, ⎬ Esquires, Magistrates - - - - -	150	—	—
T. B. PLESTOW, ⎭ - - - - - - - -	150	—	—
To Mr. R. Blakiston, Chief Clerk, (including an increase, at the rate of £.50 per annum, having served 10 years and upwards, pursuant to the Secretary of State's Letter of 13th September last - - -	62	10	—
Mr. Wᵐ Miller, Second D° - - - - - - - - -	33	10	—
Eight Constables, 13 weeks, at one guinea per week - - - -	109	4	—
Miss Reeves, Housekeeper, 3 months - - - - - -	8	15	—
Robert Dale, Messenger, 13 weeks, at one guinea - - - -	13	13	—

INCIDENTAL EXPENSES.

	£.	s.	d.
Mr. Staunton, Stationer - - - - - - - - - -	11	2	6
Mr. Downes, Printer - - - - - - - - - -	9	10	—
Mr. Bain, for Newspapers - - - - - - - - -	4	14	—
Messrs. Soulsby & Co. for Coals - - - - - - -	17	14	—
Mr. Dale, Messenger, for petty expenses of Postage, &c. - - -	3	12	9
Mr. Blakiston, for what he has paid Constables and others, on Public Service, (per order of Magistrates) - - - - -	1	7	—
Mr. Hardy, for corrected Newgate Calendars, for September and October Sessions last - - - - - - - - - -	2	2	—
S. Burgess, for posting Bills - - - - - - - -	—	10	—
Anne Allen, Wood Account to 2d November last - - - - -	—	16	—
Mr. Price, for a Coal Hod - - - - - - - - -	—	5	6
Messrs. Reed & Hunter, Law Booksellers - - - - - -	3	13	—
George Neave, for Candles - - - - - - - - -	2	11	10

NECESSARY DISBURSEMENTS:

Rent, Taxes, and Repairs of the House.

	£.	s.	d.
One Quarter's Rent, due Christmas last - - - - - -	16	—	—
Robert Southby, for sweeping Chimnies - - - - - -	—	7	6
Henry Burton, for paving and lighting, half a year's, to Michaelmas 1815 -	1	10	—
James Porter, one year's Land-Tax to Lady-day 1815 - - - -	4	2	8
Mr. Hill, for Carpenters Work, &c. - - - - - - -	1	4	—
Mrs. Burt, Smiths Work - - - - - - - - -	3	18	6
Wᵐ Tarte, Glazier - - - - - - - - - -	1	7	9
£.	764	1	—

WE certify this Account to be true, to the best of our knowledge and belief,

P. COLQUHOUN.

W. FIELDING.

Appendix, N° 8.ᵃ—An ACCOUNT of the ESTABLISHMENT of the Police

RANK OF OFFICER.	HIS NAME.	By whom Appointed.	How Appointed.	When Appointed.	Duration of Interest.	SALARY.
Three Magistrates	Thomas Evance - - - - Robert Joseph Chambers - Baker John Sellon - - -	The King.	Sign Manual.	1st Jan. 1801. 27th Aug. 1808. 17th Sept. 1814.	- -	£.600. per Ann. each, as fixed by 54 Geo. III. c. 37.
Chief Clerk - Second Clerk -	James Reeves - - - - - - George Kitson - - - - - -	Secretary of State.	Verbally.	3d Aug. 1796. 11th Feb. 1814.	- - - - - -	£.200. £.154.
Officers.	Daniel Harris - - - - - - John May - - - - - - - James Glannon - - - - - - William Collingbourn - - - - James Lockie - - - - - - John Clark - - - - - - Paul Barrett - - - - - - Thomas Aldred - - - - - -	The Magistrates, with the Approbation of the Secretary of State.	By Warrant.	21st May 1798. 21st May 1798. 12th Oct. 1799. 15th June 1802. 4th April 1803. 24th July 1811. 23d Aug. 1811. 20th July 1812.	- -	£.1. 1. per Week each.
Office Keeper - Housekeeper -	Henry Clark - - - - - - Ann Clark - - - - - - -	- Ditto - - -	Verbally.	24th June 1809.	- - -	£ 1. 11. 6. per Week.
Messenger -	James Kirk - - - - - - -	Secretary of State.	By Letter.	23d May 1815.	- - -	£. 1. 1s. per Week.
	John Carbill, Superannuated Messenger - - - - - - - -	The Magistrates, with the Approbation of the Secretary of State.	Verbally.	21st May 1798.	- - -	10 s. per Week.

The Establishment of the above Office during the Year 1815 was the same as in 1814.

of the PUBLIC OFFICE, UNION HALL; for the Year 1814.

By whom paid.	FEES.	By whom Paid.	Other Emoluments.	From Whence.	Total Receipt.	Other Employments, Places or Pensions under Government.
The Receiver.	- - - -	- - - -	- - - -	- - - -	£. 540. per Annum. each, 10 per Cent. being deducted for Income Tax.	—
The Receiver.	- - - -	- - - -	Resident in Union Hall.	- - - -	£. 180. per Annum.	—
The Receiver.	- - - -	- - - -	- - - - -	- - - -	£. 121. 7. per Annum.	—.
The Receiver.	1 s. for serving a Warrant or Summons.	The Party Prosecuted.	Rewards for apprehending Offenders	- - - -	Uncertain; depending wholly upon the Business done.	—
The Receiver.	- - - -	- - - -	Resident in Union Hall.	- - - -	- - £. 77. 7. - -	—
The Receiver.	- - - -	- - - -	- - - - -	- - - -	- - £. 54. 12. - -	—
The Receiver.	- - - -	- - - -	- - - - -	- - - -	£. 26. per Annum.	—

JAMES REEVES,
Chief Clerk.

Appendix, Nº 8.ᵇ

ACCOUNT of the CHARGES of the ESTABLISHMENT of the Public Office, Union Hall; for the different Quarters of the Years 1814 and 1815.

ESTABLISHMENT for the Quarter ending 5th April 1814.

SALARIES.	£. s. d.	£. s. d.
To Thoˢ. Evance, Esq. - - Magistrate - - - - -	150 — —	
R. J. Chambers, Esq. - - - Dᵒ - - - - -	150 — —	
Rᵈ Birnie, Esq. - - - - - Dᵒ - - - - -	150 — —	
To Mr. Jaˢ Reeves - - - - Chief Clerk - - - -	50 — —	
— John May - - - - Second Clerk - - - -	12 5 8	
— Geo. Kitson - - - - Second Clerk - - - -	14 11 8	
Nine Constables - - - - - - - - -	118 13 —	
Officekeeper - - - - - - - - -	13 13 —	
Housekeeper - - - - - - - - -	6 16 6	
Messenger - - - - - - - - - -	13 13 —	679 12 10
INCIDENTAL EXPENSES.		
Goff expenses attending the prosecution of Hopwood for Fraud	2 8 —	
Petty Disbursements - - - - - - - -	5 3 5	
Dutton - - - - - Stavemaker - - - - -	5 13 —	
Reed & Co. - - - - Booksellers - - - -	1 2 6	
Carter - - - - - Tallow Chandler - - - -	1 11 3	
Johnson - - - - - Newsman - - - -	4 4 6	
Grant - - - - - - Printer - - - - -	5 17 6	
Muggeridge - - - - Stationer - - - -	2 18 6	
Saunders - - - - Clockmaker - - - -	— 12 —	
Horne & Co. - - - Coal Merchants - - - -	9 7 —	
Handy - - - - - Lamplighter - - - -	7 18 —	
Officer's Sunday attendance - - - - - -	1 12 6	48 8 2
Ware - - - - - - Rent - - - - -	52 10 —	
Cundrick - - - - - Repairs - - - -	4 5 —	56 15 —
	£.	784 16 —

Appendix, N° 8. c.

PUBLIC OFFICE, UNION HALL.

ESTABLISHMENT, &c. for the Quarter ending 5th July 1814.

SALARIES.	£.	s.	d.	£.	s.	d.
To Thoˢ Evance, Esq. - - Magistrate - - - - - -	150	—	—			
R. J. Chambers, Esq. - D° - - - - - -	150	—	—			
Rᵈ Birnie, Esq. - - - D° - - - - - -	150	—	—			
To Mr. Jaˢ Reeves - - - - Chief Clerk - - - - - -	50	—	—			
— Geo. Kitson - - - - Second Clerk - - - -	25	—	—			
Nine Constables - - - - - - - - -	122	17	—			
Office Keeper - - - - - - - - - -	13	13	—			
Housekeeper - - - - - - - - - -	6	16	6			
Messenger - - - - - - - - - -	13	13	—			
				681	19	6
INCIDENTAL EXPENSES.						
Petty disbursements - - - - - - - -	3	18	2½			
Johnson, - - Newsman - - - - - - -	4	4	6			
Grant, - - - Printer - - - - - - -	15	6	—			
Muggeridge, Stationer - - - - - - -	2	15	4			
Officers, Sunday attendance - - - - - - -	1	12	6			
Handy, - - Lamplighter - - - - - -	37	7	—			
Carter, - - Tallow Chandler - - - - - -	2	4	3			
Hutting, - - Armourer - - - - - - -	4	16	—			
Downs, - - Stationer - - - - - - -	4	12	—			
Reed & Co. - Booksellers - - - - - -	4	4	—			
Horne & Co. Coal Merchants - - - - - -	16	8	6			
Expenses of 8 Officers attending at Whitehall, pursuant to order of Secretary of State - - - - - -	6	—	—			
May, the Officer; expenses apprehending Pitman for felony -	4	4	9			
Collingbourn and 2 other Officers; expenses apprehending Coley for felony - - - - - - - - -	1	1	—			
Goff and 2 other Officers; expenses apprehending Whiffin and 5 others for felony - - - - - - -	10	8	—			
Collingbourn and Clark; expenses going to Eltham concerning a robbery - - - - - - - - -	1	17	4			
				120	19	4½
Ware, - - - Rent - - - - - - - -	52	10	—			
Hill, - - - - Repairs - - - - - -	284	6	2½			
				336	16	2½
			£.	1,139	15	1

APPENDIX, N° 8ᵈ.

PUBLIC OFFICE, UNION HALL.

ESTABLISHMENT, &c. for the Quarter ending 10th October 1814.

SALARIES.	£.	s.	d.	£.	s.	d.
To Thoˢ Evance, Esq. - - Magistrate - - - - -	150	—	—			
R. J. Chambers, Esq. - - Dᵒ - - - - - -	150	—	—			
Rᵈ Birnie, Esq. - - - - Dᵒ - - - - -	121	12	10½			
B. J. Sellon, Serjᵗ at Law - Dᵒ - - - - - -	28	7	1½			
To Mr. James Reeves - - Chief Clerk - - - - -	50	—	—			
— Geo. Kitson - - - Second Clerk - - - -	25	—	—			
Nine Constables - - - - - - - -	122	17	—			
Officekeeper - - - - - - - - -	13	13	—			
Housekeeper - - - - - - - - -	6	16	6			
Messenger - - - - - - - - -	13	13	—			
				681	19	6
INCIDENTAL EXPENSES.						
Petty Disbursements - - - - - -	3	17	7			
Johnson - - Newsman - - - - - -	4	5	—			
Grant - - - Printer - - - - - - -	10	18	6			
Muggeridge - Stationer - - - - -	10	19	6			
Officers, Sunday Attendance - - - - - -	1	12	6			
Downes - - Printer - - - - - -	—	14	—			
Carter - - Tallow Chandler - - - - -	2	13	9			
Dutton - - Stave-maker - - - - - -	1	5	—			
Wilkinson and another; their expenses in conveying Hack to this Office for Murder - - - - - - - -	—	11	—			
May; Expenses in apprehending Tillbury and another for Felony	2	2	—			
Expenses of 20 Constables attending at Hyde Park, pursuant to order of Secretary of State - - - - - -	10	—	—			
Forged Note detained at the Bank; the same having paid to Mr. Hutting (vide last Quarter's account) from this Office	1	—	—			
				49	18	10
Ware - - - Rent - - - - - - -				52	10	—
			£.	784	8	4

Appendix, N° 8 ᶜ.

PUBLIC OFFICE, UNION HALL.

ESTABLISHMENT, &c. for the Quarter ending 5th January 1815.

	£. s. d.	£. s. d.
SALARIES.		
To Thoˢ EVANCE, Esq. - - Magistrate - - - - -	150 — —	
R. J. CHAMBERS, Esq. - - Dº - - - - - -	150 — —	
B. J. SELLON, Serjᵗ at Law - Dº - - - - - -	150 — —	
To Mr. Jaˢ Reeves - - - Chief Clerk - - - - -	50 — —	
— Geo. Kitson - - - Second Clerk - - - - -	25 — —	
Nine Constables - - - - - - - - -	122 17 —	
Officekeeper - - - - - - - - - -	13 13 —	
Housekeeper - - - - - - - - - -	6 16 6	
Messenger - - - - - - - - - -	13 13 —	681 19 6
INCIDENTAL EXPENSES.		
Officers Sunday attendance - - - - - - -	1 12 6	
Petty Disbursements - - - - - - - -	5 4 5	
Barnes & Co. - - Printers - - - - - - -	5 5 6	
Johnson - - - Newsman - - - - - -	4 4 6	
Smith & Co. - - Upholsterers - - - - - -	— 12 —	
Reed & Co. - - Booksellers - - - - - -	13 7 6	
Carter - - - - Tallow Chandler - - - - -	1 7 4	
Muggeridge - - Stationer - - - - - - -	10 6 9	
Goff and others; Expenses attending the prosecution of Swift for selling Fire-works - - - - - - -	92 10 —	
Handy - - - - Lamplighter - - - - - -	3 15 —	
May; Expenses apprehending Guston and another for Felony -	4 16 —	
May; Expenses apprehending Clark and four others for Felony -	6 8 9	
Advertisement, respecting a Bank Note supposed to be stolen -	— 6 6	149 16 9
Ware - - - - Rent - - - - - - -	52 10 —	
REPAIRS.		
Houlder - - - Glazier - - - - - - -	— 2 6	
Brettle - - - Smith - - - - - - -	1 14 6	
Hill - - - - - Carpenter - - - - - -	1 6 8	
Cundick - - - - Dº - - - - - - -	5 12 1	61 5 9
	£	893 2 —

Appendix, Nº 8ᶜ.

PUBLIC OFFICE, UNION HALL.

ESTABLISHMENT, &c. for the Quarter ending 5th April 1815.

SALARIES.	£. s. d.	£. s. d.
To Thoˢ EVANCE, Esq. - - - - Magistrate - - - -	150 — —	
R. J. CHAMBERS, Esq. - - - - Dº - - - - -	150 — —	
BAKER JOHN SELLON, Serjᵗ at Law Dº - - - - -	150 — —	
To Mr. Jaˢ Reeves - - - - - Chief Clerk - - - -	50 — —	
— Geo. Kitson - - - - - Second Clerk - - -	29 17 5	
Nine Constables - - - - - - - - -	122 17 —	
Officekeeper - - - - - - - - - -	13 13 —	
Housekeeper - - - - - - - - - -	6 16 6	
Messenger - - - - - - - - - -	13 13 —	
		686 16 11
INCIDENTAL EXPENSES.		
Officers Sunday attendance - - - - - - -	1 12 6	
Petty disbursements - - - - - - - -	4 7 8	
Reed & Co. - - Booksellers - - - - - -	3 19 —	
Johnson - - - Newsman - - - - - -	4 4 6	
Carter - - - - Tallow Chandler - - - -	1 12 9	
Hutting - - - Armourer - - - - - -	11 16 —	
Dutton - - - - Stave-maker - - - - -	4 15 —	
Putley - - - - Cutler - - - - - - -	1 10 6	
Downes - - - Printer - - - - - - -	1 1 —	
Smith & Co. - - Upholsterers - - - - - -	5 15 6	
Barnes - - - - Printer - - - - - - -	6 14 —	
Muggeridge - - Stationer - - - - - -	7 7 1	
Handy - - - - Lamplighter - - - - - -	4 3 —	
John Day, Esq. for printed Criminal Returns - - - -	4 4 —	
Glannon; Expenses apprehending Muller - - - -	2 3 6	
Dº - - Expenses apprehending Thirstole - - - -	1 — —	
Dº - - Expenses apprehending Michaelis - - - -	6 16 6	
Barrett - Expenses apprehending Drew - - - - -	— 13 6	
May - - Expenses apprehending England - - - -	— 7 —	
Horne & Co. - - Coal Merchants - - - - -	16 12 6	
		90 15 6
Ware - - - - Rent - - - - - - -	52 10 —	
REPAIRS.		
Hill - - - - Carpenter - - - - - -	23 — 5	
Houlder - - - Glazier - - - - - - -	2 15 —	
		78 5 5
	£.	855 17 10

Appendix, N° 8ᵍ.

PUBLIC OFFICE, UNION HALL.

ESTABLISHMENT, &c. for the Quarter ending 5th July 1815.

SALARIES.	£.	s.	d.	£.	s.	d.
To Tho' EVANCE, Esq. - Magistrate - - - -	150	—	—			
R. J. CHAMBERS, Esq. - - - Dᵒ - - - - -	150	—	—			
B. J. SELLON, Serjeant at Law Dᵒ - - - - -	150	—	—			
To Mr. Jaˢ Reeves - - - - Chief Clerk - - - -	50	·	—			
— Geo. Kitson - - - - Second Clerk - - - -	33	10	—			
Nine Constables - - - - - - - - -	122	17	—			
Officekeeper - - - - - - - - -	13	13	—			
Housekeeper - - - - - - - - -	6	16	6			
Messenger - - - - - - - - -	13	13	—			
Superannuated Messengers - - - - - -, -	1	10	—			
				691	19	6
INCIDENTAL EXPENSES.						
Officers Sunday Attendance - - - - - - -	1	12	6			
Petty Disbursements - - - - - - - -	3	7	5			
Johnson - - - Newsman - - - - - -	4	4	6			
Carter - - - - Tallow Chandler - - - - -	1	16	3			
Reed & Co. - - Booksellers - - - - - -	8	3	6			
Muggeridge - - Stationer - - - - - -	2	15	7			
Ware - - - - Printing - - - - - -	1	9	6			
D'Arcy, per order of Rᵈ Birnie, Esq. - - - - -	5	5	—			
May and Goff; Expenses apprehending Bailey - - -	3	10	—			
- - Dᵒ - - Expenses pursuing two men (names unknown) concerned in a footpad robbery - - - - - -	18	13	6			
May and Goff; Expenses apprehending Banks - - -	4	1	—			
- - Dᵒ - - Expenses apprehending England and 19 others, suspected of divers Felonies - - - - - -	29	6	1			
May and Goff; further Expenses in same case - - - -	21	17	4			
Mr. Reeves, for law expenses incurred in the prosecution of England and others at the Assizes - - - - -	39	16	9			
Harris; Expenses in the same case - - - - -	3	—	—			
Goff and another; Expenses apprehending Drew for Rioting -	1	—	9			
				149	19	8
Ware - - - - Rent - - - - - - -	52	10	—			
REPAIRS.						
Jackson - - - Locksmith - - - - - -	1	12	—			
Brettle - - - Smith - - - , - - -	—	19	8			
				55	1	8
	£.			897	—	10

Appendix, N° 8 ʰ.

PUBLIC OFFICE, UNION HALL.

ESTABLISHMENT, &c. for the Quarter ending 10th October 1815.

SALARIES.	£.	s.	d.	£.	s.	d.
To THOˢ EVANCE, Esq. - - Magistrate - - - - - -	150	—	—			
R. J. CHAMBERS, Esq. - D° - - - - - -	150	—	—			
B. J. SELLON, Serjᵗ at Law D° - - - - - -	150	—	—			
To Mr. Jaˢ Reeves - - - - Chief Clerk - - - - -	50	—	—			
— Geo. Kitson - - - - Second Clerk - - - -	33	10	—			
Nine Constables - - - - - - - - -	122	17	—			
Officekeeper - - - - - - - - - -	13	13	—			
Housekeeper - - - - - - - - - -	6	16	6			
Messenger - - - - - - - - - -	13	13	—			
Superannuated Messenger - - - - - - -	6	10	—			
				696	19	6
INCIDENTAL EXPENSES.						
Officers, Sunday attendance - - - - - - -	1	12	6			
Petty Disbursements - - - - - - - -	7	10	5			
Johnson - - - Newsman - - - - - - -	4	6	2			
Horne & Co. - - Coal Merchants - - - - - -	14	17	6			
Carter - - - - Tallow Chandler - - - - -	1	9	3			
Handy - - - - Lamplighter - - - - - -	9	1	1			
Barnes - - - Printer - - - - - - -	10	9	—			
Robins - - - D° - - - - - - -	19	1	6			
Downes - - - D° - - - - - - -	15	4	—			
Muggeridge - - Stationer - - - - - - -	2	19	—			
Allsop - - - - Stave Maker - - - - - -	5	12	6			
Swinden - - - Clock Maker - - - - - -	—	12	—			
Glannon, expenses apprehending Aldridge - - - -	6	19	—			
Goff and May - - D° - - Richardson - - - -	11	4	11			
D° - - - - - D° - - Healey - - - - -	20	5	8			
D° - - - - - D° - - Digby - - - - -	9	18	—			
D° - - - - - D° - - Cooper - - - -	5	11	3			
D° - - - - - D° - - Maddox - - - -	1	15	6			
Shergold and Hall, for attending as extra Constables during the Riots - - - - - - - - - }	3	—	—			
Goff and others, expenses apprehending Kees - - - -	—	12	9			
Advertisements - - - - - - - - -	2	3	—			
				154	5	—
Ware - - - Rent - - - - - - - - - - -				52	10	—
			£.	903	14	6

Appendix, N° 8ᵗ.

PUBLIC OFFICE, UNION HALL,

ESTABLISHMENT, &c. for the Quarter ending 5th January 1816.

SALARIES.	£.	s.	d.	£.	s.	d.
To Thoˢ EVANCE, Esq. - - Magistrate - - - - -	150	—	—			
R. J. CHAMBERS, Esq. - - D° - - - - - -	150	—	—			
B. J. SELLON, Serjᵗ at Law - D° - - - - -	150	—	—			
To Mr. Jaˢ Reeves - - - - Chief Clerk - - - - -	67	10	—			
— Geo. Kitson - - - Second Clerk - - - -	33	10	—			
Nine Constables - - - - - - - - -	122	17	—			
Officekeeper - - - - - - - - - -	13	13	—			
Housekeeper - - - - - - - - -	6	16	6			
Messenger - - - - - - - - - -	13	13	—			
Superannuated Messenger - - - - - - -	6	10	—			
				714	9	6
INCIDENTAL EXPENSES.						
Officers, Sunday attendance - - - - - - -	1	12	6			
Petty Disbursements - - - - - - - -	4	3	9			
Handy - - - - Lamplighter - - - - - -	25	12	9			
Reed & Co. - - Booksellers - - - - - -	3	9	—			
Johnson - - - Newsman - - - - - - -	4	11	6			
Downes - - - Printer - - - - - - -	24	6	3			
Carter - - - Tallow Chandler - - - - -	1	13	6			
Muggeridge - - Stationer - - - - - - -	4	15	6			
Smart - For repairing a Perambulator - - - - -	—	18	—			
Advertisements - - - - - - - - -	4	19	—			
May and Goff; expenses apprehending Savage - - - -	1	19	6			
Goff and another; expenses apprehending Healey - - -	5	3	6			
Goff and another; expenses apprehending Humphreys - -	1	18	6			
May and others; expenses apprehending several Vagrants on the Kent Road, at the request of the Officers of Greenwich Hospital - - - - - - - - - - -	8	5	—			
Goff and Shergold; expenses apprehending Little - - -	1	15	6			
- D° - D° - D° - D° Drew - - -	1	13	9			
Harris; expenses apprehending Bristow and others - - -	4	5	—			
Collingbourn and another; expenses apprehending Deering -	1	6	6			
May and Goff; expenses apprehending Rogers and others - -	18	4	6			
				120	13	6
Ware - - - Rent - - - - - - - - -	52	10	—			
REPAIRS.						
Houlder - - Glazier - - - - - - - -	2	7	3			
Brettle - - Smith - - - - - - - -	1	12	—			
				56	9	3
£.				891	12	3

JAMES REEVES,
Chief Clerk.

Appendix, N° 9.

Appendix, Nº 9.

THAMES POLICE OFFICE.

SIR,   Thames Police Office, 6th June 1816.

THE accompanying Return of the THAMES POLICE ESTABLISHMENT is made out as similar to the Return of the other Police Offices as the nature of our Preventive System of Police for the River will admit. I believe I omitted mentioning, what you will perceive in this Return, that besides the strength of our own Establishment for the River, we afford a Police Strength of Fifty-one Constables to the Great Commercial Docks, as well as at the King's Yard at Deptford. This is done under sanction of Government, but at no expense, as they are paid by their respective employers; their police conduct, however, is under the controul of the Magistrates.

The gross sums of the expenses of this Institution for the last three years, which I was desired to make out, I find we cannot furnish you with, as our receiver, Mr. Colquhoun, has other charges which we are unacquainted with; he, however, can readily give the whole.

I have the honour to be,

SIR,

The Hon. H. Grey Bennet,   Your very obedient humble servant,
     &c. &c. &c.   JOHN HARRIOTT.

AN ACCOUNT of the ESTABLISHMENT of the THAMES POLICE OFFICE, for the Year 1816.

RANK of OFFICER.	NAME.	By whom Appointed.	When.	Salary.	By whom Paid.	Emoluments.	
Three Magistrates	John Harriott	— — —	July - 1798		— —	Resides in the House.	
	William Kinnard	The King	Oct. - 1800	£.600 per ann. each			
	John Longley	— — —	April - 1807				
Chief Clerk	Edward William Symons	The Secretary of State	Dec. - 1809	£.200 per ann.			
Second Clerk	James Fell		Jan. - 1809	£.154 per ann.			
Chief Surveyor	John Gotty	The Magistrates with the approbation of the Secretary of State.	July - 1798	£.150 per ann			
Surveyors	James Evans		April - 1801	£.90 per ann.			The higher Salaries are intended to stimulate and reward active services and good conduct, not entirely depending upon length of service.
	Joseph Harding		Feb. - 1804	£.90 per ann.			
	Thomas Walker	— — —	Feb. - 1802	£.90 per ann.			
	Joseph Powis	— — —	April - 1811	£.80 per ann.			
	Alexander Mitchell	— — —	Oct. - 1812	£.80 per ann			
	John Herbert	— — —	Nov. - 1801	£.80 per ann.			
	John Gillman	— — —	May - 1800	£.80 per ann.			
	Richard Dalby	— — —	March 1802	£.75 per ann.	The Receiver.		
	James Craigie	— — —	Feb. - 1806	£.75 per ann.		Payment for extra trouble in serving warrants and summonses from parties prosecuting; shares of rewards and penalties.	
	James White	— — —	Oct. - 1813	£.75 per ann.			
	Thomas Piercey	— — —	Feb. - 1811				
	Thomas Moody	— — —	April - 1812				
	Daniel Blyth	— — —	Nov. - 1815	£.65 per ann. each.			
	John Robison	— — —	Nov. - 1801				
	Henry Ford	— — —	Aug. - 1807				
	Thomas Ellis	— — —	Nov. - 1814				
Constables	John Merrant	— — —	Oct. - 1801				
	John Woollard	— — —	Nov. - 1802				
	Thomas Edwards	— — —	July - 1811				
	Benjamin Blaby	— — —	June - 1814	21 s. per Week each			
Gaoler	William Warner	— — —	Sept. - 1798				
Office Keeper	William Dyball	— — —	Nov. - 1802				
Messenger	John Ansell	— — —	Oct. - 1801				

(continued)

The THAMES POLICE OFFICE—*continued.*

RANK of OFFICER.	NAME.	By whom Appointed.	When.	Salary.	By whom Paid.	Emoluments.	
	John Rye - - - -	- - - -	- - -	21 s. per Week	- -	An extra allowance of 5 s. per Week for taking care of a Sailing Cutter attached to the Establishment.	
	Robert Nichols - -						
	John Bates - - -						
	William Sherwood -						
	William Stevenson -						
	Thomas Hamilton -						
	George Faint - - -						
	Henry Larwell - -						
	James Bolas - - -						
	Mark Arnold - - -						These Men are divided into parties, each under the direction of a Surveyor, with regular periods of duty and relief. Four boats are throughout the night as well as in the day constantly moving upon the river between London Bridge and Greenwich (within which limits their general operations are at present necessarily confined) each boat's crew being out nine hours in the course of every twenty-four, exclusive of other duties. Their powers are derived from the Thames Police and other Acts of Parliament relating to the river, and the object of those powers the protection of property afloat and upon the wharfs and quays adjoining the river, from the various modes of plunder to which it is always more or less particularly exposed ; and from accidents by fire, which would arise from negligence with respect to gunpowder and combustible materials. Some of the Surveyors also act under deputations from the Commissioners of the Navy for the detection of offences committed on His Majesty's Stores.
	William Thomas - -						
	William Taylor - -						
	William Halcrow -						
	Thomas Stevens -						
	George Webster - -						
	Robert Izod - - -						
	Samuel Hill - - -						
	James Hanson - -						
	William Strong - -						
	Alexander Lamond -						
River Constables or Watermen.	Samuel Davis - - -	The Magistrates with the approbation of the Secretary of State.	- - -	20 s. per Week each.	The Receiver	Shares of Rewards and Penalties with their Surveyors.	
	James Lewden - -						
	Thomas Gillings - -						
	George Forfar - -						
	George Perren - -						
	Joseph Galloway -						
	William Rigby - -						
	William Judge - -						
	Samuel Cromarty -						The duty of the Chief Surveyor is to proceed on the river at varied and uncertain times, not only to direct his attention to the foregoing objects, but also to notice and report daily to the Magistrates the conduct and efficiency of all the other officers and men.
	Robert Young - -						
	Adam High - - -						
	John Mitchell - - -						
	Samuel Cromarty, jun.						
	Joseph Daniels - -						
	William Fortey - -						
	Thomas Grimstone -						
	David Hart - - -						
	Isaac Judge - - -						
	Thomas Morris - -						
	John Little - - -						
	William Howard - -						
	John Wynick - -						
	Thomas Oaff - - -						
Waterside Watchmen.	Robert Noaks - - -						
	John Ives - - - -						

(continued)

The THAMES POLICE OFFICE—*continued.*

RANK OF OFFICER.	NAME.	
Surveyor.	Robert Gibson - - - -	
Constables.	Francis Fairbairns - - - -	
	Telford Brearley - - - -	
	John Evans Hill - - - -	
	John Hanever - - - -	
	William Bradly - - - -	
	William Winnall - - - -	
	John Stevens - - - -	
	Thomas Morgan - - - -	These persons are servants of the West India Dock Company, and occasion no charge to the public. At the request of the Directors, and with the approbation of the Secretary of State, they are sworn and appointed by the Magistrates Constables of this Establishment, to act at the Docks for their protection, and the detection of Offences there committed.
	Samuel Floyd - - - -	
	James Moore - - - -	
	Ebenezer Teeton - - - -	
	John Parsons - - - -	
	Donald M'Phail - - - -	
	Richard Richards - - - -	
	William Fisher - - - -	
	William Taylor - - - -	
	Thomas Montagu Crump - - -	
	Thomas Latham - - -	
	Henry Schlette - - -	
	Joseph Westbrooke - - -	
	William Clarke - - - -	
	James Slater - - - -	
	Joseph Carter - - - -	
	Thomas Bolton - - - -	
	Daniel Clements - - - -	
	Richard Ellis - - - -	
	Alexander Durham - - - -	
	James Griffiths - - - -	These persons are servants of the London Dock Company, and appointed in like manner to act as Thames Police Constables in the London Docks.
	Obadiah Scott - - - -	
	Archibald Mc Donald - - -	
	John Watkins - - - -	
	Thomas Meriton - - - -	
	William Pierce - - - -	
	James Pullen - - - -	
	Joseph Hawkins - - - -	
	James Benson - - - -	
	James Murdoch - - - -	
	Richard Over - - - -	
	Francis William Wymer - - -	
	Andrew Grubb - - - -	Servants of the East India Dock Company, appointed in like manner to act at the East India Docks.
	Robert Sims - - - -	
	John Moore - - - -	
	Archibald Moncrief - - - -	
	John Little - - - -	
	John Thompson - - - -	
	Robert Myers - - - -	Servants of the Commercial Dock Company, appointed in like manner to act at the Commercial Docks.
	John Chiverton - - - -	
	Richard Hemming - - - -	Servants of the East Country Dock Company, appointed in like manner to act at the East Country Docks.
	John Field - - - - -	
	George Sherwin - - - -	Warder of His Majesty's Dock Yard, Deptford, appointed a Thames Police Constable at the request of the Commissioner.

Thames Police Office, }
6 June 1816.   }

JOHN HARRIOTT.

Appendix, No. 10.

FORM OF A RECOGNIZANCE IN A COMMON ASSAULT.

Middlesex⎱
(to wit.)⎰ *Thomas Dean*, No. 35, Threadneedle-street, Bookbinder, acknowledges himself
to be indebted to our Sovereign Lord the King, in the Sum of Ten Pounds.
John Smith, - - - Same - - - Same, Acknowledges, &c. - - Ten Pounds.
————————————————— Acknowledges, &c.   Pounds.

UPON CONDITION, That if Daniel Abbott do personally appear at the next General Sessions of the Peace to be held for the said County of Middlesex, at the Sessions-house, on Clerkenweell-Green, then and there to answer the Complaint of James Smith, for Assaulting and Beating him, against the Peace, &c.

And do not depart the Court without Leave. Then this Recognizance to be void, or else to remain in full force.

Taken and acknowledged, the 1st day of May 1816, before me

Appendix, No. 11.

[An ABSTRACT of the several ACTS OF PARLIAMENT now in force, for the Regulating of Public Houses, and of the Persons licensed to keep such Public Houses;—*was delivered in, and read.*]

BY the Act 29 Geo. III, c. 79:—Persons suffering unlawful combinations and confederacies in their houses, to forfeit Five Pounds for the first offence, and for the second offence, &c. " be deemed guilty of an unlawful Combination and Confederacy in Breach of " this Act;" in which case they will forfeit Twenty Pounds, or be liable to three months imprisonment, or may be transported; and if a Publican permits unlawful meetings in his house, or suffers seditious or immoral publications to be read therein, he will forfeit his licence.—Penalties Half to the Informer.

2.—By the Act 1 James I, c. 9; 4 James I, c. 5; 1 Charles I, c. 4:—Publicans who suffer tippling, shall forfeit for each offence Ten Shillings, and the tipplers shall forfeit Three Shillings and Four Pence for each offence.

3.—By the Act 26 Geo. II, c. 31:—Publicans suffering unlawful games in their houses, or disorders therein, shall forfeit their recognizance, and be disqualified from keeping an alehouse for three years.

4.—By the Act 30 Geo. II, c. 24:—Publicans suffering journeymen, labourers, servants, or apprentices, to game in their houses, forfeit Forty Shillings for the first offence, and Ten Pounds for every subsequent offence.—One-fourth to him or her who shall contribute to the conviction.

5.—By the Act 17 Geo. II, c. 5:—Persons who shall knowingly permit rogues and vagabonds to lodge and take shelter in their houses and premises, and shall not deliver them to the constable, or carry them before a justice, shall forfeit not less than Ten Shillings, nor more than Forty Shillings.—One half to the informer.

6.—By the Act 14 Geo. III, c. 90:—Publicans harbouring watchmen or patroles while on Duty, or suffering them to tipple, shall forfeit Twenty Shillings for the first, Forty Shillings for the second, and Five Pounds for the third offence.

7.—By the Act 41 Geo. III, c. 11:—Persons buying, receiving, exchanging, or detaining arms, clothes, or regimental necessaries, shall forfeit Five Pounds for each offence.

8.—By the Act 30 Geo. II, c. 21:—Suspected persons offering goods to sell, and refusing to give a satisfactory account how they obtained the same, may be detained and given in charge to a constable, to be carried before a justice to be dealt with according to law.

9.—By the Act 26 Geo. II, c. 31:—Publicans doing any act to forfeit their recognizance, and being convicted thereof, the licence becomes void, and they are disabled from holding any licence for three years.

10.—By the Act 7 James I, c. 10:—If any Alehouse-keeper be convicted of drunkenness, beside the other penalties of the law for this offence, he shall be entirely disabled from holding a licence for three years.

11.—By the Act 11 & 12 Will. c. 15:—Every retailer of ale or beer, who shall not sell the same in a full ale quart or ale pint, according to the standard in the Exchequer, shall, on conviction, forfeit Forty Shillings, and not less than Ten Shillings.—Half to the informer.

12.—By the Act 19 Geo. II, c. 21:—Persons convicted of profane cursing and swearing, shall forfeit One Shilling, if a labourer, soldier or seaman; and Two Shillings, if under the degree of a gentleman: and Five Shillings, if of or above the degree of a gentleman.—The second offence, double penalties, (after the conviction for the first), and the third, and every subsequent offence, treble.

510.

13.—By

13.—By the Act of 9 Geo. II, c. 23, sec. 8 :—Retailers of spirituous liquors or strong waters, who shall make any increase of such liquors after the same have been taken an account of by an officer for the duties thereby granted, by any private or clandestine addition thereto of water, or any other liquors, shall forfeit the sum of Forty Shillings for every gallon of such spirits and water, or other liquors mixed as aforesaid ; and all which liquors so mixed are to be seized for His Majesty's use.

14.—By the Act 17 Geo. II, c. 17, sec. 18 :—It is enacted, " That in any case where a " licence shall have been granted for retailing spirituous liquors to any person who shall, " at the time of granting such licence, keep a tavern, victualling-house, inn, coffee- " house, or alehouse, if such person so licensed shall afterwards, during the time of con- " tinuing such licence, exercise the trade of a distiller, grocer, or chandler, or keep a " brandy shop or shops for sale of any spirituous liquors, the licence granted in every " such case shall be void, and such persons retailing such spirituous liquors afterwards, " shall forfeit Ten Pounds for every such offence."

15.—26 Geo. II, c. 31 :—29 Geo. II, c. 12 :—32 Geo. III, c. 59, are Acts for regulating the manner of licensing alehouses in that part of Great Britain called England, and for the more easy convicting Persons selling ale and other liquors without licences.

16.—48 Geo. III, c. 143, sec. 5:—All persons neglecting to renew their Excise licences within ten days after the expiration of their former licences, shall for every such offence forfeit Fifty Pounds.

Appendix, No. 12.

PROCEEDINGS of the COMMON COUNCIL of the City of *London*, in the several Mayoralties of 1814 and 1816, for clearing the Streets of VAGRANTS, PROSTITUTES, and IDLE and DISORDERLY Persons.

DOMVILLE, MAYOR.

A COMMON COUNCIL holden in the Chamber of the Guildhall of the City of *London*, on Thursday the 19th day of May 1814;—The Committee appointed to consider the Petition of sundry inhabitant householders of the principal streets of this City, relative to common Prostitutes infesting the same, did this day deliver into this Court a Report in writing under their hands, which was read and ordered to be printed, together with the Appendixes annexed thereto, and the Petition of the said inhabitants, presented to this Court on the 16th day of December last, and a Copy thereof to be sent to every Member of this Court.

Woodthorpe.

To the Right Honourable the Lord Mayor, Aldermen and Commons, of the City of London, in Common Council assembled :—The humble Petition and Memorial of the undersigned Inhabitant Householders of the principal Streets in the City of London,—Sheweth

THAT your Petitioners having long deplored the alarming extent of the vice of Prostitution, an evil great in itself, and in its results of incalculable injury to society ; and being convinced that the removal of Prostitutes from the public streets would lessen the evil, and greatly tend to promote the welfare and peace of the City in general, respectfully entreat that in your several legislative and executive capacities, you will adopt such mea- sures as shall remedy the grievance complained of, as far as may be practicable. Your Petitioners are particularly induced to make this application to your Honourable Court, from seeing the late republication of your Resolutions of the 12th of February 1789, wherein among many other excellent Regulations, it is given in charge to the Marshals; Marshal Men, and Constables of this City, " to clear the streets of Vagrants and other " idle and disorderly characters ;" and " that the two Marshals, attended by the Con- " stables of each Precinct or Ward, do search all houses suspected of harbouring common " Prostitutes, &c. and carry any offenders they may find in such houses before the Lord " Mayor, or some other Justice of the City, to be punished according to law."

That your Petitioners do not assume that they only are aggrieved by the existence of this nuisance ; but they beg leave respectfully to represent, that, from their local situation, they have stronger reasons for complaining of it than their fellow citizens in general.

It cannot be necessary to inform your Honourable Court, that the principal streets of this City are every evening crowded with profligate women, who, by their riotous and obscene conduct, annoy or alarm the well-disposed inhabitants ; but to justify this application, your Petitioners request permission to specify a few of the injurious consequences to which they are subjected.

The audacity with which these women accost passengers, and the horrid oaths and obscene language which they are accustomed to use, your Petitioners as fathers and as masters, interested in the welfare of their families, cannot but consider an intolerable grievance, for no virtuous female however protected, can pass through the streets in the

evening

evening without witnessing these disgusting scenes; and the utmost vigilance your Petitioners can use is insufficient to preserve their sons and servants from frequent solicitations even at their own doors. Familiarity with the sight of these women who practice various arts to entrap unwary youth, gradually diminishes disgust and caution, and is too often followed with the most ruinous consequences to the health, reputation, and morals of the rising generation. The intimacy these depraved women form with shopmen and apprentices on the one hand, and the connection they have with house-breakers, pick-pockets, and receivers of stolen goods, on the other, afford facilities for plunder to a very great extent. They also themselves constitute a numerous class of pick-pockets, and petty offenders, as must be well known to your Honourable Court.

Your Petitioners confide in the wisdom of the Members composing your Court to adopt such measures as to them shall seem meet for the purpose of effecting the object of this Petition, and thereby to relieve a numerous class of citizens from a nuisance the most disgusting in itself and pernicious in its effects.

And your Petitioners will ever gratefully acknowledge the obligation.

(Signed by upwards of Two Thousand Persons.)

To the Right Honourable the Lord Mayor, Aldermen, and Commons of the City of London, in Common Council assembled.

WE, whose names are hereunto subscribed of your Committee, appointed on the 16th day of December last, to examine the allegations contained in the Petition and Memorial of the Inhabitant Householders of the principal streets of this City, complaining of the alarming extent of the vice of Prostitution, and of the great number of profligate and dissolute women frequenting the said streets, and to report our opinion thereon; Do certify, That we have considered the said Petition and Memorial with that attention which the nature and importance of the subject, and the number and respectability of the petitioners so imperiously demand; and are of opinion that the evil complained of exists to a very great degree and has much increased of late years. That its tendency is greatly to violate public decorum, and is extremely injurious to the best interests of society, and your Committee doubt not will be felt by the Court, as that which ought to be lessened and counteracted by all possible means.

We beg leave further to certify, that we have been attended by this City's Solicitor, the present Clerk to the Lord Mayor, and the Clerk to the Sitting Justices at Guildhall; as also by the upper Marshal, who readily afforded us every information in their power, relative to the evil, its great and increasing extent, and the modes which have been at various times adopted by the Magistrates, for the prevention and remedy thereof.

From all the circumstances stated by these officers respectively, as well as from our own personal knowledge and observation, we are thoroughly convinced, that the character, habits, and abandoned principles of the women, who thus infest the public streets, render them highly dangerous to the youth of this city, and the intimacy so frequently known to exist between those persons and various descriptions of offenders, has notoriously proved the occasion of many robberies and petty thefts.

From other circumstances which have been represented to us during this inquiry, we are also of opinion, that the numerous low and disreputable public-houses, and liquor-shops, in various parts, which are the places of resort for those persons, and encourage the association of other idle and disorderly characters of the very worst and most mischievous classes; as also the many houses of ill fame kept in the Metropolis, have greatly contributed to the increase of the evil complained of.

We are also apprehensive, that many of the patroles, watchmen, and night officers of this City, execute their several duties in a very negligent manner; and it is to be feared, in some instances they not only connive at, but encourage the improper conduct of these women.

Your Committee feel confident, that as the various officers above alluded to, are under the immediate controul of the Deputy and Common Council of every Ward respectively, they will, under the direction of this Honourable Court, use all possible care and attention, in the future appointment of those officers, and see that they execute their several duties in a proper manner.

We are also of opinion, that the necessity and importance of administering the laws in reference to this subject with more than ordinary attention and diligence, should be respectfully and earnestly urged upon the Magistrates of this City; (particularly as the Marshals, Marshalmen and Constables are more immediately under their authority; and that they be called upon to exert themselves in their several offices, to promote this end.) And the Right Honourable the Lord Mayor should be requested to issue a Proclamation in relation thereto.

Although your Committee encourage the hope that by such measures as they have recommended being adopted, this evil may be diminished; yet apprehending it possible, that a greater number of profligate women may be taken before the magistrates than usual, especially in the first instance;

We, your said Committee, have taken into our consideration, what means could be afforded for the confinement and employment of the characters alluded to in the Petition, that might be committed by the Magistrates, with a view as well to their reform as punishment; and Mr. Town Clerk having laid before us a printed copy of the Letters

Patent

Patent of King Edward the VIth, founding the Royal Hospital of Bridewell; extracts of which we have caused to be hereunto annexed in Appendix, No. I;—We examined the same, and it appeared to us that the said Hospital, by the pious intention of the royal founder, was every way calculated to afford the remedy so much desired. We, therefore, in order to ascertain the present means of the said Hospital, conceiving ourselves justified to make inquiry (that Hospital being a public institution) requested Mr. John Poynder, the Clerk of Bridewell Hospital, to attend us, which he did; but he stated, upon some questions being put to him, that he could not take upon himself, to give the answers required, without consulting some of the Governors, or a Committee thereon, and therefore he requested that such questions as we your Committee wished to have answered might be transmitted to him in writing, and therefore directed the Town Clerk to write to Mr. Poynder thereon, which he did to the following effect; *viz.*

Guildhall, January 29, 1814.

Sir,

I am directed by the Committee appointed by the Court of Common Council to take into consideration the Petition signed by upwards of two thousand inhabitant householders of the City of London, relative to the nuisance created by common Prostitutes frequenting the public streets (of which the enclosed is a copy) and also to consider and report what remedy can be applied for the relief of the public in respect thereof, to request you will be good enough to answer the several questions following, or submit them, if you think fit, to the Governors of Bridewell Hospital, or any Committee of the said Governors; *viz.*

Whether the afore-mentioned Committee of the Common Council, can be furnished with a copy of the Report of a Select Committee of the Governors relative to Bridewell Hospital, presented in the year 1798?

Whether any and what alterations have been made in the management of that establishment in the year 1798?

What number of idle and disorderly persons can be admitted into Bridewell at one time for the purpose of employment or punishment?

Whether any enlargement can be made in the present establishment of Bridewell, for the above purpose and to what extent?

Whether any distinction can be made in the treatment of the vicious, and those who are less profligate, in order that they might not be associated in their several employments?

What is the nature of the employments to which idle and disorderly persons, particularly females, are at present put?

Whether any other employment, than what is now used, can be adopted for idle and disorderly women committed to Bridewell, so as to preserve a distinction between the vicious and the less profligate?

What are the kinds of punishment or correction inflicted on common Prostitutes committed to Bridewell, exclusive of hard labour?

Whether the Governors of Bridewell can suggest any method by which the objects of the petitioners can be obtained, and the evil so much complained of remedied?

And generally, whether the Governors can state what good effects have been the result of the correction and labour in Bridewell?

I have the honour to be, Sir,
Your obedient servant,

H. Woodthorpe.

John Poynder, esq. ⎱
Bridewell Hospital. ⎰

That we your Committee were favoured with an answer by directions of the House Committee of the Governors of Bridewell Hospital, which is as follows:

Sir,

I have laid your Letter, written by direction of the Committee appointed by the Court of Common Council, relative to the evil of Prostitutes frequenting the public streets, and also a copy of the Petition which accompanied it, before a Committee of the Governors of Bridewell Hospital, who have directed me to inform you, in answer to your application for a copy of a Report, that however desirous they may feel of affording every possible facility to the accomplishment of the object which is at present in view, they are yet of opinion that they are not justified in delivering a copy of such Report.

I am further directed to inform you, that impressed as the Committee are, with a strong sense of the extent of the evil in question, and with every possible desire to suggest a remedy, they are yet apprehensive that the Committee appointed by the Court of Common Council, in turning their attention to the Hospital of Bridewell, are not aware of the limited accommodation which (consistently with the other objects of that Foundation) can be afforded to females of the description pointed out by the above-mentioned Petition, there being only fifteen cells on the side of the prison appropriated to females, and two rooms occupied as a night and day-room by the persons sent by the Magistrates under the authority

authority of an Act of Parliament, to be passed to their respective parishes; and although one of those rooms might be converted so as to contain about twenty-five females, yet the Committee apprehend they should not be warranted in diverting such room from its present purpose as a permanent measure, inasmuch as in time of peace, and particularly in the winter season, the number of Passes are increased far beyond the present amount.

I have the honour to be,

With great regard, Sir,

Your most obedient humble Servant,

John Poynder.

Bridewell Hospital,
New Bridge-street,
Feb. 22, 1814.

Henry Woodthorpe, esq.

Upon the reading of the answer, we your Committee were much surprised and disappointed, and Mr. Alderman Wood, and other Members, Governors of Bridewell Hospital, being present, stated they were fully convinced some misunderstanding must have taken place on the construction of the Town Clerk's letter, or such an answer would never have been directed to be sent to a Committee of the Corporation of the City of London, and there could be no pretence whatever for keeping any of the transactions of that Hospital a secret from the public; and Mr. Alderman Wood felt so assured that the Governors at large would afford every assistance to obtain the object so much desired by your Committee, that he would instantly apply for a General Court to be holden at Bridewell, to take into consideration the application of the Committee, and to give the answers required.

That at a subsequent meeting of your Committee, Mr. Alderman Wood informed us, that he had applied to Sir Richard Garr Glynn, baronet, the President of Bridewell Hospital, who most readily gave directions (even without a requisition) for a special General Court to be holden on Monday the 7th day of March instant; and it being necessary, according to the Regulations of the said Governors, that when a special General Court was called, the objects of the meeting should be expressly stated in the summons, together with the substance of the motions intended to be made upon the occasion; he had prepared the same, and transmitted them to the Clerk of the Hospital, and the following Summons was issued accordingly.

Bridewell and *Bethlem* Hospitals, February 25, 1814.

You are requested to meet at a Special Court to be holden at Bridewell Hospital on Monday, the 7th day of March next, at eleven o'clock in the forenoon, to consider of an application made by a Committee appointed by the Court of Common Council of the City of London, to the Committee of these Hospitals, relative to the nuisance of common Prostitutes frequenting the public streets, and also to consider of the answer given by the Committee of these Hospitals to such application, when the following motions, of which notice has been given by a Governor, are intended to be made; *viz.*

That the application made by the Committee appointed by the Common Council, including the Petition and the Answer by Mr. Poynder to that application, be read:

" That a copy of the Report of the Select Committee in 1798, alluded to in that Letter, be
" furnished the said Committee, together with as full and explicit an answer to the
" several questions therein as can be given:

" That this Court feel it their bounden duty to promote as far as they have the means, the
" great object proposed by the Petitioners to the Court of Common Council, and to adopt
" such regulations in Bridewell Hospital as may enable them to accommodate as many
" persons, that may be committed by the Magistrates, as they possibly can:

" That it be referred to the Committee of these Hospitals, to give answers to the ques-
" tions proposed by the Committee of the Court of Common Council, and if they see
" necessary, to confer with that Committee, and also to consider what regulations would
" be proper to be adopted agreeably to the foregoing Resolutions."

John Poynder, Clerk.

Mr. Alderman Wood further stated, that at the General Court which was held agreeably to the above Summons, he found it unnecessary to make the first of the intended questions, in consequence of the Minutes of the House Committee being according to custom read at the Court, in which were inserted the application of the Committee with the Petition presented to this Honourable Court, and the answer written by Mr. Poynder thereto, and his two following motions being rejected, the fourth was not moved.

That although we your Committee were fully aware of the nature of the Report of the Select Committee of Governors of Bridewell Hospital, appointed in the year 1798; yet we conceived that it was not only most proper, but most respectful to the Governors, to obtain the information by application to themselves, and inasmuch as they have by their measures refused us the necessary information, we have by the favour of an individual been furnished with a printed copy of the said Report, which we have caused to be copied and hereunto annexed, for the information of this honourable Court, in Appendix, No. 2.

We having therefore duly considered the Letters Patent founding the Royal Hospital of Bridewell, and the Report of the said Select Committee of the Governors, do not hesitate to declare, that it is the bounden duty of the Governors of Bridewell Hospital to carry into effect many of the recommendations contained in the said Report; it being in their power

to

to furnish sufficient and convenient places of confinement and employment for a far greater number of those profligate characters, than it is at all probable will be committed to their care and charge.

Your Committee therefore feel assured that there exists no impediment to the efficient administration of the laws regarding this description of offenders; and that should they be found persisting in their abandoned practices, the Hospital of Bridewell can afford all the facilities which the Magistrates or the public can desire, for their confinement, employment, and reform, which the laws provide for; so as the parties may be restrained, punished, or amended, and the petitioners gratified in their wishes, by a total removal of an evil from our public streets, so truly disgraceful in itself; and, as has been found, so injurious to the best interests of the youth of this City, and of society at large. All which we submit to the judgment of this Honourable Court. Dated this 23d day of March 1814.

Sam¹ Nash, Jn° Will. Goss, C. W. Hick, A. Young, Thomas Price, J. Jacks, James Pearsall, Samˡ Hale, Philip Green, Thoˢ Vallance, F. Paynter, Joseph Daw, Edwᵈ Frisby, Mʷ Wood, James Davies, Thomas Dornford, Thoˢ Harper, J. Daker, Chaˢ Foster, Willᵐ Sowerby, Chaˢ Martin, Samˡ Favell.

Appendix, N° 1.—Extracts from the Letters Patent respecting *Bridewell* Hospital.

" And also full power and authority to examine all and singular persons idly wandering
" within the City aforesaid, and the Liberties thereof, and to employ snd exercise themselves
" according to their strength in honest employment."

" And further, we give and grant for us, our heirs and successors, to the aforesaid
" Mayor and Commonalty and Citizens of our City of London aforesaid, and their
" successors for ever, that it will may and shall be lawful, as well for the aforesaid Mayor
" and Commonalty and Citizens for the time being, as for the said and such Officers,
" Ministers and Governors, which the aforesaid Mayor and Commonalty and Citizens
" aforesaid shall appoint and ordain, from time to time, to be Officers, Ministers, or
" Governors under them, of the said Manor or House called Bridewell Place, or of those
" other Houses or Hospitals assigned as aforesaid, for the Poor aforesaid; and of two or
" three of them altogether, hereafter from time to time, as well within the city of London
" aforesaid, and the suburbs thereof, as within our said county of Middlesex, diligently
" to look after and examine by all ways and means, by which they may the better know
" according to their prudence and discretion, all and all manner of suspected Houses,
" Taverns, Inns, Gaming Houses, Plays, Dancers, and others Places whatsoever and
" Liberty or Liberties, and whatsoever privileged Places within the said City and Suburbs
" thereof, and in our said county of Middlesex, by whatsoever name or titles they,
" or any of them, are or shall be named or called; and also to search and inquire after
" all and singular Houses in any manner suspected, or Places whatsoever for idle Ruffians,
" idle Rioters, Vagabonds and sturdy Beggars, or whatsoever other Persons suspected,
" and Men or Women whatsoever of bad Name and Fame, and not only to apprehend the
" said Ruffians, Rioters, Vagabonds, and Beggars, within the said suspected Houses or
" Places, Liberty or Liberties, and privileged Places being within the said City and
" Suburbs thereof, or within the said county of Middlesex; but also the Tenants,
" Masters, Owners or Keepers of such Houses or Places where any shall be found, to
" commit to the House of Correction and Bridewell, or in any other manner to punish all
" such as to them shall seem good and lawful, unless the Tenants, Masters, Owners or
" Keepers of such Houses and Places can honestly and justly excuse and acquit themselves
" before the aforesaid Mayor and Aldermen of the said City, for the time being, or before
" the Officers, Ministers, or Governors under them, of the aforesaid Houses, why they so
" maintain and support such idle Ruffians and suspected Persons and Vagabonds, or per-
" mit them to lie in and frequent their Houses. And also unless such Men so suspected,
" and being Vagabonds so taken, can sufficiently and fully declare for his honest and
" good conversation, and give a just account how they live, and for what cause they so
" wander and daily frequent such suspected Houses, and hidden or prohibited places, and
" find sufficient Security, that they and every of them behave themselves honestly for the
" future."

Appendix, N° 2.—The Report of the Select Committee appointed by a General Court of Governors of the Royal Hospitals of *Bridewell* and *Bethlem*, on the first day of March last, " To inquire and Report whether, and by what Means the Estates and " Revenues of the House of *Bridewell*, can be appropriated with greater effect than " at present, to the Benefit of its original and proper Objects, conformable to the " beneficent Intention of the Royal Founder, and our Ancestors."

To the Right Honourable the Lord Mayor, President, the Worshipful the Treasurer, and Governors of the Hospital of *Bridewell*.

My Lord and Gentlemen,

YOUR COMMITTEE in the discharge of their duty, and in order to lay the most permanent and solid foundation they are able, for the appropriation of the estates and revenues of the House of Bridewell, to the benefit of its original and proper objects, conformable to the beneficent intention of the Royal Founder, and our Ancestors; have proceeded to inquire into the nature and extent of such intention, and, in the progress of that inquiry,

inquiry, your Committee beg leave to refer to four Instruments, all of the year 1552, as the documents from which the original constitution of Bridewell is to be ascertained, *viz.*

1st.—A Supplication of the Poor, addressed to the Privy Council, in favour of the foundation of Bridewell:

2d.—A Declaration, made to the Privy Council by the Citizens of London, concerning the uses to which Bridewell was intended to be applied:

3d.—An Indenture of the 12th of June 1552, between King Edward the VIth, and the Corporation of London, concerning the intended Grant of Bridewell, for the purpose stated in the Declaration above-mentioned; and,

4th.—The Grant and Charter of Bridewell, made by King Edward the VIth, on the 26th day of June 1552, " for the furtherance, amplifying, and increase of so honest and noble " a Work."

That it appears to your Committee, that soon after the granting of this Charter, King Edward the VIth died, without any variation having been made in his intentions as expressed and explained in the said Charter, and the preceding instruments on which the same was grounded; and that no other alteration of competent authority has been since made in the constitution of Bridewell Hospital, except by an Act passed in the twenty-second year of the present reign, whereby the government of the said Hospital was declared to be vested in the Mayor and Aldermen of the City of London for the time being, and twelve Common Council of the said City, to be annually named by the Court of Common Council; together with the then acting Governors and their successors, to be elected at the general Courts of the said Hospital.

That it appears to your Committee, that the original foundation of Bridewell was " to " reform beggary, by opening an house of occupations, and by making some general pro- " vision of work wherewith the willing poor may be exercised, and whereby the froward, " strong, and sturdy vagabond may be compelled to live profitably to the commonwealth;" and that it made part of a general plan for relieving and correcting the distresses and infirmities of human nature, by different establishments within the metropolis;—One, a seminary for the education of fatherless youth at Christ's Hospital;—Another, an house of recovery at St Thomas's Hospital, " for taking out of the streets the miserable, aged, sore, and sick " persons; and the same to harbour, and by physic and surgery to cure and make whole." And the third Hospital, that of Bridewell, being the most needful and necessary of the three, an house of occupations, " wherein, first, the child, when he is brought up and grown " to years, and found unapt to learning, neither any honest person desireth, or would have " his service, may there be exercised and occupied." Secondly, " Where the sore and " sick, when they may be cured," may be protected and employed, until their entire recovery, and, " not be suffered to wander as vagabonds in the commonwealth, as " they had been accustomed:" And, Thirdly, " Where shall be brought the sturdy and the " idle, and likewise such prisoners as are quit at the Sessions, that there they may be set to " labour."

That, in the above-mentioned Declaration, it is expressed, that " the ordinary officers in " this house, shall be certain persons, to whom a convenient stipend shall be given, who shall " be called Task-masters and Task-mistresses; these shall be such honest persons as are " expert in such sciences and occupations as shall there be exercised; and they shall take " the charge of every man's task and proportion of work that shall be daily limited and " appointed for them to do; and these shall have power to correct and punish such as are " under their task, if they loiter and be found negligent: There shall also be persons elected " (one of the number of poor artificers, such as have led an honest life and of upright deal- " ing) who shall put in surety to the treasurer, for such stock of wares and stuff as shall be " delivered unto them, to be made and wrought; there shall also be other ordinary officers, " as porters, cooks, stewards, &c. to whom likewise shall be given convenient stipends."

That your Committee is of opinion, that a judicious economical use of Bridewell Hospital and its estates, according to the intentions of the Royal Founder, as expressed in the said Charter, and the other Instruments above referred to (with exception only of such legacies and benefactions as have a peculiar and appropriate application) would have a very great effect in the diminution of vice and misery, and in the increase of industry and good habits of life, within the metropolis; and that the persons, particularly and specifically marked out, as the objects of the trusts created by the Founder of Bridewell, are, at the present time, in the greatest want of it, to the greatest increase of beggary, and to the disgrace and detriment of the community; viz. idle, uneducated youth, of both sexes, who are advancing to maturity, and are becoming profligate and vicious for want of character or occupation; convalescents from hospitals, who require gentle employments and nourishing food, to recover entirely their health and strength, and the means and power of labour; and discharged prisoners, and other prisoners, who not having character, or the means of honest employment, are frequently reduced to the dreadful alternative, either to steal or starve.

That, in order to diminish the number of beggars, and of idle and dissolute persons, as well as to reform beggary, it is the opinion of your Committee, that some general plan or provision for work, should be adopted and encouraged within the walls of this Hospital, wherewith the willing poor may more usefully to themselves and to the public be employed than they are at present, and whereby the froward, strong and hardy vagabond may be induced to live with increased comfort to himself, and with increased profit to the commonwealth.

That your Committee is of opinion, that with economical management, particularly in the articles of clothing and food, a small revenue may be sufficient for great and extensive purposes; that by a marked distinction between the industrious and idle, and between the vicious

and

and the well disposed, and by affording countenance and favour to those who endeavour to do well, reform may be effected; that by example, by encouragement, and by holding forth the purposes of an improved condition of life, the energy and industry of man may be awakened and brought into action in any situation, and under any circumstances. And lastly, that by disinterested kindness and attention, the affection, the confidence, and the implicit reliance of the poor, may be obtained.

That, in carrying into execution the intentions of the founder of Bridewell, it will be necessary that a complete separation should take place between the different classes, and sexes, of the persons that have been enumerated; and first, that two separate Establishments be recommended to be made, for the employment of young persons of each sex, dividing them again according to their behaviour and improvement: Secondly, that as to convalescents from hospitals, distinct apartments be provided for each sex, and employment given to them: Thirdly, that separate places be prepared for persons of each sex discharged from prisons, or committed to hard labour, and that those persons respectively have a reasonable and liberal proportion of the profits of their labour reserved for them, on their good behaviour, and paid them on their being discharged, in order to enable them to set off in a course of honest and useful employment, subject only to a small deduction or deductions, if thought proper, on account of their diet and clothing.

That the execution of this plan would be very much assisted, and the means extended, by a system of recommending and helping such persons (as fast as they merit it) to situations in which they may find employment and a livelihood, as thereby the apartments and the funds would be sooner ready for new objects; at the same time, by a wise and liberal encouragement to labour and good conduct, and by an economical system of diet, many of the persons would nearly maintain themselves, and all would be earning something, and be supported in the house at a much less expense than they now are.

That, it is the sacred and inviolable duty of the acting Governors, to apply the funds and buildings of Bridewell Hospital, for the original purposes of the institution, as far as they will extend and are required; and in case they prove inadequate, and more is wanted for purposes so useful, the Public, being duly impressed with the idea, that the Governors are seriously and earnestly engaged in so great and necessary a work, your Committee has no doubt but that the liberality of individuals will soon supply the deficiency.

That, in the arrangement and execution of any plan for appropriating with greater effect the estates and revenues of the House of Bridewell, it will be nesessary to proceed with caution, as to the practicability of the proposed measures; and with foresight as to the competency of the means for carrying them effectually into execution, leaving the further extension of the plan to future consideration, when its practicability and expense shall have been experimentally ascertained, but so as not to extend it beyond the income of the charity.

That, upon examining Mr. Hudson, the Steward and Receiver of the rents of Bridewell Hospital, it appears, that upon an average for five years last, there has been annually received by rents, dividends, annuities, and benefactions (exclusive of Lock's and Fowke's Gifts) the sum of 4,451 l. 0s. 4d. and that there had been annually expended during the like period, upon an average, the several sums following, viz. Arts-masters and Apprentices (exclusive of their houses, repairs and taxes) 192 l. 6s. 10¾ d. Salaries, Gratuities, and clothing Beadles 1,047 l. 3s. 11¼ d. Taxes, Repairs and Rent of Burial Ground 423 l. 0s. 11d. For Printing, Coals, Stationary, Tradesmen's Bills, and two annual Feasts, 331 l. 9s. 9¼ d. And in the maintenance of Vagrants, the sum of 701 l. 3s. 10¾ d. amounting together to the sum of 2,695 l. 5s. 5d. which being deducted from the annual average Receipt, leaves a Balance of 1,755 l. 14s. 11 d. So that your Committee is of opinion that by a judicious and economical use of the funds of the Charity, not only vagrants may be maintained, but all the other beneficent intentions of our pious and benevolent ancestors may be attained, without interfering with the Funds arising from Lock's and Fowke's Benefactions.

That, in the forming any new arrangement at Bridewell, it will be proper to make use of the present existing accommodation, and of the persons now on the Establishment, as far as may be done, and not to remove any person, or vary any thing in the house, if such person or thing can be effectually and properly applied towards the execution of the original plan of Bridewell, which your Committee apprehends must be adhered to as far as is practicable, and its benefits are wanted by that part of the community for which it was intended: And, that by so making use of such accommodation and persons, the Corporation may save expense in the outset, and avoid, as to individuals who have been long on their establishment, the dismission of them, in case they prove willing and able to assist effectually and usefully in promoting the objects of the institution.

That your Committee has thought it necessary to inquire into what effects have been produced in Bridewell, by the present expenditure, but not with the view, or consequence, of criminating any individual, as they have the satisfaction of being able to say that any existing defects in Bridewell, arise from an improper system of operation, rather than from the misconduct of any person employed; and that the blame, if any, is to be imputed to the system of management and not to the persons to whom the execution has been entrusted. But, as the defects of that system cannot be properly corrected, without their being detailed and explained, your Committee has thought it necessary to go into an inquiry on that subject, and to state to the Court the effects of that inquiry.

That your Committee finds, that instead of the two classes of persons mentioned in the Declaration, viz. Task-masters and Task-mistresses to attend to the work within the house, and poor artificers to be supplied with work out of the house, certain persons have

been

been introduced into the Establishment, called Arts-masters, who have been accommodated, free of rent, repairs, and taxes, with houses and other advantages within the Hospital, on condition of their taking, and instructing, a certain number of Apprentices.

That these persons were originally useful parts of the Institution, being at one time under agreement to retain, each of them, twenty Apprentices, to be named by the Governors, viz. in the year 1708, when these Arts-masters had one hundred and forty Apprentices at one time; a circumstance that might have had very beneficial effects in providing for one of the original objects of the Charity, " idle, uneducated youth for the Metropolis, " advancing to maturity without character or occupation."

That, during the preceding period of thirty-one years, from 1767 to the 22d of December 1798, there have been one hundred and seventy-three lads Apprentices to the Arts-masters: that of these, there have been, during the same period, as many as one hundred and eleven, who have served out their time; of the remainder, fifty-eight have run away, (some of whom are at sea:) four have died; and none now remain in the House.

That, of the one hundred and eleven Apprentices who have served out their time, five only are Master-workmen, fifty-nine are Journeymen, eight are Servants, thirteen in the Army or Navy, ten in various other situations, and sixteen have died: but of them, as many as seventy-five have received from Lock and Fowke's Charity, the gifts of 20 *l.* each, under the allegation of having actually set up in business; a circumstance that has been required to entitle them to those Donations.

That the other persons in the House are Vagrants taken up in London, and committed for a month or some other period to hard labour. That the permanent average amount of such vagrant and disorderly persons (whose number are nearly equal) is fifteen men and twenty-five women, at one time with another, during the last four years. That, during the same period, the yearly average number of Vagrants committed for seven days has been 1,042. Of disorderly persons committed for a longer time 309, and that the produce of the whole of their labour, during the same period, has been on an average of the four years 19 *l.* 3 *s.* 1½*d.* a year, which at the rate above stated of the general average of forty persons containing in the house, does not amount to so much as ten shillings a head for the year's produce of the labour of each individual: That the average expense of the maintenance of these persons, amounts at present to the sum of 582 *l.* a year, being fixed at an allowance of nine-pence a day for each person; and that the salaries of the Task-master and Task-mistresses, appointed to deliver out their work, but who were discharged for misbehaviour in April 1797, amounted to 65 *l.* a year.

That no other employment is provided for the persons confined in Bridewell, except picking oakum, and beating hemp, in which they earn on an average not quite a penny a day; though there are few of them at the period of life, or in a state of health to be disabled from labour; as is the case with most of the inhabitants of Poor Houses and of other Hospitals. That this employment is not so profitable as to allow them any compensation or encouragement out of it, or of a nature to fit them to obtain their own livelihood when they are discharged from the House.

That your Committee is aware of the difficulty of obtaining labour for such description of persons as those usually confined in Bridewell, but relying on the examples of success that have been afforded in similar places, they do not despair of the consequences of an attempt to introduce into Bridewell a system of labour that shall be productive, not only of emolument to the establishment, and to all the individuals employed in it, but of benefit to the persons employed, by enabling them, when discharged, to earn their livelihood in future. Though however your Committee thinks it not proper to despair of that, which has been afforded in other instances where the attempt has been properly made, yet they conceive it is imprudent to form too great expectations of the facility of the undertaking, or of the completeness of the success that may attend it.

That a considerable loss and inconvenience is occasioned by the precise periods for which the different persons in Bridewell are fixed there, viz. the Vagrants committed for seven days, the disorderly persons generally, for a month; and the Apprentices bound to their trade for seven years: That if the Vagrants could be sent home as soon as convenient, a considerable expense of maintenance would be saved: and your Committee observes, that in so short a period, their labour is capable of little or no profit, and they cannot receive any improvement or reform: that if disorderly persons were committed for a longer period than they now are, with a discretionary power of shortening that period, in case of their good behaviour, and of the means of employment being afforded them out of the house, a greater degree of real reform, and of profitable labour would be obtained: and lastly, if Boys and Girls could be taught some easy and useful employment in a shorter period, more young persons might be endowed with the means of an honest livelihood, than can be in the present mode of an apprenticeship for seven years.

Your Committee observes with great concern, that there is no appearance, and very little prospect, of any reform or amendment being effected, upon the present system, upon any of the persons in Bridewell; and that some of them, of the women at least, are likely to continue for some time an expense to the establishment. It appears one great defect of the present system, is, that in Bridewell there is no distinction, either in food or in treatment, between the idle and the industrious, and between the profligate and the well-disposed; but that those who are capable and would be willing to work, receive the same diet, the same unprofitable task, and the same uniform measure with those who persevere in the dis-

graceful

graceful resolution of living as the drones of society, on the labour of others. It appears also that the prisoners receive no share whatever of their earnings, either given at the time as a present gratification and inducement to exertion, or husbanded for them until they quit the house, and then applied as the means of placing them in a way of livelihood. Your Committee however is aware that the present produce of their labour, is not of any amount to allow them any benefit out of it; at the same time it cannot help referring to the regulations of the Houses of Correction of Dorchester, Oxford, and Gloucester, and to those of some other well-regulated establishments of that kind, where the gradations of diet are in proportion to the earnings and good behaviour of the prisoner, and where a large and liberal share of his earnings is reserved for him to set him off, on quitting the House, in an advantageous course of industry and occupation.

That in the case of " Convalescents from Hospitals," a class of persons which was one of the original objects of its institution) and is now entitled to its protection and very deserving of attention. It is within the observation of those who have attended to the circumstances of beggars, that many of the most deserving and necessitous of them, are persons from hospitals, from which they they have been discharged without the power of labour, or the means of support; and who for want of such an asylum as Bridewell was intended to be, have been driven to solicit the charity of the public, as street beggars : That (such is the infirmity of human nature) those who have in that manner discovered a successful and easy trade, are not likely to discontinue it, and return to a course of labour, unless some assistance or encouragement is afforded them for that purpose; and from the unfortunate disposition of too many of our fellow creatures, if the pauper does not receive charitable relief under such distressed circumstances, he is in many instances induced to prey upon the public for his subsistence; and, to use the language of the rules of the House of Bridewell, drawn up in the year 1557; being " set at liberty in the highways, is made of a " sick beggar, a whole thief."

That, the expense and difficulty of providing, according to the original plan, for convalescents upon the establishment, would be inconsiderable; as they are of a description of persons who do not in general require reform or correction; but only want an asylum and reception, and that, for a short time; that being many of them artisans, instructed in a trade, and almost all of them habituated to employment, some of them might be able to earn more than the cost of their diet, if economically managed, would amount to; to whom the surplus of their earnings given them on quitting the hospital, could be an aid and support to them, until they could get into a course of employment. That the number of persons wanting this relief, would be very soon diminished by the application of it, and the hospitals in the metropolis greatly relieved; as it is a known fact, that many patients, for want of the means of entire recovery of health and strength on quitting one hospital, have soon been obliged to apply for admission into another; in any event the application of a limited annual sum for this purpose, out of the revenues of Bridewell, would in the opinion of your Committee be conformable to the intentions of the royal founder, and extremely beneficial to the public.

That there is yet another description of individuals, who are peculiar and original objects of the establishment at Bridewell, " persons discharged from prisons," who, returning into society without the habits or means of employment, without friends, without money, and without character, are driven to commit desperate crimes, in order to prolong a miserable existence : it is due to these poor creatures, to the community, to ourselves, and the memory of our royal founder, that his expressed intentions in behalf of them should be carried into effect. More difficulty and perhaps more expense, will attend the reform and management of these persons, than of the class before mentioned; but that which has been effected in other places, should not be despaired of in Bridewell. Your Committee therefore is of opinion, that another limited part of the income, and of the accommodation of the hospital, should be set apart for so important and necessary a purpose.

That in order to execute the plan intended to be recommended to the Court by your Committee, it will be proper that a General Committee be appointed by the Court; and, that in arrangement of any measures for the due application of the revenues of Bridewell, it will be essential to divide the several objects of attention between different Sub-Committees, to be elected out of such General Committee, and to be independent of each other; each responsible to the General Committee, as that Committee will be answerable to the general Court. That the Sub-Committee should consist of five persons each, one of whom should be the victor for the time, and two, sufficient for dispatch of business at the prefixed times for the meeting of the Committee. That in the appointment of these Committees, those Governors should be preferred, whose local situation, and personal inclination, would be most likely to secure a regular and convenient attendance; and, that in case of any member of the Sub-Committee declaring, that it is not convenient for him to attend, a new member be thereupon appointed from the General Committee.

That Minutes be made of every act done by such Committees respectively, with the reasons thereof; and that the Minutes of every Sub-Committee be read, for approbation, at the next meeting of the General Committee; and the Minutes of all such Committees be read (if called for) at the next General Court of the Hospital, for its approbation; and that, subject to the regulations of the Hospital, and to the orders of the General Committee, the Sub-Committee have a discretion, as to the matters committed to them in every measure, which, with the reasons, shall have been so entered on their Minutes.

That with regard to the occupation and improvement of one of the original objects of

Bridewell,

Bridewell, " uneducated Youth advancing to maturity without the means of Livelihood," it appears to your Committee, that, as to Boys, more benefit may be obtained, by preparing, clothing, and fitting them out for the navy, or for service, or for manufactures, than from any profit to be derived from their work. At the same time, as the habit of occupation leads to industry and good courses of life, it will be proper to keep them in employment ; though, in the arrangement of it, regard should be had, rather to placing them out properly and speedily, in a course of livelihood, than to producing any considerable emolument from their labour.

That upon the admission of uneducated Boys on the establishment, it will be necessary to place them, at first, in an inferior class, where some ordinary unskilled labour may be ready for them, and where they may receive preparatory instruction with an inferior order of diet; and that as soon as they manifest a desire and capacity of being removed, they be promoted to another class, from whence, as their inclinations and abilities become known, they may be removed into the naval class, or into that either for service or manufacture, in which they should be placed out as soon as opportunity offers.

That looking after either to the character or improvement of these Boys, your Committee conceive that the establishment for them should be separated from Bridewell, and be considered as a " School of Occupation," for the uneducated children of the poor of the metropolis; that from such a school, children would be placed out better, more easily, and with more credit in life, than from Bridewell, or any House of Correction.

That the application of a proportional part of the revenues of the Hospital (not specifically appropriated by the donors) to the above-mentioned purpose, would have a great effect in removing young lads, at a critical age, from scenes of temptation and profligacy ; and in thereby diminishing the source, not merely of petty thefts, but of atrocious crimes, in the metropolis. That it appears to your Committee to be unnecessary to enumerate the causes which, in London, produce objects for such a charity, as, in a very populous city in an advanced state of society and civilization, the calamities and infirmity of human nature must require continued exertion to counteract the corruption of manners, and the prevalence of vice and idleness ; that there is however one class of unhappy lads who have peculiar claims on such an establishment, the apprentices of chimney sweepers, whose apprenticeships, and means of livelihood, cease at the age of sixteen years ; when they become unfitted by their size for the only employment they have been taught; and are in too many instances driven to a profligate and vicious course of life, by the want, not only of education and protection, but of the mere necessaries of life.

That as to the Girls, who may be entitled to protection and employment in this Charity, a greater difficulty may attend the placing them out in the world, but that the establishment of a spinning, knitting and sewing school, for supplying the different persons on the establishment, and those in Bethlem Hospital, or any other Charity ; and also for selling to the poor at a reduced price, not only coarse linen and hose, but all the common and necessary articles of women's dress, and the appropriation of a limited part of the revenues of the Hospital, in the support of such an establishment, would be beneficial to the community, and at the same time conformable to the intentions expressed in the original documents respecting Bridewell. That the produce of the work of such a school would not be inconsiderable ; it appearing, by the statement of one of the members of the Committee, that the average produce of the sewing-work of the elder girls, at the Foundling Hospital, (whose ages were from eleven to fourteen years) was, in the year 1797, on an average, about 12 l. each, and that the average of all the girls employed in sewing-work, though more of them were under than above ten years of age, amounted to 5 l. 14 s. each, per annum.

That Convalescents from Hospitals constitute the next class of the original objects of Bridewell, which was intended, amongst other things, as an asylum " for the Sore and Sick until their entire recovery." For them it appears to be best that work should be provided, under the direction of the Sub-Committee, for that part of the establishment ; and that they should have the profit of their work husbanded for them respectively, against the time of their quitting the House, subject only to a small allowance for their diet. That though there would be little or no difficulty in inducing persons of this description to work, yet, as the periods of their continuance in the House of Convalescence would be short and uncertain, not exceeding in general ten days or a fortnight, the profits of their work must be inconsiderable.

That as to Convalescents, your Committee conceive that a preference should be given to those applying from St. Thomas's Hospital ; and in the next place, to those applying from any hospital within the city of London ; (and if after provision made for such cases, more vacancies occur) then for convalescents from any hospitals in or about the metropolis ; that in recommending an establishment for convalescents, your Committee has satisfaction in referring to a similar establishment at the General Hospital of Barcelona, where for convalescents (to cite Mr. Townsend's Journey through Spain, vol. i. page 132.) " A separate habitation is provided, that after they are dismissed from the sick wards, as cured of their diseases, they may have time to recruit their strength before they are turned out to endure their accustomed hardships and to get their bread by labour." Your Committee has however the satisfaction to observe, while they commend the humanity and utility of such an establishment, that, as it may be to Barcelona, it was in plan, conception and intention, anticipated by the wisdom and policy of our ancestors.

That for the third class of persons, who were the original objects of Bridewell, " the " sturdy and the idle, and likewise such prisoners as are quit at the Sessions," the local

situation

situation and the accommodation of Bridewell, seem to be well adapted: That, besides the separation of the sexes, and of the different classes of persons, it appears to your Committee to be expedient that there should be some general labour, not requiring skill or instruction, for those who are not capable and desirous of being employed in any other more profitable work: That for these there should be an inferiority of condition, as to diet, accommodation, and clothing, in order to induce them to endeavour to obtain and preserve a situation in one of the other classes, and to make them avoid, what would be the consequence of misbehaviour in the other classes, their being reduced again to the inferior class.

That there is a part of the third class, which though discredited by the general name of Vagrants, is composed of persons very different in character, conduct, and circumstances; the honest and unfortunate sufferer being confounded with the vicious and profligate, who have abandoned their families, their parishes, and the places where their labour and industry might be useful: That the sentence of a week's idleness and confinement to all of them, at the same time that it is too favourable for one part of them, is severity and injustice to the others, therefore your Committee is of opinion, that a more strict judicial inquiry ought to be made into the cases of vagrants committed to Bridewell; and, while the unfortunate and blameless passenger is favoured by a speedy and comfortable return to his or her own parish, the rogue and vagabond should receive that proper correction, which might, by its example, prevent the resort of the idle and profligate to the metropolis.

That the most essential and most difficult part of such a reform, as your Committee have the honour of being employed to consider and report upon, is the providing suitable and profitable occupation for the different persons to be employed. In the first place, they would propose a slop shop for making clothing for the men in the house, and for the boys, who should be fitted out and sent to sea, or into any other situation; and also for supplying Bethlem Hospital and other public institutions with articles of clothing.

Your Committee has to add, in the next place, the suggestion of a cheap linen shop, which might furnish sewing work for the female part of the establishments, and from whence the hospitals of Bridewell and Bethlem, and any other public bodies who approved of the plan of employment, as a measure of general utility, might be supplied with linen, and all articles of plain and useful attire for the female sex.

That for this part of the establishment, it would be expedient to solicit the protection and inspection of those ladies, whose benevolence interests them in the forlorn situation of the unemployed female poor; and if more occupation were wanting, a sufficiency might be obtained by selling to the poor at a reduced price, as is done at Hartingfordbury in Herts, and at Bamburgh Castle, in Northumberland, in both instances with as much individual charity and relief to the poor who purchase, as advantage and occupation to the charities who supply them.

That if other means of employment are wanting, your Committee would suggest the resumption of the spinning wheels, and twine wheels, the making of coarse serviceable hats and mats, the preparing of candlewicks for tallow-chandlers, and a large rope and twine yard in a convenient place within the hospital. And for that general labour which should be provided for the inferior class at Bridewell, your Committee is of opinion, that the introduction of corn hand mills into the hospital, would be a better and much more productive species of labour than that which is now used.

That your Committee is informed that the labour of one man will in four hours grind a bushel of corn, and that two persons will with ease grind the same quantity in two hours and a half. Your Committee therefore submits that this kind of labour will answer a great deal better than that of picking oakum; an employment calculated to promote habits of distress and idleness, rather than of cleanliness and exertion. That the task of corn to be ground by each person in the day, might be kept separate and distinct from his cell, and have no other communication than the handle through the wall, and that when his daily task was done, he might, if he chose, be supplied with more work, the profits of which he should have reserved for him: That by such a species of labour, not only the two united hospitals might be supplied with good and genuine flour, but such a quantity sent into the consumption of the market, as might have a tendency to reduce the price of bread.

That your Committee is apprehensive, that the Arts-masters cannot, at least in their present situation, be made useful to the establishment; your Committee however apprehends that if they and their houses can be made useful in the execution of such a plan as may be adopted, and in case they are willing and able to assist in carrying into effect such plan, it may be proper that they should have a preference in that respect: That in the trades which it may be found expedient to exercise in the hospital, Arts-masters skilled therein might be of essential service in conducting the same upon terms of contract, beneficial to themselves and also to the hospital.

That in the reform of human nature, much may be done, not only by reward and encouragement, but also by economy and gradations of diet, upon the plan adopted in the Dorchester Gaol and House of Correction; where those who do not evince a willingness to work, have an inferior degree of food and accommodation; and those whose work is profitable, receive a better diet and increase of comfort in proportion to their exertions and industry. That for the particulars of improved economy, with respect to diet, in this country, your Committee begs leave to refer the Court to the Reports of the Society for bettering the Condition of the Poor; from which it will appear that a very great saving may be made in that respect.

That considerable effect may be produced by apparent and real neatness in every object around,

around; for which purpose, your Committee recommends, in addition to personal and domestic cleanliness, the frequent and periodical whitewashing of all the apartments of Bridewell, as the means of inducing, and confirming habits of cleanliness and decency in the persons employed there; and, (your Committee thinks itself justified in adding) consequent habits of morality and industry.

That your Committee is of opinion, that the providing for the several persons who have been stated to be the original objects of this hospital, was the condition of the grant of Bridewell House, and its estates and revenues, and, (that except so far as the change of times and manners may have rendered any of the objects at present inapplicable) the Corporation is bound to apply their revenues for the benefit of reform of the three descriptions of persons above-mentioned, in proportion to their necessities and circumstances.

Your Committee submits the above Report to the Court, expressing its hopes, that if it is adopted, it may tend to appropriate the estates and revenues of Bridewell Hospital with greater effect than at present, to its original and proper objects, conformably to the beneficent intention of the Royal Founder, and our ancestors.

Thoˢ Bernard, Edward Spencer, J. Keysall, Peter Perchard, Nath. Wright, Robᵗ Precious, Martin Pearkes, W. Wallis, Walter Sterling, Ed. Bigg, Robᵗ Hunter, Richard Till, George Godwin.

Bridewell Hospital,⎫
January 28, 1799.⎭

WOOD, MAYOR.

A COMMON COUNCIL holden in the Chamber of the Guildhall of the City of *London*, on Wednesday the 17th day of January 1816;—The Committee appointed on the 16th day of December 1813, to examine the Allegations contained in the Petition of sundry Inhabitants, Householders of this City, relative to Common Prostitutes frequenting the public Streets, did this day deliver into this Court a further Report thereon, which was read and ordered to be printed, and a Copy thereof sent to every Member of this Court.

Woodthorpe.

To the Right Honourable the Lord Mayor, Aldermen and Commons, of the City of London, in Common Council assembled.

WE, whose Names are hereunto subscribed, of your Committee appointed on the 16th day of December 1813, to examine the Allegations contained in the Petition of sundry Inhabitant Householders of this City, relative to Common Prostitutes frequenting the public Streets, and to report our opinion thereon; do certify, That having made a Report which was ordered to be printed, this Honourable Court were pleased, on the 5th day of October 1814, unanimously to agree to certain Resolutions founded thereon, and to direct that they should be advertised in the London Morning and Evening Newspapers: and in compliance with the wishes of this Honourable Court, expressed in the said Resolutions, Sir William Domville, Baronet, the then Lord Mayor, issued the following Proclamation; *viz.*

DOMVILLE, MAYOR.

Mansion House, October 13, 1814.

" WHEREAS a Petition has been presented to the Court of Common Council, signed " by upwards of Two Thousand Inhabitant Householders of the City of London, com- " plaining of the great Nuisance occasioned by Common Prostitutes frequenting the public " Streets and Passages, in violation of public morals, and in breach of the Peace and " good Order of this City: And the said Court of Common Council requesting the " Lord Mayor would give such directions as would tend to prevent such violation of " Decency in future;—

" The Lord Mayor doth hereby warn such persons to avoid the commission of any of " the like Offences in future, upon pain of being proceeded against and punished with the " utmost rigour of the Law, and all Peace Officers are ordered to be aiding and assisting " herein.

" By Order of the Lord Mayor,
" *Francis Hobler.*"

WITH a view to promote the objects stated in the Resolutions of this Honourable Court, your Committee met, and directed a Copy of the said Proclamation to be put up in every Watch-house of this City, and agreed to sundry Resolutions which they sent to the Deputies and Common Council-men of the several Wards, and earnestly recommended

510.   them

them to take into their consideration the best means of carrying into full effect the said Resolutions of this Honourable Court, of the 5th day of October 1814, and particularly to procure to be appointed in their respective Wards, at the Wardmotes to be holden on Saint Thomas's Day then ensuing, Committees consisting of (in addition to themselves) two or more respectable inhabitants out of each Precinct, for the special purpose of attending to the important business of assisting the several Inquests in discovering and removing all houses of ill fame, and superintending the discharge of the duties of the Peace Officers, and also the state and conduct of Liquor Shops and Public Houses in their several Districts, and to report their proceedings from time to time to future Wardmotes; and we have the satisfaction of stating that several Wards appointed, agreeably to this recommendation, Committees, and published sundry Resolutions in the public Papers, expressive of their desire, and declaring their determination and readiness to adopt and enforce the measures recommended to them, and to carefully watch over the conduct of the Constables, Patrol, and other Night Officers, in that respect; and also that of the Liquor Shops and Public Houses, so frequently known to considerably contribute to the great evil complained of in the Petition so numerously signed, and presented unto this Honourable Court on the 16th day of December 1813.

We beg leave further to certify, that we have met repeatedly during the year, and have been attended from time to time by the Marshals, Marshalmen, and City Day and Night Patrol, who have reported to us the state of the City, and have afforded us that degree of information which has greatly assisted us in the prosecution of the desirable purpose of repressing as far as possible the evil complained of. That the several Members of this Committee have also exerted themselves in their respective Wards, and have reported to us at various times the state of their said Wards, and of the proceedings had therein, and from their information, as well as that of the Marshals, Marshalmen, and City Patrol, we have reason to believe that the evil has certainly been in a considerable degree diminished, particularly during the day-time; and by the zeal and activity of the various inquests in their respective Wards, a number of houses of ill fame have been discovered and presented to the Court of Lord Mayor and Aldermen, who with a promptitude becoming so important an object, directed them to be prosecuted by the City Solicitor at the City's expense, and in the course of the present year no less than seventeen indictments have been preferred against thirty individuals, fourteen of which indictments have already been prosecuted with effect, two remain to be tried, and in one instance only have the parties been acquitted, and this under circumstances which promise a speedy removal of the nuisance.

That notwithstanding these good effects have been already produced by the commendable exertions of the Common Council and Inquests in their respective Wards, and the prosecutions that have been carried on by the orders of the Court of Lord Mayor and Aldermen in the course of the present year, there remains much to be done; the evil yet exists so as to require those exertions to be continued with undiminished zeal, and your Committee have every reason to hope, if they are thus persevered in, the evil may be in a still greater degree removed from the City of London. For this purpose we beg to recommend that the Right honourable the Lord Mayor should be requested to issue a Proclamation in like manner as was done in the mayoralty of Sir William Domville, Baronet; and that the inquests to be appointed in the different Wards on Saint Thomas's Day next, should be urged by a consideration of the solemn oath which they take to discover and make known to the Court of Lord Mayor and Aldermen, all Houses of Ill Fame, and all disorderly Public or Victualling Houses, in order that legal steps may be taken for their removal.

We your Committee cannot conclude this Report without congratulating this Honourable Court upon the success which has already attended their unanimous Resolutions, and expressing a hope that by the decided testimony thus borne by the City of London against so great an evil, and by the continued exertions of the Magistracy, and all the subordinate Officers in their different departments, it may diminish still more and more, until (and at no distant period) it may cease to deform Society by its pernicious and dangerous influence. All which we submit to the judgment of this Honourable Court. Dated this 4th day of December 1815.

Claud° Stephen Hunter, Sam¹ Nash, Tho° Harper, Cha° Martin, James Davies, C. W. Hick, F. Paynter, Edw⁴ Frisby, Sam¹ Favell, James Pearsall, Will™ Sowerby, Thomas Dornford, James Jacks, W. Box, Edw⁴ Poynder.

Appendix, N° 13.

Accounts of COMMITMENTS to the several Prisons in the Cities of *London* and *Westminster*, and County of *Middlesex*; for the last Three Years.

(1.)—A Return of the Number of Persons COMMITTED to *Newgate* for the last Three Years; distinguishing each Year, and those committed for Felonies, Assaults, and other Misdemeanors; specifying the Number of Boys under the Age of Sixteen, and their respective Ages.

	Felony.	Misdemeanors.	Assaults.	GIRLS, 15 and under.	BOYS, of the AGE of							TOTAL.
					9.	10.	11.	12.	13.	14.	15.	
1812. December	149	9	-	5	-	-	-	1	1	—	—	
1813. January	129	2	-	3	-	-	1	-	1	3	3	
February	143	14	1	2	-	-	2	1	-	1	2	
April	218	12	-	3	-	-	-	-	-	-	4	
June	224	11	1	1	-	-	-	1	-	3	2	
July	159	8	-	2	-	-	-	1	2	1	2	
September	212	14	1	-	-	-	-	-	-	2	2	
October	218	4	-	3	1	-	-	1	-	2	3	
					1	3	3	2	5	11	18	
	1,452	**74**	**3**	**19**				43				**1,591**
1813. December	129	2	-	1	1	3	1	1	-	1	4	
1814. January	135	2	-	1	-	-	-	1	-	1	4	
February	136	11	-	1	2	1	1	5	2	2	3	
April	200	7	-	4	-	-	-	3	-	1	4 ... 1	
May	104	9	-	-	-	-	1	3	4	3	—	
July	173	9	-	1	-	-	-	-	1	3	4	
September	240	5	-	-	1	2	3	5	2	2	3	
October	194	4	-	1	-	1	-	4	1	2	1	
					4	8	12	19	11	15	20	
	1,311	**49**	**-**	**9**				89				**1,458**
1814. November	155	17	-	1	-	-	1	-	—	—	—	
1815. January	177	1	-	1	-	1	1	1	2	3	3	
February	181	10	-	1	-	1	2	2	1	2	7	
April	223	13	-	1	-	-	-	1	2	2	3	
May	130	4	-	1	-	-	1	-	4	1	1	
June	148	9	-	2	-	-	-	-	-	3	3	
September	340	21	1	2	-	1	1	1	4	6	5	
October	143	17	-	3	-	-	2	2	1	3	2	
					-	3	8	7	14	20	24	
	1,497	**92**	**1**	**12**				76				**1,678**
				Errors Excepted,			TOTAL					**4,727**

JN° A. NEWMAN,
Keeper of Newgate.

(2.)—An Account of the Number of Persons COMMITTED to the *Giltspur-street* Prison and House of Correction for the City of London (late Poultry and Giltspur-street Compters) from the 1st day of January 1816 to the 30th day of April 1816; distinguishing those committed for Felonies, Assaults and other Misdemeanors, together with the ages of such as have been committed by the Magistrates for want of Bail.

POULTRY SIDE, Taken before the Right Honble the Lord Mayor.					GILTSPUR-STREET SIDE, Taken before the sitting Alderman at Guildhall.				
	Felons.	Assaults.	Misde-meanors.	TOTAL.		Felons.	Assaults.	Misde-meanors.	TOTAL.
1816:					1816:				
January	49	28	237	314	January	50	29	70	149
February	49	21	166	236	February	38	22	54	114
March	56	21	159	236	March	36	23	88	147
April	60	10	134	204	April	25	21	78	124
	214	80	696	990		149	95	290	554
						214	80	696	990
					TOTAL	363	175	986	1,524

N. B.—The above Persons were committed by the Constables, and are called Charges in the first Instance; but their Ages are not taken, unless they are afterwards committed by the Magistrates for want of Bail, &c. as follows:

NUMBER and AGE of Persons COMMITTED to the *Giltspur-street* Prison by the Magistrates, for want of Bail, &c. within the period afore-mentioned:

Ages:	Felonies.	Assaults.	Misde-meanors.	TOTAL.
From 10 to 15	—	—	—	—
15 - 20	. .	1	1	2
20 - 25	. .	5	2	7
25 - 30	. .	7	3	10
30 - 35	. .	6	2	8
35 - 40	. .	4	3	7
40 - 45	. .	4	. .	4
45 - 50	1	1	2	4
50 - 55	. .	1	. .	1
55 - 60	—	—	—	—
TOTAL	1	29	13	43

NUMBER and AGE of Persons COMMITTED to the House of Correction within the period afore-mentioned.

Ages:	Felonies.	Assaults.	Misde-meanors.	TOTAL.
From 10 to 15	3	1	1	5
15 - 20	5	. .	. .	5
20 - 25	5	1	5	11
25 - 30	5	. .	1	6
30 - 35	1	1	2	4
35 - 40	2	. .	1	3
40 - 45	1	. .	. .	1
45 - 50	. .	. .	1	1
50 - 55	—	—	—	—
55 - 60	3	. .	. .	3
60 - 65	—	—	—	—
65 - 70	1	. .	. .	1
TOTAL	26	3	11	40

May 8th, 1816.

JOHN TEAGUE,
Keeper of the Giltspur-street Prison,
and Governor of the House of Correction.

(3.)—A Return of the Number of Persons COMMITTED to the *Poultry* and *Giltspur-street* Compters for the last Three Years ; distinguishing each Year, and those committed for Felonies, Assaults, and other Misdemeanors.

POULTRY COMPTER,		GILTSPUR-STREET COMPTER,	
1813:		**1813:**	
Felonies	454	Felonies	592
Assaults	218	Assaults	381
Misdemeanors	998	Misdemeanors	841
TOTAL	1,670	TOTAL	1,814
1814:		**1814:**	
Felonies	444	Felonies	528
Assaults	153	Assaults	335
Misdemeanors	1,101	Misdemeanors	888
TOTAL	1,698	TOTAL	1,751
1815:		**1815:**	
Felonies	472	Felonies	542
Assaults	223	Assaults	425
Misdemeanors	1,222	Misdemeanors	1,132
TOTAL	1,917	TOTAL	2,099

May 6, 1816.   JOHN TEAGUE,
                                              Keeper.

(4.)—Return to an Order of the Committee of the House of Commons, on the Police of the Metropolis; stating the Number of Persons COMMITTED to *New Prison*, at *Clerkenwell*, for the last Three Years; distinguishing each Year, and those committed for Felonies, Assaults, and other Misdemeanors.

YEAR.	Felonies.	Assaults.	Misdemeanors.	TOTAL N° of Persons Committed.
From 1 January } To 31 December } --- 1813	1,424	558	553	2,535
From 1 January } To 31 December } --- 1814	1,576	692	513	2,781
From 1 January } To 31 December } --- 1815	1,677	819	712	3,208
TOTAL	4,677	2,069	1,778	8,524

N. B.—There was no Record of the Ages of the Prisoners kept in this Prison, till the 12th January 1816.

New Prison, Clerkenwell, }   WILLIAM BEEBY,
    6th May 1816.   }   Keeper.

(5)—A Return of the Number of Prisoners COMMITTED to the House of Correction for the County of *Middlesex*, with their different Offences, during the years 1813, 1814, 1815; and from the 1st January to 2d May 1816, both days inclusive;—viz.

	For the Year 1813:			For the Year 1814:			For the Year 1815:			From 1 January to 2 May 1816:		
—	Males.	Females.	Total.	Males.	Females.	Total.	Males.	Females.	Total.	Males.	Females.	Total.
Assault	113	38	151	96	31	127	104	35	139	29	31	60
Arson	-	-	-	-	-	-	-	-	-	-	1	1
Burglary	9	-	9	16	3	19	19	3	22	7	4	11
Bastardy	33	-	33	21	3	24	45	4	49	15	-	15
Bestiality	-	-	-	-	-	-	2	-	2	—	—	—
Bigamy	1	-	1	1	-	1	—	—	—	—	—	—
Conspiracy	-	-	-	1	1	2	1	-	1	2	-	2
Cutting and Maiming	-	-	-	2	-	2	—	—	—	—	—	—
Coining	2	2	4	3	2	5	3	1	4	—	—	—
Debtors	114	16	130	82	17	99	89	17	106	44	9	53
Disorderly Apprentices	64	3	67	62	7	69	52	6	58	18	-	18
Disorderly Persons	50	144	194	23	97	120	21	68	89	15	20	35
Exposing	-	-	-	-	-	-	-	-	-	1	-	1
Fraud	6	3	9	9	6	15	12	5	17	4	-	4
Forgery, on suspicion	12	2	14	3	1	4	3	-	3	3	-	3
Felony	272	137	409	368	124	492	422	148	570	170	58	228
Highway Robbery	-	-	-	-	-	-	-	-	-	6	-	6
Juggling	-	-	-	-	-	-	3	-	3	4	1	5
Lottery Rogues & Vagabonds	14	7	21	33	.73	106	16	22	38	7	18	25
Misdemeanor	170	94	264	209	83	292	219	109	328	83	21	104
Murder, on suspicion	10	6	16	9	-	9	11	1	12	-	1	1
Nuisance	2	1	3	3	1	4	1	1	2	—	—	—
Petit Larceny	6	2	8	12	5	17	16	8	24	3	1	4
Rogues and Vagabonds to be passed	183	150	333	181	111	292	455	209	664	140	53	193
Rogues and Vagabonds leaving their Families	28	1	29	22	-	22	34	-	34	13	-	13
Rogues and Vagabonds, reputed Thieves	21	2	23	41	1	42	46	1	47	24	5	29
Riot	15	7	22	40	10	50	30	11	41	1	4	5
Rape	-	-	-	-	-	-	4	-	4	1	-	1
Sodomy	7	-	7	5	-	5	5	-	5	3	-	3
Soldiers and Marines	98	-	98	32	-	32	49	-	49	18	-	18
Uttering forged Notes	20	7	27	20	15	35	14	10	24	7	1	8
D° - base Coin	22	7	29	19	20	39	5	10	15	3	1	4
TOTALS	1,272	629	1,901	1,313	611	1,924	1,681	669	2,350	621	229	850

(6.)—A Return of the Number of Prisoners COMMITTED to *Tothill Fields* Bridewell, from the 1st day of January 1816 to the 7th day of May following, inclusive; distinguishing those committed for Felonies, Assaults, and other Misdemeanors; specifying the different Ages for each Offence, as far as can be made out.

OFFENCES:

Felonies	227
Assaults	85
Misdemeanors	144
Vagrants	45
Lottery Vagrant	1
Aliens	5
Debtors	54
Night Charges	21
TOTAL	582

Felonies.	Age.	Assaults.	Age.	Misde-meanors.	Age.	Vagrants.	Age.	Lottery Vagrant.	Age.	Debtors.	Age.
1 - at -	11	1 - at -	14	1 - at -	12	1 - at -	22	1 - at -	39	1 - at -	22
1 -	12	1 -	17	4 -	14	1 -	34			1 -	25
2 -	13	2 -	18	2 -	16	1 -	36			1 -	26
4 -	14	2 -	19	1 -	17	1 -	42			1 -	33
1 -	15	2 -	20	1 -	18	1 -	50			1 -	36
5 -	16	2 -	25	3 -	19	1 -	54			1 -	50
6 -	17	1 -	26	2 -	20	1 -	65			1 -	53
9 -	18	1 -	27	3 -	21	1 -	68			1 -	63
7 -	19	2 -	29	3 -	22	1 -	74				
4 -	20	3 -	30	2 -	23	1 -	76				
3 -	21	1 -	33	1 -	24	1 -	79				
3 -	22	1 -	35	3 -	25						
1 -	23	1 -	43	2 -	26						
2 -	24	1 -	48	1 -	27						
3 -	25	1 -	52	4 -	28						
1 -	26			2 -	29						
2 -	27			2 -	30						
2 -	28			3 -	32						
6 -	30			1 -	34						
2 -	31			1 -	35						
3 -	32			1 -	36						
1 -	34			3 -	37						
3 -	36			1 -	41						
3 -	37			1 -	42						
1 -	38			1 -	44						
1 -	40			2 -	45						
1 -	42			3 -	47						
1 -	44			1 -	53						
2 -	48			1 -	55						
1 -	49			1 -	59						
1 -	51			1 -	62						
1 -	56			1 -	66						
1 -	59										
85		**22**		**59**		**11**		**1**		**8**	

(7.)—Return of the Number of Persons COMMITTED to *Tothill Fields* Bridewell for the last Three Years, from the 1st day of January 1813 to the 31st day of December 1815, inclusive; distinguishing each year, and those committed for Felonies, Assaults, and other Misdemeanors; specifying the Number of Boys of the Age of Sixteen and under, as far as can be made out.

OFFENCES.	1813.	1814.	1815.
Felonies - - - - - - - - - -	420	529	604
Assaults - - - - - - - - - -	168	195	237
Misdemeanors - - - - - - - - - -	266	318	366
Vagrants - - - - - - - - -	195	136	166
Lottery Vagrants - - - - - - - -	2	13	2
Aliens brought from the Alien Office - - - -	10	2	—
Prisoners of War brought from the Transport Office - -	32	35	—
Debtors - - - - - - - - - -	142	117	143
Night Charges - - - - - - - -	232	167	140
TOTAL - - -	1,467	1,512	1,658
Boys Nine years of age - - - - - - - -	1	—	—
— Ten years of age - - - - - - - -	1	2	4
— Eleven years of age - - - - - - - -	-	1	4
— Twelve years of age - - - - - - - -	2	1	1
— Thirteen years of age - - - - - - - -	-	1	4
— Fourteen years of age - - - - - - - -	1	5	1
— Fifteen years of age - - - - - - - -	1	1	3
— Sixteen years of age - - - - - - - -	1	7	6
	7	18	23

Appendix, N° 14.

A Return of Persons COMMITTED to the County Gaol at *Newington,* in and for the County of *Surrey*; from January 1st, 1813, to May 1st, 1816, inclusive;—showing the Account of each Year respectively, and the Ages of BOYS under Sixteen Years.

For the Year 1813:

Felonies - - - - - - 522
Misdemeanors - - - - - 108   } Total - - - 840:
Assaults - - - - - - 210

Of whom are - - - Boys
2 - - - - aged 12 years.
1 - - - - - —- 14 years.
4 - - - - - —- 15 years.

Total - - - - 7 - - - - under 16 years.

For the Year 1814:

Felonies - - - - - - 472
Misdemeanors - - - - - 88   } Total - - - 760:
Assaults - - - - - - 200

Of whom are - - - Boys
1 - - - - aged 11 years.
3 - - - - - —- 12 years.
4 - - - - - —- 14 years.
1 - - - - - —- 15 years.

Total - - - - 9 - - - - under 16 years.

For the Year 1815:

Felonies - - - - - - 488
Misdemeanors - - - - - 114   } Total - - - 799:
Assaults - - - - - - 197

Of whom are - - - Boys
1 - - - - aged 12 years.
4 - - - - - —- 13 years.
4 - - - - - —- 14 years.
1 - - - - - —- 15 years.

Total - - - - 10 - - - - under 16 years.

Persons COMMITTED in 1813 - - - 840
D° - - - - - - in 1814 - - - 760
D° - - - - - - in 1815 - - - 799   } being
Total - - - - 2,399;

Felonies - - - -1,482
Misdemeanors - 310
Assaults - - - 607

2,399

(*continued*)

For the Year 1816, to the 1st day of May inclusive:

Felonies - - - - - - 189 ⎤
Misdemeanors - - - - - 49 ⎬ Total - - - 272:
Assaults - - - - - - 34 ⎦

Of whom are - - - Boys
5 - - - - aged 13 years.
4 - - - - — 14 years.
6 - - - - — 15 years.

TOTAL - - - 15 - - - under 16 years.

An Account of the AGES of BOYS in the foregoing Return:

	Number of BOYS Committed,	Years of Age:				
		11.	12.	13.	14.	15.
In the year 1813 - - - - - -	7	- -	2	- -	1	4
In the year 1814 - - - - - -	9	1	3	- -	4	1
In the year 1815 - - - - -	10	- -	1	4	4	1
To 1 May 1816 - - - - -	15	- -	- -	5	4	6

Total under 16 years ⎱ - 41.
of Age - - - - ⎰

PERSONS COMMITTED,

In the Year 1813;
Felonies - - - - - - 522
Misdemeanors - - - - - 108
Assaults - - - - - - 210
——— - - - 840

In the Year 1814;
Felonies - - - - - - 472
Misdemeanors - - - - - 88
Assaults - - - - - - 200
——— - - - 760

In the Year 1815;
Felonies - - - - - - 488
Misdemeanors - - - - - 114
Assaults - - - - - - 197
——— - - - 799

To the 1st May 1816;
Felonies - - - - - - 189
Misdemeanors - - - - - 49
Assaults - - - - - - 34
——— - - - 272

2,671

WILLIAM WALTER,
Keeper of the County Gaol at *Newington,*
in and for the County of *Surrey.*

EXTRACTS FROM THE EVIDENCE of the Rev. Thomas Thirlwall,

before the Select Committee on the Police of The Metropolis.

The Reverend *Thomas Thirlwall*, called in ; and Examined.

YOU are one of the Middlesex Magistrates ?—I am.

Is this Book, which the Chairman holds in his hand, purporting to be, *Rev. T. Thirlwall.* " A Vindication of the Magistrates, acting in and for the Tower Division, from the Charges contained in a printed work, entitled, ' The Report of the Committee on the State of the Police of the Metropolis, together with the Minutes of Evidence, taken before a Committee of the House of Commons,' by Thomas Thirlwall, M. A. Rector of Bowers Gifford, Essex, and Magistrate for the Counties of Middlesex and Essex," your publication ?—I am the author of the Vindication.

The next sentence in the book the Chairman wishes to pass over as concerning himself ; the last is this, " It is pretty well known, my loyalty to my King, and attachment to the Constitution, and I had almost said enthusiastic admiration of its forms. I have contributed my part in the worst of times to its safety : I hope, therefore, that my observations will not be tortured into any intentional disrespect to the Committee ; I acknowledge its authority and bow to its decisions. But when I make this declaration, it does not follow that I am bound against my conscience to admit either candour or impartiality in the proceedings, or that if the body of Magistrates are to be tried, I should not prefer Mr. Beaumont bringing his charges before my Lord Ellenborough, rather than before a Committee of the House of Commons, with even Captain Bennet in the chair. I am not partial to the Committees in the time of Cromwell, nor to the Committees in France in the time of the Revolution. I do not wish to be tried by Committees ; I protest against a trial by Committees, Inquisitions, or Star-Chambers." The Committee, considering that latter inuendo as being most clearly pointed against their proceedings, require from you an explanation of those observations : the first question they ask you is, before they require from you an explanation as to the latter inuendo ; What grounds have you for accusing the Committee, of either want of candour or impartiality ?—I deny that I have.

You wish that answer to stand as it does ?—I do.

How then do you explain those words, " But when I make this declaration," meaning the declaration of respect towards the Committee, " it does not follow that I am bound, against my conscience, to admit either candour or impartiality in their proceedings ?"—I beg it to be understood, in its plain and literal sense, that I am not bound. I have not refused the credit of candour or impartiality ; I have merely stated that I, as an Englishman, and with the rights and privileges of an Englishman, and with all the lights and advantages which an education has given me, conceive, that as a general topic it is open to discussion like that of every other institution ; the comparative merits of a Committee of the House of Commons, and that of a trial by Peers ; and I have no hesitation in stating, that I prefer the one to the other. I meant nothing disrespectful to the Committee.

The Committee wish to ask of you, as a clergyman and a magistrate, when you wrote that sentence, whether you did not mean to insinuate that the Committee was neither candid nor impartial ?— I beg to object to any questions tending to criminate myself.

231.   The

Rev. T. Thirlwall.

The last question that the Committee wish to propose, is, as to the inuendo in the conclusion of the sentence. Having stated your preference to a trial by jury, over what you are pleased to term a trial by a Committee, you add, "I am not partial to the Committees in the time of Cromwell, nor to the Committees in France in the time of the Revolution; I do not wish to be tried by Committees; I protest against a trial by Committees, Inquisitions or Star Chambers." What do you mean by that inuendo?—I mean what it states.

You mean then to assimilate, what you are pleased to term a trial by a Committee of the House of Commons, with proceedings in Committees in the time of Cromwell, to Committees in France at the time of the Revolution, to Inquisitions and Star Chambers?—No; no such thing; I had no idea of the kind.

What do you mean then by this last paragraph?—I mean it to fill up a period.

The Committee think it right to inform you, that this is likely to come before the House of Commons; and they wish seriously to ask you, whether you stand by the answer you have last given?—I do.

Have you any thing else to add upon this subject?—No, I have not.

EXTRACTS

From the Evidence of the Rev.ᵈ *Thomas Thirlwall*,
before the Select Committee on the Police of
The Metropolis.

Ordered, by The House of Commons, *to be Printed,*

2 *May* 1817.

231.